Managerial economics
ANALYSIS AND CASES

Managerial economics

ANALYSIS AND CASES

WILLIAM WARREN HAYNES, D.C.S.

Dean, School of Business
State University of New York, Albany

1969 · Revised Edition

BUSINESS PUBLICATIONS, INC.

Austin, Texas

Irwin-Dorsey Limited, Georgetown, Ontario

Revised Edition
First Printing, June, 1969

Library of Congress Catalog Card No. 69–19983
Printed in the United States of America

Preface

This text consists of three main elements: (1) an exposition of the fundamental theoretical and analytical tools of economics useful in decision making; (2) a review of empirical studies and illustrations of the applications of economic analysis in management; and (3) cases involving actual managerial situations which require the use of analysis. The book is based on certain beliefs about the subject matter of managerial economics and its teaching which deserve an explicit statement.

1. Managerial economics represents an integral set of concepts rather than a variety of divergent and independent ideas. The book presents a cumulative flow of analysis which reaches a higher degree of complexity as the learning proceeds. The book introduces basic ideas in the earlier chapters and builds upon those in the later sections. This method requires constant application, for a failure to master the earlier material will create difficulties in understanding what follows. The method also involves considerable repetition; the same ideas crop up again and again throughout the volume. The author considers such repetition an advantage, for only by considering the same ideas in different settings does the student grasp their full significance.

2. Managerial economics is not merely another course in economic theory; it requires a different approach than one would find in a theory textbook. For example, the understanding of a graph showing the theoretical equilibrium in perfect competition is less important in managerial economics than are the marginal tools of analysis incorporated in that theory. An understanding of theory *is* important; this book assumes at least an elementary training in theory. But managerial economics is concerned with bridging the gap between theory and practice, which is a special subject in itself. Whenever theoretical analysis is presented in this book, its relevance to practice is developed; nothing is more irritating to the student than to read a section on pure theory and then another on practice with little obvious connection between the two. There are important connections; this book tries to make them clear wherever possible.

3. It follows from what has just been said that a book on managerial economics must combine textbook exposition with cases. To present cases without the sections on analysis would force the student to develop the principles on his own, a useful exercise no doubt, but one that is uneco-

nomical. The problem of applying economic analysis is difficult enough in itself without requiring that the student invent the analysis himself. The accumulation of knowledge up to the present is too valuable to be ignored. To be sure, a critical attitude toward "conventional wisdom" is always in order; a student who is willing to challenge accepted generalizations will inevitably think more deeply than one who mechanically accepts what he reads.

The presentation of analysis without case material is also inadequate for the purposes of managerial economics. The very nature of managerial economics is one of application, and the best way to learn application is to apply. Anyone can learn a formula for the elasticity of demand. But the estimation of price elasticities in actual markets requires a variety of skills; and the application of the knowledge of such elasticities to decision-making problems is far from simple. To take another example, formal procedures for the treatment of uncertainty (which will be discussed in Chapter 10) cannot displace completely more subjective skills in determining how far the analysis should be carried and how much refinement is justified. A course in managerial economics without cases misses some of the judgmental skills which are an essential part of the subject.

4. The problem of deciding on how much institutional, psychological, and sociological material to introduce in a course in managerial economics is a difficult one. It is obvious that price policy, one of the major subjects of managerial economics, is governed in part by antitrust and antidiscrimination legislation. Should a book such as this attempt to teach the intricacies of such legislation and its interpretations in the courts? The author has chosen a compromise. He has decided against trying to include all there is to know about the government regulations that affect economic decision making; this is a subject in itself. But he has tried to indicate the importance of the legal environment within which decisions are made, mostly by presenting cases in which law and economics are interwoven.

Similarly, the author has avoided making this a book in psychology and sociology at the same time that he has tried to emphasize the importance of psychological and sociological forces underlying demand and influencing the decision-making process. The case method is again an excellent way of introducing such considerations; a good case is never concerned exclusively with economic variables but shows how economic factors are mixed with other variables. A case write-up must always simplify, but it should at least suggest the complexity of the "total situation" found in actual practice.

5. Recent developments in operations research (or management science) present a similar dilemma. That those subjects have a close relation to managerial economics is beyond doubt. It would be impossible, for example, to determine whether inventory theory or replacement theory is economics or operations research, nor would a controversy on this point

be very fruitful. Operations research is distinguished by its mathematical approach, but as economics becomes more mathematical this difference loses significance. This book goes this far in introducing the reader to operations research: it includes as illustrations a variety of econometric studies that move in the quantitative direction of modern management science; it also contains a number of "models" of the sort that are characteristic of these new developments; and it provides a discussion of the relation of certain standard managerial economics subjects to such topics as probability theory and linear programming.

In this revised edition, the quantitative approaches to managerial economics have been given somewhat more space than in the earlier edition. Linear programming, for example, receives a fuller treatment than previously. But this book cannot hope to go into the quantitative approaches as deeply and thoroughly as do volumes specializing in those topics. Many of the simplifying assumptions in quantitative models are like those in managerial economics, so that the overlap with books in management science is substantial.

Some readers may be tempted to de-emphasize the empirical studies and illustrative materials that are scattered throughout the volume. This would be a mistake, for, although these materials are concentrated in separate sections, they are an essential part of the subject development. Some generalizations of managerial economics seem quite obvious when stated simply but take on a different character when related to concrete reality. The managerial economist is one who can mold fundamental analytical tools to meet the needs of a specific decision-making situation; the illustrative materials, along with the cases, provide training in this kind of application.

Numerous persons have generously assisted in the development of this book. Among those who have contributed cases or have cooperated with the author in writing cases are Professor Carl L. Moore of Lehigh University; Professor Frederic A. Brett of the University of Alabama; Professors Robert N. Anthony, Stanley I. Buchin, John V. Lintner, and Henry B. Arthur of the Harvard Graduate School of Business Administration; and Bernard Davis, James L. Gibson, James Ledford, Dale Osborne, and Martin B. Solomon, Jr., all graduate students at the University of Kentucky at the time much of this book was written. Ravi Matthai, Director of the Indian Institute of Management at Ahmedabad, has kindly granted permission to reproduce cases which the author wrote or supervised while in India. Mr. K. L. Varshneya of the Indian Institute of Management, Ahmedabad, and Professor John I. Reynolds of the Harvard Business School participated in writing two of the Indian cases included in this volume. Colleagues, at the University of Kentucky and the Harvard Graduate School of Business Administration, have read parts of the manuscript and have made helpful suggestions. Graduate students, who have been subjected to the text in mimeographed form, have contributed ideas for the improvement of the exposition. Gilbert Crouse and Jimmy L. Thomas have been particularly helpful in finding research materials and in correcting errors. The author is grateful to all but takes full responsibility for the errors which remain.

Thanks are also due to Judy Shewmaker, Ruth Davis, Betty Rae King, and Anne Chaabane who not only typed the manuscript in its several successive stages but also helped improve it in many ways. The assistance of businessmen who provided materials for the cases is also gratefully acknowledged. Unless otherwise indicated by a footnote, material for the cases was gathered and prepared by the author.

Boston, Massachusetts   W. W. HAYNES
May, 1969

Table of contents

*and short-run demand. Technological substitutability. Promotional
activity. Product improvements. Population changes. Summary. Empirical studies and illustrations.* 4. Psychological and sociological influences and some current demand hypotheses: *Some current hypotheses. Empirical studies and illustrations.*

1. Gross national product model building: *The problem of consistency. Federal government expenditures. State and local government expenditures. Expenditures on plant and equipment. Residential construction. Inventory investment. The excess of exports over
imports. Consumption. Individual components: sources and suggestions. Some awkward problems. Checks for consistency. Recapitula-
tion. Empirical studies and illustrations.* 2. Econometric models: *A
model of the U.S. economy. Empirical checks on the U.S. model.
Limitations of econometric models. Empirical studies and illustrations.* 3. The lead-lag approach: *Limitations of the lead-lag approach. Diffusion indexes. Empirical studies and illustrations.* 4.
Forecasting the demand for individual products: *Forecasting demand with the manipulable variables held constant. Some useful
ideas. Forecasting when the company manipulates some of the variables. Conclusion. Empirical studies and illustrations. Forecasting
automobile sales. Orders and shipments.*

PART THREE.   Cost analysis

1. Introduction: fixed and variable costs and other cost classifications: *Fixed and variable costs. Other cost classifications. Other cost
concepts. Empirical studies and illustrations.* Corner grocery store.
Chain grocery stores. 2. Accounting costs and economic costs:
*Limitations of traditional accounting data for decision making. The
special problem of depreciation. Empirical studies and illustrations.*
3. Break-even charts: *Form of the break-even charts. Contribution
to overhead and profit. Construction of break-even charts. Scale of
the output axis. Limitations of break-even analysis. Evaluation of
break-even charts. Empirical studies and illustrations.* 4. Theoretical
cost functions: *Unit costs. Total costs. Empirical studies and illustra-
trations.* 5. A confrontation of the linear (break-even) and theoretical models: *Linear functions as approximations of curvilinear functions. Empirical evidence on constant marginal costs. A compromise.
Implications for decision making. Empirical studies and illustrations.*

1. Production functions: *A single output—isoquants. Output maximization and cost minimization. Managerial use of production func-*

esses. Increasing marginal costs. A variety of applications. 4. A review of other advanced topics: *Replacement decisions. Lease or buy decisions.*

PART ONE / Introduction to managerial economics

1 / The scope and method of managerial economics

Managerial economics is economics applied in decision making. It is a special branch of economics bridging the gap between abstract theory and managerial practice. Its stress is on the use of the tools of economic analysis in clarifying problems, in organizing and evaluating information, and in comparing alternative courses of action. While managerial economics is sometimes known as business economics, it encompasses methods and a point of view applicable both in business and in other institutions faced with optimization in decision making.

Economics is sometimes defined as the study of the allocation of scarce social resources among unlimited ends. It follows that managerial economics is the study of the allocation of the resources available to a firm or other unit of management among the activities of that unit. Such a definition implies that managerial economics is concerned with choice—with the selection among alternatives.

Managerial economics is pragmatic: It is concerned with analytical tools that are useful, that have proven themselves in practice, or that promise to improve decision making in the future. In the attempt to be practical it cuts through many of the refinements of theory. While it avoids some of the most difficult abstract issues of economic theory, it inevitably involves complications that are ignored in theory, for it must face up to the total situation in which decisions are made.

1. RELATION TO OTHER BRANCHES OF LEARNING

One way to clarify the scope of a field of study is to discuss its relation to other subjects. Managerial economics has a close connection with microeconomic theory, macroeconomic theory, the theory of decision making, operations research, and statistics. The fully trained managerial economist integrates concepts and methods from all of these disciplines, bringing them to bear on managerial problems.

Microeconomic theory

The main source of concepts and analytical tools for managerial economics is microeconomic theory, also known as price theory or Marshallian economics. This volume contains numerous references to such microeconomic concepts as the elasticity of demand, marginal cost, the short and long runs, market structures, and so on. It also makes use of well-known models in price theory, such as the model for monopoly price, the kinked demand theory, and the model of price discrimination.

In the attempt to be operational, managerial economics neglects some of the fine points that take up so much space in the theoretical literature. For example, managerial economics (at least as developed in this book) makes little use of indifference curves, which are central in the modern theory of demand. Indifference curves have helped clarify some important issues in economics, such as the separation of the income effects and substitution effects of price change. But so far they have played no part in managerial decisions, for they are remote from the level of abstraction on which decisions are made. Measurement of the variables required in a practical application of indifference analysis is improbable. This is not to claim that the kind of thought involved is completely irrelevant; but managers prefer to devote their time to concepts that have a more immediate applicability.

Macroeconomic theory

The chief debt of managerial economics to macroeconomic theory is in the area of forecasting. Post-Keynesian aggregative theory (the theory of income and employment) has direct implications for forecasting general business conditions. Since the prospects of an individual firm often depend greatly on business in general, individual firm forecasts depend on general business forecasts, which make use of models derived from theory. The most widely used model in modern forecasting, the gross national product model, is a direct product of theoretical developments in the past 30 years. Again the applications bypass some of the fine points of interest to the theorist; but the actual use of these models requires an examination of details (the inventory situation in the automobile industry, excess capacity in chemicals, consumer attitudes) that the theory necessarily ignores.

The relation of managerial economics to economic theory (of either the micro or macro varieties) is much like that of engineering to physics, or of medicine to biology or bacteriology. It is the relation of an applied field to the more fundamental but more abstract basic disciplines from which it borrows concepts and analytical tools. The fundamental theoretical fields will no doubt in the long run make the greater contribution to the extension of human knowledge. But the applied fields involve the development of skills that are worthy of respect in themselves and that require specialized training. The practicing physician may not contribute much to the advance of biological theory, but he plays an essential role in producing the fruits of progress in theory. The managerial economist stands in a similar relation to theory, with perhaps the difference that the dichotomy between the "pure" and the "applied" is less clear in management than it is in medicine.

The theory of decision making

The theory of decision making (closely related to and hardly separable from organization theory) is a relatively new subject that has a significance for managerial economics. Much of economic theory is based on the assumption of a single goal—maximization of utility for the individual or maximization of profit for the firm. It also usually rests on the assumption of certainty—of perfect knowledge. The theory of decision making, in contrast, recognizes the multiplicity of goals and the pervasiveness of uncertainty in the real world of management. The theory of decision making often replaces the notion of a single optimum solution with the view that the objective is to find solutions that "satisfice" rather than maximize. It probes into an analysis of motivation, of the relation of rewards and aspiration levels, of patterns of influence and authority.

The theory of decision making is concerned with the processes by which expectations under conditions of uncertainty are formed. It recognizes the costs of collecting and processing information, the problem of communication, and the need to reconcile the diverse objectives of individuals and interests in the organization. It requires the consideration of the psychological and sociological influences on human behavior.

Economic theory and the theory of decision making appear to be in conflict, each based on a different set of assumptions. Which theory shall we choose? It is unnecessary to make a black-and-white choice. This book is obviously based on the belief that economic analysis is useful in the achievement of better decisions. But it does not ignore the obstacles to the exact application of that analysis. It does not claim that businessmen always do or always can reach the optima indicated by theory, but it does argue that it is useful to have some idea of the direction of such optima. It admits that while economic theory is easy to apply in simple, slow-moving situations with clear-cut objectives, it is much less able to handle more complex problems with multiple goals and high degrees of uncertainty.

One of the main benefits of the case method in managerial economics is that it indicates the strengths and weaknesses of economic analysis in actual decision-making situations. One of the skills to be learned from a book of this type is the ability to evaluate the relevance of particular conceptual tools in dealing with the problems faced by management. The manager must temper the refinements of theory with the requirements of decision making.

In brief, the theory of decision making is a reminder of the complexities of decision making and the frequent need to compromise our "pure" models to make them useful in actual practice. In addition, the theory of decision making promises to contribute to the improvement of practice by focusing on new problems and suggesting new lines of attack. A modern work on managerial economics must take these developments into account.

Operations research

There is some disagreement about the proper definition of operations research, but in any case it is closely related to managerial economics. Operations research is concerned with "model building"—with the construction of theoretical models that aid in decision making. Managerial economics applies models; economic theorists were constructing "models" long before that expression became fashionable. Operations research is frequently concerned with optimization; economics has long dealt with the consequences of the maximization of profits or minimization of costs.

Some writers suggest that it is the "team approach" which makes operations research distinctive. Operations research workers have come from the natural sciences, from statistics, from mathematics, as well as from economics, and the resultant pooling of diverse talents may be its distinctive feature. Probably more important is the heavy reliance on mathematics. Most of the best-known operations research techniques are mathematical in character, as opposed to the more subjective and qualitative techniques usually used by management. Since economics is now becoming more mathematical, this suggests another parallel development in the two related fields.

The best way to describe operations research is to identify its recurrent techniques and models. The best-known method is linear programming, which is applied to a variety of problems of choice. Operations research workers have also developed inventory models indicating optimum quantities to order and optimum ordering times. In addition are waiting-line (queuing) models, bidding models, and applications of probability theory. Economic analysis involves a logic which is closely related to the logic of these models. For example, incremental or marginal reasoning of long application in economics is also applied in inventory models. Economists have also taken a great interest in the relation of linear programming to traditional theories of the firm. And some topics in operations research, such as replacement theory, have developed directly from the work of economists.

It is not important to determine where managerial economics begins and operations research ends. It is important to recognize the close relation of the two subjects and the contribution that each makes to the other. The last chapters of this book take up this connection in greater detail.

Statistics

Statistics is important to managerial economics in several ways. First, it provides the basis for the empirical testing of theory. Generalizations in economics, like generalizations in any science, are subject to empirical test. While deductive reasoning has made a central contribution to economics, the results of that reasoning can never be fully accepted until they are checked against the data from the world of reality. This volume presents statistical tests of some of the generalizations most important to managerial economics.

Statistics is important in a second way, in providing the individual firm with measures of the appropriate functional relationships involved in decision making. It is not enough, for example, to state that the firm should base its pricing decisions on considerations of demand and cost. To take such action, the firm could use statistical measurements of the shape and position of the demand and cost functions. It is not enough to know that linear programming can be used to determine the minimum costs of alternative allocations of the firm's facilities. To apply linear programming, it is necessary to measure the appropriate costs. This is not to state that statistical approaches are the only way to obtain estimates of the parameters for decision making. Later chapters will take up accounting, engineering, and subjective managerial estimates. But statistical methods no doubt provide the most reliable data for most purposes.

The theory of probability upon which statistics is based is important to managerial economics in still another way. Managers do not usually have exact information about the variables affecting decisions; they must deal with the uncertainty of future events. The theory of probability provides the logic for dealing with such uncertainty. The managerial economist is constantly faced with the choice between models ignoring uncertainty and those that explicitly incorporate probability theory.

2. NORMATIVE VERSUS DESCRIPTIVE ECONOMICS

Managerial economics is part of normative economics; it is prescriptive rather than descriptive in character. It is concerned with what decisions *ought* to be made. The main body of economic theory, on the other hand, confines itself to descriptive hypotheses, attempting to generalize about the relations among variables, without judgments about what is desirable or undesirable. For example, the law of diminishing returns is a generalization about what happens to output when variable inputs are added to fixed inputs, involving no judgments about whether the outcome is "good" or "bad."

Normative economics encompasses those branches of economics that attempt to combine descriptive economics with value judgments (or judgments about goals) to reach policy conclusions. Public policy (the economic policy of the government) is one type of normative economics; managerial economics is another.

One interesting feature of normative economics is of special signficance to managerial decision making. Some of the main propositions of managerial economics are heavily deductive. For example, the statement that profits are at a maximum when marginal revenue is equal to marginal cost is entirely a matter of logic that does not require any check against the facts. A substantial part of economic analysis is of this character, providing a system of logic that is self-contained. As was stated earlier, it is necessary to fit the correct data into this logical framework to reach specific conclusions about what should be done. And the question of whether a particular line of logic is *useful* is an empirical issue, requiring a check against the facts. Linear programming is an appropriate illustration. The logic of linear programming is deduction of a mathematical form. Given certain assumptions, linear programming indicates the logical consequences. But to use linear programming, one must have data on capacities, requirements, costs, or whatever is involved. And decisions on when linear programming is useful and profitable are sometimes difficult.

In conclusion, managerial economics is a branch of normative economics that draws from descriptive economics (sometimes called positive economics) and from well-established deductive patterns of logic. Managerial economics is, in addition, continually concerned with the separation of what will work from those lines of thought which have not proven their worth in practice. The application of managerial economics is inseparable from considerations of values, or norms, for it is always concerned with the achievement of objectives or the optimization of goals.

3. MANAGERIAL ECONOMICS AND OPTIMIZATION

As has been suggested, the concept of optimization is basic in both managerial economics and operations research. Throughout this volume are examples of models and principles based on the assumptions of profit maximization or cost minimization. The practitioner must adopt a mixed attitude towards such assumptions. He knows that as a description of actual behavior they are inaccurate and oversimplified. But he also knows that such simplifying assumptions are essential if he is to create order out of chaos.

Few managers actually seek the greatest attainment of a single goal; they settle for the partial achievement of a variety of goals, recognizing that furtherance of one objective may mean a partial sacrifice of another. Even if the manager could specify a single goal, he could not achieve the "true" optimum, for the number of relevant variables and the variety of interrelationships would be too large and complex for any system of thought. Electronic computers may permit the consideration of more variables than was ever possible before, but computer models are also abstractions from reality. Any model or theory must necessarily simplify. The result is a paradox: managerial economics often assumes a desire to optimize a given objective, but it also simplifies in ways that assure a failure to achieve the optimum.

Operations researchers have invented the term "suboptimization" to describe this process of abstraction from the total complexity of reality and the wide variety of goals. Instead of striving for perfection they construct models which reflect only part of reality and which face up to the bounds of human rationality. Such models indicate optimal positions within the limits or assumptions on which they are constructed. The result may be imperfect but should be superior to decisions based on crude rules of thumb or simple repetitions of past decisions. One great advantage of the point of view of suboptimization is its flexibility. It substitutes for rules of thumb and rigid formulas the point of view that "it depends." Decisions must be adapted to circumstances; they must be based on an analysis of the possibilities. The questions of managerial economics are always those of more or less, of this combination opposed to those combinations, or of this alternative rated against others—with adaptation to the environment and to the goals of management.

Another way of summarizing the position on optimization is to state that managerial economics requires a compromise. It involves first of all a compromise between the need for simplification to make the analysis manageable and the need to consider a variety of objectives and influences. It involves a compromise between the refinements of theory and the need to be practical. It weighs the costs of completeness against the errors of simplification. In the end, the criterion of its worth is its usefulness.

4. PROFITS: A CENTRAL CONCEPT

Although we have discussed the variety of goals of management, we must recognize that profit maximization is the central assumption in managerial economics. The reasons for the stress on profits are several. Profits are, after all, the one pervasive objective running through all business situations; other objectives are more a matter of personal taste or of social conditioning and are variable from firm to firm, society to society, and time to time. The survival of a firm depends upon its ability to earn profits. Profits are a measure of its success. Another reason for emphasizing profits has to do with convenience in analysis. It is easy to construct models based on the assumption of profit maximization; it is more difficult to build models based on a multiplicity of goals, especially when those goals are concerned with such unstable and relatively immeasurable factors as the desire to be "fair," the improvement of public relations, the maintenance of satisfactory relations with the community, the wish to perform a service to the community, the desire to increase one's personal influence and power, and so on.

It is therefore usual to proceed in the early analysis as though profits were the only goal. After the consequences of that assumption have been derived, it is possible to bring in other considerations. Economics has developed a systematic and sophisticated system of logic as long as the goal is one of profits; it becomes more awkward and cumbersome when it incorporates other objectives.

It is of interest that profit maximization is a basic theme both in descriptive and prescriptive economics. Milton Friedman argues cogently that, while profit maximization is an oversimplification as a description of actual behavior, it is the basis for generalizations which permit prediction.[1] While his position is considered one-sided by some economists, the argument for the emphasis on profit maximization in managerial economics is even stronger; it is clearly useful to know which alternatives lead to maximum profits or minimum costs if one is interested in making decisions. Profitability analysis may not provide the whole answer but it provides insight into the heart of the problem.

Theories of profit

One difficulty in defining profit is that no single theory has been able to explain profits in a simple way. Profit is a mixture resulting from a variety of influences. The result is a variety of profit theories. These theories fall into four categories: those emphasizing profit as a reward for taking risks; those stressing the effect of frictions, imperfections, and lags in producing profits; those centering on the monopoly element; and those relating profits to the flow of innovations in the economy.

The first theory of profit explains it as a reward for taking risks and bearing uncertainty. Entrepreneurs are unwilling to assume risks unless a reward compensates for the chances they take. The greater the risk the greater the profit incentive which is required. Thus one would expect a higher rate of profit in unstable and unpredictable industries such as electronics than in those with steady, dependable rates of growth, such as electric utilities.

Another theory of profit interprets it as a result of imperfections in the market mechanism. In a purely competitive economy without lags such

---

[1] Milton Friedman, *Essays in Positive Economics* (Chicago: University of Chicago Press, 1953).

profits would disappear. Any time "excess profits" (those in excess of what is required to overcome the risk and uncertainty and to cover the opportunity costs of capital) appear, the entry of new firms and expansion of existing firms would create a downward pressure on prices and the excess profits would be wiped out. In the real world of imperfections and frictions, the squeezing out of excess profits would be delayed, permitting temporary excess profits.

Monopoly is itself a source of profits. The existence of monopoly permits a curtailment of production and the establishment of prices above the competitive level. While profit can normally be considered a socially desirable guide for production, since it stimulates expansion in those parts of the economy where expansion is desirable, monopoly profit may be socially undesirable, since it is a reward for curtailing expansion where such expansion is socially beneficial. Actually the evaluation of monopoly profit is more complex than this bit of static analysis would suggest. In a world of change some degree of monopoly profit may act as an incentive to change and growth. For example, the temporary monopoly power resulting from patents may stimulate invention and innovation.

Another theory of profit warns against condemning all monopoly profit too hastily. The innovation theory notes that profits arise from the development of new products, new production techniques, and new modes of marketing. The innovator who develops these new products and methods deserves a reward for his contribution to progress. It is true that he earns excess profits from the monopoly which the superiority of his innovations provides, but this monopoly is temporary. Old innovations are replaced by new ones in a constant process of "creative destruction."[2]

The innovation theory of profit breaks away from the static equilibrium analysis which is usual in traditional economic theory. Innovation profits result from change—from the disruption of the equilibrium or status quo. Any theory which ignores innovation neglects the most important function of profits, which is to reward change and to stimulate the replacement of less valuable and productive activities with more vital ones.

Managerial economics and alternative profit theories

One paradox of managerial economics is that, while it makes use of the assumption of profit maximization, it makes little direct use of the theories of profit. Uncertainty, lags, frictions, and innovations give rise to the alternatives with which managerial economics is concerned. But most of the analysis is in terms of costs, demand, revenues, and market structure rather than directly in terms of profits. Thus we shall be concerned with the measurements of marginal revenue and incremental costs which lie

---

2 The chief writer on the innovation theory of profits is Joseph Schumpeter, especially in his *Theory of Economic Development* (Cambridge, Mass.: Harvard University Press, 1934).

behind incremental profits. We shall consider the contributions to over-head and profits which result from the alternatives under consideration. We shall compute the present value of estimated streams of profit in the future. We shall compare discounted rates of return, which are measures of profitability, with costs of capital. But none of this analysis is a direct application of one theory of profit or another.

Let us consider the risk and uncertainty theory first. Businessmen have coped with it in a variety of ways, mostly subjective in character. In re-cent years, more formal techniques for the analysis of uncertainty have developed under the titles of "decision theory," "decision trees," "Bayesian statistics," "queuing theory," "the Monte Carlo method," and "Markov processes." Modern managerial economics has recognized these important ideas and has incorporated them as part of the apparatus required for economic analysis. It is no surprise that a book entitled *Probability and Statistics for Business Decisions* should use the language of economics in many places (incremental cost, incremental gain, marginal utility, oppor-tunity cost, and so on). Nor is it surprising that a book entitled *Economic Analysis for Business Decisions* should be heavily concerned with prob-ability models.

The present volume, however, relegates the topics of risk and uncer-tainty to a secondary position, not taking them up in a formal way until Chapter 10. There are several reasons for this treatment. One is that the student should become thoroughly familiar with the basic concepts of managerial economics before complicating the analysis with probabilistic models. Some books on the subject tend to displace the important ideas of demand, cost, pricing, and capital budgeting with discussions of nor-mal curves, Bayes' theorem, and Bernoulli processes. This is unfortunate, for the concepts of managerial economics and of statistics are comple-mentary rather than competitive. Both aspects deserve attention and since probability is covered in courses in statistics and operations research, it seems appropriate that a course in managerial economics concentrate on the fundamental economic analysis.

Thus, while we recognize the importance of risk and uncertainty as a source of profits, we shall not make much direct use of this idea, except in a general way, until the last part of the book. The theory of profit as a reward for risk-taking is a useful one to keep in mind, but its direct application is better postponed for more advanced work.

We must show similar restraint in relating managerial economics to the innovation theory of profits. Economic analysis cannot produce the innovations; they are dependent upon qualities of imagination and leader-ship, and are influenced by the organizational environments and systems of incentives conducive to change. Managerial economics does evaluate new alternatives once they are developed. The entire chapter on capital budgeting is concerned with that topic. No analysis of alternatives can produce profits unless some of the alternatives are themselves profitable.

This discussion of profits has enabled us to place managerial economics in its proper perspective. Economics is not and cannot be the source of imaginative ideas for change. It does not provide the tools for determining the appropriate organization for the search for innovations. It does not deal with problems of leadership, communication, and human relations involved in carrying out decisions. It is appropriate only for the evaluation of alternatives which have somehow already been discovered.

Problems of measuring profit

The measurement of profit is full of difficulties. A considerable portion of this book is concerned with the correct measurement of costs for the purpose of determining the profitability of alternatives. The usual data on profits shown on income statements are based on historical data which do not reflect the impact of decisions on costs in an accurate way. The precise ways in which economic concepts are used to revise accounting data are considered throughout this book, especially in Chapters 2, 5, and 6.

One major deficiency of accounting profit data results from general changes in the price level. The accepted accounting practice is to value assets at original cost rather than current market value. It is also the accepted practice to compute depreciation on the basis of original cost.

These accounting conventions mean that the assets are undervalued on the books in times of inflation and overvalued in periods of deflation. More important, they mean that depreciation is understated and profits are overstated in inflation, while the reverse is true in deflation. Inflation raises replacement costs and increases the funds required for the maintenance of physical facilities. The conventions of accounting treat depreciation as a recovery of initial investment and thus do not face up to the impact of inflation on replacement costs. Price level changes also affect the market value of inventories in a way that is not accurately reflected in the accounts. The development of the LIFO method of inventory accounting or the rule of "cost or market, whichever is lower" do not overcome the problem satisfactorily.

Every manager should be aware of the impact of inflation on accounting profits. Proposals for the revision of accounting techniques would cope with the problem of inflation, but many practical problems stand in the way. Paradoxically, the remainder of this book devotes little attention to price level corrections, for it is concerned with profits for decision making rather than the reporting of profits; price level changes are more important in the reporting area.

5. SUMMARY: SOME VIEWS ON THE PLACE OF MANAGERIAL ECONOMICS

One way to conclude this chapter and summarize some of its major points is to quote from a symposium on managerial economics. In this symposium some theorists and research workers in managerial economics and operations research state their views on the present position of managerial economics. William J. Baumol notes the contributions that economic theory can make in the following statements:

> [T]he economist is an expert model builder. Indeed there are few disciplines which produce model builders with such practice and such skill. This, I think, is one of the most important things which the economic theorist can contribute to the work of management science. In management science it is important—in fact, absolutely essential—to be able to recognize the structure of a managerial problem. In order to be able to analyze it at all and to be able to do so systematically, it is necessary to do several things: first of all, to undertake a judicious simplification—an elimination of minor details which are peripheral to the problem and which, if included in the model, would prevent any successful and systematic analysis. Second, it is important to capture in a formal statement the essence of all the interrelationships which characterize the situation, because it is only after stating these interrelationships so explicitly that we can hope to use the powerful techniques of rigorous analysis in the investigation of a managerial problem. . . .[3]

Baumol suggests that a second way in which economic theory may be helpful to managerial science is to provide a set of analytical methods. He makes the interesting point that it is not the final theorems of economics that are important to management but rather the method of reasoning. Managerial economics borrows the analytical tools of theory but gives less regard to the final theorems or generalizations of theory. Baumol concludes that "a managerial economist can become a far more helpful member of a management group by virtue of his studies of economic analysis, primarily because there he learns to become an effective model builder and because there he acquires a very rich body of tools and techniques which can help him to deal with the problems of the firm in a far more rigorous, a far more probing, and a far deeper manner."[4]

Another discussant notes the ways in which managerial economics differs from descriptive theory. He states that the traditions of managerial economics are those of

> . . . specifying the technology not in generalized production functions but in specific processes; of identifying and measuring the goals of an organization rather than assuming a simple profit maximizing goal; of considering the role of information and ignorance instead of certainty; of treating the organizational attributes of the firm as a constraint or as a variable instead of collapsing the firm into a single personality; of finding statistical constructs to enable measurement with analysis rather than remaining satisfied with unmeasured concepts;

---

[3] William J. Baumol, "What Can Economic Theory Contribute to Managerial Economics?" *American Economic Review, Papers and Proceedings,* May, 1961, pp. 143–44.

[4] *Ibid.,* p. 146.

of welcoming mathematical and computer techniques to handle complex systems. . . .[5]

Other participants in the discussion review conclusions already outlined in this chapter: the close relation of managerial economics to operations research and management science, and the need of managerial economics to be operational. But perhaps enough space has been given such introductory statements. The best way to understand managerial economics is to delve into the subject itself. The chapters that follow provide the materials for such an understanding. They also provide case materials which are essential for the acquirement of skills in applying the analysis to concrete situations.

---

[5] Julius Margolis, "Discussion," *American Economic Review, Papers and Proceedings,* May, 1961, p. 155.

2 / Six fundamental concepts

As background for the remainder of the book, it is desirable to introduce six fundamental concepts which are basic to all of managerial economics. These concepts are elementary—almost self-evident. But their application is not always so self-evident. Empirical studies and illustrations at the end of each section of this chapter provide some insight into the difficulties that complicate the use of these principles in decision making.

This chapter is devoted to the six concepts: the incremental concept, the concept of time perspective, the discounting concept, the opportunity cost concept, the equimarginal principle, and the contribution concept.

1. THE INCREMENTAL CONCEPT

Incremental reasoning is easier to describe in general than it is to apply in practice. It involves estimating the impact of decision alternatives on costs and revenues, stressing the *changes* in total cost and total revenue that result from changes in prices, products, procedures, investments, or whatever may be at stake in the decision. The two basic concepts in this analysis are incremental cost and incremental revenue. Incremental cost may be defined as the change in total cost resulting from a decision. Incremental revenue is the change in total revenue resulting from a decision.

A decision is obviously a profitable one if:

1. It increases revenue more than costs.
2. It decreases some costs more than it increases others.
3. It increases some revenues more than it decreases others.
4. It reduces costs more than revenue.

16

Before the reader dismisses this analysis as too elementary for his attention, he might consider some of its implications. Some businessmen take the view that to make an overall profit they "must make a profit on every job."[1] The result is that they refuse orders that do not cover full cost (labor, materials, and overhead), plus a provision for profit. Incremental reasoning indicates that this rule may be inconsistent with profit maximization in the short run. A refusal to accept business below full cost may mean rejection of a possibility of adding more to revenue than to cost. The relevant cost is not the full cost but rather the incremental cost. A simple problem illustrates what is involved. Take a case in which a new order will bring in $10,000 additional revenue. The costs are estimated as follows:

Labor	$ 3,000
Materials	4,000
Overhead (allocated at 120 percent of labor cost)	3,600
Selling and administrative expense (allocated at 20 percent of labor and materials cost)	1,400
Full cost	$12,000

This order appears to be unprofitable. But suppose that there is idle capacity with which this order could be produced. Suppose that acceptance of the order will *add* only $1,000 of overhead (the incremental overhead, limited to the *added* use of heat, power, and light, the *added* wear and tear on the machinery, the *added* costs of supervision, and so on). Suppose also that the order in actuality requires no added selling costs since the only requirement is a signature on the contract and no added administrative costs. In addition, only part of the labor cost is incremental, since some idle workers already on the payroll will be put to work without added pay.

It is possible that the incremental cost of taking the order will be as follows:

Labor	$2,000
Materials	4,000
Overhead	1,000
Total incremental cost	$7,000

While it at first appeared that the order would result in a loss of $2,000, it now appears that the result is an addition of $3,000 in profit.

Perhaps a brief comment will minimize a common misunderstanding

---

[1] The exact words of a manager in an interview. The cases which follow contain similar statements.

about incremental reasoning. Incremental reasoning does *not* mean that the firm should price at incremental cost or should accept all orders that cover merely their incremental costs. In fact, "charging what the market will bear" is consistent with incrementalism, for it implies increasing rates as long as the resulting revenues increase. The acceptance of the $10,000 order in our illustration is conditioned upon the existence of idle capacity that would otherwise go unused and the absence of more profitable alternatives. Incremental reasoning never leads to acceptance of a less profitable order in preference to one that is more profitable; in fact it leads to the opposite.

It may be desirable to summarize the discussion in the form of a simple principle, which we can call the incremental principle: *a decision is sound if it increases revenue more than costs, or reduces costs more than revenue.*

Empirical studies and illustrations

Do managers actually use incremental reasoning? The answer is that some do and others do not. Managers are not always fully aware of the reasoning behind their own decisions; apparently many of them unconsciously do apply incremental principles. In any case, many of them are inarticulate on their decision-making processes, making it difficult to determine what logic they do apply.

Earley's study of "excellently managed" large firms suggests that progressive corporations do make formal use of incremental analysis, and make use of accounting methods that are consistent with marginalism.[2] Earley finds that most of the 88 firms covered by the study "employ marginal accounting extensively, including segmented variable-fixed cost differentiation and the determination of separable fixed costs. . . . Most of them follow essentially marginal principles, and eschew or subordinate cost allocations and full-costing, in their product selection, product investment, and both short- and long-range pricing decisions."[3]

A study of small firms in which the author has participated makes it clear that the use of incremental accounting methods is far from universal.[4] Of the 100 firms covered by the study, not one used the special accounting methods cited in the previous study. It is true that the managers were often aware of the distinction between fixed and variable costs, and it is also true that some of these managers made use of *ad hoc* cost analyses that helped them apply incremental reasoning. Other managers reached decisions consistent with incrementalism by trial and error

---

[2] James S. Earley, "Marginal Policies of 'Excellently Managed' Companies," *American Economic Review,* March, 1956, pp. 44–70.

[3] *Ibid.,* p. 61.

[4] W. W. Haynes, *Pricing Decisions in Small Business* (Lexington, Ky.: University of Kentucky Press, 1962).

or by experimentation. But none of these small firms had a programmed accounting method (a routine method automatically producing data period by period) that provided the kinds of costs figures required for decision making.[5] The item in the accounts that had the greatest impact on decision making was the profit or loss figure on the income statement. If this figure seemed "low" in relation to some predetermined standard, the manager often sought ways of improving the situation. In other words, the income figure motivated the managers to make decisions but did not provide the analysis required by those decisions. Accounting performed its stewardship function, supplying data required by the owners, creditors, or tax collectors. It also performed the control function, providing measurements of actual performance that could be compared with earlier experience or with standards. But normally it did not provide incremental data that would be useful for decisions.[6]

The failure of the accounting systems of many firms to supply incremental data is not necessarily a deficiency. In many cases *ad hoc* analyses are less expensive than programmed accounting systems that must be maintained period after period. Furthermore, what is an incremental cost varies from one decision to another, making it unlikely that a programmed incremental system would always produce the required information. A manager who is experienced in decision making may be able to make the necessary adjustments in the regular accounting data on the back of an envelope in a few minutes. Thus the absence of marginalist accounting methods does not necessarily imply the absence of incremental reasoning.

A few illustrations should help the reader picture the variety of actual practice. We start with two firms which not only fail to maintain records consistent with incrementalism but which also make decisions which appear to be inconsistent with incremental reasoning.

A laundry and dry cleaning establishment. The managers of this firm rejected an opportunity to make use of idle capacity in the summer months when business was slack. A large motel wished to make a contract

---

[5] Throughout this book will be references to the distinction between programmed and nonprogrammed accounting techniques. The programmed techniques are routine, resulting in period statements of a standard form. The nonprogrammed methods involve *ad hoc* or "tailor-made" analyses (special studies) made for particular decision-making problems.

[6] Since the first edition of this book was published, the author has traveled extensively in foreign countries, especially in Asia. The use of systematic incremental reasoning appears to be the exception rather than the rule in the areas he has visited. Traditional cost accounting, with its arbitrary cost allocations, appears to have confused far more managers than it has helped in the area of decision making. It is still the case that less than 20 percent, perhaps even less than 10 percent, of experienced managers in training programs in developing countries (and some developed countries) are able to see that the traditional accounts fail to provide the kinds of incremental data required. Thus the gap between "excellently managed" firms and the great majority of firms still remains, at least in the cost analysis area.

that would supply the laundry with business that would not cover "full costs" but which would more than cover incremental costs, leaving a contribution to overhead and profit. Apparently the managers were so certain that the full-cost figure, including allocated overhead, was the correct figure for decision making that they rejected a profitable order. They were unable to give any other reasons for rejecting the order; they did not believe that acceptance of the order would have any effect on their other business either in the present or in the future.

An air conditioning and sheet metal firm.   The managers of this firm, like those of the laundry just mentioned, rejected a large order that would have filled excess capacity and would have made a contribution to overhead and profits. Again the reliance on full costs, including allocated overhead, appears to have confused the decision-making process.

Additional illustrations from actual practice present a different pattern: the absence of marginal accounting systems but decisions consistent with incrementalism. The managers of a billboard advertising firm paid little attention to their regular financial accounting figures in making decisions on advertising rates. Instead they made up *ad hoc* income statements for future periods under alternative assumptions about rates. By this method they reached conclusions that appear to be fully in accord with incremental reasoning, even though the managers were unfamiliar with the economic jargon one might use to describe their analysis. Other companies appear to approximate incrementalism by trial and error, learning from experience what policies are likely to be conducive to increased profits.

In a study of small business, most companies appeared to fall in between the extremes already discussed. Their managers were concerned with full costs (in retailing they emphasized wholesale costs); they used these costs as a starting point in pricing. But they did not adhere to rigid markups on costs; instead they varied markups on different lines of goods and revised markups over time. Thus the most common pattern was that of "partial incrementalism," with either full cost or wholesale cost serving as a reference point or resistance point, but with considerable flexibility in adjustments to market conditions.

This review of empirical studies and illustrations supports two conclusions:

1. It is impossible to generalize on the uses of incremental reasoning, actual practice being variable.

2. Some firms could profit by giving more attention to incremental analysis, whether or not they revise their accounts to reflect this analysis.

2. INCREMENTALISM AND MARGINALISM

The reader with any familiarity with elementary economics is likely to recognize that incremental reasoning is closely related to the marginal costs and marginal revenues of economic theory. There are similarities and differences, both of which require attention.

1. While marginal costs and revenues are always defined in terms of unit changes in output, incremental costs and revenues are not necessarily restricted to unit changes.[7] If a one-unit increase in output results in an increase in cost from $700 to $710 and an increase in revenue from $800 to $815, the marginal cost is $10 and the marginal revenue is $15. If a 10-unit increase in output increases cost from $700 to $790 and increases revenue from $800 to $940, we can speak of an incremental cost of $90 and an incremental revenue of $140. Or we can state that the average marginal cost over this range is $9 and average marginal revenue is $14.

If the cost function is curvilinear, the marginal cost may change for each unit change in output; the measurement of marginal costs and marginal revenues permits a microscopic examination of such unit-by-unit changes. The decision maker may wish to avoid such refinement. He wants to know whether the decision as a whole is profitable and is willing to look at the entire increase in revenue to compare with the entire change in costs. This runs the risk of ignoring some other change in output within the range that might be even more profitable, but the cost of refinement may outweigh that risk.

2. Incremental concepts are more flexible than marginal concepts in another way. Normally, marginal cost and marginal revenue are restricted to the effects of changes in *output*. But decision making may not be concerned with changed output at all. For example, the problem may be one of substituting one process for another to produce the same output. The problem is then one of comparing the cost of the first process with that of the alternative. The marginalist language is not particularly suited to this kind of decision.[8]

One way of comparing the marginal and incremental approaches is to draw a traditional cost diagram like those that appear in all principles of economics textbooks. Figure 2–1 shows marginal cost as a curve, rising over most of its range.

Let us consider increasing output from 2,000 to 3,000 units. What is the marginal cost of this change? In terms of this traditional diagram, it is rather dangerous to give a single answer. At first the marginal cost is low, but it rises rapidly. Even to speak of an *average* marginal cost over this range is to oversimplify and to ignore the dramatic change over the range of outputs.

---

[7] Strictly speaking marginal concepts must be defined as derivatives of cost or revenue functions or, alternatively, as slopes of tangents to such functions. We wish, however, to postpone the introduction of calculus; the argument is not affected seriously by this simplification.

[8] It is possible to compare the marginal cost of one process with that of another but not of the marginal cost of the change. We can, however, use the term incremental cost to refer to the change in cost brought about by the change in process.

FIGURE 2–1

AVERAGE AND MARGINAL COSTS AS PRESENTED TRADITIONALLY

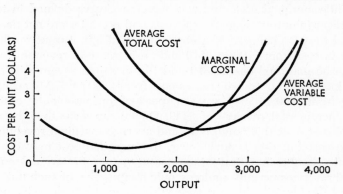

But, as we shall see, many studies of cost functions suggest that another pattern of costs is common in industry. The studies find relatively constant marginal costs over a wide range of outputs, as in Figure 2–2. In this situation no error results from using a single marginal cost figure over the whole range.

Let us assume that in the firm illustrated in Figure 2–2 the total fixed costs are $4,000 (per time period). The average variable cost is $2.75 per unit. The marginal cost is also $2.75 per unit. Suppose again that the decision involves a choice between an output of 2,000 units and one of 3,000 units. In the language of marginal cost there is no doubt about how to express the change in cost—it is $2.75 per unit. In the incremental

FIGURE 2–2

COST CURVES WITH CONSTANT MARGINAL COSTS

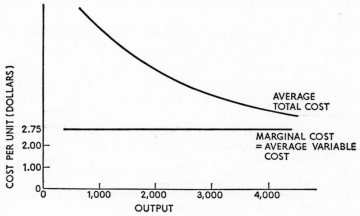

language, however, it is perfectly appropriate to speak of an *addition* to total cost of $2,750. Even if the marginal cost curve were slightly curved such a description of the change in costs might be precise enough for practical purposes.

Empirical studies and illustrations

The chief question for empirical research raised by this section is whether marginal costs are in fact constant, justifying the substitution of incremental cost measurements over large changes in output for measurements of cost changes for minute variations in output. If we could be certain of the universal linearity of short-run costs, the problem of decision making would be greatly simplified. At this point a general survey of the findings should suffice; Part 3, which is devoted entirely to cost analysis, will present more detailed findings.

The empirical studies of Joel Dean were among the first to suggest linearity of marginal costs. The studies covered a hosiery mill,[9] a leather belt shop,[10] and a furniture factory.[11] They all indicated a pattern much like that shown in Figure 2–3—a straight-line total cost curve, which means a horizontal marginal cost curve and an L-shaped average total cost curve. The reader should note how the curves were fitted to the dots representing actual observations (adjusted to remove some other influences).

Since the time of Dean's work, the preponderance of statistical studies has supported the conclusion that total costs are linear and marginal costs are constant in the short run.[12] For example, Yntema's study of costs in the steel industry resulted in the equation[13]

$$X_t = 182,100,000 + 55.73X_2$$

in which

$$X_t = \text{total cost in dollars}$$

$$X_2 = \text{weighted output, tons}$$

---

[9] Joel Dean, *Statistical Cost Functions of a Hosiery Mill* (Chicago: University of Chicago Press, 1941).

[10] Joel Dean, *The Relation of Cost to Output for a Leather Belt Shop* (New York: National Bureau of Economic Research, 1941).

[11] Joel Dean, *Statistical Determination of Costs, With Special Reference to Marginal Cost* (Chicago: University of Chicago Press, 1936).

[12] See J. Johnston, *Statistical Cost Analysis* (New York: McGraw-Hill Book Co., Inc., 1960), especially chaps. 4 and 5. Johnston's work is the most complete survey of cost studies.

[13] United States Steel Corporation, *T.N.E.C. Papers*, Vol. II (New York, 1940), p. 53.

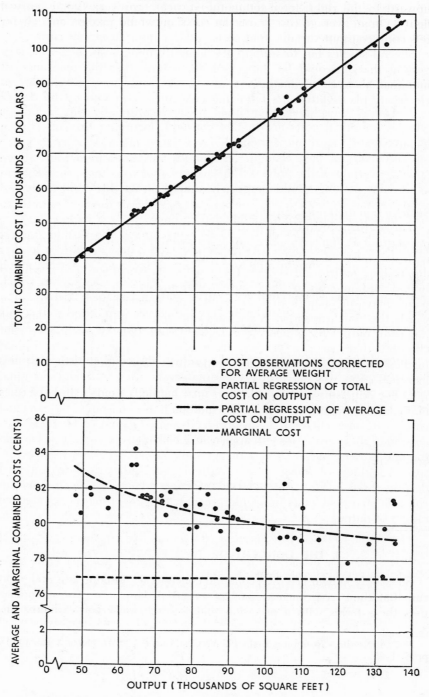

FIGURE 2–3

PARTIAL REGRESSIONS OF TOTAL, AVERAGE, AND MARGINAL COMBINED COSTS ON
OUTPUT: LEATHER BELT SHOP

• COST OBSERVATIONS CORRECTED
  FOR AVERAGE WEIGHT

— PARTIAL REGRESSION OF TOTAL
  COST ON OUTPUT

– – PARTIAL REGRESSION OF AVERAGE
  COST ON OUTPUT

- - - MARGINAL COST

SOURCE: Joel Dean, *The Relation of Cost to Output for a Leather Belt Shop* (New York: National Bureau of Economic Research, 1941), p. 27.

On a total cost graph this equation would appear as a straight line sloping upward to the right, intersecting the vertical (cost) axis at a positive figure. On an average cost graph the equation would take on an L shape, reflecting constant variable unit costs and declining fixed unit costs.

Several studies fail to support the linearity hypothesis, however, suggesting that it would be dangerous to assume that the constancy of marginal costs is universal. A study of short-run fuel costs in steam electricity plants fitted the following curvilinear equation to the data.[14]

$$Y = 16.68 + 0.125X + 0.00439X^2$$

where

$$Y = \text{total fuel cost}$$

$$X = \text{output as a percentage of capacity}$$

Such an equation implies rising marginal costs.

The statistical studies are still a matter of controversy. First, on a priori grounds, limited short-run capacity would appear to be inconsistent with constancy of marginal costs at all levels of output; at some point diminishing returns must occur. Perhaps the statistical studies have failed to find data on cases in which output was pressing on capacity, at which point increasing marginal costs might have been experienced. In other words the conclusion that costs are linear might apply only within the ranges of output for which the data were collected. An alternative conclusion is that marginal costs are constant up to capacity, at which point further increases in output are impossible (one might say that the marginal cost curve becomes vertical).

Other criticisms are that the statistical methods used in these studies may show a bias toward linearity, and that the constancy of marginal costs is inconsistent with some observed market behavior. A fuller discussion of these criticisms will appear in the chapter on costs. It is enough for our present purposes to indicate some misgivings about the widespread findings of linearity in statistical cost studies, and to reiterate, despite these misgivings, that the evidence favors the conclusion that constant marginal costs are widespread within the usually experienced ranges of output.

3. THE CONCEPT OF TIME PERSPECTIVE

So widely known are the economic concepts of the long run and short run that they have become part of everyday language. The economist uses these terms with a precision that is often missed in ordinary dis-

---

[14] J. A. Nordin, "Note on a Light Plant's Cost Curves," *Econometrica*, July, 1947, pp. 231–35.

cussion. In the parlance of economics, a decision is long run if it involves possible variations in all inputs. Such would be the case in building an entirely new plant. Decisions are short run if some of the inputs remain fixed while others may be varied. An illustration is the increase in the output of a department that requires variation in the quantity of labor and materials but not the amount of floor space or the number of machines.

Expressing the distinction between the long run and short run by emphasizing different kinds of decisions is not usual in economic theory. But it fits the purposes of managerial economics; it brings out clearly that there are a variety of short runs according to what is fixed and what is variable. The neat dichotomy between the short and long runs breaks down in actual practice. What remains is an estimate of those costs that will and those that will not be affected by the decision under consideration.

Managerial economists are concerned with the short-run and long-run effects of decisions on revenues as well as costs. The line between short-run and long-run revenue (or demand) is even fuzzier than that for costs. The really important problem in decision making is to maintain the right balance between the long-run, short-run, and intermediate-run perspectives.[15] A decision may be made on the basis of short-run considerations, but may, as time passes, have long-run repercussions that make it more or less profitable than it at first seemed. An illustration may make this clear.

Let us consider a firm with temporary idle capacity. A possible order for 10,000 units comes to management's attention. The prospective customer is willing to pay $2 per unit, or $20,000 for the whole lot, but no more. The short-run incremental cost (which ignores the fixed costs) is only $1.50. Therefore, the contribution to overhead and profit is $.50 per unit ($5,000 for the lot). But the long-run repercussions of the order must be taken into account:

1. If the management commits itself to a series of repeat orders at the same price, in time the so-called fixed costs may become variable. For example, it eventually will become necessary to replace the machinery. In fact, the gradual accumulation of orders may require an addition to capacity, with added depreciation and top-level supervision.

2. Acceptance of this order might have other kinds of long-run repercussions. If other customers find out about this low price they may demand equal treatment. Such customers may object that they are being treated unfairly and may transfer to suppliers with firmer "ethical" views on pricing. The shading of prices under conditions of excess capacity

---

[15] Another way of expressing this point is that management should take a long-range view of effects on costs and revenues rather than merely a "shortsighted" view.

may undermine the company "image" in the minds of the clientele, giving a picture of a cut-throat competitor rather than that of a stable, dependable supplier.

Again it is possible to summarize the discussion in the form of a principle, which we call the principle of time perspective: *a decision should take into account both the short-run and long-run effects on revenues and costs, giving appropriate weight to the most relevant time periods.* The real problem is determining how to apply this general principle in specific decision-making situations.

Empirical studies and illustrations

Several illustrations should suffice to indicate the rather complex interrelations between the short and long runs on both the cost and demand sides and how such considerations are important in decision making.

Tennessee Valley Authority rate reductions. The Tennessee Valley Authority introduced sharp rate reductions soon after its formation. Table 2–1 presents data on electricity consumption and revenues at a number of locations before and after the rate reductions. As the reader can verify by examining the data, consumption did rise (in fact it rose more than the national average); but the rise in consumption was not sufficient to offset the rate reduction. One might conclude from Table 2–1 that the rate reduction was unprofitable, the data indicating clearly why the private utilities which preceded the TVA did not reduce rates. A longer-run perspective might, however, lead to quite a different conclusion, for the period covered by the data is too short to allow a full adjustment to the lower rates. It takes time to wire additional homes and to install new appliances. Data for a longer period show a much greater response to the rate reduction and thus contradict the conclusion implied by Table 2–1 (though it is clear that a rapid increase in consumption would have taken place in any case, the national trend being upward; it would be necessary to correct the data for trend to obtain the true response of consumption to rates).

A printing company's refusal to price below full cost. A printing company included in a study made by the author maintained a policy of never quoting prices below full cost despite the fact that it frequently experienced idle capacity and that the management was aware that the incremental cost was far below full cost. The management had given considerable thought to the problem and had concluded that the long-run repercussions of going below full cost would more than offset any short-run gain. The reduction in rates for some customers might have an undesirable effect on customer "goodwill," especially among regular customers who might not benefit from the price reductions. Secondly, management argued that the availability of idle capacity was unpredictable and that by the time the order became firm the situation might

TABLE 2-1

AVERAGE CONSUMPTION, NUMBER OF CUSTOMERS, TOTAL REVENUE, AND AVERAGE REVENUE PER KILOWATT-HOUR, BEFORE AND AFTER INTRODUCTION OF TVA RATES

A	B	C	Average Consumption per Customer (Kilowatt-Hours)		Number of Customers		Total Consumption (Kilowatt-Hours)		Total Revenue		Average Revenue (Cents per Kilowatt-Hour)	
Contractor	Date TVA Service Began	Months TVA Rates in Effect at June 30, 1935	Month Prior to TVA	June, 1935	Month Prior to TVA	June, 1935	Month Prior to TVA	June, 1935	Month Prior to TVA	June, 1935	Month Prior to TVA	June, 1935
Tupelo, Mississippi	February 7, 1934	17	49	112	955	1,241	46,398	138,570	$3,436	$2,849	7.4	2.1
Alcorn County Electric Power Association	June 1, 1934	13	49	101	1,180	1,519	58,288	153,880	3,129	3,298	5.4	2.1
Athens, Alabama	June 1, 1934	13	51	112	521	712	26,589	79,667	1,464	1,655	5.5	2.1
Pontotoc County Electric Power Association	June 1, 1934	13	33	71	311	450	10,158	31,985	648	781	6.4	2.4
New Albany, Mississippi ..	November 12, 1934	7	43	75	539	577	22,896	43,021	1,553	1,028	6.8	2.4
Pulaski, Tennessee	January 4, 1935	6	49	84	477	531	23,581	44,431	1,370	991	5.8	2.2
Dayton, Tennessee	February 1, 1935	5	40	53	451	480	17,995	25,457	1,132	680	6.3	2.7

SOURCE: Tennessee Valley Authority, *Statistical Bulletin* No. VII, December, 1935, as reprinted in M. P. McNair and R. S. Meriam, *Problems in Business Economics* (New York: McGraw-Hill Book Co., 1941), p. 94.

change, with an interference of low-price orders with regular-price business. The management wished to avoid the "image" of a firm that exploited the market when demand was favorable and that was willing to negotiate prices downward when demand was unfavorable.

It would be difficult to demonstrate that management's reasoning on pricing was correct, but at least the argument is plausible. On the other hand there was evidence that the management did not always enforce its policy consistently. It admitted that in special cases it regretfully broke away from its policy. And sometimes it performed special services (such as editing manuscripts) without charge, a practice which amounts to a hidden form of price reduction. Despite these reservations, this illustration does point up the need to consider the long-run as well as the short-run impact of price policy.

4. THE DISCOUNTING PRINCIPLE

One of the fundamental ideas in economics is that a dollar tomorrow is worth less than a dollar today. This appears similar to the saying that a bird in the hand is worth two in the bush. This analogy might be misleading, implying that the reason for discounting the future dollars is the uncertainty about receiving them. Even under conditions of certainty it would still be necessary to discount future dollars to make them comparable with present dollars.

A simple illustration should make clear the necessity of discounting. Suppose you are offered a choice between a gift of $100 today or $100 next year. Naturally you will select the $100 today. This is true, as has been stated, even if there is certainty about the receipt of either gift, since today's $100 can be invested and can accumulate interest during the year. Let us suppose that you can earn 5 percent interest on any money you have at your disposal. By the end of the year it will accumulate interest to become a total of $105.

There is another way of putting the matter that brings out the discounting principle more forcefully. We might ask how much money today would be equivalent to $100 a year from now. Again assume a rate of interest of 5 percent. We discount the $100 at 5 percent, which means that we divide it by 1.05. Thus

$$V = \frac{\$100}{1+i} = \frac{\$100}{1.05} = \$95.24$$

where

$$V = \text{present value}$$
$$i = \text{the rate of interest}$$

As a cross check for those who are unfamiliar with the discounting principle, we can multiply the $95.24 by 1.05 to determine how much money will have accumulated during the year at 5 percent. The answer is $100.

$$\$95.24 \times 1.05 = \$100$$

This shows that $95.24 plus the interest on $95.24 will accumulate to an amount exactly equal to $100; a person who can earn 5 percent on his money should be indifferent in choosing between the two bundles of money—$100 a year from now or $95.24 today. The present value of $100 is thus $95.24.

The same kind of reasoning applies to longer periods. A sum of $100 two years from now is worth

$$V = \frac{\$100}{(1+i)^2} = \frac{\$100}{(1.05)^2} = \frac{\$100}{1.1025} = \$90.70$$

Again we can check by computing how much the cumulative interest on $90.70 would be after two years.

We can now establish a general formula for the present value of a sum to be received at any future date.

$$V = \frac{R_n}{(1+i)^n}$$

in which

$V =$ present value
$R =$ the amount to be received in the future
$i =$ the rate of interest
$n =$ the number of years elapsing before the receipt of R

If the receipts are spread over a period of years the formula becomes:

$$V = \frac{R_1}{1+i} + \frac{R_2}{(1+i)^2} + \frac{R_3}{(1+i)^3} + \cdots\cdots + \frac{R_n}{(1+i)^n}$$

Another form of the same formula is:

$$V = \sum_{k=1}^{n} \frac{R_k}{(1+i)^k}$$

when k can take on any value from 1 through n.

It will be necessary to refer to and elaborate on these formulas, especially in the chapter on investment decisions. For present purposes, however, the need is not so much the memorization of a formula as it is the grasp of a fundamental concept. The main point in this section may be summarized in a principle, which we shall call the discounting principle: *If a decision affects costs and revenues at future dates, it is necessary to discount those costs and revenues to present values before a valid comparison of alternatives is possible.*

Empirical studies and illustrations

The practice of discounting is pervasive and observable in everyday business practice. The simplest case of discounting is that when one borrows on a note at the bank. If the note is for $1,000 the borrower does not receive the full amount but rather that amount discounted at the appropriate rate of interest. If the discount rate is 6 percent and the note for one year, the borrower will receive approximately $942. One might say that the present value to the bank of the borrower's promise to pay $1,000 in a year is only $942 at the time of the loan.

The bond market also illustrates the discounting principle in operation. The market price of a particular bond reflects not only the face value of the bond at maturity and the interest payments but also the current discount rate. As the market discount rates vary, bond prices vary inversely in a definite mathematical relation to those discount rates. (One could as well say that the market discount rates reflect the changes in bond prices, for discount rates and bond prices move simultaneously with changes in the market conditions.)

Real estate prices reflect the discounting principle, though in a more complicated and less obvious way. The rational way to determine what one will pay for a piece of property is to estimate the future returns he expects, which may in the case of a home be primarily subjective in character. One will discount those future returns at the current cost of capital[16] to reflect the sacrifice of alternative earnings. The market value of the real estate is determined by the interaction of such discounted present values set on the property by the various potential buyers and sellers. Even such rules of thumb as "an apartment house should sell at ten times annual rentals" are rough approximations of the discounting principle.

The same principle of discounting should apply to the operations of an individual firm, though considerable uncertainy about the future revenues and appropriate discount rates necessarily exists. If a firm is considering buying a new piece of equipment, it should estimate the discounted value of the added earnings from that equipment. (Chapter 9 goes into this problem more fully.) If it is considering the purchase of another firm, or a merger, the same principle of valuation applies. And, as we shall see, if it produces outputs that mature at varying ages, it cannot compare the profitability of changing the product mix without invoking the discounting principle.

---

[16] A full discussion of the cost of capital appears in Chapter 9.

5. THE OPPORTUNITY COST CONCEPT

The next concept, opportunity cost, is also self-evident when stated simply but sometimes less obvious when it comes to practical application. The reflection of opportunity costs in the accounts is far from simple; in fact, it probably is impossible to devise a programmed system of accounts that will routinely provide accurate estimates of opportunity costs.

By the opportunity cost of a decision is meant the sacrifice of alternatives required by that decision. The best way to pin down the meaning of this term is to provide some specific illustrations:

1. The opportunity cost of the funds tied up in one's own business is the interest (or profits corrected for differences in risk) that could be earned on those funds in other ventures.

2. The opportunity cost of the time one puts into his own business is the salary he could earn in other occupations (with a correction for the relative "psychic income" in the two occupations).

3. The opportunity cost of using a machine to produce one product is the sacrifice of earnings that would be possible from other products.

4. The opportunity cost of using a machine that is useless for any other purpose is nil, since its use requires no sacrifice of other opportunities.

5. The opportunity cost of using idle space is obviously less than that of use of the space that is needed for other activities.

It follows from the above that opportunity costs require the measurement of *sacrifices*. If a decision involves no sacrifices, it is cost free. The expenditure of cash (for raw materials, for example) involves a sacrifice of other possible expenditures, and therefore is an opportunity cost as defined here. Under this broad definition, the only costs that are relevant for decision making are opportunity costs.

In a sense the opportunity cost concept is the most fundamental of all cost concepts. Indeed, one can argue that it should have come first in this chapter. We should include in incremental cost or marginal cost only measurements of additional *sacrifices* required by a decision. If an increase in output requires no expansion of the factory but merely uses idle space, we make no sacrifice by using that space; we need not include a charge for its use; the opportunity cost of its use is nil and therefore we exclude it from the estimate of incremental cost. Similarly, the rate of discount that we use to compute present values is really an opportunity cost rate; but this is a point which might best be postponed to later chapters.

Closely related to this discussion of opportunity costs is a useful distinction between explicit and implicit costs. Explicit costs are those that are recognized in the accounts, as would be true of payments for raw materials and, usually, for labor. Implicit (or imputed) costs are those sacrifices (such as the interest on the owners' own investment) that are not recognized in the accounts. Some writers use the term opportunity costs narrowly to refer only to the second category: the implicit costs. There are strong arguments, however, for our broader definition to include all sacrifices, whether implicit or explicit.

To complicate matters slightly, some explicit expenses may not involve sacrifices of alternatives. For example, a company may pay wages to idle labor in periods of slack activity. These wages are in the nature of a fixed cost and are not included in the opportunity cost in a decision to use that labor in producing for a special order.

The discussion in this section can be summarized in another principle, which we shall call the opportunity cost principle: *The cost involved in any decision consists of the sacrifices of alternatives required by that decision. If there are no sacrifices, there is no cost.*

Empirical studies and illustrations

The question of whether managers actually use opportunity cost reasoning is not one amenable to exact empirical test. It is obvious that most of them are continually weighing alternatives, which means that they are at least resorting to rough subjective evaluations of opportunity costs. Some modern mathematical models in use in large progressive firms either implicitly or explicitly incorporate opportunity cost considerations; this is true of linear programming allocation models and of replacement models. But casual observation indicates strongly that some managers fail to make correct analyses of opportunity costs. Traditional accounting techniques are poorly adapted to the reflection of opportunity costs. Cost accounting systems which allocate overhead on some predetermined basis, such as direct labor cost, fail to reflect varying availabilities of idle capacity. It is true that standard cost systems avoid the extreme error of increasing overhead allocations when volume is down, which would run absolutely counter to opportunity cost reasoning. But even standard overhead allocations fail to reflect the true sacrifices required by decisions. For example, such a system would not apply a lower percentage allocation to direct labor cost in a department that is half idle, even though the sacrifice in increasing the use of that department would be small.

In short, the practice in application of opportunity cost reasoning is variable. Perhaps the best that can be done here is to indicate some of the sophisticated ways in which the reasoning is being applied in management.

The simplex method.[17]   Since linear programming provides optimal solutions to the problem of choice among alternatives (assuming that the

---

[17] Perhaps the nonmathematical student should be assured that this illustration is quite simple and that it might serve as an elementary introduction to linear programming.

relevant functions are in fact linear), it follows that it must somehow take opportunity costs into account. The best known computational method for solving linear programming problems is known as the simplex method. Without going into a full exposition of the simplex method, it is possible to show how that technique does incorporate opportunity cost reasoning.

It is best for our purposes to work with a hypothetical illustration. Suppose a company has three departments, each with limited capacity. Department A has a capacity of 310 hours per week, Department B a capacity of 300 hours, and Department C a capacity of 500 hours. The firm is considering five products, each of which flows through all three departments but which requires different proportions of capacity. We need two kinds of information about these products: how much department time each product takes up per unit of output, and how much each contributes to overhead and profits. The last phrase should be of special interest, for it indicates that we are applying incremental reasoning: we need to know the *contribution* per unit *above marginal costs* (incremental costs per unit); we make no attempt to determine full cost. Table 2–2 presents the required information.

TABLE 2–2

CAPACITY REQUIREMENTS AND UNIT CONTRIBUTIONS FOR FIVE HYPOTHETICAL PRODUCTS

	Time Required per Unit			Contribution to Overhead and Profit per Unit
Product	Dept. A	Dept. B	Dept. C	
1.........................	3	4	5	$10
2.........................	5	4	10	18
3.........................	4	4	4	9
4.........................	8	4	10	15
5.........................	4	6	7	12

The optimal solution will usually involve not more than three products, equal to the number of the constraints (department capacities) in the problem. Suppose that somehow management has hit on one "feasible" solution, a solution that falls within the constraints. (A text on linear programming will supply several ways of finding such a solution.) This initial solution appears in Table 2–3. Note that all of the capacity is used up in the production of the three products. The total contribution to overhead and profit from this solution is the 20 units of product 1 times $10, plus the 30 units of product 2 times $18, plus the 25 units of product 3 times $9, which is

$$\$200 + \$540 + \$225 = \$965$$

TABLE 2–3

A FEASIBLE SOLUTION, LINEAR PROGRAMMING PROBLEM

Product	Quantity of Product in the Solution	Use of Department Capacity		
		Dept. A	Dept. B	Dept. C
1..........................	20	60	80	100
2..........................	30	150	120	300
3..........................	25	100	100	100
		310	300	500

The question now is whether a reshuffling of products will lead to an increase in profit. This is where the opportunity cost concept becomes significant. If the introduction of units of product 4, let us say, contributes more to overhead and profit than is sacrificed in terms of reduced production of the other products, it is profitable to introduce product 4. What is the opportunity cost of introducing one unit of product 4? First, it is necessary to determine physically how much of products 1, 2, and 3 must be given up to release capacity to produce one unit of product 4. The ratios indicating the amounts of sacrifice of products 1, 2, and 3 per unit of product 4 are known as *rates of substitution*. The simplex method of linear programming automatically provides these rates of substitution. Rather than go into the complexities of the computation, it is sufficient for our purpose to state that the rates of substitution for the introduction of one unit of product 4 are:

$$-\frac{18}{7} \text{ of product 1, } \frac{10}{7} \text{ of product 2, and } \frac{15}{7} \text{ of product 3.}[18]$$

Now it is possible to compute the opportunity cost of introducing one unit of product 4. This is done by multiplying each physical rate of substitution by the contribution per unit made by each of the original three products. The result is an opportunity cost of

$$-\frac{18}{7} \times \$10 + \frac{10}{7} \times \$18 + \frac{15}{7} \times \$9 = \$19.29$$

Since product 4 makes a contribution per unit of only $15, it is unprofitable to introduce it into the product mix; its opportunity cost exceeds its contribution.

The profitability of introducing product 5 can be tested in the same way. But the exposition so far is sufficient to demonstrate that opportunity cost reasoning is an integral part of linear programming.

---

[18] The negative rate of substitution means that bringing in product 4 also releases resources for a greater quantity of product 1. Readers who are impatient to learn about the computations of these ratios of substitution may wish to refer to pp. 629 ff.

Optimal use of water in a hydroelectric system. Electric utilities which own hydroelectric dams also operate steam-generating plants. They face a choice of using hydro power or steam power or some combination of the two. It is relatively easy to measure the cost of generating power in a steam plant, though the correct handling of depreciation may present some difficulty. But the cost of producing hydro power is much more troubling. After all, the dams are already built; their costs of construction are sunk and are irrelevant in making decisions for the future. The same is true of the expensive generators, on which wear-and-tear is probably a small cost relative to the original price of the generators. And water is a "free gift of nature." Why not run the water through the generators as rapidly as possible and minimize the use of the steam plants?

Merely posing the question should suggest the solution to the problem. The use of the water behind a dam is *not* cost free, for it does require a sacrifice. Water used today cannot be used tomorrow, its use today involves an opportunity cost. Looking at the matter another way, the water behind a dam has value based on its capacity to produce power in the future.

Suppose a utility owns one hydroelectric dam and three steam plants. The three steam plants vary in efficiency, the new plant burning less coal per kilowatt-hour than the old ones. To meet the peak-load requirements all three plants and the dam must operate near capacity. To meet lower loads it is possible to cut off either the high-cost plants or the hydroelectric dam, or both. Running the water through the generators in off-peak periods would run the risk of not having enough stored-up water for peak periods. The sacrifice (opportunity cost) would be a measure of the loss of revenue and customer dissatisfaction that might result. In addition, the operation of the high-cost steam plants involves a sacrifice in the inefficient burning of fuel. The flow of water should be regulated so as to minimize this sacrifice.

If the utility has additional objectives, such as flood control or maintenance of navigation (as is true of some public power systems), the analysis becomes more complex but the basic principles are the same. The stored-up water has value; its use involves an opportunity cost.

6. THE EQUIMARGINAL PRINCIPLE

One of the widest known principles of economics is the proposition that an input should be allocated so that the value added by the last unit is the same in all uses. We shall call this generalization the equimarginal principle.

Let us consider a case in which a firm has 100 units of labor at its disposal. For purposes of simplicity we shall assume this amount to be fixed, so that the total payroll is predetermined. The firm is involved in five activities which require labor services—activities A, B, C, D, and E. It can increase any one of these activities by adding more labor, but only at the sacrifice of other activities.

If we add a unit of labor to activity C, an increase in output results. Let us call the value of this added output the value of the marginal product of labor in activity C.[19] Similarly we can estimate the value of the marginal product in activities A, B, D, and E. It should be clear that if the value of the marginal product is greater in one activity than another, an optimum has not been achieved. It would be possible to shift labor from low marginal value to high marginal value uses, thus increasing the total value of all products taken together. If, for example, the value of the marginal product of labor in activity A is $10, while that in activity B is $15, it is profitable to increase activity B and reduce activity A. The optimum is reached when the value of the marginal product is equal in all activities. In terms of symbols this is when

$$VMP_{LA} = VMP_{LB} = VMP_{LC} = VMP_{LD} = VMP_{LE}$$

in which the subscript L indicates labor and the other subscripts identify the activities.

An elaboration of the equimarginal principle

We need to clarify several aspects of the equimarginal principle. First, we must note that the values of the marginal products in our formula are *net* of incremental costs (the incremental costs do not include the cost of the input which is being allocated). In activity A we may add one unit of labor, with an increase in physical output of 100 units. Each unit is worth $.25, so that the 100 units will sell for $25. But the increased production consumes raw materials, fuel, and other inputs, so that the variable costs in activity A (not counting the labor cost) are higher. Let's say that the incremental costs are $15, leaving a net addition of $10. The value of the marginal product which is relevant for our purposes is this $10.

If the revenues which result from the addition of labor are to be in the future, it is necessary to discount those revenues before comparisons in the alternative activities are possible. Activity C might not produce its revenue for five years while activity D will produce its revenue almost immediately. The discounting of these revenues will make them comparable.

The whole subject of capital budgeting, to be taken up in Chapter 9, is based on the principles just reviewed. In capital budgeting the resource

---

[19] We shall ignore certain refinements at this point, such as the distinction between the value of the marginal product and the marginal revenue product.

to be allocated consists of the funds available to the firm (rather than labor). The objective is to apply the funds where the discounted values of the marginal products are greatest, expanding the high-value activities and contracting the low-value activities until an equality of marginal values is achieved.

Implicit in the discussion up to this point is diminishing returns to the inputs which are being allocated. This point deserves closer attention. One of the most fundamental of all generalizations in economics is the "law of diminishing returns" (also known as the law of variable proportions). It states that as quantities of variable inputs are added to fixed quantities of other inputs the marginal product eventually declines. To return to our earlier illustration, as more labor is added to activity A, we expect the value of the marginal product of labor to decline, as shown in Figure 2–4.

FIGURE 2–4

DIMINISHING RETURNS TO LABOR

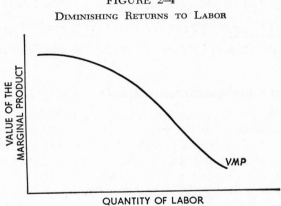

We would expect the law of diminishing returns to apply to the other activities in the same way, though each marginal product curve will have a somewhat different shape depending on technology. Figure 2–5 shows the five marginal product curves simultaneously. Suppose that we allocate twenty units of labor to each activity, as shown in Figure 2–5. Clearly we have not equated the values of the marginal products—the value in activity E is much higher than the others. It is profitable to transfer labor to E, away from A and C especially; the addition to the value of E is higher than the reductions in the values of A and C. By reshuffling labor in this way, we reach an optimum in which the values of the marginal products are equal in all activities.[20] The optimum is shown in Figure 2–6.

Several complications which are often important in practice can re-

―――――――――

[20] We assume that the labor is divisible so that fractional amounts can be allocated to the activities.

FIGURE 2–5

MARGINAL PRODUCT CURVES FOR FIVE ACTIVITIES

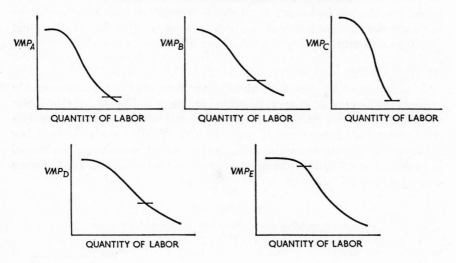

FIGURE 2–6

OPTIMAL ALLOCATION OF LABOR TO FIVE ACTIVITIES

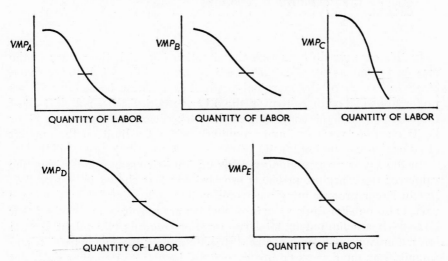

ceive only passing attention in this introductory chapter. One is that the measurement of the value of the marginal product may have to be corrected if the expansion of an activity requires a reduction in the price of the output. If activity A represents the production of radios, but it is impossible to sell more radios without a reduction in price, it is neces-

sary to adjust for the change in price. Another complication is complementarity of demand, when an increase in the availability of one product
stimulates the sales of another. Similarly if products are complementary
in production a more involved analysis is required. But the equimarginal
principle still applies after the necessary adjustments are made.

Constant marginal products

In many cases the law of diminishing returns may not operate exactly
as described so far. It may be possible for a firm to increase the quantity
of labor in one department without encountering diminishing marginal
production until some limit of capacity is reached or until all the labor
is employed. The curve for the value of the marginal product is horizontal
in such a case up to full capacity at which point it drops to zero. Figure
2–7 represents this situation for five activities.

FIGURE 2–7

CONSTANT MARGINAL PRODUCTS IN FIVE ACTIVITIES

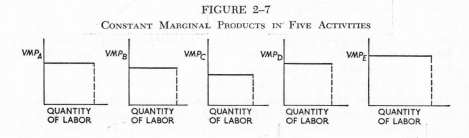

In this case we do not reach the situation in which the values of the
marginal products are equal in all activities unless there is labor to spare.
Since the value of the marginal product is greatest in activity E, we
prefer to use labor there than in the other activities. Why not shift all of
the labor to E? Some constraint, such as a limit of the capacity in E, or
limits on other variable inputs required, may set a limit on the amount
of labor that can be used in E.

In the linear programming models an implicit assumption is that the
values of the marginal products are horizontal as shown in Figure 2–7.
But in linear programming we would not be allocating labor alone; we
would also be allocating other inputs which are required along with labor
but which are limited in total supply. For example, we might have a
limited amount of floor space to distribute among the five activities, and
a limited amount of assembly capacity. Linear programming does not
equate the values of the marginal product of labor in the five activities,
but does allocate labor and the other inputs to achieve a maximum contribution to profits.

The outcome of the discussion is this. We may retain the equimarginal
principle as long as diminishing returns are relevant. But when the values
of the marginal products are constant (horizontal), we need an alterna-

tive form of the principle, making use of inequalities rather than equalities. This form of the principle would read as follows: We should apply inputs first to activities with higher marginal product values before moving to lower values.

Empirical studies and illustrations

The equimarginal principle is an extremely practical idea despite the abstract appearance of the preceding discussion. It is behind any rational budgetary procedure. The objective of budgeting is (or should be) to allocate resources where they are most productive. But it is productivity at the margin rather than average productivity which is relevant. Even when productivity is extremely difficult to measure, the equimarginal principle must be applied in at least a rough or general way if one wishes to avoid waste in useless activities.

One of the clearest cases of the application of the principle is in investment decisions. Whatever criterion is used in making such decisions —whether it is a crude measure like the payback period or a refined measure like the present value—the aim is to separate investments with high rates of return from investments with low returns, so that the funds can be allocated accordingly.

At the opposite extreme is the allocation of research expenditures. The productivity of research is notoriously difficult to measure. In fact, some research organizations deliberately avoid measurements on the grounds that too careful a supervision and too great an eagerness to achieve results may actually interfere with fundamental research. One can never tell when research that appears to be highly theoretical and remote from practicality will eventually pay off. Nevertheless, the equimarginal principle is relevant in research. After all, a company does not hire research men indiscriminately. It selects men who promise to make a contribution to the company's line of activity. The company is likely to expand research activities which are beginning to pay off and to contract activities which appear to have passed their peak of usefulness. No doubt mistakes are made in this process, but the failure to make any comparisons of potential productivity can only lead to diffusion of expenditure on nonessentials.

A recent study based on an analysis of research and development in 120 firms suggests that more systematic evaluations of research are possible.[21] While one must not expect pinpoint precision in estimating the worth of alternative lines of research—and in many cases only qualitative estimates are possible—it is nevertheless possible to rank different types of research. Many companies budget research as a given percentage of sales, others follow a rule of increasing such expenditures

---

[21] J. B. Quinn, "How to Evaluate Research Output," *Harvard Business Review,* March–April, 1960, pp. 69–80; and "Long-Range Planning of Industrial Research," *Harvard Business Review,* July–August, 1961, pp. 88–102.

by a fixed percentage, but it makes more sense to evaluate each research program individually.

The same type of reasoning is (or should be) applied in budgeting for universities. It might be objected that universities are not operated for profit and that they are engaged in relatively immeasurable activities. But surely the expansion of the budget in any department is subject to diminishing returns. And surely some rough comparisons of the value of the marginal product from department to department are possible. In one university known to the author, several departments were expanded to the point that the marginal product must have been close to zero—the evidence was that some of the faculty members did no teaching and apparently had negligible duties of any character, research or otherwise. In the same university, several other departments were in a decline because of an inability to retain key staff members. Any casual observer could see that the marginal products were quite different from department to department and that the university's resources were misallocated.

One great enemy of the equimarginal principle is the stress on averages. It is irrational, for example, to budget advertising expenditure on the basis of some average percentage of sales. Such a policy would result in lower advertising in poor times than in prosperity, when the opposite practice might be more profitable. There is no reason to suppose that advertising expenditures on one product must hold the same ratio to sales as for another product—the responsiveness may be quite different for one than for another. Similarly, the averaging of budget increases over all departments is unlikely to be consistent with the equimarginal principle. Some departments can make highly productive use of additional resources, while other departments may actually be due for cutbacks of less essential activities.

Another enemy of the equimarginal principle consists of a variety of sociological pressures. Inertia is one—activities are continued simply because they exist. Empire building is another—activities expand to fulfill the needs of managers for power. Unfortunately, departments which are already overbudgeted often use some of their excess resources to build up propaganda machines (public relations offices) to win additional support. Perhaps governmental agencies, which are less subject to constant tests in the market, are more prone to distortions in the allocation of resources due to an overstress on averaging, to inertia, and to bureaucratic self-perpetuation.

7. THE CONTRIBUTION CONCEPT

The concepts presented so far are not independent of each other; we have already seen how the opportunity cost concept overlaps several others. This is also true of the contribution concept, which is merely a convenient way of presenting ideas discussed earlier in this chapter. In fact the expression "contribution to overhead and profits" has already been used several times. Since one of the most important innovations in the language of management in recent decades has been the introduction of the idea of contributions, it deserves special attention despite the duplication which results.

The simplest case to consider is that of a product the price of which is determined by outside forces—by competition or by regulatory agencies. Let us assume this price is $95. Within the firm, the total cost, including allocated overheads is $103, but the incremental cost is only $75. The "loss" on the item appears to be $8 and the temptation is to drop the product. But the contribution to overhead and profits is $20. Some further analysis is in order.

The mere fact that the contribution is positive does not prove that the product should be retained. If the company has a backlog of orders on products requiring the same production time per unit and if these products earn contributions of $50 or $40 or $30, we certainly won't wish to sacrifice these larger contributions in favor of a $20 one.[22] But it is the comparison of contributions which is important, not the comparison of profits or losses based on full costs.

Most products vary one from another in production requirements; the simple comparison of contributions in the above illustration is inadequate in such a case. An item which contributes $50 may be less profitable than one which contributes only $20 if it uses up much more of the company's capacity. This suggests that the measurement of contribution per unit of output is inappropriate in most cases.

If a company has only one bottleneck in production, let us say in machine hours available, we can convert the contributions per unit of output into contributions per machine hour. Table 2–4 presents such a situation in a company producing five products.

TABLE 2–4

CONTRIBUTIONS ON FIVE PRODUCTS IN A SINGLE PLANT

Product	Price	Incremental Cost	Contribution per Unit	Machine Minutes Requirements
A	$15.00	$10.00	$5.00	60 minutes
B	14.00	8.00	6.00	80
C	13.00	9.00	4.00	40
D	12.00	7.50	4.50	30
E	6.00	2.50	3.50	15

---

[22] Other factors will influence the decision, such as the desire to maintain a complete "product line" or to retain the goodwill of an old customer.

At first glance Product B appears to be best; it produces a contribution larger than elsewhere and presumably deserves the first priority in allocation of capacity. But Product B uses up more capacity for each unit produced. Clearly we must convert the contributions to make them comparable. One way to do this is to convert them into contributions per hour of machine time. The results are as follows:

Product A .... $ 5 per machine hour
Product B 5
Product C 6
Product D 9
Product E 14

These results indicate the Product E, which at first appeared to be the lowest contributor, is in fact the largest. The priorities should be almost the opposite of those which appear at first glance. If this illustration seems farfetched, it should be stated that in actual practice the order of contributions are frequently quite different from those suggested by casual observation.

Suppose, however, that more than one capacity bottleneck appears. If all five products pass through four processes, each of which can be the bottleneck, it is no longer possible to compute simple contributions in terms of one of the bottlenecks. The problem becomes one in linear programming.

Normally the application of contributions to overhead and profits rests on an assumed linearity of revenues and costs. As in the above illustration, the price and unit cost are assumed to be independent of output. The unit incremental cost remains the same until the demand is satisfied or the capacity is used up. If the quantity demanded increases at lower prices or if the incremental cost varies at different levels of output, the problem becomes more complicated but the contribution idea is still useful. For example, one can compare Product E's contribution of $3.50 at a price of $6 with its contribution of $3 at a price of $5.50. If sales at the higher price are 10,000 units and at the lower price are 30,000 units, the total contribution from Product E increases from $35,000 to $90,000. It may be desirable to accept the lower unit contribution to obtain the higher volume even if other lower contribution products are sacrificed.

Empirical studies and illustrations

Twenty years ago the expression "contribution to overhead and profits" was almost unknown, although many managers were in fact using the idea without giving it a name. Today the term has become part of the vocabulary of management; one can say that a manager who does not understand contributions is probably not very proficient in modern cost analysis. Probably the term is used most widely in product mix decisions and pricing decisions, but it is also applicable to make or buy and other decisions. The "cash flows" which are estimated in capital budgeting are closely related to the contribution concept, as we shall see in the chapter on capital budgeting.

As has been stated, the contribution concept is applicable when linear programming is used to solve product mix problems. A mathematical friend of the author's confesses that he applied linear programming in solving a textile mill's production problems without knowing the difference between full cost and incremental cost. The profitability estimates he used in the solution were profits above full costs rather than contributions above incremental costs. His solution was wrong, for no mathematical technique can correct for incorrect data.

It may be useful to push the linear programming illustration a little further. By introducing the elements of linear programming in bits as the economic aspects are introduced, the reader will be in a better position to study the more comprehensive treatment of linear programming in later chapters. It is important to recognize that linear programming is not a subject completely independent of the concepts of incremental cost, contributions, or opportunity costs, but is in fact a sophisticated way to incorporate those concepts in a mathematical form.

The initial step in linear programming is to set up the fundamental equations of the problem. Let us use the same contributions shown in Table 2–4 but this time assume four bottleneck departments rather than one. These are the four constraints. The basic data are shown in Table 2–5.

TABLE 2–5

DATA ON FIVE PRODUCTS TO BE PRODUCED IN FOUR DEPARTMENTS

Product	Contribution per Unit	Machine Hours per Unit			
		Dept. 1	Dept. 2	Dept. 3	Dept. 4
A	$5.00	1.00	.50	1.00	.50
B	6.00	1.33	.60	1.00	1.00
C	4.00	.67	.70	1.00	.50
D	4.50	.50	.80	1.00	1.00
E	3.50	.25	.90	1.00	.50

We are now in a position to set up the "objective equation." If the objective is to maximize the contribution to overhead and profits from the products, the objective equation is

$$Z = 5.00X_A + 6.00X_B + 4.00X_C + 4.50X_D + 3.50X_E = \text{maximum}$$

in which

$$Z = \text{total contribution}$$
$$X_A = \text{output of Product A}$$
$$X_B = \text{output of Product B}$$
$$X_C = \text{output of Product C}$$
$$X_D = \text{output of Product D}$$
$$X_E = \text{output of Product E}$$

Next we set up a series of inequations for each of the constraints—for each of the bottleneck departments. Suppose that the capacities in the four departments are:

Department 1 . . . . 18,000 machine hours
Department 2 15,000
Department 3 24,000
Department 4 20,000

The number of hours used up by each product in each department cannot exceed the capacity of that department. This condition can be expressed mathematically in the form of four inequations,

$$1.00X_A + 1.33X_B + .67X_C + .50X_D + .25X_E \leqq 18{,}000$$
$$.50X_A + .60X_B + .70X_C + .80X_D + .90X_E \leqq 15{,}000$$
$$1.00X_A + 1.00X_B + 1.00X_C + 1.00X_D + 1.00X_E \leqq 24{,}000$$
$$.50X_A + 1.00X_B + .50X_C + 1.00X_D + .50X_E \leqq 20{,}000$$

Each of these inequations states that the sum of the machine hours used up by the five products must be "less than or equal to" the capacity of each department.

It is not necessary for our purpose here to show how to reach a solution. The task from this point is a mechanical one which can be turned over to a clerk who is familiar with the simplex method, computer programming, or other methods of solving the problem. The point to note here is that the objective equation makes use of the same contribution concept which is applied in other applications of managerial economics. But one cannot maximize the contributions without taking all of the constraints into account. Linear programming provides a method of solving such problems when the outputs are independent because they use the same capacities.

8. SOME IMPORTANT APPLICATIONS

This entire volume is devoted to applications of the foregoing analysis to a variety of decisions. It is possible at this point to introduce some elementary but significant applications of the basic concepts: incremental costs, opportunity costs, the long and short runs, discounting, and the equimarginal principle.

Make or buy

Decisions to make or buy are among the most pervasive in industry. The question of purchasing on the outside or producing within the firm requires a direct application of the principles discussed so far, but the issues are complicated by a wide variety of considerations, as we shall see.

The advice that one should make or buy depending on which alternative is cheaper is not very helpful; the term "cheaper" is ambiguous. The costs of making or buying can be measured in a variety of ways; the following is only a partial list of the possible cost measurements.[23]

The Cost to Make	*The Cost to Buy*
1. Labor and materials.	1. The purchase price.
2. Labor, materials, and other variable expenses.	2. Purchase price plus delivery expense.
3. Labor, materials, other variable costs, and factory overhead.	3. Purchase price, delivery expense, plus receiving and handling expense.
4. Labor, materials, other variable costs, factory overhead, and selling expense.	4. Purchase price, delivery expense, receiving and handling expense, plus buying costs.
5. Labor, materials, other variable costs, factory overhead, selling expense, and general overhead.	5. Purchase price, delivery expense, receiving and handling expense, buying costs, plus costs of inspection.

The fact is that some of these measurements are appropriate part of the time and others are needed under different circumstances. The problem is to determine the impact of the decision on costs—the estimation of the incremental costs. Professor Culliton, the leading writer on make or buy, suggests three alternative methods of determining the impact of the decision; all three are variations on the incremental approach developed in this volume.

Complete budgets. This method projects the costs of the entire firm under the two alternatives. This would reveal the difference in costs, which is, of course, what is required in incremental reasoning. The method is rather cumbersome for decision-making purposes; time can be saved by narrowing attention to the cost areas most likely to be affected by the decision.

Localized budgets. This method restricts attention to the area of the business directly affected by the decision to make or buy. When the analysis within this area is complete, it is possible to adjust for changes in costs in other segments of the business.

Incremental cost method. This method requires estimates of changes

---

[23] Adapted from James W. Culliton, *Make or Buy* (Harvard University, Bureau of Business Research, 1942), p. 8.

in costs brought about by the decision to make or buy. It differs from the other methods in that it starts at the beginning with estimates of changes in particular costs, rather than totaling up costs before computing the differences.

All three methods, if properly interpreted and adjusted, result in the same conclusion. Professor Culliton prefers the second method, but this preference results from his interpretation of the incremental method as ignoring possible changes in the so-called fixed expenses. In this volume we define incremental costs to include *all* changes in costs and even require that it take into account both long-run and short-run impacts. Under this interpretation the distinction between the second and third methods becomes blurred and we shall treat them as one.

Professor Culliton recommends that the analysis concentrate on changes in total costs rather than unit costs. Unit costs require an averaging that often obscures what is happening to the totals and thus confuses the decision maker.

The chief source of confusion in the analysis of costs is in the treatment of burden or overhead. In all probability some of the so-called overhead costs will be affected and others unaffected, creating the necessity of determining which fall into the changing or unchanging categories. To increase the complexity of the problem, some costs may be unaffected in the short run but may increase in the long run. For example, a decision to make a part may absorb some short-run capacity; but if this capacity is needed for other purposes in the future, restriction of attention to the short run is in error. To put the matter in another way, it is necessary to consider the opportunity costs of each alternative, and one opportunity cost of making is the absorption of capacity that may in the future be useful for other products.

Decisions to make or buy should take into account a variety of special considerations which complicate the analysis.

Quality. The firm may be able to achieve greater control over quality by manufacturing the part itself. The result is a reduction in assembly costs or an increase in customer goodwill and future sales which should be a part of a complete incremental analysis. Alternatively, the firm may not require as high a quality as outsiders are supplying and can bring quality and costs into line by manufacturing itself. On the other hand, the specialized knowledge of outside suppliers may exceed the know-how within the firm, so that the firm cannot match the outside quality.

Assurance of supply. The firm may be able to coordinate the flow of parts more effectively by producing at home. Some suppliers are undependable and others are unable to keep up with demand. If the firm has access to several or many suppliers, this argument for making the part becomes less persuasive. In any case the total impact on costs, including the costs of disrupted production, and the total impact on revenue, including the effect of changed customer goodwill, should be estimated.

Defense against monopoly.   A firm may manufacture parts to protect itself against a monopoly in supply. A mere threat to manufacture may in some cases suffice to restrain suppliers from overcharging, but threats must be backed up with demonstrations that the firm is competent to do the job.

The argument that a firm should make parts to fill in the excess capacity created by cyclical or seasonal fluctuations in demand is simply a special application of incremental-opportunity cost reasoning. Excess capacity means that the incremental overhead costs of manufacturing are small and that the sacrifices of alternative opportunities are limited. But the effect on supplier goodwill and the resulting difficulties of obtaining supplies in good times must be reckoned with.

Thus, complete incremental reasoning requires the evaluation of a number of subtle considerations that might at first be overlooked: customer goodwill, supplier goodwill, internal know-how, administrative and technical skills, and the risk that the costs of unimportant sidelines in manufacture might not be controlled satisfactorily. Students of the problem think that there may be a tendency to overlook some of the less measurable advantages of outside supply and to exaggerate the economies of internal manufacture.

Slowly maturing products[24]

Economic analysis usually rests on the assumption that the firm uses inputs and produces the corresponding outputs simultaneously. In most cases this is a useful simplification, but for slowly maturing products the assumption is inappropriate. In the production of wines, cheese, timber, or garden nursery materials, time must elapse before the product leaves the firm. This fact means that the management must decide when the product is mature, which is a question of economics. In addition, decisions on pricing and even the choice of products are more complex because of the introduction of the time element.

Suppose that the decision to produce a maturing item has been made. The issue is when to bring maturation to a halt and to sell. As might be expected, this problem raises questions of opportunity costs, discounting, and incremental analysis.

The first point is that the economic life is *not* at the point at which revenue from a product is highest. If this were the case, one would never cut redwood trees, for they should continue to grow and add value for centuries. Obviously one must recognize that postponement of harvest

---

[24] Because of the difficulty of this topic, it may be desirable to read this section at first for a general understanding and to return to it after a study of Chapter 9 on capital budgeting.

involves a sacrifice of the earnings that could be made on the cash received from sale now. Or putting the matter another way, it is necessary to discount long-distant dollars if we are to compare them with revenues in the nearer future.

Unfortunately, two competing principles of maximization are available, each based on different assumptions:

1. The principle that the life of the product should be determined at the point at which the percentage rate of increased revenue is equal to the opportunity costs of capital. This principle will maximize the *present value* of the product.

2. The principle that the optimum life is at the point at which the percentage increase in revenue is at a maximum. This principle will maximize the *rate of return*.

Figure 2–8 compares the two approaches. The vertical scale representing dollars of revenue or cost, is semilogarithmic to show *percentage rates* of change rather than absolute amounts of change. The horizontal axis shows time on an arithmetic scale. Thus a curve that is concave upward is one with increasing percentage rates of growth; and one that is concave downward is increasing at a decreasing percentage rate. The solid curve *CRT* represents the revenue to be derived from the product at different points in time. It is drawn here to show first increasing returns to age and then decreasing marginal returns, which would appear to be the appropriate assumption. For example, the value of cheese should increase more rapidly as it approaches the age at which it becomes palatable. But beyond that point further aging has a decreasing effectiveness and eventually may even cause the value to decline.

The broken lines represent growth curves. On semilogarithmic paper they are straight parallel lines, indicating equal rates of increase throughout. This results from the assumption of a given cost of capital (the rate of return that can be made on alternative investments). Let us assume that this rate is 8 percent; the slopes of all the lines are 8 percent per time period. The broken line through *C* indicates the path along which the initial sum *OC* grows if it is invested in other alternatives and earns profits at the rate appropriate to those alternatives. In the early periods the increase in revenue from the particular product under consideration exceeds the accumulation that would have taken place otherwise. At any point in time it would be possible to stop the aging of the product, sell it, and invest the funds in alternatives, in which case the growth of the funds would be a broken line higher than the initial one.

Marginal principles suggest that the optimum life is at *N*, at which point the rate of increase in revenue is equal to the rate of increase on the alternative growth lines. Beyond that point an investment in alternatives would lead to a larger increase in earnings. We may look at this solution in another way: the life of *N* produces a revenue *NR*, which, when dis-

FIGURE 2–8

GROWTH CURVE AND DISCOUNT CURVES

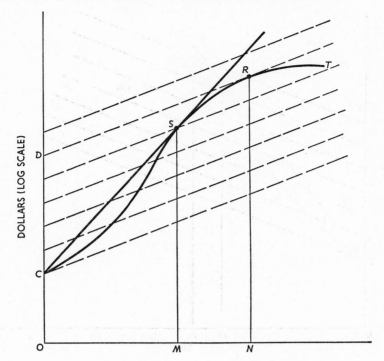

counted, gives the highest present value, *OD*. The present value of the aging asset can always be found by tracing back to the vertical axis along one of the broken discounting lines.

The other solution to this problem brings up a factor which we have neglected up to this point. The growth curves do permit us to compare this alternative with the earnings of other opportunities. But they do not force us to compare the aging of one batch with the alternative of selling it off and starting a new batch of the same product. The highest average percentage rate of growth in revenue is not at *R* but rather at *S*. The slope of the line *CS* is the discounted rate of return (marginal efficiency of capital) if the product is aged to a life of *M*. Continuing to age the product up to a life of *N* results in a lower discounted rate of return.

The literature on the subject is full of debate as to whether the *N* or *M* is the correct solution. Actually, it is wrong to say that either is always correct, for each is based on a special set of assumptions. The solution *N* is based on the assumption that the only alternatives are investments

FIGURE 2–9

GROWTH CURVE AND DISCOUNT CURVES (LIMITED SCOPE FOR PROPER AGING)

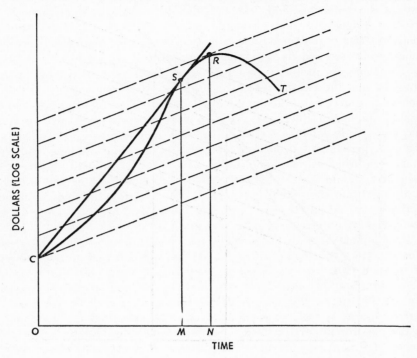

in other products. The solution M recognizes the possibility of shortening the aging cycle and concentrating on the higher growth early periods of life.

As Boulding has suggested, the difference between these two alternatives may be less important in practice than Figure 2–8 has suggested.[25] If, for example, the revenue curve has the shape shown in Figure 2–9, as would be the case if technology or public taste places rather definite limits on what can be considered a "properly aged" product, the two methods give approximately the same solution. In any case, both methods indicate a length of life shorter than would be found if discounting were completely ignored.

Product-line decisions

Most firms produce more than one product. They sometimes face the problem of deciding whether to add new products, to drop old products

[25] K. E. Boulding, *Economic Analysis* (3d ed.; New York: Harper & Bros., 1955), pp. 862–72.

from the product line, to change the relative proportions of products, to farm out part of the production to other firms, and so on. In the discussion at this point we shall deal with the short run, in which capacity is fixed; a longer run analysis would require a discussion of investment analysis which is postponed to a later chapter. But we must not ignore the longer run repercussions of the short-run decisions.

The short-run problem itself includes a number of variations. Let us consider first the case in which the firm has excess capacity: its present line of products is not absorbing the capacity. The question is whether to add another product. The first step is to compute the contribution of the new product to overhead and profits. This requires an estimate of the added revenue and of the incremental costs of the product. The normal overhead allocations should be avoided in such estimates; instead the estimates should measure the increase in each cost, direct or indirect, resulting from adding the product. If the contribution, the difference between the added revenue and the incremental cost, is positive, the analysis is favorable to adding the product.

A complete analysis, however, must check for other considerations. For example, the management should not introduce the new product if an even better new product is available. A search for all the available opportunities should precede making the final decision. Another way of expressing this idea is to say that the opportunity costs of alternative uses of the excess capacity must be estimated. Another factor is the possible impact of the new product on the products already produced. In some cases it may complement or "round out" the product line, increasing the sales of the other products. In such a case the contribution to overhead and profits of the new product is greater than the direct contribution of the product itself. In other cases the product may compete with items in the present line, so that the initial contribution estimates must be adjusted downward. Such adjustments in estimates should recognize both immediate and longer run impacts of the new product. If, for example, the excess capacity is temporary, management must face the question of whether the new product can be abandoned when the demand for the other products recovers, or whether an expansion of facilities will be justified. Often it may be preferable to accept temporary excess capacity than to create production bottlenecks when the excess disappears. In addition, management must determine whether it has the know-how to produce and distribute the product.

If the situation is one of full use of capacity the analysis becomes even more complex. In this case management must not only determine the contribution of each product (and of products that might be introduced into the product mix) but must also determine how much the opportunity cost of increasing the output of one product is in terms of the reduction of the contributions of the other products. This is exactly the kind of estimate made in the simplex method of linear programming, as we have already seen. The linear programming method of determining which products belong "in the solution" assumed limited capacity and makes use of both contribution estimates and estimates of opportunity costs. A management which does not use linear programming must nevertheless run through estimates analogous to those in the simplex method if it is going to approximate an optimal use of its resources.

Now we come to an even more complex situation: allocation of resources to a variety of slowly maturing products. An example would be a garden nursery with a fixed acreage of land and a wide variety of planting opportunities. Such a nursery faces the problem of determining which plants to propagate and grow, what ages to assume in such choices, what future prices should be assumed as well as what prices to charge now on plants which are already mature. In addition, the nursery must determine when to mark down prices on plants tying up land needed for other uses, and when to destroy plant materials that are in the way. The solution to such a problem requires an estimate of the contributions of the various plants over time, which requires in turn estimates of revenues and incremental costs. It also requires the discounting of future revenues, costs, and contributions to arrive at the present value of such contributions at the time decisions on the use of the land are to be made. Estimates of the present value of the contribution for all plants on an acre basis would provide a basis for rational decisions. These estimates would make it possible to compare the contribution from rapidly maturing plants with those of slowly maturing plants.

Such complex models for decision making are open to the criticism that they are "impractical"; most managers do not have the data or the knowledge to apply the models. The trend, however, is towards a more systematic analysis of product mix problems. And even in firms where decisions continue to be qualitative and subjective, it can do management no harm to think through the logic required for rational decisions on which products to expand, which to contract, and which to abandon.

Other applications

The principles in this chapter apply to many other decisions, some of which we shall list briefly.

Decisions on allocation of space in a retail store. The correct procedure would measure the contributions to overhead and profit above incremental cost for each commodity. The analysis is complicated by the fact that the space is not homogeneous; the space where the traffic flows is more valuable than space in remote parts of the store. The turnover of each product depends not only on its price but also upon its location.

Decisions on advertising expenditures. While many firms have applied simple rules of thumb in their advertising expenditures, more refined techniques reflecting economic reasoning are coming into use.

FIGURE 2–10

RELATIONSHIP OF REVENUE AND PROFITS TO ADVERTISING OUTLAYS

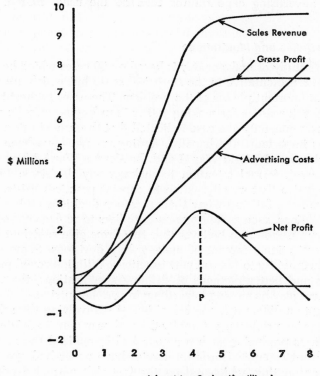

Advertising Outlay ($ millions)

It doesn't make sense to budget advertising as a percentage of sales or on the level of the rival's expenditures. What is needed is a measure of responsiveness of sales to advertising along with measures of the added cost of production of a larger volume.

Figure 2–10 shows how sales and profits might respond to increased advertising outlays. This diagram assumes diminishing returns to advertising—a reasonable assumption. The problem of measurement is extremely difficult in this case. Advertising has effects spread out over time. Competitors may change their advertising. Consumer tastes may change independently of the advertising. Research techniques are being developed which may overcome some of these problems.[26] But even in

---

[26] R. J. Jessen, "A Switch Over Experimental Design to Measure Advertising Effect," reprinted in R. E. Frank, A. E. Kuehn, and W. F. Massy, *Quantitative Techniques in Marketing Analysis* (Homewood, Ill.: Richard D. Irwin, Inc., 1962) pp. 190–230.

the absence of exact measurements, it is clear that the principles outlined in this chapter provide a more flexible and rational basis for determining advertising expenditures than do the usual rules of thumb.

Empirical studies and illustrations

Culliton's study of make or buy is based on 50 cases which he does not claim to be representative in the statistical sense but which are sufficient to indicate important phases of the problem. The cases suggest that some of the textbook reasons for making rather than buying may be unimportant. For example, only one case indicated that the fear of interruption of supply was important. (Perhaps his findings would have been different if they had covered World War II and the Korean War.) Many firms fail to give enough formal attention to make-or-buy decisions; they often fail to recognize that an alternative to current practices exists. Furthermore, these firms fail to review their previous decisions and fail to look for new solutions, such as finding new suppliers to replace old ones.

Professor Culliton also believes that few firms give sufficient attention to the organizational impact of make-or-buy decisions. Some managers overrate their ability to take on new functions. With improved purchasing techniques and better methods of defining specifications, the weight of the argument may be moving toward buying on the outside.

Turning to a different kind of decision, that involving the selection of slowly maturing products, a study by the author and an associate suggests that few firms producing such products had formalized their analysis to any significant extent.[27] Garden nurseries have never had great success with cost accounting, which reflects the fact that normal overhead cost allocations are not helpful in such an industry. Perhaps most nursery managers attempt by evaluation of past experience and trial and error to apply the discounting principle and incremental reasoning. It would be interesting to see whether they could improve their decisions by a more mathematical approach with the use of electronic computers. In time, a more formal application of the principles in this chapter may replace the present more intuitive procedures in determining which plants to propagate and grow, when to sell the product, when and how much to mark down prices, and when to clear off the land.

---

[27] J. L. Gibson and W. W. Haynes, *Accounting in Small Business Decisions* (Lexington: University of Kentucky Press, 1963).

Cases for part one

The case method provides the most convenient way of acquiring skill in applying managerial economics short of actual decision making itself. The learning of economic analysis abstracted from actual decisions does not provide the skills required to bridge the gap between theory and practice. Cases reveal the complexity of the environment in which decisions are made. Cases force the student to leave the ivory tower of abstract theory, to face up to the uncertainties of the "real world," and to make the simplifications required to create order out of the multitude of facts faced by management.

Almost all of the cases in this book are based on actual situations; a few are synthesized from the experience of several firms. Obviously none of the cases supplies "all of the facts." Management never has all the facts, though management is in a better position than is the student to search for answers to questions that arise during the decision-making process. Trying to make sense out of a situation without full knowledge may be frustrating; but it is part of the essence of management.

The case method

Many readers of this book will be unfamiliar with the case method. The best way to learn this method is to use it, but a few introductory comments may be helpful. The case method requires the development of an orderly analysis of the given situation. It involves the evaluation of facts, the organization of such facts into meaningful patterns, the weighing of important facts against unimportant or irrelevant information, the formulation of alternative courses of action, the evaluation of those alternatives in terms of the facts and the goals of the undertaking, and the final choice of a solution.

Normally there is no single "correct" solution to a case. Two managers of equal ability might select different alternatives; it is often difficult to say that one alternative is better than the other. It is possible to say, however, that some case analyses and some recommendations are superior to others. The criteria for making this determination are:

1. The extent to which the analysis and solution show an understanding of the real issues involved.

2. The extent to which the analysis is based on the particular facts in the situation.

3. The degree to which the solution appears to be workable under the circumstances.

4. The extent to which the analyst is able to support his position.

Procedure in analyzing a case.   *The steps in analyzing a case may vary from one student to another and one case to another. It would be wrong to claim that only one procedure is appropriate. The following outline of steps should be taken merely as suggestive of one way of going about the analysis.*

DEFINITION OF THE CENTRAL ISSUE OR ISSUES.   *A case may contain a variety of issues from the trivial to the significant. The analyst should focus on the key problems. The separate superficial issues are often symptoms of a deeper problem; the analyst can often organize his thoughts around a central theme that clarifies the total situation.*

ORGANIZATION OF THE EVIDENCE.   *When the analyst has determined what he considers to be the central issue or issues, he can then proceed to organize the facts around topics related to those issues. This requires the separation of the unimportant from the significant and the irrelevant from the relevant. Often it is necessary to organize the facts in a new form: in the form of a break-even chart or flow of funds statement, for example. The construction of charts and tables that clarify the situation requires imagination; it is one of the chief tools of orderly decision making.*

DETERMINATION OF THE ALTERNATIVES.   *In some cases the alternatives are clear; in others the analyst must invent alternatives appropriate to the situation. Sometimes a new alternative which was not evident at first reveals new possibilities for a solution. The analyst cannot remain content with predetermined alternatives; he must strive for new and better solutions.*

EVALUATION OF THE ALTERNATIVES.   *This step is normally simultaneous with the second step. One of the best ways to organize the facts in a case is to relate them to the alternatives. Some facts become arguments in favor of or against an alternative; some of them suggest the probable consequences of choosing one alternative over another.*

It is necessary finally to appraise each alternative—to weigh its strengths and weaknesses. Weak alternatives are discarded in favor of strong ones.

THE DECISION.   *The manager must not evade making a final choice of the alternative which seems best to him. He must be decisive. He should*

be aware of the limitations as well as strengths of his choice, and he
should beware of overstating his case. But the manager must decide, for
inaction itself involves a choice.

The case method applied in managerial economics. The cases in a
managerial economics book have a special character; they are not the
same as cases in accounting, finance, or policy. The cases are intended to
provide an opportunity to apply the concepts of economics to the problems of management. Rather than being "representative" of all managerial
decisions, they are chosen from those areas of management most amenable to economic analysis.

Nevertheless, these cases should be approached in the same way as
other policy cases. The initial effort should go into determining the problems or issues, with secondary regard to whether or not these are economic problems. Some students make the mistake of organizing their case
analysis around economic concepts instead of using the concepts as tools
where appropriate in the analysis of the case. The objective is not to find
out whether the case is one in opportunity costs or demand elasticities or
valuation, but rather to determine the issues and then use whatever
analysis is appropriate. Some of the cases, however, are intended as
simple exercises in the use of economic analysis.

This chapter consists of elementary cases. The fundamental concepts
discussed in Chapter 2 should be helpful in making decisions in these
cases. The objective should be to size up each situation, to organize and
analyze the facts, to evalute the alternatives, and to reach a solution—
and to use economic concepts when they are helpful.

NEWVILLE BRANCH OF AJAX CLEANERS*

Mr. B. Fraley was manager of the Newville branch of the Ajax
Cleaners. In this position he had considerable autonomy in making decisions affecting the branch. The central office of the company developed
the accounting reports for each branch and occasionally made suggestions
to the individual managers.

In June, 1961, the ratio of wages and salaries of the Newville branch
to sales was 46 percent. The company suggested that as a rule of thumb
this ratio should never exceed 33⅓ percent. The president of the company
recommended that Mr. Fraley discontinue the shirt laundry service, a
minor adjunct to the dry cleaning business, in order to bring labor costs
into line.

Mr. Fraley consulted the accounting reports which he received from
the central office in considering his decision. These financial reports

---

* This case was prepared by W. W. Haynes of the Harvard Business School and
J. L. Gibson of the University of Kentucky as a basis for class discussion. All names
and locations have been disguised. The case is a by-product of research for the Small
Business Administration, which agency is in no way responsible for the discussion.

provided broad aggregates which were not helpful in evaluating the profitability of the shirt laundry. Mr. Fraley made an estimate of costs and revenues resulting from the shirt laundry in June. He accumulated data on labor costs and supplies. (He consulted Mr. Frederick, an accountant friend, who suggested the basis for allocating overhead. Exhibit 1 shows the estimate of overhead costs and direct costs for the shirt laundry department.) The result showed a small loss on the shirt laundry as follows:

Revenue	$740
Full cost	745
Loss	$ 5

Mr. Frederick was not certain that the full cost figure was the appropriate one for Mr. Fraley's problem. He had been reading some articles on "marginal income accounting" and suggested that a variation on that approach might be helpful in clarifying the problem at hand and future decision-making issues. Obviously such an approach would have to be kept extremely simple and inexpensive to deal with Mr. Fraley's small operations.

The steps in establishing a system of marginal income accounting are as follows:

1. Segmentation of the business. Mr. Fraley's business might be broken into two segments—dry cleaning and shirt laundry.

2. Segregation of costs between fixed and variable costs. This would require that Mr. Fraley make qualitative judgments as to which costs

EXHIBIT 1

COST COMPUTATIONS ON THE LAUNDRY—JUNE, 1961
(including overhead allocation bases)

Manager's salary—Average time spent in the department	$155
Advertising—Sales	22
Telephone—Sales	16
Heat, light, power—Ratio of departmental heat, light, power costs	5
Employer's payroll tax—Ratio of departmental salary costs	9
Rent—Floor space	16
Amortization—Floor space	23
Insurance—Sales	24
	$270

Add direct costs		
Salaries	$200	
Supplies	140	
Heat, light, power	25	
Payroll tax	10	
Depreciation	100	
		475
Total cost		$745

were fixed and which were variable. A more elaborate statistical approach for segregating costs would be too expensive.

3. Separation of the fixed costs into assigned fixed costs and unassigned fixed costs. The assigned fixed costs would be those which were fixed for short period fluctuations in activity but which were avoidable if the segment were permanently discontinued. Examples would be depreciation on specialized equipment and salaries of supervisors in the particular segment. The unassigned fixed costs would be those which did not vary with output and which could not be avoided by discontinuance of one segment.

The result of such an analysis would be a chart of accounts which would appear as in Exhibit 2. Such a system of accounts would break the data into four categories: revenue, variable costs, assigned fixed costs, and unassigned fixed costs. Mr. Fraley could easily prepare this report once the system had been established. The report indicated the "contribution" each segment was making to assigned and unassigned fixed costs and to profits.

Some particular expenses might overlap several categories, requiring an allocation. For example, heat, light, and power would fall into both the variable cost and unassigned fixed cost categories. Mr. Fraley would have to determine which labor costs would in fact vary with output, which would be fixed as long as the segment was maintained, and which

EXHIBIT 2
CHART OF ACCOUNTS
MARGINAL INCOME ANALYSIS

Laundry
1. Sales revenue
2. Variable costs
   a) Salaries
   b) Supplies
   c) Heat, light, power
   d) Employer's payroll tax
   e) Repair and maintenance
   f) Clothes lost and repaired
3. Assigned fixed costs
   a) Depreciation of equipment

Dry Cleaning
1. Sales revenue
2. Variable costs
   a) Salaries
   b) Supplies
   c) Heat, light, power
   d) Employer's payroll tax
   e) Repair and maintenance
   f) Clothes lost and repaired
3. Assigned fixed costs
   a) Depreciation of equipment

4. Unassigned fixed costs
   a) Salaries
   b) Advertising
   c) Repairs and maintenance of plant
   d) Taxes
   e) Telephone
   f) Heat, light, power
   g) Employer's payroll tax
   h) Rent
   i) Depreciation of building, fixtures
   j) Amortization of leasehold improvements
   k) Insurance

would be attributable only to the total operation. One danger of such a system is that it might not reflect the fact that a cost which had been variable had become fixed, or vice versa.

Mr. Frederick offered to assist Mr. Fraley without charge in preparing a report for June, 1961, based on such a system of accounts because of his interest in the accounting problem it presented. The result is shown in Exhibit 3.

EXHIBIT 3
MARGINAL INCOME ANALYSIS REPORT FOR JUNE, 1961

	Dry Cleaning		Laundry	
Sales		$2,800		$740
Variable costs:				
Salaries	$ 790		$200	
Supplies	760		140	
Heat, light, power	150		25	
Employer's payroll tax	43	1,743	10	375
Contribution to assigned and unassigned fixed cost		$1,057		$365
Depreciation		200		100
Contribution to unassigned fixed cost	$1,122	$ 857		$265
Unassigned fixed costs:				
Salaries $650				
Advertising 88				
Telephone 66				
Heat, light, power 35				
Employer's payroll tax ... 36				
Rent 100				
Depreciation 183				
Amortization 140				
Insurance 95	1,393			
Net loss for the period		$ 271		

Mr. Fraley was then faced with consideration of both the full cost report and the marginal income report in making his decision about abandonment of the shirt laundry. Exhibit 4 presents a summary of the income statement for the entire operation in June.

1. *Was the rule of thumb helpful? Why or why not?*
2. *Was the full cost estimate helpful? Why or why not?*
3. *Did the marginal income analysis help in making the decision? Why or why not?*
4. *What is accomplished by separating the assigned fixed costs from the variable costs? From the unassigned fixed costs?*
5. *Are the allocation bases in Exhibit 1 reasonable? Do they contribute to decision making in this firm?*
6. *What is the relation between the variable costs in this case and the incre-*

EXHIBIT 4
NET INCOME STATEMENT FOR JUNE, 1961

Sales		$3,540
Salaries	$1,640	
Supplies	900	
Heat, light, power	210	
Employer's payroll tax	89	
Advertising	88	
Telephone	66	
Rent	100	
Depreciation	483	
Amortization of leasehold improvements	140	
Insurance	95	
Total expenses		$3,811
Net Loss		($ 271)

mental cost concept? What is the relation of the contribution to the unassigned fixed costs in this case to the incremental cost concept?

7. *Which is relevant in this case: the contribution to the unassigned fixed cost or the contribution to the assigned and unassigned fixed cost? Explain.*
8. *Are the costs properly classified in Exhibit 3?*
9. *Was the shirt laundry profitable?*
10. *What decision was correct on the shirt laundry business?*

WHAT PRICE PROGRESS*

EFFICIENCY EXPERT: Joe, you said you put in these peanuts because some people ask for them, but do you realize what this rack of peanuts is *costing* you?

JOE: It ain't gonna cost. 'Sgonna be a profit. Sure, I hadda pay $25 for a fancy rack to holda bags, but the peanuts cost 6 cents a bag and I sell 'em for 10 cents. Figger I sell 50 bags a week to start. It'll take 12½ weeks to cover the cost of the rack. After that I gotta clear profit of 4 cents a bag. The more I sell, the more I make.

EFFICIENCY EXPERT: That is an antiquated and completely unrealistic approach, Joe. Fortunately, modern accounting procedures permit a more accurate picture which reveals the complexities involved.

JOE: Huh?

EFFICIENCY EXPERT: To be precise, those peanuts must be integrated into your entire operation and be allocated their appropriate share of business overhead. They must share a proportionate part of your expenditures for rent, heat, light, equipment depreciation, decorating, salaries for your waitresses, cook . . .

JOE: The *cook?* What's he gotta do wit'a peanuts? He don' even know I got 'em!

---

* Reprinted from *Lybrand Journal* (Lybrand Ross Brothers & Montgomery) whose editors note: "We have been unable to locate the source of this paper. If any of our readers can provide us with this information, we shall be delighted to acknowledge our indebtedness."

EFFICIENCY EXPERT: Look Joe, the cook is in the kitchen, the kitchen prepares the food, the food is what brings people in here, and the people ask to buy peanuts. *That's* why you must charge a portion of the cook's wages, as well as a part of your own salary to peanut sales. This sheet contains a carefully calculated cost analysis which indicates the peanut operation should pay exactly $1,278 per year toward these general overhead costs.

JOE: The peanuts? $1,278 a year for overhead? The nuts?

EFFICIENCY EXPERT: It's really a little more than that. You also spend money each week to have the windows washed, to have the place swept out in the mornings, keep soap in the washroom and provide free cokes to the police. That raises the total to $1,313 per year.

JOE: (*Thoughtfully*) But the peanut salesman said I'd make money . . . put 'em on the end of the counter, he said . . . and get 4 cents a bag profit . . .

EFFICIENCY EXPERT: (*With a sniff*) He's not an accountant. Do you actually know what the portion of the counter occupied by the peanut rack is worth to you?

JOE: Ain't worth nothing . . . no stool there . . . just a dead spot at the end.

EFFICIENCY EXPERT: The modern cost picture permits no dead spots. Your counter contains 60 square feet and your counter business grosses $15,000 a year. Consequently, the square foot of space occupied by the peanut rack is worth $250 per year. Since you have taken that area away from general counter use, you must charge the value of the space to the occupant.

JOE: You mean I gotta add *$250 a year more* to the *peanuts?*

EFFICIENCY EXPERT: Right. That raises their share of the general operating costs to a grand total of $1,563 per year. Now then, if you sell 50 bags of peanuts per week, these allocated costs will amount to 60 cents per bag.

JOE: *What?*

EFFICIENCY EXPERT: Obviously, to that must be added your purchase price of 6 cents per bag, which brings the total to 66 cents. So you see by selling peanuts at 10 cents per bag, you are losing 56 cents on every sale.

JOE: Somethin's crazy!

EFFICIENCY EXPERT: Not at all! Here are the *figures*. They *prove* your peanuts operation cannot stand on its own feet.

JOE: (*Brightening*) Suppose I sell *lotsa* peanuts . . . thousand bags a week 'stead of 50.

EFFICIENCY EXPERT: (*Tolerantly*) Joe, you don't understand the problem. If the volume of peanuts sales increases, our operating costs will go up . . . you'll have to handle more bags with more time, more depreciation, more everything. The basic principle of accounting is firm on that subject: "The Bigger the Operation the More General Overhead Costs that must be Allocated." No, increasing the volume of sales won't help.

JOE: Okay, You so smart, *you* tell *me* what I gotta do.

EFFICIENCY EXPERT: (*Condescendingly*) Well . . . you could first reduce operating expenses.

JOE: How?

EFFICIENCY EXPERT: Move to a building with cheaper rent. Cut salaries. Wash the windows biweekly. Have the floor swept only on Thursday. Remove the soap from the washrooms. Decrease the square foot value of your counter. For example, if you can cut your expenses 50 percent, that will reduce the amount allocated to peanuts from $1,563 to $781.50 per year, reducing the cost to 36 cents per bag.

JOE: (*Slowly*) That's better?

EFFICIENCY EXPERT: Much, much better. However, even then you would lose 26 cents per bag if you only charge 10 cents. Therefore, you must also raise your selling price. If you want a net profit of 4 cents per bag you would have to charge 40 cents.

JOE: (*Flabbergasted*) You mean even after I cut operating costs 50 percent I still gotta charge 40 cents for a 10 cents bag of peanuts? Nobody's that nuts about nuts! Who'd buy 'em?

EFFICIENCY EXPERT: That's a secondary consideration. The point is, at 40 cents you'd be selling at a price based upon a true and proper evaluation of your then reduced costs.

JOE: (*Eagerly*) Look! I gotta better idea. Why don't I just throw the nuts out . . . put 'em in a ash can?

EFFICIENCY EXPERT: Can you afford it?

JOE: Sure. All I got is about 50 bags of peanuts . . . cost about three bucks . . . so I lose $25 on the rack, but I'm outa this nutsy business and no more grief.

EFFICIENCY EXPERT: (*Shaking head*) Joe it isn't that simple. You are *in* the peanut business! The minute you throw those peanuts out you are adding $1,563 of annual overhead to the rest of your operation. Joe . . . be realistic . . . *can you afford to do that?*

JOE: (*Completely crushed*) It'sa unbelievable! Last week I was a make money. Now I'm in a trouble . . . just because I think peanuts on a counter is a gonna bring me some extra profit . . . just because I believe 50 bags of peanuts a week is a easy.

EFFICIENCY EXPERT: (*With raised eyebrow*) That is the object of modern cost studies, Joe . . . to dispel those false illusions.

THE HARRISS GIFT STORE

Mrs. G. W. Harriss was owner and manager of a small gift and food shop in a town with a population of 10,000. The store specialized in gifts, greeting cards, various types of dry goods, jewelry, and similar items. It also maintained a department for the sale of foods prepared by several women in the town.

Price policy

Mrs. Harriss's pricing policy was very much like that of similar stores in other locations. Her usual markup on wholesale cost varied from 50 percent on "competitive" items, such as household goods, inexpensive linens, and low-price gifts to 100 percent on higher quality goods, such as china, glass, high-quality linens, and expensive handkerchiefs. Sometimes she followed a price suggested by the manufacturer, as was true in the case of greeting cards, on which the markup was about 100 percent.

Mrs. Harriss was probably less flexible than most store managers in varying prices over time. She never held special sales. She had never marked down the price on greeting cards. Occasionally she would "give someone a price" on an item that had been sitting on the shelves for a long time. She believed that higher prices would lead to a loss of business because of a reputation for overcharging, but she doubted that reduced prices would have much effect on volume. On a few items—napkins, paper cups, and cheap stationery—she followed the price set by 5-and-10 cent stores.

The food was handled on a commission basis. Mrs. Harriss received 20 percent of the retail price. The individual cooks preparing these foods determined the price; Mrs. Harriss recommended a formula of double the cost of ingredients and fuel to arrive at the price before the commission. Unsold foods were returned to the supplier. One of Mrs. Harriss's competitors had abandoned a similar food line because of the low markup; he believed that the line was not covering the overhead costs.

History of the store

Mrs. Harriss started her store in 1931 in a rented location. Her objective was to supplement her husband's income to provide for the college education of her three children. While she had an excellent education, employment opportunities for people of her age (45) and background were practically nonexistent, especially in the small southern town where she lived. Wage levels in this region were far below the national average. Mrs. Harriss probably could have found a clerical or sales job but nothing that would have made full use of her talents.

In 1937 Mrs. Harriss purchased the building where her store was located for $6,900. The building was 40 years old and was located in one of the best blocks in the town. Even in this block vacant store space was frequently available. Previous to the purchase of the building Mrs. Harriss had paid $35 per month for the store space. The building also included an upstairs apartment, which rented at $50 per month.

In 1946 Mr. Harriss retired from his job, going onto a company pension which provided a moderate monthly income. At that time he joined Mrs. Harriss in operating the store, though his activity was limited by his poor health. He served as cashier and helped maintain the records. Both Mr. and Mrs. Harriss worked a long week: from 9 A.M. to 6 P.M. on weekdays and from 9 A.M. to 9 P.M. on Saturday. They employed part-time help in the peak periods.

Income from the store

Exhibit 1 shows the income earned from the store operations in a fairly representative year in the 1940's. In the 1950's the net income was slightly higher, varying from $3,000 to $4,000 per year.

EXHIBIT 1

INCOME STATEMENT, 194—

Sales (including commissions on food)		$31,243.65
Inventory, Jan. 1	$ 2,304.37	
Merchandise bought for sale	25,291.48	
Materials and supplies	99.96	
Travel to market	24.15	
	$27,719.96	
Inventory, Dec. 31	2,480.68	
Cost of merchandise sold		25,239.28
Gross profit		$ 6,004.37
Other deductions		
Wages, part-time employees	$ 1,630.77	
Taxes	149.86	
Depreciation on building	150.00	
Depreciation on counters	35.00	
Other depreciation	12.34	
Other expenses	774.84	
		2,752.81
Net income from the store		$ 3,251.56
Rent from the apartment		235.00
		$ 3,486.56

Contemplated sale of the business

In 1954 Mrs. Harriss decided to sell her business. She was eligible for social security and no longer needed the extra income from the store. She planned to retain ownership of the building but to sell the shop itself. She considered the terms on which she would sell the business. She believed she should charge the full cost of the inventory, which by 1954 had risen to $7,800. She thought a charge of $1,000 for the equipment (a large refrigerator, a furnace, cases, shelving, scales, and cash register) would be reasonable; she did not have accurate records of what this equipment had originally cost but it was considerably more than $1,000. She also planned to charge $1,000 for goodwill. She thought a rental of $100 per month for the store would be reasonable.

1. *Was Mrs. Harriss's price policy sound?*
2. *Was it profitable to stock foods even though they carried only a 20 percent markup?*
3. *Does Exhibit 1 show the economic profit of the store? Does it reflect all the opportunity costs? If not, what is a corrected estimate of profits?*
4. *In your opinion which of the following estimates comes closest to the economic value of the business itself (not the building): (a) $1,000, (b) $2,000, (c) $5,000, (d) $10,000?*
5. *What concepts are involved in determining its value?*

SELECTED DECISION-MAKING RULES AND PRACTICES

The following examples of practices, policies, and rules of thumb are taken from case studies of actual firms. Some of the examples may be consistent with the principles of managerial economics; others may represent a practical compromise with those principles, while still others are difficult to reconcile with incremental reasoning.

1. Some firms follow the rule that the annual budget for the replacement of equipment should equal the annual depreciation charges on equipment. The vice-president of one manufacturing firm, for example, was considering such a policy to accelerate the replacement of equipment which he believed was lagging behind.[1] Many of this company's machines were over 10 years or even 20 years old.

2. The owner-manager of a small printing firm follows the rule: "To make a profit, you must make a profit on every job." By this he means that each job must be priced to cover all the costs, including allocated overhead, and return a profit above those costs.

3. A dry cleaning and laundry firm considered the possibility of filling in its off-peak excess capacity with laundry service for motels. The company management, however, turned down this opportunity when it learned that the motels would not pay a high enough price to cover the overhead as well as the direct costs.

4. The plant manager of a branch of a large national firm was faced with a decision on making or buying a component. Up to the time of the decision the plant manufactured the part, but a potential supplier was willing to sell at a price below the plant's full cost. In spite of this low price the manager decided to continue manufacture within the plant. His reasoning was as follows:

   a) The overhead presently absorbed by manufacturing the component would have to be reallocated to other parts manufactured within the plant.

   b) The reallocation of overhead would result in higher unit costs for other parts.

   c) These higher unit costs would require higher prices for the company's products, placing it in a less-favorable competitive position.

5. One owner-manager of a furniture company made the following statement: "Overhead must come first." By this he meant that price must cover the overhead costs and then cover as much of the variable costs as possible.

6. A garden nursery and landscaping firm refused to develop plants or trees which took more than eight years to mature. The management

---

[1] See Paul E. Holden and Frank R. Shallenberger, *Selected Case Problems in Industrial Management* (Englewood Cliffs, N.J.: Prentice-Hall, Inc., 1953), pp. 55–57.

reasoned that the high prices of the slower maturing plants didn't compensate for the longer period they tied up the land.

7. Many firms maintain a policy of not buying new equipment or replacing old equipment unless the investment will pay for itself in less than three years (or some other predetermined number of years). This rule is known as the payback criterion.

8. The author of this book sometimes feels under pressure to attend athletic events because he already has tickets in his possession.

9. The Empire Room of the Waldorf Astoria Hotel in New York City is similar to other dining, dancing and entertainment facilities in the Hilton Hotels chain. In 1955 the Empire Room was less profitable than its counterparts in the other Hilton hotels, with only a 5.7 percent return on sales (a loss of 5.5 percent in 1954) as compared with returns of from 7.1 percent to 34.4 percent in the other hotels.[2] In spite of this low profit level, Hilton Hotels spent more proportionately on advertising the Empire Room than it spent on the other rooms. In January and February, 1954, the advertising budget for the Empire Room was $11,779 and total sales amounted to $143,308. Similar figures for other Hilton hotels in New York were:

Room	Advertising Costs	Sales
Rendezvous Room (Plaza Hotel)	$1,905	$ 88,826
Persian Room (Plaza Hotel)	7,803	98,340
Grill Room (Roosevelt Hotel)	5,779	249,378
Cafe Rouge (New York Statler)	2,747	111,688
Lounge Room (Mayflower Hotel)	3,800	59,047

1. *How do the rules and practices of these companies hold up under analysis in terms of the concepts in Chapter 2: incremental reasoning, time perspective, discounting, opportunity costs, and the equimarginal principle?*

ATHERTON COMPANY*

Early in January, 1956, the sales manager and controller of the Atherton Company met for the purpose of preparing a joint pricing recommendation for Item 345. After the president approved their recommenda-

[2] See *Hilton Hotels Corporation* (*BR*), a case published by the Harvard Graduate School of Business Administration, copyright 1960, p. 15. The data are reproduced by permission of the President and Fellows of Harvard College and Professor John D. Glover.

* Case material of the Harvard Graduate School of Business Administration is prepared as a basis for class discussion. Cases are not designed to present illustrations of either correct or incorrect handling of administrative problems. Copyright, 1956, by the President and Fellows of Harvard College.

tion, the price would be announced in letters to retail customers. In accordance with company and industry practice, announced prices were adhered to for the year unless radical changes in market conditions occurred.

The Atherton Company was the largest company in its segment of the textile industry; its 1955 sales had exceeded $6 million. Company salesmen were on a straight salary basis, and each salesman sold the full line. Most of the Atherton competitors were small. Usually they waited for the Atherton Company to announce prices before mailing out their own price lists.

Item 345, an expensive yet competitive fabric, was the sole product of a department whose facilities could not be utilized on other items in the product line. In January, 1954, the Atherton Company had raised its price from $1.50 to $2 per yard. This had been done to bring the profit per yard on Item 345 up to that of other products in the line. Although the company was in a strong position financially, considerable capital would be required in the next few years to finance a recently approved long-term modernization and expansion program. The 1954 pricing decision had been one of several changes advocated by the directors in an attempt to strengthen the company's working capital position so as to insure that adequate funds would be available for this program.

Competitors of the Atherton Company had held their prices on products similar to Item 345 at $1.50 during 1954 and 1955. The industry and Atherton Company volume for Item 345 for the years 1950 to 1955, as estimated by the sales manager, is shown in Exhibit 1. As shown by this exhibit, the Atherton Company had lost a significant portion of its former market position. In the sales manager's opinion, a reasonable forecast of industry volume for 1956 was 700,000 yards. He was certain that the company could sell 25 percent of the 1956 industry total if the $1.50 price was adopted. He feared a further volume decline if the competitive price was not met. As many consumers were convinced of the superiority

EXHIBIT 1

ATHERTON COMPANY

(prices and production, 1950–1955, Item 345)

Year	Physical Volume of Production (Yards)		Price Charged by Most Competitors	Atherton Company Price
	Industry Total	Atherton Item 345		
1950	610,000	213,000	$2.00	$2.00
1951	575,000	200,000	2.00	2.00
1952	430,000	150,000	1.50	1.50
1953	475,000	165,000	1.50	1.50
1954	500,000	150,000	1.50	2.00
1955	625,000	125,000	1.50	2.00

of the Atherton product, the sales manager reasoned that sales of Item 345 would probably not fall below 75,000 yards, even at a $2 price.

During the pricing discussions, the controller and sales manager had considered two other aspects of the problem. The controller was concerned about the possibility that competitors would reduce their prices below $1.50 if the Atherton Company announced a $1.50 price for Item 345. The sales manager was confident that competitors would not go below $1.50 because they all had higher costs and several of them were in tight financial straits.

The controller prepared estimated costs of Item 345 at various volumes of production (Exhibit 2). These estimated costs reflected current labor and material costs. They were based on past experience except for the estimates of 75,000 and 100,000 yards. The company had produced more than 100,000 yards in each year since World War II, and prewar experience was not applicable due to equipment changes and increases in labor productivity.

EXHIBIT 2

ATHERTON COMPANY

(estimated cost per yard of Item 345 at various volumes of production)

	75,000	100,000	125,000	150,000	175,000	200,000
Direct labor	$ .400	$ .390	$ .380	$ .370	$ .380	$ .400
Material	.200	.200	.200	.200	.200	.200
Material spoilage	.020	.020	.019	.019	.019	.020
Department expense:						
Direct*	.060	.056	.050	.050	.050	.050
Indirect†	.400	.300	.240	.200	.180	.150
General overhead‡	.120	.117	.114	.111	.114	.120
Factory cost	$1.200	$1.083	$1.003	$ .950	$ .943	$ .940
Selling and adminis-						
trative expense§	.780	.704	.652	.618	.613	.611
	$1.980	$1.787	$1.655	$1.568	$1.556	$1.551

* Indirect labor, supplies, repairs, power, etc.
† Depreciation, supervision, etc.
‡ 30 percent of direct labor.
§ 65 percent of factory cost.

1. *How, if at all, did the company's financial condition relate to the pricing decision?*
2. *Which price, $1.50 or $2, should have been recommended?*

FINCH PRINTING COMPANY

In December, 1954, William Welch agreed to become a director of the Finch Printing Company, located in an eastern city with a population of over 300,000. He was a cousin of three majority stockholders in the company—Miss Mabel Finch, the company vice-president, and her sister and brother, both of whom were inactive. He understood that one of his responsibilities was to represent the interests of these stockholders.

Background

The Finch Printing Company was founded in 1901 by Jacob Finch, father of the three major stockholders just mentioned. The company engaged in job printing of a high quality. The company had a city-wide reputation for fine workmanship, dependability, and strong managerial ethics. The firm did considerable printing for religious organizations, but its main customers were commercial firms. It printed several journals or trade magazines with a wide geographical circulation, but most of its business was local. The firm never reached a large size; maximum employment was 50.

Jacob Finch maintained several policies which undoubtedly limited the profits of the firm. He refused to do any printing for liquor firms even though opportunities to print for them were numerous. He tried to maintain employment for most of his employees during the depression of the 1930's despite the low level of business, a fact that weakened the financial structure of the company in that period.

Upon Jacob Finch's death in 1941, his daughter, Mabel Finch, took over the management of the company as president. It was not her intention to remain in that position, but she was unable to find a successor until 1953. The company was not particularly profitable during her presidency, despite the general improvement in business activity during World War II and the years that followed. Wartime restrictions limited the ability of the company to make profits.

In October, 1953, Miss Finch succeeded in employing a new president, Mr. Arthur Yount, who was thoroughly familiar with the printing industry. Mr. Yount received a salary and was to share in the company profits on a prearranged basis. One of Mr. Yount's first acts was to sign a contract with a correspondence school, resulting in a 40 to 50 percent increase in sales (see Exhibit 1).

In 1954, when William Welch became a director, the firm was still located in an antiquated four-story building not entirely suited to modern printing techniques. The building had been largely written off; most of the balance sheet item "Building and building improvements" represented land and a new elevator installed in conformance with safety requirements. The building was located near the center of the city and undoubtedly was worth over $40,000 because of that location.

Developments in 1954, 1955, and 1956

In spite of the improvement in profits from 1953 to 1954 (see Exhibit 1), the company prospects did not appear favorable to Mr. Welch. He found that a serious difference had arisen between Mr. Yount, the president, and the vice-president, Miss Finch. Miss Finch believed that Mr. Yount was not living up to certain agreements made orally when he was employed and that he was not carrying out some of the long-standing policies of the firm. Furthermore, she believed that he was limiting her authority to much narrower confines than was originally intended. Mr. Yount apparently believed that Miss Finch was interfering with his management of the business and that she was cutting across organizational channels. There was evidence of the formation of factions at lower levels in the firm.

The board of directors met once a month. In 1955 and 1956 it consisted of five members: Mr. Yount (the president), Mr. Welch, two members who represented the Bettsville Industrial Foundation which held mortgage bonds in the company, and Mr. Oswald (a minority stockholder). Miss Finch preferred not to hold a position as a director, but she attended meetings as secretary of the board. The majority of the directors appeared to be satisfied with the new presidency, partly because of the improved profit position which offered greater protection to the creditors.

The approximate division of the common stock in the company was as follows

Mabel Finch	25%
Her sister	18
Her brother	17
Mr. Yount	10
Mr. Oswald	20
Others	10

The company had paid no dividends to the stockholders for over ten years up to late 1955, when the board voted a dividend of $1 per share. Mr. Welch had at first favored a larger dividend but was convinced that this would be unwise after examining a cash budget for the near future. The payments due on the mortgage, the accrued taxes, and the bonus due the president, and other obligations seemed to preclude a larger dividend at that time.

Miss Finch had always worked at a low salary, both as president and vice-president. In 1956 the board approved an increase in her salary from $3,500 to $5,000. She had felt an obligation to her family to keep her father's business going. She also felt the same responsibility to the company employees that her father had exhibited in earlier years.

The situation in 1956

Mr. Welch became increasingly concerned with the company's situation as the years passed. The profit position deteriorated after 1954. The company appeared to be too dependent on a single customer, the corre-

EXHIBIT 1

COMPARATIVE PROFIT AND LOSS STATEMENT FOR THE FISCAL YEARS ENDED SEPTEMBER 30, 1953, 1954, 1955, 1956

	1953 Amount	1953 Percent to Net Sales	1954 Amount	1954 Percent to Net Sales	1955 Amount	1955 Percent to Net Sales	For the 6 Months Ended March 31, 1956 Amount	For the 6 Months Ended March 31, 1956 Percent to Net Sales
Net sales								
Correspondence school	$ 0	0	$ 64,712	27.55	$100,058	36.60	$ 25,530	20.08
Other	174,625	100.00	170,141	72.45	173,306	63.40	101,594	79.92
Total net sales	$174,625	100.00	$234,853	100.00	$273,364	100.00	$127,124	100.00
Cost of sales								
Materials cost	$ 72,228	41.36	$ 87,591	37.30	$102,677	37.56	$ 50,867	40.01
Change in work in process	(508)	(.29)	(735)	(.31)	46	.02	(1,039)	(.82)
Direct department expenses	2,030	1.16	4,552	1.94	4,618	1.69	2,664	2.10
Wages—Direct	44,970	25.75	61,823	26.32	64,866	23.73	32,074	25.23
Wages—Indirect	15,266	8.74	14,244	6.07	15,383	5.63	7,454	5.86
Wages—Maintenance	3,449	1.98	3,234	1.37	3,469	1.27	1,878	1.48
Spoilage	1,155	.66	2,409	1.03	1,794	.66	720	.57
Payroll taxes	1,594	.91	2,043	.86	2,356	.86	895	.70
Power and light	1,256	.72	1,108	.47	1,141	.42	624	.49
Insurance—General	699	.40	765	.33	278	.10	—	—
Water	81	.05	130	.06	105	.04	36	.03
Fuel	747	.43	1,097	.47	991	.36	870	.68
Building maintenance	460	.26	1,377	.59	833	.30	147	.12
Depreciation—Building	655	.38	655	.28	655	.24	480	.38
Depreciation—Machinery	5,015	2.87	5,256	2.23	6,124	2.23	3,045	2.40
Cost of sales	$149,097	85.38	$185,550	79.01	$205,336	75.11	$100,715	79.23
Gross profit	$ 25,528	14.62	$ 49,303	20.99	$ 68,028	24.89	$ 26,409	20.77

EXHIBIT 1—Continued

	1953		1954		1955		For the 6 Months Ended March 31, 1956	
	Amount	Percent to Net Sales	Amount	Percent to Net Sales	Amount	Percent to Net Sales	Amount	Percent to Net Sales
Expenses								
Administrative, general	$ 22,339 ⎱		$ 25,896 ⎱		$ 31,382 ⎱		$ 13,388 ⎱	
Selling and delivery	12,295 ⎰	19.84	12,807 ⎰	16.48	19,570 ⎰	18.64	11,450 ⎰	19.54
Operating profit (loss)	$ (9,106)	(5.22)	$ 10,600	4.51	$ 17,075	6.25	$ 1,571	1.23
Other income	1,640	.94	8,999	3.83	1,377	.50	533	.42
Total	$ (7,466)	(4.28)	$ 19,599	8.34	$ 18,452	6.75	$ 2,104	1.65
Other deductions	+1,748	+1.00	−2,071	−.88	−2,068	−.75	−913	−.71
Profit (loss) before provision for taxes on income	$ (9,214)	(5.28)	$ 17,528	7.46	$ 16,384	6.00	$ 1,191	.94
Provision for taxes—Estimated	0	0	−2,561	−1.09	−5,356	−1.96	−389	−.31
Net profit (loss)	$ (9,214)	(5.28)	$ 14,966	6.37	$ 11,028	4.04	$ 802	.63

spondence school, and sales to that customer showed evidence of declining in 1956 (see Exhibit 1). The tension between the president and vice-president continued, and disharmony spread through the company. For example, the plant superintendent spoke rudely to Miss Finch and refused to let her "interfere" in his department even when it seemed necessary to her to check on the progress of some orders for which she was responsible. Several employees resigned, including one who showed considerable promise as a manager.

Mr. Welch was concerned about several risks facing the company: the risk of losing the correspondence business, with a resultant loss of profits; the risk of declines in "other sales"; the risk of the president's resignation with a probable loss of the correspondence business; and the risk that the internal friction would result in greater inefficiency and higher costs. Mr. Welch believed that most of the stockholders had long before assumed that their stock was almost worthless, and there was a possibility that Mr. Yount (who owned about 10 percent of the stock) might eventually be able to buy up a majority interest at low prices.

Several alternatives occurred to Mr. Welch as he thought about the problems of the company:

1. The company might lower prices to get fuller use of its idle capacity and labor force. Mr. Welch suspected that a high proportion of the costs were fixed, especially wage costs. Printing firms did not normally hire and fire printers as business increased and decreased; they found it necessary to maintain the work force during the lulls, with resultant idle labor during a substantial part of the year.

2. The company might raise prices to improve its margins, though Mr. Welch noted that there were at least 50 competitors in the city, some of which might win customers away if prices were raised.

3. The company might invest in improved equipment in order to cut costs. Mr. Welch knew little about printing equipment. The only proposal for new equipment that he could recall during his period on the board was one for a press like one the company owned. When Miss Finch pointed out to the directors that the existent press was idle a good part of the time, this proposal was abandoned.

4. The company might build or lease a new one-floor plant which would result in lower handling costs. Mr. Welch did not know what this would cost, but he learned from an acquaintance in the printing business that simply moving and rewiring the equipment might cost $60,000.

5. The company might add to its sales force, which consisted in 1956 of the part-time efforts of the president, the vice-president, plus the sales manager, and one additional salesman. The sales manager and salesman were paid a 10 percent commission on sales.

Mr. Welch was not completely satisfied with any of these alternatives.

EXHIBIT 2
COMPARATIVE BALANCE SHEET

| | Year Ending March 31 | | |
ASSETS	1954	1955	1956
Current			
Cash	$ 15,028	$ 19,073	$ 4,152
Accounts receivable	16,188	18,467	29,995
Inventories			
Raw materials	10,598	10,361	9,682
Finished goods	329	537	189
Supplies	2,038	1,941	1,962
Work in process	4,329	4,284	5,322
Total current assets	$ 48,511	$ 54,662	$ 51,302
Other			
Cash surrender value—Life insurance (pledged)	$ 4,518	$ 4,750	$ 4,750
Accounts receivable—Officers and employees	119	739	44
Claim for refund of federal income taxes		892	892
Property, plant and equipment—(Mortgaged)			
Building and building improvements	23,637	24,291	24,291
Machinery and equipment	121,285	118,916	119,168
Delivery equipment	53	53	53
Office furniture and fixtures	6,544	6,667	6,707
Total depreciable assets	$151,517	$149,927	$150,219
Less reserve for depreciation	104,818	111,491	115,161
	$ 46,699	$ 38,436	$ 35,059
Land	9,115	9,115	9,115
Deferred charges	2,623	1,561	1,643
	$111,586	$110,155	$102,805

LIABILITIES AND CAPITAL

	1954	1955	1956
Current			
Notes payable (due within one year)			
Bettsville Industrial Foundation	$ 3,000	$ 3,000	$ 3,000
For equipment purchased	7,400	3,125	2,192
Accounts payable	21,310	20,534	21,062
Accrued expenses	1,084	1,363	1,861
Provision for taxes on income—Estimated	2,688	5,523	401
Provision for bonuses—Estimated			433
Total current liabilities	$ 35,482	$ 33,545	$ 28,950
Deferred indebtedness			
Mortgage notes payable maturing subsequent to September 30, 1954			
Bettsville Industrial Foundation	$ 17,000	$ 12,750	$ 10,500
For equipment purchased	3,200		
American Type Founders, Inc.		806	
Capital stock and surplus			
Common stock authorized and issued (500 shares—No par value)	$ 48,480	$ 48,480	$ 48,480
Surplus	7,423	14,573	14,875
	$111,586	$110,155	$102,805

But he believed that inaction could result in complete failure for the company.

Exhibit 2 presents a comparative balance sheet for the years 1954 through 1956.

1. *Do the profit and loss statements in Exhibit 1 show the economic profits of the firm? Do they reflect the full opportunity costs? Explain.*
2. *Break the expenses in Exhibit 1 into fixed and variable categories. (It may be necessary to split some categories. It will be necessary to use rough judgments in some of the separation of costs.)*
3. *What is the ratio of incremental cost to revenue (sales) according to your fixed-variable cost breakdown? What is the significance of this fact?*
4. *Does the capital stock and surplus category on the balance sheet show the economic worth of the firm? Explain.*
5. *What is the major issue in this case? (Beware of ignoring issues which are not listed in the case.)*
6. *Miss Finch continued to insist on the policy of refusing liquor business. Was she correct in this insistence? Was she rational? Was she ethical?*
7. *What action should Mr. Welch recommend?*

PART TWO / Demand

3 / Demand

Economic analysis usually starts with demand or the consumer side of economic activity and then transfers attention to the supply or cost side. After a treatment of both demand and supply it is possible to bring the two sides together in the discussion of pricing and other types of decisions. This book follows this traditional procedure.

Demand analysis is important to decision making in two ways: (1) it provides the basis for analyzing market influences on the firm's products and thus helps in the adaptation to those influences; and (2) it provides guidance in the manipulation of demand itself. Some decisions require a passive adaptation to market forces while others require the active shifting of those forces.

1. SOME BASIC CONCEPTS

Even though most readers of this chapter are familiar with the terminology of demand analysis, a brief review is in order. Standard usage is essential to full communication on the subject. It is important to recognize that the layman and the professional economist sometimes use the term "demand" in different ways. To the layman demand frequently means simply the quantity sold or to be sold. For example, one often hears an expression such as: "The demand for automobiles may be 7.25 million in the coming year." The economist instead uses the term to mean a functional relationship between a dependent variable, the quantity of purchases, and several independent variables, such as price, income, the prices of substitutes, and so on.[1]

---

[1] If the reader is unfamiliar with the distinction between a movement along a demand curve and a shift in a demand curve, he should review the pertinent sections of any elementary economics textbook.

Quantitative expressions of demand

The economist may express his knowledge of demand in several ways. At the most abstract level he may use mathematical notation to indicate the functional relationship under study, such as:

$$Q_d = f(X_1, X_2, X_3, \ldots, X_n) \tag{3-1}$$

in which

Q_d is the quantity purchasers are willing to buy, and
X_1, X_2, etc. are the influences on Q_d.

Normally the Q_d in such an equation represents the quantity of a particular product (such as shoes), and the X's represent specific influences such as price, advertising expenditures, income, population, the availability of credit, and the prices of substitutes.

Such a functional notation is of limited use to the manager, for it indicates the existence of a relationship without specifying the nature or magnitude of the influences of the independent variables on quantity. One cannot even tell from such an abstract equation whether the relationship is positive or negative—whether, for example, an increase in price has a stimulating or dampening effect on the quantity of sales. It is therefore desirable to express the relationship in concrete form, such as:

$$Y = -2812.8 + 34.4X_1 + 35.6X_2 + 2024.3X_3 \tag{3-2}$$

in which

Y = thousands of refrigerators sold
X_1 = disposable income in billions of 1939 dollars
X_2 = change in disposable income from the preceding year
X_3 = logarithm of time (1925 = 1)

This equation is based on an actual statistical study of refrigerator sales.[2] The parameters of the equation (the constants or coefficients) must of course come from some empirical source—in this case multiple correlation analysis. Such an equation may be useful for forecasting, though projection of an equation based on past data provides a risky basis for predictions in the future.

The economist may express the demand relationship in the form of a demand schedule or demand curve. In this case attention is restricted to one independent variable, usually price. The other variables are held constant. Table 3–1 presents a hypothetical demand schedule.

The same information may be shown on a graph as in Figure 3–1. The

---

[2] *Survey of Current Business,* June, 1950, p. 8. An evaluation of this study appears in Joel Dean, *Managerial Economics* (Englewood Cliffs, N.J.: Prentice-Hall, Inc., 1951), pp. 213–14.

TABLE 3–1

DEMAND SCHEDULE

Price	Quantity (Units per Month)
$10	100
9	120
8	150
7	200
6	260
5	340

economist is quite aware that such a table or graph is a simplification, excluding information about all other influences on the quantity sold. But he often desires to focus attention on one relationship, traditionally the price-quantity relation.

In business practice actual quantification of the demand function is probably the exception rather than the rule. The manager does make subjective estimates of the influence of price and the other variables on sales; without such estimates any rational approach to decisions would be impossible. The present trend is toward quantification, but the cost of the statistical analysis required may in some cases exceed the benefits, especially when uncertainty is great or when the volume is too small to provide a reasonable return on the cost of the research.

FIGURE 3–1

DEMAND CURVE

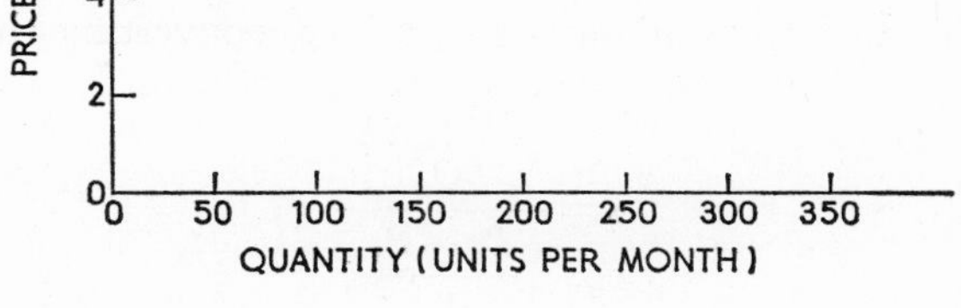

The elasticity of demand

One of the best-known concepts in economics is that of the elasticity of demand. More fully the term is known as the price elasticity of demand to distinguish it from other elasticity measures. The elasticity of demand is an extremely simple idea. It is a measure of the *responsiveness* of the quantity sold to price change (assuming all other variables constant). More specifically the price elasticity is roughly a measure of the ratio of the *percentage* response of the quantity sold to a *percentage* change in price. Such a comparison of percentages with percentages is a great convenience, for it is independent of the particular units in which prices or quantities are measured; it is an abstract number that may be compared with elasticities on other products at other times.

Several formulas for computing elasticities of demand are available, varying in accuracy and sophistication. A crude but simple formula is

$$\eta = \frac{\dfrac{Q_2 - Q_1}{Q_1}}{\dfrac{P_2 - P_1}{P_1}} \tag{3-3}$$

where

η = the elasticity of demand
Q_1 = the quantity sold before the price change
Q_2 = the quantity sold after the price change
P_1 = the price before the price change
P_2 = the price after the price change

The numerator of this expression is the change in the quantity as a ratio of the original quantity. The denominator expresses the change in price as a ratio of the original price. The result is usually a negative number, since the change in quantity should be opposite in sign to the change in price. Often the minus sign is omitted from the result; it is taken for granted.

Formula (3–3) is useful for rough estimates. Its most serious limitation is that it expresses the changes in quantity or price as ratios of the *original* quantity or price, introducing a bias, as can be seen from comparing its results with those from alternative formulas. The computations could just as well be based on *final* quantities or prices, converting the formula to

$$\eta = \frac{\dfrac{Q_2 - Q_1}{Q_2}}{\dfrac{P_2 - P_1}{P_2}} \tag{3-4}$$

The result will differ in most cases from the answer provided by Formula (3–3).

A slightly more complicated formula overcomes the bias resulting from computing the percentages on the basis of the original prices and quantities alone by expressing the changes as ratios to the sum of the original and final amounts as in

$$\eta = \frac{\dfrac{Q_2 - Q_1}{Q_2 + Q_1}}{\dfrac{P_2 - P_1}{P_2 + P_1}} \qquad (3\text{--}5)$$

The formulas so far provide measures of *arc* elasticity. They measure the responsiveness of quantity change to price change over a *finite* movement of price and quantity. Since they cover the entire distance from Q_1 to Q_2 and from P_1 to P_2 they average together elasticities at points in between. Another measure of elasticity is available, known as point elasticity. It measures the responsiveness of quantity to price at a given point and requires calculus in its computation. The formula is

$$\eta = \frac{dQ}{dP} \cdot \frac{P}{Q} \qquad (3\text{--}6)$$

in which

P = the price at a given point on the demand curve
Q = the quantity at that price
$\dfrac{dQ}{dP}$ = the derivative of quantity with respect to price at that point

Those familiar with calculus will have no difficulty with this formula. For others it may be sufficient to state that it measures the limit that is approached as the change in quantity and change in price are made smaller and smaller. To make the computation, an equation for the demand curve is necessary. It is then possible to take the required derivative of quantity with respect to price and to multiply this derivative by $\dfrac{P}{Q}$.

Most readers will recognize that the elasticity of demand is not the same as the slope of the demand curve. The slope is given by

$$\text{Slope} = \frac{Q_2 - Q_1}{P_2 - P_1} \text{ or Slope} = \frac{dQ}{dP} \qquad (3\text{--}7)$$

While the slope of a straight-line demand curve is the same at all points, the elasticity for such a curve varies from one point to the next.

An elasticity of zero (perfectly inelastic demand) means there is no response to price change. An elasticity of infinity (perfectly elastic demand) means that the firm can sell any quantity it wishes at the prevailing price, but none at all at slightly higher prices. An elasticity of one (unitary elasticity) means that the percentage change in quantity equals the percentage change in price. Figures 3–2, 3–3, and 3–4 illustrate demand curves with such elasticities throughout the range of the price-quantity relationship.

If the elasticity is one, the total revenue is unaffected by price change.

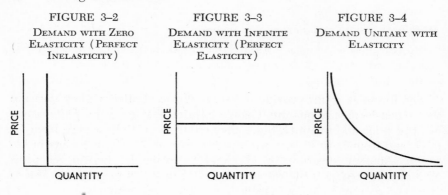

FIGURE 3–2

DEMAND WITH ZERO ELASTICITY (PERFECT INELASTICITY)

FIGURE 3–3

DEMAND WITH INFINITE ELASTICITY (PERFECT ELASTICITY)

FIGURE 3–4

DEMAND UNITARY WITH ELASTICITY

The change in price is exactly offset by the change in quantity. A demand curve with unitary elasticity through its range would have an equation such as

$$R = Q \cdot P \qquad (3\text{–}8)$$

in which R represents total revenue, in this case a constant. It would be unusual to find a demand curve which would even approximate unitary elasticity throughout its range. But many demand curves are elastic in one part of their range and inelastic in another part, which means they include a point at which elasticity is one. Such is the case for a straight-line demand curve sloping downward to the right, as shown in Figure 3–5.

If the elasticity is less than one, total revenue falls as price decreases. If the elasticity exceeds unity, total revenue increases as price decreases. It is important to learn this simple relationship between elasticities and revenue changes.

FIGURE 3–5

LINEAR DEMAND CURVE WITH VARYING ELASTICITIES

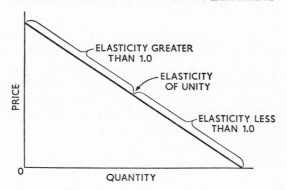

Marginal revenue and incremental revenue

By marginal revenue is meant the addition to total revenue resulting from an additional unit of output (sales). Alternatively, it may be defined as the addition to total revenue divided by the addition to output, if one wishes to obtain an average figure over a range of output greater than one unit. The concept of marginal revenue is closely related to that of elasticity. Its measurement assumes that the position of the demand curve is fixed—that all the influences on quantity other than price are held constant to permit concentration on the price-quantity relation. Or, putting it another way, it assumes that the influence of price can be separated from that of the other variables affecting quantity.

The formula for marginal revenue is

$$MR = \frac{R_2 - R_1}{Q_2 - Q_1} = \frac{\triangle R}{\triangle Q} \tag{3-9}$$

in which R_1 represents the total revenue before the price change that brought about the change in quantity and R_2 the total revenue after this change. The reason for dividing by the difference between the old quantity and the new quantity is to convert the total change in revenue to a change in revenue per *unit* change in output. In terms of calculus the formula for marginal revenue becomes

$$MR = \frac{dR}{dQ} \tag{3-10}$$

which is simply the derivative of the total revenue curve with respect to quantity.

If one knows the elasticity of demand and price he can compute the marginal revenue. It is obvious, for example, that an elasticity of unity means a marginal revenue of zero, for the price change brings no change in total revenue. If the demand is perfectly elastic, the marginal revenue is equal to the price. A general formula for the relation between marginal revenue and demand elasticity is

$$MR = P \left(1 - \frac{1}{\eta} \right) \tag{3-11}$$

Instead of presenting a proof, we urge the reader to test the formula with a few examples.[3]

---

[3] A geometric proof appears in George J. Stigler, *Theory of Price* (New York: Macmillan Co., 1952), pp. 37–38. A simpler and more complete proof using calculus appears in R. G. D. Allen, *Mathematics for Economists* (London: Macmillan & Co., Ltd., 1938), p. 257–58. Please note that the negative sign of η is ignored in this formula. An alternative formulation is $MR = P \left(1 + \frac{1}{\eta} \right)$ in which the negative sign is recognized.

For demand curves sloping downward to the right (which is true of most demand curves), the marginal revenue is less than the price. The reason for this is clear. If the price is reduced from $10 to $9 and sales increase from 1,000 units to 1,500 units, the marginal revenue is not $9. It is true that revenue increases by $9 for each of the added 500 units. But it is also true that the revenue is reduced by the fact that the original 1,000 units now sell for $1 less. The marginal revenue is computed, as indicated in Formula (3–9), by dividing the change in revenue of $3,500 by the change in quantity of 500 units. The result is $7. Another way of arriving at the same figure of $7 is to recognize that for every additional $9 on added units one must in this case deduct a loss of $1 of revenue on each of two units formerly selling at $10.

The incremental revenue concept also has to do with changes in total revenue. Its formula is

$$IR = R_2 - R_1 = \triangle R \qquad (3\text{–}12)$$

It differs from the marginal revenue in two important respects:

1. Incremental revenue is not necessarily converted into changes in revenue per *unit* of output change. It simply measures the difference between the old and new total revenues.

2. Incremental revenue is not restricted to the effects of a change in price. It is a versatile measure of the effect of any kind of managerial decision on total revenue.

Income elasticity of demand

The income elasticity of demand is a measure of the responsiveness of the quantity of purchases to changes in income. The purchases of some commodities respond very little to income changes. An example would be potatoes. The sales of other commodities increase or decrease rapidly with increases or decreases in income. The industries subject to such rapid shifts in demand are known as "feast and famine" industries. The steel industry is a good example. In general, durable consumer goods suffer from higher income elasticities than do nondurable goods.

The income elasticity of demand for most commodities is positive, indicating higher purchases at higher incomes. The income elasticity for a few commodities is negative; such commodities are known as "inferior goods." An example is pork and beans, which are used extensively in periods of low income, but, which give way to more expensive foods in more prosperous periods.

The formula for income elasticity is

$$\zeta = \frac{\dfrac{Q_2 - Q_1}{Q_2 + Q_1}}{\dfrac{Y_2 - Y_1}{Y_2 + Y_1}} \qquad (3\text{–}13)$$

in which Y_2 and Y_1 represent the new and old incomes. In terms of calculus the formula is

$$\zeta = \frac{dQ}{dY} \cdot \frac{Y}{Q} \qquad (3\text{-}14)$$

in which Y and Q are the income and quantity at a given point on the demand function. Disposable personal income is the most common measure of income for such purposes, but other measures of income are also in use.

Knowledge of income elasticities is useful in forecasting the effects of changes in business activity on particular industries. If one has made a forecast of national income or disposable personal income, he can then apply income elasticities in estimating the changes in the purchases of individual commodities. Such forecasting is limited by the same difficulties to which the price elasticities are subject: sales are influenced by other variables not covered by the elasticity measure; and past relationships may not persist in the future.

Cross elasticity of demand

The cross elasticity of demand measures one of the most important demand relationships, the closeness of substitutes or the degree of complementarity of demand. The quantity of sales of one commodity or service is influenced by the prices of substitutes; the lower the prices of substitutes the lower the quantity sold of the commodity under consideration. The formula for cross elasticity is

$$\theta = \frac{\dfrac{Q_2 - Q_1}{Q_2 + Q_1}}{\dfrac{P_{s2} - P_{s1}}{P_{s2} + P_{s1}}} \qquad (3\text{-}15)$$

in which P_{s1} and P_{s2} represent the new and old prices of the substitute commodity.

A high cross elasticity means that the commodities are close substitutes. A cross elasticity of zero means that they are independent of each other in the market. A negative cross elasticity means that the goods are complementary in the market—a decrease in the price of one stimulates the sales of the other.[4] An example would be the sale of high-fidelity components and the prices of records. The lower prices of records have no doubt stimulated the sale of high-fidelity components.

This ends the discussion of demand elasticity concepts. The concept of elasticity is a flexible tool that may be used to measure the influence of

---

[4] We avoid more complex definitions of complementarity, such as those which appear in J. R. Hicks, *Value and Capital*.

changes of any variable on another. The reader probably could work out himself the formulas for total cost elasticity (responsiveness of total cost to changes in output), average cost elasticity, market share elasticity (responsiveness of the percentage share one firm has of the market to changes in the ratio of its prices to industry prices), and promotional elasticity (responsiveness of sales to changes in advertising or other promotional expenditure).

Empirical studies and illustrations

Economists have long experimented with the statistical measurement of demand. In the past half century they have refined their procedures to the point that the econometric treatment of demand has become a rather specialized subject. The leading figure in demand measurement before World War II was Henry Schultz, whose *The Theory and Measurement of Demand*[5] is a classic. Schultz's findings on the demand for sugar are representative of his results. For the period from 1875 to 1929 he found that the price elasticity of the demand for sugar remained fairly constant, in the area of −0.40 or −0.30, with slight evidence of a downward trend in elasticity. That the demand for sugar is inelastic should not surprise the reader; the result is very much in line with what one would expect. Schultz also found that the increase in per capita consumption of sugar had slowed down in the 55 years covered by his study, suggesting a low income elasticity and the absence of a shift in tastes towards sugar and products incorporating sugar.

Schultz's findings on other agricultural commodities are of interest, even though they are based on prewar data and on statistical methods that have since been refined. The elasticities in Table 3–2 are based on

TABLE 3–2

ELASTICITIES OF PER CAPITA DEMAND FOR SELECTED AGRICULTURAL COMMODITIES

Commodity	Price Elasticity with Standard Errors	Comments
Corn	−0.4924 ± 0.1563	Earlier periods show somewhat higher elasticities.
Cotton	−0.1248 ± 0.0570	Considerable change in elasticity over time, partly because of the international character of the market.
Wheat	−0.1854 ± 0.0372	
Potatoes	−0.3073 ± 0.0285	Earlier periods show somewhat higher elasticities.
Barley	−0.3870 ± 0.2361	Earlier periods show somewhat lower elasticities.
Rye	−2.4444 ± 0.4569	Earlier periods show much lower elasticities.

SOURCE: Henry Schultz, *The Theory and Measurement of Demand* (Chicago: The University of Chicago Press, 1938), pp. 551–53.

[5] Chicago: University of Chicago Press, 1938.

the period from 1914 or 1915 through 1929, often with the elimination of the years 1917 through 1921.

Schultz is careful not to attribute too much accuracy to his findings. He notes that the standard errors are relatively large, making it impossible to say with a high degree of probability that the difference between two elasticities is significant. The evidence, with a few exceptions like that of rye, suggests strongly that the demand for agricultural commodities is inelastic, a conclusion supported by more recent studies. This inelasticity means that a small crop has greater value to farmers as a whole than a large crop, a fact that accounts for various attempts to restrict agricultural output.

Richard Stone has conducted a similar study based on more recent British experience.[6] Table 3–3 presents selected elasticities from his study, including income elasticities and cross elasticities, as well as price elasticities. The reader might find it an interesting exercise to try to estimate the elasticities before looking at Table 3–3, or at least to separate those commodities that he thinks will have extremely low price elasticities or low income elasticities from those with higher elasticities.

The low price elasticities for bread, margarine, tea (remember this is a study in the United Kingdom), and tobacco are what one would expect. The positive price elasticity for coffee and the negative cross elasticity of coffee related to tea prices run contrary to all expectations, and indeed Stone rejects them as unacceptable (note that the standard errors are high). That flour and margarine are "inferior commodities" (ones with negative income elasticities) is understandable. To Americans the high positive income elasticity of demand for fish may seem strange. The high substitutability of butter for margarine, of imported mutton and lamb for pork, or carcass meat for bacon and ham, and of other fresh fruit for apples are consistent with the usual observations. It is reassuring that most of these elasticities (but not quite all of them) come so close to a priori expectations, suggesting that it is possible to develop judgment about such matters even without statistical measurements.

Empirical measurements of price elasticities, income elasticities, and cross elasticities for manufactured commodities are less common than for agriculture. Studies of automobile demand both before and after World War II indicate that its price elasticity is not much more than 1.0, a fact that helps explain the reluctance of automobile manufacturers to reduce price to offset declines in demand.[7] The evidence is overwhelming that the elasticity of demand for cigarettes is extremely low in Western countries; in Great Britain, for example, enormous tax and price increases on

---

[6] Richard Stone, *The Measurement of Consumers' Expenditure and Behaviour in the United Kingdom, 1920–1938* (Cambridge, Eng.: Cambridge University Press, 1954), Vol. I.

[7] See, for example, C. F. Roos and V. von Szelski, *The Dynamics of Automobile Demand* (New York: General Motors Corporation, 1939), pp. 21 ff.

TABLE 3-3

Demand Analyses for Selected Products Based on Budget Surveys, 1937–39, or Time Series, 1920–38

Commodity	Income Elasticity	Own Price	Substitution Elasticity with Respect to	
			Price of Specified Commodities	
Flour (1924–38)	−0.15 (±0.11)	−0.79 ± 0.21		
Bread	−0.05 (±0.04)	−0.08 ± 0.07		
Home-produced beef and veal	0.34 (±0.06)	−0.41 ± 0.18	Imported mutton and lamb price	0.50 ± 0.15
Pork	0.58 (±0.24)	−0.67 ± 0.18	Home-produced and imported mutton and lamb price	0.85 ± 0.48
Bacon and ham	0.55 (±0.09)	−0.88 ± 0.12	Carcass meat price	1.45 ± 0.43
Poultry	1.17 (±0.22)	−0.27 ± 0.23	Home-produced mutton and lamb price	0.86 ± 0.35
Eggs	0.54 (±0.07)	−0.43 ± 0.12		
Fish, fresh and cured	0.88 (±0.07)	−0.74 ± 0.15	Carcass meat price	0.49 ± 0.22
Fresh milk	0.50 (±0.18)	−0.49 ± 0.13	Home-produced beef and veal price	0.73 ± 0.15
Butter	0.37 (±0.08)	−0.41 ± 0.13	Flour price	−0.21 ± 0.11
Margarine	−0.16 (±0.11)	0.01 ± 0.17	Butter price	1.01 ± 0.17
Home-produced potatoes	0.21 (±0.06)	−0.56 ± 0.06	Imported potatoes price	0.09 ± 0.06
Home-produced apples	1.33 (±0.21)	−1.67 ± 0.20	Other fresh fruit price	2.77 ± 0.66
Oranges	0.92 (±0.17)	−0.97 ± 0.24	Dried fruit price	0.63 ± 0.32
Sugar	0.09 (±0.04)	−0.44 ± 0.10	Chocolate and confectionery price	1.06 ± 0.34
Tea	0.04 (±0.04)	−0.26 ± 0.07	Coffee price	0.14 ± 0.08
Coffee	1.42 (±0.30)	0.55 ± 0.42	Tea price	−0.54 ± 0.39
Beer	−0.05 (±0.09)	−0.87 ± 0.06		
Tobacco as a whole	0.25 (±0.07)	−0.27 ± 0.06		
Cigarettes	0.22 (±0.10)	−0.39 ± 0.10		
Coal	0.26 (±0.07)	−0.50 ± 0.19		
Electricity	0.15 (±0.11)	−0.60 ± 0.14		

Source: Richard Stone, *The Measurement of Consumers' Expenditure and Behaviour in the United Kingdom, 1920–1938*, pp. 322–27, 390, 400. The elasticities Stone has selected as most reliable are shown, by permission of the Cambridge University Press.

cigarettes have done little to curtail the volume of purchases.[8] Both the price elasticity and the income elasticity of demand for public utility services are low, as one might expect. The income elasticity of demand for clothing and furniture is probably slightly greater than unity; the income elasticity of expenditures upon rent is probably less than unity.[9]

The best known of the U.S. demand studies of the 1960's was that of H. S. Houthakker and L. D. Taylor.[10] Their findings are not easily summarized since they applied a variety of approaches to the different commodities in their study. In most cases they tried to apply a dynamic model which recognizes that current expenditures depend upon preexisting inventories and upon habit formation. The long-term effect of price or income changes is distinguished from the short term. For durable commodities for which inventories are maintained the short-term effect of a change in income will be greater than the long-term effect. For habit-forming commodities, the long-term effect is larger than the short-term effect, and income changes have a smaller effect than they do on durable commodities.

One illustration of the Houthakker-Taylor study is the demand for new cars and net purchases of used cars. The equation reached after considerable experimentation was:

$$f_t = .5183\, f_{t-1} + .1544\, \triangle\, y_t + .0148\, y_{t-1} -$$
$$.4749\, \triangle\, p_t - .0457\, p_{t-1} + 14.0725\, d_t$$

in which

f_t = per capita personal consumption expenditures on new and used automobiles in the year t (1954 dollars)

y_t = total per capita consumption expenditure in year t

p_t = relative price in year t of the good in question (1954 = 100)

d_t = dummy variable used to separate post–World War II years from earlier years; takes a value of 0 for 1929–41 and 1 for 1946–61.

According to this equation, the short-run relative price elasticity was −.9578, while the long-run relative price elasticity was −.1525. The short-run total expenditure elasticity (somewhat like the income elasticity) was .1937 while the long-run total expenditure elasticity was .0308. An attempt to include consumer credit as a variable did not improve the equation.

The Houthakker-Taylor study covered 83 commodities. The authors do

---

[8] A statistical study of the demand for tobacco in 14 countries found low price and income elasticities, but a high response to population growth. A. P. Koutsoyannis, "Demand Functions for Tobacco," *The Manchester School of Economic and Social Studies.* January, 1963.

[9] Summaries of studies of the demand elasticities for these and other commodities appear in Aaron W. Warner and Victor R. Fuchs, *Concepts and Cases in Economic Analysis* (New York: Harcourt, Brace & Co., 1958), pp. 144–69.

[10] H. S. Houthakker and L. D. Taylor, *Consumer Demand in the United States, 1929–1970* (Cambridge, Mass.: Harvard University Press, 1966).

not claim a high degree of accuracy for many of their equations and suggest ways in which research methods could be improved. It is clear that the study of consumer demand is still in the developing stages.

These various measurements of demand are all subject to error. Obviously they do not reach the degree of precision and accuracy of prediction sometimes achieved in the physical sciences. The difficulty of conducting controlled experiments in which one could test the response to given changes in price or income is a great handicap. Furthermore the statistical methods which are applied to the data on quantities and prices are a matter for criticism and improvement. One British study which measured the predictive accuracy of demand analysis came to rather negative conclusions on the subject.[11] That we shall see an improvement in the statistical methods used in measuring demand is beyond doubt.

2. MARKET STRUCTURE

It is time to be quite explicit about a point which is implicit in the preceding discussion, the distinction between two kinds of demand schedules or curves: the industry (market) demand and the demand facing the individual company. It is possible to compute price elasticities and income elasticities for either.

In general, one would expect the price elasticity of company demand to be greater than that of industry demand, for the individual company faces competition from the products of rival firms. These products are substitutes for the company's products; an increase in the company's price will lead to a shift of sales to the rival firms. The precise elasticity of company demand depends on the nature of competition within the industry—on the structure of the market.

A classification of markets

The most elementary breakdown of types of market structures is into four categories:
1. Monopoly
2. Pure competition
3. Monopolistic competition
4. Oligopoly

The case of single-firm monopoly is rare. It is approximated in public utilities, such as electric utilities, which are usually granted a monopoly privilege by government issuance of franchises within a market area. It should be noted that even an electric utility faces some competition from substitutes (gas, fuel oil). In some cases it is difficult to determine where one industry begins and the other ends. Thus the concept of monopoly is

---

[11] Mark B. Shupack, "The Predictive Accuracy of Empirical Demand Analysis," *The Economic Journal,* September, 1962, pp. 550–75.

not a neat one. When a single firm controls an entire industry, the company demand curve and the industry demand curve are the same.

The case of pure competition is equally rare. The conditions for pure competition are: (1) a homogeneous commodity for all firms in the industry; (2) numerous sellers and buyers, so that none has a perceptible influence on the total market; (3) free entry into and exit from the industry. The theory of pure competition also assumes perfect knowledge of the prevailing price on the part of buyers and sellers. Under these conditions the product of one firm is indistinguishable from that of another. Advertising, patents, brand names, and other features that separate one firm's product from that of another do not exist. While cases which meet all of these requirements are exceptional, some markets approach pure competition closely enough that the theory is a useful approximation. Under such conditions, the demand for the individual firm's product approaches perfect elasticity. A perfectly elastic demand implies that the firm can sell all it wishes at the market price. It can sell nothing at a price that is higher, for buyers will transfer to other sellers.

Monopolistic competition refers to markets in which (1) the sellers are numerous and (2) the product of each firm is differentiated from that of the competitors. In such a situation the firm's demand curve slopes downward to the right, with an elasticity greater than that of the industry demand. There is some question whether one may refer to the industry demand curve at all in such a case, for the product of each firm is to some degree different from that of the next. Nevertheless, it is useful to retain the concept of the industry as long as one recognizes its limitations.

Oligopoly refers to markets with small numbers of firms; the Greek base of the word means "few sellers." Two kinds of oligopoly may be distinguished: homogeneous oligopoly in which the product is standardized; and differentiated oligopoly in which the product of each firm is somewhat distinct from that of the next. The markets for steel and cement approximate the conditions of homogeneous oligopoly, for most buyers of those products care little about who is the supplier but are interested in minimizing the cost of an approximately standard product. Differentiated oligopoly is more widespread (automobiles, machinery, household appliances). In such conditions products are differentiated physically; advertising, salesmanship, trade names, and other devices also distinguish the product of one firm from that of another. It is more difficult to generalize about the shape or elasticity of the demand curve in oligopoly than in the preceding market situations. In fact, the interdependence of the price policies of competing firms in oligopoly may preclude drawing a simple demand curve, showing the relationship between a firm's own price and the quantity it sells. Economists have dealt with this problem of interdependence in a variety of ways, some of which will be discussed shortly.

The foregoing four category breakdown of markets will suffice for most purposes. It may be useful, however, to recognize several other categories:

1. Monopsony—markets with one buyer.
2. Bilateral monopoly—markets with one buyer and one seller.
3. Oligopsony—markets with few buyers.

Demand in oligopoly: the kinked demand curve

The relation of market structure to the elasticity of demand is easily summarized for the cases other than oligopoly. As has been stated already, the monopolist's demand is the industry demand. Its elasticity depends on the overall elasticity of demand for the product, which in turn depends on the availability and closeness of substitutes and other characteristics soon to be discussed. In pure competition the firm's demand is perfectly elastic. In monopolistic competition the demand is less than perfectly elastic but is likely to be highly elastic because of the competition from substitutes within the industry. The exact degree of elasticity depends in part on the extent to which the firm's product is differentiated from substitute products in the minds of consumers. It also depends on the ease with which new competitors can enter the industry; easy entry makes the demand for the product of individual firms more elastic, for high prices and high profits will attract new firms into the industries.

The case of oligopoly is less susceptible to generalization, which is unfortunate since oligopoly covers a large proportion of American industry. This difficulty results from the interdependence of the demands facing the individual firms within an industry. In the case of homogeneous oligopoly the interdependence of demand is more pronounced than it is in differentiated oligopoly, in which brand names, advertising, packaging, and the physical differences in the products provide some insulation from competition.

In the late 1930's several writers hypothesized that the demand curve of the firm in oligopoly is kinked. The kinked demand theory is still controversial but is worthy of consideration. According to the theory the firm's demand curve appears as in Figure 3–6. The kink is at the existing price. Above that price the demand is highly elastic. Below, it is less elastic. The result is a sharp break in the marginal revenue curve, as is illustrated in the figure.

It should be made clear that the kinked demand is the demand as perceived by the seller who, on the basis of past experience, predicts the probable reactions of competitors to his price changes. He expects that if he raises price the competitors will not follow, resulting in an elastic demand as his customers transfer to other suppliers. He expects that if he reduces price, the competitors will retaliate, taking away most of the gains

FIGURE 3–6
A KINKED DEMAND CURVE

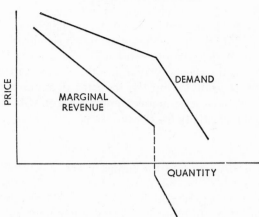

of the lower price. As a consequence, the incentive to change price is reduced, which should mean that prices in oligopoly are relatively sticky.

The empirical studies that will be cited raise doubts about the relevance of the kinked demand theory. Nevertheless, it is clear that the demand curves of the firms in oligopoly *are* interdependent. The individual entrepreneur will not normally change price without evaluating the probable reactions of competitors.

Price leadership and collusion

The kinked demand theory is based on the assumption that each management reaches its own conclusions on price without direct communication with the other firms. In a sense the firms are both independent and interdependent. They set price without consultation with anyone else in the industry, but they evaluate the probable reactions of others. The question is whether in fact this degree of independence is met in industry. Empirical studies suggest two important ways in which the fear of retaliation is actually reduced:

1. Price leadership is one device for minimizing retaliation. Price leadership permits the firms to achieve price flexibility without running the risks suggested by the kinked demand curve. Price leadership is not necessarily inconsistent with the kinked demand theory, for it might be interpreted as a method by which the kink can be shifted in an orderly way. Price leadership may, however, help account for the failure of empirical studies to support the prediction of the kinked demand theory that prices will be stickier in oligopoly than in other market structures.

It should be noted that price leadership does not require direct communication among the firms. It merely requires the establishment of a tradition or custom of following the leader. It does not require that one dominant firm act as the leader. Some studies suggest a pattern of "barometric price leadership" in which a smaller firm changes price and, if this change is confirmed by the larger firms, the new price level prevails.

2. Collusion, in which direct communication among the firms influences price policy, is the second way of limiting intercompany rivalry. The effect of collusion is to divide up the industry demand among the firms, each of which will have a company demand curve with an elasticity of demand close to the elasticity for the industry.

Conditions of entry

The conditions of entry into the industry are another important influence on the oligopolist's demand. In some industries there are considerable barriers to new competition, which provide some protection to the firms already in the industry. In other industries, entry may be relatively easy, making the long-run demand much more elastic and limiting the control of the existing firms over price policy.

What are the barriers to entry that are significant in protecting oligopolists from new competition? Bain suggests four types of barriers:[12]

1. Absolute cost advantages of established firms due to economies in securing inputs or to patented production techniques.

2. Product differentiation advantages resulting from consumer loyalty to the established products.

3. Economies of large scale that make it difficult for a new firm to finance the size or build up a market that permits a minimization of costs.

4. Large capital requirements which exceed the financial resources of potential entrants.

To take some specific examples, entry into the automobile industry is limited by both the requirement of large scale in production and marketing and by loyalty to the existing brands. Entry into the aluminum industry is limited by the difficulty of finding new sources of bauxite. Entry into the newspaper business is limited by the difficulty of building up large enough circulations to attract adequate advertising revenues and sometimes by difficulties in obtaining access to the national news services.

If oligopoly has received a disproportionate amount of space in this discussion of market structure, it is because oligopoly is the most complex and also because it best illustrates the significant influence of market structure on demand. Market structure is a major determinant of the position and elasticity of the individual firm's demand; it is also a determinant

---

[12] Joe S. Bain, *Barriers to New Competition* (Cambridge, Mass.: Harvard University Press, 1956), pp. 1–25.

that is difficult to quantify. The decision maker will find that evaluation of his market structure is one of the most difficult problems that he faces.

Empirical studies and illustrations

Until the 1930's little attention was paid to the relative occurrence of different market structures. The traditional classification of industries was into two categories, competition and monopoly, with neglect of the shadings in between, except for some pioneer studies in oligopoly. Joan Robinson's *Economics of Imperfect Competition* and Chamberlin's *Theory of Monopolistic Competition* argued that pure competition and pure monopoly were exceptions rather than the rule. This led the way to a study of other market structures. The current view is that oligopoly and monopolistic competition are the predominant market forms, though disagreement on their relative prevalence remains.

The statistical tools for measuring degrees of monopoly power are not entirely satisfactory. The usual approach is to measure the concentration of production, by which is meant the percentage of the total industry output contributed by two, three, four, or some other small number of firms. Economists insist that bigness and monopoly power are two different things; a relatively small firm may have considerable control over price if the market is small and competitors few. And there may be pockets of monopoly or oligopoly in industries in which exist thousands of firms.

Table 3–4 presents data on the concentration in 20 leading manufacturing industries. Studies show that changes in concentration are slow; the figures in Table 3–4 for 1947 are still representative of the situation today. The industries shown are not, however, representative of the entire economy; rather they are all manufacturing industries in which concentration is especially pronounced.

A general view in the 1930's and 1940's was that the concentration of ownership in American industry was becoming higher, with a trend towards monopoly and oligopoly. This view wins little support in statistical studies, which show no pronounced trend and which even suggest some deconcentration.

A controversial study of Stigler runs counter to the usual opinion, for his findings indicate a great predominance of competition. According to Stigler the situation in 1939 measured in terms of originating income was:

Competition 55.2%
Compulsory cartels 2.5
Monopoly 24.4
Not allocable .... 17.9[13]

---

[13] George J. Stigler, *Five Lectures on Economic Problems* (New York: Macmillan Co., 1950), p. 50.

TABLE 3–4

Seller Concentration in 20 Manufacturing Industries

Industry	Percentage of Industry Value Product Supplied by 4 Largest Firms in 1947
Passenger automobiles	90*
Meat packing	41†
Steel	45‡
Petroleum refining	37
Flour milling	29
Shoes	28
Canned fruits and vegetables	27
Tires and tubes	77
Cigarettes	90
Soap and glycerine	79
Tractors	67
Farm machinery, except tractors	36
Distilled liquors	75
Rayon	78¶
Metal containers	78
Copper	92‖
Cement	30
Typewriters	79
Fountain pens	57
Gypsum products	85

* Refers to 1951 national passenger car registrations.
† Refers to value added for wholesale fresh meat packing only. Inclusion of retail slaughter and farm slaughter would reduce the figure perceptibly.
‡ Refers to value added figures.
§ Includes all synthetic fibers.
‖ Refers to the control of copper refining capacity in the U.S. in 1947.
Source: Data are from the 1947 *Census of Manufacturers*, except as noted, as republished in Joe S. Bain, *Barriers to New Competition* (Cambridge: Harvard University Press, 1956), p. 45.

Disregarding the unallocable sector, these estimates become:

Competition	67.3%
Compulsory cartels	3.1
Monopoly	29.7

Stigler has avoided the categories of oligopoly and monopolistic competition, apparently including most of oligopoly in the monopoly sector and monopolistic competition in the competitive sector. Stigler's study is a warning against generalizing from a few well-known cases, such as aluminum, steel, and automobiles. At the same time many observers would disagree with part of Stigler's classification, noting, for example, that within industries he lists as competitive are pockets of oligopoly and monopoly.

Such studies of economic concentration developed by social economists for purposes of overall analysis and control, are of limited value in managerial economics. The manager needs to know the impact of the market structure on his own demand, including the probable effects of his price policy on the policies of his rivals. It is possible to discover cases in which the seller has little or no control over price; he must accept the market price. Examples include most of agriculture and the stock market. It is also possible to find firms with such considerable monopoly power that the industry demand curve and the firm demand curve can be taken to be the same. Such is the case of the telephone companies and some of the other utilities, and is also even true of some small service outlets in communities not large enough to support rivals.[14] But the really interesting problems in managerial economics fall in between these extremes. Most firms have some control over price; their demand curves have a downward slope. And among these are firms that must be conscious of existing or potential rivalry.

Unfortunately current research does not provide many helpful generalizations on market structure or on the relation of market structure to demand. We are not even certain about the relevance of the kinked demand theory. Stigler finds that sticky prices are less prevalent in oligopoly, where theory would lead one to expect them, than in monopoly, where the reasons for price stability are less clear.[15] But, as already noted, much of the flexibility of prices in oligopoly no doubt arises from price leadership, which rather than being inconsistent with the kinked demand theory might be interpreted as a way of moving the kink from one price to another. Similarly the adoption by members of an industry of common formulas for estimating prices is probably largely a means of limiting price competition and avoiding the risks of price warfare.

Interviews with managers in oligopolistic industries, including some industries characterized by small firms, suggests that kinked demand thinking may be fairly common. A Danish study of pricing finds evidence of kinked demand reasoning, but the author admits considerable difficulty in interpreting the interview findings. One example is a tannery which continued to charge a higher markup on dyed leather than on black leather, even though technological change had reversed the relative costs of production on the two lines. The author quotes management as stating: "Perhaps we ought to raise the price of black leather somewhat and lower the price of dyed leather to a corresponding degree, but we dare not do so. The fact is that we shall then run the risk of being unable to sell black leather shoes whereas our competitors will also reduce their prices for

[14] As Schumpeter has stressed, even these monopolies may be temporary, since they must face competition from new products and a constant revision of tastes in a continual process of "creative destruction."

[15] George J. Stigler, "The Kinky Demand Curve and Rigid Prices," *Journal of Political Economy*, October, 1947, pp. 432–49.

dyed shoes."[16] A research project led by the author of this textbook has found similar cases and also cases in which the fear is not so much that of price retaliation on the particular commodity under consideration but on other products. One firm, for example, hesitated to reduce price on septic tanks because of fear that its chief rival would retaliate by breaking into the firm's monopoly on burial vaults.[17] In addition are cases of apparent kinked demand reasoning when it no longer appears applicable. For example, such reasoning is widespread in the printing industry, even in cities with large numbers of firms in which the impact of the price policy of one firm on the total market would appear to be small.[18] Such printing markets would seem to be characterized by monopolistic competition rather than oligopoly; one might expect that each firm would set prices without attention to possible reactions of competitors. Yet the continual agitation in the industry for full-cost pricing and for the adherence of individual firms to such a policy suggests that the line between oligopoly and monopolistic competition is blurred. Even more troubling are the cases of some small retailers who seem to believe that customers will react much more strongly to price increases, transferring business elsewhere, than to price decreases, which they feel may have little success in pulling customers from competitors. The psychological basis for this asymmetry of behavior, if it exists, is not easy to see. Such reasoning may be merely a rationalization for inertia in pricing rather than a conclusion based on observation and experience.

Another subject for empirical research is the prevalence of price leadership in oligopoly. Studies have clearly established that leadership patterns do exist in a number of industries, though as one might expect, borderline cases are rather difficult to classify. A pattern of price leadership is, or has been, fairly well established in the oil industry, in steel, in fruit jars, cement, cigarettes, sulphur, and various metal alloys and metal products. The practice would appear to be best suited to conditions of homogeneous oligopoly, but may appear even with considerable differentiation of the product. In the case of differentiation the result of leadership may not be adoption of the *same* price throughout the industry but rather a structure of prices that move together. As has already been noted, price leadership does not imply collusion among the firms, nor does it require that the largest firm or any single firm act consistently as the leader.

Among the most important recent empirical studies of market structure are those of Bain, concentrating on the conditions of entry into various

[16] B. Fog, *Industrial Pricing Policies* (Amsterdam: North Holland Publishing Company, 1960), p. 130.

[17] J. L. Gibson and W. W. Haynes, *The Role of Accounting in Small Business Decisions* (Lexington: University of Kentucky Press, 1962), pp. 57–58.

[18] *Ibid.*, pp. 70–89.

industries.[19] As mentioned earlier, Bain classifies the barriers to new competition into four categories: (1) scale-economy barriers, which make it difficult for new firms to enter because of the problem of reaching the optimal size; (2) product differentiation barriers, which consist of established consumer preferences and control of product designs and distributive channels that make entry difficult; (3) absolute cost advantages, such as control of patents or of raw materials and other productive factors; and (4) capital-requirement advantages of established firms. Table 3–5 pre-

TABLE 3–5

RELATIVE WEIGHTS OF SPECIFIC ENTRY BARRIERS IN 20 INDUSTRIES
(higher numbers denote higher entry barriers)

Industry	Scale-Economy Barrier	Product Differentiation Barrier*	Absolute Cost Barrier	Capital-Requirement Barrier
Automobiles	III	III	I	III
Canned goods	I	I to II	I	I
Cement	II	I	I	II
Cigarettes	I	III	I	III
Copper	n.a.	I	III	n.a.
Farm machinery	II	I to III	I	n.a.
Flour	I	I to II	I	Φ
Fountain pens	n.a.	I to III	I	I
Gypsum products†	n.a.	I	III	I
Liquor	I	III	I	II
Meat packing	I	I	I	Φ or I
Metal containers	n.a.	II	I	I
Petroleum refining	II	II	I	III
Rayon	II	I	I	II
Shoes	II	I to II	I	Φ
Soap	II	II	I	II
Steel	II	I	III	III
Tires and tubes	I	II	I	II
Tractors	III	III	I	III
Typewriters	III	III	I	n.a.

* Alternative ratings refer generally to different product lines within an industry.
† Product differentiation rating refers to the period subsequent to 1950. A rating of III is probably indicated for earlier periods.
SOURCE: Joe S. Bain, *Barriers to New Competition*, p. 169.

sents his findings for 20 leading manufacturing industries. In each case, a III connotes a great or important barrier to entry, while I indicates a low barrier. In the case of capital requirements, there are four ranks, the smallest indicated by Φ. On the basis of these rankings, Bain concludes that the industries with very high entry barriers are:

Automobiles	Liquor
Cigarettes	Tractors
Fountain pens ("quality grades")	Typewriters

[19] Joe S. Bain, *op. cit.*, pp. 15–16.

and those with substantial entry barriers are:

Copper	Shoes (high-priced men's and specialties)
Farm machines (large, complex)	Soap
Petroleum refining	Steel

Firms in the remaining industries, with moderate or low entry barriers, must take into account the long-run effects of price policy on new competition. Bain finds high excess profits among firms with very high barriers to entry, suggesting that they benefit from the long-run as well as the short-run inelasticity of demand.

It would be possible to cite many more studies on market structure, including intensive studies of individual industries. But perhaps enough space has been devoted to that subject. The manager is faced with the problem of determining for himself the market structure in which his firm operates and then determining its implications for demand and for company policy.

3. OTHER INFLUENCES ON DEMAND ELASTICITIES AND DEMAND LEVELS

The preceding section establishes the influence of market structure on demand. It is now appropriate to review a variety of factors affecting demand. Most of these have to do with industry demand, but some of them operate directly on company demand.

Closeness of substitutes

Many of the influences on demand elasticities can be summarized under the heading of "closeness of substitutes." The factors of market structure and differentiation of the product that have already been discussed are aspects of the closeness of substitutes. It might be argued, therefore, that the case of substitution is not a separate topic but rather a catchall for a variety of influences.

The manager can manipulate the closeness of substitutes or degree of differentiation to some extent through advertising and other forms of sales promotion. Sometimes the objective may be to increase the degree of differentiation, with an increase in the monopoly power of the firm. But maximization of differentiation is not, and should not be, the objective of every firm. Many firms indeed profit from making their products as similar as possible to competing products. Some furniture firms, for example, send representatives to the furniture shows to copy the designs of the higher priced leading firms. The objective in such cases is to minimize the degree of differentiation so that the firms can take advantage of the resultant high elasticity of demand with somewhat lower prices. In such cases advertising may aim at increasing rather than decreasing demand elasticities.

Derived demand: producers' goods and consumers' goods

Some commodities and services are produced for direct consumer purchase. Others are materials, parts, services, or components that are eventually incorporated in the final product. The demand for the latter is derived from the demand for the ultimate consumer goods and thus is known as derived demand. The demand for steel is a derived demand, for consumers do not buy steel directly, but buy products incorporating steel or requiring steel somewhere in the productive process. Similarly, the demand for labor services is usually derived from the demand for the products resulting from those services.

The line between what is and is not a derived demand is hazy. One might say that the demand for automobiles is not a direct demand but is derived from the demand for transportation services, and this way of looking at the problem may be useful. Similarly, the demand for new houses is derived from the demand for housing services. But it probably would not be useful to say that the demand for asparagus is derived from the demand for calories, vitamins, and other food values.

In general, derived demands are less elastic than final demands. The less costly the component in relation to the total cost of the final good, the more likely this is to be the case. For example, the demand for glue in binding books is probably quite inelastic, since a large percentage change in the price of glue will have little effect on the total cost of production. Some labor unions may try to take advantage of this principle in demanding high wages for special skills that are a small proportion of total costs. But a demand may be derived and still be subject to competition from close substitutes. If it is easy to replace union labor with machinery, for example, the elasticity of demand for that labor may be high.

The demand for consumer goods may or may not be derived. The demand for producers' goods, however, is always derived; producers' goods are not valuable for their own sake but because they aid in the production of other goods and services. Thus in analyzing the demand for any producers' goods it is necessary to investigate the markets for final or intermediate products using those producers' goods.

Another factor distinguishes the demand for producers' goods from that for consumer goods. The buyers of producers' goods are usually experts, less influenced by promotional activity and more influenced by a careful evaluation of the characteristics of the commodity. Such buyers are often sensitive to small price differences.

Since we are concerned here not only with demand elasticities but also with shifts in demand, this is the appropriate point to introduce a well-known concept: the acceleration principle, also known as the principle of intensified fluctuations in derived demand. If the demand for a final good increases, the demand for the relevant producers' goods may rise more rapidly. The reason is that the demand for increased capacity is likely to be large in ratio to the normal replacement demand. The reader may wish to refer to an elementary text to find numerical illustrations of how this principle works in theory. In the real world of business the assumptions lying behind those simple illustrations are not met fully, but the acceleration principle does provide a partial explanation of the greater volatility of the markets for producers' goods.

Durable and nondurable goods

Another influence on both demand elasticity and demand volatility is the durability of the good. The demand for a durable good, consumer or producers', is likely to be more volatile for two reasons:
1. It can be stored.
2. Its replacement can be postponed.
In addition, the demand for a durable good is more likely to be a derived demand, the volatility of which is high for reasons already developed.

The storability of durable goods makes possible the expansion or contraction of inventories. In the recessions since World War II, the decrease in the size of inventories in billions of dollars has been almost the same magnitude as the decrease in the entire Gross National Product, which means that those industries dependent upon the build-up of inventories as an important part of total demand suffer disproportionately in recessions. If a producer of durable goods wishes to forecast his demand he must give some attention to the probability that the inventories of his product will be increased or decreased. This may require an evaluation of the current inventory-sales ratio and of buyers' attitudes towards increased inventories.

The storability of the commodity also affects the short-run price elasticity of demand. If buyers believe that a reduction of price is temporary, they will tend to build up inventories. A price increase may have the opposite effect. If, on the other hand, the buyers forecast that the price decrease is merely a beginning of a trend, they may wait for even lower prices and use up their inventories. The last point suggests that expectations are a central influence on demand. Customers buy not for the past or present but for the future and must make predictions of the state of future markets. Expectations of price changes are perhaps less important in practice than expectations of shortages, which clearly motivate buyers to stock up now and to avoid shutdowns in the future.

Another influence on the demand for durable goods is the postponability of replacement. In periods of recession, consumers postpone the replacement of automobiles, furniture, and other durable consumer goods.

In the great depression of the thirties, especially in 1932 and 1933, there was little replacement of producers' goods, as is indicated by the fact that the net investment was small or even negative. But in periods of expected shortages, such as the period just after the beginning of the Korean War, replacement demand takes an upward leap.

Long-run and short-run demand

No clear line divides long-run from short-run demand. But demand elasticity does vary according to the amount of time that is permitted for reactions to price change. In general, the short-run elasticity of industry demand is less than the long-run elasticity (unless the cut in price is considered to be temporary). The reasons for this are:

1. It takes time for buyers to become familiar with the new price and to adjust to it, and to make the required changes in their consumption habits.

2. It may take time to finance the purchase of new equipment that is required to use the commodity the price of which is changed. For example, the full effect of a reduction of electricity rates will not be felt until consumers have had time to buy new refrigerators, freezers, and electrical heating devices.

If the short-run change in price is temporary—or, more important, if it is expected to be temporary—the short-run elasticity may be quite high. In such a case, an increase in price encourages the postponement of purchases, and a decrease motivates buyers to stock up on the item. This kind of expectational effect is a short-run rather than long-run phenomenon. As has already been noted, the effect on expectations might be the opposite of that just discussed, with an increase in price leading to the expectation of further increases. Such expectations are more characteristic of speculative markets. The forecaster has a difficult problem in separating those situations in which the elasticity of expectations (to use the technical phrase for this kind of relationship) is positive from those in which it is negative.

Technological substitutability

This list of factors influencing demand would be incomplete without mentioning the physical or technological characteristics of the commodities themselves. Technological substitutability of commodities contributes to substitutability in the market place and to higher demand elasticities. The fact that fuel oil can take the place of coal in generating electricity has increased the elasticity of demand for both oil and coal.

In the modern world, the constant flow of innovation—the development of new products, new distribution and selling techniques, and new modes of production—has a tendency to create new substitutes for old products. The result is what Schumpeter has called "creative destruction," which includes the destruction of demands for old goods and services. No evaluation of demand is complete until the analyst has examined the possible encroachment of new products on old markets. Since the forecasting of technological change is quite hazardous, innovation is another factor creating uncertainty in predictions of demand.

Promotional activity

Management does not necessarily take the demand as given. It can act to shift the position and shape of the demand curve. A sales force can promote the product through personal selling. Advertising can create a greater awareness of a product and its attributes; it may help create tastes which were formerly unknown or unexpressed. Changes in distribution channels or in the service provided may help shift the demand curve upward.

Product improvements

Changes in the product itself will bring a change in its demand. The theoretical economist tends to treat the product as a given, stable entity. But the manager can of course change the product and in many industries is in fact constantly in the process of doing so. A large part of research and development activity is devoted not only to the creation of new products but also to modifying products which already exist.

Population changes

Population growth is another important influence on demand. More specifically, shifts in the age distribution of population bring about substantial changes in markets for a wide range of products. In most parts of the world the proportion of the population below 20 years of age and over 65 years of age is increasing sharply. The proportion of income under the control of these age groups is increasing even more rapidly. Demography, the study of population, will become increasingly significant in demand studies in the future.

Summary

No doubt the foregoing discussion of demand factors is incomplete. Some writers would add that it makes a difference whether the good or service is a luxury or necessity, with the demand for necessities being more inelastic. Whether or not a particular commodity is a necessity depends in part on whether substitutes are available. The economist is more hesitant to use the luxury-necessity classification than is the layman, for the issue is largely one of taste and culture. Some goods which appear now to be essential to life were unknown 60 years ago: the refrigerator is an example. Nevertheless, the analyst may find it useful to consider whether under present conditions the good is likely to be considered a necessity in his evaluation of demand. This will force him to consider some of the sociological influences on demand.

Another hypothesis is that the demand for inexpensive items—items that take up only a small part of the purchaser's income—is less elastic. The reason is that consumers pay less attention to price changes on such insignificant items. This is another factor making the demand for salt inelastic, it is claimed. At the same time, many low-priced items are ones purchased frequently by the consumer, who therefore may be more aware of price change on such purchases than he is on less frequent purchases. Perhaps the way to resolve this issue is to consider these two different influences on demand: the ratio of the price of the item to income, and the frequency of purchase of the item.

It may be useful to review the various demand influences listed so far. A later section will go more fully into the psychological and sociological determinates of demand, but the factors stressed so far are:

1. Market structure, including the extent of differentiation of the product from competitive products. This factor includes the influences of sales promotion, advertising, brand names, etc. It also includes conditions of entry into the industry and the likelihood of retaliation to price change.

2. The availability of technological substitutes for the product.

3. The directness of demand. (Is it a derived demand?)

4. The durability of the commodity.

5. The length of time permitted for adjustments to price change.

6. The degree of consumer urgency for the commodity or service. (Is it a luxury or necessity?)

7. The ratio of the price of the item to the income of the buyer or to the budget of the producer.

8. The frequency with which the item is purchased, with the resultant familiarity with its characteristics and price.

9. Promotional activity.

10. Population change.

Reflection on these influences (some of which overlap) should contribute to skills in the evaluation of demand. But the subjective character of such analysis is obvious. How close is a substitute? How does one measure degrees of differentiation? When does a luxury become a necessity? Until it is possible to quantify these influences it will be impossible to forecast the elasticity or position of demand with precision. Quantification of these behavioral factors will inevitably lag behind quantification of technological and cost factors, which means that the analysis of demand still requires considerable art as well as skill.

Empirical studies and illustrations

Considerable empirical material on the determinants of demand is available. This section will concentrate on studies of the volatility of demand, and studies of the acceleration principle.

Studies of demand volatility.   The Department of Commerce recently studied the effects of income changes on the demands for various commodities. Instead of measuring the income elasticity of demand, these studies focus on income sensitivity, a slightly different concept. As we have seen, income elasticities measure the ratio of percentage changes in *quantity* demanded to percentage changes in income; indexes of income sensitivity measure the ratio of percentage changes in *expenditure* (in dollars) to percentage changes in income. The study covers both prewar and postwar conditions. Some of the main findings are summarized in Table 3–6.

TABLE 3–6

INCOME SENSITIVITY OF SELECTED CONSUMER EXPENDITURES

(based on disposable personal income)

Commodity Group	Prewar	Postwar
Total personal consumption expenditures	0.8	1.0
Durable goods	2.1	1.2
Nondurable goods	.7	.9
Services	.5	1.0
Automobiles and parts	2.8	1.1

SOURCE: U.S. Department of Commerce, Office of Business Economics, as published in L. J. Paradiso and M. A. Smith, "Consumer Purchasing and Income Patterns," *Survey of Current Business,* March, 1959, pp. 21–28.

These data support the conclusion already stated that the demand for durable goods is more volatile than for nondurables, but the differences between durables and nondurables since the war are much less than before. Probably the increased liquidity of consumers and the greater stability of business activity accounts for these changes in sensitivity; consumers are no longer at the mercy of current income in allocating their expenditures. A few comments on the income sensitivity of demand for individual commodities may be of interest. The postwar demand for street railway and bus services has shown a negative income sensitivity, suggesting that these are considered to be inferior services for most consumers, who prefer to use more expensive automobile services if their income allows. The income sensitivity of the demand for gas, electricity, water, and telephone services has shown a sharp increase from the prewar to the postwar period (from 0.2 to 1.3 and over), suggesting that public utilities are no longer insulated from the business cycle. The demand for physicians and dentists has shown an increased income sensitivity (from around 0.8 to 1.1 and over) while that for alcohol has declined, perhaps indicating a shift in consumer attitudes on what are luxuries and what are necessities.

Unfortunately, comparable data are not available on the sensitivity of the demand for producers' goods. But casual observation shows a great decline in the volatility of the demand for such goods as compared with the prewar period, a change which one can hope is permanent since fluctuations in this demand were the primary influence in the major depressions of earlier history. An improvement in investment planning by business helps account for the greater stability of the demand for producers' goods.

Status of the acceleration principle.   Do statistical studies support the famous principle of intensified fluctuations in derived demand? The answer depends on how strictly one wishes to interpret that principle. If he expects it to lead to precise predictions of demand fluctuations, he is going to be disappointed. Several factors complicate the operation of the principle:

1. If the demand for the final good increases but under conditions of excess capacity, no stimulation of derived demand may take place.

2. If expectations are optimistic, the demand for the producers' good may increase even without an increase in final demand.

3. The addition of extra shifts or overtime work makes it possible to increase output without adding to facilities.

4. Technological developments may stimulate the purchase of producers' goods without any change in ultimate demand; furthermore, technological progress may bring a change in the capital-output ratio because of a change in the intensity of the use of capital in producing a particular output.

Thus it should be no surprise that the empirical support for the acceleration principle is meager. Econometricians have been engaged in testing the principle since the pioneer work of Tinbergen in 1938; their findings have been mostly negative.[20] Recent studies have attempted to verify more flexible interpretations of the acceleration principle, relating investment to changes in output over a series of previous periods and making an allowance for excess capacity.[21] These modifications, plus a recognition of the role of expectations, place the acceleration principle in a more favorable light.

One leaves the study of the acceleration principle with mixed feelings. Despite the failure of most empirical studies to support the principle, it is a matter of common sense that changes in the demand for final output must require varying levels of investment. It is also common sense to

---

[20] See J. Tinbergen, "Statistical Evidence on the Acceleration Principle," *Economica*, May, 1938, pp. 164–76; T. Hultgren, *American Transportation in Prosperity and Depression* (New York: National Bureau of Economic Research, 1948), pp. 157–69; and J. R. Meyer and E. Kuh, *The Investment Decision* (Cambridge, Mass.: Harvard University Press, 1957).

[21] L. M. Koyck, *Distributed Lags and Investment Analysis* (Amsterdam: North Holland Publishing Company, 1954), chap. iv, and Robert Eisner, "A Distributed Lag Investment Function," *Econometrica*, January, 1960, pp. 1–29.

recognize that in a world of changing technology, shifting expectations, and excess capacity the principle could not work out in a neat, mathematical way. It probably is wise to retain the acceleration principle as a hypothesis on the behavior of the demand for producers' goods; but it is unwise to use the principle as a total explanation or as a mechanical device for predicting changes in demand.

4. PSYCHOLOGICAL AND SOCIOLOGICAL INFLUENCES AND SOME CURRENT DEMAND HYPOTHESES

Traditional demand analysis takes price, income, and the availability of substitutes as the independent variables and the quantity purchased as the dependent variable. Economists are aware that human beings are involved in this relationship but they usually give little attention to the psychological and sociological motivations of these human beings. Or, when they do give attention to the psychology of consumer behavior, they use concepts usually unfamiliar to the psychologists and sociologists, such as marginal utility and indifference curves.

Utility analysis has an important position in theoretical economics. It has helped clear up some troubling issues in theory, such as the "paradox of value." It has assisted in the construction of welfare economics (which, however, remains in an unsatisfactory state). Marginal utility and indifference curves have so far made little contribution to managerial economics. This is natural, for managerial economics is concerned with the analysis of particular markets rather than with consumer behavior or price structures as abstractions. It would appear that managerial economics requires a more concrete basis for studying the motives and decision-making processes of consumers and businessmen. It is natural that we should turn to psychology and sociology for this kind of analysis.

The question is whether the behavioral sciences are yet prepared to supply the generalizations that might prove helpful in the analysis of demand. In this book it is possible only to list some of the major findings and some of the current directions of research in this area.

1. One of the basic propositions of psychology is that there is much more to human choice than the careful evaluation of alternatives. People make choices for a great variety of reasons, some of which are observable (such as a reaction to a change in price), some of which the individual may not wish to reveal in an interview, and some of which the decision maker may not realize himself. No simple cause-and-effect pattern can describe consumer behavior.

2. Behind patterns of consumer behavior that appear on the surface to be straightforward are deeper causes and motives which are difficult to observe and to measure. Accordingly, research into such behavior is a difficult task, involving techniques that go behind and beyond the simple correlation of prices, incomes, and quantities purchased.

3. Consumer behavior is socially conditioned. Economists themselves have long recognized the inadequacies of the traditional approach of adding together individuals' demand curves to obtain market demand curves. This approach implicitly assumes the independence of each individual's demand for a product. Such an assumption ignores such notions as:

a) Veblen's "conspicuous consumption," which views people as buying not merely to satisfy inner wants but also to impress others.

b) Duesenberry's "demonstration effect," which portrays individuals coming under the influence of the consumption patterns of those with whom they come into contact. A family moving into a wealthy neighborhood is running the risk that the "demonstration" of higher consumption patterns there will set a higher goal of spending. Studies have shown, for example, the major importance of neighborhood influence in the purchase of air conditioners.

c) The notion that commodities serve as status symbols. The drop in automobile sales and the introduction of compact cars in the late 1950's was attributed by some to the reduced prestige value of the automobile. Some observers argued that homes were taking the place of automobiles as status symbols.

4. Interviews may reveal shifts in consumer expectations and attitudes which help explain changing consumption patterns. In particular, it is claimed that attitudes of optimism or pessimism about the future will determine the level of purchases of durable consumer goods, such as furniture, appliances, and automobiles.

At the present state of knowledge of the psychology or sociology of consumption, a great deal of controversy remains. For example, the expression "motivation research" is likely to set off strong differences of opinion—with one camp stressing the deeper Freudian reasons for buying convertible automobiles or smoking cigarettes, while the opposite camp continues to stress the more obvious reasons for purchases, such as the simple enjoyment of acquiring things.

In the near future, research may help reduce such controversy by establishing a firmer basis for our understanding of consumer behavior. In the next decade or two we can expect a more complete synthesis of the economics, the psychology, and the sociology of consumption. At the present time a number of lines of research are in progress.

1. Statistical studies which try to relate data on actual purchases with other observable data, such as liquid asset holdings, age groupings of the population, the extent of consumer debt, marital status, buying plans, price expectations, and income expectations. Electronic computers should make possible a more complete study of the interrelations among these variables.

2. The use of survey techniques based on structured interviews which will provide a larger volume of data on consumer attitudes and behavior.

The Survey Research Center at the University of Michigan has led in the development of such surveys.

3. The use of open-end interviews which may provide knowledge about consumer behavior that the structured interviews cannot reveal. The open-end interview permits the respondents to develop the reasons for their answers in a way that may go beyond "yes" and "no" answers to predetermined questions.

4. The development of projective techniques which attempt to probe deeply into the reasons for consumers' choices. They require long depth interviews extending over several hours. They make use of Rorschach ink-blot tests, sentence completion tests, the interpretation of pictorial representations, and similar devices for discovering the basic causes of consumer behavior. Such techniques may reveal, for example, that some consumers unconsciously connect the consumption of milk and other dairy products with obesity—a fact which may be more important than price or income in explaining their low level of purchases of such products. Projective techniques thus try to discover the deeper psychological reasons for choice, reasons of which the consumer himself may be unaware.

Some current hypotheses

At the present time competition continues between two approaches to consumer behavior. One approach tries to avoid the rather undefined area of psychology and sociology by relating purchasing outcomes to relatively measurable variables, such as income or price. The other approach makes a more direct attack on the intervening psychological and sociological variables. The managerial economist takes an interest in these alternative attacks on the problem despite the inconclusive state of present research, for in the long run these studies should increase our ability to predict demand outcomes.

Earlier sections have developed measures (such as income elasticities) which relate purchases to income. Some economists are dissatisfied with such measures, which are based on the assumption that the *absolute* level of income governs consumption. Two alternatives to the *absolute income hypothesis* have been proposed: the *relative income hypothesis*, which stresses the relative position of the consumer on the income scale, and the *permanent income hypothesis*, which suggests that consumption is related to average income or anticipated income over a number of periods.[22]

The permanent income hypothesis has important implications for the purchase of durable consumer goods. It separates current income into two components: "transitory" income and "permanent" income. The transitory income includes any fluctuations in short-run income that are not expected

---

[22] See Robert Ferber, "Research on Household Behavior," *American Economic Review*, March, 1962, pp. 19–63, for an excellent survey of the literature. Much of the present section is based on Ferber's survey.

to persist in the long run. An increase in transitory income, according to this hypothesis, is more likely to flow into durable goods purchases which are intermittent in character. Transitory income appears to be closely related to the concept of "discretionary" income which has long been used in studies of the demand for durable goods. Discretionary income is that part of income left over after deduction of regular, recurrent expenses; it is available for the purchase of durable goods. One weakness in this approach is the difficulty of drawing the dividing line between that part of income which is permanent and that part which is transitory or discretionary. Nevertheless, the permanent income hypothesis promises to lead to a deeper understanding of consumer behavior.

Other studies are attempting to relate consumption variables to recent changes in income, to increases in household wealth, and to the size of liquid assets. The heavy purchases of durable goods after World War II, for example, are claimed to relate not only to the difficulties of purchasing such goods during the war, but also to the high levels of liquid assets.

To turn away from the hypotheses stressing income, wealth, and liquid assets, we come now to the hypotheses focusing on expectations, attitudes, and other psychological and sociological variables. George Katona has long argued that attitudes such as optimism about the future, and the willingness to buy are important determinants of consumer behavior. These changes in attitudes may bring about shifts in consumption patterns long before income and wealth changes take place. Data on attitudes provide an insight into underlying motives and thus lead to a deeper understanding of behavior.

At the same time that Katona and his associates at the Survey Research Center were collecting attitudinal data, they were also surveying consumer intentions-to-buy, which are on a somewhat different plane from the underlying psychological motives. Close relations between intentions-to-buy and actual purchases were discovered. Some observers have argued that the success of the findings on intentions-to-buy makes the deeper probing into motives unnecessary, since the data on expectations and attitudes appear to add little to the predictive power of this type of analysis.

Other research workers are focusing attention on consumer decision-making processes. For example, attention is being devoted to the extent to which consumers deliberate on the purchase of durable goods. Deliberation appears to be more frequent among consumers with more education and higher incomes.

Such a wide variety of hypotheses and research approaches is confusing to the practitioner. In time this type of analysis should lead to a deeper understanding of consumer behavior and a higher predictive power in dealing with broad consumption aggregates and with the demands for individual commodities.

Empirical studies and illustrations

The recent upsurge of research in consumer behavior is voluminous; only a few examples may be presented here. It is hoped that these examples will reveal the nature of findings in this field of endeavor. The following studies focus attention on the psychological and sociological demand influences:

1. A study of the purchases of instant coffee, reported by Mason Haire,[23] suggests the difficulties of structured interviews. A questionnaire included the question, "Do you like instant coffee?" Those who answered no were asked, "What do you dislike about it?" Most of those with negative responses stated that they didn't like the flavor. The research workers were skeptical of this answer. They found upon deeper probing that many of the respondents thought that the purchaser of instant coffee was lazy. To housewives who place a high value on the art of making coffee, such considerations are probably more important than the simple matter of flavor. But it is difficult for housewives to verbalize these motives; they find it difficult to say that they reject instant coffee because they wish to avoid being classified as lazy.

2. Sociological studies indicate that buying habits are correlated with social positions and conceptions of role. Isolated city dwellers prefer to buy in small stores because of the personal contacts possible there. Concepts of "fashion" vary from one social class to another. Sewing at home has a higher value as a prestige symbol in some social classes than in others.

3. Cartoon devices have been used by psychologists to probe into the deeper reasons for consumer behavior. Such an approach was used to determine the reasons for the decline of a grocery store's sales.[24] A cartoon showed two women drinking coffee at a table. The balloon above the first woman shows her saying: "Well, I feel I have to buy food where the price is lower—that's the main thing as far as I'm concerned." The second woman answers: "Art and I agree that I should shop where . . . ." The respondent is supposed to fill in the rest of the statement, thus indicating attitudes about grocery stores. In this case, a series of seven cartoons produced a pattern indicating the high importance of the quality of meat in the selection of a grocery. The store in question had in fact sold meat of variable quality when it opened, giving an unfavorable first impression.

---

[23] Mason Haire, "Projective Techniques in Marketing Research," *Journal of Marketing*, April, 1950, pp. 649–56. Republished in Robert Ferber and Hugh G. Wales, *Motivation and Market Behavior* (Homewood, Ill.: Richard D. Irwin, Inc., 1958), pp. 93–103.

[24] Martin Zober, "Some Projective Techniques Applied to Marketing Research," *Journal of Marketing*, January, 1956, pp. 262–68. Reprinted in Ferber and Wales, *op. cit.*, pp. 197–206.

As a result of the survey, the store concentrated on advertising the high quality of its meats.

4. An interesting study of the market for air conditioners supports the importance of sociological influences on demand. Some neighborhoods have gone in for air conditioning on a large scale; other neighborhoods with the same socio-economic status have not experienced this upsurge in demand. The demand for air conditioners spreads by means of neighborhood contact, with certain families taking a role of leadership. Thus neighborhood group pressures serve as a major influence on the purchase of these durable goods; "it is the group that determines when a luxury becomes a necessity."[25]

5. Unfortunately validity tests on some of the devices used to probe into psychological motives do not support a high level of confidence in the findings. The best-known of all the projective techniques, the Rorschach inkblot test, has shown little validity as a personnel screening device.[26] Validation experiments involving the Thematic Apperception Test, another well-known projective technique, have also shown low correlations. While such tests have not involved the study of consumer behavior, they suggest extreme caution in using these techniques in forecasting demand. Recent developments in projective techniques indicate that progress in the future is likely. A more careful experimental foundation is required before the validity of this approach can be assured.

The last study to be cited is in the area of durable consumer goods. Durable goods offer an especially difficult challenge to the research worker, since the consumer is able to build up or contract his stock of durables at various rates over time. The problem is one of determining the major influences on these rates of change in purchasing. One must decide at the outset whether he is going to measure the influences on the consumption of the *services* produced by durable goods or is going to try to measure influences on the final purchases. In addition, the researcher faces the following problems:

1. There are no well-defined units in which the quantity of durable goods can be measured. The quantity of wheat is measured in bushels, but in what units do we measure the quantity of automobiles?

2. Great differences exist in the quality of durables and quality changes over time, complicating the measurement problem.

3. Related to the preceding problems is the difficulty of obtaining adequate price data for durables. What is the price of an automobile? The problem is compounded by the fact that the published "suggested prices" are not always the prices at which the goods are sold.

---

[25] W. H. Whyte, Jr., "The Web of Word of Mouth," in L. H. Clark (ed), *The Life Cycle and Consumer Behavior* (New York: New York University Press, 1955).

[26] For a review of statistical study of the Rorschach test see D. B. Lucas, "Can the Clinical Techniques be Validated," in Ferber and Wales, *op. cit.*, p. 127.

4. The existence of a second-hand market for durable goods creates a problem of relating the demand for new units to the demand for old units. It is necessary to consider both the "stock demand" (such as the demand for automobiles both new and old) and the "flow demand" (the demand for new automobiles). But the data on the stocks of durable goods are usually inadequate.

5. The most difficult problem in measuring the stock of existing durable goods is that of depreciation. Only rough approximations of depreciation are possible. The possibility of repairing the durable good means that there is more than one way to increase the stock.

All of these difficulties are illustrated in a study of the demand for household refrigeration.[27] The researcher, M. L. Burstein, attempted to overcome the inadequacies of the suggested list prices by constructing a price index based on the Sears, Roebuck mail order catalog data. He considered a variety of depreciation patterns, both of the declining balance and straight-line varieties, with a preference for assuming a depreciation rate of 10 percent per annum.

Burstein used two different measures of income in his analysis· (1) disposable personal income, which is in line with the absolute income hypothesis and (2) expected income (based on a complicated weighted average of income over a period of eight years), which reflects the permanent income hypothesis. Thirty-eight different equations were fitted to the data, to reflect different income concepts, different treatments of depreciation, different statistical techniques, and so on. The equations were of the form:

$$S = a\, P^{\beta_1}\, Y^{\beta_2}(10)^u$$

where S = per capita consumption of services, P = real income per capita, and u the stochastic variable (a disturbance term, reflecting the inability of the other variables to measure all of the variations in demand influences). Another way of writing the equation is:

$$\log S = a + \beta_1 \log (P) + \beta_2 \log (Y) + u$$

which is linear in logarithms. One great convenience of this type of equation is that β_1 is a measure of the price elasticity of demand and β_2 of the income elasticity. The problem is to find the magnitude of these parameters by "fitting" the equation to the data.

While each of the 38 equations gave somewhat different estimates, Burstein concluded that the price elasticity for refrigeration was between -1.0 and -2.0 and that the income elasticity was between 1.0 and 2.0. It is interesting to note that Burstein made no use of psychological or

[27] M. L. Burstein, "The Demand for Household Refrigeration in the United States," in Arnold C. Harberger (ed.), *The Demand for Durable Goods* (Chicago: The University of Chicago Press, 1960), pp. 99–145.

sociological concepts or data in his analysis, placing his analysis in sharp contrast with the studies discussed earlier in this section. We can expect a continued development of these two kinds of research. While the economist may continue to prefer approaches stressing variables (such as price and income) which can be expressed in monetary units, Burstein's study shows that the measurement of such variables may be every bit as difficult as the measurement of psychological or sociological factors.

4 / Forecasting demand

Forecasting is one of the chief activities of the managerial economist; perhaps it has become his predominant responsibility. We have already commenced our study of forecasting, for the demand studies in the preceding chapter are useful in predicting the effects of changes in the independent variables.

A distinction between conditional and nonconditional forecasts may be useful in relating the present chapter to the preceding one.[1] Conditional forecasting is the less conjectural activity; it involves less uncertainty. It may be defined as the estimation of the impact of certain *known or assumed* changes in the independent variables on the dependent variables. For example, if we know the demand schedule for a particular commodity, we can estimate the effect of a change in price on the quantity of sales. We do not try, in this case, to forecast the change in price itself; we take this change as given. But we do try to predict its effects. Two kinds of uncertainty surround such predictions; we cannot be certain that we have measured the past price-volume relationship correctly; and we cannot be certain that the past relationship still holds (for "all other things" do not remain equal). Nevertheless, we are not asked in this type of prediction to estimate the change in the price itself.

Nonconditional forecasting, in contrast, requires the estimation of the changes in the independent variables themselves. Most of this chapter is concerned with nonconditional forecasting. Such forecasting involves all of the risks of conditional forecasting already mentioned; it also runs the risks of inaccurate estimates of the independent (exogenous) variables.

In practice, forecasters almost always treat some variables as "exog-

---

[1] This distinction is made by H. Theil in *Economic Forecasts and Policy* (Amsterdam: North Holland Publishing Company, 1958), p. 6.

enous," or determined outside the particular model being used. For example, it is usual to treat government expenditure as exogenous, with the view that decisions on such expenditures are determined by political rather than economic forces. The forecaster takes a great interest in such exogenous variables; he may devote considerable time to estimating defense expenditures, for example, but his analysis at this point involves little, if any, economic theory.

Much economic forecasting is concerned with estimating changes in general business conditions. Economic forecasters estimate the level of the gross national product, or national income, or the index of industrial production for some forthcoming period. The techniques for short-term forecasting (usually limited to one year or, at the most, two years in the future) are quite different from those used in long-run forecasting. We shall focus attention on short-run forecasting, which makes greater use of economic analysis.

Forecasts of general business conditions make possible forecasts of the sales of particular industries or individual firms. In converting macroeconomic forecasts into forecasts of details we can make use of the measurements of demand elasticities already discussed. For example, if a forecast indicates a 5 percent increase in national income and the income elasticity of demand for a product is 2.0, we can forecast a 10 percent increase in the sales of that product. Unfortunately, we shall see that forecasting particular demands is usually more complicated than this illustration would suggest.

This chapter starts with techniques for forecasting general business conditions and then transfers attention to forecasting the demand for particular commodities. In forecasting general business, we shall stress the three methods that predominate: (1) gross national product model building of a qualitative-quantitative character; (2) econometric model building; and (3) the lead-lag approach.

1. GROSS NATIONAL PRODUCT MODEL BUILDING

The gross national product is a measure of the value of the production of goods and services within a particular period. For the purposes of forecasting it may be also considered a measure of aggregate demand, of the total spending taking place in the economy. The basic assumption in GNP model building is that demand governs business activity; if total spending increases, business activity increases. The problem of forecasting is thus one of forecasting the components of aggregate demand.

For this purpose it is desirable to break the GNP into several parts, each of which represents an important segment of total expenditure. Some of these components are much larger than others, as is shown in the data for 1967 in Table 4–1. In forecasting, however, the time spent on analyzing a component is not proportional to its dollar magnitude; inventory investment and the consumption of durable consumer goods require attention out of proportion to their share of the total.

The problem of consistency

The procedure is to forecast the components of the GNP and to sum. But the components are interdependent, so that much more than simple addition is involved. The level of consumption, for example, depends

TABLE 4–1

GROSS NATIONAL PRODUCT, 1967
(in billions of dollars)

Personal consumption expenditures		$492.2
Durable goods	$ 72.6	
Nondurable goods	215.8	
Services	203.8	
Gross private domestic investment		114.3
New construction		
Residential nonfarm	$ 24.6	
Other	27.9	
Producers' durable equipment	55.7	
Change in business inventories	6.1	
Net exports of goods and services		4.8
Exports	$ 45.8	
Imports	41.0	
Government purchases of goods and services		178.4
Federal	90.6	
State and local	87.8	
Total gross national product		$789.7

in large part on the level of the gross national product itself. The level of purchases of plant and equipment depends on many factors, but among them is the rate at which the GNP is increasing or the extent to which demand is exerting pressure on capacity. Inventory investment depends on the rate of current purchases as well as on the accuracy with which this rate has been anticipated. Net foreign investment depends in part on the rate of growth in the domestic gross national product as compared with that of foreign national products.

It might be objected that the problem is circular and is insoluble. If each component depends on others or on the total, where does one start? A mathematician would find no difficulty with such a situation; he could construct a series of simultaneous equations to reflect the kinds of interdependence under discussion. In fact, this is exactly what the econometrician does. Even if one does not resort to mathematics, he can make adjustments in one component to bring it in line with a forecast of another, making succeeding adjustments of this sort until he reaches a whole that appears consistent.

Federal government expenditures

The forecaster usually starts with estimates of government expenditures because they are more likely to be independent of the other components. While it is true that the government sometimes adjusts its spending according to the level of business activity, most government spending must be planned in advance; the forecaster can make use of the budgets, proposed legislation, and presidential messages that indicate the direction of federal spending.

The simplest procedure for the untrained forecaster is to start with the latest figure on federal government expenditures and to concentrate on probable increases or decreases in that figure. By concentrating on *changes* in anticipated spending on current production the amateur forecaster avoids some problems of definition and refinement that the professional forecaster would go into more fully. Some government payments, such as social security payments and interest on the federal debt, do not enter into the gross national product, for they are not considered to be payments for current services rendered; they are not earnings from current production. It is necessary to focus attention on federal spending on newly produced goods and services.[2]

What are the sources of information on such changes in government spending? The President's budget message and state-of-the-union message early in the year provide information on what he proposes for the next budget period. The Bureau of the Budget publishes reports on government spending plans.[3] Newspapers and weeklies provide information on how the President's program is progressing in Congress and on other changes in expenditure that may emanate from Congress. Commentators try to evaluate in advance the probabilities of certain programs succeeding in getting through the legislative mill and others failing. Again, it should be stressed that the forecast must be one of *spending on current production.* The mere appropriation of funds by Congress does not assure that those funds will be spent in the period under consideration.

Forecasting federal government spending requires political as well as economic astuteness. In the cold war, one main difficulty is in predicting sudden shifts in military requirements. But, as demonstrated in the Korean War, even shifts in military spending under crisis conditions may be slow.

---

[2] At the same time the forecaster must recognize that government "transfer payments" are an important element in disposable personal income and thus exert an influence on consumption.

[3] A list of these and similar sources appears in Table 4–2.

State and local government expenditure

The task of aggregating the expenditures of thousands of separate state and local governments is beyond the resources of most forecasters. The simplest solution is to deal with probable changes in the aggregate. Since World War II, state and local government expenditures have exhibited an upward trend so consistent from year to year that forecasters are prone simply to project the trend into the future. The projection of past trends is normally a risky venture, for the structural forces that accounted for the trend in the past may not endure in the future. In the case of state and local government expenditures, however, the pressures for the expansion of the road program and for the building of schools would appear to guarantee a continued yearly increment in spending. The trend projection would recognize that state and local government expenditures are increasing at an increasing rate; the increment in spending tends to grow over the years.

Expenditures on plant and equipment

If one knew nothing about the recent levels of spending, forecasting the expenditures on new plant and equipment would be extremely hazardous. Again it is simpler to forecast *changes* in the total based on knowledge of current attitudes, plans, and conditions. At the same time, it is well to remember that this category of spending has in the past shown rather dramatic fluctuations. Investment is based on expectations of future sales and profits, and expectations are prone to change sharply. Investment is also sensitive to the rates of change in the other categories of spending and in current or expected pressures on capacity.

Fortunately, several surveys of business plans for investment are available to assist the forecaster. The McGraw-Hill Book Company publishes (in *Business Week* and elsewhere) a survey of plans for spending on plant and durable equipment. While the survey covers only a part of industry, it has shown a rather close correlation with actual expenditures except in several unusual periods. One of these periods was 1951, in which the unexpected Korean War had pronounced effects on investment. The Commerce Department and the SEC make a similar survey of planned business investment. It is too much to expect that these surveys will always provide an accurate estimate of expenditures on plant and equipment; businessmen may change their minds as actual events unfold. Figure 4–1 shows that the Commerce-SEC estimates have been highly satisfactory, except for 1950. The figure shows percentage increases and decreases in investment forecasts and actual investment. If the comparisons had been ones of the absolute level of investment the errors would have appeared to be much smaller; the deviations between actual and planned investment have averaged only 3 percent in absolute terms in the period from 1948 to 1961.[4] The largest error occurred when the Korean War broke out; investment in 1950 rose 2 percent instead of declining 11 percent as planned.

The forecaster of investment must be aware of a wide variety of influences on investment and try to evaluate their impact. Current profits and stock prices no doubt influence future expectations. Current monetary conditions help determine the ability of firms to finance expansions (though heavy reliance on plowed back earnings blunts this influence). The availability of excess capacity at present helps form expectations of the need for new plant and equipment. The rate of technological change determines the obsolescence of old equipment and thus influences the rate of replacement. It is no use pretending that analysis of such diverse influences is easy; and a high degree of accuracy is not to be expected. Fortunately, the supply of data for investment forecasting is constantly increasing. *The Survey of Current Business,* for example, now publishes data on anticipated changes in sales, on manufacturers' evaluations of their capacity, and on the carryover of plant and equipment projects.

Residential construction

An evaluation of monetary conditions—of the availability of credit, of interest rates, and of the terms on which mortgage loans may be obtained—is more important in forecasting residential construction than for any other sector. The size of down payments required in purchasing new homes, and the length of time for repayment influence the magnitude of construction. The pegged Federal Housing Administration and Veterans Administration interest rates have been major factors in fluctuations in new housing. When those rates are far below current market rates, the availability of FHA and VA loans diminishes sharply. Privately financed housing starts have been much more stable. Among the other influences are: the level of vacancies in homes and apartments already built, the rate of formation of new families which depends on the age structure of the population, and consumer attitudes towards future income prospects.

The forecaster of residential construction should give regard to several statistical series. The F. W. Dodge Corporation publishes data on construction contract awards which give an idea of building that is in prospect about five months in the future. Data are also available in the *Survey of Current Business* and elsewhere on housing starts and on construction already under way. Since it takes a number of months to complete buildings that have been started, figures on housing starts

---

[4] See Arthur M. Okun, "The Predictive Value of Surveys of Business Intentions," *American Economic Review,* May, 1962, p. 220.

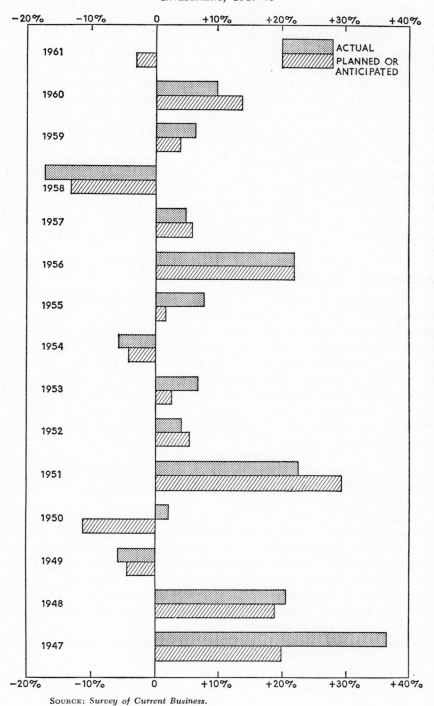

FIGURE 4–1

COMPARISON OF PERCENT CHANGES IN PLANNED INVESTMENT AND ACTUAL
INVESTMENT, 1947 56

ACTUAL
PLANNED OR
ANTICIPATED

SOURCE: *Survey of Current Business.*

provide some insight into the level of construction in the future. The problem of seasonal variations plagues the interpretation of data on construction awards and starts. A rise in one of these indexes may merely reflect the usual spring and summer increase in building activity. It is desirable to correct data for seasonal, but the means for such corrections are not always available. Without such corrections the forecaster will have difficulty in separating cyclical from seasonal influences. It would be desirable if all data were corrected for seasonal; in the area of construction activity such corrected data are especially important, but there is no systematic way of correcting for an unusually severe winter or cool summer.

Inventory investment

The forecaster should not grapple with inventory investment until he has dealt with most of the other sectors, for inventories are peculiarly sensitive to the rate of consumer and investment purchases. Inventory investment is highly volatile, sometimes rising to a positive $10 billion (annual rate) in prosperity and falling to a negative $10 billion in recession. Since World War II no other sector has had a greater influence in determining the pace of expansion or contraction in short-run business activity.

One important influence on inventory investment is the existing ratio between inventory levels and sales. In short-run forecasting it is reasonable to assume that the businessman intends to maintain a certain ratio of stocks to sales. Inventories below this level are inadequate to meet customer requirements. Inventories above this level involve unnecessary interest and storage expenditures and risks of obsolescence. Over long periods, technological change and improvements in inventory management may permit a change in these ratios, but in short-run forecasting such trends can be ignored.

The level of inventory investment depends also on the expectations of businessmen. If they expect sales to increase they will build up inventories, and vice versa. Thus the forecasting of inventory investment must rest in part on an evaluation of business expectations, which in turn depends on expected changes in the other sectors. *Fortune* magazine and other publications attempt to evaluate inventory-sales ratios and sales expectations and to convert these into estimates of inventory changes.

Some forecasters find it useful to distinguish between voluntary and involuntary inventory investment or disinvestment. Inventories may increase because businessmen want them to increase to take care of anticipated improved business. In such a case, a present rise in inventory investment is a favorable indicator of future levels of investment. An increase in inventories may, however, result from a failure of sales to reach anticipated levels, in which case an eventual contraction of the inventory build-up may be expected as firms cut back their orders for replacements. Similarly, inventories may contract because managers planned it so or because of an unexpected increase in sales; the one cause has the opposite significance of the other. It is true that the data on inventory investment do not reveal whether the investment or disinvestment is voluntary or not. But it is not difficult in practice to determine whether the present inventory expansion or contraction is one planned by business or instead one that is likely to experience a reversal in the near future.

The big problem in estimating inventory investment is one of timing. One may know that the present expansion of inventories is temporary but may be unable to specify exactly when the reversal will take place. He may be aware that the present inventory disinvestment results from a desire to bring stocks back in line with sales, but he may not know how long the correction will continue, especially if a continued decline in sales means a continued failure in the restoration of the desired ratio.

The excess of exports over imports

Normally the forecaster will not devote a great deal of attention to the excess of exports over imports, for it is small in magnitude and is not subject to the sharp fluctuations which occur in inventory investment. A thorough analysis of this segment could be extremely complex, involving an evaluation of both the import and export situations, which requires an investigation of the progress of foreign economies as well as the domestic scene, international comparisons of price and wage changes, revisions in tariffs and other policies affecting trade, and the study of the markets for particular commodities important in international trade. A background in international economics would be helpful in analyzing this sector.

Consumption

The Keynesian tradition is to consider consumption to be relatively passive. If the main determinant of consumption is income, then the forecast of the other segments should lead to the required forecast of consumption. One need merely apply the multiplier theory, which says that a given change in the other segments (investment and government spending) should result in an induced change in consumption because of the changes in income that result. We do not yet have a precise idea of what the magnitude of the multiplier is, though we are quite certain that it is less for decreases in nonconsumption spending than it is for increases in such spending.

One simple rule which provides fairly accurate forecasts of consumption is as follows: In normal recoveries from mild recessions the increase in consumption is approximately equal to the increase in nonconsumption spending; in mild recessions consumption remains at the prerecession level or increases slightly. This rule requires modification for more severe recessions or depressions and for inflationary periods or periods (like the beginning of the Korean War) when shortages are expected. In any case, the forecaster should modify his estimates for special influences on consumption in the period under study. In particular he should make a separate study of the demand for durable consumers' goods, which tends to be more volatile and more subject to the special influences which will be discussed shortly.

A more sophisticated approach would make the forecast of consumption a part of the solution of at least two simultaneous equations which would reflect the relations between disposable personal income and the GNP, between consumption and disposable personal income, and which might treat the increase or decrease in nonconsumption spending as an independent variable. This approach begins to move in the direction of the econometric models to be discussed shortly. These approaches to handling the problem of induced changes in consumption will be developed more fully in a few pages.

No one (and certainly not Keynes himself) ever really believed that the forecasting of consumption was a simple matter of estimating income. The forecaster must contend with autonomous as well as induced changes in consumption. There is reason to believe that consumer attitudes and expectations influence the level of their expenditures. And a multitude of factors help determine the level of spending on particular types of commodities and services.

The forecaster may find it convenient to forecast the consumption of durable goods separately, for durable goods more than nondurables are subject to special influences. In fact, the careful forecaster will break durable goods into subcomponents, such as purchases of automobiles, of household appliances, of furniture, and so on. No one could have made an accurate forecast of conditions in 1958 without considering the automobile market, and no one could have come close on automobile sales if he merely assumed that they are governed entirely by income. In the forecasting of the consumption of durable consumer goods one should take into account the present levels of installment debt; a high debt may mean a reluctance of lenders to permit rapid increases in indebtedness and also a reluctance of consumers to obligate themselves further. One should also evaluate the present levels of holdings of consumer durables. One factor depressing the 1958 automobile market was the larger number of fairly new cars already in the hands of the consumers.

In the late 1960's a new type of consumer survey was added to the forecaster's tool kit. It is known as the survey of consumer buying expectations. Every quarter a sample of 15,000 households is questioned on its anticipated spending on automobiles, houses, appliances, and furniture. The results are published quarterly by the Bureau of the Census and the U.S. Department of Commerce in a publication called *Consumer Buying Indicators*. In late 1968 the reliability of these consumer buying indicators was reduced by the introduction of a surtax on the federal income tax, which was likely to have an impact not yet reflected in the survey of consumer buying plans.

Individual components: sources and suggestions

The sketch of gross national product model building presented so far provides a framework for the forecaster. Filling in the detail requires a knowledge of sources of information, supported by skills in using that information to best effect. Table 4–2 lists some of the most important sources of data and indicates their uses.

None of the sources in Table 4–2 should be used mechanically; each requires an evaluation in terms of the other variables and the total business situation. For example, the series on construction contracts awarded does not consistently lead actual construction by an exact number of months. The lead varies from period to period, and erratic fluctuations in the contract awards are difficult to interpret. The chief distinction between the professional and amateur forecaster is in the skills in interpreting such data.

Some awkward problems

In using the gross national product model, the forecaster must face up to some difficulties which are mentioned here only briefly. The two most serious problems are those of price changes and of the induced effects of changes in one segment of the economy on other segments.

Price changes. Forecasting would be much simpler if one could assume stability in prices. But in some years the increase in the gross national product in current dollars may be as much a result of inflation as of changes in the "real" product. The forecaster should provide separate estimates of changes in production and changes in prices.

One simple procedure is to make an initial forecast, using the framework already described, without any attention to potential price changes, temporarily making the assumption of stable prices. The forecaster can then examine the implications of the initial forecast, making adjustments where necessary. If, for example, the initial forecast is one of a great increase in aggregate demand which will place considerable pressure on capacity, the forecaster may anticipate considerable inflation resulting from the competition for scarce resources. In any case, the forecaster must take care in separating his analysis in real terms from that in terms of current dollars. An extrapolation of past increases in state and local government spending which reflect both inflation and increases in volume does not make sense if one is forecasting only the physical increases in output.

TABLE 4–2

SOURCES AND USES OF KEY FORECASTING INFORMATION

Component of GNP	Type of Information	Source and Date	Uses of the Information
Federal government spending	1. President's budget message to Congress.	Newspapers carry summaries in January. Also published by government.	Provides the most important information on federal expenditures for the next fiscal year, starting on July 1. Is subject to revision by Congress.
	2. Summary of the budget message.	*The Budget in Brief* (Government publication in January).	Presents a summary of the budget message.
	3. Review of the economic situation with emphasis on the federal budget.	President's *Economic Report* (Government publication in late January).	Presents an interpretation of the budget and its economic implications.
	4. Review of the economic situation with emphasis on the federal budget.	*Midyear Budget Review* (Government publication in August).	Presents a review of the federal spending program for the current fiscal year, reflecting congressional revisions of the budget.
	5. Reports on congressional action on presidential spending plans.	Newspapers and weekly magazines throughout the sessions of Congress.	Provides information on the success or failure of the President's program in Congress, as well as predictions of future plans both of the President and Congress.
State and local government spending	1. Data on the levels of state and local government spending in recent periods.	The national income accounts in the *Survey of Current Business* (monthly).	The usual procedure is to extrapolate the recent trend into the future, with possible revisions based on newspaper reports on expedited programs or on financial difficulties.
Investment in plant and equipment	1. Surveys of intentions to invest.	McGraw-Hill Book Company (*Business Week* in November); also Department of Commerce and SEC (*Survey of Current Business*, November, March, and other issues).	These surveys provide excellent information in business investment plans for the coming year (or quarter). The past record of these surveys is good for most periods.

TABLE 4–2— Continued

Component of GNP	Type of Information	Source and Date	Uses of the Information
	2. New orders for durable goods.	*Survey of Current Business* (monthly).	Since orders usually lead actual production and sales, this series provides suggestions on future changes in investment.
	3. Nonresidential construction contracts (F. W. Dodge Index).	*Survey of Current Business* (monthly) and *Business Conditions Digest* (monthly).	Since construction awards should normally lead actual construction, this series suggests potential changes in the building of factories, office buildings, stores, etc.
Residential construction	1. Family formation.	Intermittent projections by the Bureau of the Census.	Provides information of a key segment of the potential market for new housing.
	2. Residential construction contracts awarded or housing starts.	*Survey of Current Business* (monthly) and *Business Conditions Digest* (monthly).	Provides an indication of potential changes in housing construction before those changes take place.
	3. Mortage terms and ease of securing loans (down payments, interest rates, monthly payments).	Newspapers provide intermittent reports. *Federal Reserve Bulletin* (monthly).	Information on the terms on FHA, VA, and regular mortgages indicates the financial restraints on the purchase of new homes.
	4. Vacancy rate.	Bureau of Labor Statistics.	Indicates the extent of saturation of the housing market.
	5. Home-building survey.	*Fortune* magazine (monthly).	Indicates developments in residential construction.
Inventory investment	1. Ratios of inventories to sales on the manufacturing, wholesaling, and retailing levels (requires computations involving series on inventories and series on sales).	*Survey of Current Business* (monthly).	Indicate whether inventories are high or low in relation to a "normal" ratio. Must be interpreted with caution in the light of recent changes in final sales and the attitude of businessmen toward inventories.
	2. Manufacturers' inventory expectations.	*Survey of Current Business* (monthly)	Indicate extent to which businessmen expect to expand or contract inventories.
	3. Inventory surveys.	*Fortune* magazine (monthly).	On the basis of sales expectations and assumed inventory-sales ratios, estimates amount of inventory change.

TABLE 4-2— *Continued*

Component of GNP	*Type of Information*	*Source and Date*	*Uses of the Information*
Consumer durable goods	1. Surveys of consumers' intentions to spend and save (including intentions to buy automobiles).	Survey Research Center, University of Michigan and Federal Reserve Board. *Federal Reserve Bulletin* (quarterly).	Indicates intentions to purchase durable goods. There is considerable correlation between these intentions and actual purchases.
	2. Rate of housing construction.	*Survey of Current Business* (monthly).	The building of new houses has an important influence on sales of furniture and appliances.
	3. Installment credit outstanding (in relation to the disposable personal income).	*Federal Reserve Bulletin* (monthly).	A high level of installment credit already outstanding may mean a lower willingness to incur new debt or a lower willingness to lend.
	4. Buying-plan surveys.	National Industrial Conference Board *Business Record*.	Suggests potential changes in the purchase of consumer goods.
	5. Projected consumer outlays on durable goods and housing.	*Consumer Buying Indicators* (quarterly).	Covers surveys of plans of consumers to purchase automobiles, appliances, furniture, and housing.
Nondurable consumer goods and services	1. Regression lines relating the past consumption of nondurable goods and services to the past disposable personal income.	Past issues of the *Survey of Current Business* provide the necessary data. Special articles in the *Survey of Current Business* review findings on such relationships.	Past relationships to disposable personal income show considerable stability, though the rate of sales to income rises in recession.
Comprehensive collection of indicators	1. Charts covering most of the best known indicators.	*Business Conditions Digest* (monthly).	A compact collection of charts covering indicators of income, production, prices, employment, and monetary conditions.

Induced effects on other segments. As has already been noted, the various segments of the gross national product are interdependent. Forecasted changes for one segment may have important implications for another. The econometrician gets around the problem by using simultaneous equations reflecting these interdependencies. The forecaster using the more qualitative model under discussion must somehow make adjustments in his initial forecasts which will perform, at least roughly, the function served by the simultaneous equations.

The two most important kinds of induced effects are (1) the effects of changes in investment and government spending on consumption and (2) the effects of the changes in the demand for total output on investment. The first is the problem of the multiplier; the second the problem of the acceleration effect. The present discussion will concentrate on the multiplier.

The multiplier may be defined as the ratio of a change in income to the change in investment or government spending which brought about the change in income. It may be expressed as:

$$m = \frac{\triangle Y}{\triangle (I + G)}$$

where $\triangle (I + G)$ is the cause, the change in investment and government spending, and $\triangle Y$, the effect, the change in income. As those who have studied elementary economics know, the multiplier is concerned with induced changes in consumption. The initial change in investment, let us say, brings about increases in national income and in disposable personal income which induce changes in consumption.

The forecaster may proceed as follows. He may initially make an estimate of consumption based on the assumption that disposable personal income remains the same. At this stage he takes into account surveys of consumer attitudes and intentions to buy, financial considerations such as the size of liquid assets and the extent of consumer debt, and any other influences on consumption which he is able to uncover. In later stages of his forecast he drops the assumption of the constancy of income. He examines his estimates of changed nonconsumption spending (investment and government expenditure) to see whether these indicate a rise or fall in incomes which will induce a change in consumption.

The crudest way to handle this problem is to make a rough estimate of the multiplier effect based on past experience and apply it to the data. If the change in nonconsumption spending is positive (an increase), the forecaster may take the multiplier to be approximately 2.0, which would suggest induced increases in consumption approximately equal to the increases in nonconsumption spending.[5] If, instead, the forecast indicates

---

[5] This approach neglects the possibility that part of the induced consumption may be lagged in time. But it is necessary to make some simplifications.

a decline in nonconsumption spending, he will apply a much smaller multiplier, for the evidence is strong that short-run declines in income do not affect consumption as much as increases in income. Consumption is "sticky" in the downward direction; in fact, consumption has declined very little in each of the recessions since World War II, suggesting that the multiplier is closer to 1.0 than to 2.0 in such periods. A major decline in investment or government spending would probably have a greater multiplier effect, for consumers would find it more difficult under such circumstances to resist a decline in their standards of living.

A more sophisticated approach would involve the use of several simultaneous equations which will treat the gross national product and consumption as unknowns and will take investment and government expenditures as exogenous variables. On the basis of past experience one might assume that consumption is 80 percent of disposable personal income and that disposable personal income is 69 percent of the gross national product. In such a case the simultaneous equations would appear as follows:

$$GNP = I + G + C$$
$$C = .69 \ (.80 \ GNP)$$

where

GNP = gross national product
I = investment (including the excess of exports over imports)
G = government spending (including state and local spending)
C = consumption

These two equations contain two unknowns (both I and G having been estimated already) and are easy to solve. More advanced approaches would use more complex equations, which might include marginal propensities to consume rather than average propensities, which would separate the effects of increases in nonconsumption spending from the effects of decreases, and which would separate the purchases of durable consumer goods from those of nondurable goods and services.

Any further elaboration of the use of simultaneous equations would bring us to econometrics, the next major topic of this chapter.

Checks for consistency

The final step in gross national product model building is to check the various components for consistency. Among the questions that are appropriate are: [6]

----

[6] See John P. Lewis, and Robert C. Turner, *Business Conditions Analysis* (New York: McGraw-Hill Book Co., 2d ed., 1967), chap. xxiv, for a fuller discussion of these issues.

1. Is the forecast level of government expenditure consistent with the total forecast? If the overall forecast indicates heavy unemployment, a reduction in taxes or an increase in public works might be in prospect. If the overall forecast indicates inflationary pressures, an increase in taxes or curtailment of spending might be imminent.

2. Are the assumptions on monetary sector consistent with the overall forecast? If the overall forecast indicates heavy unemployment, an easing of money by the Federal Reserve System may be imminent, with possible repercussions on residential construction or other sectors.

3. Are prospective profits consistent with other parts of the forecast? We have not discussed the forecasting of profits, but the thorough forecaster will check to see that prospective profits are in line with estimates of investments.

4. Is the level of personal saving consistent with the rest of the forecast? Again, we have not developed the forecast of personal saving, though it is directly related to the forecast of consumption. A complete forecast would devote special attention to the savings forecast.

5. What magnitude of government surplus or deficit is likely under the conditions indicated? Some forecasters pay particular attention to the prospective deficit or surplus. A large deficit would be a stimulant to the economy that should already be reflected in government expenditure. But one can argue that the real point of interest is the *net* contribution of the government above its intake of taxes. If government expenditures are increasing but tax collections are increasing even faster, the stimulating effect of expenditures will be much less than they seem at first.

6. Is the forecast of total output and prices consistent with the available capacity? A strong pressure on capacity might mean that some investment or consumption plans might not materialize and that inflationary pressures will exceed those in the initial forecast.

Recapitulation

The foregoing discussion of gross national product model building has deliberately avoided some of the technical issues the forecaster must face in practice. But an understanding of this approach should be a big step in the evaluation of published forecasts by the decision maker. The reader should now be aware of the kinds of assumptions that go into such forecasting and, consequently, of the limitations of the forecasts. This is not to say that this kind of forecast is deficient. It is the author's view that in the hands of a skilled economist the qualitative type of model under discussion has the most to offer, partly because its limitations are glaringly obvious.

Empirical studies and illustrations

How accurate are the GNP model forecasts? The forecasts of the *United States News and World Report* serve as a starting point. Even though this publication is a popular news magazine, its forecasts have a reputation for sophistication. Each January the *United States News and World Report* forecasts the GNP and related magnitudes. A review of these forecasts from 1957 through 1962 should give some idea of their accuracy.

1. The forecast published on January 4, 1957, for the next 12 months did well in estimating a peak in the GNP in midyear with a downtrend toward the year's end. The actual GNP reached a peak in the third quarter, which is as close to midyear as quarterly data can come. The *United States News and World Report* was low in its estimate of the difference between the 1957 and the 1956 GNP's—the actual increase was $23.6 billion as compared with the predicted increase of $13.8 billion. Apparently the forecast underestimated the amount of inflation in early 1957. The forecast was correct in predicting that 1957 investment would be slightly below that in 1956, though it overestimated the amount of inventory disinvestment, an easy error to make in view of the volatility of inventory investment. All in all, the forecast for 1957 was helpful in predicting the direction of change, though not completely accurate in predicting the amount of change.

2. The forecast on January 3, 1958, was remarkable in that it predicted a turning point in the GNP in the first quarter which actually took place. The forecast underestimated the rate of decrease in the GNP in the recession of early 1958; it also underestimated the rate of recovery. The largest errors appear to have been in the estimates of the fluctuations in investment, which were more violent than the predictions indicated. Again the main errors were in inventory investment. Apparently the forecast also underestimated the rate of increase in government spending.

3. The forecast of January 2, 1959, was more accurate than the two previous ones, with an estimated increase in the GNP of $26.0 billion from the fourth quarter of 1959 to the fourth quarter of 1960 as compared with the actual increase of $27.7 billion. An error in underestimating the increase in consumption was offset by an error in predicting an increase in government spending which did not take place. Most of the other component forecasts were as accurate as could be expected.

More remarkable than the accuracy of the overall fourth-quarter-to-fourth-quarter forecast was the forecast's insight into the pattern during 1959. The *United States News and World Report* predicted that the recovery would continue throughout 1959, interrupted only in event of a steel strike at midyear. It predicted a slowing down of output in the third quarter, with a rather severe decline in the case of a strike. It predicted new highs in activity in the fourth quarter. Figure 4–2 compares the actual changes in the GNP (solid line) with the forecast (broken line). It was necessary to translate some qualitative statements into quantities to make this comparison. It should be noted that Figure 4–2

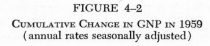

FIGURE 4-2

CUMULATIVE CHANGE IN GNP IN 1959
(annual rates seasonally adjusted)

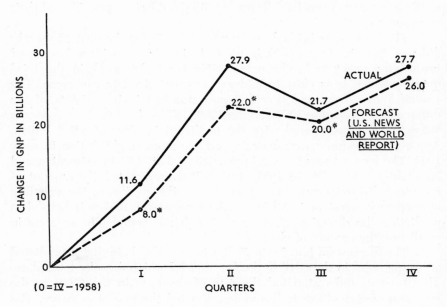

plots the *changes* in the GNP; a graph for the absolute amount of GNP would appear much more accurate. The forecast for 1959 deserves a very high mark.

4. The forecast on January 4, 1960, was again commendable in predicting the pattern during the year. The *United States News and World Report* predicted that most of the increase would come in the first half of the year but that total spending would level off in the third quarter and possibly dip in the fourth. It is true that the expressions "level off" and "may dip" are ambiguous, but the actual decline in the GNP in late 1960 was so small that stronger language would have been misleading.

Figure 4-3 presents the comparison between actual and forecast change in the GNP for 1960. The *United States News and World Report* overestimated the increase in the GNP from fourth quarter to fourth quarter; nevertheless the forecast must be considered a success.

5. The forecast on January 2, 1961, was again overly modest in its estimate of recovery, but it was correct in its timing of the recovery. The GNP actually increased by $34.0 billion compared with the forecast of $20.3 billion. In particular the forecast was overly cautious in esti-

FIGURE 4–3

CUMULATIVE CHANGE IN GNP IN 1960
(annual rates seasonally adjusted)

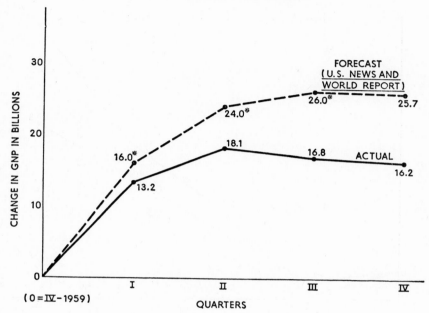

mating the recovery in construction, in inventory investment, and in federal government spending. But the forecast of modest recovery was perhaps more useful to businessmen than the frequent forecasts of boom published in this period. Figure 4–4 presents the comparison of actual changes with the forecast.

6. The forecast on January 8, 1962, was less satisfactory than those already reviewed. Like most forecasts in this period, that of *United States News and World Report* greatly overestimated the rate of recovery in 1962, as can be seen in Figure 4–5. Both consumption and investment fell short of expectations, and even the rate of government expenditure fell below that predicted.

The record of the *United States News and World Report* in this period of six years would encourage confidence in GNP model building as a forecasting tool, despite the error of overoptimism in 1962. Further study would be necessary to determine whether other GNP model builders have done as well.

It is quite clear that most forecasters were in error in overestimating the economic growth in 1962. For example, the Council of Economic

FIGURE 4–4

CUMULATIVE CHANGE IN GNP IN 1961
(annual rates seasonally adjusted)

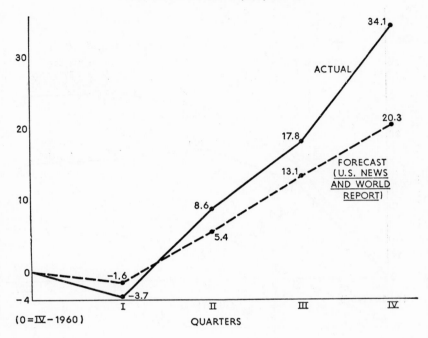

Advisors grossly overestimated the amount of investment and consumption in 1962.[7] The failure of the actual growth to reach the predicted levels was a source of considerable concern to the Kennedy Administration in early 1962 and accounts for the Administration's proposals for sharp tax reductions. But the failure of forecasts in 1962 were failures in predicting the *amount* of change and not failures in forecasting the *direction* of change. All in all, the evidence suggests that forecasting is a worthwhile undertaking, even though it is still subject to substantial risks of error.

The record of forecasting from 1962 to 1968 has been much like that for the period already surveyed. It seems unnecessary to review this more recent period in detail since it contains no turning points; the GNP progressed year after year with some periods of acceleration and deceleration. Forecasting the direction of change has been a relatively mechani-

---

[7] See "What Went Wrong?" *The Conference Board Business Record,* January, 1963, for an analysis of errors in the 1962 forecasts.

FIGURE 4–5

CUMULATIVE CHANGE IN GNP IN 1962
(annual rates seasonally adjusted)

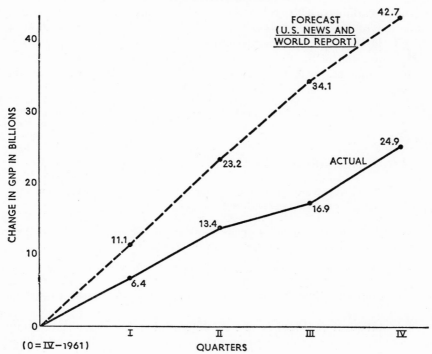

cal operation in this period. The largest error made in the late 1960's was in the magnitude of Vietnam War expenditures which grew much more rapidly than was expected. The result was much stronger inflationary pressures in the period from 1966 to 1968 than some forecasters had recognized.

2. ECONOMETRIC MODELS

Econometrics involves the combination of economic theory, mathematical model building, and statistics. The econometric models used in forecasting general business consist of systems of simultaneous equations which show the pattern of interaction among the specified economic variables, such as income, saving, employment, prices, and output. Statistical methods, such as the method of least squares, are applied to determine the parameters (the constants or coefficients) which provide the best fit of the model to the actual data. Such models are often dynamic in that they relate variables at one moment of time to other variables in other periods. The models include both exogenous and endogenous variables. The endogenous variables are those which require a solution of the simultaneous equations; an example is consumption, which is dependent upon other variables in the model.

The equations of the model consist of two types. Some are identities—equations that are true by definition of the terms. An example is the equation:

$$GNP = C + I + G$$

in which

GNP = gross national product
C = consumption
I = gross private domestic investment plus net foreign investment
G = governmental expenditure

Other equations are behavioral statements, indicating how some variables react to other variables.[8] An example would be:

$$C = 190 + .65Y$$

in which consumption in billions of dollars is related to the disposable personal income (Y).

The statistical problem is one of determining the magnitude of the parameters, so that the equations give a "good fit." In the consumption function equation just presented, the problem is in determining whether the constants of 190 billions and .65 are appropriate in terms of past experience. One of the major limitations of econometrics is that of necessity it must extrapolate past relationships into the future. It must assume that the recent structure of the economy is stable enough that parameters based on past experience are relevant in the future. Another limitation is that it is never possible to introduce enough variables to reflect the full complexity of the economy.

Econometricians do not use their models rigidly in obtaining forecasts. They use judgment in introducing outside information in the form of exogenous variables and even in modifying some of the equations to suit current conditions. For example, they have adjusted consumption function equations to reflect the introduction of compact cars.

The following discussion of econometrics requires no more than an elementary understanding of algebra; the actual construction of econo-

---

[8] A finer breakdown would recognize four types of equations: definitional, behavioral, institutional, and technical. Our behavioral category includes the last three types.

metric models requires considerable advanced work in economic theory, mathematics, and statistics. The objective here is a broad understanding rather than a detailed discussion of technique.

A model of the U.S. economy

The best way to develop the discussion of econometric models is to introduce an actual model now in use. The model used here for illustrative purposes was developed by the office of Business Economics, Department of Commerce, under the influence of the earlier work of Lawrence R. Klein. The model consists of 49 equations, of which 13 are definitional identities. Before discussing the complex model, it is desirable to introduce a simple six-equation model to give an overall view of this approach.[9]

$$C_t = \alpha_0 + \alpha_1 Y_t + \alpha_2 C_{t-1} + u_{1t} \tag{1}$$
$$I_t = \beta_0 + \beta_1 P_t + \beta_2 K_{t-1} + u_{2t} \tag{2}$$
$$W_t = \gamma_0 + \gamma_1 Y_t + \gamma_2 t + u_{3t} \tag{3}$$
$$Y_t = C_t + I_t + G_t \tag{4}$$
$$P_t = Y_t - W_t \tag{5}$$
$$K_t = K_{t-1} + I_t \tag{6}$$

The variables included in the above equations are defined as:

C = Consumption
Y = Income (net product)
W = Wage income
P = Nonwage income
I = Net investment
K = Net capital stock at end of period
t = time
G = Government expenditures on goods and services
u_1, u_2, u_3 = disturbance terms

The subscript t refers to a given time period; $t-1$ to the previous period.

The first equation in this simple model states that consumption in a given period depends on that period's income and on consumption in the previous period. The second equation states that investment depends upon nonwage income and on the stock of capital inherited from the previous period. Wages in the third equation depend upon income and time. The remaining three equations are definitional identities.

The more complete 49-equation model is a variation on the simple model. It includes some *predetermined* variables which are known ahead of time, such as the prior period's consumption and capital stock. It also includes other *exogenous* variables which are not to be predicted

---

[9] A more complete description of the model appears in M. Liebenberg, A. H. Hirsch, and J. Popkin, "A Quarterly Econometric Model of the United States: A Progress Report," *Survey of Current Business*, May, 1966, pp. 13–20.

by the model but introduced on the basis of an independent analysis. An example is government expenditure. Lastly, it includes a large number of endogenous variables the values of which are obtained by solving the 49 simultaneous equations. The disturbance terms are assumed to be zero in the solution of these equations.

The 49 equations are as follows (an explanation of the symbols will be found on page 148):

I. GNP Component Equations

1. Personal consumption expenditures, automobiles and parts

$$C_a = -134.0 - 11.0 \frac{p_a}{p_c} + .104 \frac{Y-T}{p_c} + 129.0(h_w)_{-1} + 1.85 d_a$$
$$ (.14) \quad (6.4) \qquad (.006) \qquad (19.4) \qquad\qquad (.30)$$

2. Personal consumption expenditures, durables other than automobiles and parts

$$C_{od} = 28.0 + .060 \frac{Y-T}{p_{od}} - 65.2 \frac{P}{W} + .060 \left(\frac{L_n}{p_{od}}\right)^{dev}_{-1}$$
$$\phantom{C_{od} =} (.07) \quad (.002) \qquad\qquad (15.2) \qquad (.008)$$

3. Personal consumption expenditures, nondurables

$$C_n = 31.1 + .252 \frac{Y-T}{p_n} + .210 \frac{1}{8} \sum_{t=-1}^{-8} (C_n)_t$$
$$ (.15) \quad (.025) \qquad\qquad (.083)$$

4. Personal consumption expenditures, services (except housing)

$$C_s = -44.2 + .069 \frac{Y-T}{p_s} + .476 \frac{1}{8} \sum_{t=-1}^{-8} (C_s)_t + .347N$$
$$ (.06) \quad (.015) \qquad\qquad (.161) \qquad\qquad (.118)$$

5. One-family housing starts, private nonfarm

$$HS_s = -768 + .622\,(HS_s)_{-1} - .113\,(HS_s)_{-3}$$
$$ (7.9) \quad (.137) \qquad\qquad (.081)$$

$$-43.9\,(r_m)_{-1} + 1530 \left(\frac{R_h}{q_h}\right)_{-1} - .0216 V^{dev}_{-2}$$
$$(13.9) \qquad\qquad (486) \qquad\qquad (.0235)$$

6. Residential structures, nonfarm

$$I_h = -.14 + .001022 \left[.41 \left(\frac{c_h}{q_h} HS\right) + .49 \left(\frac{c_h}{q_h} HS\right)_{-1} \right.$$
$$ (1.06) \quad (.000060)$$

$$\left. + .10 \left(\frac{c_h}{q_h} HS\right)_{-2} \right] - .19 d_1 + .0 d_2 + .38 d_3 + I_{hr}$$
$$ (.21) \quad (.23) \quad (.24)$$

7. Fixed investment, nonresidential

$$I_p = 11.0 + .804 I^e_p + .108(\Delta X)_{-1} + .524(I^a_p - I^e_p)_{-2} + .163t + .14 C_a$$
$$ (1.5) \quad (.045) \quad (.026) \qquad (.126) \qquad\qquad (.012)$$

8. Change in business inventories

$$I_i = 49.9 + .232(X - I_i - C_s) + .363(I_i)_{-1}$$
$$\quad\; (0.2)\; (.044) \qquad\qquad\qquad (.084)$$

$$- .354 \sum_{j=-\infty}^{-1} (I_i)_j + .215(U_d)_{-1} + .72t + 4.34d_i$$
$$(.053) \qquad\qquad\quad (.064) \qquad\quad (.18)\; (.86)$$

9. Imports other than crude materials and foodstuffs

$$F_{if} = 15.5 + .0573\; \frac{Y - T}{p_i} - 49.4\; \frac{P}{W}$$
$$\quad\;\; (0.1)\; (.0026) \qquad\quad (17.0)$$

10. Imports of crude materials and foodstuffs

$$F_{im} = 3.94 + .0027 \left(\frac{pX}{p_i}\right)_{-1}$$
$$\quad\;\; (.03)\; (.0005)$$

II. Price and Wage Rate Equations

11. Implicit price deflator, gross private output, except housing services

$$p = .226 + 1.305\; \frac{1}{3} \sum_{i=0}^{-2} \left(\frac{W - W_g}{X}\right)_i$$
$$\;\; (.0006)\; (.076)$$

$$+ .00208 \left(\frac{X}{X_c}\right)^{9.2} \sum_{j=0}^{-1} \triangle (X - I_i)_j + .00113t$$
$$(.00042) \qquad\qquad\qquad\qquad\qquad (.00018)$$

12. Implicit price deflator, personal consumption expenditures, durables other than automobiles and parts

$$p_{od} = -.095 + .77\triangle p + 1.08\; (p_{od})_{-1} + .000154\; (U_d)_{-1}$$
$$\quad\;\; (.0004)\; (.18) \qquad (.04) \qquad\quad (.000045)$$

13. Implicit price deflator, personal consumption expenditures, nondurables

$$p_n = -.019 + .95\triangle p + 1.016(p_n)_{-1}$$
$$\quad (.0005)\; (.18) \qquad (.012)$$

14. Implicit price deflator, personal consumption expenditures, services (except housing)

$$p_s = -.118 + .155w + 1.56\; \frac{C_s}{C'}$$
$$\quad (.002)\; (.005) \qquad (.41)$$

15. Implicit price deflator, residential structures, nonfarm

$$q_h = .491 + .115w$$
$$\quad (.002)\; (.003)$$

16. Implicit price deflator, fixed investment, nonresidential

$$q_p = .023 + 1.39\triangle p + .976(q_p)_{-1}$$
$$\quad (.0006)\; (.23) \qquad (.008)$$

17. Wage rate (private sector)

$$\frac{w - w_{-4}}{w_{-4}} = \underset{(.002)}{-.015} + \underset{(.0016)}{.0106} \left[\sum_{t=0}^{-3} \left(\frac{N_L - N_w - N_e}{N_L} \right)_t \right]^{-1}$$

$$+ \underset{(.293)}{.877} \sum_{i=0}^{-3} \left(\frac{p_c - p_{c-1}}{p_{c-1}} \right)_i + \underset{(.00047)}{.00128}(P_c - P_{c-4}) - \underset{(.119)}{.311} \frac{w_{-4} - w_{-8}}{w_{-8}}$$

III. Employment, Weekly Hours, and Labor Force Equations

18. Average weekly hours (employees)

$$h_w = \underset{(.0005)}{.821} + \underset{(.018)}{.223} \frac{X}{X_c} - \underset{(.00004)}{.00041t}$$

19. Man-hours per unit of capacity output

$$\frac{h(N_w - N_g + N_e)}{X_c} = \underset{(.0002)}{.1684} - \underset{(.00008)}{.00109t} + [\underset{(.013)}{.125} - \underset{(.00059)}{.00148t}] \frac{X^* - X_c}{X_c}$$

$$+ \underset{(.0121)}{.0579} \frac{X - X^*}{X_c}; X^* = \frac{1}{6}(3X_{-1} + 2X_{-2} + X_{-3})$$

20. Civilian labor force

$$\frac{N_L}{N'} = \underset{(.0030)}{.5753} + \underset{(.126)}{.183} \frac{N_w + N_e}{N'} + \underset{(.00023)}{.00047t} + .83(\hat{u}_{N_L})_{-1}$$

IV. Nonwage Income Components Equations

21. Nonwage personal income

$$P = \underset{(.2)}{55.6} + \underset{(.062)}{.149P_c} + \underset{(.035)}{.794t} + DIV$$

22. Corporate profits and inventory valuation adjustment .

$$P_c = \underset{(.2)}{215.0} + \underset{(.053)}{.275} \left[\frac{CGP}{pX} \right] pX - \underset{(11.4)}{19.4} \frac{w}{p}$$

$$- \underset{(140)}{550} \frac{h(N_w - N_g + N_e)}{X} - \underset{(7.6)}{40.0} \frac{X_c}{X} - D_{ac}$$

23. Dividends

$$DIV = \underset{(.038)}{-.576} + \underset{(.0102)}{.0418P_c} + \underset{(.033)}{.897DIV_{-1}}$$

V. Monetary Equations

24. Interest rate (short-term), 4–6 month commercial paper

$$r_s = \underset{(.03)}{1.06} - \underset{(.102)}{.214R_{-1}} + \underset{(.087)}{.977r_d}$$

25. Yield, corporate bonds (Moody's)

$$r_L = .243 + .082r_s + .885(r_L)_{-1}$$
$$(.017) \quad (.030) \quad (.039)$$

26. Mortgage yield, FHA-insured new homes

$$r_m = .591 + .198r_L + .739(r_m)_{-1}$$
$$(.015) \quad (.070) \quad (.077)$$

27. Liquid assets of households

$$L_h = -154 + 1.084p_c(C' + C_r) + 152\,\frac{1}{r_L} + .85(\hat{u}_{L_h})_{-1}$$
$$(2.4) \quad (.047) \qquad\qquad\qquad (50)\,r_L$$

VI. *Miscellaneous Equations*

28. Capital consumption allowances, constant dollars (fixed nonresidential capital stock)

$$D_p = -4.89 + .0340(K_p)_{-1}$$
$$(.04) \quad (.0010)$$

29. Gross private output at capacity

$$X_c = 3.734(10)^{.00223t}[(K_p)_{-1}]^{.305}[.97(N_L - N_g)]^{.695}$$

30. Personal tax and nontax payments

$$T_p = a_0 + a_1 Y$$

31. Corporate profits tax liability

$$T_c = b_0 + b_1 P_c$$

32. Indirect business tax and nontax liability

$$T_i = -9.39 + .125_p(X - I_i) + .112t$$
$$(.10) \quad (.011) \qquad\qquad (.050)$$

33. State unemployment insurance benefits

$$TR_u = -1.60 + 1.11(N_L' - N_w - N_e)$$
$$(.05) \quad (.06)$$

34. New orders, manufacturers' durables

$$O_d = -1.10 + .955\,\frac{P_c}{p_{wd}}$$
$$(.33) \quad (.052)$$

35. Shipments, manufacturers' durables

$$S_d = 13.8 + .917\triangle(O_d)_{-1} - .202\triangle\left(\frac{U_d}{S_d}O_d\right)_{-1} + .715(O_d)_{-2}$$
$$(.3) \quad (.142) \qquad\qquad (.076) \qquad\qquad\qquad (.048)$$

36. Unfilled orders, manufacturers' durables

$$U_d = -.38 + .92(O_d - S_d) + (U_d)_{-1}$$
$$(.11) \quad (.04)$$

VII. Identities

37. $\quad h = \dfrac{h_w(N_w - N_g) + h_e N_e}{N_w - N_g + N_e}$

38. $\quad HS = HS_s + HS_m$

39. $\quad p_a C_a + p_{od} C_{od} + p_n C_n + p_s C_s + p_r C_r + q_h I_h$
$$+ I_{hf} + q_p I_p + p I_i + e_i - p_i(F_{if} + F_{im}) + F_e + G = GNP$$

40. $\quad GNP = pX + W_g + p_r C_r$

41. $\quad W + P + P_c - DIV - i_c - i_g + T_b + TR_b + D_{ac}$
$$+ D_{anc} + T_i - S_g + SD = GNP; \; |\,SD\,| \leqq 4.0, \,|\,SD - SD_{-1}\,| \leqq 1.0$$

42. $\quad Y = W + P$

43. $\quad T = T_p - TR_u - TR_o + T_e$

44. $\quad w = \dfrac{W - W_g}{h_w(N_w - N_g)}$

45. $\quad p_c = \dfrac{p_a C_a + p_{od} C_{od} + p_n C_n + p_s C_s + p_r C_r}{C' + C_r}$

46. $\quad C' = C_a + C_{od} + C_n + C_s$

47. $\quad S_p = Y - T - p_c(C' + C_r) - i_c - TR_f$

48. $\quad S_c = P_c - T_c - DIV$

49. $\quad K_p = (K_p)_{-1} + .25 I_p - D_p$

The symbols are defined as follows (variables preceded by * are exogenous):

C'	Personal consumption expenditures, except housing services, billions of 1958 dollars.
C_a	Personal consumption expenditures, automobiles and parts, billions of 1958 dollars.
*c_h	Average cost per new private nonfarm housing unit started, in thousands of dollars.
CGP	Corporate gross product, billions of dollars (ratio CGP/pX is assumed exogenous).
C_n	Personal consumption expenditures, nondurables, billions of 1958 dollars.
C_{od}	Personal consumption expenditures, durables other than automobiles and parts, billions of 1958 dollars.
*C_r	Personal consumption expenditures, housing, billions of 1958 dollars.

C_s	Personal consumption expenditures, services (except housing), billions of 1958 dollars.
d_1, d_2, d_3	Seasonal dummy variables, housing expenditures equation; d = 1 in quarter corresponding to subscript, 0 otherwise.
$^*d_a$	Dummy variable for auto equation (−1 during strike quarter; +1 following strike quarter; +1 in 1955 to reflect abrupt credit and taste changes; 0 otherwise).
$^*d_i$	Dummy variable for inventory equation (−1 during strike quarter; +1 before and after strike; 0 otherwise).
$^*D_{ac}$	Capital consumption allowances, corporate sector.
$^*D_{anc}$	Capital consumption allowances, noncorporate sector.
dev	Deviation from least squares linear trend.
DIV	Dividends, billions of dollars.
D_p	Capital consumption allowances, constant dollars, fixed nonresidential capital stock, quarterly rate, billions of 1958 dollars.
e_i	Discrepancy in jumpoff quarter between change in business inventories in current dollars and pI_i.
$^*F_e$	Exports, billions of dollars.
F_{if}	Imports other than crude materials and foodstuffs, billions of 1958 dollars.
F_{im}	Imports of crude materials and foodstuffs, billions of 1958 dollars.
$^*G$	Government purchases of goods and services, billions of dollars.
GNP	Gross national product, billions of dollars.
h	Average weekly hours index, private sector (1957–59 = 1.000).
$^*h_e$	Average weekly hours index, self-employed (1957–59 = 1.000).
h_w	Average weekly hours index, private employees (1957–59 = 1.000).
HS	Private nonfarm housing starts, in thousands at annual rate.
$^*HS_m$	Number of new 2 or more family units started, in thousands at annual rate.
HS_s	Number of new single-family units started, in thousands at annual rate.
$^*i_c$	Interest paid by consumers, billions of dollars.
$^*i_g$	Net interest paid by government, billions of dollars.
I_h	Residential structures, nonfarm, billions of 1958 dollars.
$^*I_{hf}$	Residential structures, farm, billions of 1958 dollars.
$^*I_{hr}$	Residential construction expenditures on other than new units (additions and alterations, etc.), billions of 1958 dollars.
I_i	Change in business inventories, billions of 1958 dollars.
I_p	Fixed investment, nonresidential, billions of 1958 dollars.
I_p^a	Actual plant and equipment outlays in billions of dollars deflated by q_p.
$^*I_p^e$	Anticipated plant and equipment outlays; first anticipations in billions of dollars deflated by q_{p-2}.
K_p	End of quarter net stock of plant and equipment, billions of 1958 dollars.
L_h	End of quarter liquid assets held by households (currency + demand and bank savings deposits + savings and loan shares), in billions of dollars.

$*N$	Total population in millions.
$*N'$	Population, ages 18–64 in millions.
$*N_e$	Self-employed, millions.
$*N_g$	Civilian government employment, millions.
N_L	Civilian labor force, millions.
N_w	Civilian wage and salary employment, millions.
O_d	Durable manufacturers' new orders, billions of dollars deflated by p_{wd}.
p	Implicit price deflator, gross private output, except housing services $(1958 = 1.000)$.
P	Nonwage personal income (sum of proprietors' income, rental income of persons, dividends, and personal interest income), billions of dollars.
$*p_a$	Implicit price deflator, personal consumption expenditures, automobiles and parts $(1958 = 1.000)$.
p_c	Implicit price deflator, personal consumption expenditures $(1958 = 1.000)$.
$*p_i$	Implicit price deflator, imports $(1958 = 1.000)$.
p_n	Implicit price deflator, personal consumption expenditures, nondurables $(1958 = 1.000)$.
p_{od}	Implicit price deflator, personal consumption expenditures, durables other than automobiles and parts $(1958 = 1.000)$.
$*p_r$	Implicit price deflator, personal consumption expenditures, housing $(1958 = 1.000)$.
p_s	Implicit price deflator, personal consumption expenditures, services (except housing) $(1958 = 1.000)$.
$*p_{wd}$	Wholesale price index, durable goods $(1957–59 = 1.000)$.
P_c	Corporate profits and inventory valuation adjustment, billions of dollars.
q_h	Implicit price deflator, residential structures, nonfarm $(1958 = 1.000)$.
q_p	Implicit price deflator, fixed investment, nonresidential $(1958 = 1.000)$.
$*R$	End of quarter excess reserves as percent of total reserves.
$*r_d$	Federal Reserve average discount rate (percent).
R_h	BLS consumer rent index $(1957–59 = 1.000)$.
r_L	Percent yield, corporate bonds (Moody's).
r_m	Percent yield, secondary market, FHA-insured new homes.
r_s	Rate, 4–6 month commercial paper (percent).
S_c	Undistributed profits and inventory valuation adjustment, billions of dollars.
S_d	Manufacturers' shipments, durable goods, billions of dollars deflated by p_{dw}.
SD	Statistical discrepancy, billions of dollars.
$*S_g$	Subsidies less current surplus of government enterprises, billions of dollars.
S_p	Personal saving, billions of dollars.
t	Time in quarters $(1953 - 1 = 1.0)$.

*T_b	Employer contributions for social insurance, billions of dollars.
T_c	Profits tax liability, billions of dollars.
*T_e	Personal contributions for social insurance, billions of dollars.
T_i	Indirect business tax and nontax liability, billions of dollars.
T_p	Personal tax and nontax payments, billions of dollars.
*TR_b	Business transfer payments, billions of dollars.
*TR_f	Personal transfer payments to foreigners, billions of dollars.
*TR_o	Transfer payments to persons, except state unemployment insurance benefits, billions of dollars.
TR_u	State unemployment insurance benefits, billions of dollars.
U_d	Unfilled manufacturers' orders, durable goods at end of quarter, billions of dollars, deflated by p_{wd}.
$(\hat{u}_{L_h})_{-1}$	Estimate of lagged disturbance, liquid assets equation.
$(\hat{u}_{N_L})_{-1}$	Estimate of lagged disturbance, labor force equation.
V	Number of vacant nonfarm housing units, end of quarter, in thousands.
w	Annual wage rate, private sector, in thousands of dollars.
W	Wage and salary disbursements and other labor income, billions of dollars.
*W_g	Government compensation, billions of dollars.
X	Gross private output, except housing services, billions of 1958 dollars.
X^*	Planned private output, billions of 1958 dollars.
X_c	Gross private output at capacity, billions of 1958 dollars.
$Y - T$	Disposable personal income, billions of dollars.

Figure 4–6 classifies the variables in this model into three categories: Exogenous variables, current endogenous variables, and lagged endogenous variables.

Empirical checks on the U.S. model

An econometric model cannot be expected to produce perfect forecasts. The exogenous variables which are estimated outside the model and introduced as inputs into the model may be in error. For example, actual government expenditures may vary from the estimates. Secondly, the parameters in the equations may be somewhat in error; they were obtained by complex regression analysis applied to data for previous years and cannot be expected to be completely accurate, especially for future years. Thirdly, the system of equations is necessarily incomplete and cannot take into account all influences on the endogenous variables. Lastly, statistical analysis of even the most sophisticated variety cannot separate out the influence of each variable from that of the next. Nevertheless there is much to be said for a method which states explicitly what relationships it is postulating; this virtue does not apply to the same extent to the more "judgmental" methods discussed earlier in this chapter.

FIGURE 4–6
CONDENSED FLOW DIAGRAM

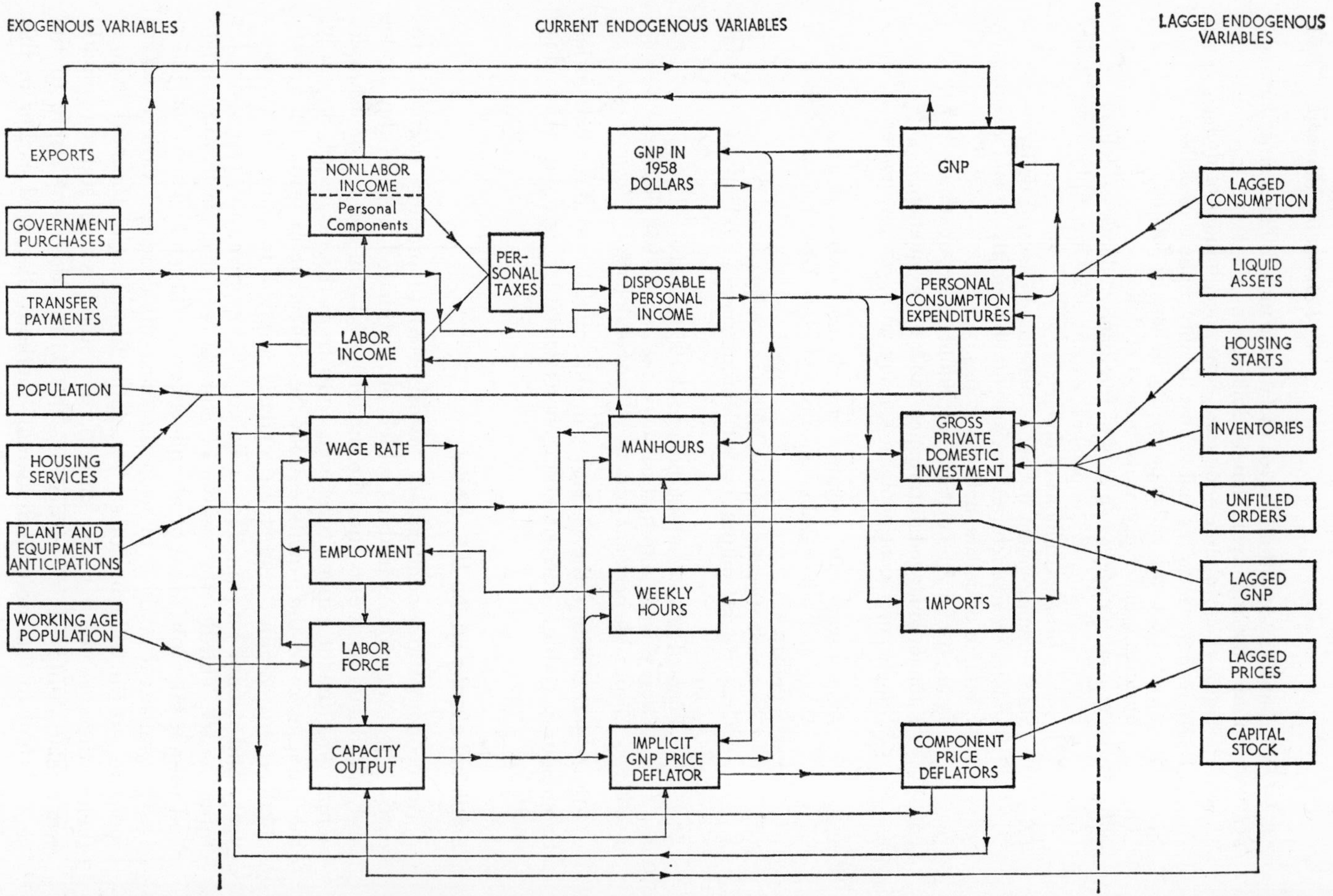

SOURCE: U.S. Department of Commerce, Office of Business Economics.

To test the model's performance, *ex-post* forecasts of economic activity were made for the years from 1953 through 1965. The results are shown in Figure 4–7. It should be stated, however, that the values of the exogenous variables were known in this test; a forecaster of the future economy must make his own estimates of these variables and cannot expect to be completely correct in these estimates. The model was also fairly accurate in predicting the turning points; of 18 forecasts, all but three came within one quarter of the actual turning points. But when the forecasts were made three quarters ahead of the turning point, rather than one or two quarters, the accuracy fell considerably.

FIGURE 4–7
PREDICTED VERSUS ACTUAL GNP, 1953–65

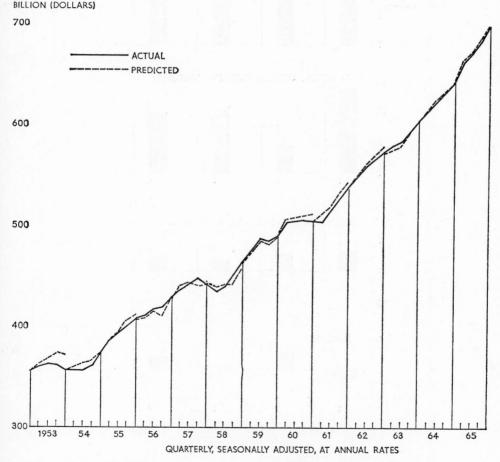

NOTE: Each four-quarter sequence of forecasts starts from actual GNP in the fourth quarter of the preceding year.
SOURCE: U.S. Department of Commerce, Office of Business Economics.

The model was used in a forecast for 1965, a year beyond the period for which the equations were fitted. A comparison of the forecasts with the predictions is shown in Figure 4–8.

FIGURE 4–8

PREDICTED VERSUS ACTUAL QUARTERLY CHANGES IN
GNP AND MAJOR COMPONENTS, 1965

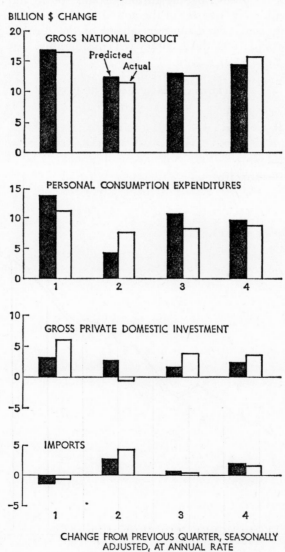

SOURCE: U.S. Department of Commerce, Office of Business
Economics.

Limitations of econometric models

Econometric models are subject to several limitations. Frequently they depend on relatively small samples even though the methods applied assume large samples of accurate data. They incorporate data which may reflect the different economic structures or institutions of earlier periods. They cannot reflect all of the changes in economic structure that may be occurring at the time of the forecast.

New variables may grow in importance, replacing old variables, but there is a lag before the econometrician can incorporate all such changes in emphasis into his model. Often the data are less accurate than would be desired. As Lawrence Klein points out, most of these limitations are problems of any kind of economic analysis.[10]

Econometric models require hard work, with long hours of data collection, months of experimentation, and years of testing. Finally the models require revision every few years. Not every forecaster can afford such an expensive and time-consuming approach. It seems clear, however, that with the refinement of these models and the increased capacity of computers, the econometric approach to forecasting will gain wider acceptance.

Empirical studies and illustrations

How well do econometric models forecast? Perhaps it is too early to give a definitive answer, but the evidence is beginning to accumulate. The use of econometrics certainly does not assure the accuracy of forecasts, as is well demonstrated by Colin Clark's forecast of a major depression in the United States in 1954.[11] But recent evidence is encouraging.

We might start with the accuracy of the forecasts made at the University of Michigan based on variations of the well-known Suits' model.[12] Table 4–3 presents a detailed comparison of the forecast and actual data for 1961, showing a remarkably small error for most components. Figure 4–9 compares the forecast and actual for the period from 1953–61. In each year the forecast of the direction of change was borne out by events as is shown by the fact that the dots appear in the first and third quad-

---

[10] L. R. Klein, *An Introduction to Econometrics* (Englewood Cliffs, N.J.: Prentice-Hall, Inc., 1962), p. 269.

[11] In a series of articles entitled "Danger Signs of An American Recession" in the *Manchester Guardian*. See the *Manchester Guardian Weekly*, November 19 and November 26, 1953. Clark writes of the possibility of six or seven million unemployed and even makes comparisons with the situation in 1929. He proposes a tax cut of $20 billion to offset the tendency toward depression.

[12] Daniel B. Suits, "Forecasting and Analysis With an Econometric Model," *American Economic Review*, March, 1962, pp. 104–32.

TABLE 4–3

REVIEW OF 1961

(monetary figures are billions of 1954 dollars)

	1961	
	Forecast	Actual*
Gross national product	450.1	446.8
Consumption expenditures		
Automobiles and parts	14.6	14.3
Other durables	25.1	24.8
Nondurables	144.7	142.7
Services	119.9	119.6
Private gross capital expenditure		
Plant and equipment	39.0	37.3
Residential construction	19.9	17.7
Inventory investment		
Durables	⎱ 2.4	0.0
Nondurables	⎰	1.7
Imports	24.8	22.2
Exports	24.6	26.4
Government expenditure on goods and services	84.7	84.5
Corporate profits	40.3	39.6
Dividends	12.4	12.3
Civilian labor force† (millions of persons)	71.3	71.6
Private wage and salary workers	⎱	46.9
Govt. employees (civilian)	⎰ 67.0	8.8
Self-employed	⎰	11.0
Unemployed†		
Number (millions)	4.3	4.9
Percent of civilian labor force	6.0	6.8

* Preliminary.
† Annual average.
SOURCE: Daniel B. Suits, "Forecasting and Analysis with an Econometric Model," *American Economic Review*, March, 1962, p. 121.

rants. The largest errors were for 1955 and 1959; in both periods (which were recoveries) increases in consumption far exceeded the estimates. These University of Michigan forecasts were especially conservative in estimating the recovery in 1961, and turned out to be more accurate than the usual highly optimistic forecasts.

A more elaborate model, that of the Econometric Institute, developed from the earlier work of Colin Clark, appears to have improved in forecasting accuracy. This model consists of 79 equations, of which 49 are identities, 3 are tax equations, and the remaining 27 are behavioral or technical equations. According to Spencer, Clark, and Hoguet, this model "predicted the downturn in the middle of 1957 with great accuracy, and the beginning of the recovery of early 1958."[13]

---

[13] M. H. Spencer, Colin G. Clark, and P. W. Hoguet, *Business and Economic Forecasting: An Econometric Approach* (Homewood, Ill.: Richard D. Irwin, Inc., 1961), p. 397.

FIGURE 4–9

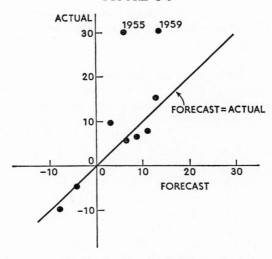

Source: Daniel B. Suits, "Forecasting and Analysis with an Econometric Model," *American Economic Review,* March, 1962, p. 122.

A comparison of forecast and actual data for the Klein-Ball-Hazelwood-Vandome United Kingdom model appears in Table 4–4. This table is in terms of index numbers. As can be seen, the forecast of a decline in production and employment was correct, but errors on some details were considerable, especially on the price level. The increase in unemployment turned out to be considerably greater than that in the forecast. Perhaps use of the more refined quarterly model now available would reduce the magnitude of some of these errors. It must be kept

TABLE 4–4

1958 Forecast of Endogenous Variables

		1957 Actual	1958 Forecast	1958 Actual
Production	P	138	136	135
Industrial employment	E_p	110	105	108
Imports	I	138	131	136
Final demand	F	125	123	127
Consumption	C	119	118	120
Wage rate	w	176	174	181
Employment	E	108	103	107
Price level	p	147	144	151
Nonwage income	D	151	146	160
Interest rate	r	155	150	155
Unemployment	U	89	130	153

Source: L. R. Klein, *op. cit.,* p. 243.

in mind that this forecast for 1958 was for a turning point in business conditions, which is almost inevitably subject to more error than a forecast of continued movement in a given direction. In any case, this forecast is more accurate than most of the qualitative forecasts of earlier decades.

A careful study of econometric forecasts in the Netherlands (1949–57) and Scandinavia (1949–52) indicates that the results were superior to naive extrapolations of past changes, but also shows that the actual changes were underestimated by 50 percent.[14] Apparently there has been a widespread tendency of econometric models to underestimate changes, though this would hardly be true of the Colin Clark forecast for 1954 already mentioned.

There is considerable room for improvement in the econometric approach to forecasting. The most hopeful feature of the approach is that research workers are continually working on refinements in the models. It seems reasonable to expect higher degrees of accuracy in econometric forecasts as the data and research techniques improve.

3. THE LEAD-LAG APPROACH

The two approaches to general business forecasting discussed so far are firmly rooted in macroeconomic theory. The approach we shall now study, the lead-lag approach, has a less clear relation to theory.[15] It is based on the observation that certain series of economic data usually turn up or down before general business turns, that other series usually move up and down with general business, and that still other series generally lag. These three types of series are known as leading series, coincident series, and lagging series.

If a single leading series were completely dependable in turning up a certain number of months before general business recoveries and turning down before general contractions, a large part of the forecasting problem would be solved. Forecasting turning points would become a mechanical skill; it could be delegated to a clerk. Unfortunately, no such series exists. Some series may lead 80 percent of the time, but none has a perfect record. Consequently, the modern practice is to observe a group of leading series in the hope that a general consensus in their upturns or downturns will signal changes in business activity.

The National Bureau of Economic Research is responsible for the most thorough study of leading, coincident, and lagging series. In 1966

---

14 Theil, *op. cit.,* p. 83.

15 The approach might be viewed as the inevitable outcome of the views (theories) of the leading American economist, W. C. Mitchell, who took the position that a detailed understanding of the sequence of events based on a study of individual time series was prerequisite to a full understanding of the cyclical process.

the National Bureau released a revised list of the 25 series which appeared most consistent in performance. Twelve of these are leading series, seven roughly coincident, and six lagging. The present discussion emphasizes the 12 leading series, which are:

Average hours worked per week, manufacturing
Nonagricultural placements
Contracts and orders for plant and equipment
New orders, durable goods industries, value
Housing starts authorized by local building permits
Price per unit of labor
Index of net business formation
Corporate profits after taxes
Common stock price index, 500 common stocks
Change in manufacturing and trade inventories
Industrial materials price index
Net changes in consumer installment debt

The seven coincident series are:

Employment in nonagricultural establishments
Unemployment rate, inverted
Industrial production index
Gross national product, in constant prices
Personal income
Sales by retail stores
Manufacturing and trade sales

The lagging group consists of:

Plant and equipment expenditures
Wage and salary cost per unit of output,
    nonfinancial corporations
Manufacturing and trade inventories
Unemployment rate, 15 weeks and over
Bank interest rates on short-term loans
Commercial and industrial loans outstanding

There is, of course, some theoretical basis for these leads and lags. One would expect leads in series reflecting commitments for the future, such as new orders, construction contracts, housing starts, and new business formation. Other leading series such as stock prices and sensitive prices relate to businessmen's profit expectations. But the lead-lag approach does not integrate these series into a theoretical model, such as the gross national product model.

As has been noted, none of the leading series is perfectly consistent in its behavior. For example, the average hours worked led 11 times in the period studied by the National Bureau, but lagged twice, and coincided 6 times. While its lead averaged 6 months, the range was from a 20 months' lead to a 5 months' lag. Similarly, stock market prices, which have been used for many decades as indicators of business change, have led 31 times, but have coincided 16 times and even lagged 5 times. This explains why forecasters prefer to observe a number of these series rather than depend on one or two.

The best sources on the leading and lagging series is the monthly publication of the Bureau of the Census called *Business Conditions Digest*. This journal, started in October, 1961, publishes each series as currently as possible, charted in a way to point up current developments. One great advantage of this source is that it supplies data which are corrected for seasonal fluctuations.

Limitations of the lead-lag approach

The preceding discussion has already suggested some of the limitations of the lead-lag approach. The amount of lead or lag varies from cycle to cycle. Some of the series require seasonal adjustments, but such adjustments are not always accurate. Even when a series is corrected for seasonal it is not easy to determine when it experiences a significant turn; each series runs through erratic fluctuations from month to month. A one-month or two-month decline in the data may represent a temporary slip without any great significance.

Another possible criticism is that the lead-lag approach provides only limited insight into the magnitude of a recession or an expansion. The National Bureau, however, has done some interesting work relating the sharpness of the declines in certain series, or composites of series, to the severity of the recession. We probably will see a fuller development of this type of analysis.

Diffusion indexes

Diffusion indexes are a variation on the lead-lag approach. They attempt to measure the extent to which an expansion or contraction is coming to an end by counting the directions of change in a group of indicators. The computation of the index involves a count of the number of expanding series and expresses this as a percentage of the total number in the group. For example, if 12 out of 30 series are expanding, the diffusion index is 40; if 24 are expanding, the index is 80.

Some forecasters follow the rule that when the index crosses the 50 percent line in a downward direction, a contraction is imminent, and that when it crosses the 50 percent line in an upward direction, expansion will soon follow. Some temporary fluctuations in the index must be ignored, putting a burden on the forecaster to determine when this is the case.

Diffusion indexes overcome the danger of relying too heavily on a small number of indicators. They reflect the extent to which an expansion or contraction has spread through the economy. But they are limited by some of the same factors that limit the usefulness of the individual indicators—the problem of adjusting for seasonal, the elimination of erratic movements from consideration, and the failure to give a clear indication of the magnitude of the impending development.

The National Bureau and other agencies are experimenting with variations on the lead-lag and diffusion approaches. We can expect further developments in this direction, with higher degrees of refinement and reliability.

Empirical studies and illustrations

The National Bureau of Economic Research has taken great care in the selection of its leading series to concentrate on those that have been most consistent in the past. For example, its index of 8 leading series led at 14 turning points and coincided at only 2 in the period from 1920 to 1960.[16] The comprehensive diffusion indexes led at every turning point—usually by seven or more months. The question is how dependable these same indicators are in forecasting changes beyond the period in the original studies.

A closer look at some of these indexes shows that they are far from perfect in their performance. Figures 4–10 and 4–11 show the behavior of five composite indexes at the trough in April, 1958, and at the peak in May, 1960. In January, 1958, one would not have obtained a clear indication of impending recovery. In April the index of eight leading series and the diffusion index based on leading series did show an upturn, though not in clearcut fashion. Only three months after the trough are the indicators definite. In fairness, one should point out that it is an accomplishment to know a recovery is underway even if the news is three months late. Turning to Figure 4–11, the leading indexes did turn down before the contraction, though erratic movements make interpretation somewhat difficult.

Unfortunately, the indicators sometimes have given false signals. In 1951 they suggested a recession which never occurred.[17] Also, in some periods, the turns in the leading series have been spread over such a long period—even longer than a year—that the forecast of the timing of the turn in general business was extremely difficult. For example, six out of eight leading series did turn before the peak in general business in July, 1957. But five of these series led by over a year, including two which led by over two years. The result was considerable uncertainty about when the turning point would actually come. The National Bureau

---

[16] Julius Shiskin, *Signals of Recession and Recovery: An Experiment with Monthly Reporting* (New York: National Bureau of Economic Research, Occasional Paper No. 77, 1961), p. 90.

[17] Frank E. Morris, "The Predictive Value of the National Bureau's Leading Indicators," in G. H. Moore (ed.), *op. cit.*, p. 114.

FIGURE 4–10

APRIL, 1958, TROUGH

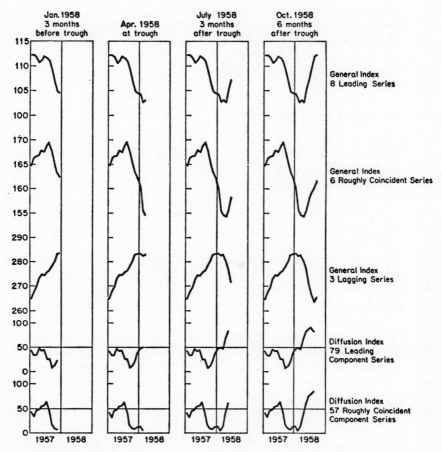

SOURCE: Julius Shiskin, *Signals of Recession and Recovery: An Experiment with Monthly Reporting* (National Bureau of Economic Research, Occasional Paper No. 77, 1961), p. 90.

and other research organizations are developing a variety of ways in which these difficulties may be overcome.

4. FORECASTING THE DEMAND FOR INDIVIDUAL PRODUCTS

We turn now from general business forecasting to forecasting the demand for a single product. This chapter and the preceding one have reviewed a number of concepts that should be useful in such an analysis. First, management must determine just what it is that it wishes to forecast: simply the quantity demanded (with the price, advertising, and

FIGURE 4–11

MAY, 1960, PEAK

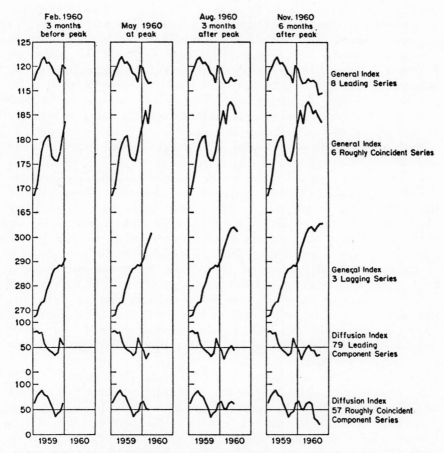

| Feb. 1960 3 months before peak | May 1960 at peak | Aug. 1960 3 months after peak | Nov. 1960 6 months after peak |

General Index 8 Leading Series

General Index 6 Roughly Coincident Series

General Index 3 Lagging Series

Diffusion Index 79 Leading Component Series

Diffusion Index 57 Roughly Coincident Component Series

NOTE: The figures available at the times indicated were slightly different from those shown above because of revisions. See *Business Cycle Indicators,* chap. xviii, pp. 610–14. The latest figures plotted above are those that became available in the month specified and cover the preceding month. The diffusion indexes are measured over 3-month spans.

SOURCE: Julius Shiskin, *Signals of Recession and Recovery: An Experiment with Monthly Reporting* (National Bureau of Economic Research, Occasional Paper No. 77, 1961), p. 99.

other controllable variables assumed to be constant); or, in addition, the response of demand to changes in the manipulable variables.

Forecasting demand with the manipulable variables held constant

Suppose management merely wishes to forecast the quantity of sales without attempting to manipulate the results. The discussion in this chapter does not suggest that this is an easy task. The problem is to forecast changes in income and the effects of those changes, changes in competitive strategies and their effects, and changes in tastes and technology that might influence demand. Several techniques are in use in making such forecasts; each deserves a critical evaluation against the analytical background of the chapter.

Leading series.   We have already seen how various leading series are used to indicate changes in general business conditions. The same approach may be used in forecasting the demand for a particular product. Suppose that historically a certain series has led sales of the product by four or five months. An upturn in the leading series then could be used to indicate an upturn in sales, and the lead in time would give management an opportunity to prepare for the change.

Such an approach to forecasting is in actual use. One example is the use by a plumbing fixture manufacturer of series on residential construction contract awards. It seems logical that construction contracts should be awarded before the actual construction takes place, and that there should be a correlation between construction and the purchases of plumbing (though we should not neglect the replacement market for plumbing fixtures). Such a procedure leaves several gaps. While it may be fairly accurate in predicting turning points, it gives little information on the magnitude of the increase or decrease, unless one can assume a fixed ratio of changes in plumbing sales to changes in construction activity. This approach also runs the risk of ignoring changes in the construction mix or in the technology of plumbing that would outdate past historical relationships. No doubt a careful forecaster would be aware of these dangers and would correct for such imminent changes as he obtains information about them.

Simple correlation techniques.   Almost as simple is the use of correlations between certain broad aggregates, such as the gross national product or the index of industrial production, and sales of the product. A high correlation would indicate that a forecast of the aggregate should also provide a forecast for the particular item, giving not only the direction of the change but also its magnitude. This technique, like the first one, is based on the assumption that past patterns will persist in the future. More serious, it requires a forecast of the broad aggregate itself, which is subject to all of the difficulties of general business forecasting already noted.

The company may be supplying only a part of the total sales of the commodity, sharing the market with competitors. If the company's share of the market is about the same, good times and bad, this complication should create no difficulty. Or if the company's share shows a steady upward or downward trend, one might simply project the percentage of the total market into the future and multiply it by the total sales that have been estimated; again this runs the risk that past trends may not persist.

Some useful ideas

Forecasting the demand for individual products requires special techniques adapted to meet the peculiarities of the special market involved. A number of interesting ideas which have been applied in actual forecasting deserve attention.

Saturation levels.   Some forecasters give attention to a limit or saturation level in the particular market. This consideration is especially important for durable consumer goods, such as automobiles or household appliances. As we approach the point at which close to 100 percent of the households have refrigerators, the potential market for additional refrigerators becomes limited; the demand becomes mainly a replacement demand (which may be bolstered by planned obsolescence through the use of new designs and colors).

Population changes.   Some demands are closely related to population growth and demographic changes. The producer of baby foods profits from projections of birth rates. The publisher of textbooks studies the potential bulge in college enrollment in the near future. Real estate investors pay attention to the growing proportion of the population over 65 in age and the special housing needs of this group. Forecasters are making estimates of the rate of family formation to help determine the potential market for residences.

Discretionary income.   Some forecasters make use of measurements of discretionary or supernumerary income rather than the usual measures of GNP or disposable personal income. There is evidence that the sale of consumer durables relates more closely to income after the deduction of certain regular expenses than it does to total income. Discretionary income is disposable personal income (personal income after income tax but including transfer payments) less necessary living costs (such as food and clothing) and less fixed commitments (payments on debt). The National Industrial Conference Board has developed a discretionary income series.

Discretionary buying power.   Indexes of discretionary buying power start with discretionary income and add cash balances, near liquid assets, and new consumer credit. Obviously a wide variety of such measurements is possible. (The purist may raise questions about the addition of flows, such as income, to stocks, such as cash, but both stocks and flows are sources of liquidity that may influence consumption.)

Consumer credit outstanding.   A forecaster may wish to consider the status of consumer debt outstanding before estimating the demand for a durable consumer good. A high ratio of outstanding consumer debt to current income may suggest a slowing down of purchases based on new debt for two reasons: lenders will become more cautious about risks, and the consumers themselves will reduce additions to debt. The forecaster may also take into account any changes in the regulation of installment debt by the Federal Reserve Board.

The size and age distribution of existing stocks. For many consumer durables the size of existing stocks must have a considerable influence on additions to stocks. In a way this repeats the point already made about saturation levels. The age distribution of the outstanding durables may be of considerable importance. For example, the automobile market in 1957–58 was depressed by the existence of large numbers of automobiles of recent vintage resulting from the peak sales of 1955–56.

Replacement demand versus new-owner demand. The demand for durables falls into two parts: the demand for replacements on the part of those who already own the item and the demand of entirely new owners. Some forecasters separate these two demands, recognizing that the influences on each are different. New household formation, for example, will have little effect on replacement demand, but may be a major influence on new-owner demand.

More complex pattern of behavior. While it seems that the expectation of price increases may stimulate the purchase of consumer durable goods, such is not always the case. Katona's studies at the University of Michigan show that bad news about the rising cost of living, as in 1966 and 1967, may discourage discretionary purchases.[18] Increases in disposable income resulting from one-time tax cuts are likely to have an impact different from increases which may be expected to be repeated. Katona's studies also suggest that studies of consumer sentiment will improve forecasts of their discretionary expenditures.

Consumer attitudes and plans. Forecasters of the demand for individual products are beginning to make use of the surveys of consumer plans made at the University of Michigan. These are published in *Consumer Buying Indicators* by the Census Bureau.

The preceding suggestions relate mainly to consumer durable goods. Similar suggestions may be helpful to the forecaster of the demand for producers' goods. Such a forecaster may want to examine the extent of excess capacity in the industry using the producers' good, as well as the age distribution of existing assets, the rate of obsolescence, the effect of tax provisions on reequipment, and the availability and cost of funds.

A forecast of the demand for capital goods or intermediate goods must often rely on a thorough analysis of end uses. Then each of the end uses must be analyzed in detail in terms of its own growth prospects and short-term factors influencing its rate of activity.

---

[18] George Katona, "On the Function of Behavioral Theory and Behavioral Research in Economics," *The American Economic Review*, March, 1968, pp. 146–49.

Forecasting when the company manipulates some of the variables

If management wishes to know more than the effects of outside forces on demand, if it wishes to evaluate the impact of its own actions as well as the forces of the market, it must bring to bear the whole set of analytical tools described in these two demand chapters on the problem. If management intends to revise prices, it must determine by whatever means are available—experience, statistics, experiment, or common sense —what the elasticity of demand is likely to be. If it intends to change the level of advertising or other sales promotion activity, it must evaluate long-run as well as the short-run effects.

It would be impossible to offer a single analytical procedure; each situation presents its own challenge. In fact the major conclusion of this section is that one must adapt the tools to the problem, avoiding too much dependence on one approach to the exclusion of others. A manager who has relied on his "feel" for the problem may find that a statistical or experimental approach opens new opportunities for improved decisions. And the mathematical model builder should be aware of the value of the subjective know-how of experienced managers. It seems likely that managers in the future will rely more heavily on the kinds of econometric studies and predicting equations that have been reviewed in these chapters.

Conclusion

No single technique for forecasting the demand for a product can meet the problem of each individual market. The previous discussion has summarized a wide variety of possible approaches. Even so, the discussion is incomplete, for it has neglected some widely known methods. Among these is the "sales force composite method," which relies on estimates of the company's own salesmen. A similar approach is the "jury of executive opinion," which coordinates the estimates of forecasts of top executives familiar with the market. Since these techniques involve little economic analysis, the failure to elaborate on them is justified in a book on managerial economics. Perhaps more serious is the failure to stress the importance in oligopolistic industries of forecasting the policies of competing firms. No doubt one of the major considerations in forecasting the demand for Fords is the prospective offerings and prices of General Motors cars. We shall return to this kind of consideration in the chapter on pricing.

Empirical studies and illustrations

Two actual demand analyses illustrate two different attacks on the problem of estimating demand and illustrate also the difficulties of such analysis. The first illustration is one of estimating the demand for coal produced by a single coalfield. The second is a procedure for forecasting the demand for refrigerators.

The demand for West Kentucky coal.[19]   The author was employed as a consultant in 1954 to estimate the demand for coal produced in the West Kentucky coalfield for the period through 1960. Several points were obvious from the outset: (1) the demand is a derived demand, so that the forecast of coal demand requires a forecast of activity in the industries using coal; (2) the demand for West Kentucky coal is not merely a fractional part of total national demand, for West Kentucky is far from representative of the industry as a whole; and (3) the analysis required an estimate of the future relative costs of coal from different fields, along with the costs of competing fuels, such as oil and gas.

The production of coal in West Kentucky had been between 20 and 21 million tons in 1952 and 1953. The first problem was to determine where the coal was being sold, both geographically and by use. This investigation of destinations proved to be a difficult task in view of the paucity and inaccuracy of the data. Figure 4–12 shows the geographical destinations as determined by a careful cross-checking of various sources of information, which sometimes required considerable subjective judgment when the data were contradictory. The breakdown by use categories is shown in Table 4–6. The determination of the use breakdown required another close scrutiny of a wide variety of sources and considerable judgment.

It was also necessary to relate the use breakdown to the geographical breakdown, so that one could tell where the retail markets or railroad markets, for example, were located. An attempt was made to break the "other industrial" category into specific categories, which included the paper industry, food processors, chemicals, heavy equipment, cement, and distilleries.

One of the most important findings was that West Kentucky coal covered a wide market, but that it supplied only a small portion of the total demand in most of this market. This meant that the demand for West Kentucky coal was highly elastic in most markets. The one exception to this conclusion was the market for coal in the TVA territory and in West Kentucky itself; the transportation cost and production cost advantage of West Kentucky in that area provided some insulation against competition from other fields. The market for most of West Kentucky's coal is best classified under the heading of monopolistic competition; the product is differentiated both by quality and by selling and distributive contacts. But in the TVA–West Kentucky area the situa-

---

[19] W. W. Haynes, *Present and Prospective Markets for West Kentucky Coal* (Lexington: Bureau of Business Research, University of Kentucky, 1955).

FIGURE 4–12

COAL MOVEMENTS FROM THE WEST KENTUCKY COALFIELD TO FINAL
DESTINATIONS 1952
(in tons)

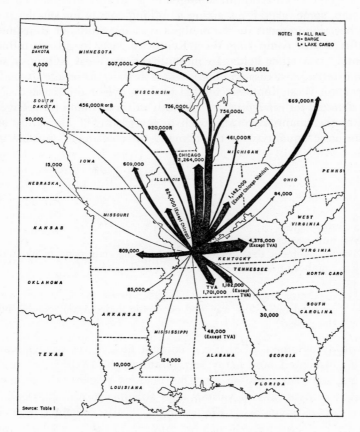

TABLE 4–6

BREAKDOWN OF WEST KENTUCKY COAL PRODUCTION BY USE CATEGORIES, 1953

Use	Approximate Proportion of Total Production Going to That Use	Tons (Thousands)
Electric utilities	50.0%	10,250
Railroads (U.S. and Canada)	12.5	2,489
Retail (for domestic and commercial use)	12.5	2,500
Other industrial	25.0	5,231
Total	100.0	20,470

tion approaches oligopoly, for a few companies dominate the market. Three groups of firms controlled 41 percent of West Kentucky production in 1953 (the tendency since then has been toward greater concentration). The concentration in selling is undoubtedly greater than that in production, some large firms acting as selling agents for smaller ones.

Another requirement in the analysis was the study of transportation cost differentials, comparing West Kentucky costs to given destinations with costs from other fields. In most directions West Kentucky was at a transportation cost disadvantage; when that disadvantage exceeded 40 cents per ton West Kentucky tended to drop out of the market.

The demand for refrigerators.   A study of the demand for refrigerators illustrates the quantitative approach to forecasting.[20] The study started with the basic equations for the demand for consumers' durable goods:

$$S = N + R \qquad (4\text{-}1)$$
$$N = \Delta y / \Delta t = ay[M(t) - y] \qquad (4\text{-}2)$$

where

S = total sales
N = new-owner demand
R = replacement demand (measured by the scrappage of old units)
y = number in use at the beginning of each period
t = time
$M(t)$ = maximum ownership level (largest number of units that would be used under the specified economic and cultural conditions of the period)

The study assumed a 25-year maximum life for refrigerators and on this basis estimated how many refrigerators would still be in use after five years, ten years, and so on. This made it possible to estimate the number of refrigerators of various ages still in use in a particular year (the consumers' inventory). For example, it was estimated that 45.953 million refrigerators were in use on January 1, 1957, of which approximately 1,000 had been produced in 1933, with larger numbers in succeeding years including the 3.7 million sold in 1956.

These estimates of the consumers' inventories of refrigerators made possible the calculation of scrappage volumes. By the use of "survival coefficients" based on the ages of the refrigerators it was possible to estimate the number which would be scrapped in a particular year. For example, it was estimated that of the 42.104 million refrigerators on hand on January 1, 1955, only 40.114 million would survive until January 1, 1956. The difference, 1.99 million, would be the theoretical scrappage

---

[20] This study by B. Slatin is presented in greater detail in Spencer, Clark, and Hoguet, *op. cit.*, pp. 252–79.

TABLE 4–7

ESTIMATE OF WEST KENTUCKY COAL SALES BY USE CATEGORIES, 1955–60
(cyclical fluctuations ignored)

Use Category	1955	1956	1957	1958	1959	1960
TVA	6,800,000	7,600,000	7,900,000	8,600,000	9,700,000	10,500,000
OVEC	—	400,000	1,000,000	2,000,000	2,200,000	2,200,000
Five electric utilities	2,120,000	3,280,000	3,420,000	3,500,000	3,730,000	3,830,000
Other electric utilities	5,064,000	5,343,000	5,637,000	5,947,000	6,274,000	6,619,000
Railroads	1,700,000	1,400,000	1,100,000	900,000	700,000	500,000
Retail demand	2,200,000	2,100,000	2,000,000	1,900,000	1,800,000	1,700,000
Other industries	5,000,000	5,000,000	5,000,000	5,000,000	5,000,000	5,000,000
Total	23,884,000	25,123,000	26,057,000	27,847,000	29,404,000	30,349,000

during 1955. The methods applied in obtaining the actual forecast recognized a cyclical element in scrappage.

The method of forecasting was based on the fundamental proposition that the increase in the number of units in use is directly proportional to the number already in use. The calculation of the factor of proportionality required an estimate of the maximum ownership level M. The change in the number of units in use, $\triangle y / \triangle t$, was expressed as

$$\triangle y / \triangle t = ay[M(t) - y] \qquad (4\text{--}3)$$

The maximum ownership level, M, was not a constant but varied with economic conditions. Estimates of the maximum ownership level depended on four variables: (1) the number of wired dwelling units; (2) the level of supernumerary income; (3) the net extension of installment credit excluding automobile credit; and (4) a price index of household furnishings. It was recognized that the parameter a in equation (3) was different for the postwar and prewar periods, mainly because of a change in the distribution of income.

The result of this analysis was the following equation for the new sales of refrigerators:

$$N = \triangle y / \triangle t = y \left\{ H_w \left[.0045 + .011 \left(\frac{I + 3C/P}{10^{.02169T} + 1.0355} \right) \right] - .000016y \right\}$$

where

$$
\begin{aligned}
N &= \text{new sales} \\
H_w &= \text{wired households} \\
I &= \text{supernumerary income (discretionary income)} \\
C &= \text{credit} \\
P &= \text{price}
\end{aligned}
$$

The equation for the prewar period was somewhat different.

The results of the forecasting equations are plotted against actual sales in Figure 4–13. The largest deviations for 1950–51 were probably due to the Korean War, in which shortages were anticipated. The authors provide similar interpretations of the other deviations.[21]

This formula, plus the analysis of scrappage rates, has been used to project long-range forecasts. The estimate is for a slight upward trend in sales over the 1960's starting from the 4 million annual volume at the beginning of the decade. Such a forecast would help refrigerator producers prepare for the markets of the 1960's. The approach is also intended to provide short-range forecasts of refrigerator sales; such forecasts would require forecasts of supernumerary income, which takes us back to the forecasts of general business conditions, with which this

---

[21] *Ibid.*, p. 277.

FIGURE 4–13

REFRIGERATORS: MANUFACTURERS' SALES AND DEMAND ESTIMATES

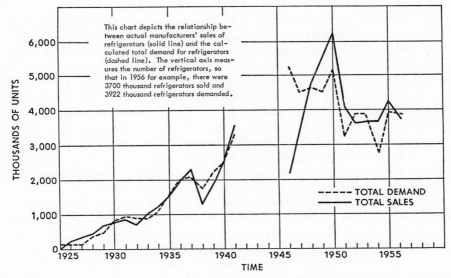

SOURCE: M. H. Spencer, C. G. Clark, and P. W. Hoguet, *Business and Economic Forecasting: An Econometric Approach* (Homewood, Ill.: Richard D. Irwin, Inc., 1961), p. 276.

chapter started, and forecasts of the prices of household furnishings, as well as the extension of installment credit.

Forecasting automobile sales

Automobile producers are interested in both long-run and short-run forecasts. Eggert and McCracken have described the procedures for both types of forecast.[22] A long-term forecast starts with the growth prospects of the economy as a whole, a subject which is in itself a specialized one. The next step is to compute the rate of new car registrations per million dollars of GNP, which on the basis of 1958 to 1963 was about 12.1 at 1962 prices. This would suggest that the "normal volume" (volume unaffected by short-run economic fluctuations) would be about 9.2 million automobile sales in 1970. A more sophisticated approach would be to separate the replacement demand from the growth demand, and to stress the total stock of automobiles rather than merely new registrations. About 7.5 percent of the cars in use at the beginning of a year are scrapped during the year. This indicates replacement of about 6.3 million cars in

---

[22] R. J. Eggert and Paul W. McCracken, "Forecasting the Automobile Market," in W. F. Butler and R. A. Kavesh (eds.), *How Business Economists Forecast* (Englewood Cliffs, N.J.: Prentice-Hall, Inc., 1966).

1970 plus a growth of another 3 to 3½ million. This estimate gives a total sales estimate of around 9.5 million, or slightly more than the cruder estimate.

Refinements of this approach take into account the age distribution of automobiles already in use. The ages of automobiles are not evenly distributed, so that rates of scrappage should vary from year to year. The distribution of income is another consideration. High-income families spend far more on automobiles than low-income families.

Automobile sales also depend on the rate of family formation and on the number of older children in the family. Families living in the country are more dependent on automobiles than those in New York or Chicago, but those in Los Angeles are influenced by its wide geographical spread. Studies show that automobile sales are also influenced by education levels, by the availability of public transportation, the growth of the suburbs, and by road and parking conditions.

On the basis of this kind of analysis, the Ford Motor Company forecasters estimated in 1964 that the 1970 demand for automobiles would be about 9.5 million, with a possibility of sales as high as 12 million or as low as 8 million depending upon business conditions.

Short-run forecasts are complicated by the irregular relationship between automobile sales and general business conditions. In 1957–58 automobile sales fell well after the general downturn and failed to recover until six months after the upturn. But in other periods automobile sales have led rather than followed general business. As a result the companies watch very closely the week-by-week pattern of sales as related to normal seasonal patterns, with particular attention to used car prices as an indication of strength in the market. Attention is also given to used car stocks in relation to sales.

The University of Michigan quarterly surveys of "Buying Intentions" and similar studies of consumer confidence help supplement the data on actual sales and stock levels. Especially important are studies of how consumers are reacting to new automobile styles. Studies of credit conditions, the amount of installment credit already outstanding, and the rate of repayment of automobile loans provide insight into the capacity of consumers to purchase.

According to Eggert and McCracken, statistical demand functions have not fared well so far in estimating demand. No doubt statistical methods will improve, but forecasting automobile sales remains partially judgmental and "requires an open-minded willingness to approach the problem from various directions."[23]

Orders and shipments

Another technique in forecasting the shipments of a particular commodity or group of commodities is to analyze data on new orders. For

[23] *Ibid.*, p. 333.

example, an elaborate model has been constructed to relate sales of machinery and equipment to new orders for such machinery and equipment.[24] This example will serve as an illustration of this approach.

Observations of past data show that new orders for machinery and equipment fluctuate more widely than shipments; they also show that the turning points in new orders tend to lead those in shipments. Unfortunately the lead of new orders has varied from four to seven months for both peaks and troughs. A statistical study of 45 quarterly observations from 1953 to 1964 resulted in the following estimating equation:

$$S_t = 2.409 + 1.035 \,\triangle N_{t-1} - 0.390 \,\triangle \left(\frac{U}{S}\,N\right)_{t-1} + 0.717 \,N_{t-2}$$

in which

$$S = \text{shipments}$$
$$N = \text{new orders}$$
$$t = \text{current quarter}$$
$$t - 1 = \text{previous quarter}$$
$$U = \text{unfilled orders}$$

It was found that while this equation gave a fairly good fit it was weak at the turning points. Several modifications in the equation were tried. One of them involved shortening the lag by one month. This was done by making the quarters for the independent variable consist of the last two months of one quarter and the first month of the next. Another refinement was in the introduction of corrections for price change. These modifications are not introduced here since the equation already shown gives the basic idea of the approach. The most important feature of this approach is the introduction of variable coefficients data. The larger the unfilled orders, the larger this coefficient, a reflection of the common-sense idea that unfilled orders create a pressure to ship.

---

[24] Joel Popkin, "The Relationship between New Orders and Shipments: An Analysis of the Machinery and Equipment Industries," *Survey of Current Business,* March, 1965, pp. 24–32.

Cases for part two

This chapter includes two kinds of case material. The first consists of cases in which the considerations in Chapter 3 such as elasticity of demand are paramount. The second concentrates primarily on the concepts in Chapter 4 on forecasting. The two kinds of analysis are interwoven in some of the cases. The cases vary from extremely broad ones in national economic forecasting to ones dealing with specific problems in small firms.

There was a temptation to include material calling for the statistical estimation of demand. It was decided, however, that the emphasis here, as throughout the book, should be on decision making. Thus material is introduced in some of the cases on some statistical findings on demand; these findings should be useful in making the required decisions. But no advanced statistical techniques are required; the student must interpret certain statistical results but is not required to do computations of his own.

FIVE CASES IN THE ELASTICITY OF DEMAND

The five short cases presented here provide an opportunity to evaluate the significance of the elasticity concept in a variety of business decisions. In some of the cases the objective is to estimate the demand elasticity and to use this estimate in arriving at a decision on price. The other cases supply information on the actual decisions on price made by management; the question is whether the managers made a sound analysis of their particular demand situations.

176

1. A bowling alley's pricing problem

In 1960 a partnership had decided to build a bowling alley to supplement the other business activities in which the partners were engaged. One of the problems the partners faced before the alley opened was the appropriate price policy. Bowling alley charges were set on the basis of "lines" played, the price being expressed as so much per line.

The partners made a survey of the rates charged within the state and in nearby states. They found that the rates usually varied from 40 cents per line at the minimum to 48 cents at the maximum, with 45 cents per line the most common figure. Some of the surveyed alleys were in towns comparable in size (15,000 population) to that in which the new alley was being built. Others were in larger towns or cities. The tendency was for the rates to be higher in the cities, where wage costs and incomes were higher.

This particular alley would have some advantages. It would be the first alley in the town and would thus hold a monopoly position. The town appeared to be large enough to support a 16-lane alley, but not so large as to attract competition. No town within 20 miles was large enough to support an alley, so that customers would be attracted from a fairly large area.

The survey of other alleys suggested that 45 cents per line was a viable rate—high enough to cover the costs and return a profit but not so high as to discourage customers. The question was whether a higher rate would be even more profitable.

2. Interstate telephone rates[1]

In 1962 the Federal Communications Commission turned its attention to the problem of interstate telephone rates. Chairman Emanuel Celler (D., N.Y.) of the House Judiciary Committee had been a frequent critic of the regulation of these rates. In November, 1962, in the midst of meetings on telephone rates, FCC Chairman Newton N. Minow announced that he had started discussions with the American Telephone and Telegraph Company, with special attention to the possibility of "after 9" rates.

The "after 9" rates would incorporate an extra reduction in telephone rates between 9 P.M. and 4:30 A.M. beyond the reductions already in effect at 6 P.M. The aim of this extra reduction would be to stimulate more nonbusiness use of telephone facilities in off-peak hours. It was estimated that between 10 percent and 15 percent of total interstate long-distance calls are made between 9 P.M. and 4:30 A.M. The proposed rates would increase this percentage.

---

[1] This case is based mainly on reports in *Telecommunications* from September 24, 1962, to February 4, 1963.

An experiment with "after 9" rates had been tried out in 10 states on an intrastate basis. An AT&T vice-president, Edward B. Crosland, reported that there was little response to the reduced rates. A study of 800,000 messages from 20 central offices provided no clearcut evidence of the stimulation of calls after 9 P.M. He added that the evidence was inadequate in estimating the long-range effect of the "after 9" plan. Customer calling habits change slowly and the publicity given the rates may have been inadequate.

One possible effect of the "after 9" rates might be a transfer of traffic from the "after 6" discount period to the "after 9" discount period, with a consequent reduction in revenues. Another effect would be a transfer from person-to-person calls, which formerly had been underpriced in relation to cost, to station-to-station calls.

After a series of meetings, the Bell System and the FCC on January 29, 1963, announced plans for an "after 9" nationwide interstate plan, along with slight increases in person-to-person rates up to 800 miles. The new rates would become effective April 1, 1963. The maximum charge for the initial period of a call would be $1 anywhere in the continental United States. At the same time a slight increase in interstate person-to-person rates up to 800 miles would make up for some of the loss in revenue. The estimated reduction in station-to-station revenues to the Bell System was $55 million per year. The 5 and 10 cent increases in person-to-person calls would bring increased revenues of $25 million, leaving a net loss of $30 million on the 1962 traffic base.

The new interstate rates would result in reductions of from 8 percent to 43 percent. In terms of mileage bands, the new "after 9" rates would be 60 cents for 221–354 miles; 65 cents for 355–600 miles; 70 cents for 601–800 miles; 75 cents for 801–1,050 miles; 80 cents for 1,051–1,360 miles; 90 cents for 1,361–1,910 miles; and $1 for all continental calls above 1,910 miles. Some comparisons with earlier years were dramatic— a call from the East Coast to the West Coast would have cost $4.25 in 1940 but would cost only $1 under the new rates.

The Chairman of the House of Representatives Interstate and Foreign Commerce Committee gave his immediate approval to the new rates. He suggested that the increased utilization at the lower rates might be so great as to permit a reduction of rates at other hours of the day. Apparently he doubted that the rates would result in the reduction of $30 million revenues which were estimated above. In fact his position implied an increase in revenues.

3. The pricing of automobiles

In 1958, Walter Reuther, the President of the United Automobile Workers suggested a reduction in the price of automobiles averaging $100 a car. The automobile market was weak in 1958, with resultant unemployment; lower prices would lead to greater sales and would stimulate employment. Mr. Reuther believed that a $100 reduction in prices, about 4 percent, would increase sales by 16 percent.

In testimony before the Senate Subcommitte on Antitrust and Monopoly, Mr. Theodore O. Yntema, Vice President of the Ford Motor Company, disagreed with Mr. Reuther's estimation.[2] Mr. Yntema cited studies which indicated price elasticities ranging from 0.5 to 1.5. Mr. Yntema made it clear that he was referring to the elasticity of demand in response to a permanent price change of all manufacturers; he admitted that the elasticity to a temporary price cut might be greater. The studies to which Mr. Yntema referred included the well-known prewar volume by Roos and von Szeliski, which found elasticities ranging from .65 to 1.53. (Apparently the Roos-Szeliski findings are interpreted in somewhat different ways by various students of automobile demand, but all interpretations fall within the range of .65 to 1.53.)

Perhaps more recent studies would be more relevant than that of Roos and Szeliski. A Department of Commerce study of automobile demand resulted in several estimating equations, one of which was

$$Y = 0.0003239 \, X_1^{2.536} \, X_2^{2.291} \, X_3^{-1.359} \, 0.932^{X_4}$$

where

Y = new private passenger car registrations per million households
X_1 = disposable personal income per household in 1939 dollars
X_2 = current annual disposable income per household as a percentage of the preceding year in 1939 dollars
X_3 = percentage of average retail price of cars to consumer prices measured by consumer price index
X_4 = average scrappage age in years[3]

Similar equations based on slightly different assumptions resulted in price elasticities close to the one implied by the above equation, as do studies by Chow.[4]

4. Price cutting at Macy's[5]

A United States Supreme Court decision in 1951 freed many firms from the restriction of "fair trade" legislation and opened the way to

---

[2] Statement before the Subcommittee on Antitrust and Monopoly, Committee on the Judiciary, U.S. Senate, February 4–5, 1958. Extracts from this statement appear in A. W. Warner and V. R. Fuchs, *Concepts and Cases in Economic Analysis* (New York: Harcourt, Brace & Co., 1958), pp. 147–48.

[3] *Survey of Current Business*, April, 1952, p. 20. This study is cited in F. E. Nemmers, *Managerial Economics: Text and Cases* (New York: John Wiley & Sons, Inc., 1962), pp. 102–7.

[4] G. C. Chow, "Statistical Demand Functions for Automobiles and Their Use for Forecasting," in A. C. Harberger (ed.), *The Demand for Durable Goods* (Chicago: University of Chicago Press, 1960).

[5] This case is based on Ralph Cassady, Jr., "New York Department Store Price War of 1951: A Microeconomic Analysis," *Journal of Marketing*, national quarterly publication of the American Marketing Association, July, 1957, pp. 3–11.

more aggressive price policies.[6] This Schewegmann decision freed firms that had not signed state "fair trade" contracts on merchandise which had been transported in interstate commerce. R. H. Macy and Company was a nonsigner firm and was also a proponent of free pricing. Macy's slogan was: "We endeavor to save our customers at least 6 percent for cash, except on price-fixed goods." Therefore it is not surprising that Macy's proceeded to cut prices only eight days after the Schewegmann decision. Macy's ran a two-page advertisement announcing 6 percent price reductions on 5,978 items which were formerly fixed in price under the "fair trade" legislation.

Macy's faced strong competition from other department stores, including Abraham and Straus, Bloomingdale's, Namm's and Gimbel's, whose motto was "Nobody—but nobody—undersells Gimbel's." These stores took retaliatory action against Macy's. One hour after the Macy's reductions took effect, Gimbel's began to cut prices. Abraham and Straus followed a few hours later with cuts of 10 percent or more. As Macy's learned of this retaliation, it proceeded to cut to 6 percent under the new low prices of competitors. By the end of the day all the other stores mentioned were engaged in a full-scale price war. Some price cuts were as much as 30 percent in the first day.

The price cuts involved well-known branded items, such as Underwood typewriters and Palm Beach suits. Only a small percentage of the original 6,000 items on which Macy's had originally cut price became involved in the deeper price cuts. A few items were cut below wholesale cost (Bayer aspirin slipped in price from 59 cents to 4 cents). The tempo of price cuts varied from item to item. Price cuts in the competing stores were not identical but tended to be similar.

The volume of business done by the stores engaged in price cutting increased sharply. While normally Macy's sold less than 3.5 percent of Sunbeam Mixmasters sold in New York, its proportion rose to 56 percent in the 10 weeks following the beginning of the price war. Abraham and Straus increased its share of Brooklyn sales from 2.5 percent to 60 percent. In June, 1957, the total sales of 13 New York and Brooklyn department stores were 14 percent above those of the previous June, with one store recording a 33.4 percent increase. The largest increases in volume were in major appliances and housewares.

The Fifth Avenue stores did not participate in the price cutting. Many neighborhood hardware stores did cut prices, and price reductions spread to the Bronx and to Jersey City. But the price war came to a close in August, 1951, about six weeks after it started. The impact of the price cuts on volume began to diminish rapidly, and the stores wished to bring

---

[6] *Schewegmann Bros.* v. *Calvert Distilleries Corporation*, 314 U.S. 384 (1951).

the war to an end. Gradually prices were restored to their former levels. One way this was done was for the aggressor to run out of stock until competitors restored the old price.

The chief question raised by the events of 1951 is whether the executives of Macy's made a correct evaluation of the elasticity of demand in initiating its price reductions. Some observers have suggested that Macy's might have done better to cut price-fixed items by 6 percent without publicizing this cut.

5. The Boston and Maine Railroad

On Sunday, January 6, 1963, the Boston and Maine Railroad instituted a new rate schedule for commuters into Boston. A federal and state subsidy of $2.2 million, part of a program to aid mass transportation, made this experiment with reduced fares possible. The objective of the federal program of subsidies was to determine whether lower commuter rates would relieve the problem of congestion on highways. The Boston and Maine experiment was to last one year, unless the railroad became discouraged with the results and terminated the program in six months.

In 1946 the Boston and Maine had carried 40,000 commuters a day to and from branches to the west, north, and east of Boston. In the following years it had modernized commuter equipment but had lost passengers steadily. It raised fares to cover the higher costs per passenger, with the result of further reductions in traffic and the curtailment of schedules. Expressways into Boston had stimulated commuting by automobile but had also accentuated traffic and parking problems in downtown Boston. By January of 1963 the Boston and Maine passenger count had fallen to 11,000 per day and the passenger deficit had reached $3.8 million per year.

The federal and state subsidies (two-thirds federal and one-third Massachusetts) made possible the reduction of fares from 25 percent to 40 percent and the increase in the number of daily trains from 187 to 391. The railroad spent $170,000 cleaning and refurnishing 101 diesel cars and an additional $43,000 to set up a canopy at North Station in Boston. The railroad hoped to reduce passenger revenue deficits despite the reduction of fares and the improvement in service.

Exhibit 1 presents passenger counts for comparable weeks in 1962 and 1963, before and after the fare reduction. Each passenger is counted both on inward and on the outward trip; this explains the fact that the totals for 1962 are about double the figure of 11,000 passengers mentioned above.

Exhibit 2 shows some of the fare changes from selected points on the Boston and Maine. The rates are quoted for 20-ride commuter books.

EXHIBIT 1

PASSENGER COUNTS, BOSTON AND MAINE RAILROAD
(comparable weeks in 1962–63)

NEW HAMPSHIRE DISTRICT (BOSTON TO WOBURN)

	Week Ending Feb. 15, 1962			*Week Ending Feb. 14, 1963*	
Day	*No. of Trains*	*Passenger Count*	*Day*	*No. of Trains*	*Passenger Count*
Fri. 9th	37	2,758	Fri. 8th	55	2,833
Sat. 10th	29	794	Sat. 9th	36	1,132
Sun. 11th	21	285	Sun. 10th	19	397
Mon. 12th	37	2,616	Mon. 11th	55	3,163
Tues. 13th	37	2,660	Tues. 12th	55	3,186
Wed. 14th	37	2,627	Wed. 13th	55	3,280
Thur. 15th	36	2,325	Thur. 14th	55	2,981

PORTLAND DISTRICT (W) READING

	Week Ending Feb. 15, 1962			*Week Ending Feb. 14, 1963*	
Day	*No. of Trains*	*Passenger Count*	*Day*	*No. of Trains*	*Passenger Count*
Fri. 9th	54	6,765	Fri. 8th	112	7,535
Sat. 10th	36	1,575	Sat. 9th	36	1,846
Sun. 11th	24	447	Sun. 10th	20	808
Mon. 12th	54	6,625	Mon. 11th	112	8,121
Tues. 13th	54	6,693	Tues. 12th	112	7,872
Wed. 14th	54	6,939	Wed. 13th	112	8,087
Thur. 15th	54	6,830	Thur. 14th	112	8,022

NEW HAMPSHIRE DISTRICT

	Week Ending Feb. 15, 1962			*Week Ending Feb. 14, 1963*	
Day	*No. of Trains*	*Passenger Count*	*Day*	*No. of Trains*	*Passenger Count*
Fri. 9th	25	3,159	Fri. 8th	46	3,868
Sat. 10th	22	1,080	Sat. 9th	27	1,467
Sun. 11th	16	1,052	Sun. 10th	18	1,199
Mon. 12th	25	2,543	Mon. 11th	46	3,699
Tues. 13th	25	2,478	Tues. 12th	46	3,876
Wed. 14th	25	2,686	Wed. 13th	46	4,978
Thur. 15th	25	2,450	Thur. 14th	46	3,703

FITCHBURG DIVISION

	Week Ending Feb. 15, 1962			*Week Ending Feb. 14, 1963*	
Day	*No. of Trains*	*Passenger Count*	*Day*	*No. of Trains*	*Passenger Count*
Fri. 9th	24	2,221	Fri. 8th	42	3,112
Sat. 10th	10	449	Sat. 9th	22	1,060
Sun. 11th	8	200	Sun. 10th	8	331
Mon. 12th	24	2,456	Mon. 11th	42	3,368
Tues. 13th	24	2,318	Tues. 12th	42	3,419
Wed. 14th	24	2,426	Wed. 13th	42	3,414
Thur. 15th	24	1,380	Thur. 14th	42	3,175

EXHIBIT 1—*Continued*

PORTLAND DISTRICT—EASTERN ROUTE

Week Ending Feb. 15, 1962			*Week Ending Feb. 14, 1963*		
Day	No. of Trains	Passenger Count	Day	No. of Trains	Passenger Count
Fri. 9th 41		5,169	Fri. 8th 92		6,855
Sat. 10th 33		1,299	Sat. 9th 35		1,969
Sun. 11th 21		644	Sun. 10th 19		1,188
Mon. 12th 41		4,690	Mon. 11th 92		6,939
Tues. 13th 41		4,841	Tues. 12th 92		6,803
Wed. 14th 41		4,991	Wed. 13th 92		6,924
Thur. 15th 41		4,526	Thur. 14th 92		6,786

PORTLAND DISTRICT—WESTERN ROUTE

Week Ending Feb. 15, 1962			*Week Ending Feb. 14, 1963*		
Day	No. of Trains	Passenger Count	Day	No. of Trains	Passenger Count
Fri. 9th 26		2,817	Fri. 8th 40		3,221
Sat. 10th 25		1,212	Sat. 9th 27		1,813
Sun. 11th 15		869	Sun. 10th 13		870
Mon. 12th 26		2,590	Mon. 11th 38		3,041
Tues. 13th 26		2,518	Tues. 12th 38		2,786
Wed. 14th 26		2,528	Wed. 13th 38		2,909
Thur. 15th 26		2,282	Thur. 14th 38		2,836

EXHIBIT 2

COMMUTER FARE CHANGES, SELECTED POINTS
BOSTON AND MAINE RAILROAD

	1962	After Jan. 6, 1963
New Hampshire District		
North Chelmsford, Mass.	$16.80	$11.13
Lowell, Mass.	15.82	10.72
Woburn	9.83	7.70
Portland District (Reading)		
Reading	10.69	8.12
Portland District—Eastern		
Salem	12.75	8.88
Portland District—Western		
Andover	14.85	10.13
Fitchburg Division		
Fitchburg	23.60	15.47
Concord	14.20	9.70

1. *What is your estimate of the elasticity of demand in the bowling alley case at prices from 40 cents to 45 cents per line? From 45 cents to 48 cents per line? From 48 cents to 50 cents per line? What reasoning underlies your estimates?*

184 Managerial economics

2. Is there great uncertainty about your elasticity estimates?
3. What are the implications of your elasticity estimates for pricing in the bowling alley? Explain.
4. In what way is the elasticity of demand involved in the telephone case?
5. On the basis of your impressions of consumer behavior, estimate the elasticity of demand for "after 9" telephone services.
6. What considerations other than the elasticity of demand would influence the impact of the "after 9" rates on company profits?
7. In the automobile case, what is the significance of Mr. Reuther's demand estimate? Of Mr. Yntema's demand estimates?
8. What is the price elasticity of the demand for automobiles according to the Department of Commerce estimating equation?
9. Did Macy's make a sound evaluation of the elasticity of demand in its 1951 pricing decisions? Was the analysis of competitors' reactions an essential part of elasticity estimates?
10. Would a nonpublicized price cut of 6 percent have resulted in a different elasticity of demand? Discuss.
11. What were the sources of uncertainty about the elasticities of demand facing Macy's in 1951?
12. Was the short-run elasticity of demand greater or less than the longer-run elasticity of demand in the case of the 1951 price war? Explain.
13. Estimate the elasticity of demand for the commuter services of the Boston and Maine Railroad.
14. Do the reductions in rates on the Boston and Maine appear to be profitable? Discuss in terms of the demand elasticities.
15. Do the data in Exhibits 1 and 2 provide a sound basis for estimating the elasticity of demand? Discuss.

THE STATE UNIVERSITY PRESS (A)

The State University Press published a work in American history in November, 1962. It priced the book at $8.50 and estimated that sales would approximate 1,800 copies. After discounts by distributors the Press expected to receive about $5.70 per copy—barely enough to cover its unit costs.

The manager of a retail store claimed that the price of $8.50 was too high. He believed that at a price of $5 the Press could expect substantial gift sales of the book, with perhaps a doubling or tripling of volume. The editors of the Press believed, however, that sales would be only 50 percent higher at the lower price.

The costs of publishing the book are shown in Exhibit 1. These costs were accumulated after publication but include some estimates. (A pre-publication forecast of costs had estimated them at $4,881; the higher actual costs resulted from a substantial number of author's changes in the galley proof and page proof stages.)

EXHIBIT 1

ESTIMATED COST OF HISTORY BOOK
(publication date—November 28, 1962)
Quantity—1,000 bound copies plus 1,000 unbound sheets

Text

Stock	$ 774.50	
Composition	2,305.90	(354.8 hours)
Press	740.40	(106.9 hours)
Ink	22.34	
Art	40.00	
Cuts	64.66	
Miscellaneous	36.50	
Overhead (15% of above)	597.00	
Total text costs		$4,581.30

Jacket

Stock	$ 28.50	
Composition	13.00	(2 hours)
Press	58.30	(8.3 hours)
Ink	7.26	
Art	107.00	
Cuts	39.00	
Overhead (15% of above)	38.00	
Mailing	3.94	
Total jacket costs		$ 300.00
Binding (1,000 copies)		724.00
Freight (estimated)		120.00
Total cost		$5,725.30

1. *Estimate the elasticity of demand and incremental or marginal revenue under the following assumptions: (1) a doubling of sales at the lower price; (2) a tripling of sales; (3) a 50 percent increase in sales. (Assume that the proportion of the retail price going to the Press is about the same at various prices.)*
2. *Assuming that the demands can be approximated by straight lines, estimate the marginal revenue at a number of prices between $8.50 and $5—for example at $8, $7.50, $7, etc. Is the assumption of straight-line demands reasonable?*
3. *Estimate the marginal cost or incremental cost per book for quantities exceeding 1,800. For this purpose assume that the press run would be increased upward from 2,000 to take care of the extra demand at the lower prices. Note that the composition costs are fixed for a single run. Binding costs include a fixed element of, say, $150 per lot, but the remaining binding costs are proportional to volume. Make any other assumptions which seem appropriate. (While a full discussion of costs appears in Chapter 5, the incremental reasoning presented in Chapter 2 should suffice for this purpose.)*
4. *Would a price of $5 be sound if the Press were a private company operated for profit? Discuss.*

5. *Would a price of $5 be sound for the University Press recognizing that the objective is not maximum profit but that heavy losses on this book would cut down on funds available for other books?*
6. *What do you think the appropriate objectives of a University Press should be? What price policy is consistent with those objectives?*

GNP FORECAST FOR 1969*

Part I

Prepare a forecast of the GNP and its principal components for each quarter through 1969, using the data for 1968, second quarter (*Survey of Current Business,* September, 1968) as follows:

Gross National Product	$852.9
Change in GNP from previous period	21.7
Personal income	678.1
Disposable personal income	586.3
Personal outlays	542.3
Personal consumption expenditures	527.9
Interest paid by consumers and transfer payments to foreigners	17.8
Change in business inventories	10.8
Corporate profits before tax (adjusted)	84.2
Corporate profits taxes	41.1
Corporate profits after taxes	48.1
Capital consumption allowances (depreciation)	73.7
Indirect business taxes, etc.	73.8
Contributions for social insurance	46.5
Transfer payments, etc.	84.0
Dividends	24.4
Change in dividends from previous period	0.8

It is important to know the following relationships: Net national product = GNP − Capital consumption allowances. National income = Net national product − Indirect business taxes. Personal income = National income − Corporate profits + Dividends − Contributions for social insurance + Transfer payments. Disposable income = Personal income − Personal income taxes.

Assume that the following data are given:

---

* Note: This case is a modification of one written by Professor John Lintner of the Harvard Graduate School of Business Administration. The case has been influenced greatly by the Duesenberry-Eckstein-Fromm econometric model. This simplified form of the latter material was developed for classroom use to illustrate some of the more fundamental relationships which need to be taken into account in forecasting in the simplest possible way. In itself, it was not intended to provide a model which would be fully adequate for forecasting business conditions in practice.

	Annual Rates in Billions of Dollars				
	1968:4	*1969:1*	*1969:2*	*1969:3*	*1969:4*
Government expenditures on goods and services					
Total	$203.0	$206.0	$209.5	$213.0	$216.0
Federal	102.5	103.0	104.0	105.0	105.0
Defense	81.0	81.5	82.0	83.0	83.0
Nondefense	21.5	21.5	22.0	22.0	22.0
State and local	100.5	103.0	105.5	108.0	111.0
Gross private domestic investment					
total[1]	121.0	121.0	121.0	124.0	128.0
Fixed nonresidential					
investment	91.0	91.0	90.0	91.0	92.0
Residential investment	30.0	30.0	31.0	33.0	36.0
Net exports	2.0	2.5	3.0	3.5	4.0

1 Excluding net change in inventories.

Assume also that:

1. Personal outlays in each quarter are equal to .95 of disposable income in the preceding quarter. The portion of personal outlays represented by interest paid by consumers and personal transfer payments by foreigners increases by $0.3 billion in each quarter and the balance represents consumer expenditures on goods and services. Personal consumption expenditures are "personal outlays" less such "transfers."

2. Examine past inventory behavior and make your own estimates, taking into account what you know, or can find out, about current conditions in the economy.

3. The quarter-to-quarter change in corporate profits before taxes in billions of dollars is equal to:

$$0.4 \, (\triangle \text{GNP})_t + 0.3 \, (\triangle \text{Inv.})_t - 0.2 \, (\triangle \text{GNP})_{t-1} - 1.0 \text{ billion}$$

except that for the first quarter of 1969, alone, the net change in corporate profits should be adjusted downward by an additional $1.5 billion to account for the increase in social security contributions of employers which takes effect as of January 1, 1969.

4. The change in corporate profits taxes equals 45 percent of the current change in the corporate profits before taxes.

5. Dividends change by 30 percent of the current change in corporate profits after taxes plus 50 percent of the change in dividends in the previous quarter.

6. The change in contributions to social security (payroll taxes) amounts to 4 percent of the change in GNP, except that for the first quarter of 1969, *alone,* an additional $1.5 billion increment in these contributions will occur because of the new level of payroll taxes effective as of January 1, 1969.

7. The change in indirect business taxes is equal to 10 percent of the change in GNP.

· 8. The change in transfer payments by government and certain interest payments increases $1.3 billion per quarter.

9. The change in personal income taxes is equal to 15 percent of the change in personal income.

10. Capital consumption allowances increase by $1.2 billion in each quarter.

Part II

After you have completed mechanical projections based on the above assumptions, consider how reasonable they seem in the light of *all* the other information you have at your disposal. What assumptions, including the data for government expenditures and investment expenditures, do you believe should be changed? How, how much, and for what reasons? What would be the order of magnitude of the changes induced in your first projection? Has this approach given adequate attention to the multiplier? Explain the basis for your conclusion.

Part III

Compare your forecast for 1969 with the actual changes in the GNP and its components during that year. How great was the error in your forecast? What are the apparent reasons for those errors?

(Note: Statistical data will be found in issues of the *Survey of Current Business* and in *Economic Indicators*. Current business literature such as *Business Week, Fortune,* monthly letters of the leading commercial banks and Federal Reserve Banks, the monthly issues of *Economic Indicators,* and the publications of the leading investment services will supply information which may enable you to form an opinion on the reasonableness of the given assumptions and data to be used in the mechanical projections.)

Forecast for the coming year: mechanical model

The "mechanical" model used in the GNP forecast for 1969 may be adapted for use for any short period in the 1970's. This approach would start with forecasts of federal expenditures quarter by quarter using the sources mentioned in Chapter 4. Next the forecast would move on to state and local government expenditures and to the components of investment. The forecast of inventory investment would proceed as in the 1969 forecast. Then the most tedious task is to forecast consumption using the assumptions listed in the 1969 forecast (except for the change in social security contributions).

After this forecast is made, the results may be compared with those in the more subjective approach in the preceding case. The question which then arises is whether the extra work required by the "mechanical" model produces results in the form of superior forecasts which compensate for the extra effort.

Forecast for the coming year: GNP "judgmental" model

On the basis of the discussion in Chapter 4, you may forecast the GNP and its principal components for the coming year. In such a forecast you will wish to use many of the sources mentioned in Chapter 4. This exercise is best done as a team effort, with part of the team concentrating on plant and equipment, part on residential construction, part on government expenditure, and so on. After preliminary estimates are made of the investment and governmental components, the team as a whole can cooperate in making estimates of consumption which will take the multiplier into account. Various degrees of mathematical sophistication are possible. The simplest approach is to assume that the induced increase in consumption will be roughly equal to total increase already estimated for all the other components; but, as Chapter 4 points out, consumption is stickier in the downward direction and is influenced by factors other than income change.

Forecast for 1969: leading indicators

In late 1968, the 12 most important leading indicators shown in *Business Conditions Digest* appeared as in Exhibits 1 and 2.

What kind of forecast for 1969 would you make on the basis of movements in these indicators in 1968? How much confidence would you have in this forecast?

By examining the same exhibits for earlier years, you may evaluate the success of these 12 leading series in forecasting the upper and lower turning points from 1948 to 1961. Also you may examine the movements in these series in the last half of 1966 and early 1967 and determine whether they gave a correct forecast of events in the following year. The GNP in 1966 and 1967 rose steadily as follows:

1966	$747.6 billion
1967—Qtr. I	772.2 billion
Qtr. II	780.2 billion
Qtr. III	795.3 billion
Qtr. IV	811.0 billion

EXHIBIT 1
LEADING INDICATORS

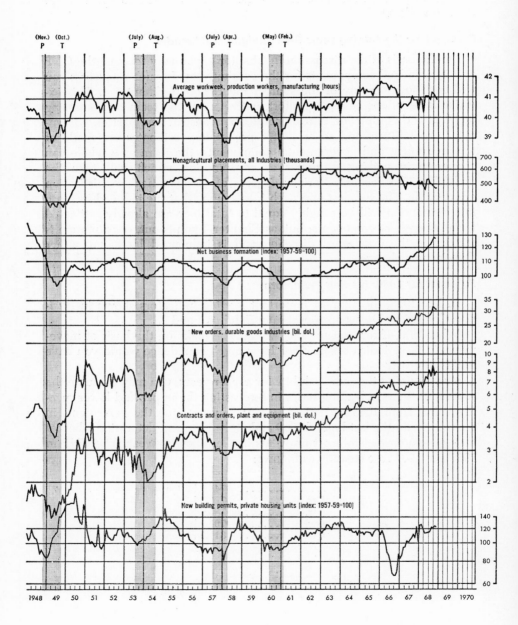

EXHIBIT 2
LEADING INDICATORS—CONTINUED

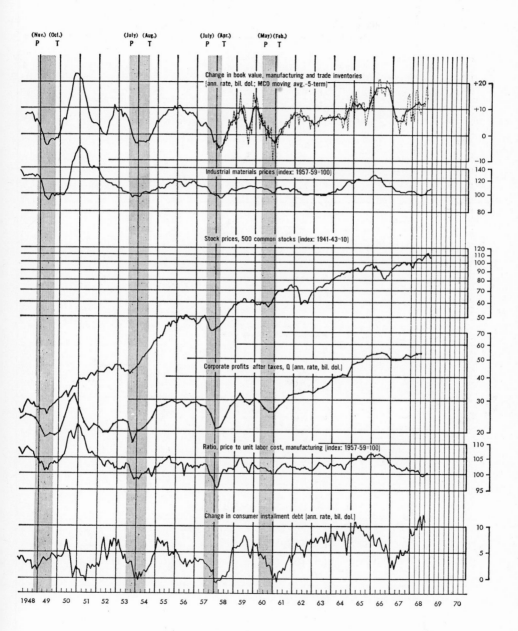

PART THREE / Cost analysis

5 / Short-run cost analysis

1. INTRODUCTION: FIXED AND VARIABLE COSTS AND OTHER COST CLASSIFICATIONS

Short-run cost analysis is concerned with the behavior of costs when some of the inputs are fixed and others are varied in quantity. Interpreted narrowly, such analysis deals exclusively with the relationship of total costs to output—with the way in which total costs increase as more variable inputs are added to provide a greater output. But this chapter is concerned with more than cost-output relationships; it covers the cost effects of a wide variety of decisions under conditions in which some inputs are fixed and others variable.

Short-run cost analysis incorporates one of the most useful toolkits in managerial economics. It is indispensable in the discussions of pricing which come later in this book. It is necessary for rational decisions on abandoning a product line or on establishing a new product line with existing facilities. It is useful in determining whether or not to increase the volume of specific outputs, to use idle capacity, or to rent facilities to outsiders. It even is important in decisions on new capital investments, which would appear to be long-run decisions but which sometimes must be analyzed in a short-run framework (as is the case in introducing a new machine into an existing department).

Fixed and variable costs

At the most elementary level, short-run cost analysis starts with the distinction between fixed costs and variable costs. Most readers of this chapter are already familiar with this distinction which separates costs unrelated to changes in volume from those dependent upon volume. Yet it is desirable to warn against several misunderstandings.

1. The dividing line between what is a fixed cost and what is variable is *not* the same for all decisions. Elementary treatments include material costs and direct labor costs in the variable cost category; they relegate the depreciation expense and, usually, the indirect labor and administrative charges to a fixed cost category; and they leave little scope for judgment. A few illustrations should make it clear that such an approach is far too simple. Take direct labor cost, for example. It makes a difference whether a decision to accept a particular order requires the addition of overtime or can be managed with the use of available idle time. It is often assumed that depreciation is entirely a fixed expense, running on regardless of the level of output. But a little reflection will suggest that the wear-and-tear component of depreciation is related to the output; this component of depreciation is known as user cost. Depreciation expense is peculiarly difficult to analyze. It may be that in some industries the assumption that it is completely fixed is a helpful simplification. But it is also possible that the decision under consideration may increase depreciation not only by increasing user cost but also by requiring the purchase of additional machinery on which additional depreciation will be incurred.

It is desirable to repeat a point made in the second chapter that there is a great variety of "short runs," each depending on the decision under consideration. It follows that there must also be variety in the way in which expenses are segregated into the fixed and variable categories. The decision maker must select the classification suited to his purposes.

2. A second warning is against the assumption that an expense must be either fixed or variable. Some expenses are a mixture of both fixed and variable elements; for decision-making purposes it may be desirable to recognize this complication. We have already noted the case of depreciation in this respect. The obsolescence component of depreciation is a function of time and thus runs on regardless of decisions about the level of output from the plant and equipment already on hand. This element of depreciation is "sunk"—it involves an investment already made and thus an expense that will run on regardless of the decision (ignoring the salvage value that might be gained from sale of such assets). The wear-and-tear element of depreciation is partly related to output, often in a complicated way. Depreciation may be accelerated by the use of overtime or extra shifts. Some types of equipment on the other hand may actually deteriorate faster when not in use. It is claimed, for example, that an automobile left in a garage for a long period suffers deterioration.

Other expenses are also a mixture of fixed and variable components. Such costs may be called semivariable expenses. Utility bills, for example, frequently include both a fixed charge and a charge based on consumption; this is known as a two-part tariff. Salesmen may be paid both a straight salary and commissions based on volume. Supervisors may be paid bonuses based on output, in addition to the fixed salaries.

Some expenses may increase in a stairstep fashion, remaining fixed over a range of outputs, but jumping to a new higher level when output passes a given level. For example, foremen's salaries may remain constant as output increases up to the point at which management will add an additional foreman, causing the expenses of supervision to rise in a single step. Stairstep costs are probably not usual in practice, for there are many ways in which management can overcome the sudden jumps in cost. For instance, it is possible to change the ratio between foremen and labor, or to put foremen on overtime.

Figures 5–1 through 5–5 illustrate different cost-output relationships for different kinds of expenses. The charts do not exhaust the possibilities. And it must be repeated that other kinds of decisions—ones not concerned simply with increasing or decreasing output—may require an entirely different analysis of what is fixed, what is variable, and what is semivariable.

3. Experience with misunderstandings in the past suggests that other elementary warnings are in order. Some students interpret the expression "variable cost" to mean any cost that varies over time. For example, they

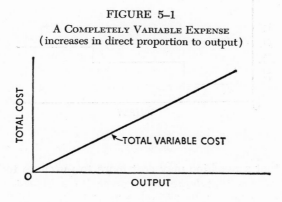

FIGURE 5–1

A COMPLETELY VARIABLE EXPENSE
(increases in direct proportion to output)

FIGURE 5–2

A COMPLETELY FIXED COST
(remains the same without regard to output)

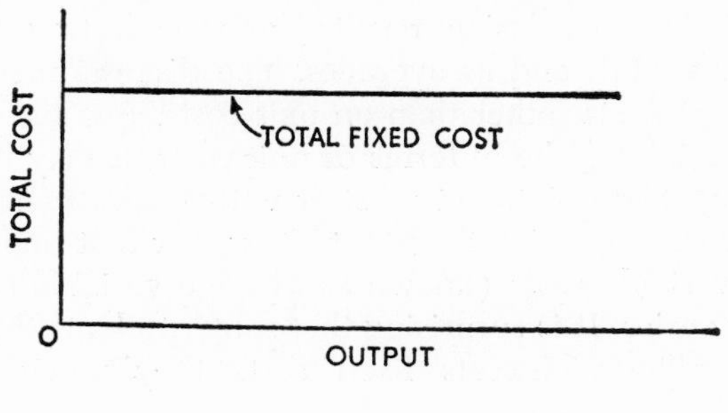

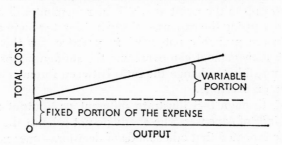

FIGURE 5–3
SEMIVARIABLE EXPENSE
(a combination of fixed and variable components)

FIGURE 5–4
A STAIRSTEP VARIABLE COST

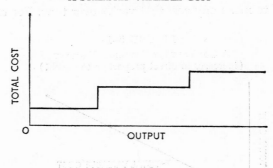

take the fact that a machine may cost more to purchase today than five years ago as evidence that depreciation on such machines is variable. This is a complete misinterpretation of what "variable" means. The term does not refer to variations in prices over time, but rather to cost-output (or decision-cost) relationships at given moments in time. In classifying costs into the fixed and variable categories, the issue is whether a change in output affects the cost.

Another primitive confusion results from neglecting the difference between costs as totals and as averages. The discussion so far has concentrated on total costs rather than on unit costs. But since much of the following discussion will be in terms of unit costs, it may be desirable to be explicit about this point. Let us start with the extreme case of costs that vary in direct proportion to output. It is clear that under such conditions the unit variable costs (known as average variable costs) are constant as output varies. It is surprising that some students therefore fall into the error of calling such costs "fixed" costs—they *are* constant per unit.

FIGURE 5–5

A More Complicated Semivariable Expense
(for example, an electric utility expense on which there is a
fixed charge and quantity discounts for greater volume)

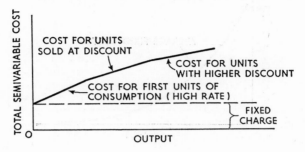

FIGURE 5–6

A Completely Variable Expense

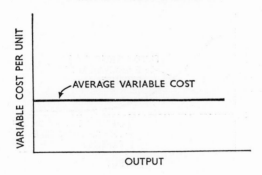

In fact some early business and engineering literature used the term just this way. It is desirable, however, to follow the standard usage of contemporary economics.

It may be instructive to draw five charts similar to Figures 5–1 through 5–5, but this time showing *unit costs* on the vertical axes. Figures 5–6 through 5–10 translate the total costs of the earlier figures into unit costs. The reader should become familiar with both types of diagrams.

4. The expression "completely fixed expense" is open to diverse interpretations. We need to distinguish among the following kinds of costs:

a) Costs which are fixed as long as operations are going on, but which are escapable if operations are shut down. An example might be the salaries of the supervisory staff.

b) Costs which run on even if production is halted but which are escapable if the company is liquidated. These costs are inescapable in the

FIGURE 5–7

A COMPLETELY FIXED EXPENSE

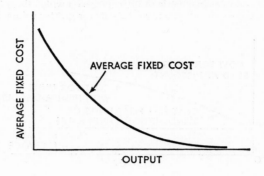

FIGURE 5–8

A SEMIVARIABLE EXPENSE

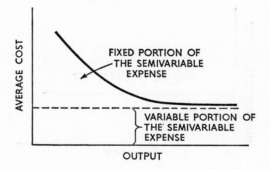

short run but escapable in the long run. An example might be the wages of watchmen or the minimum heating expense required to prevent the freezing of pipes. We shall call these expenses "stand-by fixed costs."

c) Costs which cannot be escaped even if the company is dissolved and the assets sold. Such would be true of the depreciation on equipment which has no market value. Strictly speaking these costs are not economic costs at all (the opportunity costs are nil), but they may appear in the accounts. Perhaps these costs should be called "completely sunk costs," since they are not escapable under any circumstances.

d) Costs which are not the result of output but which are at the discretion of management. Examples are advertising expense, research expense, and consultants' fees. This category may sometimes include a substantial part of wages and salaries. These expenses go under the names of "programmed fixed costs" or "discretionary expenses."

FIGURE 5–9

A Stairstep Variable Cost

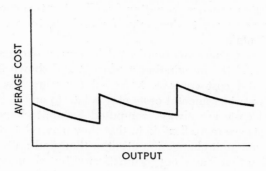

FIGURE 5–10

A More Complicated Semivariable Expense

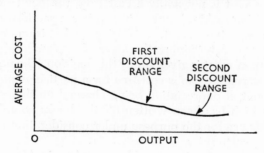

Other cost classifications

It will become increasingly clear as we proceed that the fixed-variable classification is inadequate to deal with all of the cost relationships involved in managerial decisions. It is appropriate at this point to review a wider range of cost terminology. Throughout our study of managerial economics the following classifications will be useful, each classification pointing up a different aspect of the decision-making problem.[1]

Incremental costs versus sunk costs. Chapter 2 has already introduced the incremental cost concept, but it is of such central importance that it should be reviewed here. A cost is incremental if it results from a decision; costs which do not arise from the particular decision but which run on anyway are excluded from incremental costs. A decision to drive an extra 1,000 miles should consider the extra fuel costs and wear-and-tear on tires

---

[1] This section is heavily influenced by Joel Dean, *Managerial Economics* (New York: Prentice-Hall, Inc., 1951), pp. 257–72.

but can ignore the portion of depreciation which marches on regardless of usage. A decision to buy a second car, in contrast, must reckon with the added depreciation expenses resulting from having two cars aging rather than one.[2] It is necessary to determine for each decision which costs are actually incremental.

Marginal costs versus costs unaffected by output changes. Chapter 2 has also introduced the marginal cost concept and shown its relationship to the incremental cost concept. Marginal costs are always related to changes in output; incremental costs may relate to any decision affecting costs. Marginal costs are always computed for unit changes in output; incremental costs are more flexible in that they may relate to any change, whether it is a one unit change in output, a thousand unit change in output, or a decision that leaves output unaffected but changes costs in other ways. Marginal costs are in contrast to costs which are unaffected by output.

Opportunity costs versus "costs" requiring no sacrifice. Chapter 2 has suggested that a cost is not really a cost from the point of view of economics (or decision making) unless it requires a sacrifice of alternatives —unless it is an opportunity cost. Determining what is an opportunity cost or, more important, determining the *level* of opportunity costs, requires the measurement of what is given up by the decision. The use of idle space which has no alternative use is cost-free for a particular purpose, regardless of the amount of depreciation being charged on the space.[3] The use of a machine which has been written off the books completely does involve a cost if its use for the purpose under consideration requires giving up alternative opportunities.

Escapable costs versus inescapable costs (avoidable versus unavoidable costs). A cost is escapable if the decision frees the enterprise from an outflow of funds that would have been required otherwise. If cutting back production by 10 percent will free the firm from material costs of $10,000 per month and labor costs of $5,000 per month, those costs are escapable. But if no foreman can be laid off as a result of this decision, formen's salaries do not enter into the escapable costs.

Whether certain costs are escapable varies according to the decision. Some costs that cannot be escaped as a result of reductions in output may be escaped by closing down the department completely. The part of depreciation which relates to wear and tear (the user cost) is escaped by reducing output, but the part which flows on over time regardless of out-

---

[2] This illustration is developed by W. J. Vatter in "Tailor-Making Cost Data for Specific Uses," *N.A.C.A. Bulletin*, 1954 Conference Proceedings as reprinted in W. E. Thomas (ed.), *Readings in Cost Accounting, Budgeting and Control* (Cincinnati: South-Western Publishing Company, 1955), pp. 316–18.

[3] This statement must be qualified to recognize that a user cost may result from putting the idle space to work.

put is escapable only if the machine or building is sold, and even then only if there is a market for such assets. (A fuller discussion of depreciation must be postponed until the next section.)

The antithesis of the escapable cost is the inescapable or sunk cost—the cost that runs on whether the alternative is chosen or not. Again what is or is not sunk depends on the decision under consideration. If I am considering leasing my house during the summer while on leave, I must consider the depreciation on the house (exclusive of wear and tear)—the payment for mowing the lawn and the fixed charge in my telephone and other utility bills—to be inescapable. But I can escape from all of these expenses by selling the house, at the cost of incurring considerable inconvenience and expenses of other types. The terms avoidable and unavoidable are often used as substitutes for escapable and inescapable. These terms will be used interchangeably in the discussion which follows.

Short-run costs versus long-run costs.   As explained briefly at the beginning of this chapter, short-run costs have to do with costs when some of the inputs are fixed in quantity. The usual illustration is that of the costs in a plant that is already built; labor and materials may be varied but not the size of the plant itself. Long-run costs have to do with variations in cost when enough time is allowed to vary the size of the plant itself. Actually, there are degrees of short run, depending on how many of the inputs are fixed. As Dean states: "The conventional dichotomy of long-run versus short-run cost curves needs to be expanded . . . to envision a whole family of cost curves that differ in degree of adaptation, so that the conventional long-run cost curve is the limiting case of perfect adaptation."[4]

Common costs versus separable costs.   Most firms produce more than one product and thus run into the problem of common costs. Often it is difficult to attribute costs to particular products since they result from the mix of products rather than from one product taken at a time. In decision making much of the confusion of trying to determine which costs are common and which are traceable to a particular product can be resolved by applying incremental reasoning. It is often easier to determine how much a change in the output of a single product brings a change in a particular kind of cost than it is to determine a product's "fair share" of that cost.[5] In any case, it is the change in cost rather than the traceability of cost which is relevant. But it is necessary to face up to more complex situations in which an increase in the output of product A brings an increase (or decrease) in the marginal cost of product B. Such problems

---

[4] Dean, *op. cit.*, p. 262.

[5] Once the accountant has adopted a routine for allocating overhead costs it may be easy to determine the "full cost" of a product. But the result of this computation is not relevant for decision making. It may be important to determine traceable costs for other purposes.

are important in determining the product mix in the oil industry or other industries in which the same raw materials or processes result in a variety of end products.

Other cost concepts

To be complete it is desirable to introduce a few additional terms that appear in business literature. Frequently businessmen refer to *out-of-pocket costs,* but their use of the term is inconsistent. Strictly speaking the term should refer to cash outlays to outsiders. The payments for raw materials are an out-of-pocket cost, but depreciation is not. Often managers use the term to mean incremental costs. But the salary of a supervisor requires a cash outlay which may not be incremental for a given increase in output. Often the out-of-pocket usage is ambiguous on what is really intended.

A similar confusion surrounds the term *direct cost.* Some accountants apparently define direct costs to be the same as variable costs. One accounting research study states, "Direct costs are those costs which vary directly with volume (raw material, direct labor, and direct supplies) plus certain costs which vary closely with production and can be allocated to a product or group of products on a reasonably accurate basis."[6] But the expression "direct" seems to refer more to the ease with which a particular expense may be traced to an individual department or product.[7] Traceability and variability are not the same thing; the ambiguity on just which is being measured results in confusion. And, as we have seen, even if we restrict direct costs to mean variable costs, its meaning depends on just what decision is being made. A completely programmed system of direct costing cannot provide the exact incremental cost figure required for every kind of decision.[8]

The distinction between *controllable* and *noncontrollable* costs is important in management, which must be concerned with fixing responsibility for keeping costs in line with predetermined standards. This book, however, is less concerned with control than it is with decision making, so that there will be few, if any, references to this dichotomy on the pages which follow.

The term *imputed* or *implicit* costs refers to costs which are relevant in decision making but which are not recorded in the accounts. In the earlier discussion of the opportunity cost concept, it was apparent that

---

[6] N.A.A. Research Report No. 37, January 1, 1961, p. 11.

[7] In fact, Gordon Shillinglaw, *Cost Accounting: Analysis and Control* (Homewood, Ill.: Richard D. Irwin, Inc., 1961), p. 102, defines a direct cost as one "that is specifically traceable to a particular costing unit." Some books appear to relate "direct costing" to the collection of variable costs but use "direct costs" to mean traceable costs, a distinction which is confusing to the layman.

[8] Support for this position appears in Howard C. Greer, "Alternatives to Direct Costing," in William E. Thomas (ed.), *Readings in Cost Accounting, Budgeting, and Control* (Cincinnati: South-Western Publishing Co., 1955), pp. 300–312.

such costs may be crucial in the choice among alternatives. Frequent examples of implicit costs are the interest and dividends that could be earned elsewhere—the salary a sole proprietor might earn in an outside position, and the rental that could be earned on property in other undertakings. A student is incurring the imputed cost of the wages he is not earning; such costs may often exceed the explicit costs.

The term *differential* cost appears in some accounting literature to mean approximately the same thing as *incremental* cost in this volume. The differential cost may be computed as a total or on a unit of output basis.

Recent articles and books on accounting have stressed the need for *relevant* costs—that is costs which are needed to reach an optimal decision.[9] It is clear that this literature is working toward the same objective sought here in focusing attention on those costs that are affected by the particular decision under consideration.

It is probably undesirable to complicate the terminology any further at this point. It will, however, be necessary to introduce some variations in these terms as they are required on later pages.

Empirical studies and illustrations

One way to illustrate the classification between fixed and variable costs, and the relevance of some of the other cost concepts, is to consider an operation familiar to everyone. Even this simple example shows the difficulties of classifying costs; it demonstrates the need for flexibility in adapting cost measures to particular problems.

CORNER GROCERY STORE

The independent corner grocery store would seem to offer the simplest situation for the analyst. Yet even it presents a number of borderline issues. Let us consider some particular expenses to see whether they fit into the fixed or variable categories.

Cost of goods sold. The sums paid at wholesale for the groceries are the clearest illustrations of variable costs. The greater the volume of sales the greater these expenses. The complications are relatively insignificant: The firm may benefit from quantity discounts which would keep this cost from being exactly constant per unit of sales; changes in the sales mix, with various commodities selling at different markups, might cause a shift in the cost of goods sold per unit of sales; the sale of an item that has become obsolete and has been sitting on the shelves a long time may involve no real sacrifice, or at least not one equal to the original wholesale cost.

---

[9] See Charles T. Horngren, "Choosing Accounting Practices for Reporting to Management," *N.A.A. Bulletin,* September, 1962, pp. 3–15; and G. R. Crowningshield, *Cost Accounting: Principles and Managerial Application* (Boston: Houghton Mifflin Co., 1962), pp. 481–82.

Rental on the building.   Rental expense would appear to be the clear-est case of a fixed expense, running on without regard to the level of sales. Yet a decision to close down would affect costs in different ways depending on the length of the rental contract and on possible alternative uses of the property. The availability of convenient storage space on the outside might enable the firm to vary warehousing rentals according to volume. If the firm actually owns the store property, the analysis becomes more complicated, for the true rental expense is the sacrifice of opportuni-ties for earnings from alternatives. The opportunity cost concept indicates how one might measure such costs.

Employees' wages.   The variability of wages in such a store depends on how short a run one has in mind. If one is looking at the variation in wages within a day, such costs are only partially variable. The store may be able to employ extra help for the anticipated rush hours, but may have to keep on help to meet unpredictable peaks in activity. Under contempo-rary employment conditions it is doubtful that clerks will work only dur-ing peak periods and it is certain that they will not make themselves available on call as the need arises unless they are relatives of the owner. Grocery stores meet this problem in part by shifting clerks from jobs at the cash registers to stocking tasks; their ability to transfer workers from jobs that have to be done at particular (but not always predictable) times to fill-in jobs helps control costs. The opportunity to keep employees on overtime also increases the ability to adjust wages to volume but, of course, produces the complication of time-and-a-half for overtime.

Storage costs.   The interest expense on inventories does not always follow the usual generalization that interest is a fixed cost, though the interest on minimum inventories does take on a fixed character. The inter-est costs, along with handling costs, and the costs of deterioration and obsolescence might in some cases be treated as a variable cost dependent on volume, since many firms vary the size of inventory with the volume of sales and output. The cost of the storage space, on the other hand, would be included in the rental expense already discussed—usually a fixed cost. One complication is that handling costs, deterioration, and obsoles-cence depend on the mix of products, which might vary from time to time.

Utilities.   The cost of heating, lighting, and water are probably as close to fixed costs as one could find. Even if the charges for electricity include both fixed and variable components (as is true in the case of a two-part tariff), the manager of a grocery store will have little oppor-tunity to relate the total charges to volume; he will not turn off the lights simply because the traffic is low.[10] At the same time, they are costs that

---

[10] A decision to carry or abandon frozen foods will affect the electricity bill. This is another illustration of the variety of short runs encountered in practice since the electricity consumed by frozen foods is fixed in the extremely short run but may be varied by changing the physical facilities.

are escapable if the store is closed down completely, for the utilities can be disconnected. In manufacturing, utility expenses are more likely to include a considerable variable component, especially if gas or electricity is used in the manufacturing process itself.

Depreciation on equipment. The depreciation on refrigerators and other specialized grocery equipment is handled as a fixed expense in the usual accounting practice. From the standpoint of short-run decisions it might be ignored almost completely, for the resale or salvage value of this equipment is probably negligible. No sacrifice is involved in its continued use. In either treatment the cost is excluded from the short-run variable costs and from incremental cost.

Advertising expense. Advertising presents a peculiarly difficult conceptual problem in the classification of costs. Suppose management were to adopt the policy of varying advertising with sales volume; it might then appear that advertising is a variable cost, rising and falling directly with sales. But advertising expense is not a result of volume; it involves an attempt to manipulate volume. Furthermore the policy of basing such expenses on volume is arbitrary and usually unsound. One aim of advertising is to increase volume, acting as a cause rather than a result of volume. Two solutions present themselves: (1) treat advertising as a fixed expense budgeted by management in advance and thus unrelated to short-run volume or (2) leave such expenses out of the fixed-variable classification, placing them in a special category of manipulable expenses, which we have called "programmed expenses." The literature does not give as much attention to the distinction between such programmed costs and fixed costs as seems warranted.

CHAIN GROCERY STORES

The preceding discussion has covered the classification of costs in a hypothetical corner grocery store. It should be of interest to turn now to a study of short-run costs in actual chain grocery stores.[11] This study breaks costs into three categories: fixed costs, discretionary fixed costs, and variable costs. Table 5–1 summarizes the findings on one of the stores. Both sales and cost of goods sold are used as bases for the breakdown of costs.

The discretionary fixed costs in Table 5–1 are costs which are fixed with respect to volume but are subject to managerial decisions. Maintenance is controlled by management. Services which include trash and garbage haulage, utilities, and legal and accounting services, could be curtailed at a zero level of output. The most important item in this category, labor costs, are clearly not variable costs in supermarkets. Scatter

---

[11] Bob R. Holdren, *The Structure of a Retail Market and the Market Behavior of Retail Units* (Englewood Cliffs, N.J.: Prentice-Hall, Inc., 1960), pp. 28–42.

TABLE 5–1

INCOME STATEMENT AND OPERATING RATIOS FOR A CHAIN GROCERY STORE
(July, 1953–June, 1954)

	Dollars	Percentage of Sales	Percentage of Cost of Goods Sold
Sales	543,416	100.00	117.91
Fixed costs	13,537	2.49	2.94
Rent	2,400	.44	.52
Interest paid	882	.16	.19
Imputed interest	1,405	.26	.30
Depreciation	5,117	.94	1.11
Insurance	1,678	.31	.36
Taxes	2,055	.38	.45
Discretionary fixed costs	66,683	12.28	14.47
Maintenance	1,552	.29	.34
Services	5,356	.99	1.16
Payroll	59,308	10.91	12.87
Miscellaneous	467	.09	.10
Total variable costs	470,321	86.55	102.05
Cost of goods sold	460,864	84.81	100.00
Gross income tax	2,717	.50	.59
Delivery	294	.05	.06
Supplies	4,272	.79	.93
Labor (estimated)	2,174	.40	.47
Advertising	5,879	1.08	1.28
Long-run profits	−13,004	−2.39	−2.82
Short-run profits	533	.10	.12
Gross profit	82,552	15.19	17.91

SOURCE: Bob R. Holdren, *The Structure of a Retail Market and the Market Behavior of Retail Units* (Englewood Cliffs, N.J.: Prentice-Hall, Inc., 1960), p. 29.

diagrams and tests of significance show that they have little, if any, relation to the volume of sales.

The evidence in this study indicates that the average variable costs in supermarkets are equal to marginal costs and are horizontal over a wide range of volume. The cost of goods sold makes up close to 99 percent of the marginal costs—almost all the other costs fall into the fixed or discretionary fixed categories.

The distinction between short-run profits and long-run profits depends on the inclusion or exclusion of the fixed costs. The store under consideration is making a slight contribution to fixed costs but is clearly unprofitable if long-run profits continue to be negative over an extensive period. Other stores included in the study show higher long-run profits and higher short-run contributions to fixed costs and profits but nevertheless show an extremely high ratio of marginal costs plus discretionary costs to total revenue.

This discussion has not covered all the categories of cost but should suffice to illustrate the way in which one might in actual practice go about classifying costs and to indicate that the variety of possible "short-runs" makes it impossible to use the same classification for all purposes.

2. ACCOUNTING COSTS AND ECONOMIC COSTS

Sometimes managerial economists play a little game which involves setting up a straw man called "accounting costs," and then knocking it down. Such a game is useful, for it stresses the variety of meanings that may be attached to cost, but it is a little unfair. Accountants did not originally develop their cost concepts for the same purposes that the economists have in mind; the difference in purpose means a difference in definition. There is plenty of room for a variety of interpretations of cost that depend on the purposes at hand. Indeed, when it comes to analysis for decision making, the economists and accountants are in close agreement. The simultaneous development of "managerial economics" and "managerial accounting" has profited from a mutual contribution of each subject to the other, so that the two are now almost inseparable.

Limitations of traditional accounting data for decision making

Originally accounting had only an indirect relationship to decision making. The main function of accounting has been that of *reporting*— of recording what *has happened*. The profit and loss statement (income statement) attempts to tell how well the firm has done. The data required to determine past profitability are not those needed to select optional alternatives for the future. Another main function of accounting closely related to that of reporting is *stewardship*—the presentation of information that will protect the interests of the stockholders, creditors, or tax collectors. But again stewardship and decision making are quite different objectives.

Accounting has had still another objective—that of *control*—of providing standards against which performance can be judged. The classification of accounts according to areas of responsibility and the collection of data most suitable for control purposes are not necessarily what is required for the choice among alternatives for the future.

The main principle followed in the collection of data for reporting, stewardship, or control has been that of recording *past or historical costs*. In measuring the cost involved in the use of resources such as materials or equipment, the accountant concerns himself with the *acquisition cost* of those resources. But decision making is necessarily concerned with future costs and revenues; the past is not always an accurate guide for the future. In fact some accountants are concerned that in a period of inflation the use of historical costs may be inadequate even for reporting purposes. The charges for depreciation based on the acquisition of assets ten years ago may fail to reflect the costs of reproducing those assets today (or other estimates of opportunity costs) and thus may result in an overstatement or understatement of profits. This is a controversial issue which becomes especially pronounced in the area of public utility regulation, for regulatory commissions customarily approve rates which provide a "fair" return on the assets of the firm. In a period of inflation, a considerable difference between the historical cost and reproduction cost of such assets may arise. Public utilities prefer reproduction cost for two reasons: it results in higher depreciation expenses, and it provides a higher value of assets to serve as a rate base in regulation. In addition, most companies would prefer that corporate income taxes be assessed on the basis of the lower profits that would result from reproduction cost depreciation.

It may be useful to review the reasons that the traditional accounting procedures for reporting or control are often deficient for decision making:

1. The historical cost data do not always reflect the opportunity costs of decisions. Raw materials acquired at $1,000 last month may be worth more today because of the higher costs of replacing them; a true measure of sacrifices must recognize such increased replacement costs. Or, to take another illustration, the use of idle floor space may involve no opportunity cost despite the depreciation the accountant charges on such space, for no sacrifice is required. In fact, it would appear that historical costs would seldom measure the true opportunity costs. In periods of slack business, the opportunity costs fall far below the depreciation based on historical costs; in periods of high activity, the sacrifice in selecting one alternative over another may be far above depreciation.

2. Closely related to the point just made is the fact that accounting valuations of assets may not reflect their true economic values. The traditional accounting procedure for valuing assets on the balance sheet is at acquisition cost minus depreciation. Accountants have always known that these values may have little relation to current market values. The managerial economist's approach to valuation is to take a look at the *future* revenues and costs that will result from an asset and to discount those future cash flows. A firm which offers an asset for sale at $1,000 because this is the book value of that asset may be sacrificing an opportunity of selling at a higher price to someone to whom the discounted present value is higher. On the other hand, to insist on the $1,000 when the asset is actually worthless to the firm (its internal discounted present value is nil) may mean the failure to cash in on a chance to sell at $700.

3. The traditional accounting procedures ignore certain items which are costs from the economic point of view. The most obvious examples, discussed in Chapter 2, are the failure of accounting for sole proprietorships or partnerships to record the sacrifice of the owners' time which may be useful for other purposes, or to record the earnings possible if the funds were invested elsewhere.

4. The traditional accounting classifications do not usually provide the required breakdown between costs affected by decisions and costs that are not. In other words, they do not measure exactly the incremental costs or escapable costs required in the analysis of a decision-making problem. The breakdown between fixed costs and variable costs moves in this direction, as we have seen, but the accounts are sometimes inadequate on such breakdowns, giving, for example, no insight into which of the overhead costs are fixed and which are variable.

Even when the accounts provide a distinction between fixed and variable costs, they may not provide the flexibility in classification required by decision making. As already noted, a cost that may be fixed or sunk for one kind of decision may be variable or escapable for another. Most accounting procedures are programmed—they are routinized to cut the costs that might be required by more flexible procedures—but decision making requires tailor-made cost classifications.

5. Traditional procedures for overhead allocation often result in more confusion than clarification as far as decision making is concerned. Accountants may allocate overhead on the basis of direct labor costs in a department, or some similar basis. Perhaps past results or budgets for the future suggest that overhead should be allocated at the rate of 150 percent of direct labor cost. Suppose that management is considering introduction of a labor-saving machine which will result in a cut of direct labor costs of $12,000 per year. One might be tempted to assume that overhead costs will be cut by $18,000 (150 percent of $12,000). But the overhead allocation rate is totally irrelevant. The real need is a determination of how much overhead is actually affected by the decision. For example, management should estimate the change in power requirements resulting from the new machine.

The accountants themselves recognize that the bases for overhead allocations are arbitrary. One classical statement on the subject is: ". . . cost allocation at best is loaded with assumption and in many cases, highly arbitrary methods of apportionment are employed in practice. Certainly it is wise not to take the results of the usual process of internal cost computation too seriously."[12]

This list of the limitations of accounting may appear to be formidable and to serve as the basis for an indictment of accounting. But remember that the traditional accounting procedures under discussion were developed for purposes other than what we have in mind. Remember also that the accounts are our main source of data for decisions. The skilled manager must learn how to interpret those accounts and to ask the accountants for data and classifications of data which suit his needs.

---

[12] W. A. Paton and A. C. Littleton, *An Introduction to Corporate Accounting Standards* (Chicago: American Accounting Association, 1940), p. 120.

The special problem of depreciation

Conceptually the most difficult problem in relating the accountant's concept of cost to that of the economist is depreciation. As already noted, the accepted accounting practice is to base depreciation on original cost and to allocate that original cost over time. The objective is to spread the acquisition cost over the time periods in which the asset is to be used. Depreciation in accounting is thus "a procedure for spreading the cost of a long term asset over its useful life in a more or less equitable manner." Many students believe that the accountant's depreciation charge is aimed at providing a fund for the replacement of assets, but this is not the purpose, as the examination of any accounting textbook will show.

The economist's objective is to compute a depreciation figure which reflects the sacrifices in selecting one alternative over another. The measurement of this sacrifice requires considerable judgment (accountants traditionally try to avoid such judgment) and varies according to the decision. The best procedure is to consider some situations in which quite different depreciation concepts are required.

1. Suppose that a machine has broken down completely, beyond any hope of repair. The management wishes to decide whether it should buy a new machine or to purchase on the outside the parts for which the machine was required. In this case, the reproduction or replacement cost of the machine is the relevant basis for depreciation—the historical cost of the old machine is irrelevant. Perhaps this illustration is trivial, for no one in his right mind would consider depreciation on the old machine if he is considering the purchase of a new machine. But extreme cases help to clarify the issue.

2. Suppose that an old machine is on hand which appears to have four years of physical life remaining. The issue is whether to sell the machine now and start buying the parts on the outside at once. The original cost of the machine was, let us say, $50,000. The book value net of depreciation is $20,000 and the annual depreciation for accounting purposes is $5,000 per annum. The measurement of depreciation required for the analysis of this problem is the expected loss in the market value of the machine in the future. If the machine is worth $7,000 now, but is expected to be worth $5,500 a year from now, the sacrifice in retaining it a year is $1,500. The economic depreciation is $1,500 rather than $5,000—it measures the sacrifice of an opportunity of selling the machine now rather than later.

3. Suppose the machine has no market value but still is productive. The depreciation is nil regardless of the book value or the accountant's depreciation charge.

4. Now consider a decision to increase output by 50 percent. What is needed is a measure of the *increase* in depreciation resulting from the increased activity. Managerial economists often assume that this increase

is negligible, for obsolescence is unaffected by use and machines or buildings tend to deteriorate over time whether used or not. A more refined
approach is to try to measure the added wear and tear resulting from use
—to measure the *user cost*. In many cases this user cost may be safely
ignored, but in others it may be a significant consideration.

Variations on these situations appear in practice, sometimes requiring
a complex analysis. Some cases may require a mixture of short-run and
long-run considerations. Taxes complicate the issue. But enough has been
said to indicate the opportunity cost basis for the economist's measurement of depreciation and to indicate that financial accounting is usually
concerned with quite a different problem. The manager must use judgment in determining which definition of depreciation is appropriate for
the purpose at hand; the accountant prefers to adopt a strict definition
which limits the scope of such judgment.

Empirical studies and illustrations

We have seen that the traditional techniques of financial and cost
accounting often are at variance with the requirements of economics. But
accountants have developed special approaches for the purposes of decision making which go under various names, such as direct costing,
marginal income analysis, differential costing, merchandise management
accounting, cost-volume-profit analysis, and contribution accounting.

The question is how extensive these approaches are in actual practice.
Chapter 2 cited a study by James S. Earley of a sample of large firms
which suggests that differential accounting is becoming widespread.
Earley states that "leading cost accountants and management consultants
are currently advocating principles of accounting analysis and decision
making that are essentially 'marginalist' in character and implications."[13]
Earley finds a widespread separation of fixed and variable costs and other
procedures moving in the direction of incremental reasoning. It appears
doubtful, however, that all of the firms in his sample face up to the full
implications of managerial economics. Do they tailor-make costs to meet
the varying requirements of different decisions? Do they adjust cost estimates to reflect changes in opportunity costs with variations in the use of
capacity?

Earley's study appears to concentrate mainly on programmed accounting techniques—on routinized procedures resulting in periodic reports.
The frequent nonprogrammed (*ad hoc*) analyses in business are more
certain to reflect the economic reasoning under discussion, for *ad hoc*
analysis is flexible in applying the concepts required in the particular
situation.

---

[13] James S. Earley, "Marginal Policies of 'Excellently Managed' Companies," *The
American Economic Review*, March, 1956, p. 44.

A study of small businesses suggests that their accounting procedures seldom reflect incremental reasoning.[14] Chapter 2 has reviewed cases in which the accounting systems encouraged the managers to use full costs (including allocated overhead) when incremental costs would have been more appropriate. But this study suggests that most managers of small firms make little use of the accounts in decision making. Most of them resort to highly subjective *ad hoc* analyses varying in thoroughness, while some make fairly careful pencil-and-paper estimates which may use some of the accounting data but which are flexible in adapting the analysis to the situation.

Actual practice, therefore, appears to vary from situations in which accounting and economics are closely interwoven in providing the information required for decisions to the opposite extreme in which overhead allocations, past costs, historical depreciation, and similar accounting conventions actually confuse management. Every manager would profit from thinking through this relationship between accounting and economics.

3. BREAK-EVEN CHARTS

Up to this point we have been mainly concerned with the classification of *particular expenses* (salaries, depreciation, etc.). We now turn to the aggregation of these expenses for the firm as a whole or for departments. Again it is possible to examine these costs as totals or as averages.

Form of the break-even charts

A widely used portrayal of costs for the firm or department as a whole is the break-even chart. The usual construction of this chart is based on the assumption that costs are either completely fixed or completely variable. It is possible, however, to draw charts showing more complicated relationships.

Figure 5–11 illustrates a typical break-even chart. The horizontal axis on such a chart represents output; the purpose of the chart is to show the effects of changes in output. It should be noted that revenues as well as expenses are shown on the vertical axis, usually with total revenue drawn as a straight line through the origin. A linear revenue function assumes that the price is unrelated to output. This assumption is appropriate under conditions of pure competition, in which the firm may sell any quantity at the market price, but it is not suitable when the demand curve slopes downward to the right. Total cost is also usually shown as a straight line; it is the sum of the fixed costs which are horizontal on the chart and the variable costs which are assumed to rise linearly.

---

[14] J. L. Gibson and W. W. Haynes, *Accounting in Small Business Decisions* (Lexington: University of Kentucky Press, 1963).

The student should not jump to the conclusion that the sole objective of the break-even chart is to determine the break-even point—the point at which total revenue equals total cost. The break-even point is of some interest, but the chart also shows what happens to profits (or losses) at outputs greater or less than the break-even volume. The objective of the chart is to indicate what happens to total costs and total revenues as output and sales change from one level to another.

Contribution to overhead and profit

Sometimes the information shown on Figure 5–11 is presented in an alternative form, with the variable costs shown first on the vertical axis, and with the addition of the fixed costs to the variable costs. Such a

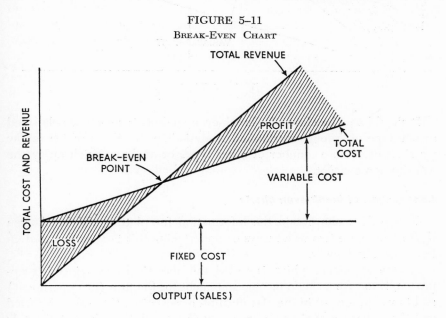

FIGURE 5–11

BREAK-EVEN CHART

form is shown in Figure 5–12. Figure 5–12 has the advantage that one can read on it the *contribution to overhead and profit* quite readily. Decision making in the short run is more concerned with this contribution to both overhead and profits than it is to the profit figure alone. This form of the break-even chart is closely related to the incremental reasoning described in Chapter 2. The stress is on the changes in total revenue and changes in total cost as output varies. The fixed costs appear in a subordinate position. The interesting point about an increase in output and sales of 10 percent, for example, is the additional contribution to overhead and profit that results; this involves a simple comparison of the increase in revenue with the increase in cost.

FIGURE 5–12

BREAK-EVEN CHART: CONTRIBUTION TO PROFIT FORM

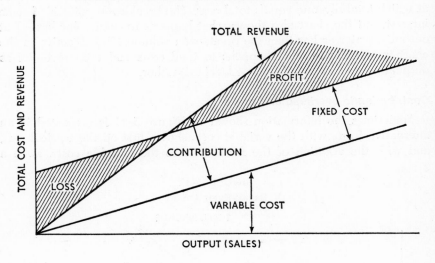

It should now be clear why break-even analysis is sometimes classified as one type of "profit contribution analysis." In the pages which follow we shall examine a number of other types of analysis which apply the contribution concept.

Construction of break-even charts

Where does one obtain the information for plotting the break-even chart? There are two usual ways of undertaking this task, both based on the income statement.

1. One approach, which is called the analytical or engineering approach, is to take a single income statement for the firm (or department) and to use judgment in the classification of costs into those that are fixed and those that are variable. A manager of a small firm who is intimately familiar with output-expense behavior should have little difficulty with such a classification, though there are inevitably some borderline problems, as in the case of semivariable expenses already described. The manager simply asks himself whether he would actually increase this expense if output were to increase and he estimates the amount of the increased spending. He may find it necessary to abandon the linearity assumption upon which break-even charts are usually constructed and introduce stairstep costs and other semivariable expenses. The resultant chart might look like Figure 5–13 rather than take the usual linear form.

2. A second approach, the statistical or historical approach, compares a series of income statements for succeeding periods which reflect vary-

FIGURE 5-13

A COMPLEX BREAK-EVEN CHART

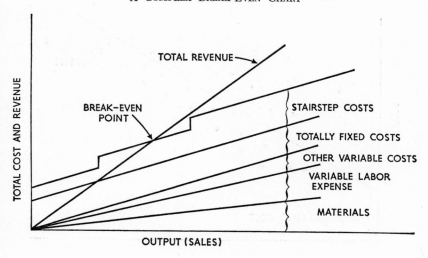

ing levels of output and costs. By plotting the output-cost relationship on a scatter diagram, one can estimate the position of the total cost line. If one assumes that the costs are linear, he can extrapolate the total cost line back to the vertical axis (at which output is zero), thus determining the level of the fixed costs.

Figure 5-14 illustrates this approach. The dots on the diagram show the relation between the cost and output for particular periods. These dots will not fall exactly on a single line, for other influences inevitably affect costs. It is hoped, however, that the dots will arrange themselves in enough of a pattern that a line of best fit may be located. The slope of this line is a measure of the marginal costs (or unit variable costs under conditions of linearity). The intercept on the vertical axis is the estimate of the fixed cost. It is then possible to draw in an appropriate total revenue line and to find the break-even point.

More refined statistical techniques for estimating the total cost line are possible. One may wish for example to correct the data for changes in input prices over time. In most cases, very simple procedures are used, though these procedures fail to separate the influence of volume from the influence of other variables.

Scale of the output axis

The discussion so far has failed to define precisely what measure of output is plotted on the horizontal axis of the break-even chart. If the firm produces one standard product, one simply plots the volume of physical output (in pounds, tons, cubic feet, or whatever the appropriate

FIGURE 5–14

Estimating the Total Cost Line from a Scatter Diagram

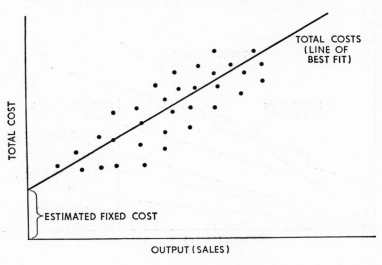

unit is). The total cost line then provides an estimate of the cost at any level of physical output.

If, however, the output is not homogeneous, the measurement of output is more complex. How can one add together quantities of refrigerators and stoves? One solution is to compute an index number of output which will give proper weight to the various products. Another solution is to measure output as a percent of capacity. A simpler, and more widely known, approach is to use sales dollars as a measure of output. Sales dollars automatically weight the various products according to their sales value. In this case, the total revenue line becomes a 45-degree diagonal, provided that the same scale is used on both axes of the break-even chart. The use of sales dollars does not completely overcome the conceptual difficulties involved in measuring output. Suppose, for example, that the price of one product is increased and another decreased. Does it follow that the relative importance of the two products is actually different as far as costs are concerned?

Limitations of break-even analysis

Some of the major limitations of break-even analysis are clear from the preceding discussion.

1. The charts usually are not corrected for changes in factor prices. If a break-even chart is based on past data, those data should be adjusted for changes in wages and for changes in the prices of raw materials. Such

adjustments are cumbersome. The analytical approach avoids the necessity of making these adjustments.

2. The charts usually assume that the price of the output (or prices of the outputs) is given. In other words, they assume a horizontal demand curve that is realistic only under conditions approximating pure competition. A simple way of attempting to overcome this limitation is to draw a series of total revenue lines on the chart, each based on the assumption of a different price. One can then estimate the volume that will be sold and produced at each price and can read from the diagram the expected profits. Figure 5–15 illustrates this form of the chart. Of the

FIGURE 5–15

BREAK-EVEN CHART WITH ALTERNATIVE REVENUE LINES
FOR ALTERNATIVE PRICES

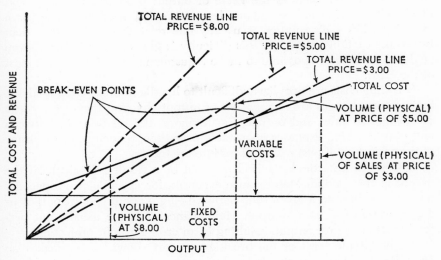

prices shown, that of $5 is the most profitable. Unfortunately, the estimation of the volume at various prices is itself difficult and subject to error.

3. The charts ignore other influences on profits. They assume that profits are a function of output, neglecting the obvious fact that they are also a result of technological change, improved management, changes in the scale of the fixed inputs, and many other forces.

Break-even charts are static. They are drawn on the assumption of given relationships between costs and revenues on one side and output on the other. Costs and revenues may, however, shift over time in such a way that projections based on past data may be misleading.

4. As has already been indicated, break-even charts are based on rather arbitrary assumptions as to the relative importance of different

products in multiproduct firms. A change in the sales mix may mean that the revenue-output relationship shown on the chart is no longer applicable. As Dean says: "Changes in the composition of demand impair the accuracy of the static sales line and may vitiate the profit projection. Whenever products differ in contribution margin and there is variation in product-mix from period to period, profits will vary at a given output rate. . . . Under these circumstances, the constant-price sales line is inaccurate, even as a static function."[15]

5. When break-even charts are based on accounting data, as they usually are, they suffer from all the limitations of such data, such as neglect of imputed cost, arbitrary depreciation estimates, and inappropriate allocations of overhead costs.

6. The carryover of inventory from one period to the next presents another difficulty. What is the value of output produced in one period to be sold later? The accountants have struggled with this issue for a long time, but their solution is usually one related to past rather than future transactions. Normally this difficulty is glossed over in break-even analysis, though it is possible to make adjustments that will correct most of the error.

7. Selling costs are peculiarly difficult to handle in break-even analysis. Selling cost changes are not a *result* of output changes; they are a *cause* of changes in sales and output. Furthermore, the relationship between output and selling expenses is unstable over time, reducing the accuracy of the projection of past relationships into the future.

8. Costs in a particular period may not be a result exclusively of the output in that period. Maintenance expenses, for example, are especially hard to attribute to a given time period, being a result of past output or a preparation for future output. Maintenance costs are usually not perfectly matched with output, resulting in an error in profit projections.

9. The simple form of the break-even chart shown so far makes no provision for taxes, particularly the corporate income tax. One may develop the chart to show part of the profit going to the government in taxes and the remainder going to the stockholders or being retained for expansion. If the company suffers alternating years of profit and loss or if it falls into varying tax brackets, this adjustment for taxes is somewhat difficult to show on the chart.

Evaluation of break-even charts

It is easy to build up a formidable list of limitations of break-even charts. Some writers are skeptical of their usefulness unless they are made much more complex than is usual.[16] At the same time, break-even

[15] Joel Dean, *Managerial Economics* (Englewood Cliffs, N.J.: Prentice-Hall, Inc., 1951), p. 334.
[16] *Ibid.*, pp. 337–38.

analysis is simple, easy to understand, and is inexpensive. The question is what degree of simplification is justified.

The usefulness of break-even charts undoubtedly varies from industry to industry. Those industries experiencing frequent changes in input prices, rapid improvements in technology, and constant shifts in product mix, will profit little from break-even analysis. In other industries, break-even analysis may be quite useful to managers who are familiar with their limitations and simplifications. Management depends heavily on analytical tools that cut through the complexity of reality and focus attention on the fundamental relationships. The problem is that what may be a useful simplification for one manager can be a misleading over-simplification for another.

Empirical studies and illustrations

1. Two pioneers in the application of break-even analysis to actual firms are Walter Rautenstrauch and Raymond Villers, who have published a series of books illustrating their approach.[17] They studied over a hundred firms and generally found a linear relationship between cost and output. As their work progressed, they distinguished carefully between what they called a profit-and-loss chart, which records the actual relation between expenses and sales over the years, and the break-even chart, which holds certain inputs fixed and prices constant. Figure 5–16 shows both a profit-and-loss chart and a series of break-even charts for an actual firm. The dots representing the actual profits and expenses for each year are taken directly from the income statements. The total expense trend line was fitted to these observations; it is claimed that the high level of the 1946 and 1947 dots shows that the firms had over-expanded in that period. The solid lines are the short-run total cost lines usually found on break-even charts. They were located by a judgmental analysis of expenses into those that were fixed and those that were variable.

2. Many authors have adapted break-even analysis to the situation of the multiproduct firm. They construct break-even charts for the individual product, individual department, or "sector." One variation is what Bergfeld, Earley, and Knobloch call the profit-volume (P/V) technique or cost-volume-profit analysis.[18] They adopt a terminology on individual

---

[17] See Walter Rautenstrauch, *The Economics of Business Enterprise* (New York: John Wiley & Sons, Inc., 1939); Walter Rautenstrauch and Raymond Villers, *The Economics of Industrial Management* (New York: Funk & Wagnalls Co., 1949); and Raymond Villers, *Dynamic Management in Industry* (Englewood Cliffs, N.J.: Prentice-Hall, Inc., 1960).

[18] Albert J. Bergfeld, James S. Earley, and William R. Knobloch, *Pricing for Profit and Growth* (New York: McGraw-Hill Book Co., 1957). Modern cost accounting books frequently include a chapter on this type of analysis.

FIGURE 5–16

PROFIT-AND-LOSS CHART AND BREAK-EVEN CHARTS FOR AN ACTUAL CONCERN

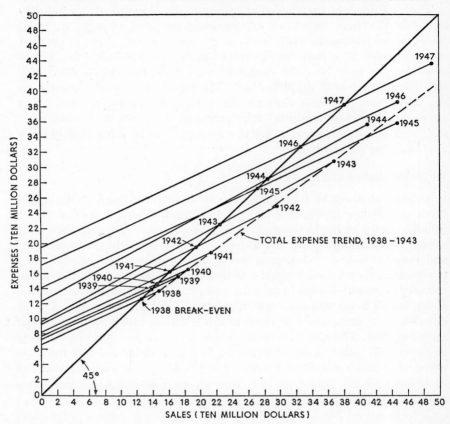

SOURCE: Walter Rautenstrauch and Raymond Villers, *The Economics of Industrial Management* (rev. ed.; New York: Funk & Wagnalls Co., 1957), p. 161.

sectors that is useful, being an application of the incremental approach stressed throughout this book. The main terms are:

P/V Income = Sector's sales volume in dollars minus sector variable costs
Profit Contribution = P/V income minus specific programmed costs
Specific Programmed Costs = Cost of selling the output of the sector or other costs of promoting that sector (as opposed to programmed cost for the firm as a whole)
P/V Ratio = The ratio between the unit P/V income and unit price

This variation on the break-even chart is shown in Figure 5–17. It shows the specific programmed cost below the zero contribution line. The up-

FIGURE 5–17

PROFIT CONTRIBUTION CHART

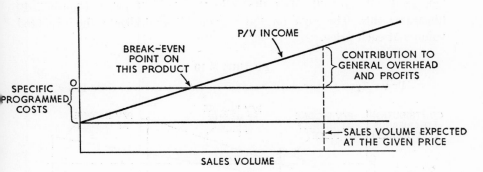

ward sloping line shows the *P/V* income; its slope is the *P/V* ratio. One moves along the sloping line to the point representing the expected sales volume. The vertical distance between this point and the zero line is the profit contribution for the sector. Such a chart ignores overheads that cannot be definitely allocated to this sector. It shows whether a product is covering its own variable and programmed costs; it shows what contribution the product is making to overall company overhead and profit. The chart thus permits an evaluation of product profits at varying levels of sales, and also provides information for the comparison of contributions from one product to another.

Figure 5–18 shows two products, permitting a comparison of both the break-even points and contributions. Product B on this chart has a lower break-even point and makes the greater contribution. This approach is helpful in making decisions on the product mix.

3. Break-even analysis is applicable to still other decision-making problems. The charts may be modified to analyze the impact of price

FIGURE 5–18

PROFIT CONTRIBUTIONS ON TWO PRODUCTS

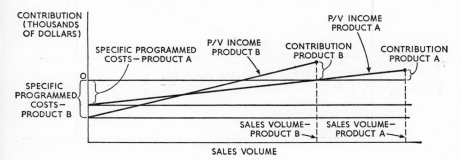

changes by showing different revenue lines for different prices. Suppose a price decrease is under consideration. The chart will show whether the increased volume will offset the reduction in unit price. Figure 5–19 illustrates this. The dots on the revenue lines indicate the expected volume at each price.

FIGURE 5–19

BREAK-EVEN CHART WITH ALTERNATIVE ASSUMPTIONS ABOUT PRICE

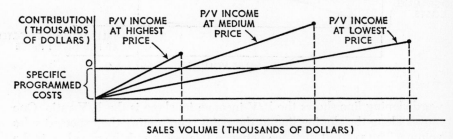

Another form of the chart is useful in evaluating the impact of new investment in equipment. Figures 5–20 through 5–22 show three different possibilities. The first, Figure 5–20, illustrates a case in which the investment leads to increased fixed costs and decreased variable costs, with a resultant higher break-even point. This chart suggests that the investment should not be undertaken unless a high volume is relatively certain, for costs are less flexible and profits are lower at small volumes and it takes

FIGURE 5–20

PROFIT CONTRIBUTION CHART FOR INVESTMENT WHICH RAISES
THE BREAK-EVEN POINT

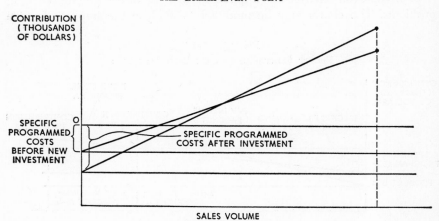

a larger volume to break even. Figure 5–21 shows a case in which the investment is so effective in reducing variable costs that the break-even point is actually lowered, a situation more favorable to the investment under conditions of uncertainty. Figure 5–22 illustrates a capital-saving investment which results in a reduction of fixed costs and a lower break-even point, an extremely favorable situation since the flexibility of costs to volume changes is actually increased and profits are higher at all volumes.

FIGURE 5–21

PROFIT CONTRIBUTION CHART FOR INVESTMENT WHICH REDUCES
THE BREAK-EVEN POINT

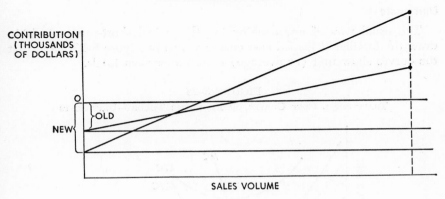

FIGURE 5–22

PROFIT CONTRIBUTION CHART FOR CAPITAL SAVING INVESTMENT

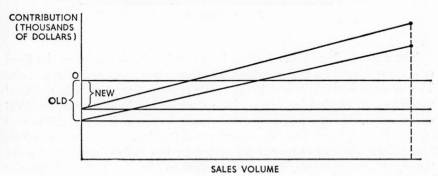

Similar modifications in break-even charts can show the impact of changes in wages or other input prices. None of these modifications completely overcomes the static character of break-even charts.

4. THEORETICAL COST FUNCTIONS

The reader with some familiarity with the usual treatment of costs in textbooks may be somewhat confused by the preceding discussion. The graphs illustrated so far do not look much like those in the textbooks. The fact is that the traditional treatment of short-run costs in economic theory is somewhat at variance with the linear type of model exemplified by the break-even chart. The student of managerial economics should be familiar with both the traditional and linear models, for both have their place.

Unit costs

The usual way of approaching the theoretical short-run costs is to draw the familiar U-shaped cost curves shown in Figure 5–23. Note that the curves show unit (or average) costs rather than totals.

FIGURE 5–23

TRADITIONAL COST CURVES OF ECONOMIC THEORY—UNIT COSTS

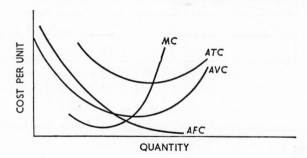

The average fixed costs (*AFC*) falls steadily to the right as the fixed cost is spread over a larger output. The curve is a rectangular hyperbola. The average variable cost (*AVC*) curve is more complex. It is the total variable cost divided by output. The theorist has long drawn the *AVC* curve with a U shape. The initial decrease in the average variable cost results, it is claimed, from increased specialization. Complete specialization at low levels of output is precluded by the indivisibility of some of the inputs. For example, it is uneconomical to hire a skilled setup man at low levels of output, and a fraction of a setup man is unavailable. Therefore, the firm permits the less skilled operators to perform their own setups.

Traditional economic theory is insistent that the average variable cost curve must eventually slope upward. This increase in unit costs follows from one of the basic generalizations of economic theory: the law of diminishing returns. According to the law of diminishing returns, as variable inputs are added to fixed inputs, average output per unit of variable input must eventually decline. (The law is also expressed in terms of an eventual decline in marginal product, but at present we are more interested in averages.) If the average product resulting from increasing variable inputs declines, it follows that the average variable cost must rise, as any simple arithmetic illustration will demonstrate.

The average total cost curve (*ATC*) is the sum of the average variable cost and the average fixed cost. The average total cost will decline at first because of the spreading of fixed costs over larger outputs and also, perhaps, because of the greater specialization in the variable inputs. Eventually the increase in average variable cost resulting from diminishing returns will offset the decrease in average fixed cost and the average total cost will rise. The result is a U-shaped average total cost curve.

The marginal cost curve (*MC*) traces the *change* in total cost as output changes. In the language of the calculus, it is the derivative of the total cost curve. In more elementary arithmetic language, it is simply the change in total cost divided by the change in output—$\triangle TC \div \triangle$ output. The marginal cost curve passes through the minima of the average variable cost curve and the average total cost curve.[19]

Total costs

The same cost data may be plotted on a total cost graph that is closer in form to the break-even charts we have already discussed. Figure 5–24 presents the same data shown in Figure 5–23 in the total cost form. The

FIGURE 5–24

TRADITIONAL COST CURVES OF ECONOMIC THEORY—TOTAL COSTS

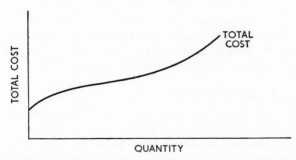

[19] A simple illustration of this relation between average and marginal quantities is as follows: the average falls if the marginal quantity is lower than the average; the average rises if the marginal quantity is higher than the average; the average remains the same if the marginal quantity is equal to the average. At the minimum, the average remains the same so that the marginal quantity must be equal to the average at the minimum. Calculus can be used to give a more sophisticated proof.

only difference as compared with the break-even chart is that total cost curve (and thus the variable cost curve) is no longer a straight line. It increases at first at a decreasing rate (decreasing marginal costs) and then increases at an increasing rate (increasing marginal costs).

So far, the theoretical graphs in this chapter have neglected the revenue side, since this chapter is primarily concerned with cost. But to complete the comparison with the break-even charts a brief word on revenue is in order. If the firm operates under conditions of pure competition, or if for some other reason the price is predetermined so that management is not concerned with the downward slope of the demand curve, the total revenue curve is a diagonal straight line as shown on the break-even charts—no new complication is introduced. If, however, the firm faces a downward slope in demand, total revenue no longer is described by a straight line but is a curve, reflecting the fact that increased sales are possible only at lower prices. Figure 5–25

FIGURE 5–25

A Break-Even Chart Drawn Consistent with Traditional Economic Theory

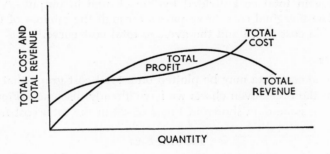

combines the cost curves of Figure 5–24 with such a total revenue curve, thus showing how a break-even chart would appear if it were made completely consistent with economic theory, assuming competition is imperfect. Note that two break-even points are possible.

Empirical studies and illustrations

Is the U-shaped short-run cost curve found in empirical studies? In view of statistical difficulties it is probably too early to generalize on how pervasive the U shape is in actual firms. Some economists argue that the widespread findings of linearity reflect the inadequacies of the statistical techniques and that the U shape is more pervasive than the studies show.

Some statistical studies do show the U-shaped curves, with gradually rising marginal costs. This is particularly true in agriculture; perhaps the predominance of agriculture in the 19th century, when economics was in its development stages, helps account for the tradition of U-shaped cost curves. One well-known study of fertilizer and output shows the typical theoretical relationship, as indicated in Figure 5-26. In this case

FIGURE 5-26

UNIT COST CURVES RELATING FERTILIZER INPUT AND POTATO PRODUCTION ON A SINGLE ACRE, AROOSTOOK FARM, MAINE, 1927–41

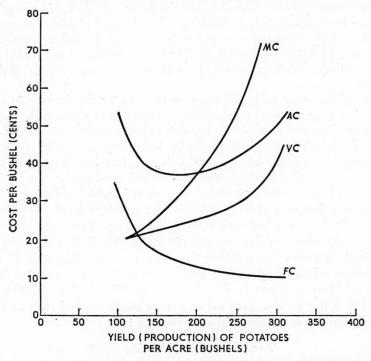

SOURCE: Maine Agricultural Experiment Station Bulletin 414, Potato Fertilizer-Rotation Studies on Aroostook Farm, 1927–41 as reported in Early Heady, *Economics of Agricultural Production and Resource Use* (Englewood Cliffs, N.J.: Prentice-Hall, 1952), p. 36 and p. 324. (Because of the discontinuous units of output, the *MC* does not intersect the *AC* at the lowest cost point.)

the fertilizer is the variable factor and the land is the fixed factor. The results indicate diminishing returns to fertilizer applications resulting in rising marginal costs and, eventually, rising average costs. Similar results appear in other fertilizer studies, such as one showing the effects of varying amounts of nitrogen fertilizer applied to corn.[20] Note, however, that these studies consider only the variation of one input, fertilizer;

---

[20] See Earl Heady, *Economics of Agricultural Production and Resource Use* (Englewood Cliffs, N.J.: Prentice-Hall, Inc., 1952), p. 328.

experiments permitting the variation of more inputs might show different results.

Not all agricultural research is in agreement on the gradually rising marginal cost curve. Some observers argue that typically in agriculture the marginal curve is close to horizontal over a wide range with a sharp upturn as capacity is approached,[21] a finding which comes close to the usual findings in manufacturing.

The controversy over the shape of short-run cost curves in manufacturing continues unabated. A British study of five factories, for example, found that the variable cost per unit fell, slightly and unevenly, over the range of output.[22] Similar studies in the 1960's raised doubts about the unwillingness of textbook writers to revise their traditional U-shaped curves.

Though constant marginal costs up to capacity are the rule in studies in business, as opposed to agriculture, such is not universally the case. A study of several automobile laundries shows strong evidence of gradually diminishing marginal products, indicating gradually rising marginal costs.[23] A study of the production of transformers shows similar evidence of gradually diminishing marginal products to the increased numbers of hours worked per day in a plant in which machinery, supervision, and the plant size itself are held constant.[24] Again the diminishing marginal product indicates gradually rising marginal costs.

An earlier study of the fuel costs in an electric light and power plant also indicates curvilinear rather than linear costs.[25] Figure 5–27 shows the results of the study; each cost figure has been multiplied by the same arbitrary constant to disguise the exact level of costs. The study found that a second degree curve gave a significantly better fit than a straight line. The equation of the fitted curve is:

$$Y = 16.68 + 0.125X + 0.00439X^2$$

where Y is total fuel cost for an eight-hour period, and X is eight-hour total output as a percent of capacity. It should be noted that this study does not cover labor costs and other elements of short-run cost.

The evidence of such empirical studies plus the theoretical argument for the gradualness of the rise of marginal cost suggests that one must be cautious about assuming that marginal costs are constant. Further

[21] *Ibid.,* p. 325.

[22] F. Troughton, "The Teaching Concerning Costs of Production in Introductory Economics," *The Journal of Industrial Economics,* April, 1963, pp. 96–115.

[23] M. H. Spencer and L. Siegelman, *Managerial Economics: Decision Making and Forward Planning* (Homewood, Ill.: Richard D. Irwin, Inc., 1959), pp. 204–7.

[24] E. A. Nemmers, *Managerial Economics* (New York: John Wiley & Sons, Inc., 1962), pp. 166–67.

[25] J. A. Nordin, "Note on a Light Plant's Cost Curves," *Econometrica,* July, 1947, p. 231–35.

FIGURE 5–27

TOTAL FUEL COST RELATED TO OUTPUT IN AN ELECTRIC LIGHT AND POWER PLANT

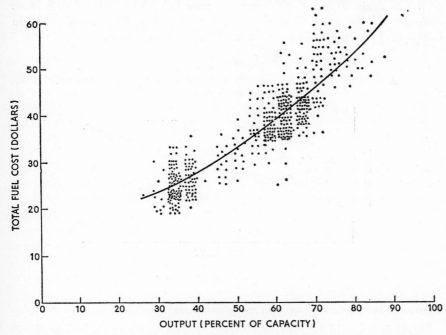

SOURCE: J. A. Nordin, "Note on a Light Plant's Cost Curves," *Econometrica*, July, 1947, p. 231.

research is needed before it is possible to separate the cases of constant marginal costs from those of rising marginal costs.

5. A CONFRONTATION OF THE LINEAR (BREAK-EVEN) AND THEORETICAL MODELS

It is the contention of this chapter that both the linear type of cost behavior described by the break-even chart and the curvilinear types of relationships found in economic theory are worthy of consideration as hypotheses of how costs might behave in the particular firm under consideration. But it is no use pretending that both types of analysis are saying the same thing. It is now desirable to compare and contrast the approaches, noting their strength and weaknesses.

Linear functions as approximations of curvilinear functions

Even if one admits that the curvilinear graphs of theory are correct, with their U-shaped curves the rising marginal costs, he may be justified in using a straight-line model as an approximation to the correct curvilinear one. Management is a process of constant approximation anyway. The question is whether the error is so great as to destroy the usefulness of the analysis. Figure 5–28 presents a case in which a line gives a close estimate of the curved total costs. The straight line would provide fairly good projections of profits at various levels of output.

FIGURE 5–28

A Case in Which a Straight Line Gives a Fairly Accurate
Estimate of Total Costs

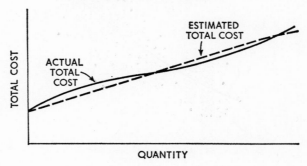

Empirical evidence on constant marginal costs

Statistics should be able to provide the answer as to whether short-run costs are linear or curvilinear. Indeed, for several decades statisticians and econometricians have been concerned with measurements of the short-run cost functions. In the main their studies have supported the linear model. As a recent survey of statistical cost functions concludes, "the various short-run studies more often than not indicate constant marginal cost and declining average cost as the pattern that best seems to describe the data that have been analyzed."[26] The reader should recognize that such findings are consistent with the simplest form of the break-even chart.

The fact that the statistical studies often support the linear model has not ended the controversy about the shape of the short-run cost curve. Theorists have been unwilling to abandon the law of diminishing returns which implies a rise in marginal cost. They have noted a number of deficiencies in the statistical studies, claiming that the methods employed impart a bias toward linearity. The fact is that the statistical work on short-run cost functions is incomplete.

If there are some fixed factors with which larger and larger quantities

---

[26] J. Johnston, *Statistical Cost Analysis* (New York: McGraw-Hill Book Co., 1960), p. 168.

of variable factors are combined, it is inevitable that diminishing returns set in. The constant marginal costs found in many statistical studies suggest that diminishing returns present no problem until the facilities are operated at some fixed limit (called "capacity") beyond which production cannot be increased. In other words, it is possible to increase output without any increase in unit variable costs up to a point at which no more can be produced or at which the costs of added output become enormous. Figure 5–29 presents such a situation.

FIGURE 5–29

CONSTANT MARGINAL COST UP TO CAPACITY

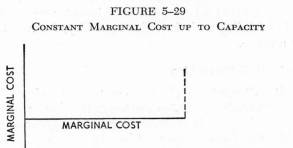

A compromise

Perhaps the way out of the difficulty is to avoid oversimplified generalizations about how short-run costs must behave. It would appear reasonable to suppose that in some industries such costs would approximate the shapes indicated in theory; in other industries they probably are close enough to linearity that the break-even type of analysis can be used without any great error. But this raises a new question: When is the linear model appropriate and when is it inappropriate? At our present state of knowledge only partial answers to this question are possible.

Stigler has introduced the useful concepts of divisibility and adaptability in this connection.[27] The orthodox economic theory rests on the assumption that the capital equipment or other fixed facilities are indivisible but highly adaptable. By indivisible is meant that one must use the entire capital facilities or none. By adaptable is meant that the facilities can be combined with varying quantities of variable inputs, such as labor and materials. Under indivisible and adaptable conditions the addition of variable inputs must result in diminishing returns and rising marginal costs.

---

[27] G. J. Stigler, "Production and Distribution in the Short Run," *Journal of Political Economy*, June, 1939, pp. 305–27.

Probably a great deal of modern manufacturing is done under quite different conditions. The capital equipment is often divisible. In a textile mill, for example, it is possible to use only part of the spinning machines or all of them as one desires. But the equipment is not adaptable, since each row of spinning machines requires a given quantity of labor and a given quantity of materials per time period. Under such conditions, a doubling of output simply means the use of twice as many machines, with double the variable cost. Output can be increased at constant marginal cost until the capacity of the plant is reached. The statistical cost studies suggest that a large portion of industry operates under such conditions of divisibility with limited adaptability, the result being linear costs within a range.

Implications for decision making

The preceding discussion of short-run cost functions has taken us somewhat off the main track of decision making in the short run. What are the implications of this analysis of linear versus curvilinear cost curves for decision making? Perhaps the greatest benefit to management is to create an awareness that there are no firm generalizations about cost behavior and that each firm and each industry must measure and predict its own cost patterns.

One reasonable way for a manager to go about estimating the impact of a decision on cost is to use his own judgment and experience in determining how the different categories of cost will react to the decision. This kind of down-to-earth estimation of cost changes is easy to apply in practice and provides the needed flexibility to handle a variety of decisions. Decision making is no longer restricted to consideration of increases or decreases in output (the only independent variables normally introduced in either the break-even analysis or in the theorists' short-run cost curves). It is then possible to consider problems of make-or-buy, introduction of new product lines, abandonment of an old product, increases in the size of the sales force, and many other decisions not easily diagrammed on the conventional graphs.

But the theoretical arguments against the linearity of costs along with the existence of some studies showing gradually rising marginal costs suggest that the manager must be especially careful not to overlook the possibility of diminishing returns as volume is increased. The causes of rising marginal costs may be rather subtle—gradual declines in labor productivity as the work force is increased, growing managerial inefficiencies as the plant becomes more crowded, almost imperceptible increases in the waste of materials, and increases in the user costs and maintenance costs of machinery as the pressure of production increases. Many managers may overlook such possible causes of rising costs; when they do so they may make decisions which do not reflect the true cost situation.

Empirical studies and illustrations

Previous sections of this chapter have presented findings from selected individual short-run cost studies. It is now appropriate to present an overall view of such cost studies, relying primarily on J. Johnston's volume, *Statistical Cost Analysis*, the most complete survey of the subject.[28] Johnston starts with Joel Dean's pioneer studies in a furniture factory, a leather belt shop, and in a hosiery mill, all of which indicate constant marginal costs. A similar study by Dean in a department store is inconclusive on whether total costs are linear, though Dean thought that the curvature, if any, would be slight. Johnston also reports two studies in the steel industry, one of which shows constant marginal cost while the other suggests a *decline* in marginal cost throughout the output range. There is doubt that the last study was successful in separating short-run costs from long-run factors, such as an increase in capacity.

Johnston also reviews a study of railway operating costs in Great Britain and a study of costs in the American rayon industry, both of which are consistent with the constant marginal cost findings in most of the other studies. Johnston's conclusion is that constant marginal costs predominate in short-run cost studies.[29]

Various critics have cast doubt on the findings of these short-run cost studies. Some have alleged that the statistical methods show a bias toward linearity; Johnston denies that such is the case and even suggests that the bias, if any, may be toward curvilinearity. Stigler has argued that the finding of constant marginal costs up to capacity are inconsistent with observed market behavior, for he finds that most of the short-run variation in output over business cycles consists of a variation in the rate of output of plants rather than a variation in the number of plants.[30] In competitive markets constant marginal costs imply variations in the number of firms. This point is controversial, but the details of the controversy are beyond the scope of this chapter; interested readers should examine the discussion in Stigler and in Johnston.[31]

Another criticism of these cost studies is that they ignore the user cost element of depreciation. Unfortunately, user cost is difficult to measure, so that we do not know whether this element of depreciation is linear or instead rises sharply at high outputs.

---

[28] Johnston, *op. cit.*
[29] *Ibid.*, p. 168.
[30] G. J. Stigler, *The Theory of Price* (rev. ed.; New York: Macmillan Co., 1952), p. 167.
[31] Johnston, *op. cit.*, p. 183.

It is still too early to be general about the shape of the short-run cost function; both the linear and curvilinear hypotheses have support. As stated earlier, it is appropriate for the manager to keep both hypotheses in mind, using judgment in relation to his own operations to determine whether he should estimate marginal cost to be constant or to be rising.

6 / Production functions and cost behavior

The preceding chapter introduced short-run cost analysis, which is one of the basic bodies of concepts in marginal economics. Before proceeding with long-run cost analysis, it is desirable to go behind costs and examine the physical relationship between inputs and outputs by which cost behavior is largely determined. This subject is known as the study of *production functions*. After examining production functions it is possible to return to the subject of costs in a more fundamental way.

1. PRODUCTION FUNCTIONS

A production function is a statement about the relationship between the inputs used in production and the resulting output or outputs. It describes a technological relationship: with a given technology certain combinations of inputs will make possible a given level of output. Usually a number of alternative combinations of inputs are available to management to produce any level of output. The production function incorporates only the optimal outputs resulting from given combinations of inputs; other technologies producing lower outputs must be eliminated as irrelevant.

A single output—isoquants

The simplest production function relates one output to two inputs. If q represents the quantity of the output, and x_1 and x_2 the quantities of the inputs, q is a function of x_1 and x_2, which in mathematical notation appears as:

$$q = f(x_1, x_2)$$

237

This function is assumed to be single valued—a given quantity of X_1 and X_2 produces a single quantity of output, which is the maximum quantity possible from such amounts of inputs. In other words, it is assumed that the entrepreneur makes the best possible use of the inputs. Economic theory usually takes the function to be continuous and smooth.

Graphing such a function will help clarify its properties. The most suitable graph is the isoquant diagram, which plots the inputs (x_1 and x_2) on the axes and shows the output in a series of curves known as isoquants. Each curve connects the various combinations of the inputs that result in a given output. For example, the isoquant q_{500} in Figure 6–1 connects all combinations of quantities of X_1 and X_2 that result in 500 units of output.

FIGURE 6–1

TYPICAL ISOQUANT DIAGRAM

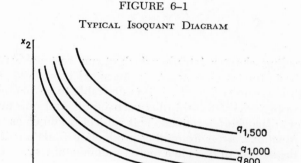

One may think of the isoquants as contour lines similar to the contours on a geographical map. Each isoquant shows a different height on a hill of production, but connects all points of the same height. As one moves upward to the right he climbs to higher levels (greater outputs), using up greater quantities of inputs.

A production function is sometimes called a production surface since it is concerned with the upper surface of the hill of production. Even with the extremely simplified example of one output and two inputs, it is difficult to draw this surface, which requires three dimensions. Figure 6–2 shows what is involved, though all attempts to show three dimensions on two-dimensional paper are necessarily limited.

The production surface is like a bandshell. The isoquants in Figure 6–1 may be looked upon as contour lines on this surface—each contour line representing a different level of output.

One important assumption in such a diagram is that the inputs are substitutable for each other. Take a particular combination of x_1 and

FIGURE 6-2

PRODUCTION SURFACE

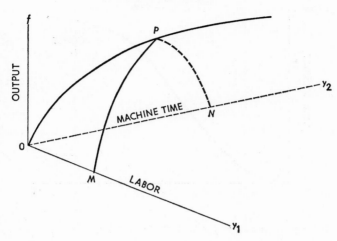

x_2 resulting in an output of 300 units. By moving along the isoquant q_{300} one finds other quantities of the inputs that result in the same output. Let us suppose that x_1 represents quantities of labor and x_2 quantities of machinery. If the quantity of labor is reduced, the quantity of machinery must be increased if one is to produce the same output. A tangent to the isoquant measures the marginal rate of substitution between the two inputs at the point of tangency. (The marginal rate of substitution is the quantity of one input which must be substituted in place of one unit of another input in order to leave the output unchanged.)

The reader may have doubts that in actual practice the curves will be smooth as shown in the graph. Let us postpone this issue for the time being, focusing attention on the implications of the curves as presented. We shall continue to assume that X_1 and X_2 are the only inputs required, a convenient assumption from the diagrammatic point of view, but unrealistic in business practice since no firm operates with only two homogeneous inputs.

The reader may well ask at this point whether Figures 6-1, 6-2, and 6-3 are long run or short run in character. Since X_1 and X_2 are the only inputs, and since each may be varied in magnitude, the diagram is long run in character. But both long-run and short-run relationships may be read from the diagram. If, for example, we draw a horizontal line on Figure 6-1 at a given quantity of X_2, the result is a short-run relationship in which x_2 (the quantity of machinery) is held constant while X_1 (the quantity of labor) is varied. This is equivalent to taking a vertical slice

FIGURE 6–3

SHORT-RUN TOTAL PRODUCT CURVE

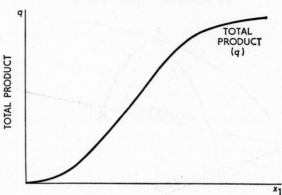

through the three-dimensional production surface—a slice parallel to the X_1 axis. The result is varying amounts of output. We may replot this short-run input-output relationship on another type of diagram, one that shows the quantities of the variable input (x_1) on the horizontal axis and the quantities of the output (q) on the vertical axis. Figure 6–3 presents such a diagram; many readers will recognize the typical short-run total product curve. If this diagram is converted into a diagram showing the average product and marginal product for varying amounts of X_1, the result (shown in Figure 6–4) is the familiar average product and marginal product curves of elementary economics.

Figure 6–4 illustrates the law of diminishing returns, which generalizes that as the quantity of the variable input is increased, holding other inputs constant, the marginal product and the average product must eventually

FIGURE 6–4

SHORT-RUN AVERAGE PRODUCT AND MARGINAL PRODUCT CURVE

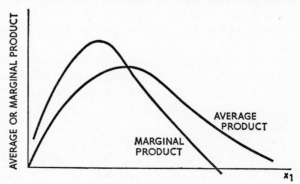

decrease. The law of diminishing returns is often called the law of eventually diminishing marginal productivity. A simple example is the addition of labor to land in producing a farm commodity. As more and more labor is added, the additions to total product must eventually decline and may even drop to zero as the workers get in each other's way. It is well to note that the law of diminishing returns is consistent with the isoquants as they were drawn originally in Figure 6–1.

Output maximization and cost minimization

So far the discussion has dealt with the production function itself, which is purely physical or technological in character. The production function does not indicate which input relationships are optimal; for that purpose input prices are required. We turn to a new diagram on which the axes again represent quantities of the inputs X_1 and X_2. Let us assume that the prices of the inputs are given, there being no quantity discounts or other reasons for the firm to be able to obtain greater quantities at lower prices. We now plot the various quantities of X_1 and X_2 that may be obtained from given monetary outlays. Figure 6–5 presents

FIGURE 6–5

Isocost Curves

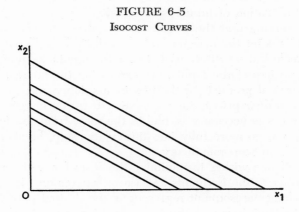

the resulting isocost curves (which are straight lines under the assumption made here), one isocost curve showing the amounts of X_1 and X_2 that can be purchased for $1,000, another isocost curve representing an expenditure of $2,000, and so on.

It should be noted that the axes in Figure 6–5 (the isocost curve diagram) represent the same variables as the axes in Figure 6–1 (the isoquant diagram). It is, therefore, an easy matter to superimpose one diagram on the other, resulting in Figure 6–6 which shows both the isoquants and the isocost lines.

FIGURE 6-6
ISOQUANTS AND ISOCOST CURVES

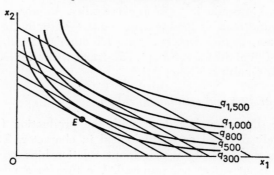

On such a diagram, it is possible to find the maximum output for a given outlay. Let us consider an outlay of $1,000. If we move along the isocost curve representing that outlay, we cross isoquants representing varying quantities of output. The highest output that is possible for this outlay is represented by the isoquant tangent to the isocost curve. The optimum combination of inputs is represented by point E, the point of tangency, assuming that the lowest isocost curve on this diagram is at $1,000. At this point the marginal rate of substitution (sometimes called the rate of technical substitution) between the inputs is equal to the ratio between the prices of the inputs. Or, expressing the point in a different way, the marginal products of the two inputs, labor and machinery, are proportional to their prices. Such a relation between marginal products and input prices is necessary to obtain the most from the input. If the reader wishes to go more fully into this relationship, he should refer to standard works in economic theory.

Similarly, if one wishes to minimize the costs for a given output, he may again refer to the isoquants and isocost curves on Figure 6-6. This time move along the isoquant representing the desired output. It should be clear that the minimum cost for this output is represented by the isocost line tangent to the isoquant.

It is not usual for management to start out, as we have in the illustrations just presented, with a given expenditure for which it wishes to determine the maximum output or with a given output for which it wishes to find the minimum cost. More commonly expenditures and outputs are considered simultaneously, the optimum depending on output price as well as on the input prices. As indicated in Figure 6-6, there are many points of tangency between isoquants and isocost lines; the line connecting these points is known as the "scale line." If the price of the output is known, it is possible to find the most profitable position on the scale line.

In any case, the optimum will be a point of tangency between an isoquant and an isocost curve—all other points involve a wasteful use of inputs.

Managerial use of production functions

Production functions may appear to be extremely abstract and remote from reality. But further reflection should convince the reader that such an analysis is, in fact, quite logical and close to common sense. If the price of one input falls while that of another rises, one would expect the substitution of the first for the second, just as is indicated by the shifts in points of tangency along the isoquants. Two objections to the analysis so far are in order: (1) It has restricted itself to the case of two inputs and one output. Mathematically, there is no great difficulty in extending the analysis to multiple inputs and outputs, but our two-dimensional diagram cannot illustrate such cases. (2) The analysis has assumed smooth, continuous curves, while in the real world discontinuities in the production function may appear. It may not always be the case that one input may be substituted for another over a continuous range, permitting minute shifts from one position to another. The economist defends his continuous curves as statements of tendency, but the practitioner must deal with the discontinuities.

An example may help illustrate the relevance of production functions. Students of dairy economics have been interested in the minimization of the cost of feeding cows in the production of milk. Let us consider a single cow to be the firm, and grain and roughage to be the inputs. The question is the economical proportions of grain and roughage to feed the cows. In the past there has been some tendency to prescribe a fixed ratio, but economic analysis suggests that the optimal ratio depends on the prices of the inputs. Studies suggest that the isoquants relating various quantities of grain and roughage to various milk output levels are like those in the diagrams we have drawn, though limited at the extreme right and upper edges by a "stomach capacity line" which shows the limits of the input that a cow can consume. If we superimpose isocost lines on the cow's isoquant diagram, it becomes clear that the optimum—the point of greatest output for a given outlay or of least outlay for a given output—depends on the prices of the inputs and shifts as these prices change. The dairy farmer could use such an analysis in increasing the return from his expenditures on feed.

In more complicated problems, with larger numbers of inputs and outputs, the mathematics of optimization becomes complex. However, in recent years the development of linear programming has made it possible to handle such complex problems. A later section of this chapter will concern itself with applications of linear programming in this area. Fortunately, linear programming can overcome some of the problems of dis-

Managerial economics

continuities mentioned before, but it also rests, as must all analysis, on a number of simplifying assumptions.

Empirical studies and illustrations

Attempts to measure production functions go back at least a century to some pioneer studies in agriculture.[1] Over the years both the economic concepts and statistical estimating techniques have been improved, but the great majority of the work is still in agriculture, in which the inputs and outputs are relatively homogeneous and research funds are plentiful. Much of the early work concerned itself with an entire industry or even the economy as a whole, rather than with the individual firm. The best known of the production function equations is known as the Cobb-Douglas function, though it may be traced back to Knut Wicksell, an outstanding Swedish economist. The Cobb-Douglas function relates output in American manufacturing industries to labor and capital inputs, taking the form

$$P = bL^aC^{1-a}$$

where

P = total output
L = an index of employment of labor in manufacturing
C = an index of fixed capital in manufacturing

This form of production function has the convenient characteristic that the exponents a and $1-a$ are the elasticities of production; that is a and $1-a$ measure the percentage response of output to percentage change in labor and capital respectively. The restriction that the two exponents add to 1 implies constant returns to scale; this restriction may be relaxed in more complex studies.

In their research, Cobb and Douglas estimated the function from times series data. The result was

$$P = 1.01L^{.75}C^{.25}$$

for the United States, with somewhat different results in other countries.[2] A review of the criticisms of these studies and of the improvements of the statistical techniques over the years lies beyond the scope of this book. However, a survey of some findings will suggest the kind of work that is being done.

Tintner derived a Cobb-Douglas type production function for 609 Iowa farms:

$$P = aA^{.29}B^{.16}C^{.05}D^{.21}E^{-.01}F^{.16}$$

---

[1] An excellent history of production function measurements appears in Earl O. Heady and John L. Dillon, *Agricultural Production Functions* (Ames: Iowa State University Press, 1961), pp. 1–29.

[2] Charles W. Cobb and Paul H. Douglas, "A Theory of Production," *American Economic Review*, Supplement (March, 1928), pp. 139–65 and later articles by Douglas and his associates. These studies are reviewed in Heady and Dillon, *op. cit.*

in which

P = crop and livestock products
A = land
B = labor
C = farm improvements
D = liquid assets
E = working assets
F = cash operating expenses[3]

Nicholls fitted a somewhat different type of function to the operations of a midwestern meat packing firm. The result for one department was:[4]

$$X = -15.30 + 4.73N - .79N^2 + 5.02H - .44H^2$$

in which

X = output (hogs processed)
N = man-hours per man per week
H = total man-hours per week

This function is short run in character, with plant size and department capital held constant.

Another recent short-run study is of an auto laundry in which the production function took the form:

$$Y = -0.8 + 4.5X - .3X^2$$

in which

Y = total output in cars washed per hour
X = number of men employed.[5]

As in the meat packing study, the subtraction of the squared terms, N^2, H^2, and X^2, indicates diminishing returns to the variable inputs.

Some of the economists studying production functions have given particular attention to the applications of their findings. For example, Earl Heady and his associates have developed a mechanical device called the Pork Costulator which helps the farmer determine the most profitable ration for feeding hogs under various price conditions.[6] The development of electronic computers means that it is becoming easier to make use of complex production functions in managerial decisions.

---

[3] G. Tintner, "A Note on the Derivation of Production Functions from Farm Records Data," *Econometrica*, Vol. 12, No. 1 (January, 1944), pp. 26–34.
[4] W. H. Nicholls, *Labor Productivity Functions in Meat Packing* (Chicago: University of Chicago Press, 1948), p. 12.
[5] Spencer and Siegelman, *op. cit.*, p. 204.
[6] Earl O. Heady, Damon V. Catron, Roger Woodworth, and Gordon C. Ashton, "Pork Production Functions for Hogs Fed in Drylot," in Heady and Dillon, *op. cit.*, pp. 300–301.

2. PRODUCTION POSSIBILITY CURVES: AN INTRODUCTION TO LINEAR PROGRAMMING

The isoquants of the previous section relate two inputs to one output. They showed q as a function of x_1 and x_2, that is $q = f(x_1, x_2)$. We may now introduce production possibility curves (also known as transformation curves) which relate one input (or one package of inputs) to two outputs. Production possibility curves relate the quantity of the input to several outputs:

$$x = g(q_1, q_2)$$

or

$$h(x_1, q_1, q_2) = 0$$

We now construct a graph to show this relationship. In Figure 6–7, the quantities of two outputs are shown along the axes. Let us examine a single production-possibility curve. It tells us that a given package of inputs will produce a relatively large amount of product Q_1 with little Q_2; but we may sacrifice Q_1 to obtain more Q_2. The production possibility curve is normally drawn concave to the origin. Its curvature reflects diminishing returns as we try to get more Q_2 at the sacrifice of Q_1 or more Q_1 at the sacrifice of Q_2.

Let us consider a hypothetical illustration. A farmer owns 100 acres which he plans to devote to growing corn or grazing sheep. The land is not uniform in quality throughout—some of it is rich soil and some is hilly and less fertile. The farmer could conceivably put all of the land into corn or he could graze sheep on the entire plot. Various combinations in between are possible. In this situation it seems reasonable to suppose that the production possibility curve will have a shape something like that in Figure 6–7. As the farmer attempts to devote more and more land to corn, he must sacrifice relatively greater quantities of sheep. He gradually moves onto land which is relatively less suited to corn and thus encounters diminishing returns. If the land were homogeneous, the production possibility curve might be a straight line—which is an extreme case of the relationship under discussion.[7]

Optimal positions

What is the optimal position on a given production possibility curve? It clearly depends on the relative prices of the outputs. If corn prices are high enough and the prices of sheep low enough, the farmer might

---

[7] Curvature might also result from the application of more units of the cooperating inputs to the land in the production of one of the products (diminishing returns).

FIGURE 6–7

PRODUCTION POSSIBILITY CURVES

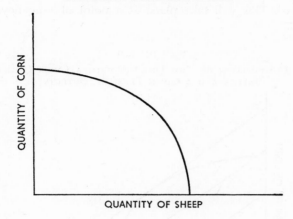

specialize completely in corn. We can construct a series of lines similar to the isocost curves in the discussion of isoquants; but these lines now reflect ratios of the prices of outputs rather than the prices of inputs. We shall call these new lines isocontribution lines. They are straight lines on the assumption that the output prices (and marginal costs) are independent of the particular firm's output. Figure 6–8 shows a set of such isocontribution lines. They are parallel, reflecting the fact that the prices of the outputs are given. The higher isocontribution curves result from greater quantities of the two outputs.

We can now superimpose such isocontribution curves on our pro-

FIGURE 6–8

ISOCONTRIBUTION LINES: TWO OUTPUTS

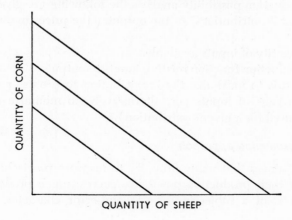

duction possibility curve diagram, since in both cases the axes represent quantities of output. The objective is to get onto the highest isocontribution curve. This will take place at a point of tangency, as shown in Figure 6–9.

FIGURE 6–9

OPTIMAL COMBINATION OF TWO OUTPUTS WITH A GIVEN QUANTITY OF INPUTS AND A GIVEN PRICE OF OUTPUTS

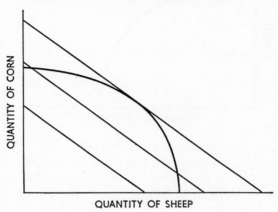

The parallel with the previous isoquant analysis deserves a review. In the isoquant analysis the following factors were given:

1. The prices of the inputs.
2. The desired quantity of output.
3. The production function relating inputs to output.

The objective was to minimize the cost of the output (or, alternatively, to maximize the output for a given outlay).

In the production possibility analysis the following are given:

1. The unit "contributions" of the outputs (the prices minus the incremental costs).
2. The quantity of inputs available.
3. The production function relating inputs to outputs.

The objective is to maximize the "contribution to profits" possible with the given package of inputs (or, alternatively, to minimize the amount of input required for a given contribution).

A linear programming approach

It is not claimed that many firms try to measure precisely the shapes or heights of their production possibility curves; much production function analysis is of a subjective or trial-and-error character. But larger

numbers of firms are applying the modern technique of linear programming which does solve the problem we have been discussing in a mathematical form. The following discussion of linear programming is introductory and nontechnical; it is aimed at showing the relationship between
production analysis in economics and linear programming and in helping
develop skills in determining when linear programming is relevant.

Figure 6–10 introduces the linear programming approach in a graphic

FIGURE 6–10

LINEAR PROGRAMMING: TWO OUTPUTS AND FIVE CAPACITY CONSTRAINTS

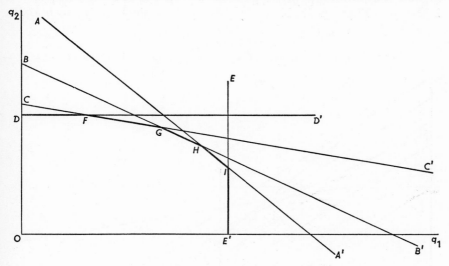

form. All of the lines on the graph are straight. Nevertheless, the heavily
shaded portions of those lines make up what looks very much like a
production possibility curve. In fact it might well be given that name.

The lines on Figure 6–10 represent the capacities of various functions
(departments) in a given plant. Consider the line AA'. It shows the
maximum quantities of products Q_1 and Q_2 that can be produced as far
as the capacity of Department A is concerned. The fact that it is a
straight line reflects the assumption that there are no diminishing returns
as more Q_1 and less of Q_2 are produced, or vice versa. This assumption
is reasonable in many manufacturing situations in which the marginal rate
of substitution in switching from one product to another is constant or
close to constant.

The lines BB' and CC' represent the capacities of other departments
through which both products flow. The lines DD' and EE' represent
capacities of departments which are required for only one of the products:

DD′ limits the quantity of the second product and *EE′* limits the quantity of the first.

The area *ODFGHIE′* on the diagram represents all the feasible combinations of the two outputs. The question is: What point on this area represents the optimum? It is clear that the optimum must lie somewhere on the boundary of *ODFGHIE′*. Linear programming provides a mathematical way of finding the optimum, but we shall apply a graphic technique. All that is necessary is as before—to superimpose a set of isocontribution lines on the graph. The point on the graph which touches the highest isocontribution line represents the optimum. Such an optimum is shown in Figure 6–11. Normally this will be a single point, such as *H*.

FIGURE 6–11

Optimum: Two Outputs and Five Capacity Constraints

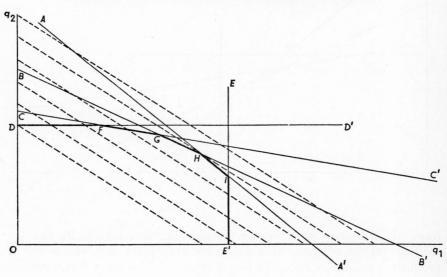

It is possible, however, that an isocontribution line will lie on top of the capacity lines, in which case any combination of q_1 and q_2 along the feasible portion of that constraint will be optimal.

Some simple mathematical notation

The linear programming approach just described can be expressed in the form of a set of equations and inequations. The reader should become familiar with the mathematical notation; such a familiarity will enable him to set up linear programming problems even if he cannot solve them. If the setup is correct, he can turn the problem of solution over to a technician. The following discussion is a development of ideas introduced in Chapter 2.

The capacities of each department are expressed in the form of an inequality. Each inequality states that the total usage of capacity must be less than or equal to the capacity available. If product Q_1 requires amount a_{11} of the capacity of Department 1 for each ton produced, while product Q_2 requires amount a_{21}, it follows that a_{11} times the quantity of Q_1 plus a_{21} times the quantity of Q_2 must not exceed the capacity of the department. The inequation appears in this form:

$$a_{11}\, q_1 + a_{21}\, q_2 \leqq b_1$$

in which

a_{11} = the rate of usage of capacity per unit of Q_1
a_{21} = the rate of usage of capacity per unit of Q_2
q_1 = the quantity of Q_1
q_2 = the quantity of Q_2
b_1 = the capacity of Department 1

The other departmental constraints can be expressed in the form of similar inequalities, as follows:

$$a_{12}\, q_1 + a_{22}\, q_2 \leqq b_2$$
$$a_{13}\, q_1 + a_{23}\, q_2 \leqq b_3$$

In these inequations, b_2 represents the capacity of Department 2, b_3 the capacity of Department 3, and b_n the capacity of the nth department.

Let us use some specific numbers to illustrate. Suppose that Q_1 requires five units of Department 1 capacity per ton of output, three units of Department 2 capacity, ten units of Department 3 capacity, six units of Department 4 capacity, and no units of Department 5 capacity. The similar requirements for Q_2 are five, six, five, none, and nine. These requirements are summarized in Table 6–1.

TABLE 6–1

CAPACITY REQUIREMENTS FOR TWO PRODUCTS

Product	Department	Capacity Requirement per Ton of Output
Q_1	1	$a_{11} = 5$
Q_1	2	$a_{12} = 3$
Q_1	3	$a_{13} = 10$
Q_1	4	$a_{14} = 6$
Q_1	5	$a_{15} = 0$
Q_2	1	$a_{21} = 5$
Q_2	2	$a_{22} = 6$
Q_2	3	$a_{23} = 5$
Q_2	4	$a_{24} = 0$
Q_2	5	$a_{25} = 9$

The capacities of the five departments are as follows:

$$b_1 = 100$$
$$b_2 = 120$$
$$b_3 = 150$$
$$b_4 = 78$$
$$b_5 = 135$$

The inequalities may now be expressed with the numerical coefficients and capacities:

$$5q_1 + 5q_2 \leqq 100$$
$$3q_1 + 6q_2 \leqq 120$$
$$10q_1 + 5q_2 \leqq 150$$
$$6q_1 \leqq 78$$
$$9q_2 \leqq 135$$

The reader may wish to draw a graph expressing these inequalities and to follow the remaining discussion on his graph.

We now have two unknowns and five inequalities. No solution is possible yet, since the objective has not yet been specified. Let us suppose that product Q_1 returns a contribution to overhead and profit of $125 per ton, while product Q_2 returns a contribution of $111 per ton. Note that we are interested only in the contribution above incremental costs; these "contributions" figures are the excess of the prices over the incremental expenses. Let us suppose also that the objective is to maximize profits (which is the same thing as to maximize the contribution to overhead and profits). We can now construct what is known as the objective function, which states how much total contribution to overhead and profits results from various combinations of Q_1 and Q_2. The function is

$$Z = c_1 q_1 + c_2 q_2 = \text{maximum}[8]$$

in which

    Z = the total contribution to overhead and profit from both products
    c_1 = the contribution per unit of q_1
    c_2 = the contribution per unit of q_2

By substituting the known quantities for the symbols, we get:

$$Z = 120q_1 + 111q_2 = \text{maximum}$$

To summarize, we now have five inequalities and one equality:

---

[8] It may be helpful to note that the equation $Z = c_1 q_1 + c_2 q_2$ gives a series of parallel lines one for each value Z. These are the isocontribution lines already discussed. The problem is to find the highest isocontribution line—the highest value of Z.

$$5q_1 + 5q_2 \leqq 100$$
$$3q_1 + 6q_2 \leqq 120$$
$$10q_1 + 5q_2 \leqq 150$$
$$6q_1 \qquad \leqq 78$$
$$9q_2 \leqq 135$$
$$Z = 120q_1 + 111q_2 = \text{maximum}$$

The techniques of linear programming (such as the simplex method) determine the optimal q_1 and q_2. The reader may reach this result by the graphic technique or by trial and error. The answer is 10 units of Q_1 and 10 units of Q_2, which produce a profit of \$1,200 + \$1,110 or \$2,310. No other feasible solution provides as large a profit.

A general statement of the linear programming setup

The approach we have described may be generalized to the case of m constraints (departmental capacities) and n products as follows:

$$Z = c_1q_1 + c_2q_2 + \cdots + c_nq_n = \text{maximum}$$
$$a_{11}q_1 + a_{21}q_2 + \cdots + a_{n1}q_n \leqq b_1$$
$$a_{12}q_1 + a_{22}q_2 + \cdots + a_{n2}q_n \leqq b_2$$
$$\cdot \quad \cdot \quad \cdot \quad \cdot \quad \cdot \quad \cdot \quad \cdot \quad \cdot$$
$$a_{1m}q_1 + a_{2m}q_2 + \cdots + a_{nm}q_n \leqq b_m$$

These additional inequalities must also hold:

$$q_1 \geqq 0; q_2 \geqq 0; \cdots\cdots\cdots; q_n \geqq 0$$

While these last inequalities were implicitly assumed in the earlier discussion, they must be stated explicitly for the mathematical solution of the problem.

The graphic technique breaks down if both m and n are greater than 2 and trial and error becomes increasingly inefficient as the number of variables and constraints increases. But as long as one can express the problem in the appropriate form of equalities and inequalities, he can turn the details over to a specialist for a solution. The important things are to understand the assumptions underlying the linear programming method, to develop skills in setting up the equalities and inequalities, and to interpret the results correctly.

Linear programming and some basic economic concepts

That linear programming has a close relationship to traditional economic analysis should now be apparent. In the two-product example the boundary of the feasibility area not only looks like a production possibility curve; that is precisely what it is. The isocontribution lines are the same isocontribution lines that appeared before. The difference is that a curvilinear production possibility curve now is made up of straight-line segments.

Linear programming relates to traditional economic analysis in other ways:

1. Linear programming recognizes the irrelevance of fixed costs and focuses attention on the excess of incremental revenue over incremental costs—and in particular on the contribution to overhead and profits. In this way it is consistent with the principles of incremental reasoning introduced in Chapter 2.

2. Implicitly linear programming takes opportunity costs into account. This is quite clear in the simplex method (not described here), in which the procedure is one of comparing the additional revenue resulting from bringing a new product into the solution with the sacrifice of earnings from the products that must be given up.

3. Linear programming also provides a basis for estimating the value of the marginal products of the inputs required. This is done by solving the "dual" of the original linear programming problem, a procedure which lies beyond the scope of this book. It is interesting that this modern mathematical technique, which developed independently of economics, supplies those measures of marginal product which economists all along have insisted provide the correct criterion for decisions on the quantities of inputs to employ.

Joel Dean's pioneer book in managerial economics (published in 1951) ignored linear programming, which was then in its infancy. It is now apparent that linear programming provides a means for bridging the gap between traditional theory and the needs of management.

Empirical studies and illustrations

Perhaps the oil industry has gone farther than any other in the application of linear programming techniques. The four main categories of the oil business are: (1) exploration, (2) drilling and production, (3) manufacturing, and (4) distribution and marketing. Linear programming has made important contributions to the last three. In production, linear programming is used to find the optimal use of alternative reservoirs available to a company along with the use of crude oil from the outside.[9]

Applications in manufacturing (refining) are more numerous. For example, it is used to find the optimal combination of products to be produced from given crude oil, to find the optimal blend of crude oils with varying characteristics to produce certain end products, or to solve some combination of these problems. Similarly, linear programming is used to determine the blend of various stocks coming from a refinery which will give the minimum cost of gasoline with required specifications. This

---

[9] W. W. Garvin, H. W. Crandall, J. B. John, and R. A. Spellman, "Applications of Linear Programming in the Oil Industry," *Management Science*, July, 1957, reprinted in E. H. Bowman and R. B. Fetter, *Analyses of Industrial Operations* (Homewood, Ill.: Richard D. Irwin, Inc., 1959), pp. 3–27.

blending program is complicated by the fact that the relation between tetraethyl lead content and octane rating is nonlinear, but a method of getting around the problem has been developed.

Oil companies have also used linear programming to minimize transportation costs from refineries to bulk terminals and to determine which refineries and bulk terminals should be expanded. They have also used the method to reduce costs from bulk terminals to service stations.

Similar applications are spreading to other industries, including scheduling of railway freight movements, the allocation of aircraft to alternative routes, and the determination of the optimum mix of products within a given plant. Each application presents its special difficulties, requiring considerable versatility in adapting the general method of linear programming to the specific problems at hand.

3. RELATION OF PRODUCTION FUNCTIONS TO COST CURVES

The preceding introductory discussion of linear programming is a diversion from the usual discussion of production functions, which concentrates on the case of one output and several inputs, rather than on several outputs related to various combinations of variable inputs combined with fixed inputs (capacity constraints). It is clear that linear programming is a special subtopic under the general heading of production functions; it is now appropriate to return to the main stream of analysis of production functions and cost behavior.

Production functions and short-run cost curves

We have already seen the results of holding one input fixed while we vary the other input. This is equivalent to taking a vertical slice through the production surface shown in Figure 6–2. The slice is taken parallel to one of the axes, since one of the inputs is held constant while the other is varied. The traditional result is the **S**-shaped total product curve like that shown in Figure 6–3. This curve suggests that at first the average and marginal products rise and then decline as shown in Figure 6–4. It is now desirable to show how these total product, average product, and marginal product curves are related to the cost curves.

Two kinds of cost are involved. One is the fixed cost of the constant amount of x_2—the input which is held constant. The other is the cost of the variable input, x_1, which of course increases as the quantity of the variable output increases. If the price of the variable input is given (independent of the quantity used) the total variable cost will rise in proportion to the quantity of the variable input. It does not require either a mathematical or arithmetic illustration to see that if the total product curve has the **S** shape shown in the diagrams, and if consequently the average product curve and marginal product curve decline, the result must eventually be the rising marginal cost and average cost curves of traditional theory.

If on the basis of material presented in Chapter 5 we doubt the universal relevance of U-shaped marginal and average cost curves, we are forced also to doubt the S-shaped total product curve derived from the production surface. Such doubts may raise questions about the usefulness of traditional production functions in dealing with practical decision-making problems.

Production functions and long-run cost curves

Long-run cost curves also are related logically to production functions. In this case, both of the inputs are variable. If we are given the prices of the inputs, we find the optimum combination of inputs for each level of output at the points of tangency between the isoquants and isocost curves already shown. It is then a simple matter to convert the results into an average long-run cost curve.

In the discussion which follows we shall deal directly with measurements of long-run costs rather than to refer to the underlying production functions. For most practical problems this is the simplest and clearest procedures. Those who wish to know more about production functions may wish to read Henderson and Quandt, R. G. D. Allen, or Baumol on the subject. All of these works are extremely clear on the theoretical aspect but give no attention to managerial applications of the theory.

4. LONG-RUN COSTS

This book devotes less space to long-run costs than to the short-run analysis of the preceding chapter. The relevance of long-run cost analysis for decisions is less clear than is true of short-run analysis. Technological considerations are more important in the long run; the economics of the choice among alternative technologies falls under the heading of "capital budgeting" to which an entire chapter is devoted later.

Long-run cost analysis is concerned with the economies or diseconomies of scale facing a single firm.[10] In some industries the economies of scale may be insignificant past a minimum size, in which case it is possible for large and small firms to compete on relatively equal terms. Such is apparently the case in a great deal of agriculture and retailing, in which the survival of small firms is at least partial evidence that their average costs are not sharply different from those of larger firms. In other industries the inability of small firms to persist suggests that they do not benefit from some cost advantages available to larger firms. An example is the

---

[10] By "economies of scale" we mean the savings in unit costs which result from larger size plants or from larger size firms.

automobile industry in which the past 50 years have marked the disappearance of dozens of small firms unable to compete with the giants. In still other industries the situation may be a combination of economies of scale at low levels of output and diseconomies at large sizes, with the optimum at some intermediate size.

Long-run costs in theory

Traditional economic theory usually assumes that the long-run cost curve has a **U** shape, reflecting increasing returns to scale at small outputs and decreasing returns to scale after output passes a certain point. Figure 6–12 illustrates such a curve.

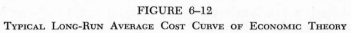

FIGURE 6–12

TYPICAL LONG-RUN AVERAGE COST CURVE OF ECONOMIC THEORY

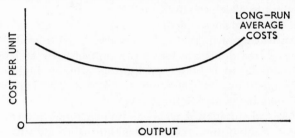

A wide variety of reasons for the downward slope of the curve in the initial stages is available:

1. Economies in the purchase of raw materials and supplies. As is well known, large purchasers frequently get the advantages of quantity discounts. They also may gain from lower freight rates on larger lots.

2. Economies in the sale of the firm's output. The larger firm is likely to have more information about the market. It also may get some advantage from the economies of advertising—the small firm could hardly afford national magazine or television advertising which may be more effective per dollar of expenditure.

3. Greater specialization in the use of manpower. A small firm is dependent on the jack-of-all-trades. The large firm can afford to hire men suited for specialized tasks. Such specialization may contribute to greater proficiency, for each employee or manager will learn his narrow task well by repetition.

4. Greater specialization of equipment. Some large machines are clearly more productive than small ones, but are too large for firms with a small volume of output. For example, large-scale electricity generators

are more economical of fuel and manpower than small generators, but they require a large market.

5. Economies of large-scale research. Small firms often cannot afford expensive research teams. Fundamental research requires the possibility of applications in a wider variety of product lines than is available to small firms.

6. Economies of large-scale finance. Large incorporated firms have access to sources of finance not available to small firms, such as the stock market. Furthermore lenders and investors may have more confidence in the financial stability of large firms.

7. Advantages of diversification. Large firms are more likely to sell in diversified markets. For example, a large electric utility may sell to a wide variety of consumers in different locations and with different patterns of demand. Such a firm can average the demand pattern of one kind of customer against those of another, thus improving its load factor (a measure of the extent to which the fixed facilities are used).

This list is no doubt incomplete. P. Sargant Florence adds such economies as the spreading of market research over large outputs.[11] He claims that the costs of bad debts are lower per unit of sales at larger outputs. Large firms may be in a better position to employ highly skilled top management and to use its abilities to the fullest. The bargaining power of large firms may be greater in the market place.

Most of these advantages of scale can be explained in terms of indivisibilities of some of the inputs. If large machines were divisible into equally efficient smaller parts, or if skilled labor or management were divisible into equally skilled smaller units, these economies of scale would disappear. In fact some economists take the position that economies of scale are entirely a result of indivisibilities, a position which is too extreme for others.[12]

This is an appropriate point at which to introduce the distinction between the plant and the firm. Economic theory often concerns itself with the firm as a whole, and with economies and diseconomies of scale for the firm. The internal management of the firm must also consider economies of plant size and distinguish between those economies available to the firm as it increases in size and those available to the plant as it increases in size.

Within the individual plant, economies of scale may result from lower unit costs of maintenance or the lower costs of moving products from one operation to another. A larger plant may be able to take advantage of the

---

[11] P. Sargant Florence, *The Logic of British and American Industry* (London: Routledge and Kegan Paul, 1953), pp. 50–60.

[12] See E. H. Chamberlin, *Theory of Monopolistic Competition* (7th ed.; Cambridge, Mass.: Harvard University Press), Appendix B, for a discussion of this issue.

line (product) principle of plant layout, with its greater specialization of equipment and shorter lines of transportation; the smaller plants may be dependent on the functional principle of layout with its greater flexibility but more complex problems of transportation and production control.[13]

Having considered the factors accounting for the downward slope of the long-run cost curve, we now turn to the argument that the curve will eventually turn upward. Let us consider plant size first of all. One large plant as compared with four smaller ones, has the disadvantage of longer distances to the market if the market is scattered geographically, and thus larger transportation costs. It is possible that the larger plant runs into managerial inefficiencies due to a more cumbersome organizational structure.

Are there diseconomies of scale for the firm? The economist points to one important bit of indirect evidence that such diseconomies exist—the fact that more than one firm is able to survive in most industries. If economies of scale persisted throughout all ranges of output, one firm would drive out all others to gain advantages of lower unit costs. Such persistent economies apparently prevail in the public utilities, which are often known as "natural monopolies" in recognition of the inability of small firms to compete against the low costs of large enterprises. Even if the long-run cost curve were to become horizontal, it would appear that the horizontal portion of the curve would be lower for some firms than for others, resulting in a tendency toward monopoly. Thus, some economists deduce from the absence of monopoly in most industries the conclusion that most cost curves must eventually rise.

What are the underlying causes of diseconomies of scale for the firm? The usual reasons given for diseconomies are related to management. Some writers argue that even in the long run management is a relatively fixed factor; it is impossible to increase management as rapidly as the other inputs, so that eventually it is spread too thin and organizational effectiveness declines. Other writers provide quite a different analysis. They claim that the managerial staffs must increase more rapidly than output because of the growing cumbersomeness of the firm and greater problems of communication and coordination.

The critics of such generalizations about the inefficiency of management for larger scales point out that the industry has many ways of overcoming the problems of communication and coordination just noted. Large firms can decentralize, providing a great deal of autonomy for smaller units within the firm.

---

[13] Discussions of line versus functional layout appear in most production management textbooks. A line layout is one planned around a single product (or group of closely related products); a functional layout is one planned around various types of equipment.

This controversy leaves us with two competing generalizations about long-run cost curves:

1. The traditional view that they are U-shaped, with definite diseconomies at large and small outputs. In most cases the U will take on a saucer shape with a long stretch of constant costs.

2. The view that the curves are L-shaped, declining at first and then becoming horizontal. Under such conditions large and small firms exist together, the mixture of the firms' sizes depending on the history and growth of the industry.

The case of constant returns to scale may be considered a special case of this second view, for surely if size is made small enough the average costs must rise because of the indivisibility of certain inputs.[14]

Relation to short-run cost curves

It is time to be somewhat more explicit about the relation between short-run and long-run costs. The long-run cost curve is sometimes known as the "planning" curve, since in theory it could be used by management to plan the economical scale of operations. Once the manager has determined the scale of output, he must then operate along a short-run cost curve consistent with that scale.

Figure 6–13 illustrates the relationship between the U-shaped short-run and U-shaped long-run cost curves found in economic theory. It should be clear why the long-run cost curve (planning curve) is sometimes called an envelope curve. Only a few short-run cost curves are shown—in theory

FIGURE 6–13

LONG-RUN AND SHORT-RUN COST CURVES ACCORDING TO TRADITIONAL THEORY

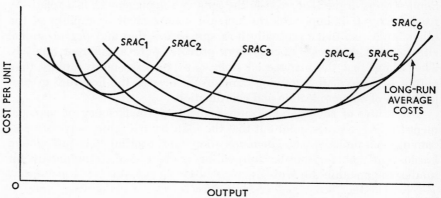

[14] Still another type of long-run cost curve is the "cork-screw" cost curve which declines at first but then encounters bumps or hills due to indivisibilities. See H. Leibenstein, *Economic Theory and Organizational Analysis* (New York: Harper & Brothers, 1960), pp. 297–312.

an infinite number of such curves exist, each reflecting a slightly different size. Indivisibilities in some of the inputs might limit the variety of possible sizes in actual practice.

Another way of describing the relationship under consideration is to state that the long-run cost curve (*LRAC*) is the curve tangent to all of the possible short-run cost curves. In the long run the manager can select whatever size will minimize the costs for the output that he forecasts in the future. In the short run he must operate along the short-run curve he has selected, even though some of the other short-run cost curves would permit lower costs.

One complication is worthy of consideration. The manager knows that his forecast of future sales and output is uncertain. Rather than select a technology that gives the lowest cost for a given output, he might select a more flexible technology that will minimize costs over a range of outputs.[15] Figure 6–14 shows two cost curves, one of which gives the lowest

FIGURE 6–14

SHORT-RUN COST CURVES FOR PLANTS DIFFERING IN FLEXIBILITY

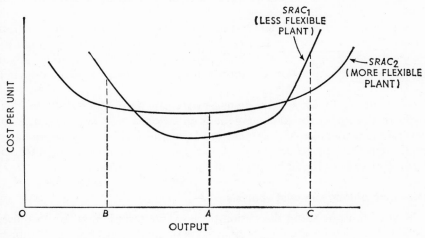

cost for output *OA*, but which because of the inflexibility of the plant means high costs at outputs *OB* or *OC*. The other curve is more horizontal, so that the penalties for wrong guesses about the appropriate scale are less severe. The fact that managers will often select the second type of curve over the first may help account in part for the empirical findings of constant short-run marginal costs that have already been noted.

---

[15] The choice between these technologies is a long-run decision. After the choice is made, the firm must operate along the short-run curve it has selected.

If the majority of the empirical studies are correct and if short-run costs are linear (with constant marginal costs) and if long-run costs do not rise at high outputs, a revision in Figure 6–13 is in order. Figure 6–15 presents such a revised graph, showing downward sloping short-run cost

FIGURE 6–15
LONG-RUN AND SHORT-RUN COST CURVES ACCORDING TO THE
MAJORITY OF EMPIRICAL STUDIES

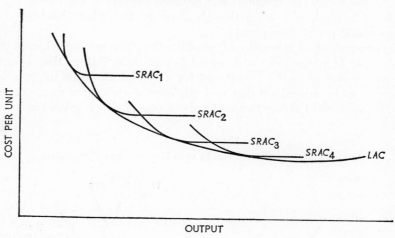

curves tangent to an L-shaped long-run cost curve. According to this graph the problem for management is to reach a size large enough to provide the economies of scale that are available (which may require the stimulation of demand to justify larger scales) and then to operate as close as possible to the full capacity of the short-run curve.

Relevance of long-run cost analysis

Most of the preceding discussion of long-run costs is familiar to those who have studied economic theory. A book on managerial economics must raise questions about the relevance of such an analysis in decision making. Management must be concerned with whether it has achieved a scale of operations that will permit it to compete and to make profits. The failure of many small firms is surely a failure to achieve a size that is economical; conceivably, the difficulties of some large firms are due to the expansion of size beyond manageable limits. It has been claimed that the U.S. Steel Company was uneconomically large when it was formed in the early 1900's, and one of the perennial arguments against government enterprises is their unmanageable size.

One might look upon the merger movement in many industries as an attempt to gain the economies of scale not available to the formerly independent units, though tax considerations and questions of market control also enter in. One might also interpret the policy of decentralization of management in such firms as General Motors, General Electric, Westinghouse, and Sears, Roebuck as attempts to overcome managerial diseconomies resulting from size by instituting internal organizational changes that would reduce these diseconomies. With the introduction of automation, electronic computers, and improved communication devices, the tide might turn toward greater decentralization in the decades ahead.

How does a firm determine what scale of operations is optimal? No doubt the usual approach is one of trial and error. The measurement of long-run costs is no easy matter, and most managers rely on rough estimates drawn from experience. In some industries the existence of economies of scale is pretty clear. No one would enter the automobile industry unless he were prepared to operate on a scale that would provide the economies of production and marketing available to General Motors and Ford. The failure of Kaiser-Fraser to survive in the automobile industry resulted from its inability to achieve a viable size, especially in the marketing function.

Another way of finding an optimal scale would be to measure the long-run cost curve statistically. The next section presents some illustrations of such measurements. The problem of isolating the effect of scale from other influences on cost is not easily overcome; much more research on this topic is needed.

Sometimes the economies of scale become a public issue. For example, an important question in a government suit to break the A & P grocery chain into smaller units was whether these units could produce grocery services as cheaply as the larger firm. Similarly there is controversy over whether the General Motors Company would suffer any diseconomies if it were broken into several smaller, independent firms. Perhaps the division of such firms into smaller units would make industry more competitive; but if the individual units were less efficient than the giants, the consumers might not benefit from the competition.

Management must take an interest in the economies of scale within the firm's operations as well as the economies for the firm as a whole. Some plant sizes are more efficient than others. The General Electric Company has found that a much larger size plant is required for producing appliances than for manufacturing light bulbs; it has concentrated its appliance manufacture in one huge plant at the same time it has spread light bulb manufacture over a large number of small units.

The difficulty of measurement of the optimal scale of operations for the individual plant is similar to that for the firm as a whole. A large firm may, however, be able to learn from experience the consequences of varying plant size and to use this information in planning for the future.

Empirical studies and illustrations

Most of the empirical evidence on long-run costs favors the **L**-shaped curve, though a few studies show a rise in costs at high outputs and other studies are inconclusive on this point. Wiles, in a summary of 44 sets of data on long-run costs, concludes that decreasing costs with size are pervasive and that increasing costs at high outputs are rare.[16] A third of his cases might be consistent with slight increases in cost at high outputs, but the margin of statistical error makes it impossible to determine that such is the case. The majority of his cases present no evidence of increasing costs, thus supporting what Wiles calls the "law of **L**-shaped costs." Bain reaches similar conclusions in his study of 20 American manufacturing industries.[17]

A more recent survey of statistical cost functions by J. Johnston also lends support to the "preponderance of the **L**-shaped pattern of long-run average cost."[18] Johnston's survey does include a few cases that suggest rising costs at large scales or, at least, uncertainty about whether the costs are increasing or not.

A study of long-run costs in the Eastern Kentucky coal industry suggests that the economies of scale are relatively small but that the large firms are on the average more profitable.[19] Figure 6–16 shows the long-run cost curve, though the results vary somewhat depending on the definition of costs, the treatment of depletion expenses, and other variables. The data indicate that the medium-size firms may be at a cost disadvantage when compared with both the small and large firms, a finding which is opposite to the traditional **U**-shaped curve. One of the great advantages of the small firms is lower daily wage costs (a fact which applies to even some of the unionized firms which have been able to circumvent the normal union scales). The large firms apparently gain from technological, managerial, and marketing advantages, leaving some of the middle-size firms paying full union scales without all of the technological advantages of the largest size. If the United Mine Workers were to enforce the union scale throughout, the costs of many small producers would rise sharply and substantial numbers of them would fail. Thus the shape of the long-run cost curve in the coal industry is strongly affected by differential wage scales.

---

[16] P. J. D. Wiles, *Prices, Cost and Output* (Oxford: Basil Blackwell & Mott, 1956), chap. 12 and pp. 227–51.

[17] Joe S. Bain, *Barriers to New Competition* (Cambridge, Mass.: Harvard University Press, 1956), chap. iii. Bain reviews the opinions of many earlier writers on the economies of scale.

[18] J. Johnston, *Statistical Cost Analysis* (New York: McGraw-Hill Book Co., 1960).

[19] Mary Jean Bowman and W. Warren Haynes, *Problems and Potentials of a Lagging Economy* (Baltimore: Johns Hopkins Press, 1963), chap. xvi.

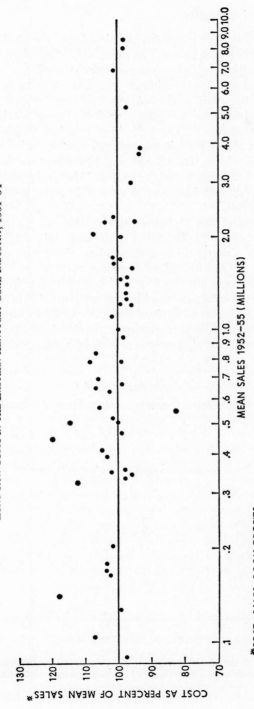

FIGURE 6-16

LONG-RUN COSTS IN THE EASTERN KENTUCKY COAL INDUSTRY, 1951–54

MEAN SALES 1952–55 (MILLIONS)

COST AS PERCENT OF MEAN SALES*

*COST=SALES−BOOK PROFITS

NOTE: Some of the small firms would show lower costs and higher profits if the data were adjusted for executive salaries. The evidence suggests that small firms may often pay out profits in the form of salaries.

Many economists have noted the deficiencies of the statistical measurement of the long-run cost curve. The most serious problem is in obtaining adequate data on the costs of productive services. Historical cost data are inappropriate and yet cross-sectioned cost data on firms of different sizes may be difficult to obtain and interpret.[20] George Stigler has attempted to overcome this problem by replacing cost studies with what he calls the "survivorship technique."[21] The technique requires the following steps: (1) classification of the firms in the industry under study by size and (2) determination of which size classes are increasing or decreasing their share of the total output. As Stigler states: "If the share of a given class falls, it is relatively inefficient, and in general is more inefficient the more rapidly the share falls."[22]

Stigler has applied this technique to the study of the making of steel ingots by open-hearth or Bessemer processes. His findings appear in Table 6–2. He translates these findings into the long-run average cost curve of Figure 6–17. This figure does not pretend to measure exactly how much higher costs are at lower and higher scales, but it reflects the smaller shares of the total produced by the small and large companies.

Stigler makes a similar analysis of the automobile industry. In this case the smallest companies show a consistent decline in their share of output but there is no evidence of diseconomies of large size (at least in normal peacetime).

FIGURE 6–17

LONG-RUN COST CURVE CONSISTENT WITH DATA ON STEEL INGOTS

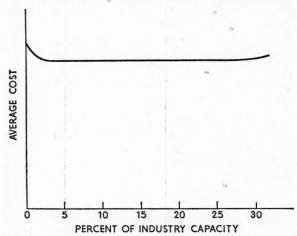

PERCENT OF INDUSTRY CAPACITY

---

[20] One problem is that firms having an advantage due to size may have a higher value (and thus higher costs) as a result of that advantage. A circularity arises which cannot be overcome statistically.

[21] George J. Stigler, "The Economics of Scale," *The Journal of Law and Economics,* October, 1958, pp. 54–71.

[22] *Ibid.,* p. 56.

TABLE 6–2

DISTRIBUTION OF OUTPUT OF STEEL INGOT CAPACITY BY
RELATIVE SIZE OF COMPANY

Company Size (percent of industry total)	1930	1938	1951
Under ½	7.16	6.11	4.65
½ to 1	5.94	5.08	5.37
1 to 2½	13.17	8.30	9.07
2½ to 5	10.64	16.59	22.21
5 to 10	11.18	14.03	8.12
10 to 25	13.24	13.99	16.10
25 and over	38.67	35.91	34.50

SOURCES: *Directory of Iron and Steel Works of the United States and Canada*, 1930, 1938; *Iron Age*, January 3, 1952, as reprinted in Stigler, *op. cit.*, p. 58.

Having reviewed empirical studies of economies of scale for firms as a whole, we now turn to a few studies of economies at the plant level. Joel Dean's investigation of a chain of retail shoestores was a pioneer attempt to measure the economies of scale statistically.[23] The findings are summarized in Figures 6–18 and 6–19, which show the total costs and average costs in 1938 in stores of different sizes. Dean and his associate, R. Warren James, used correlation analysis in fitting curves to the total costs and average costs. The evidence indicates clear economies of scale at small store sizes. The diseconomies at large store sizes are not clear, since so few stores appear in the upper range of sizes. It should be noted that in this type of study of long-run costs all the data are for one period, in this case 1938. Normally studies of short-run cost functions require data over a number of periods, while those of long-run costs require data in one period for plants (or firms) of different sizes.

Dean and James recognized that the use of output as a measure of size was deficient, for different stores are subject to different relative variations in sales over the seasons and business cycles. Stores are built to handle peak loads and to provide flexibility for variations in sales. Nevertheless the studies show strong evidence of economies of scale as sales increase from 5,000 pairs to 25,000 pairs of shoes.

A study of milk-processing plants is of special interest because it shows the relation between short-run and long-run costs.[24] The study covered 12 butter-powder plants located in Washington, Oregon, and Idaho. The

---

[23] Joel Dean and R. Warren James, *The Long-Run Behavior of Costs in a Chain of Shoe Stores: A Statistical Analysis* (University of Chicago Studies in Business Administration, Vol. XII, No. 3 [Chicago: University of Chicago Press, 1942]).

[24] S. H. Walker, H. J. Preston, and G. T. Nelson, *An Economic Analysis of Butter-Nonfat Dry Milk Plants*, University of Idaho Agricultural Experiment Station Research Bulletin No. 20, June, 1953. An excellent summary of this study appears in M. H. Spencer and L. Siegelman, *Managerial Economics: Decision Making and Forward Planning* (Homewood, Ill.: Richard D. Irwin, Inc., 1959), pp. 260–64.

FIGURE 6–18

Simple Regression of Total Cost on Output

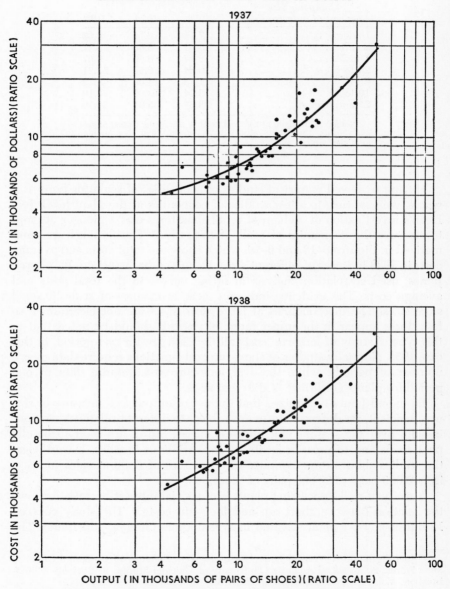

Source: Joel Dean and R. Warren James, *The Long-Run Behavior of Costs in a Chain of Shoe Stores: A Statistical Analysis* (Chicago: University of Chicago Press, 1942).

FIGURE 6–19

SIMPLE REGRESSION OF AVERAGE COST ON OUTPUT

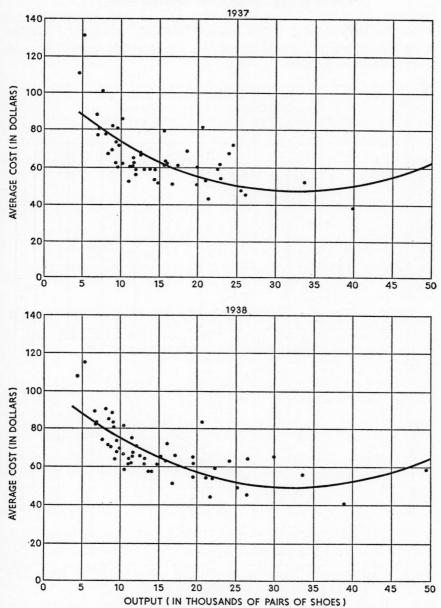

SOURCE: Dean and James, *The Long-Run Behavior of Costs in a Chain of Shoe Stores: A Statistical Analysis, ibid.*

plants were of two types: roller plants and spray plants. The findings
appear in Figure 6–20. The variations in cost along a single curve are the
result ⁻f seasonal variations in output in a single plant. The movement
from one curve to the next shows the variation of costs in different size
plants. The evidence shows clear economies of scale; it would be possible
to draw an envelope curve encompassing the short-run curves, showing
lower costs for larger sizes.

FIGURE 6–20

SHORT-RUN COST OUTPUT FUNCTIONS FOR
12 BUTTER-POWDER PLANTS OF DIFFERENT SIZES

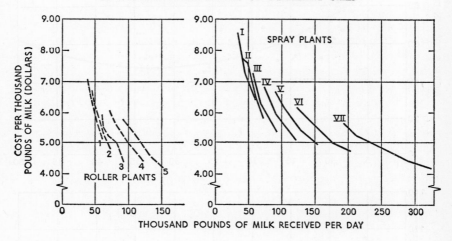

Cases for part three

Cost analysis is necessary in a variety of problem-solving situations. The cases in this chapter require such a cost analysis in pricing decisions, decisions on product mix, decisions on abandonment of activities or expansion of activities or the establishment of new branches.

It is not possible to find cases which isolate cost considerations from other economic variables. The cases in this chapter require some attention to the demand concepts covered in Chapters 3 and 4. Some of the cases foreshadow the discussions of pricing and capital budgeting which are treated more formally later in this book. Marketing considerations are important throughout. No attempt is made here to isolate one aspect of the analysis from the rest of the business considerations.

SHORT CASES IN COST ANALYSIS*

The following case extracts illustrate a variety of ways in which cost analysis enters into some managerial policies and decisions.

1. The owner-manager of a small printing firm maintained a policy of cost-plus pricing. He computed the full cost of each order by adding an overhead allocation to the direct labor and material expenses. When asked what he would do if a recession were to hit his sales, with a resultant increase in overhead costs per unit of production, he replied that he would increase price to meet the higher overhead costs. In subsequent interviews he insisted that he would maintain such a policy. His firm began operations just after World War II and he had never faced a serious decline in sales.

2. The best known of the questionnaire studies on pricing is that of R. L. Hall and C. J. Hitch.[1] They found that the majority of the 38 firms

---

* Most of these cases are concerned with the use of costs in pricing, a subject which comes up later in the book. It is believed that the study of the role of costs in pricing at this point will help the reader get more out of the later pricing material.

[1] "Price Theory and Business Behavior," reprinted in T. Wilson and P. W. S. Andrews, *Oxford Studies in the Price Mechanism* (Oxford: Oxford University Press, 1951).

in their survey followed a full-cost policy. The reasons for the emphasis on full cost were as follows:

   a) The desire to be fair.
   b) Ignorance of demand and marginal revenue conditions.
   c) Uncertainty about the potential reaction of competitors.
   d) Belief that the elasticity to price decreases is low.
   e) Belief that higher prices would encourage new entrants.
   f) Administrative difficulties of a more flexible price policy.

One of the full-cost cases was a firm which refused to supply below cost. It computed average overheads on the basis of "conventional output" (output under normal business conditions). It added a margin for profit which was smaller on competitive lines and higher on specialties and novelties which resulted from the firm's research and development activity. The managers believed experience showed that price cuts below full costs did not pay because the demand was inelastic. Furthermore, price changes were a nuisance to distributors and an annoyance to customers. A trade association set minimum prices on a few lines. In depression conditions the management found that demand shifted to more popular, competitive lines and that timely price reductions on such lines alone were successful in increasing revenue.

3. A box manufacturing firm owned five printing presses to print labels on boxes. These presses varied in size and in the capacity to print multicolored labels. Some of the presses were better suited to printing large volumes than others. In the past management had been uncertain about the allocation of orders to the presses. In many cases it was clear that a certain large order or a certain multicolored label should be assigned to a particular press. But there was uncertainty about the desirability of printing some small, simple orders on the large, complex presses when those presses were idle, especially when there was a backlog of small orders. An accounting firm was called in to advise the printing firm on this issue. Its advice was to compute an hourly rate on each press which would include an allocation of overhead. The hourly rate on the large, complex presses would be higher because of the higher labor costs (more pressmen per press), the higher depreciation charges on the press, and the higher allocation of plantwide overhead. These hourly rates would help prevent the use of expensive presses on low-value jobs.

4. Paul T. Norton, Jr. describes a case of a furniture company which abandoned a machining operation in its main plants.[2] The four spindles which had been used were now idle. The four employees who had done the machining for the company had rented a shed in another part of town and had rented four second-hand spindles. They were supplying the parts

---

2 Paul T. Norton, Jr., "Engineering Economy" in William G. Ireson and Eugene L. Grant, *Handbook of Industrial Engineering and Management* (Englewood Cliffs, N.J.: Prentice-Hall, Inc., 1955), pp. 151–52.

formerly produced by the company at a price below the former internal cost to the furniture company. The reason that they were able to do this was that the overhead costs in their shed were far below the overhead rate in the main plant. The overhead costs in the main plant were allocated on the basis of direct labor cost. The direct labor cost on this operation was especially high because the men were highly skilled and the job was less mechanized than other jobs in the plant.

5. A trade association official stated that the pricing practices of its members lacked uniformity and objectivity. Many of the members made their pricing decisions in a highly subjective way. The trade association was trying to convert its members to a "scientific approach" to pricing which would base prices on costs.

6. The owner-manager of a garden nursery firm claimed that he could not determine the cost of his individual plants and therefore could not price on the basis of costs. Some of the costs could be attributed to the individual items—for example, the labor cost of digging up the plants could be measured. It was fairly easy to compute the labor and transportation costs of a landscaping job. But the costs of propagating and growing a plant were uncertain. How much was the cost of the land occupied by the plant? How could the general expenses of the company be charged against particular items? The variable weather and plant diseases created uncertainty about the losses and damage which would occur before the plants had matured.

7. The cost of east-bound and west-bound traffic on a railroad is a joint cost. Every freight car hauled east must eventually be hauled west even if it is empty. The railroads are therefore faced with the problem of determining the costs to be attributed to the return trip. In 1951, for example, the loaded car-miles for Class I American railways were 20.6 billion while the empty car-miles were 10.6 billion, with a predominance of traffic eastward.[3]

1. *In each case evaluate the use of costs in the decisions with which the firm or firms are faced.*
2. *Is the company described in the second case a full-cost pricer? Discuss.*
3. *Which cost concepts are most pertinent in these case situations?*

RANDOLPH STONE COMPANY*

The Randolph Stone Company was a partnership engaged in stone quarrying and the paving of roads. The company sold primarily to state

---

[3] M. Beckmann, C. B. McGuire, and C. B. Winsten, *Studies in the Economics of Transportation* (New Haven, Conn.: Published for the Cowles Commission for Research in Economics by the Yale University Press, 1956), p. 195.

* This case is an exercise in the construction of break-even charts rather than one involving a choice among alternatives.

EXHIBIT 1

Profit and Loss Statement 1956 through 1961

	1956	1957	1958	1959	1960	1961
Net sales	$131,758.71	$248,025.45	$404,037.72	$196,432.41	$84,574.65	$433,658.51
Operating expenses						
Salaries and wages	19,186.50	35,196.48	41,484.90	24,543.03	17,379.57	46,598.01
Travel expense	114.00	529.26	308.79	171.96	54.90	204.60
Stationery and office supplies	67.35	126.12	78.18	78.66	.36	94.14
Auditing and legal	1.89	469.50	226.14	40.50	4.20	4.59
Dues and subscriptions	325.32	1,541.10	2,248.77	582.39	489.92	1,499.46
Repairs of equipment	2,157.24	2,933.19	7,496.79	4,475.01	1,294.83	9,559.05
Freight, in	8,104.29	13,779.39	10,270.02	5,315.64	2,763.69	12,542.07
Hired truck expense	13,513.08	27,204.21	39,039.69	15,553.44	7,897.17	42,546.69
Miscellaneous expense	508.41	424.59	1,621.26	569.10	4.65	606.00
Truck repair expense	207.42	456.24	1,981.56	1,082.22	317.94	1,814.10
Gas, oil, and lubricants	8,127.39	6,222.00	12,842.70	5,502.57	3,135.36	6,805.20
Stone purchased and sand	26,895.42	46,092.93	94,143.48	58,066.53	16,924.95	134,154.18
Oils and asphalt	29,425.35	53,740.89	80,837.55	22,336.02	11,076.18	46,041.87
Rent	514.29	.....	6,972.51	6,804.60	2,345.34	3,682.26
Insurance expense	300.27	1,135.08	8,874.36	4,402.89	245.19	1,057.95
Utilities	814.38	1,706.19	2,123.79	464.82	245.55	333.18
License and fees	90.66	471.00	739.14	1,033.71	563.25	766.98
FICA expense	342.54	763.98	1,004.40	670.38	451.05	1,375.62
Kentucky unemployment contributions	344.01	831.39	1,345.29	744.48	452.91	1,249.77
Interest expense	1,592.01	4,795.50	4,852.20	3,533.55	1,863.54	1,350.84
Bonding expense	520.35	1,156.05	256.89	713.64	371.19	2,420.46
Depreciation of equipment	6,075.39	12,144.33	15,988.59	17,354.13	17,221.83	31,498.68
Telephone and postage	.....	84.69	36.99	42.42	15.39	6.00
Taxes	.....	3.81	33.15	263.55	15.75	315.00
Commissions	.....	750.00	.....	.....	.....	.....
Advertising	.....	.....	402.15	440.43	37.50	52.89
Federal unemployment insurance	.....	.....	74.16	80.94	73.35	91.77
Sales tax	.....	.....	.....	2,260.89	2,319.72	6,926.25
Bad-debt expense	.....	.....	.....	1,042.41	42.18	274.80
Road construction supplies	.....	.....	.....	.....	.....	911.31
	$119,227.56	$212,557.92	$335,283.45	$178,169.91	$87,557.46	$354,783.72
Net profit (loss)	$ 12,531.15	$ 35,467.53	$ 68,754.27	$ 18,262.50	$(2,982.81)	$ 78,874.79

and local governments; its gravel was purchased for road construction in nearby sections of the state.

The company owned and operated five stone quarries located within 100 miles of each other. In addition, it owned a paving operation in the same vicinity.

The quarries were generally profitable, returning on the average a book profit of from 10 to 20 percent of the book value of the partners' property. Occasionally one of the quarries operated at a loss, though this resulted partly from the fact that special repairs were charged off as a current expense.

The most unstable part of the business was the paving operation. Its instability resulted from the variations in road construction activities of the state government involved. In election years paving activity was high; in other years it tapered off. The result was that the paving activities of the firm fluctuated sharply from high to low profits.

Exhibit 1 covers data on paving revenues and expenses for the years from 1956 through 1961.

1. *Classify the expenses into fixed expenses and variable expenses based on the 1961 profits and loss statement. Use judgment in determining whether the expense is fixed or variable. Some expenses, such as advertising and rent, might be classified in a separate category, since they are more in the nature of programmed or manipulable expenses which are neither fixed nor a result of changes in output.*
2. *On the basis of your answer to Question 1, construct a break-even chart.*
3. *Plot a scatter diagram relating total cost to sales. Complete a break-even chart based on this approach.*
4. *Compare your two break-even charts (the one based on the classification of accounts; the other on a rough "statistical" analysis). Do they provide approximately the same estimate of fixed costs? How do you account for the differences in the two charts?*
5. *What limitations would a statistician find in the "statistical" chart constructed as an answer to Question 3?*

M AND H COMPANY (A)*

In 1967 M and H was a relatively new firm engaged in the billboard advertising business. In the period from July 1 to December 31, 1967, the company suffered substantial losses of $40,611.11 on a total income of $780,585.18. While company officials realized that the losses were a result in part of the relatively newness of the firm, they wished to learn more about the causes of the losses and about ways of increasing the profitability of the business.

---

* All names and locations and to some extent the character of the business in this case have been disguised.

The company's business was concentrated in two locations—Boonville and Dorchester. Boonville appeared to be the more profitable of the two locations according to a breakdown of income and sales by location as follows:

	Boonville	Dorchester
Income	$642,853.96	$ 137,731.22
Operating expense	$212,103.99	$ 38,366.67
Direct selling expense	122,820.78	19,327.14
General administration and selling expense	166,376.88	97,294.64
Cash flow profit	$141,552.31	$− 17,257.23

EXHIBIT 1

M AND H COMPANY (A)

(schedule of direct operating expenses, July through December, 1967)

Particulars	Boonville	Dorchester	Combined Total
Labor	$ 56,051.15	$13,895.77	$ 69,946.92
Materials	12,304.63	4,974.93	17,279.56
Lease rental expense	67,794.75	3,134.07	70,928.82
Illumination	22,845.56	2,977.53	25,823.09
Travel expense	—	2,568.63	2,568.63
Repairs and maintenance	3,771.39	1,246.86	5,018.25
Plant removal expense	—	269.65	269.65
Special treatment	2,481.05	—	2,481.05
Other direct operating expense	2,488.37	1,345.57	3,833.94
Write-off special treatment	3,967.99	—	3,967.99
Amortization covenant not to compete	—	150.00	150.00
Outright sales cost	34,387.28	7,753.84	42,141.12
Write-off cost of leased signs	—	49.82	49.82
Write-off cost of installment sale	6,011.82	—	6,011.82
Total	$212,103.99	$38,366.67	$250,470.66
Amortization leaseholds	$ 26,370.86	—	$ 26,370.86

EXHIBIT 2

M AND H COMPANY (A)

(schedule of direct selling expense, July through December, 1967)

Particulars	Boonville	Dorchester	Total
Agency commission	$ 84,545.28	$15,081.50	$ 99,626.78
Association fees	2,316.00	536.64	2,852.64
Salesmen's salaries	20,393.15	3,516.09	23,909.24
Salesmen's commission	15,566.35	192.91	15,759.26
Total direct selling expense	$122,820.78	$19,327.14	$142,147.92

By "cash flow profit" the firm's accountants meant profit before deduction of depreciation and amortization of leaseholds. The company officials realized that no outflow of cash resulted from such expenses. Since one of the objectives of such accumulations of data was to help plan cash inflow and outflows, company officials were accustomed to such cash flow concepts.

EXHIBIT 3

M AND H COMPANY (A)
(schedule of general administration and selling expense,
July through December, 1967)

Particulars	Boonville	Dorchester	Combined Total
Gasoline and oil	$ 3,845.01	$ 4,891.44	$ 8,736.45
Insurance—Trucks	3,299.32	1,634.36	4,933.68
Repairs—Auto and trucks	2,303.04	1,022.66	3,325.70
Tires and tubes	687.99	401.14	1,089.13
Taxes & license—Auto & trucks	1,473.69	404.76	1,878.45
Other auto and truck expense (painting)	1,956.19	1,121.52	3,077.71
Dues and subscriptions	4,300.63	1,816.04	6,116.67
Group insurance	728.84	1,640.58	2,369.42
Payroll taxes	12,038.39	3,695.94	15,734.33
Workmen's compensation fees	2,805.81	745.96	3,551.77
Employees' welfare and pension expense	715.08	—	715.08
Insurance—Fire and liability	610.03	547.40	1,157.43
Legal and audit	4,021.53	2,093.28	6,114.81
Damage claims	19.50	—	19.50
Donations cash	15.00	179.85	194.85
Donations—Service	505.10	20.26	525.36
Repairs—Machinery and equipment	1,296.33	961.43	2,257.76
Postage	776.07	493.97	1,270.04
Stationery and office supplies	2,405.90	2,752.21	5,158.11
Telephone and telegraph	2,890.53	3,433.25	6,323.78
Freight and express	372.66	290.44	663.10
Amortization of organization cost	848.34	424.17	1,272.51
Building supplies	293.26	242.30	535.56
Heat, light, and water	1,473.15	1,275.51	2,748.66
Building repairs	505.77	619.11	1,124.88
Taxes—Real estate	378.08	93.96	472.04
Salaries: officers	11,250.00	12,750.00	24,000.00
supervision	10,758.84	4,567.50	15,326.34
general office	14,025.12	6,866.48	20,891.60
others	5,483.72	6,020.50	11,504.22
art and photo	9,792.96	615.33	10,408.29
janitors	676.84	918.13	1,594.97
Advertising	878.67	1,190.55	2,069.22
Other selling expenses	3,080.27	978.06	4,058.33
Travel and entertainment	4,382.07	6,299.40	10,681.47
Other taxes and license	1,151.47	201.51	1,352.98
Sales and use tax	2,514.72	300.61	2,815.33
Interest expense	51,350.79	25,785.03	77,135.82
Provision for bad debt	406.17	—	406.17
Gain or loss on sale assets	60.00	—	60.00
	$166,376.88	$97,294.64	$263,671.52

EXHIBIT 4

M AND H COMPANY (A)

(schedule of depreciation, July through December, 1967)

Particulars	Boonville	Dorchester	Combined Total
Buildings	$ 2,340.00	$ 975.00	$ 3,315.00
Poster	78,235.38	12,633.74	90,869.12
Paint	23,892.90	4,068.31	27,961.21
Autos and truck	5,400.00	2,850.00	8,250.00
Machinery and equipment	4,950.00	877.50	5,827.50
Furniture and office equipment	787.50	600.00	1,387.50
Illumination equipment	—	975.00	975.00
	$115,605.78	$22,979.55	$138,585.33

Unfortunately, while the accounts showed a breakdown of revenues and costs between Boonville and Dorchester, the company officials were not fully confident that the breakdown was accurate. They suspected that some expenses were charged against Dorchester which were in fact a result of Boonville operations or were common costs which could be allocated only on an arbitrary basis.

The company was engaged in three main types of activity in each location: posters, paint, and commercial. The poster business consisted of leasing large billboards, of a standard size, on which preprinted posters were pasted. The "paint" activity consisted of nonstandard billboards on which specially painted material was pasted. The "commercial" business included various special jobs of a miscellaneous nature usually involving heavy use of the workshops of the company.

The company officials were convinced that an expansion of volume would improve the profitability of the business. They were not certain whether that expansion should stress the poster business, the paint business, the commercial business, or a mixture of the three. Nor were they certain of the extent to which increased volume would result in increased profits. One official suggested that it might be useful to construct a break-even chart and to determine the volume of sales at which the business would break even. This exercise would require a separation of the company's fixed costs from the variable costs. Other officials believed it would be more useful to separate costs by activity.

In addition to learning more about the impact of sales volume on profits, the company officials wished to know whether it would be desirable to abandon or sell off any part of its business. It might well be that some of the departments were not carrying their full part of the load. Also the officials wanted to know whether it would be profitable to buy up additional poster plant, paint plant, or commercial activities in other locations. The question was what format for the allocation of the company's costs would provide the most information for such key decisions faced by the company.

Exhibit 1 presents the direct operating expenses at both Boonville and Dorchester for the period from July 1, 1967 to December 31, 1967. Exhibits 2, 3, and 4 present similar breakdowns of direct selling expenses, general administration and selling expense, and depreciation.

M AND H COMPANY (B)

The M and H Company (B) invited a management consultant to advise them on the use of the company's accounts in decision making. The consultant's report* is reproduced below:

This report presents the accounts of the M and H Company in the form of marginal income accounting—also known as differential accounting, cost-volume-profit analysis, or incremental analysis. The method is closely akin to direct costing, but does not require the tie-in with the day-to-day financial accounts or the change in inventory valuation required by direct costing.

Purposes of marginal income accounting

The objective of marginal income accounting is to aid in decision making rather than the reporting of past performance. It supplements the financial reports. If M and H were to adopt a permanent system of marginal income accounting, it would need special analyses of the accounts only twice a year. These could be kept in a form which is relatively inexpensive—the work could be done in slack periods in the accounting department.

In the case at instance, marginal income accounting would help achieve the following objectives:

1. Separation of the results of the Boonville and Dorchester operations: As we have seen there has already been a tendency to mix the Boonville and Dorchester accounts in such a way that the results are confusing and misleading. It is imperative for a business man to know how much each operation is contributing to the business.

2. Separation of the results of the poster, paint, and commercial departments: At present one cannot tell whether any of these departments is contributing adequately to the business to justify its existence. Nor can one tell which branches are the most profitable and thus the most appropriate for expansion.

3. Determination of the incremental costs of each activity: While at the present time one has a notion that the variable costs are much less than the fixed costs—and that the incremental costs are perhaps only 30 to 40 percent of the billings—that such is the case has not been determined in a systematic way. The incremental costs vary from one activity to another. In fact, they vary from one type of decision to another. Any system which helps to determine incremental costs should assist the executives in future decisions about the business.

---

* Editorial changes are made in the original version for the purpose of classroom discussion and to disguise the original company.

It might be noted here that marginal income accounting tries to avoid arbitrary allocations of overhead. If some costs are common costs of the company as a whole, and are not a result of any particular activity (Boonville or Dorchester) as such, these costs are marked as company overhead. If some other costs are clearly related to Boonville activity or Dorchester activity but cannot be shown to be a result of a particular department (poster, paint or commercial), such costs are marked as Boonville overhead or as Dorchester overhead. One of the primary objectives of marginal income accounting is to determine how much Boonville and Dorchester are separately contributing to the company's overhead and profits and how much poster, paint, and commercial departments are contributing to local overhead, company overhead and profits. Thus a central concept throughout is the *contribution to overhead and profits*.

Arrangement of the accounts

I have identified each major account classification in a way which should be almost self-explanatory. The classes are shown in Exhibit 1. A code has been established for each class.

Marginal income analysis for July, 1967 through December, 1967

The operational results for the six months from July through December, 1967, appear in Exhibit 2. These results are based on a close study of each individual expense item to determine whether it is fixed or variable, sunk or escapable, and attributable to Boonville, Dorchester or the company as a whole.

Break-even charts: Boonville

The results can also be shown in the form of a series of break-even charts. Rather than construct a break-even chart for the company as a whole it makes more sense to construct individual charts for each segment of the business separately. An overall break-even chart would add together differing elements, thereby obscuring the outcome of particular operations.

The special break-even chart required to be constructed is known as the profit/volume chart. On it is plotted first of all the fixed costs (both sunk and escapable) resulting from the particular segment. Then is plotted what is called the P/V line (the profit-volume line) which is the incremental income at various volumes of sales. It is, in other words, the added income *minus* the added (variable) costs. The slope of the P/V line is the P/V ratio—the added contribution per unit of sales. Where the P/V line crosses the zero horizontal line is the break-even point. At this point, the income less the variable costs is enough to cover the segment's fixed costs. *But* at this point the segment makes *no* contribution to the company's overhead and profits.

Take Exhibit 3, for example. The specific fixed costs of the Boonville poster department amount to $185,806.65. The P/V ratio is .70, which means that every $1 of Boonville poster sales adds $.70 more income. It takes billings of $266,580 in each six-month period to break even in the poster plant—that is, to cover the specific fixed costs. Beyond that point the contribution to profit

EXHIBIT 1
M AND H COMPANY (B)
(marginal income—classification of accounts)

B–PO–1	Boonville income from poster plant
B–PO–2	Boonville variable costs in poster plant
B–PO–3	Boonville poster plant contribution to poster fixed costs, local and company overhead, and profit.
B–PO–4	Boonville poster plant fixed costs
B–PO–4A	(Part of B–PO–4) Boonville poster plant sunk costs.
B–PO–4B	(Part of B–PO–4) Boonville poster plant escapable fixed costs.
B–PO–5	Boonville poster plant contribution to local and company overhead and profit (after deduction of poster plant fixed costs).

B–PA–1
B–PA–2
B–PA–3
B–PA–4 } The same for the Boonville paint plant
B–PA–4A
B–PA–4B
B–PA–5

B–C–1
B–C–2
B–C–3
B–C–4 } The same for the Boonville commercial plant
B–C–4A
B–C–4B
B–C–5

D–PO–1   D–PA–1   D–C–1
D–PO–2   D–PA–2   D–C–2
D–PO–3   D–PA–3   D–C–3   The same for the Dorchester poster plant,
D–PO–4   D–PA–4   D–C–4 }   Dorchester paint plant, and Dorchester com-
D–PO–4A   D–PA–4A   D–C–4A   mercial plant, respectively.
D–PO–4B   D–PA–4B   D–C–4B
D–PO–5   D–PA–5   D–C–5

In addition there are three overhead accounts, two local contribution accounts, and one company profit account.

B–OH	Boonville overhead
D–OH	Dorchester overhead
B–6	Boonville contribution to company overhead and profit
D–6	Dorchester contribution to company overhead and profit
O	Company-wide overhead
P	Company profit

increases rapidly, reaching a level of $61,803.08 at billings of $355,230.92. At billings of $450,000 it would appear that the contribution would be over $127,500.

However, one qualification is necessary. Exhibit 3 probably exaggerates the added profits *beyond* present levels of sales in one respect. Remember that the salesmen's earnings have been treated partly as a fixed cost and partly as a variable cost. As billings push on beyond present levels and the salesmen become relatively more dependent upon commissions, the proportion of variable

EXHIBIT 2

M AND H COMPANY (B)

B–PO–1	$355,230.92	B–PA–1	$206,261.48
Less B–PO–2	107,621.19	Less B–PA–2	72,305.19
Equals B–PO–3	247,609.73	Equals B–PA–3	133,956.29
Less B–PO–4A	96,155.16	Less B–PA–4A	32,343.98
Less B–PO–4B	89,651.49	Less B–PA–4B	51,502.33
Equals B–PO–5	61,803.08	Equals B–PA–5	50,109.98

B–C–1	$81,361.56
Less B–C–2	54,718.73
Equals B–C–3	26,642.83
Less B–C–4A	—
Less B–C–4B	2,299,83
Less B–C–5	24,343.00

D–PO–1	$99,898.50	D–PA–1	$23,318.21
Less D–PO–2	40,619.18	Less D–PA–2	3,866.94
Equals D–PO–3	59,279.32	Equals D–PA–3	19,451.27
Less D–PO–4A	13,608.73	Less D–PA–4A	4,068.32
Less D–PO–4B	15,937.68	Less D–PA–4B	5,517.93
Equals D–PO–5	29,732.91	Equals D–PA–5	9,865.02

D–C–1	$14,514.51
Less D–C–2	9,883.79
Equals D–C–3	4,630.72
Less D–C–4A	—
Less D–C–4B	591.66
Equals D–C–5	4,039.06

Total Boonville contribution to local and company overhead and profits ($61,803.08 + $50,109.98 + $24,343.00)	$136,256.06
Less B–OH (Boonville overhead)	89,482.10
Equals B–6 (Boonville contribution to company overhead and profits)	$ 46,773.96

Total Dorchester contribution to local and company overhead and profits ($29,732.91 + $9,865.02 + $4,039.06)	$ 43,636.99
Less D–OH (Dorchester overhead)	31,011.46
Equals D–6 (Dorchester contribution to company overhead and profits)	$ 12,625.53

Total contribution to company overhead & profits	$ 59,399.49
Less O (Company-wide overhead)	100,011.60
Equals company's loss	(40,611.11)

costs will rise, with a reduction in the P/V ratio. Thus, a completely accurate drawing of the charts would show a kink in the P/V ratio line somewhere beyond the present level of sales. This error is probably not serious—it might reduce the ratio from .70 to .65 beyond the sales level of $420,000 (or something of that magnitude).

Which of the three Boonville departments is the most profitable? The paint

EXHIBIT 3

M AND H COMPANY (B)
(P/V [break-even] chart, Boonville poster department—
July through December, 1967)

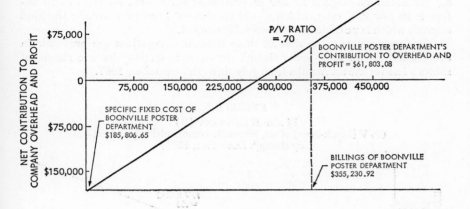

department made the largest contribution in ratio to its revenue in the six months under study. (See Exhibit 4.) The contribution of $50,109.98 on sales of $206,261.48 appears to be more favorable than the poster department's contribution of $61,803.08 on revenues of $355,230.92. This comparison is misleading, however. The results for the poster department are for its poorest six months. It will make a much larger contribution in the other six months, while the paint department will remain relatively stable. In addition, the

EXHIBIT 4

M AND H COMPANY (B)
(P/V [break-even] chart, Boonville paint department—
July through December, 1967)

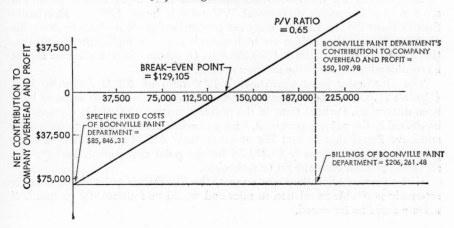

poster department's P/V ratio is somewhat higher, which means that its contribution will respond rapidly to sales increases.

The Boonville commercial department's high ratio of contribution to sales certainly indicates that it is a desirable adjunct of the business. (See Exhibit 5.) Its main advantage is its low proportion of fixed costs. Its main disadvantage is its low P/V ratio, which would preclude it from ever making the kind of profit which is possible in the poster department.

The fact appears to be that all three Boonville operations are profitable in every sense of the word—even though the overall company income statement shows a loss for the six months from July through December, 1967.

EXHIBIT 5

M and H Company (B)
(P/V [break-even] chart, Boonville commercial department—
July through December, 1967)

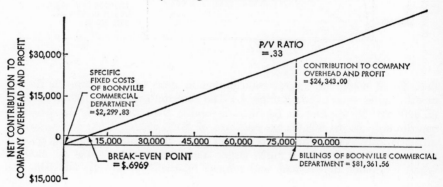

Break-even charts: Dorchester

The analysis for the Dorchester operations runs along similar lines. For some reason the poster department P/V ratio is lower (.59) in Dorchester than in Boonville—its variable costs are proportionally higher than in Boonville (Exhibit 6). But the billings are high enough to give a high ratio of contribution ($29,732.91) to billings ($99,898.50). Of course, the contribution should be considerably higher in the summer months.

The Dorchester paint department's P/V ratio of .83 is extremely high (Exhibit 7). One wonders whether all the variable costs for this segment have been discovered. Perhaps some of the poster department's variable costs should be shifted to the paint department. I have checked over the original worksheets and have found that M and H's accounts show $12,714.21 of labor for the poster department but only $1,181.56 for the paint department. Perhaps this allocation of labor costs should be rechecked.

If the present allocations are correct, the Dorchester paint department is extremely profitable in relation to sales and would be fantastically profitable if volume could be increased.

EXHIBIT 6

M and H Company (B)

(P/V [break-even] chart, Dorchester poster department—
July through December, 1967)

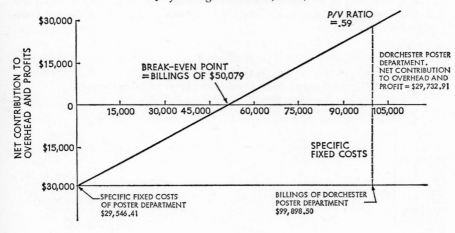

EXHIBIT 7

M and H Company (B)

(P/V [break-even] chart, Dorchester paint department—
July through December, 1967)

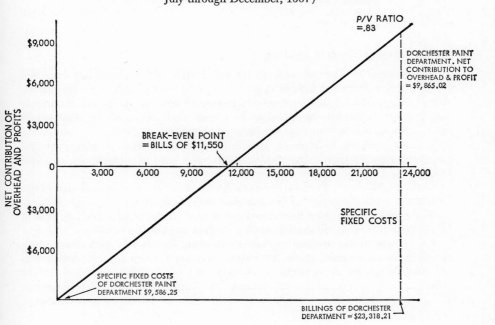

The Dorchester commercial department also makes a satisfactory contribution to overhead and profit (Exhibit 8). In this case the contribution results from the high volume in relation to fixed costs rather than to the P/V ratio which is relatively low. The low P/V ratio of .32 results, of course, from the fact that commercial work takes proportionally more labor and materials (outright sales cost).

EXHIBIT 8

M AND H COMPANY (B)

(P/V [break-even] chart, Dorchester commercial department—
July through December, 1967)

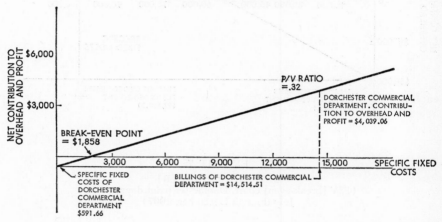

Future marginal income reports

I have tried to think of methods by which the analysis could be simplified so that future marginal income reports could be constructed with less effort. Accountants often use shortcuts which assume all costs of one type are variable and of another type are fixed, and so on. I think that such simplifications would not be appropriate in your business for several reasons:

1. It is desirable to separate specific fixed costs from local overhead and company-wide overhead. It is unlikely that any simple formula will do this exactly.

2. Costs which are fixed in one period may become variable and vice versa. Therefore a periodic review of the classification is desirable.

3. As you change your business—buying new property and perhaps selling off old property—you will need flexibility in changing the classification.

I am returning the original worksheets showing the classification of accounts. It will serve as a useful guide for future marginal income reports. But it will not provide automatic answers to all problems of classification which might arise.

(S) ⸻

Consultant

1. *What is the purpose of separating sunk fixed costs from escapable fixed costs? What is the meaning of these terms? How is this breakdown relevant?*
2. *What is the meaning of the term "specific fixed costs" as used in the consultant's report?*
3. *Would an overall break-even chart for the company as a whole serve the purpose just as well as the individual P/V charts?*
4. *What is the meaning and significance of the break-even points shown on the P/V charts?*
5. *Three types of "contribution" are shown in Exhibit 2. What is the significance of each?*
6. *What purposes could be served by this type of analysis?*
7. *What are the limitations of this type of analysis?*

JANET LEE'S DEPARTMENT STORE*

Janet Lee's store was a moderately small department store, with annual sales of $5,000,000. The store was organized into 60 departments, each of which is expected to contribute to the profitability of the entire operation. The merchandise ranged from candles and ready-to-wear goods to home furnishings and heavy appliances.

In the years from 1958 to 1961, the managers of the store had read and heard a great deal about a new system of accounting for retail stores, Merchandise Management Accounting. They doubted that this system would be suited to their business. They used the Contribution Plan Accounting system, and saw no reason to change it. In any case, management made little use of the accounts for the analysis of alternatives in decision making. The managers believed that the successful operation of a department store depended on the accumulated knowledge and subjective judgment of store officials and that no programmed system of data collection could be very helpful. The managers admitted that they did not always understand the information provided by their present system of accounting and that much of this information was probably irrelevant for decisions. However, the accounting system was important for indicating areas which require management's attention.

The present accounting system

The Contribution Plan Accounting system used by the store accumulated and recorded expenses of the individual departments. Exhibit 1 illustrates a standard department statement. The top part of the statement shows the computation of the cost of sales and the gross margin for the department. The next section shows the so-called direct expenses, which are the expenses that were attributable directly to the department. For

---

* This case was prepared by W. W. Haynes and J. L. Gibson of the University of Kentucky as a basis for class discussion. It is a synthesis of the situations in several stores rather than a case based on a single store. All names are disguised.

EXHIBIT 1
DEPARTMENT STATEMENT
Merchandise Statement

1. Inventory at cost—First of period
2. Merchandise received at invoice cost
3. Transportation cost ($\% = 3 \div 2$)
4. Transfers at cost ($+$ in, $-$ out)
5.   Cumulative cost ($\% = 5 \div 10$ for year)
6. Inventory at retail—First of period
7. Merchandise rec'd at retail ($\% = 2 \div 7$ from 100%)
8. Additional markups, less cancellations
9. Transfers at retail ($+$ in, $-$ out)
10.   Cumulative retail (markon $\% = 5 \div 10$ from 100%)
11. Gross sales
12. Less returns ($\% = 12 \div 11$)
13.   Net sales
14. Markdowns, less cancellations ($\% = 14 \div 13$)
15. Employee discounts ($\% = 15 \div 13$)
16. Shrinkage—Estimated or actual ($\% = 16 \div 13$)
17.   Total retail deductions (13 to 16 incl.)
18. Inventory at retail—End of period ($10 - 17$)
19. Inventory at cost—End of period ($18 \times \%\,5$ yr. to date)
20.   Gross cost of goods sold ($5 - 19$) ($\% = 20 \div 13$)
21. Cash discounts on merchandise ($\% = 21 \div 13$)
22. Net cost of goods sold ($20 - 21$) ($\% = 22 \div 13$)
23.   Workroom and other costs ($+$ or $-$) ($\% = 23 \div 13$)
24. Total cost of sales ($22 +$ or $- 23$) ($\% = 24 \div 13$)
25.   Gross margin ($13 - 24$) ($\% = 25 \div 13$)

Expense Statement

Direct—Fixed plant and equipment charges
Newspaper space costs
Other direct advertising
Buying salaries
Other direct buying
Selling salaries
Delivery—Prorate (sales)
Other direct
Interest expense (.5% on inventory investment)
Travel
Total direct (also as % of 13)
Indirect—Administrative
Occupancy
Handling
Publicity
Buying
Selling
Total indirect (also as % of 13)
Total expenses (direct and indirect) (also as % of 13)
Net profit (gross margin—total expenses) (also as % of 13)

example, the item "fixed plant and equipment charges" refers to depreciation on such furnishings as display counters in the particular department. Therefore, the expression "direct expense" in this store did not necessarily mean "variable expense," for some of the expenses were fixed in the short run. The item "delivery expense" was included among the direct expenses, even though it was prorated on the basis of sales.

The sections of the report discussed so far provided two important percentages: (1) the gross margin as a percentage of net sales; and (2) the direct expenses also as a percentage of net sales. Subtracting (2) from (1) gave the "contribution" of the department to the indirect expenses and profit.

The last section of Exhibit 1, called the "indirect expenses," involved such items of administrative costs, occupancy, publicity, and indirect buying and selling expenses. These expenses were obtained by prorating the company-wide expenses to each department on the bases shown in Exhibit 2. Deduction of the indirect expenses plus the direct expenses from the gross margin resulted in the net profit for the department. This figure, like the others, appeared both in dollars and percentages and could be compared with similar figures for other departments. In addition, trade association literature included average percentages of similar stores which could be used for comparison.

EXHIBIT 2

BASES FOR ALLOCATING INDIRECT EXPENSES

Expense	*Bases for Allocating**
Administrative offices	Sales
Sales audit branch	Sales transactions
Personnel division	Average number of employees
Store maintenance	Area occupied
Buying and stock control	Purchases
Advertising	Sales
Credit branch	Credit transactions
Accounts payable branch	Number of invoices
Plant and equipment	Dollar value of space occupied
Heat, light, and water	Area occupied
Window display	Space points used
Institutional advertising	Radio time used
Receiving, checking, marking	Invoices handled
Contributions	Equally to all departments

* Expense distributions are made according to suggestions of *Standard Expense Center Accounting Manual*, NRMA, 1954.

Merchandise management accounting

In the late 1950's several experts on accounting for retail stores developed a more elaborate system called Merchandise Management Accounting—M.M.A. Some writers claim that this is an inappropriate title for an accounting system which aims at providing information for decisions in the future rather than the recording of historical data. One critic suggests that a more appropriate name might be *Merchandising Cost Analysis* or *Controllable Profit Merchandising*.

The central tool of M.M.A. is the cost pattern. In theory such a pattern might be constructed for each commodity carried by the store; in practice it may be desirable to combine some items to reduce the amount of record keeping. It is possible to maintain the system by departments rather than by commodities, reducing the cost of the system with a loss of detailed information. But one of the objectives of M.M.A. is to give more attention to individual items rather than to treat departments as homogeneous units.

Exhibit 3, taken from an article by one of the developers of M.M.A.,[1]

EXHIBIT 3
MAJOR APPLIANCE DEPARTMENT
(variable cost centers—unit computations)

Receiving	$ .37	$ .50	$ .65	$ .78	$ .92
Warehousing	$ .75	$1.19	$1.45	$1.80	$2.25
Selling	6.0%	...	...	...	...
Advertising	2.5%	...	...	...	...
Carrying charges	(1.05%)	(1.95%)	(2.75%)	(3.77%)	(4.90%)	(8.25%)
Credit expense	$1.35	$1.60	$2.00	$2.40	$2.90	$4.25
Delivery	$1.40	$2.20	$2.95	$3.63	$4.40	$5.10
Installation	$3.50	$5.10	$5.50	$6.40	$7.25	...*
Warranty	$ .75	$1.20	$1.82	$2.10	$2.95	$5.25
Markdowns	3.50%	4.00%	4.50%	10.00%	...	...
Other costs	.70%	.90%	1.17%	...	...	...

* Customer pays.

illustrates a hypothetical cost pattern on one item in a major appliance department. The cost of receiving this item was estimated at $.65 per unit, and the cost of warehousing at $1.45 per unit. Some costs vary with dollar sales rather than with physical volume and are thus shown as percentages; illustrations are selling (if salesmen are paid on a percentage commission) and markdowns. The other cost estimates may be read from the chart.

Some duplication of cost patterns would exist within a department. There might be only 12 basic patterns in an appliance department because of similarities in items. This fact reduces the amount of record keeping.

Exhibit 4, also taken from Jones' article shows how one might use

---

[1] Robert I. Jones, "Merchandise Management Accounting in Practice," Arthur Andersen & Co., 1957.

EXHIBIT 4

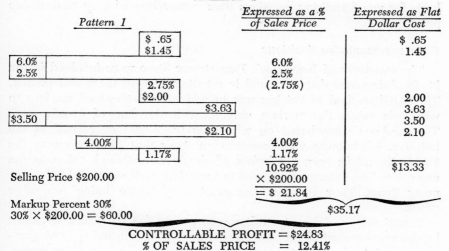

	Pattern 1	Expressed as a % of Sales Price	Expressed as Flat Dollar Cost
	$ .65		$ .65
	$1.45		1.45
6.0%		6.0%	
2.5%		2.5%	
	2.75%	(2.75%)	
	$2.00		2.00
	$3.63		3.63
$3.50			3.50
	$2.10		2.10
4.00%		4.00%	
	1.17%	1.17%	
		10.92%	$13.33
Selling Price $200.00		× $200.00	
		= $ 21.84	

Markup Percent 30%
30% × $200.00 = $60.00 $35.17

CONTROLLABLE PROFIT = $24.83
% OF SALES PRICE   = 12.41%

the cost pattern on an appliance with a $200 selling price. Some of the expenses are expressed as percentages of the $200, others as "flat" dollar costs. The markup on the retail price of 30 percent ($60) can then be compared with the expenses obtained from the cost pattern of $35.17, leaving a "controllable profit" of $24.83.

Mr. Jones suggests a number of ways in which the cost patterns would be useful. The analysis (1) could indicate the effects on profit contribution of an increase in markup, or of carrying a more expensive item with the same markup; (2) could be useful in negotiating cost prices with suppliers by indicating the profit contribution on each individual item; (3) could aid in the analysis of alternative methods of buying (direct shipment versus warehouse handling, for example); (4) could indicate which items might receive more sales emphasis because of their high profit contributions; (5) could suggest areas in which handling costs are excessive, stimulating investigation of why such costs are out of line; and (6) could lead to elimination or reduction of some services. In fact, any decision requiring consideration of variable costs could be aided by the information developed by this system.

One additional refinement in M.M.A. is the computation of the return on invested capital. Exhibit 5 shows how the controllable profit may be converted into percentage returns, depending on the inventory turnover rate. For example, the 12.41 percent of sales price on the $200 appliance in Exhibit 4 would provide a 20.9 percent (actually slightly higher) return on investment if the turnover were four times per year. The comparison of returns on investment provides a sounder basis for merchandising decisions than comparison of only controllable profit.

Some representative decisions

The managers of Janet Lee's Department Store were involved in the kinds of decisions that are usual in retailing. One of these was pricing. The usual method of pricing was to add a predetermined markup to wholesale price, the markup varying with the line of merchandise. The markups were based on what was traditional or normal in the industry. Markdowns were common on items that did not move; the final price might even fall below wholesale cost, though this was the exception. The managers adhered to manufacturers' suggested prices on many items. They followed the practice of "price lining" on other goods.

Sometimes special cost studies were made for particular decisions by the management of the store. For example, an unusual type of glassware was introduced in the store; the managers had no previous experience with such merchandise. They estimated the incremental costs of handling the glassware, finding that delivery expense would be unusually large. On the basis of the cost estimates, a price was initiated and a small bonus was paid to sales clerks whose customers carried the glassware out of the store rather than have it delivered.

Another kind of decision problem was the opening and closing of a department or the change of its location. One example was the candies department, which in 1957 was located on the main floor. The managers believed that more profitable items could be located in that space and moved the candy counter to the basement. Later the store made an agreement with a national firm which handles high quality, high price candies to carry its merchandise on the main floor. The national firm guaranteed the sale of the candy, agreeing to take back all unsold candy. It also agreed to pay 50 percent of the advertising cost. The manufacturer's representative prepared a "profitability study" which compared the costs and revenue of the candies with that of the merchandise then occupying the space. This study was instrumental in persuading the management to invest in the required refrigerator cases and to move the candy department back to the first floor.

1. *Would Janet Lee's Department Store benefit from introduction of M.M.A.?*
2. *Should the store make greater use of accounting in decision making?*
3. *What are the deficiencies of the present accounting methods used in the store?*
4. *Discuss the bases of indirect expenses allocation shown in Exhibit 2.*
5. *Evaluate the cost pattern used in M.M.A. Does it give an estimate of incremental cost? Should it do so?*
6. *Does M.M.A. give all the information required for pricing?*

EXHIBIT 5

Conversion Table of Controllable Profit to Return on Total Investment

Controllable Profit as a Percent of Cost	Return on Total Investment at Indicated Inventory Turnover Rates									Each Turnover of .1 Equals
	2	3	4	5	6	7	8	9	10	
2%	1.7 %	2.6 %	3.5 %	4.3 %	5.2 %	6.1 %	7.0 %	7.8 %	8.7 %	.09%
4	3.5	5.2	7.0	8.7	10.4	12.2	13.9	15.7	17.4	.17
6	5.2	7.8	10.4	13.0	15.7	18.3	20.9	23.5	26.1	.26
8	7.0	10.4	13.9	17.4	20.9	24.3	27.8	31.3	34.8	.35
10	8.7	13.0	17.4	21.7	26.1	30.4	34.8	39.1	43.5	.44
12	10.4	15.7	20.9	26.1	31.3	36.5	41.7	47.0	52.2	.52
14	12.2	18.3	24.3	30.4	36.5	42.6	48.7	54.8	60.9	.61
16	13.9	20.9	27.8	34.8	41.7	48.7	55.7	62.6	69.6	.70
18	15.7	23.5	31.3	39.1	47.0	54.8	62.6	70.4	78.3	.78
20	17.4	26.1	34.8	43.5	52.2	60.9	69.6	78.3	87.0	.87
24	20.9	31.3	41.7	52.2	62.6	73.0	83.5	93.9	104.3	1.04
28	24.3	36.5	48.7	60.9	73.0	85.2	97.4	109.6	121.7	1.22
32	27.8	41.7	55.7	69.6	83.5	97.4	111.3	125.2	139.1	1.39
36	31.3	47.0	62.6	78.3	93.9	109.6	125.2	140.9	156.5	1.57
40	34.8	52.2	69.6	87.0	104.3	121.7	139.1	156.5	173.9	1.74
44	38.3	57.4	76.5	95.7	114.8	133.9	153.0	172.2	191.3	1.91
48	41.7	62.6	83.5	104.3	125.2	146.1	167.0	187.8	208.7	2.09
Each 1% of cost equals	.87%	1.30%	1.74%	2.17%	2.61%	3.04%	3.48%	3.91%	4.35%	

This table, together with the preceding table, gives an evaluation of item profitability in terms of controllable profit return on total investment. For instance, by reference to the preceding table, it is found that a $100 item with a 50 percent markup earns $18 controllable profit or a return of 36 percent on the merchandise cost. From this table, it is found that the item which earns 36 percent on merchandise cost (assuming a stock turn of 5) returns 78.3 percent on total investment. For illustrative purposes, this table is based upon a "total investment to inventory" ratio of 230 per cent. This ratio of 230 percent is the average relationship for a number of large retailers for 1956.

Source: Robert I. Jones, "Objective and Basic Principles of M.M.A.," Journal of Retailing, Spring, 1958, p. 4.

DIRECT COSTING*

One of the most controversial issues in the accounting profession in recent years has been that concerning direct costing. The concept of direct costing was first developed in 1936 but was not placed into use in many firms until the 1950's. A survey in 1953 revealed only 17 companies using the method; by 1962 the number had increased to over 250.[1]

The controversy over direct costing has centered on two major issues: the measurement of period income for purposes of financial accounting; and the use of accounting data in decision making. This case is more concerned with the decision-making aspects since they are closer to the subject matter of managerial economics.

The measurement of income

The advocates of direct costing like to think of costs as falling into two categories: direct costs and period costs. The direct costs are those which vary with volume; the period costs are constant for a given period. The main effect of direct costing in the area of financial accounting is on the valuation of inventory. A change in the valuation of inventory means a change in the reporting of period income. Direct costing would eliminate the allocation of fixed overhead costs to inventory which is characteristic of absorption accounting. In periods of excess production over sales, the effect would be to avoid including overhead in inventory values and thus to prevent the "overstatement" of income. In periods when sales exceed production, the effect is to prevent the "understatement" of income.

An illustration from an article in *Business Week*[2] on direct costing shows how standard absorption accounting might distort income. (See Exhibit 1.) In this case sales increased by 50 percent from January to February, but the absorption accounting system showed a profit of $2,000 in January and a loss of $5,000 in February. The reason for this was the inclusion of $6,000 of period costs in the January inventory—costs which were charged to the cost of sales in February. Direct costing resulted in a restatement of profits, with a $4,000 loss in January and a $1,000 profit in February. The supporters of direct costing would claim that the second result is more reasonable, since February is the kind of

---

* Most of this case is based on Wilmer Wright and Felix P. Kollaritsch, "A Management Consultant and a Professor of Accounting Look at the Concept of Direct Costing," *The Controller* (now known as *Financial Executive*), July, 1962, pp. 322–29, 354–57. The case is intended as an introduction to direct costing and to its relation to economic analysis. For a full discussion of the issues the reader is referred to texts on cost accounting and to research bulletins of the National Association of Accountants.

[1] *Business Week*, March 24, 1962, p. 46.

[2] "Direct Costing to the Rescue," *Business Week*, March 24, 1962, p. 45.

month which is profitable, while a long sequence of months like January could only lead to bankruptcy.

The advocates of absorption accounting would uphold the allocation of overheads to production. They insist that the production process involves a conversion not only of material and labor into the values of the product but also a conversion of overhead into such values. They argue that machines as well as labor produce values. It seems to them illogical that replacement of labor by machines should lead to a neglect of part of the conversion costs. According to one writer on the subject, "a product is the result of all expenditures made in its manufacture. In establishing accountability, the product should be charged with those expenses."[3] The same writer notes that it is possible to convert depreciation from a period cost to a direct cost by shifting from straight-line depreciation to unit production depreciation; it seems unreasonable to him that such an arbitrary change in costing should determine whether or not depreciation should enter into unit cost. He also notes that the shortening of the length of the accounting period results in a higher proportion of period costs—if the period is made short enough even wages become a period cost.

One strong argument against direct costing applies when inventories are deliberately built up in one period for sale in another period. It seems logical that a substantial part of the overhead should be deferred until the final sale of the product. Direct costing would not permit the deferment of overhead in the period of inventory build-up and thus, as shown in Exhibit 1, would avoid any recognition of the values in the

EXHIBIT 1

TWO METHODS OF MEASURING INCOME

1. *Standard Absorption Accounting*	*January*	*February*
Sales @ $10	$20,000	$30,000
Cost of sales @ $8 per unit	16,000	24,000
($5 direct cost plus $3 standard overhead)		
Unabsorbed "burden" or overhead	—	9,000
($12,000 minus $3 per unit produced)		
Gross profit	4,000	(3,000)*
Selling and administrative expenses	2,000	2,000
Net operating profit	2,000	(5,000)*

2. *Direct Costing*	*January*	*February*
Sales @ $10	$20,000	$30,000
Direct cost of sales @ $5	10,000	15,000
Gross profit	10,000	15,000
Overhead expenses	12,000	12,000
Selling and administrative expenses	2,000	2,000
Net operating profit	(4,000)*	1,000

* Loss.
SOURCE: *Business Week*, March 24, 1962, p. 45.

---

[3] Felix P. Kollaritsch, *op. cit.*, p. 325.

inventories other than the direct cost. It would seem important to determine the cause of excess production in any particular period. If the purpose of the excess production in one period is to provide for seasonally high levels of sales in the future the absorption of overhead would appear to be reasonable; values in the production period do exceed the direct costs and should be recognized on both the balance sheet and income statement. If, however, the excess production is due to an error of scheduling the absorption of overhead might seem improper.

The movement to direct costing for the reporting of income has been slowed by the opposition of the public accounting profession and by the requirements of the Securities and Exchange Commission. The Internal Revenue Service requires the use of full costs in the valuation of inventory for tax purposes. It seems unlikely that these agencies will soon change their opposition to direct costing for financial reporting.

Decision making

Even if one agrees that direct costing is not appropriate for the reporting of income, he may still recommend it for decision-making purposes. It is possible to adopt direct costing and then to convert the final figures to a full-cost basis in the financial reports.

The advocates of direct costing claim that it is better suited to providing data for decisions than is absorption accounting. For example, the system shows the effects of an increase in the volume of sales on costs and on profits. In combination with information about price-volume relationships, it indicates the effects of price change on profits. Wilmer Wright, one of the best-known consultants on direct costing, has contructed a comparison of direct costing and absorption costing for a single product (Model #1971) in the form of a table. (See Exhibit 2.) He claims that the information provided by direct costing is much more useful for profit planning, pricing, make-or-buy decisions, or for decisions on product mix. Note that Exhibit 2 shows that direct costing does not preclude the allocation of overhead (period costs). In fact the overhead is allocated in two parts: those costs which would be eliminated if the product line were dropped (specific period expense) and those which would continue on even if the line were dropped. The period costs are not allocated to particular units but are handled as totals.

Some accountants and other authorities deny that direct costing has these advantages. The Committee on Distribution Costs and Efficiency of the American Marketing Association had this to say:

> If all overhead is not absorbed, it will not be possible to show net profits by products or customer classes. Without these net profit figures, it is difficult to make full application of the results to management decisions.[4]

[4] The Committee on Distribution Costs and Efficiency, The American Marketing Association, "The Values and Uses of Distribution Cost Analysis," *Journal of Marketing,*

EXHIBIT 2

Cost Analysis—Model 1971
(direct costs)

	Dollars per Unit	Profit Plan
Planned volume—units		5,000
Net sales	$165.00	$825,000
Direct cost		
Material	$ 46.00	$230,000
Variable labor	45.50	227,500
Other direct expense	24.00	120,000
Total direct cost	$115.50	$577,500
Margin	$ 49.50	$247,500
Percent P/V	30%	30%
Specific period expense		150,000
Model contribution		$ 97,500
Allocated period expense		90,000
Operating profit		$ 7,500

Cost Analysis—Model 1971
(absorption costs)

	Dollars per Unit	Profit Plan
Planned volume—units		5,000
Net sales	$165.00	$825,000
Manufacturing cost		
Direct labor	$ 35.00	$175,000
Material	46.00	230,000
Manufacturing overhead	58.50	292,500
Total manufacturing cost	$139.50	$697,500
Gross profit	$ 25.50	$127,500
Percent	15.4%	15.4%
Selling and administrative costs	$ 24.00	$120,000
Operating profit	$ 1.50	$ 7,500

Source: Wilmer Wright and Felix P. Kollaritsch, "A Management Consultant and a Professor of Accounting Look at the Concept of Direct Costing," *The Controller* (now known as *Financial Executive*), July, 1962, p. 326.

One writer on the subject has argued that fully allocated costs are superior to direct costs in pricing. His argument is as follows:

If the full unit cost is not recovered in the price, production will be abandoned. . . . Intelligent pricing necessitates full unit cost information. The establishing of prices without the inclusion of the related pro rata fixed manufacturing expenses would appear to be unrealistic and complicated. *How much, for instance, should a regular price be set above the marginal cost? 10 percent, 20 percent, or more?* Without the knowledge of the pro rata fixed expenses applicable to a product, any price decision would be arbitrary and probably unsound. In pricing products, consideration should be given to the amount of capital invested in production facilities, particularly in the case of multiproduct plants where varying capital investments are needed for different products.[5]

The same author has also criticized the emphasis of direct costing on contribution margins in these words:

Under direct costing only those items which sell below their direct cost are considered actual loss items. The higher the contribution margin the more profitable is the item, say those who believe in direct costing—without further analysis of those fixed expenses originated with the production of the item. It is doubtful whether the true profitability of a product or department can be measured without first determining its corresponding fixed expenses. Contribution margins and profit are not synonymous. The product with the highest contribution margin could easily be responsible for the incurrence of fixed expenses far in excess of the returns that the price of this product yields above direct costs. On the other hand, a product with a small contribution margin might not only cover its direct fixed expenses but may also render a satisfactory profit. Under direct costing it would be possible for some truly profitable items to be neglected by management because of low contribution margins.[6]

Conclusion

The debate over direct costing has also gone into the issue of cost control, a subject which is of less interest in this case. The position in favor of direct costing can be summarized in the following quotation:

[I]t may be stated with little fear of contradiction that the use of direct costing will continue to grow because it meets the needs of operating executives for internal management accounting and at the same time can accommodate almost any requirement for external reporting. Controllers who have taken the lead in converting their accounting system to direct costing are extremely enthusiastic. They report that since the conversion operating people have been turning to them more and more for guidance before important decisions are made. Operating executives, on the other hand, report that their financial men have learned to talk in terms that nonaccounting people can understand.[7]

The position against direct costing has been summarized in the following statements:

Its effectiveness is limited to special purposes which cannot be considered as the primary functions of cost accounting.
The exclusion of fixed manufacturing expenses from inventories is unrealistic. Fixed expenses are as much a part of the creation of new values as are labor and material.

---

[5] Felix P. Kollaritsch, *op. cit.*, p. 329.
[6] *Ibid.*, p. 357.
[7] Wilmer Wright, *op. cit.*, p. 357.

Intelligent pricing and aggressive competition can only be exercised when complete information as to the cost of a product, product line, or department is available.

Profitability cannot be measured by the contribution margin.

Fixed costs are not best controlled in total, but rather in their relationship to the unit.

Simplifications, although a desirable objective in accounting, must be foregone where they lead to a distortion of facts or result in vagueness.[8]

1. *What production schedule is implicit in Exhibit 1? What number of units is produced in January? In February?*
   a) *Is this production schedule likely in actual business operations?*
   b) *Could such a schedule ever be a reasonable adaptation to conditions?*
   c) *Would it make any difference whether the excess production in January was deliberately planned for February sales or was a result of erroneous scheduling?*
2. *When is income or wealth created: at the time of production or at the time of sale? What bearing does this have on the issue of direct costing versus absorption accounting?*
3. *Would reported profit fluctuate more widely under direct costing or absorption accounting? Discuss.*
4. *Why might the U.S. Treasury oppose direct costing for tax purposes?*
5. *Is direct costing more useful and appropriate for income reporting or for decision making? Discuss.*
6. *Does direct costing bring the costs of idle capacity to the income statement more promptly than absorption accounting? Explain.*
7. *Do the advocates of direct costing maintain that fixed costs are unimportant?*
8. *Do you agree that profitability cannot be measured by the contribution margin? Does your answer depend upon whether it is short-run or long-run profitability which is under consideration?*
9. *Does direct costing lead to lower prices? Discuss.*
10. *Could direct costing lead to investment in unprofitable equipment and unprofitable products? Discuss.*
11. *What is your position on the direct costing controversy? Explain.*
12. *One writer has argued that instead of emphasizing direct costing or conventional costing, we should stress "relevant costing." (C. T. Horngren, Cost Accounting: A Managerial Emphasis, 1962.) What do you suppose he has in mind?*

FULGRAVE PRINTING COMPANY*

Mr. Prescott, President of the Fulgrave Printing Company, believed that few printers had an accurate method of determining the cost of an individual job. He felt that the result was price cutting and deteriora-

---

[8] Felix P. Kollaritsch, *op. cit.*, p. 357.

* This case was prepared by W. W. Haynes and J. L. Gibson of the University of Kentucky as the basis for class discussion. All names and locations have been disguised.

tion of industry profits, which in 1959 averaged 2½ percent of sales. The Fulgrave Printing Company had installed a modern cost system which combined forecasted and actual costs and developed data to serve as a basis for pricing. Mr. Prescott believed that other firms should adopt a similar system.

Background

The Fulgrave Printing Company, one of over 100 firms in a metropolitan area of over an 800,000 population, employed over 300 and was located in a modern air-conditioned plant. Competition was intense, though printers tended to specialize in particular kinds of work. On some kinds of printing the Fulgrave company competed with printers in other cities. The company was a "commercial printer," producing a wide variety of jobs, but avoiding short runs and small volumes that were of interest to smaller firms. Exhibit 1 illustrates the production process of job order print shops and is applicable to the Fulgrave Printing Company.

EXHIBIT 1

PRODUCTION FLOW DIAGRAM FOR JOB ORDER PRINTING

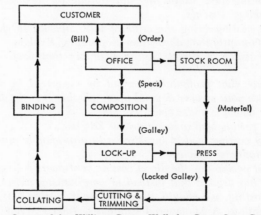

Suggested by William Green, *Wellesley Press, Inc., Case Study*, Harvard Business School, 1958.

The company's cost system: hourly machine rates

The budgeted cost system required the estimation of hourly machine costs for the coming period. The company accountants estimated total labor and overhead costs for the next year; they also estimated the volume of sales and the number of machine-hours required for those sales. These cost and hour estimates became the basis for the hourly machine rate on each machine, group of machines, or other cost centers in the plant. The hourly machine rates included overhead costs which were distributed to the various machines. Exhibit 2 shows how hourly costs were estimated for one press.

EXHIBIT 2

DETERMINATION OF HOURLY COST FOR VERTICAL PRESS

Investment: $10,000
Floor area: 300 square feet
52 weeks × 40 hours = 1 full-time man = 2,080 hours to be paid for
52 weeks × 40 hours = 2,080 maximum possible working hours
Less: 10 days vacation = 80 hours (10 days × 8 hours)
Less: 6 days holidays = 48 hours (6 days × 8 hours)
100 percent production = 2,080 hours − 128 hours = 1952 hours

1. Direct costs

Labor: 2 men at $1.75 × 2,080 hours	$ 7,280.00
F.O.A.B. Unemployment (percent of labor)	254.80
Workmen's compensation	21.84
Power (1,600 K.W.H. at $.04)	64.00
Depreciation (10% of investment)	1,000.00
Repairs (1% of investment)	100.00
Total direct costs	$ 8,720.64

2. Indirect costs

Rent (300 sq. ft. × $3)	$ 900.00
Insurance (½% of investment)	50.00
Taxes (1% of investment)	100.00
Administrative costs (80% of direct costs)	6,976.51
Total indirect costs	$ 8,026.51

3. Total cost for one year (next 12 months) $16,747.15

4. Hourly rates

100% production (1,952 hours)	$ 8.58
80% production (1,562 hours)	10.72
60% production (1,171 hours)	14.30
40% production (781 hours)	21.44
20% production (390 hours)	42.94

The budgeted cost system required 45 different hourly machine rates. These rates were sometimes revised during the year to bring them in line with actual experience. In theory the rates might be revised slightly every 60 or 90 days. In the 12 months preceding June, 1960, however, only ten rates had been revised. In June, 1960, itself, Mr. Green, the company vice-president, revised 14 additional rates. Mr. Green had the primary responsibility for rate revisions.

In the establishment of the hourly machine rates, seasonal fluctuations in sales were ignored. The objective was to set rates for the year as a whole. Mr. Green stated that it did not make sense for the company to set higher rates in the low season simply because the fixed costs had to be distributed over a smaller volume; nor was it reasonable to compute lower hourly machine rates in the peak seasons.

Costing individual jobs

The hourly machine rates were the chief but not the only factor in pricing individual jobs. In estimating the cost of a job, specialized estimators accumulated the costs on a job for each machine or other cost center through which it would pass. For this purpose time standards were required. In 1960 the company was engaged in estimating time standards on the basis of its own experience. Prior to this time it had relied on time standards or norms published by national agencies. Even when internal time standards were established, the company maintained records showing comparisons with the outside norms to see how its own experience measured up.

Thus the estimated cost in each cost center consisted of the time standard multiplied by the predetermined hourly cost. The full cost of the total job was the sum of such costs on every process used in the production of the order, plus the cost of materials. The charge for materials depended on the quantity used in the individual order. The company usually did not pass on to the customer any savings resulting from consolidating orders in the purchase of materials; quantity discounts were not passed on to the customer unless his order was large enough in itself to result in such a discount. An estimated price for a job is illustrated in Exhibit 3.

EXHIBIT 3*

PRICE ESTIMATE FOR AN INDIVIDUAL JOB

Materials (including the markup on materials)

1,000 sheets 17 × 22, 20 lb. white Howard Bond 50 lbs. @ $.30	$ 15.00
½ lb. Bronze blue ink @ $1.90	.95

Production

Composition—2 hours × $7.86 hourly cost	15.72
Lock-up—½ hour × $8.15 hourly cost	4.08
Press, vertical—5 hours × $10.72 hourly cost	53.60
Cutting—1 hour × $5.60 hourly cost	5.60
Total cost	$ 94.95
Markup on total cost (20%)	19.00
Selling price	$113.95

* This exhibit does not represent any actual job priced by the firm on which this case is based.

Pricing individual jobs

In principle the company followed the practice of pricing on the basis of full cost plus a predetermined markup. A special markup was applied to outside materials before their inclusion in the total cost of the work to which the profit markup was added. However, a certain amount of judgment entered into pricing; it was not merely a mechanical procedure. The authority over pricing was delegated to the sales department, though Mr. Green sometimes had an influence over pricing decisions.

The company officials believed firmly in pricing on the basis of full costs. They believed the failure of some companies to adhere to this practice accounted for the severe competition in the industry. In fact, they believed other pricing procedures were unethical and referred to price-cutters as "chiselers."

The predetermined markups varied from one category of business to another. The Fulgrave company divided its business into five categories, each with a different markup percentage as indicated by Exhibit 4.

EXHIBIT 4

MARKUP SCHEDULE*

Type of Job	Markup on Cost
Class #I: The first run of any job requiring speculative creative work. Any job requiring outside purchases of over 60 percent of the final price.	20 percent markup on outside materials plus 20 percent markup on the total cost including outside materials.
Class #II: Reruns of jobs originally in Class #I. First runs of jobs not requiring speculative creativity.	15 percent markup on outside materials plus 20 percent markup on total cost.
Class #III: Reruns of jobs originally in Class #II.	15–15 percent
Class #IV: Jobs which are a part of a total program and which will result in additional business.	10–15 percent
Class #V: Magazines and other special publications.	10–10 percent

* Although the job classes are those of Fulgrave Printing Company, the markups are hypothetical.

Company officials did not apply the markups mechanically. They used judgment in modifying the estimates. Sometimes the estimators themselves had an influence over the final price; they might estimate a low machine cost on a particular job because a fast worker would be assigned to it. Mr. Green, the vice-president, did not approve of this practice, which was based on the estimators' misunderstanding of company policy. He argued that the time standards on any job should be based on average performance, not on the speed of the particular employee who might work on a job. He believed that the sales force sometimes put pressure on the estimators to come up with low estimates. In some cases judgment on the part of the estimators was justified. For example, they might know that a particular customer's job would flow expeditiously through the plant and that a reduction in actual cost would result.

Higher markups on brokering

Class No. 1, with the highest markups, included what is known in the printing business as "brokering." This consisted of jobs which were produced largely on the outside, with only a minority of the work done by the Fulgrave company. Not all printing companies charged a higher markup on such jobs; in fact some companies reduced their markups to get such jobs. Mr. Green was certain that the Fulgrave policy was sound, even though the higher markup was applied to the entire job and not merely to the "value added." He gave the following reasons for this position:

1. Since brokering jobs require a relatively small amount of machine time, they absorb only a small amount of overhead. (As noted earlier, the overhead is allocated through the hourly machine rates.) A high markup was needed to assure that the sales commissions were covered.

2. Brokering jobs usually require more work on design and more special contact with the customer.

3. Brokering jobs are frequently speculative; an extra charge would help compensate for the extra risk.

Price competition versus nonprice competition

Mr. Green stated that a high proportion of printing costs were fixed for short-run changes in volume. For example, labor costs did not vary greatly in proportion to volume because of the difficulty of retaining printers if they were laid off during the lulls in business. Mr. Green estimated that only 45 or 50 percent of the costs were variable. He recognized that the low level of variable costs created a temptation to cut prices; in fact, this was one reason for the cutthroat competition in the industry. Nevertheless, the Fulgrave company resisted pricing below full cost. Mr. Green stated several reasons for this policy:

1. Prices below full cost depress the market and result in low industry profits. Such prices are unethical.

2. Regular customers might be offended by special prices on irregular business. They preferred to deal with a company with consistent and stable price policies.

3. While it might seem desirable to get "fill-in" business to make use of idle capacity, there was no assurance that the capacity would in fact be idle when the jobs were ready to be run. Delays in starting jobs were frequent and unpredictable. Low-price jobs might interfere with the flow of regular work.

Mr. Green also stated that if the volume of business were down for a considerable period, it would be possible to pare some of the so-called fixed costs. For example, the labor force would be contracted. It was true that other costs such as depreciation would run on anyway, but these were a small percentage of the total. The president of the company, Mr. Prescott, admitted that the company might have to adjust to competition if idle capacity became a serious problem. In the period of the 1940's and 1950's, however, there had been no prolonged periods of substantial idle capacity.

The company preferred to rely on nonprice competition to win customers. The company stressed good customer relations. For example, if a customer's order turned out to be for a larger volume than was originally intended, the company would pass on half of the savings in unit costs. Mr. Green believed that such a practice helped retain customers. Sometimes the company provided special services to the customer without charge. For example, Mr. Green spent part of his evenings doing editorial work on a customer's manuscript.

1. *Evaluate the hourly machine rates on the company's presses.*
2. *Should the hourly machine rates have been revised more frequently?*
3. *Should the hourly rates be higher, lower, or the same in low seasons?*
4. *Does the Fulgrave Printing Company engage in full-cost pricing? Discuss.*
5. *Is the company's pricing completely cost oriented?*
6. *Would the company be better off to transfer attention from hourly machine costs to incremental costs?*
7. *What is the significance of the high proportion of fixed costs in the company's operations?*
8. *Evaluate the reasons for not pricing below full cost.*
9. *The bottom part of Exhibit 2 indicates higher hourly costs the lower the production rate. Discuss the significance of this fact.*

THE MINERVA OXYGEN VENT VALVE*

In March, 1959, Mr. H. R. Deming, president of Dem-A-Lex Dynamics Corporation of Lexington, Mass., called a meeting of the executive committee to consider a proposal which would establish improved quality control over an item produced by Dem-A-Lex as subcontractor for several prime contractors. The item was an oxygen vent valve used in the "Minerva," a rocket powered missile.

This valve had been adopted by several large missile manufacturing companies during 1958 for use in the recently developed Minerva missile. In early 1959, however, the Department of Defense announced that the Minerva missile had been designated as an operational first line weapon and that all prime contractors of the Minerva missile were to enter crash production programs. Because of the increased urgency of the program and the importance of the oxygen vent valve to the Minerva's proper func-

---

* This case was prepared by Andrew McCosh under the direction of Stanley I. Buchin of the Harvard University Graduate School of Business Administration as a basis for classroom discussion rather than to illustrate either effective or ineffective handling of administrative situations. Copyright © 1965 by the President and Fellows of Harvard College. Used by specific permission.

tioning, an executive committee meeting had been called to consider a proposal, submitted by Mr. Massey, the company's production manager. Mr. Massey's proposal recommended the utilization of a newly introduced piece of testing equipment which would greatly reduce the number of defective vent valves delivered by Dem-A-Lex to the various prime contractors.

Company history

Mr. Deming, a graduate electromechanical engineer, had left his position with a large electrical products manufacturing company in 1948 and started a small research service organization in an Army surplus Quonset hut. He stated, "I had always wanted to tinker around with my own ideas and push them to completion, and when I saw the chance to obtain a research grant for the development of a high temperature pressure indicator, I couldn't resist the temptation to apply for the grant. I was completely fed up with all the red tape, required reports, and voluminous records associated with my previous job."

Since 1948, the company had grown rapidly and net sales in 1958 had exceeded $6 million (see Exhibits 1 and 2). As the company had expanded, Mr. Deming, considered by most of his associates as an inventive genius, decided to devote his time and energy to research and development of new products and had turned the actual operating management of the business over to his son Stephen Deming, a former Air Force jet pilot and a recent graduate of a well-known business school. Mr. Deming, Sr., had developed several unique and commercially saleable products since 1948, among which were: metal and fabric strain gauges which signaled a condition of overload on the material; special high pressure intensifiers and pressure transducers; solenoid triggered butterfly valves; ultralow temperature liquid pumps and flow regulators; high tension circuit breakers; and most recently the oxygen vent valve. Patents had initially been obtained on each of these items, but after a few years on the market, similar devices, but different enough to avoid patent infringement, had been developed by the larger manufacturing companies in the industry. Because of their size and volume production methods, these companies could generally produce the item more cheaply than could Dem-A-Lex.

As a result of this, Dem-A-Lex did not attempt to compete on a volume-price basis with the larger firms in the industry, but instead, exploited each product as fully as possible before the larger concerns developed a similar item. After the loss of the high volume customer to the larger producers, Dem-A-Lex then concentrated its efforts on modification and adaption of the item to the customer with unique or special requirements who could not obtain the special adaptation from the high

EXHIBIT 1

THE MINERVA OXYGEN VENT VALVE

(balance sheet as of December 31, 1958, in thousands of dollars)

ASSETS

Cash and marketable securities	$378	
Accounts receivable (net)	954	
Inventories	685	
Notes receivable (employees)	126	
Total current assets		$2,143
Land and buildings (net)	$360	
Machinery and equipment (net)	680	
Prepaid expenses	6	
Other assets	13	
Total fixed assets		1,059
Total assets		$3,202

LIABILITIES AND NET WORTH

Accounts payable	$250	
Notes payable to bank @ 6%	700	
Dividends payable	35	
Other accruals	315	
Total current liabilities		$1,300
Mortgage payable on real estate	$120	
Long-term bonds (7% coupon)	500	
Common stock (40% owned by		
Mr. Deming, Sr., and his son)	410	
Earned surplus	872	
Total fixed liabilities and net worth		1,902
Total liabilities and net worth		$3,202

volume producer, or whose requirements were too small to interest such a producer.

Flexible production scheduling and the ability of the research department to modify standard production models to meet unusual product specifications, had given Dem-A-Lex the ability to capture a specialized portion of the total market for most of its products. Mr. H. R. Deming commented, "We are not trying to butt heads with the big boys. Our policy is to sell our real assets—our research and development skills, and our productive flexibility."

Sale of vent valves accounted for nearly 25 percent of Dem-A-Lex's total sales during 1958, while the other 75 percent was made up of the sale of strain gauges, pressure gauges, intensifiers, and transducers, various types of electrically and hydraulically operated valves, regulators, circuit breakers, and other electrical and mechanical devices. Sales revenue from these items had been increasing at an annual rate of 8 percent since 1951. All of these items were manufactured in the general produc-

EXHIBIT 2

THE MINERVA OXYGEN VENT VALVE

(statement of profit and loss for year ending December 31, 1958,
in thousands of dollars)

Gross sales	$6,193	
Less allowances given for defective valves	143	
Net sales		$6,050
Cost of goods sold:		
Direct labor	$1,010	
Materials	2,030	
Factory burden	1,362	
Cost of goods sold		4,402
Gross profit		$1,648
Operating expenses:		
Selling expense*	332	
Administrative expense*	198	
Research expense*	350	
Interest expense	93	
Total operating expenses		$ 973
Net profits before tax		$ 675
Federal taxes (52%)		350
Net income after tax		$ 325
Dividends on common stock		30
Net addition to retained earnings		$ 295

* See Exhibit 3 for an analysis of this expense.

tion department with general purpose equipment, while the vent valve was produced in a separate department on specialized equipment. This specialized equipment had been purchased or built by Mr. Deming himself during 1957 and 1958 at a cost of about $525,000. However, Mr. Deming commented that if he had to replace all this equipment today by purchase from outside vendors, it would probably cost him over $950,000.

Oxygen vent valve

In November, 1956, Mr. H. R. Deming had begun work on the development of an improved oxygen vent valve. He had been motivated to experiment with this type of valve because of the high number of failures (nearly 60 percent defective) of valves which were then being used by missile producers. By January, 1958, he had designed a valve which was lighter in weight and more resistant to extreme temperature and pressure than any valve then on the market. A new missile designated the Minerva was also introduced in early 1958, and by coincidence

Dem-A-Lex's new vent valve met the missile's more rigid technical requirements. Because of this, Dem-A-Lex received subcontracts from several missile manufacturers to produce the oxygen vent valve for the Minerva missile.

The oxygen vent valve was a critical component to the proper functioning of any liquid rocket engine. A liquid rocket engine was basically a very simple mechanism. It consisted of a fuel tank, an oxygen tank, a pressure tank, a combustion chamber, and a number of valves for regulating the flow of material from the various tanks into the combustion chamber. Nitrogen gas from the pressure tank was used to force liquid oxygen and a liquid fuel (generally alcohol or kerosene and LOX) through propellent control valves into injector nozzles and thence into the combustion chamber where the mixture was ignited to provide the rocket's thrust.

Most missiles had four vent valves located on either side of the airframe just below the nose cone or warhead; the Minerva missile, however, had eight vent valves. In order to fill the oxygen tank these vent valves were opened and liquid oxygen at −220° F. was pumped into the oxygen tank through filler valves at the base of the tank until the tank was full. When the tank was completely filled, liquid oxygen spewed out the four vent valves in heavy white streams. These valves then had to be closed before the system could be pressurized. Pressurization was accomplished by pumping nitrogen gas through a second chamber of the oxygen vent valve into the oxygen tank. If the vent valves did not close (because of the very low temperature), all pressure would be lost, and no oxygen could be forced into the combustion chamber.

These valves had to withstand not only temperatures of −220° F., but also those of +500° F. generated by the missile in flight as well as the great pressure caused by the expansion of nitrogen gas as it was forced through the valve chamber into the oxygen tank. Mr. Deming had developed an alloy of beryllium and titanium, referred to as "Berylitt," which was designed to withstand both extreme temperature and pressure. Mr. Deming felt the vent valves had been quite successful because only 450 vent valves had proved defective out of the total 1958 sale of 1,500 valves. Previous valves had failed, on the average, 60 percent of the time.

Under the terms of various subcontracts which Dem-A-Lex held, the prime contractor was permitted to charge Dem-A-Lex $300 for each vent valve which was found defective. Of this, $250 was the cost of removing the defective valve from the missile and the installation of a new valve, while $50 was allowed for repairing the defective valve with parts supplied by Dem-A-Lex. These repair parts had cost Dem-A-Lex an average of $25 per defective valve in 1958 and had been charged to the burden account (Exhibit 4) by the accounting department, while the charge of $300 for each defective valve was recorded as a deduction from

EXHIBIT 3

THE MINERVA OXYGEN VENT VALVE

(analysis of selling, administrative, and research expenses
for year ending December 31, 1958, in thousands of dollars)

Selling expense
Advertising .... $ 33
Salesmen's salaries and commissions 251
Traveling expenses 24
Supplies 7
Heat, light and power (allocated on basis of floor space
    utilized by sales department) 2
Samples 13
Depreciation (allocated on basis of floor space
    utilized by sales department) 2

    Total Selling Expense $332

Administrative expense
Officers' salaries (included half of
    Mr. Deming, Sr.'s, salary) .... $ 62
Office wages 81
Office expenses 14
Legal and accounting 6
Telephone and telegraph 3
Miscellaneous expenses 7
Depreciation (allocated on basis of floor space
    utilized by the office. Also included direct depreciation
    computed on various articles of office equipment) 4
Bad debt losses 16
Heat, light, and power (allocated on basis of
    floor space utilized by the office) 5

    Total Administrative Expense $198

Research expense*
Officers' salaries (included half of Mr. Deming,
    Sr.'s, salary) .... $ 25
Laboratory supplies and expendable equipment 45
Depreciation (allocated on basis of floor
    space utilized by the research laboratory) 4
Heat, light, and power (allocated on basis of
    floor space utilized by the research
    laboratory) 4
Salaries of research personnel 186
Materials used in development of operational
    prototypes 79
Machinery and equipment depreciation 4
Liability insurance 3

    Total Research Expense $350

* During 1958, the research staff spent approximately 75%–80% of its time on the development and testing of an oxygen vent valve constructed of "Berylitt," a metal alloy recently perfected by Dem-A-Lex.

gross sales (Exhibit 2). Thus, each defective valve cost Dem-A-Lex an additional $325. Because of the urgency of the missile program, the prime contractor repaired the valves at the missile site, rather than sending them back to Dem-A-Lex for replacement.

EXHIBIT 4

THE MINERVA OXYGEN VALVE

(analysis of projected factory burden for fiscal 1959 in thousands of dollars)

	Budgeted for 1959 Assuming No Change in Production Procedures	Budgeted for 1959 Assuming Plating-Polish-ing Operation Added for 2,000 Vent Valves	Budgeted for* 1959 Assuming Testing Equip-ment Rented
Fringe benefits†	$ 354	$ 358	$ 359
Supervision	213	213	213
Inspection	147	150	149
Purchasing and receiving	123	128	128
Repair to tools and equipment	99	102	100
Clerical, trucking, and cleanup	90	90	90
Maintenance	43	43	48
Valve replacement parts	$ 17	$ 0	$ 5
Small tools	41	43	40
Spoiled work	69	65	67
Supplies	83	84	85
Department indirect	52	54	54
Heat, light and power	23	26	26
Test machine rental			24
Depreciation (allocated on basis of floor space utilized by the production facilities)	44	44	44
Total Factory Burden	$1,403	$1,400	$1,432

* These budgeted figures did not include any expected change in overhead costs associated with the addition of the plating-polishing process to the vent valve production operation.
† This item was composed of the cost of unemployment compensation, social security, a company sponsored health insurance plan, and vacation payments, for all direct and indirect labor. It averaged 20% of labor costs annually.

The standard price which Dem-A-Lex received for each oxygen vent valve was $975. The cost accounting department computed the factory cost of each vent valve as follows:

Direct materials		$139
Direct labor:		
Machining time	$175	
Assembly time	100	
Inspection and packaging time	25	
Total direct labor		$300
Overhead: 135% of direct labor		405
Total product cost per valve		$844

The 135 percent overhead rate was based on the relationship of overhead costs to direct labor costs in 1958 (Exhibit 2). The factory cost accountant itemized the costs charged to the factory burden account as shown in Exhibit 4.

Quality control of the oxygen vent valve

Dem-A-Lex, in early 1959, had no way of subjecting its vent valves to operational temperatures and pressure before the valve was assembled into the missile. Each component part of the valve was carefully inspected for size, required tolerances, and surface before assembly, and the assembled valve was hydraulically tested before shipment to the missile manufacturer, but this did not prevent valve failure when the rocket engine was statically fired at the launching site (a test firing with the missile securely fastened to its launching pad).

One of two types of failure might occur when the engine was statically fired; first, the valve might freeze in the open position due to the frigid temperature of the liquid oxygen, or second, after it was closed, a butterfly valve (inside the vent valve) might freeze in the closed position and as the nitrogen gas was forced into the chamber of the vent valve, pressure would build up until the vent valve ruptured thus depressurizing the oxygen tank. If either of the above conditions occurred, the valve had to be removed and rebuilt by the replacement of tension springs, the butterfly valve, and various pressure seals and diaphragms. Both types of valve failure were caused by a common factor, the expansion or contraction of the metal components in the valve as it was subjected to operational temperatures. Even the most accurate measurement of specified tolerances could not eliminate these failures, since the internal molecular structure of the metal in each valve was slightly different and thus each valve would be affected differently by the operational temperatures. Mr. Stephen Deming stated that it was much cheaper to have the prime contractor repair the defective valve than it was to junk it and that the cost of a valve failure ($300) charged by the prime contractor did not depend upon the type of defect that occurred. The subcontract did not permit the prime contractor to charge Dem-A-Lex $300 for the failure of a valve which had been rebuilt by the prime contractor. Thus, Dem-A-Lex could never be held financially responsible for more than one failure on each valve produced.

Mr. Stephen Deming pointed out, however, that the research department had developed a vanadium electroplating and polishing process which, if used, would guarantee that every vent valve would function perfectly. This process would eliminate all defects by reducing the expansion or contraction of any metal surface which had been treated with vanadium. The plating and polishing procedure would require $110 of material and three hours of labor at $3 per hour for each valve produced.

The company currently had excess capacity on the electroplating and polishing equipment located in the general production department and thus would not have to purchase additional equipment to perform this operation. However, there was no excess labor time available in the department, and Mr. Deming estimated that two or three new men would have to be hired to run the plating and polishing equipment. Mr. Massey stated that this equipment was currently being used by the general production department about 20 hours per week and that the processing of the vent valves on this equipment would consume another 14 to 15 hours per week, thus loading the equipment to nearly 90 percent of its total capacity. These pieces of machinery occupied approximately 800 square feet of the total factory space of 20,000 square feet and were being depreciated at the rate of $2,100 per year. This equipment would be fully depreciated by December 31, 1963. However, Mr. Deming, Sr. commented that he did not feel the additional cost was justified since he thought it was cheaper to "let your customers do your testing for you, and then all you have to do is pay for *just* those valves that have to be repaired. It's nonsense to incur the cost of plating when we don't have to!"

Mr. Massey, on the other hand, was in favor of renting a "revolutionary" piece of testing equipment which had just been put on the market. He had recently been approached by the National Machinery and Testing Equipment Co., of Zanesville, Indiana, about newly developed testing equipment which could be used to test each valve before its shipment to the prime contractor. Mr. Massey had loaned National Machinery 100 vent valves to test on this new equipment and had been told that 40 of these valves were defective while 60 were operationally perfect. The 60 valves which had tested "good" were especially marked and sent to one of the prime contractors by Dem-A-Lex. Later this prime contractor informed Dem-A-Lex that twelve of the valves which had tested "good" failed to operate and hence had to be rebuilt. The 40 vent valves which tested defective were sent to the general production department for electroplating and polishing. The National Machinery and Testing Co. stated that they could not guarantee complete accuracy in that a few valves which tested good would prove defective, while some which tested bad, would in fact be operationally perfect. However, the equipment was reliable in that it would produce consistent readings on successive tests for any given valve. Mr. Massey was very much in favor of renting the testing equipment because he stated "It's obvious that it's going to save us money. By testing the valves we had only 12 rejects in a hundred, while if these same valves had been shipped directly to the prime contractor we would have incurred the cost of making good on about 42 (30 + 12) rejects. Thus, you see, the testing equipment would reduce our number of rejects by 70 percent; this would mean a cash saving of $300 as well as a reduction in the cost of repair parts for each potential reject which could be detected before shipment."

The testing equipment would cost Dem-A-Lex $24,000 a year for rental, and this figure would be a flat rate. There would be no additional installation charge, and the shakedown testing that would be required would be done at the expense of National Machinery. Mr. Massey proposed that the testing equipment be installed in a room recently vacated by the office staff. "If we do this," he said "we won't have to charge any overhead to the testing operation, since the space was vacant anyway." The office staff had just recently moved to quarters (2,400 square feet) which rented for $250 per month, across the street from the factory in order that the supplies storeroom could be expanded for the purpose of increasing its operational efficiency. The space which was vacated by the office staff consisted of 2,000 square feet of the total factory area of 20,000 square feet. The valve department occupied approximately 5,000 square feet of the total factory area. However, expansion of the storeroom was not critical and thus could be delayed for an extended period of time. This testing equipment would require the addition of two men to the payroll who would operate and load the equipment as a team. Because of union regulations these men would not be permitted to perform any other operation in their slack time. These specially trained employees would be paid $3.50 per hour. The National Machinery and Testing Equipment Co. estimated that the testing equipment could handle 2,500 vent valves annually working a 40 hour week. The machinery was also capable of operating under overtime conditions. The period of the initial rental contract would be one year, though this could be extended at Dem-A-Lex's option. The company also estimated that an annual expense of $3,500 could be expected for normal maintenance of the testing equipment including bimonthly replacement of the freon gas used in the equipment. Mr. Massey had also been informed that National Machinery was working on an improved testing machine which would probably be put on the market in 1961 or 1962.

Neither Mr. H. R. Deming nor his son, Stephen, was at all convinced of the advisability of renting the special testing machine. Mr. H. R. Deming did not feel that the anticipated volume of vent valve production would be enough to justify the rental charge, and further was concerned over the possibility that one of the large manufacturing companies might develop an improved oxygen vent valve which would replace Dem-a-Lex's valve. However, since solid fuel rockets were expected to make their entrance by 1965, at which time the production of liquid fuel rockets would be drastically curtailed, Mr. Sears (sales manager) did not feel that any competitor would be interested in spending a lot of time and money developing an improved oxygen vent valve unless he was specifically requested to do so by a major prime contractor. He did not think that any competitor was working on an oxygen vent valve at that time, and he estimated it would take at least two years and $400,000 for a competitor to develop an improved valve. Mr. Sears further pointed out that the increased urgency of the missile program might encourage missile manufacturers to look elsewhere for more reliable vent valves, but he did not think this too likely as long as the number of defective valves did not exceed a "reasonable" level. Dem-A-Lex was well liked by its prime contractors and had built up good rapport with them in past associations. Mr. Sears estimated that 2,000 oxygen vent valves would be demanded annually through 1965. Because of the complexity of the vent valve and because of expected increases in labor and material costs, Mr. Sears could foresee no reason for the biannually negotiated price of the valve to fall below the current contract price of $975. All of Dem-A-Lex's vent valve two-year subcontracts came up for renewal in January to April, 1960.

Stephen Deming was not sure whether the rental of the testing equipment could be justified, but he felt very strongly that all vent valves should be vanadium plated and polished by the newly developed production process. He commented, "Why should we spend $2,000 a month on fancy testing equipment when all we really need to do to solve our problem is to just plate the valves on existing equipment with only a small additional cost per valve?"

After extensive discussion of each of the above points of view, Mr. Deming adjourned the executive committee meeting until the afternoon of the following day when he expected Mr. Swen's (the company controller) return from an out-of-town trip. He instructed Stephen Deming to fill Mr. Swen in on the discussion which had taken place at the committee meeting and to ask him to be prepared to submit his recommendations relative to quality control of the vent valve to the committee the following afternoon.

PART FOUR / Pricing

7 / Pricing

The best place to start a discussion of pricing is with price theory. This theory consists of abstract analysis which aims at the prediction of the effects of broad economic changes and the evaluation of social controls. The theory of price is more concerned with the allocation of a society's resources than it is with the formation of particular prices. It is too much to expect that tools that are useful for social economics would be exactly those suitable for managerial economics; managerial economics requires an adaptation of the analysis to meet the needs of the individual undertaking. Nevertheless the theory is a convenient starting point.

1. THE THEORY OF PRICE FROM THE VIEWPOINT OF THE INDIVIDUAL FIRM

The basic assumption of the theory is the desire of entrepreneurs to maximize profits. Another assumption, which may be removed in more complete models, is that the firm produces but one output. It is also assumed that the managers know the shapes and positions of their demand and cost functions. Under these conditions determination of the optimal price is complicated only by a variety of market structures.

Pure competition

In pure competition the firm can have no price policy. It must sell at the market price over which it has no control. The market price has a tendency to move to a position that will clear the market—that will equate the quantities sellers are willing to sell with quantities buyers are willing to buy. The process of moving towards such an equilibrium is one in which the individual firm participates but in which its influence

319

is insignificant. The demand curve facing the firm is horizontal. At the market price the firm can sell all it desires; at any higher price it can sell nothing.

Figure 7–1 illustrates the situation in pure competition. The demand curve (average revenue curve) is also the marginal revenue curve. The only decision to be made by the firm is one of determining the quantity to produce. Under the conditions that have been specified, the firm will produce the quantity that equates marginal cost with price. Up to this point an increase in output adds more to revenue than to cost. Beyond this point it adds more to cost than to revenue.

FIGURE 7–1

DEMAND AND COST CONDITIONS IN PURE COMPETITION

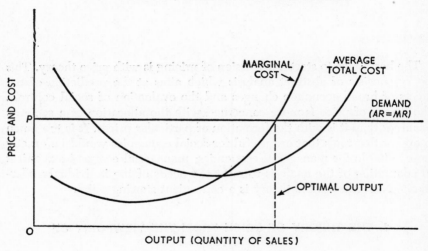

The price shown in Figure 7–1 is one permitting the firm to earn profits exceeding normal profit (the opportunity cost of capital). Figure 7–1 shows a short-run solution, for in the long run the excess profits will attract additional firms into the industry, and will encourage the existing firms to expand, thus exerting a downward pressure on price. In the long run, price tends to be equal to the minimum average cost of each firm. The firm would prefer the prices to be higher, but the forces determining price tend to squeeze out any excess profits.

Few firms operate under conditions of pure competition. The stock market and the market for grains approximate these conditions. The seller of a common stock on the New York Stock Exchange cannot hope to influence the price at which he sells. He can sell all he likes at the quoted price. It is true that a large corporation, like the American Telephone and Telegraph Company, is in somewhat a different position in floating a new issue of common stock, for the issue may be large enough to have an impact on the market. But this is the exception; in most cases the individual stock buyer or seller is at the mercy of the market. The problem of the stock speculator is to outguess the market rather than to manipulate price.

In a discussion of the price policy of the individual firm, the theory of pure competition has limited relevance; it does emphasize the impersonal market forces that play a role even under semimonopolistic conditions. The theory is useful in social economics, for it permits the kinds of broad prediction needed there, such as the effect of an excise tax, of price control, or of rationing. But a chapter on price policy must focus on the more usual market situations in which firms have some control over price.

Monopoly

The theory of monopoly is more pertinent in discussions of price policy, not because monopoly is prevalent but because the theory is a convenient starting point in dealing with more complex markets. In monopoly the demand curve slopes downward to the right, for it is the industry demand curve. The negative slope such as that shown in Figure 7–2 reflects the fact that purchasers take more at lower prices than at high. The marginal revenue curve lies below the demand (average revenue) curve, for reasons already developed. The way to maximize profits is to equate marginal revenue and marginal cost. The firm may

FIGURE 7–2

PRICE DETERMINATION UNDER CONDITIONS OF MONOPOLY

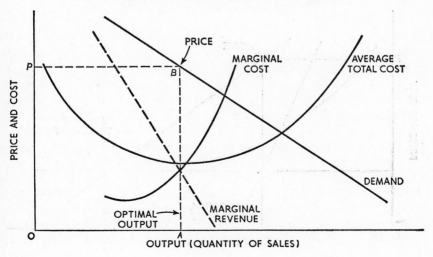

reach this position in two ways: it may throw onto the market the quantity *OA* which will sell at the price *AB;* or it may set the price at *AB* and let the buyers decide how much they will take at this price, which turns out to be quantity *OA.* In actual practice it is more usual for the firm to establish the price, and let the market set the quantity, than it is to let the market clear the quantity that is produced. In the "real world" the situation is more complex, for the firm does not know the exact position and shape of the demand curve. Furthermore it can manipulate the position of this curve through sales activity. Management must make simultaneous decisions on price and on promotional activity.

Under conditions of monopoly excess profits are probable, but not inevitable. Presumably barriers to the entry of new firms protect the position of the monopolist from an erosion of profits. If, however, the demand curve is tangent to the cost curve, the firm must remain content with normal profits (which are included in the average cost curve).

So far, the diagrams have shown the cost curves in their traditional U shapes. The chapter on costs presented evidence that the marginal cost curves are often horizontal, with a consequent decline in average costs over the whole range of outputs. Such a redrawing of the graph, as in Figure 7–3, does not change the theory, for the optimum is still at the point at which marginal cost equals marginal revenue. It is possible under such conditions that the optimal price is *below* the average cost, meaning that under no circumstances can the firm meet all of its costs. Such a situation would be a temporary, short-run phenomenon, for in the

FIGURE 7–3

PRICE DETERMINATION UNDER CONDITIONS OF MONOPOLY—CONSTANT
MARGINAL COSTS

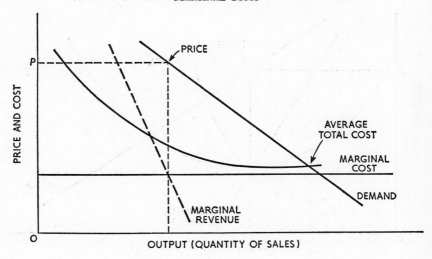

long run, the firm would choose to dissolve rather than to continue operating at a loss.

The theory of monopoly price like all theories, is a simplification. No firm has complete protection from the entry of substitutes. No firm has exact information on the position and shape of its demand curve. The theory of monopoly is therefore only a step in understanding pricing even in those industries in which the monopoly position is strong.

Monopolistic competition

Chamberlin's theory of monopolistic competition, which has become part of the orthodox theory of price since its formulation in the 1930's, starts by considering each firm a monopoly with a downward sloping demand curve and marginal revenue curve. The demand curve does not have a steep slope, for each product faces the competition of close substitutes. But differentiation of the product assures that the demand is not perfectly elastic, thus providing scope for price policy.

Where does competition enter into this theory? As already suggested, the competition of substitutes makes the demand curve more elastic than it would be otherwise. In addition, barriers to entry are absent, so that excess profits attract new competition, with a consequent long-run tendency for excess profits to diminish. Lastly, the firm faces such a large number of competitors that it ignores any impact its price policy may have on others, for its actions are imperceptible to competitors. The result is price competition that tends to wipe out excess profits despite the individual firm's control over price.

Rather than develop the intricacies of the theory of monopolistic competition (the reader may wish to read Chamberlin on the subject) it will suffice for our purposes to indicate the final equilibrium suggested by the theory. Figure 7–4 shows the long-run equilibrium for the individual firm, which cannot earn excess profits because of the entry of new competitors and because of price competition with close substitutes. Chamberlin did not insist that the equilibrium must necessarily be of the tangency variety shown in Figure 7–4, with zero excess profits. Discontinuities in the chain of substitutes, special advantages of patents and trademarks that cannot be wiped out completely by competition, may permit a situation as in Figure 7–5 in which the demand curve is not pushed completely back to a tangency with the cost curve. In any case, the firm equates marginal revenue and marginal cost, the only position consistent with the objective of maximizing profit.

The relevance of the theory of monopolistic competition is sometimes questioned. The tangency solution, with a long term tendency toward excess capacity, is disputed by some economists. We have already seen in earlier chapters on cost reasons for doubting that the cost curves will have the U-shape usually assumed in the theory. The theory in the usual

FIGURE 7–4

EQUILIBRIUM UNDER CONDITIONS OF MONOPOLISTIC COMPETITION

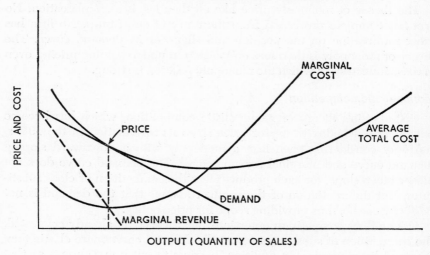

FIGURE 7–5

PRICE IN MONOPOLISTIC COMPETITION—NONTANGENCY CASE

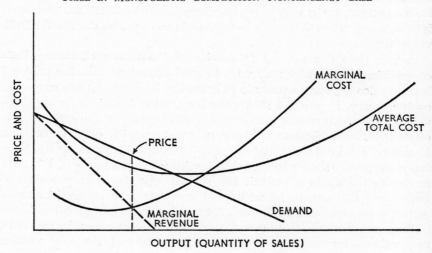

form is static and ignores the constant changes in product characteristics and shifts in marketing activity and competition which characterize markets for differentiated products. Most firms produce a line of products rather than the single product shown on the graphs. Many firms, rather than settling for a comfortable tangency equilibrium, appear to be engaged in a constant struggle to reduce excess capacity through marketing effort, through changes in the product mix, and through the introduction of new products.

Nevertheless, several features of the theory are clearly relevant. Most firms do face downward sloping demand curves; they can sell more at lower prices than higher ones. They have scope for price policy. Their products are differentiated from the products of competitors but substitutes are close enough to reduce or completely undermine monopoly positions. They may at times enjoy demand curves lying considerably above costs and leaving unusually high profits. But they face the constant erosion of profits by the entry of competitive products and by the marketing tactics of other firms. They are not perfect competitors with no control over price; but also they are not monopolists who can earn comfortable profits without facing competition.

Oligopoly

Oligopoly is a situation less amenable to broad theorizing. The complexity of the problem seems to preclude simple generalizations. Basically the problem is one of interdependence among the sellers. Any change in price on the part of one seller may set off a chain of reactions among other sellers. The decision maker will take into account the probability of such reactions.

The inadequacies of the kinked demand theory have already been discussed. But perhaps the kinked demand is the simplest way to bring out the essence of oligopoly pricing. Management must consider the probable repercussions to an increase or decrease in price. The firm is no longer so insignificant in the total picture that its decisions go unnoticed. Other firms will feel the impact of those decisions and may react. Each firm will consider potential reactions before changing price.

Rather than present a survey of the various theories of oligopoly, it might be better to list some patterns of behavior that have been observed in oligopolistic markets.

Price wars. In price wars each competitor shades price below that of the other, sometimes to the point that price falls below variable costs. Normally price wars are not planned but are a consequence of one firm cutting price and starting off a chain of reactions.

Price cuts to drive out competition. A financially strong firm, disliking the insecurity of oligopoly, may try to drive out competitors by deliberately cutting price. A classic example was the reduction of price on kerosene by John D. Rockefeller. In practice, this variety of behavior may be difficult to distinguish from the first.

Price leadership. One way of avoiding the unpleasantness of price retaliation is to develop a pattern of price leadership, in which competitors follow the price changes of one firm established as the traditional leader. Price leadership may take several forms: leadership by a dominant firm or barometric price leadership in which a smaller firm tries out a new price, which may or may not be confirmed by the larger firms.

Collusion. Another way of avoiding price retaliation is to agree formally on price or to divide up the market. Such arrangements convert oligopoly into monopoly, though there is always a risk of a firm breaking the agreement. Collusion is usually illegal under the antitrust laws but is still with us, as is evidenced by recent suits against manufacturers of electrical equipment.

Nonprice competition. Because of the dangers of price competition, the firms in oligopoly may prefer to compete in advertising, style, sales activity, brand names, and so on. No doubt competitors retaliate to such activity but presumably the danger of destructive competition is less.

Secret price concessions. It may be safer to engage in secret price concessions for selected customers than to reduce price openly, with the possibility of retaliation.

All past attempts to generalize such a variety of behavior have fallen short. This is true of the Stackleberg solution, which assumes that oligopolists explicitly recognize the interdependence of their actions, the kinked demand theory, which claims that the seller will distinguish the reactions to a price increase from those to a price decrease, or the theory of games, which tries to apply sophisticated mathematical models to oligopoly. These theories all provide insights into oligopoly behavior, but none can claim to be "the" theory of oligopoly.

Traditional theory: Its strengths and weaknesses

All of the foregoing theories of pricing behavior, with the possible exception of the theories of oligopoly, fall under the heading of marginalism. All of them assume an entrepreneur who weighs the penalties and rewards of price decisions. He compares the added gain and added cost of increasing output, or of changing price, and works toward the position at which the added gain and loss are equal. Such theories recognize that both cost and demand conditions do influence pricing. They portray the firm as adjusting to changes in market forces, revising price as demands shift or as costs change. They picture the manager, not as a simple-minded automaton who rigidly follows mechanical rules of thumb, but rather as a rational human being who can analyze the implications of changes in conditions. Throughout this book we accept the viewpoint of marginalism as a useful way of organizing one's thoughts about pricing decisions.

At the same time, the managerial economist must learn to distinguish between what the traditional theory can and cannot do. The theory suffers from serious limitations when it comes to the analysis of individual firm behavior.

1. The theory usually rests on the assumption of profit maximization. In the real world profit maximization is no doubt a primary objective, but research indicates clearly that entrepreneurs are guided by other motives. Some managers may be more interested in maximizing sales or increasing the market share than in profits. Some may strive for personal power or prestige. Many managers are guided by strong convictions of what is ethical and what is not. Managers of small firms often care a great deal about how the community reacts to their practices. Managers of large firms are often aware of their responsibilities to the public. The cynic may claim that the alleged ethical motives are merely rationalizations of long-run profit-making; that the managers are really trying to avoid costly antitrust suits or other forms of regulation; or that they are endeavoring to build up public goodwill which gradually reflects itself in increased demand. It is difficult to draw the line between profit-seeking and other goals, but there can be little doubt that some managers sacrifice profits, even long-run profits, to maintain policies they feel are fair and just.

Increasingly, the view of social scientists is that businesses do not and cannot take profit maximization as the single objective. Several writers like R. A. Lester, and R. A. Gordon challenged the profit maximization assumption in the 1940's, but the major attack on the assumption came in the 1950's and 1960's under the leadership of H. A. Simon and his associates at the Carnegie Institute of Technology (now Carnegie-Mellon). They have argued that the appropriate assumption is a goal of satisfactory profits which represent levels of managerial aspiration influenced by the organization and a variety of influences on management.[1] They would replace the profit maximization assumption with a more complex study of decision-making process, on organizational structure, on corporate strategies, and on decision rules.

2. The theory does not distinguish clearly between the long- and short-run effects of price change. Putting the matter in another way, traditional economic theory does not deal adequately with the dynamics of pricing. In particular, the theory has little to say about the effect of today's prices on future profits. The usual graphs for short-run pricing show today's demand curve (and marginal revenue curve) and today's cost curves (including the marginal cost curve) and suggest that the manager prices to equate marginal revenue and marginal cost. The manager may, however, try to consider the discounted effect of today's price on future revenues. If he wants to build up an image of a low-price outlet, he may avoid charging as much as the immediate market would permit, sacrificing current profits for future profits. The economic theorist

[1] Representative of the literature on the subject is J. G. March and H. A. Simon, *Organizations* (New York: John Wiley & Sons, Inc., 1958), and R. M. Cyert and J. G. March, *A Behavioral Theory of the Firm* (Englewood Cliffs, N.J.: Prentice-Hall, Inc., 1963).

has always known this to be the case, but the formal tools of analysis that he has developed do not usually deal with this problem explicitly.

3. The theory usually assumes a single-product firm. The real world is made up of firms producing several or many products. The theorist has good reasons for concentrating on the one-product case, but in managerial economics these reasons no longer dominate. The managerial economist must deal explicitly with the problem of the interdependence of products both in sales and in production.

4. The theory does not face up to the problem of uncertainty. As we have seen, economic theory usually assumes that the entrepreneur knows his demand and cost functions. In the world of business this is hardly ever the case. The tools for dealing with uncertainty are still under development. But whether or not the managerial economist makes formal use of the modern statistical and operations research techniques for dealing with uncertainty, he must take uncertainty into account.

5. The theory fails to view the firm as an organization in which pricing decisions are influenced by a variety of persons with varied objectives and motives. The information influencing prices comes from many directions: the firm's accounting system, the firm's sales forces, news about competitors' actions and plans, and various policies and decision rules established within the firm.[2]

In conclusion, the theory of pricing in the individual firm is an important step in the understanding of pricing. The managerial economist is, however, faced with the problem of bridging the gap between theory and practice, which means he must constantly check the relevance of theory against the actual facts with which he is working and must revise the analytical tools to meet the particular needs at hand.

Two shortcuts in pricing

The prescriptive literature on pricing sometimes contains two shortcuts that seem to bypass the difficulties of applying marginalism in the uncertain world of business. The better known of these alternatives is full-cost pricing; the other is "going rate" pricing. Each deserves attention as a possible way of simplifying the pricing problem; each has serious limitations.

Full-cost pricing. One difficulty in discussing full-cost pricing is the absence of a consistent definition of what it means. In this book full-cost pricing means pricing at a level covering total costs, including overhead, plus a predetermined markup. Sometimes the expression "cost plus" pricing is used to describe the same approach. But some of the literature uses these two terms to cover cases in which variable markups are added to full costs.

---

[2] These criticisms and others are reviewed in Cyert and March, *op. cit.*

The view that full-cost pricing must assure profitable business operations is widespread. Some writers and trade associations consider the approach to be the "scientific approach" to pricing, presumably because it substitutes a formula for subjective judgments. Other writers claim that the method is a reasonable way of dealing with uncertainty and ignorance. If the manager does not know the shape or position of his demand curve, he may find it convenient to adopt a method that does not require such knowledge. If he is strongly motivated by questions of fairness and justice in pricing, he may adopt a formula that treats all categories of customers alike at all times regardless of the particular conditions of the market. Full-cost pricing may help assure prices that are related to long-run cost in such a way as to discourage the entry of new competition into the industry. Lastly, full-cost pricing may, if adopted by all members of the industry, help protect the firms against price wars and cutthroat price competition, at the same time providing some flexibility in adjusting prices to cost changes.

It might be contended that the overhead allocations and profit mark-ups of full-cost pricing reflect a recognition of opportunity costs. They help assure that facilities are not allocated to products that fail to carry their share of the overhead and produce their share of the profit. If firms always operated at full capacity, and always with the same relation between demand and capacity, the logic of this argument would be more appealing. In the world of cyclical change, of seasonality in demand, of varying price elasticities, and of complementary relations in demand, it is difficult to see how full-cost pricing can assure anything approaching optimal profits.

The best way to point up the weaknesses of full-cost pricing is to contrast it with the marginalist theory of pricing already presented.

1. Marginalism describes firms as adjusting to conditions of demand. Full-cost pricing does not permit such adjustments.

2. Marginalism implies that marginal costs are the relevant costs. Full-cost pricing ignores marginal or incremental costs and uses average costs instead.

3. Marginalism recognizes that the nature of competition, or the structure of the market, is a major determinant of pricing behavior. The advocates of full-cost pricing usually ignore market structure.

In addition, it should be noted that full-cost pricing accepts the accountant's definition of costs, with its stress on original costs, with its questionable treatment of opportunity costs, and with its arbitrary allocations of overhead. It seems unlikely that a price formula based on an inflexible and (for economic purposes) an erroneous view of costs can lead to profitable operations.

This discussion of full-cost pricing does not state that the method is entirely without its merits. It does suggest, however, that the manager should consider carefully whether it meets the needs of his situation before accepting it as the sole answer to the pricing problem.

"Going rate" pricing.   Another shortcut to pricing, avoiding the effort of analysis, is to charge the "going rate." As is true of full-cost pricing, this approach is not necessarily unsound; in an oligopolistic price leadership situation it may be a reasonable way to stabilize prices. But analysis is necessary to indicate when such an approach to pricing is justified. The trouble with some of the literature on the subject is that it does not tell the manager when he should adopt the going rate and when he should make exceptions.

The distinction between "price takers" and "price makers" is related to the topic of going rate pricing. Some sellers—those who operate in highly competitive conditions approaching pure competition—cannot determine prices but must accept those established by relatively impersonal market forces. Such sellers are "price takers"—they must take prices which are given. Examples are sellers of shares in the stock market, farmers selling their crops, or those who sell basic commodities like tin, rubber or copper in world markets. The sellers with which we are mainly concerned in this chapter are "price makers"—those who have scope for discretion about prices. Since this book is concerned primarily with decision making, it inevitably focuses on enterprises which can make choices. Therefore, the remainder of this chapter will ignore "price takers" and "going rate pricing."

Empirical studies and illustrations

The major issue in research on pricing has been the extent to which practice has followed mechanical procedures such as full-cost pricing, or, alternatively, has followed the more flexible and more demand-oriented precepts of marginalism. The findings are mixed and still somewhat a matter of controversy.

The best-known questionnaire survey on pricing is that of R. L. Hall and C. J. Hitch, who were concerned primarily with oligopoly.[3] They found a great majority of the 38 covered firms applying a full-cost policy. Most of them started with direct cost, added a percentage to cover overhead, and then added another percentage for profit. Hall and Hitch suggest a variety of reasons for adoption of full-cost pricing, among which are considerations of "fairness," ignorance of demand, ignorance of potential reactions of competitors, the belief that the short-run elasticity of market demand is low, the belief that increased prices would encourage new entrants, and the administrative difficulties of a more flexible price

---

[3] R. L. Hall and C. J. Hitch, "Price Theory and Business Behaviour," *Oxford Economic Papers*, No. 2 (May, 1939), pp. 12, 18–22, 25–27, 29–33. Reprinted in T. Wilson and P. W. S. Andrews, *Oxford Studies in the Price Mechanism* (Oxford: Clarendon Press, 1951), pp. 107–38.

policy. Hall and Hitch use the kinked demand analysis to help explain full-cost pricing: this analysis emphasizes the belief that competitors follow a decrease in price, reducing the profitability of such decreases, but do not follow an increase. Hall and Hitch summarize their findings as follows:

1. A large proportion of businesses make no attempt to equate marginal revenue and marginal cost in the sense in which economists have asserted that this is typical behaviour.

2. An element of oligopoly is extremely common in markets for manufactured products; most businesses take into account in their pricing the probable reaction of competitors and potential competitors to their prices.

3. Where this element of oligopoly is present, and in many cases where it is absent, there is a strong tendency among businessmen to fix prices directly at a level which they regard as their "full cost."

4. Prices so fixed have a tendency to be stable. They will be changed if there is a significant change in wage or raw material costs, but not in response to moderate or temporary shifts in demand.

5. There is usually some element in the prices ruling at any time which can only be explained in the light of the history of the industry.[4]

The Hall and Hitch conclusions have come under attack. Critics have noted that the firms in the study varied margins from product to product; this suggests some attention to market forces. The critics have also suggested that an inability to measure marginal revenue and marginal cost precisely does not require an abandonment of marginalism, which must be interpreted to include subjective estimates and approaches to maximum profits by trial and error.

George J. Stigler's study of price statistics raises doubts about the kinked demand theory.[5] Stigler finds, for example, greater price stability in monopoly than in oligopoly, contrary to the implications of the kinked demand theory.

A study in the 1950's by James S. Earley lends support to marginalism.[6] Earley's study covers large firms which are claimed to be "excellently managed," and thus is not necessarily representative of practice in general. Earley finds that these firms are adopting accounting methods that move in the marginalist direction, with breakdowns between fixed and variable costs and the separation of those fixed costs that can be attributed directly to particular segments. He also finds differentiation of

---

[4] *Ibid.*, p. 125.

[5] George J. Stigler, "The Kinky Oligopoly Demand Curve and Rigid Prices," *The Journal of Political Economy*, October, 1947, pp. 432–49.

[6] James S. Earley, "Marginal Policies of 'Excellently Managed' Companies," *The American Economic Review*, March, 1956, pp. 44–70; and James S. Earley, "Recent Developments in Cost Accounting and the 'Marginal Analysis,'" *The Journal of Political Economy*, June, 1955, pp. 227–42.

margins on different product lines, with attention to competitive pressures and demand elasticities.

It is impossible to review all of the literature on this subject, but it is desirable to turn to another approach—the case study. The best-known collection of case studies, that of Kaplan, Dirlam, and Lanzillotti, covers 20 of the largest industrial corporations in the United States.[7] The authors stress these patterns:

1. Considerable concern with the "fairness" of prices, with attention to public responsibilities.

2. Establishment of "target returns," stated as percentage returns on investment, consistent with what is considered "fair."

3. Attention to market share, with improvement in the firm's market position a major objective.

4. A preference for stable prices or for stable margins.

5. Stress on full costs in the mechanics of pricing, with widespread use of standard costs as the relevant full-cost data.

6. Adjustment of margins on particular commodities to market conditions.

7. Price leadership of both the dominant firm and barometric varieties.

8. Restraint in charging what the market will bear in periods of market shortages.

9. The occasional use of simple and crude rules of thumb in determining price changes such as doubling the increase in labor costs in a new wage agreement.

The individual cases show considerable diversity in behavior. Some firms, like International Harvester, may give especially strong attention to target returns, but still compute incremental costs when faced with severe competition. Other firms, such as the A & P, may place the maintenance or improvement of market share ahead of target returns. The firms vary in willingness to delegate discretion over prices to subordinate officials. One firm follows a policy of pricing to meet competition: the National Steel Corporation follows prices set by U.S. Steel, with stress on control of costs to return a profit at those prices.

Kaplan, Dirlam, and Lanzillotti recognize certain limitations in their approach. They have difficulties in evaluating information released by company officials; they cannot be certain, for example, that the stated objectives are not sometimes rationalizations rather than descriptions of the actual goals. Critics of the study are particularly unconvinced by the authors' dismissal of profit maximization as a useful concept; they doubt that the firms are as bound by "target returns" as the authors sug-

---

[7] A. D. H. Kaplan, Joel B. Dirlam, and Robert F. Lanzillotti, *Pricing in Big Business* (Washington, D.C.: The Brookings Institution, 1958). Also see Robert F. Lanzillotti, "Pricing Objectives in Large Companies," *The American Economic Review*, December, 1958, pp. 921–40.

gest; they note evidence that the "targets" may be estimates of what the traffic will bear, which means that they are subject to market forces.

A study of small firms conducted by the author reaches conclusions somewhat different from those already cited.[8]

1. It does not find adherence to full-cost pricing, but rather some flexible attention to costs as resistance or reference points. Small businesses do adjust prices to market forces. They seek, through subjective evaluations of demand and through trial and error, prices that will help them achieve their objectives, one of which is profit maximization.

2. On the other hand, small firms have not adopted the incremental accounting techniques mentioned by Earley. Accounting appears to have a limited role in their pricing decisions, and when it does play a role it leads to stress on full costs and averages, rather than on incremental costs. The extent to which small businessmen are marginalists results not from their use of accounting but from their experimentation in the market, their willingness to evaluate demand and costs subjectively, or their imitation of the practices of other firms.

3. Small firms do not appear to give the attention to "target returns" found in big business.

4. Small firms are often concerned with the ethics of pricing, and with community relations, as well as with the impact of prices on profits.

A more complete review of the literature would reveal even greater diversity of practice. This is what one would expect when he examines decision making in detail, for pricing must be adapted to the structure of the market, to the availability of information, to the competence of management, and to the variety of goals and community pressures. This survey of empirical studies indicates that short generalizations about pricing behavior are oversimplified. Probably the widest generalization possible is that most firms appear to practice "partial marginalism," but this covers a wide variety of behavior.

2. INCREMENTAL REASONING IN PRICING

The argument of this chapter up to this point is that neither the traditional theory of the firm, with its high level of abstraction and generalization, nor the widely known short-cut formulas, with their inflexibility, provide the complete answer to the pricing problem.

The present section attempts to provide a general framework within which the manager can formulate a pricing policy. This framework does not provide all of the answers, but it supplies a point of view from which

[8] W. W. Haynes, *Pricing Decisions in Small Business* (Lexington: University of Kentucky Press, 1962).

the manager can start to apply logic to his pricing problem. This framework or point of view might best be called incremental reasoning. It obviously leans heavily on economic theory, but it reformulates the theory in a form more suitable for decision making.

In this section we shift from description to prescription. Traditional theory has attempted to be descriptive—to generalize on what actually happens in the market. Managerial economics is prescriptive. On the basis of logic and of an understanding of markets, managerial economics attempts to suggest ways in which individual enterprises can best set prices in terms of their objectives. Marginalism has certain limitations as descriptive theory, as has been suggested in the preceding section. But marginalism or incrementalism provide the most useful system of logic in dealing with prescriptions for pricing.

Incremental reasoning in its most general form states: If a pricing decision leads to a greater increase in revenue than in costs it is sound; if it leads to a greater reduction in costs than in revenues it is favorable. What incremental reasoning amounts to, therefore, is the comparison of the impact of decisions on revenues and costs. Such reasoning does not, however, require a restriction of attention to revenues, costs, and profits; it permits, indeed it requires, consideration of the extent to which the decision contributes to or detracts from other goals. The recognition of multiple goals requires the weighting of objectives, and, at the present state of knowledge, considerable subjective judgment. One way of handling this difficulty is to concentrate first on the impact of the decision on profits and later to adjust for other considerations.

Incremental reasoning requires a full play of the imagination to make certain that all repercussions of the decision are taken into account. The following guides should be useful:

1. In evaluating the cost impact of the pricing decision, the stress should be on the *changes* in costs rather than on average costs. Overhead allocations are irrelevant and should be ignored. Incremental reasoning requires the statistical measurement of incremental costs or judgment about which costs are affected by the decision and by how much.

2. The method requires attention to the long-run as well as the short-run impact of the decision. A decision to increase prices now may increase immediate profits, but it may gradually undermine the firm's reputation for low prices and destroy customer goodwill. Or it may attract new competition. The decision maker should discount the expected changes in future revenue, applying the discounting principle discussed in Chapter 2, but this does not mean that he should ignore those changes.

3. The method requires consideration of possible complementary relations in demand between one product and another. The major reason for "loss leaders" in retailing is that they attract customers who will purchase

other items. Any time the price decision on one item has an impact on the sale of other items, these additional effects on revenue must be evaluated.

4. The method also requires the careful evaluation of opportunity costs. It may at first appear that a reduction in price is justified by the fact that the incremental costs are below the added revenues. But it should be determined whether the incremental costs include a full measure of any sacrifices of profits required by the decision. For example, a printing firm may reduce price to get some additional orders, recognizing that the materials cost and added labor cost of such orders are low. But if the policy means the use of space that is also required by business at higher prices and if it leads to delay in that business, the total impact on profits may be much less than was at first anticipated. In fact, this very reason is given by some printers in their refusal to price below full cost.

5. The incremental method means that attention must be given to demand elasticities or, more simply, price-volume relationships. The decision maker must develop some way of determining the impact of price change on volume. Sometimes a statistical or experimental approach to measuring demand may be justified. Other times, the manager may make an estimate of the responsiveness of sales to price by evaluating past experience and by considering the various factors that might influence the elasticity of demand for this particular kind of product.

6. The method requires attention to market structure. As has already been noted, no estimate of demand elasticities facing the individual firm is possible without attention to the nature of competition. In some cases, the closeness of a large number of substitutes may mean that the firm has little control over price. In other cases, differentiation of the product may provide some scope for price policy, though it may require a careful coordination of pricing with sales promotion activity. In still other cases, the possible retaliation of competitors should be taken into account.

7. The method requires some way of dealing with uncertainty. The manager never knows the exact consequences of his pricing decisions. The degree of uncertainty may vary from one decision to another. No general rules govern optimal behavior in such circumstances, for the attitude toward risk varies from one individual to the next. In a large impersonal corporation the individual attitudes toward uncertainty may best be ignored, with decision making based on the aim of maximizing *expected profits* (average profits). In small firms, the greater willingness of some managers than others to take chances is often a perfectly reasonable reflection of different attitudes toward possible gains or losses in income. Thus it is impossible to generalize that a manager should always say "yes" to a decision that offers a 0.7 probability of adding $100,000 to profits with a 0.3 probability of losses of $120,000. One manager may be attracted by the fact that this is better than a fair gamble. Another man-

ager may be concerned that it offers the possibility of complete bankruptcy.

8. Incremental reasoning requires attention to changing business conditions. Instead of a mechanical application of formulas through good times and bad, it suggests the possibility of flexibility of prices to meet changing markets. This is not to say that flexibility is always wise, but rather to stress that it is always worthy of consideration.

9. Incremental reasoning implies the individualization of pricing on the various products of a multiproduct concern. It is true that mechanical formulas simplify pricing decisions. In a firm with thousands of products such a simplification may cut managerial costs. But the demand and competitive conditions facing the products are likely to be diverse; rigid pricing formulas prevent adjustment to that diversity. This is again a question of benefits versus costs. Will the firm gain enough in added profits or in furtherance of its other goals to justify the added management costs?

One way of summarizing part of what has been said is to note that incremental reasoning implies both cross-sectional flexibility and flexibility over time. By cross-sectional flexibility is meant the willingness to adapt prices to the special conditions of demand and cost facing each product. Cross-sectional flexibility thus means the same thing as the individualization of pricing. Flexibility over time has to do with the ability to adapt pricing to changing market conditions, to shifts in demand, to changes in price elasticities, and to the availability of excess capacity.

It is more important to develop a way of reasoning about pricing than it is to learn specific rules. Correct reasoning can be tailor-made to particular circumstances; rules frequently are applied when they no longer fit. Some managers who have never heard of incremental costs or demand elasticities no doubt reach decisions that are at least roughly consistent with incremental reasoning. Others appear to be bound by rules of thumb and mechanical formulas that get in the way of such reasoning.

Empirical studies and illustrations

The major empirical issue that the preceding section raises is whether business does in fact follow the kind of incremental reasoning that has been outlined. The obvious answer is that some approximate such reasoning and others do not. Studies previously cited indicate that some firms adopt accounting methods that will help them apply marginal reasoning; others tend to apply mechanical full-cost formulas. The study of small firms conducted by the author indicates considerable variation in the degree of sophistication in pricing policies and practices.

That firms with small staffs can apply incremental reasoning with only a minimum familiarity with the formal principles involved is illustrated by one case from this study, the case of a billboard advertising firm. This firm is aggressive in raising rates on its billboards to the level that traffic will bear. The managers seek information on what other firms are charging. They are not content with imitation, however, for they experiment with pricing to determine whether higher rates actually lead to lower volume. By such a procedure they find the point at which advertisers are likely to abandon billboard advertising in the towns in which this firm is located. The managers have bought out other firms with the intent of raising rates to the range that they have found feasible. The evidence suggests that the managers have been highly successful in increasing profits from their undertaking through price policy.

At the same time many other firms are engaged in pricing practices that appear to fall far short of the incremental approach. While adherence to full-cost pricing is relatively rare in small business, many firms consider full cost to be a *floor* below which they should not reduce prices. They accept the view that making a profit on every job assures profits for the firm as a whole. On the other hand, most small firms that claim to base prices on full costs do in fact take demand into account in their actual pricing. They adjust their prices to changing market conditions as long as the prices are above full cost. Other firms, such as garden and landscape nurseries which find it extremely hard to determine costs of individual products, make no formal reference to cost in their pricing. Still other firms simply imitate the prices of others, not necessarily those of competitors but even those of firms in other markets. Many firms prefer to follow the suggestions of manufacturers or wholesalers rather than to make their own decisions on prices. Thus a great variety of behavior is observable, falling into the following patterns:

The rigid adherence to full-cost pricing.   The pattern is rare in small business and is probably less prevalent in large firms than some writers assume.

Full costs plus variable markups.   This pattern is much more common than is the extreme type of full-cost pricing. It is clear that the determination of the markups requires an evaluation of market conditions.

Pricing using programmed costs other than full costs.   In retailing, prices are seldom related to full costs but rather to the wholesale cost, delivered cost, or cost of goods sold. Predetermined markups are used widely in retailing but they are markups on this wholesale cost; furthermore, such markups are variable from commodity to commodity, and are often flexible over time.

In large firms pricing decisions are often related to estimates of marginal or incremental costs. Sometimes these estimates are obtained from programmed systems of accounting which provide direct costs, differential costs, or other approximations to marginal costs.

Pricing based on ad hoc *estimates of costs and demand.* Few small firms make extensive use of their accounting data in pricing decisions. When they do make analyses for the purposes of pricing, they usually rely on *ad hoc* (back-of-the-envelope) estimates. Large firms also frequently make use of special studies, but are more likely than small firms to depend on technical specialists or consultants to aid them in analyzing pricing situations.

Pricing with little reference to costs. In some industries costs are so nebulous that they have little meaning to management in determining prices. An example is the garden nursery industry in which it is impossible to determine the "cost" of a particular plant or variety of plants. In such cases, managers may claim they consider costs in pricing, but in practice they refer only to the overall costs and profits on their income statements. Their pricing is based more on an evaluation of competition and the prices customers are willing to pay.

Perhaps the main point to stress is that even small firms with limited staffs and training can, if they wish, apply incremental reasoning in pricing, if they are willing to accept the fact that such reasoning is consistent with the subjective use of past experience, the rough estimation of the impact of price changes, and the experimentation with prices to determine the results of change.

3. SOME SPECIFIC GUIDES

The reasoning presented so far in this chapter has been general, providing an analysis applicable in a wide variety of situations. It is desirable now to review some more specific ideas which have been suggested as guides to pricing. Such guides do not enable the manager to bypass incremental reasoning; he still must determine when and where the ideas are applicable. The guides do, however, provide hints that may aid in bridging the gap between the theory and its application.

Loss leaders

The use of loss leaders, which is widespread in retailing, is an application of ideas already discussed. It is a little difficult to define the expression "loss leader," for the idea is not, of course, to produce losses but rather to increase profits. One might define it as a product priced below wholesale cost, but such a definition might be both too broad and too restrictive. It is too broad in that it would cover pricing to clear the counter of unsold style goods and other special sales of overstocked items. It is narrow in excluding the possibility of a price that does cover wholesale cost but which nevertheless is "low" in its direct contribution to overhead. As a result, a complicated definition is required: a loss leader is an item the price of which produces a less than customary contribution or a negative contribution to overhead but which is expected to create profits through its effect on future sales or sales of other items.

An illustration of a loss leader might be coffee sold by a grocery at wholesale cost. The objective is to attract customers to the store in the hope that they will buy other items. Another illustration is reduced magazine subscription rates aimed at creating familiarity with the magazine, leading to future subscriptions at regular rates. Holdren lists some characteristics desirable in commodities which are to serve as loss leaders in a grocery store.[9]

1. The buyer should know the prices of the commodity in other stores.
2. The price differential should be large enough to be perceptible.
3. The buyer's purchases of the commodity should be large enough to make a price cut important to him.
4. The buyer's demand for the commodity should be inelastic.
5. A price reduction should not signify a reduction in quality.

Turnover and pricing

One widely accepted view is that high turnover items should carry lower markups than those with lower turnover. One reason for such a view is that high turnover items are probably also high frequency-of-purchase items on which the customer is familiar with prices and willing to transfer trade if he sees better bargains elsewhere. The correlation is not exact, however, for turnover is measured from the point of view of the seller while frequency of purchase concerns the buyer. Nails may be a high turnover item for the hardware store but a low frequency purchase for the ordinary amateur carpenter.

A second reason for lower markups on high turnover goods is related to opportunity costs. High turnover goods occupy space for a shorter period of time and thus require a lesser sacrifice of space that could be devoted to other goods. Furthermore, high turnover items may require less selling effort per dollar of sales, with a lower opportunity cost of selling time. If the firm has excess space and excess selling time, these reasons become less compelling.

It would be a mistake to rely on a formula relating markup to turnover alone. Turnover is itself a function of price. It might be possible to increase the turnover, and thus reduce the unit opportunity cost of space and selling effort, by reducing price. Furthermore, there is not a close correlation between turnover and space occupancy; jewelry may

[9] Bob R. Holdren, *The Structure of a Retail Market and the Market Behavior of Retail Units* (Englewood Cliffs, N.J.: Prentice-Hall, Inc., 1960), p. 140.

turn over slowly but occupies little space. The decision maker should consider the whole range of effects of price change and not just a single factor such as turnover.

Pioneer pricing: skimming price versus penetration price

Joel Dean's *Managerial Economics* is a rich source of useful distinctions worthy of consideration in pricing. Some of these distinctions are concerned with the life cycle of the product. Dean argues that the analysis of pricing in the early stages, when the product first appears on the market, is quite different for that in the late stages, when the product is suffering from encroachment from new products and from shifts in taste. But he wisely does not generalize about each stage, finding diversity within each of the stages of the life cycle. The problem is to determine for each product at each stage of its cycle both the short-run and long-run elasticities of demand.

Consider first a new product. Dean distinguishes between two kinds of policy for such a product: (1) a *skimming price* policy, with initial high prices; and (2) a *penetration price* policy, with low prices at the beginning. Each deserves separate attention.

The strategy of *skimming price* is most suitable when (1) the short-run demand is relatively inelastic and (2) when undesirable effects of high present prices on future sales or sales of other products are not large. The demand is more likely to be less elastic for a product that is sharply differentiated from previous products, so that the possibility of substitution and of price comparisons is limited. In such a case, a high level of promotional activity may be appropriate, for it is necessary to make the public aware of the product.

It requires considerable judgment to determine when initial high prices are appropriate. Hula hoops sold initially at high prices to that segment of the market that cared enough for the novelty to buy anyway. It is doubtful that those who purchased hula hoops later on at lower prices were at all deterred by the previous high prices; if anything the effect was the opposite, one of feeling that the low price was a real bargain. Similarly a high price on a "spectacular" movie in its first year should have little negative impact on those customers who can afford only the lower price and are willing to wait.

Dean makes the point that skimming price policy is safer. It gives the firm an opportunity to sell the product on a small scale at a price that is almost certain to cover costs. Later the firm can explore the possibility of tapping lower price segments of the market. Perhaps this kind of reasoning influenced the setting of tolls on the San Francisco Bay Bridge, on which the initial rate was 60 cents per automobile, followed by a reduction to 50 cents, 40 cents, and finally to 25 cents. At each rate the traffic exceeded expectations, reducing the risk of lower rates. It is necessary to point out, however, that the objective of the bridge was not to maximize profits—the short-run demand was probably inelastic enough that a rate of 50 cents or 40 cents would have produced more revenue than the lower rate. The high revenues at high rates did reduce the risk of exploring the effects of lower rates.

A *penetration price* policy sacrifices the maximization of short-run profits for long-run objectives. Some products are introduced at prices below those intended for the long run to create familiarity with the product. Such apparently was the case with Tang, a powdered substitute for orange juice which appeared at first at cut-rate prices (two jars for the price of one, coupons offering discounts, etc.). After the public had gained familiarity with the product these special price cuts were removed. Apparently the producers of Tang believed that the initial price elasticity was high, but that those who tried out and liked the product would be willing to pay a higher price.

The conditions most favorable to penetration pricing are: (1) high short-run price elasticities with lower long-run elasticities, as in the case just discussed; (2) economics of scale in production; (3) the threat of new substitutes which may require restraint in profit making to discourage entry (Dean calls this *stay-out pricing*); and (4) a favorable impact of sales of the product under consideration on the sales of other company products and on customer goodwill.

In the selection of a skimming price or penetration price (or some compromise), the firm might well consider the prices of substitutes. If the prices of substitutes permit pricing of the new product at a high profit or if substitutes are too remote to be worthy of consideration, a skimming price may be appropriate. If the problem is one of taking business away from fairly close substitutes, a penetration price may be necessary to establish the new product on the market.

Pricing mature products

In an economy of rapid innovation and changing tastes such as ours, many products can expect a limited life on the market. The market for hula hoops and Davy Crockett caps may last a year or less; passenger services on the railroads are suffering curtailment after a century of consumer acceptance. The length of the life cycle is not easily predicted. Even when the deterioration has clearly set in, no general rules govern the optimal policy. In some cases a low price policy may delay the encroachment of new substitutes. In other cases low prices may instead set off price retaliation. Let us consider the case of motion picture theaters in the 1950's. That the market had declined was incontestable. But it does not follow that the appropriate reaction was price reduction. It may be that the demand had shifted to the left without any pronounced change in elasticity. In other words, the availability of television has cut into the market, but it does not follow that consumers' decisions to go or not to go to a movie were more price oriented than before. It seems unlikely that movies would enjoy a great revival if their prices were halved; in fact, the practice in the 1960's seems to have been to raise prices substantially.

A case in which a low price policy seems to have delayed market decline is that of books. If book prices had increased as much as prices in general in the last two decades with novels selling at $7 to $10 rather than $3.50 to $5, the book industry might well be in great difficulty. Indeed, the appearence of high-quality paperbacks selling from $.75 to $2.50 has helped a great deal to bolster the industry, though this development is better considered as an introduction of a new product than a price reduction. Perhaps it is wrong to classify book publishing as a mature industry, but the book industry does appear to be adjusting both price and product to the changing times and taste.

Odd-number and round-number pricing

Some sellers believe that odd-number prices are more attractive to buyers than even numbers. A price of 43 cents may, for some strange reason, be more appealing than 42 cents or even 40 cents. Such a situation would indicate a jagged demand curve. The problem for management would be to determine which numbers have the greater appeal. Research so far provides little help on this score.

More widespread and plausible is the belief that demand is quite elastic to price reductions slightly below some round number. The sale of gasoline at 28.9 cents or 32.9 cents, the pricing of long-playing records at $3.98, $4.98, or $5.98, and similar practices give evidence that customers are heavily influenced by reductions of price below round numbers or, at least, a widespread belief that such is the case. Again, present research is inconclusive on the effectiveness of such pricing. Perhaps the real impact is in price comparisons among products: the customer may be quite sensitive to the difference between 32.9 cents on one gasoline and 33.0 cents on another, but insensitive to the difference between 32.8 and 32.9. This creates an incentive to settle at 32.9

Some sellers follow the opposite policy, with a preference for round numbers. For example, the management of a nursery with a reputation for quality believes that prices of $4 or $4.50 are more consistent with that reputation than prices like $3.99 or $4.23 that have a cut-rate appearance. This nursery does experiment with special prices at its annual sale, but, in general, resists pricing practices that might give the impression of a low-quality, mass volume operation.

Imitative pricing and suggested prices

Another approach to pricing is simply to imitate the prices of others. The reasons for such a policy in oligopoly are already familiar to the reader. But the practice appears even when the oligopolistic reasoning no longer applies, as when the imitator is in an entirely different location from the imitated. Imitation is easy on the decision maker. He may get the benefit of another firm's market analysis without worrying himself about demand elasticities and incremental costs.

Similarly the practice of following the suggested prices of manufacturers or wholesalers gives the manager time to devote to other decisions. Some managers prefer to minimize the time devoted to pricing decisions and go out of the way to find prepriced items. The suggested price is probably one that the manufacturer or wholesaler has found feasible under the market conditions and thus permits the retailer to gain the benefit of analysis without having to engage in it himself. This policy limits flexibility in meeting local conditions, but some sellers prefer to escape the pain of analyzing those conditions.

In the case of resale price maintenance, especially when it is supported by legislation, the choice of the seller is limited. He can sell the item only at the price established by the manufacturer. Some small retailers believe that such practices protect them from unfair competition from large outlets. Some manufacturers apparently prefer the control and stability of price that resale price maintenance provides. But in recent years, especially with the advent of discount houses and with court rulings unfavorable to price maintenance, the hold of this pricing practice has diminished.

Price lining

Another practice that is claimed to simplify the pricing problem is that of price lining, which consists of deciding for a considerable period of time (at least several years) on a limited number of price levels for different qualities of the same product. For example, a store may carry lines of summer dresses at $12.95, $15.95, $19.95, and $24.95. As each new season approaches, the buyers must decide on which dresses to fit into those predetermined price lines.

Department store managers apparently believe that price lining simplifies the setting of prices, releasing time for sales promotion, inventory control, and other activities. Some writers deny that such a simplification results, for the buyers must still decide on which qualities to fit into the lines.[10] Maximization of profits still requires equating

---

[10] See Milton H. Spencer and Louis Siegelman, *Managerial Economics: Decision Making and Forward Planning* (Homewood, Ill.: Richard D. Irwin, Inc., 1959), pp. 286–87 for a more complete discussion.

marginal cost and marginal revenue, which in this case requires recognition of the fact that improved qualities normally increase volume but also increase the cost not only on the last unit but also on the intramarginal units. Figure 7–6 illustrates this reasoning. The marginal cost curve lies above the average cost curve for the same kind of reason that the marginal revenue curve lies below a downward sloping demand curve. Suppose, for example, that management is considering a choice between a dress the cost of which is $11 against one which costs $12. The selling price is predetermined to be $15.95 whichever dress is selected. It is expected that the $11 quality will sell in a volume of 200 dresses; The $12 quality in a volume of 300. The marginal cost (unit incremental cost) of the added dresses is $14, which is still below the selling price. Marginal reasoning would lead the manager to a higher quality that would equate the marginal cost to the price of $15.95.

Spencer and Siegelman take the view that the analysis required to fit the quality to price is just as difficult, requiring marginal reasoning as complete as that required to fit price to quality.

Empirical studies and illustrations

Only one of the pricing devices just described will be illustrated from empirical findings—the use of loss leaders. Holdren's outstanding study of supermarkets presents evidence on the commodities selected as price leaders. His study is limited to one city at one period of time, so that the findings may not be exactly reproduced in similar studies elsewhere. Table 7–1 reproduces his data on the average price, wholesale list price, and percentage margin in eight supermarkets.

FIGURE 7–6

PRICE LINING

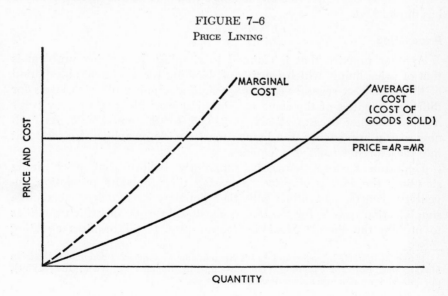

TABLE 7–1

PRICES IN EIGHT SUPERMARKETS ON SELECTED ITEMS
(July, 1954, prices)

Items	Average Price (in cents)	Average Deviation as a Percent of Average Price	Average Price of Customary Purchase Unit (in cents)	Wholesale List (in cents)	Percentage Margin of Wholesale List
Cereals and bakery products					
Flour, wheat, 5 lbs.	52	4	5⁰	49.5	4.8
Biscuit mix, 20 oz.	24	7	24	21.5	10.4
Corn flakes, 12 oz.	24	4.5	24	18.1	24.6
Rolled oats, 20 oz.	18.5	3	18.5	15.0	18.9
Corn meal, 1 lb.	14	11.5	14	13.5	3.6
Rice, 1 lb.	45	2	45	34.04	24.4
Meats, poultry and fish					
Round steak, lb.	85	10	85	....	....
Rib roast, lb.	55	0	55	....	....
Canned luncheon meat	4ᵇ	0	49	39.6	19.2
Canned salmon	75	2	75	61.4	18.1
Canned tuna fish	39	12	39	29.6	24.1
Dairy products					
Milk, evaporated	13	3	78	12.5	3.8
American cheese, lb.	67	2	67	....	....
Other fruits and vegetables					
Canned orange juice, 46 oz.	34	7	34	30.3	10.9
Peaches, #2½	29	13	29	25.96	10.5
Sliced pineapple, #2½	33	3	33	26.9	18.5
Fruit cocktail, #2½	31	21	31	32.9	.3
Cream style corn, #303 ...	17	4	34	14.7	13.5
Peas, canned, #303	21	4	21	16.6	21
Tomatoes, canned, #2	23	7	23	19.1	17
Strained baby food, 4½–5 oz.	10	6	60	9	10
Dried prunes, lb.	33.5	7	33.5	25	25.4
Navy beans, lb.	16	6	16	12.8	20
Other foods					
Vegetable soup, 11 oz.	14.5	18	29	11.97	17.4
Beans with pork, 16 oz. ...	15	13	30	14.90	.7
Tomato catsup, 14 oz.	26	20	26	16.10	38.1
Coffee, lb.	118	3	118	123.50	− 4.7
Tea, ½ lb.	39	6	39	30.20	22.6
Vegetable shortening, lb. ..	30	3.5	90	33.4	−11.3
Peanut butter, lb.	48	12	48	45.1	6
Sugar, white, 5 lbs.	51.5	4	51.5	50	2.9
Corn syrup, 24 oz.	32	3	32	17.5	45.3
Grape jelly, 12 oz.	25	14	25	16.75	33
Chocolate bars, 1 oz.	5	0	5	3.50	30
Flavored gelatin dessert, 3–4 oz.	8.5	6	34	7.3	14.1

SOURCE: Bob R. Holdren, *The Structure of a Retail Market and the Market Behavior of Retail Units* (Englewood Cliffs, N.J.: Prentice-Hall, Inc., 1960), pp. 76–79.

Several products are quite clearly loss leaders, for their prices do not even cover wholesale cost. These are coffee, selling at that time at five cents below wholesale cost, and vegetable shortening, selling at over 10 percent below cost. But the low margins on a number of other commodities qualify them for inclusion as loss leaders, such as flour, corn meal, evaporated milk, fruit cocktail, strained baby food, beans with pork, peanut butter, and sugar.

Coffee is apparently a "natural" loss leader, being relatively high in price and purchased frequently, so that the consumer is quite aware of price differentials. Holdren points out, however, that the margin was unusually low in 1954 because of the high level of wholesale coffee prices at that time; in fact, coffee prices had fallen to as much as 30 percent below wholesale cost and margins were undergoing a recovery at the time the study was made.

4. THE ENVIRONMENT OF PRICING DECISIONS

The discussion up to this point has stressed the logic required by pricing decisions. But practical pricing decisions are made in a complex environment in which the central logic is often obscured. The pricing decision is, first of all, only one phase of the total marketing strategy; the reduction of price is only one of a great variety of sales promotion devices. The decision maker cannot determine price without reference to other ways of manipulating sales. He must simultaneously consider pricing, product development, advertising, packaging, personal selling, servicing facilities, delivery service, and a variety of other means of promotion.

Pricing objectives

The objectives of pricing are not as clear-cut as the previous discussion might imply.[11] The models of economic theory usually assume profit maximization. But sometimes survival of the firm itself is at stake. As we have noted many times already, short-run profit maximization and long-run maximization are sometimes at odds. Under conditions of uncertainty, pricing decisions may take the form of minimizing the risks of loss; the emphasis on this factor depends on the entrepreneur's attitudes toward risk and the financial resources at his disposal. Some firms may be motivated by the desire to get their products to their customers at a reasonable cost. Many may restrain their profit seeking in the fear of

---

[11] The following discussion makes considerable use of ideas in Alfred R. Oxenfeldt, *Pricing for Marketing Executives* (Belmont, Calif.: Wadsworth Publishing Co., Inc., 1961).

prosecution for monopolistic or discriminatory practices.[12] Some feel a sense of obligation to their communities; or they may wish to avoid being known as "gougers" or "chiselers." Firms may hold down prices to gain a larger share of the market, sometimes even at the expense of profits. They may price in a way to limit their clientele to those with whom it is pleasant to deal.

Parties involved in pricing

The manager responsible for pricing decisions must consider a variety of individuals concerned with price. Oxenfeldt lists seven main parties to the pricing process: those responsible for sales promotion, the ultimate customers for the product, rival sellers, potential rivals, middlemen, suppliers, and the government. Economic theory usually stresses only two of these parties: the buyers and the sellers. The pricing process in practice must take all of them into account, for they all are involved in the pattern of communication and influence which determines the final outcome.

The case of the middleman is a good one to bring out the complexity of the pricing environment. Most manufacturers distribute their products through middlemen rather than directly. The interests of the manufacturer and the middleman are often in conflict. The manufacturer would like the middleman to carry his product at a minimum markup; but the margin must be large enough to stimulate a desire to carry and "push" the product. The manufacturer would like a variety of middlemen to provide a wide coverage of the market; but middlemen often want to handle products on an exclusive basis. The manufacturer may wish to control the prices charged by the middlemen and even the retail price; but the middlemen may wish to expand their sales by cutting price or to obtain a larger margin than the suggested price provides. A reduction of price by the manufacturer may reduce the value of middlemen's inventories, a fact that may lead to resentment unless some adjustment is made. Many of these issues are resolved by reference to trade policies and customs.

The relation of the government to pricing decisions is an especially painful one to many businessmen. Especially difficult is the problem of avoiding price discrimination of the sort deemed illegal under the Robinson-Patman Act. Most multiproduct firms, especially those with widespread markets, engage in price discrimination in a broad sense. The problem is to determine when such discrimination becomes illegal in the

---

[12] Some of these objectives can be interpreted as aspects of long-run profit maximization. For example, avoidance of antitrust suits and public disapproval may contribute to the profitability of the firm in the long run.

sense of the statutes. The criteria of legality require a determination of whether the pricing practices injure rivals or tend to lessen competition. They also require consideration of whether price differences reflect cost differences—for example, the lower costs made possible by supplying large quantities to certain customers. Similar difficulties arise in the interpretation of statutes and court decisions governing resale price maintenance, sales below cost, basing point systems of pricing, and a variety of other pricing practices.

A book in economic analysis such as this cannot develop fully all of these sociological, psychological, and legal influences on price. We have chosen to stress the central economic concepts required by pricing, leaving to the practitioner the task of adapting the analysis to the needs of each particular situation.

Internal organization for pricing

In small firms there is no great problem in organizing for pricing. The pricing decisions like the other major decisions are the responsibility of top management. The danger in the small firm is that the managers will be so engrossed in the day-to-day activities of handling customers, ordering supplies, and so on that they will neglect to think about pricing at all. In fact, some small firm managers admit that they avoid pricing decisions whenever possible, preferring to depend on suggested prices, mechanical formulas, or on price followership. Such practices may often be appropriate, but managers should consider from time to time whether a more flexible or analytical approach can be justified.

In larger firms, in which specialization and delegation are inevitable, the problem is often one of coordinating pricing decisions with other marketing and production decisions. In recent years, the marketing literature has stressed the "new marketing concept," which calls for teamwork in coordinating advertising, personal sales effort, and decisions on distribution channels with pricing. Some firms use committees to assist communication among the various executives involved, though it is probably unwise to give the final decision-making authority to a committee; it is usually better to fix responsibility on a single individual or department. The recent stress on the position of "vice president in charge of marketing" reflects the recognition of the need for a central direction of marketing activities.

Information required for pricing flows from many specialized branches of the firm. The salesmen feed back information on customer reactions to price and on the prices of competitors. The cost accountants supply data on costs. Specialized analysts, such as marketing researchers, provide the results of experiments and statistical studies. Often representatives from the treasurer's department and the production departments participate in the pricing process.

The degree to which pricing decisions are routinized varies from company to company and product to product. A programmed routine for pricing makes it possible to delegate pricing decisions to subordinates, but it reduces the flexibility required to adapt to particular circumstances. The degree of routinization should depend upon the following factors:

The number of pricing decisions.   A firm which must make thousands of pricing decisions on a wide range of products, none of which provides a substantial proportion of sales, may find it economical to adopt relatively mechanical routines for pricing. The costs of separate analyses on each product are too high.

The speed required by pricing decisions.   Mechanical formulas, such as a predetermined markup on full cost, have the advantage of speed, with a loss of flexibility and adaptation to special conditions.

The variety of markets served by the firm.   Substantial differences in the character of the market may make it profitable to analyze each market separately to determine the appropriate prices.

The quality of the available information.   If the data on demand and costs are highly conjectural, the best the firm may be able to do is to rely on a mechanical formula such as cost plus.

Personnel considerations.   The ability to make appropriate analyses for pricing depends upon the training and competence of the company's personnel.

Market structures.   If the firm's markets are highly competitive, allowing little pricing discretion, there is little need for analysis for pricing. The same is true if the firm has adopted the policy of following the price moves of a leader in the industry. In markets permitting pricing discretion it may be profitable to devote considerable attention to demand elasticities, the probable reactions of competitors, and so on.

In a large undertaking a decision must be made as to the degree of decentralization permitted in pricing decisions. In retail chains pricing is usually centralized in the headquarters, though sometimes authority to mark down prices in special sales is delegated to local managers. In large department stores considerable authority for pricing is delegated to departmental buyers, though apparently decision rules and customs limit the discretion of the individual buyer. Large manufacturers vary in the extent to which they decentralize pricing authority to product divisions. Decentralization has the advantage of placing the authority for pricing in the hands of those close to the local problems and familiar with local needs. It is probably conducive to greater flexibility in pricing. Centralization assures greater control at the center and reduces competition among divisions of the same company.

A multistage approach to pricing

A. R. Oxenfeldt has outlined what he calls a "multi-stage approach to pricing," which helps assure that the environmental conditions surrounding pricing decisions are taken into account.[13] This approach breaks the pricing process into a series of successive steps; decisions on the early stages facilitate subsequent decisions. Oxenfeldt outlines six stages, as follows:

Selection of market targets. The firm should determine the character of the market it expects to reach with the product under consideration. It may try to find segments of the market in which it has a special advantage, such as some insulation from competition. It may decide it wishes to sell to a particular income group or to those with special tastes. It may stress winning a larger share of the market. It may wish to develop markets which are complementary to those for the company's existing products. Such a decision requires an evaluation of the firm's capabilities, goals, and resources.

Selection of the firm or brand image. Management should decide what kind of reputation for the firm and brand names it is trying to build up in the public's mind. Some firms establish a reputation for high quality which may justify their high prices. Others may wish to be known as economical outlets for mass-produced commodities. Still others may wish to be known as innovators. The point is that management should make product, packaging, advertising, and pricing decisions which are consistent with the image they are trying to create.

Composition of the marketing mix. Management must coordinate advertising decisions with pricing. For example, if it is trying to increase sales by reducing price, its advertising should aim at increasing the elasticity of demand to such price decreases. Such advertising would stress the price advantage of the company's product. On the other hand, an increase in price might be accompanied by advertising which stresses the quality and distinctiveness of the firm's product. Similarly, decisions on the quality of service, styling, and packaging should relate to the pricing decisions.

Selection of the specific price policy. The firm should next determine an overall price policy within which it can establish individual prices. Some illustrations of such policies are: follow the price of the leader; set prices at 10 percent below those of the leader; determine the best price for each product individually; follow the practice of marking up by a predetermined percentage on full cost; follow the prices suggested by manufacturers or wholesalers; maintain uniform prices throughout all

---

[13] Alfred R. Oxenfeldt, "Multi-Stage Approach to Pricing," *Harvard Business Review* (July–August, 1960), pp. 125–33. Oxenfeldt's discussion is similar to Dean's "Steps in Pioneering Pricing" in *Managerial Economics, op. cit.,* pp. 413–19.

markets; or differentiate price according to the characteristics of particular markets.

Selection of a price strategy.   The firm should choose prices today that are consistent with its long-term objectives. We have already presented illustrations of such strategies. For example, a penetration price strategy may aim at the creation of familiarity with the product as rapidly as possible, with subsequent dominance of the market. Prices may aim at discouraging the entry of new competition into the market. In other situations the strategy may be one of avoiding "rocking the boat," with restraint in changing prices in a way that will provoke retaliation.

Setting specific prices.   The previous steps provide a framework for establishing the prices of individual products. Some of the previous steps reduce this final step to a mere mechanical routine which can be delegated to clerks. But the choice of policies and strategies which call for flexibility will require considerable high-level analysis before prices are determined.

It would be easy to expand this list of steps. For example, Dean treats the selection of distribution channels as a separate step. The seller must determine what margins will cover the distributors' costs and create an incentive to promote the product. He must compare high margin, high selling effort channels with the possibility of lower margins and lower prices.

Two steps in full-cost pricing

Some of the controversy over full-cost pricing results from confusion about what it really means. In its extreme form it means the rigid application of a single predetermined markup on full cost for all commodities. This variety of full-cost pricing is rare. In a somewhat more flexible form it means starting with full cost but with addition of variable markups, the particular markup depending on the demand conditions facing the particular product.

When the more flexible variety of full-cost pricing is adopted, its application may fall into two steps, the first of which requires considerable flexibility while the second is rigid and mechanical. The two steps are:

1. Determination of the percentage markup.
2. Application of this markup to particular products within a category of products.

In determining the appropriate markup for a particular category of commodities (within which the individual commodities have similar characteristics), the firm should use great care in evaluating the cost, demand, and competitive factors facing such products. At this stage management should give great attention to demand elasticities, as well as to questions of brand image and long-run strategy. But once this markup has been determined it may be safe to apply it fairly mechanically to particular products within the category, at least until some significant change in market conditions takes place. In this way it is possible to reach a compromise between the need to adapt to the particular market situations on one hand and the desire to hold down decision-making costs on the other. Whether this type of compromise is appropriate depends on the structure of the market and the volatility of market conditions.

Some pricing prescriptions

One way of concluding this chapter is to list a series of suggestions on pricing which reflect the analysis presented in this chapter. These prescriptions are based on several works on pricing which attempt to bridge the gap between abstract theory and the needs of the individual firm.[14]

Sound reasoning on pricing includes the following elements, with different emphases depending on the industry and market structure:

1. Consideration of price-volume relationships (elasticities of demand) to determine what happens to total revenue at various prices.

2. Comparison of those price-volume relationships with incremental costs to determine the most profitable price on each item.

3. Estimation of the contribution to overhead and profits on each product that can be produced with the given facilities.

4. Selection of those products and sale at prices that will assure the largest contributions to overhead and profits.

5. Investment in new facilities according to the estimated profits in the future of alternative products at optimum prices, taking costs into account.

6. Flexibility of prices over time to meet changing market and cost conditions, unless there are strong arguments against flexibility (possible retaliation, high costs of changing decisions, etc.).

7. Consideration of the impact of price changes on the "image" of the company in the market, on customer goodwill, and on the firm's reputation for "fair" prices.

8. Consideration of the impact that price changes on one commodity may have on the sales of other items.

9. Experimentation with price changes, when this is not too costly, to determine what customer responses are likely to be.

10. Determination of how much customers will benefit from price reductions, for this will give some clues as to the response to price changes.

11. Comparison of the long-range implications of price changes against the immediate impact of those changes.

---

[14] This list is based primarily on the following works: Joel Dean, *Managerial Economics;* A. R. Oxenfeldt, *Pricing for Marketing Executives;* and W. W. Haynes, *Pricing Decisions in Small Business.*

12. Consideration of the life cycle of the product, with different price strategies for new products than for mature products facing a decline in demand.

13. Consideration of competitors' reactions to price changes.

14. Evaluation of the impact of price changes on the entry or exit of competitive rivals.

15. Coordination of price policies with other marketing policies, so that these are consistent and complementary.

16. Determination of the incremental costs or marginal costs of each product, even when full-cost pricing is applied, in order to evaluate the impact of full-cost pricing from time to time.

17. Avoidance of overestimating how much can be accomplished by pricing alone. It is only one phase of management and cannot guarantee profitable operations.

Empirical studies and illustrations

A good illustration to demonstrate the importance of organizational structure and decision-making processes comes from a study of department store pricing.[15] This study concentrates on the ordering and pricing practices in one department of a store with over 100 departments. The analysis of pricing in this department enabled the researchers to construct models with which they could predict normal prices, sales prices, and markdowns with an amazing degree of accuracy.

The study found that in the department under study the normal markup was 40 percent. It was also customary to establish prices ending in $.95. Thus the normal rule for pricing was: "Divide each cost by .60 and move the result to the nearest 95 cents." Different but similar rules applied to exclusive items and imports.

In establishing sales prices, the managers followed a series of simple rules, operating within a set of constraints to ensure consistency with prices in other departments. Rather than develop these rules and constraints in detail here, it is preferable to focus on the procedures for markdowns, which were similar to those for sales prices.

Markdowns occurred when the feedback of information indicated that sales were unsatisfactory or inventories were overextended. The store merchandise manager planned store-wide clearances throughout the year, though departments could schedule special clearances in some circumstances (such as a large shipment of new merchandise without the capacity for storing the additional inventory).

---

[15] R. M. Cyert, J. G. March, and C. G. Moore, "A Model of Retail Ordering and Pricing by a Department Store," in R. E. Frank, A. E. Kuehn, and W. F. Massy, *Quantitative Techniques in Marketing Analysis: Text and Readings* (Homewood, Ill.: Richard D. Irwin, Inc., 1962); also Richard M. Cyert, James G. March, A *Behavioral Theory of the Firm* (Englewood Cliffs, N.J.: Prentice-Hall, Inc., 1963).

FIGURE 7–7
FLOW CHART FOR MARKDOWN ROUTINE

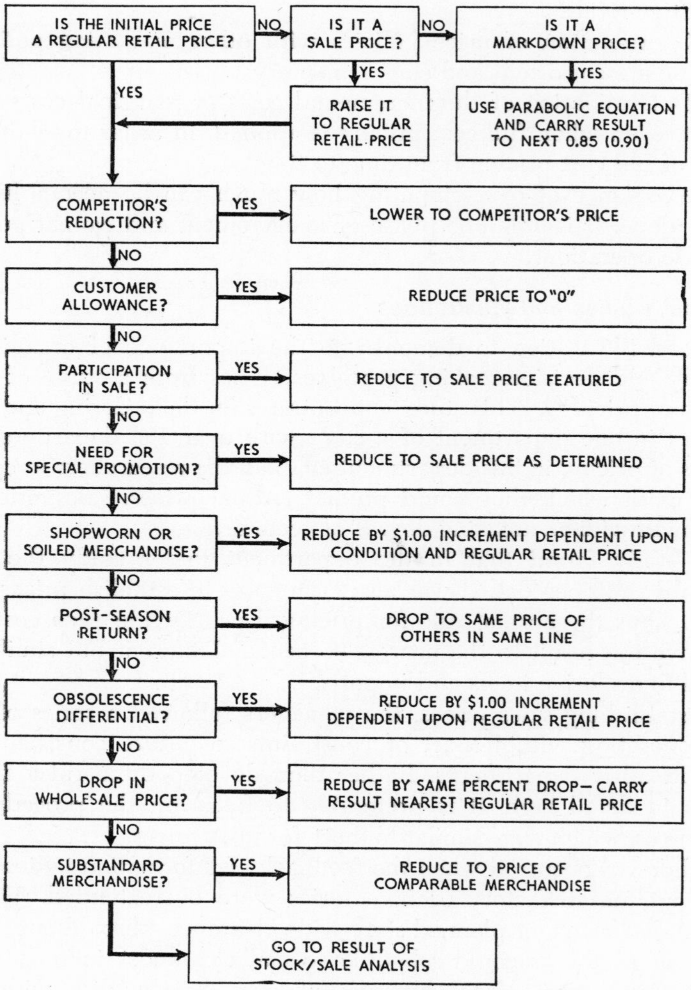

IS THE INITIAL PRICE A REGULAR RETAIL PRICE?	NO →	IS IT A SALE PRICE?	NO →	IS IT A MARKDOWN PRICE?

↓YES (under "IS IT A SALE PRICE?") → RAISE IT TO REGULAR RETAIL PRICE

↓YES (under "IS IT A MARKDOWN PRICE?") → USE PARABOLIC EQUATION AND CARRY RESULT TO NEXT 0.85 (0.90)

↓YES (under initial price)

COMPETITOR'S REDUCTION?	YES →	LOWER TO COMPETITOR'S PRICE
↓NO		
CUSTOMER ALLOWANCE?	YES →	REDUCE PRICE TO "0"
↓NO		
PARTICIPATION IN SALE?	YES →	REDUCE TO SALE PRICE FEATURED
↓NO		
NEED FOR SPECIAL PROMOTION?	YES →	REDUCE TO SALE PRICE AS DETERMINED
↓NO		
SHOPWORN OR SOILED MERCHANDISE?	YES →	REDUCE BY $1.00 INCREMENT DEPENDENT UPON CONDITION AND REGULAR RETAIL PRICE
↓NO		
POST-SEASON RETURN?	YES →	DROP TO SAME PRICE OF OTHERS IN SAME LINE
↓NO		
OBSOLESCENCE DIFFERENTIAL?	YES →	REDUCE BY $1.00 INCREMENT DEPENDENT UPON REGULAR RETAIL PRICE
↓NO		
DROP IN WHOLESALE PRICE?	YES →	REDUCE BY SAME PERCENT DROP— CARRY RESULT NEAREST REGULAR RETAIL PRICE
↓NO		
SUBSTANDARD MERCHANDISE?	YES →	REDUCE TO PRICE OF COMPARABLE MERCHANDISE
↓NO		

GO TO RESULT OF STOCK/SALE ANALYSIS

SOURCE: R. M. Cyert, J. G. March, and C. G. Moore, "A Model of Retail Ordering and Pricing by a Department Store," in R. E. Frank, A. E. Kuehn, and W. F. Massy, *Quantitative Techniques in Marketing Analysis: Text and Readings* (Homewood, Ill.: Richard D. Irwin, Inc., 1962). Also published in Richard M. Cyert, James G. March, *A Behavioral Theory of the Firm* (Englewood Cliffs, N.J.: Prentice-Hall, Inc., 1963). Reprinted by permission.

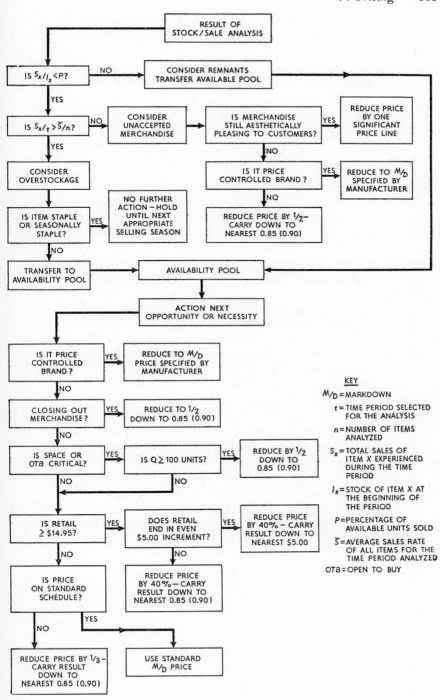

RESULT OF STOCK/SALE ANALYSIS

IS $S_x/I_x < P$? — NO → CONSIDER REMNANTS TRANSFER AVAILABLE POOL

YES

IS $S_x/t > \bar{S}/n$? — NO → CONSIDER UNACCEPTED MERCHANDISE → IS MERCHANDISE STILL AESTHETICALLY PLEASING TO CUSTOMERS? — YES → REDUCE PRICE BY ONE SIGNIFICANT PRICE LINE

YES

CONSIDER OVERSTOCKAGE

NO

IS IT PRICE CONTROLLED BRAND? — YES → REDUCE TO M/D SPECIFIED BY MANUFACTURER

NO

IS ITEM STAPLE OR SEASONALLY STAPLE? — YES → NO FURTHER ACTION – HOLD UNTIL NEXT APPROPRIATE SELLING SEASON

REDUCE PRICE BY 1/2 – CARRY DOWN TO NEAREST 0.85 (0.90)

NO

TRANSFER TO AVAILABILITY POOL → AVAILABILITY POOL

ACTION NEXT OPPORTUNITY OR NECESSITY

IS IT PRICE CONTROLLED BRAND? — YES → REDUCE TO M/D PRICE SPECIFIED BY MANUFACTURER

NO

CLOSING OUT MERCHANDISE? — YES → REDUCE TO 1/2 DOWN TO 0.85 (0.90)

NO

IS SPACE OR OTB CRITICAL? — YES → IS $Q \geq 100$ UNITS? — YES → REDUCE BY 1/2 DOWN TO 0.85 (0.90)

NO

NO

IS RETAIL $\geq \$14.95$? — YES → DOES RETAIL END IN EVEN $5.00 INCREMENT? — YES → REDUCE PRICE BY 40% – CARRY RESULT DOWN TO NEAREST $5.00

NO

NO

IS PRICE ON STANDARD SCHEDULE?

REDUCE PRICE BY 40% – CARRY RESULT DOWN TO NEAREST 0.85 (0.90)

YES

NO

REDUCE PRICE BY 1/3 – CARRY RESULT DOWN TO NEAREST 0.85 (0.90)

USE STANDARD M/D PRICE

KEY

M/D = MARKDOWN
t = TIME PERIOD SELECTED FOR THE ANALYSIS
n = NUMBER OF ITEMS ANALYZED
S_x = TOTAL SALES OF ITEM X EXPERIENCED DURING THE TIME PERIOD
I_x = STOCK OF ITEM X AT THE BEGINNING OF THE PERIOD
P = PERCENTAGE OF AVAILABLE UNITS SOLD
$\bar{S}$ = AVERAGE SALES RATE OF ALL ITEMS FOR THE TIME PERIOD ANALYZED
OTB = OPEN TO BUY

The rule for the first markdown was usually to reduce retail price by one third and carry the result down to the nearest $.85. A 40 percent markdown was taken on higher-priced items. The rule for second markdowns was not explicit, but, in general, the greater the first markdown the greater the second. The researchers found that the equation

$$Y^2 = 5(X - 2)$$

where

$$Y = \text{second markdown}$$
$$X = \text{initial markdown}$$

provided a good prediction of second markdowns.

Figure 7–7 presents flow charts which outline the model for markdowns. This figure covers a number of special cases and exceptions to the general rules we have discussed. For example, if the commodity was price controlled, the markdown was specified by the manufacturer. If the store was closing out merchandise, the markdown was one half.

The researchers tested their models against actual prices. In the case of normal prices, they predicted 188 out of a random sample of 197 prices to the exact penny. In the case of sales prices, they predicted 56 out of a sample of 58 prices to the exact penny. And they predicted 140 of a sample of 159 markdowns with complete accuracy. It is important to realize that these predictions followed from a stress on "decision rules" and standard practices rather than on the traditional tools of economic analysis, such as demand elasticities and marginal costs. It is true that the usual economic considerations entered into the models in various ways —in the attention to competitors' price reductions, for example. And it seems reasonable to suppose that the rules themselves were an adaptation to the underlying economic influences. The researchers agreed that the markups were a result of long-run learning, but they noted that in the short run such markups were highly stable. It is claimed that some markups in department stores have remained the same for 40 or 50 years. Thus, a complete understanding of pricing would appear to require a study of organizations and behavior patterns as well as the use of economic analysis.

8 / Selected topics in pricing

It has been impossible in previous chapters to ignore the fact that most firms produce and sell more than one product and often sell each product at more than one price. In economic theory the abstraction of the single-product firm is useful; in managerial economics we must face up to the fact of multiple products. The earlier treatment of complementarity of demand, of loss leaders, of product-line decisions, and of linear programming decisions on product mix are all concerned with aspects of this fact. The present chapter deals more systematically with the whole subject of multiple products and multiple prices on individual products.

This chapter starts with the simplest topic involving multiple prices: price discrimination (sometimes known as differential pricing). It then transfers attention to the theory of production involving multiple products. This analysis will permit us to sort out the complex problem of joint products, by-products, and common costs. It will then be necessary to consider complementary and substitutionary relationships on the demand side. The next topic is public utility rate regulation which can be evaluated in terms of the economic analysis developed throughout this book. The chapter concludes with a section on peak-load pricing, which is related to the two earlier topics in the chapter, though in ways which are difficult to analyze with precision.

1. PRICE DISCRIMINATION

Two definitions of price discrimination are necessary for our purposes. One is a strict, narrow definition, useful for analytical purposes. The other is looser and broader, but closer to the realities of business. The two definitions are:

1. The practice of charging different prices to different segments of the market for the same commodity or service.[1]

2. The practice of charging prices that are not proportional to the marginal costs of slightly differentiated goods or services.

The first definition presumes a homogeneous commodity. The second definition recognizes that differentiation of price is likely to accompany differentiation in characteristics of the commodity. To determine whether price discrimination exists one must compare cost differentials with price differentials. The absence of price differentials may be discriminatory, as is the case when the same commodity is sold at the same price over a wide territory in which transportation costs vary. The existence of price differentials may, on the other hand, be nondiscriminatory, as would be the case if the prices are related to transportation costs.

Some writers prefer the term "differential pricing" to "price discrimination," for the latter term may carry special connotations. Price discrimination is intended to be a neutral, objective term describing a business practice rather than something that is evil by definition.

Conditions necessary for price discrimination

Two conditions are necessary for profitable price discrimination:

1. Segmentation of the market. It must be possible to segment the market and to prevent resale from one segment to another.

2. Differences in the elasticity of demand. The elasticity of demand in one segment of the market must be lower than in another if discrimination is to be profitable.

Segmentation of the market and differences in elasticity both imply that competition must be imperfect. In a highly competitive market, new sellers would move rapidly into those market segments in which high prices are charged, undermining price differentials and destroying the segmentation. Specialists would engage in speculation—buying in the cheap segments and selling in the dear markets until the price differentials disappear.

How is segmentation of the market achieved? A great variety of methods are in use. It is best to present specific illustrations.

1. Doctors are able to separate patients with high incomes from those with low. The fact that the product is a direct personal service prevents its resale.

2. Railroads separate high-value commodities from those with low value per unit of volume or weight. A simple inspection of the commodities insures that they do not travel at the wrong rate.

---

[1] Joan Robinson's classic definition of price discrimination is "the act of selling the same article, produced under a single control, at different prices to different buyers." See *The Economics of Imperfect Competition* (London: Macmillan & Co., Ltd., 1933), p. 179.

3. Manufacturers frequently offer quantity discounts, thus separating large purchasers from small ones. If the quantity discounts are proportional to the marginal costs of selling to large and small buyers, no discrimination results. If the quantity discounts also reflect the differences in bargaining power of the buyers or the urgency of their demand, price discrimination is present.

4. State universities usually charge higher tuition rates to out-of-state students than to residents of the state. Such universities require evidence of residence, sometimes calling in legal advice in borderline cases.

5. Some firms sell approximately the same product under different brand names at widely differing prices. Consumer ignorance of the similarity in quality prevents a large-scale transfer of customers from one brand to the other.

6. Some producers charge different prices to different trade channels. For example, they may charge more in the replacement market than in the original-equipment market. The replacement demand is likely to be less elastic, permitting a higher charge.

7. Firms sometimes sell abroad at prices lower than domestic prices, a practice known as "dumping." Tariffs and the cost of shipping the product back to the exporting country help maintain segmentation of the market.

8. One simple way of segmenting customers, with some leakage to be sure, is to offer the commodity at a "regular" price most of the year and then reduce the price in the form of special sales. Some customers are not patient enough or price conscious enough to wait for the sales; others are bargain hunters and will wait. Such a policy makes it possible for the seller to tap both kinds of market.[2]

9. Professional journals usually carry lower student subscription rates. They require evidence of a student status. The presumption is that the student demand for journals is more elastic; in addition, students may acquire a long-run desire for the journal, adding to the long-run demand.

10. Faculty members can buy books at discounts below student prices. Their demand is more elastic for books they do not use directly in their courses; furthermore they may adopt the books in the future. The elasticity of student demand is reduced by the practice of "required" texts.

11. Theaters usually charge children lower prices even though they occupy just as much space as adults and may actually be somewhat more costly in wear and tear. In most cases it is easy to determine the age category of the customer, but some leakage seems likely on children at ages close to the dividing line.

---

[2] This illustration may be controversial as an example of price discrimination. One might argue that the service provided at a sale is quite different from that in normal periods so that two different "commodities" are involved. One might even argue that the marginal costs are widely different in the two periods, especially if the items on sale are ones threatening to become obsolete in the near future. In such a case, the original wholesale cost is not a good measure of opportunity cost.

The reader can no doubt supply other illustrations. We might classify these examples into broad categories:

1. Segmentation by income and wealth.
2. Segmentation by quantity of purchase.
3. Segmentation by social or professional status of the customer.
4. Segmentation by geography.
5. Segmentation by time of purchase.
6. Segmentation by preferences for brand names and other sales promotion devices.
7. Segmentation by age of the customer.
8. Segmentation by convenience to the buyer.

The theory of price discrimination

For purposes of the exposition of the theory of price discrimination, it is desirable to start with a homogeneous commodity. This makes it possible to consider only one marginal cost curve. Once this basic problem is understood it is not difficult to extend the theory to differentiated products.

Figure 8–1 presents the standard diagram of price discrimination. The market consists of two segments, one with a more elastic demand curve than the other. Demand in the more elastic segment is indicated by D_1; in the less elastic segment by D_2. The corresponding marginal revenue curves are indicated by MR_1 and MR_2. The aggregate marginal revenue curve sums horizontally the quantities in both markets at each marginal revenue. The reader should note that it is the quantities that are summed and not the marginal revenues themselves.[3]

On the cost side of the analysis only the marginal cost is relevant; the other cost curves are not shown. It should be clear that only one marginal cost curve exists under the conditions specified; it makes no difference from the cost point of view whether the product sells in market 1 or market 2, since it is the same product. The marginal cost is governed by the total output.

The problem in maximizing profits is one, as before, of equating marginal revenue and marginal cost. Such an equality exists when the aggregate marginal revenue curve intersects the marginal cost curve.[4] The horizontal line from this point of intersection intersects the two marginal revenue curves, thus indicating how the total output should be allocated between the two markets. The prices are found on the demand

---

[3] This point is stressed to distinguish price discrimination from the pricing of joint products in which the *vertical* addition of marginal revenues is appropriate.

[4] The solution would not be affected by redrawing the marginal cost curve to be horizontal. Earlier chapters have presented evidence of horizontal marginal cost curves; but it is clearer for purposes of exposition to draw a rising marginal cost curve.

FIGURE 8–1

PRICE DISCRIMINATION WITH TWO MARKET SEGMENTS

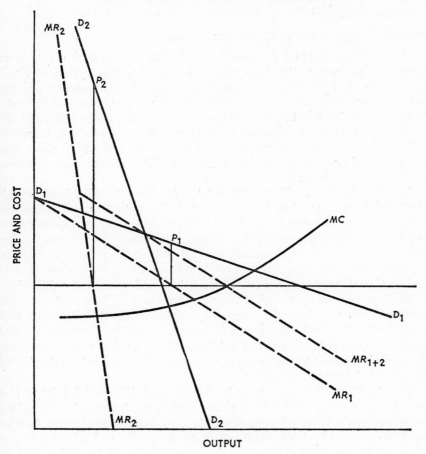

curves, directly above the intersection of the horizontal line with the marginal revenue curves. As one would expect, the price in the first segment, P_1, is considerably lower than the price in the second, P_2.

As a check on his understanding of the diagram, the reader might note that the solution equates the marginal revenue in the two segments, as well as equating marginal revenue to marginal cost. If MR_1 were greater than MR_2, or *vice versa,* the firm could increase profits by transferring units from one segment to the other. This is an illustration of the equimarginal principle. If either MR_1 or MR_2 were greater than marginal cost, an expansion of output would be profitable. Optimization requires that $MR_1 = MR_2 = MC$.

362   *Managerial economics*

The two prices, P_1 and P_2, provide different margins of contribution to profit and overhead. The case of differentiated products involves the same principle; the prices are not proportional to the marginal costs.

Price discrimination in practice: legal issues

An understanding of the fundamental theory presented above is an essential (and a practical) step in understanding the myriad of applications. At the same time, it is not always possible to determine whether a particular case is one of price discrimination or not. The first difficulty is in determining whether two or more products are really differentiated versions of the same product or, instead, two different products on which price comparisons are inappropriate. A second difficulty is in measuring the marginal costs of the various products, which requires some way of dealing with common costs.

The legal status of differential pricing is uncertain. This book avoids the legal intricacies of antitrust and price discrimination legislation and rulings. In general, the Federal Trade Commission and the courts have permitted price differentials that reflect differences in cost; our earlier discussion of costs should explain why this criterion has been so troublesome in such cases. The courts tend to rely on average costs rather than marginal costs in measuring cost differentials, with consequent difficulties in the treatment of overhead. The courts have upheld larger discounts to retailers than to wholesalers and have upheld quantity discounts that could be justified in terms of cost differentials. But the courts have ruled against basing point systems of pricing and have ruled against quantity discounts that may injure or suppress competition. A major criterion of illegality is injury to competitors.

The position of the manager in this area of differential pricing is a complex one. On one hand he is challenged to use imagination in finding more profitable ways of adjusting prices to market conditions. But he may be concerned with his obligations to the public and with avoidance of price differentials that might be considered unfair or harmful to competition. A cash discount, rewarding those who make prompt payments, is easily justified on welfare grounds and probably is not a true case of discrimination since the costs of cash sales are lower. Load factor differentials, which offer price incentives to use capacity in off-peak periods, may actually reduce unit costs and thus permit lower prices for everyone.[5] But discounts to large purchasers may reflect the bargaining power of those purchasers rather than real differences in cost and may encourage the further concentration of economic power. In addition, the manager must consider the legal consequences of his pricing behavior, with the possibility, in view of the complexity of the problem, that his

---

[5] As we shall see later in this chapter, load factor price differentials are not necessarily discriminatory.

ideas of equity may not always conform to those of the Federal Trade Commission or the courts.

Discrimination and economic welfare

A technical analysis of the effect of price discrimination on economic welfare appears in books on economic theory. It is sufficient for our purposes to summarize the arguments; it is becoming increasingly important that managers become familiar with welfare considerations, even though strictly speaking they are a part of social economics rather than managerial economics. The economist's main argument against such discrimination is that it hinders the attainment of equal marginal values among uses and among users. If one consumer pays $5 for commodity A and $10 for commodity B while a second consumer pays $8 and $6 respectively, it can be shown that both will benefit by exchanging units of the one for units of the other. The first consumer will be willing to give up a unit of commodity A which at the margin is worth only $5 to him to gain a unit of commodity B worth close to $10. The second consumer will agree to this exchange for he gives up a unit worth $6 to him to gain one worth close to $8. Under conditions of price discrimination there are barriers to this kind of exchange—if not, the discrimination will be unprofitable. Both consumers are restrained from reaching a higher level of satisfaction. If price discrimination did not exist, if each consumer paid the same price for the commodities, this particular barrier to welfare would not exist.[6]

Perhaps an easier example to follow is the case in which a single consumer is charged two different prices for the same service applied to two different uses. An example would be a higher rate for electricity used in lighting than the rate for heating water, both to be used the same time of the day. Let us assume that the marginal costs of those services are the same. The consumer will hold back in purchasing the high-price service and will extend the use of the low-price service. He will not achieve an optimum in the use of the services, since the marginal value of one is higher than that of the other. In the absence of price discrimination, he would tend toward equal marginal values in both uses.

Another argument against price discrimination—one that gets closer to the legal issues—is that it can be used to drive out competitors. A price below cost, even below marginal cost, may benefit the seller in the long run by driving out competition and creating a monopoly. The consumer may benefit from the initial low price but will suffer from the later higher monopoly price.

Nevertheless, most economists agree that price discrimination may be acceptable in certain cases. If a particular service can be produced profitably only under conditions of discrimination, all consumers may benefit

---

[6] This is merely an introduction to the issues involved. Even if the first customer were to pay a higher price for both commodities, there could be gains from trade.

from having a wider range of choice in their purchases. If a public utility is able to reach new pools of demand at discriminatory low prices, and to achieve economies of scale which otherwise would be unattainable, the additional contribution to overhead and profits will permit a general reduction in rates, to the benefit of all consumers.[7]

When the distribution of income is taken into account, additional, but more nebulous, arguments for discrimination appear. A doctor may be justified in charging higher rates to wealthier patients on the grounds that they can "afford" to pay more. The assumption here is that the marginal utility of money is less to the rich than to the poor. Although economists prefer not to make such interpersonal comparisons of utility, this argument is a basis for much social legislation and for the progressive income tax. The doctors by charging high rates to some and low rates to others are helping to redistribute the national income and are subsidizing the low-income groups. Whether this basis for discrimination is acceptable to the reader will depend more on his value judgments about the "correct" distribution of income than it will on economic analysis alone.

A fuller discussion of the welfare aspects of price discrimination would take us beyond the scope of managerial economics. A footnote refers the reader to several outstanding discussions of the topic.[8]

Empirical studies and illustrations

An almost endless series of illustrations of price discrimination could be presented, for it is a widespread practice. To save space, it seems appropriate to restrict attention to price discrimination in the public utilities. The utilities are usually "natural monopolies," subject to decreasing long-run costs, and thus are particularly prone to seek price discrimination to achieve economies of scale.

Water supply. An outstanding study of water supply indicates that price discrimination is widely practiced by municipal water companies, both public and private.[9] In New York City some users are unmetered, which means that they pay a flat rate with no extra charge for the heavy use of water. Obviously there is discrimination between such users and those who pay according to volume of consumption. This discrimination encourages the waste of water. It means that consumers pay more for water used in the production of food (the producer must pay for the

---

[7] Even when price discrimination can be justified on such grounds it may be argued that each consumer should pay the same *marginal* price. See J. Hirshleifer, J. C. DeHaven, and J. W. Milliman, *Water Supply: Economics, Technology, and Policy* (Chicago: University of Chicago Press, 1960), p. 92.

[8] Tibor Scitovsky, *Welfare and Competition* (Chicago: Richard D. Irwin, Inc., 1951); J. De V. Graaf, *Theoretical Welfare Economics* (Cambridge: Cambridge University Press, 1957); J. Rothenberg, *The Measurement of Social Welfare* (Englewood Cliffs, N.J.: Prentice-Hall, Inc., 1961).

[9] J. Hirshleifer, J. C. DeHaven, and J W. Milliman, *op. cit.*, pp. 44–45.

water and will pass on the cost) than they pay for direct use. The result is a disparity in the value of the marginal uses of the water. In Los Angeles, on the other hand, lower rates are charged for irrigation water than for water in urban use, and the rate differentials are clearly not in proportion to the marginal costs. The result is a subsidy to farm production.

Some of the water rate differentials are undoubtedly related to costs and thus are not discriminatory in the strict definition of price discrimination. For example, most systems charge less per unit for greater volumes, a fact that may reflect the lower cost of delivering and metering the increments in volume. In Los Angeles (and many other cities) a differential exists between firm service and service the water department may curtail at its convenience. Since the cost of water delivered at peak periods is greater than delivered at other times, this differential is not necessarily discriminatory—it is a way of charging for the extra load that peak users place on the system.

The system of block rates in water utilities may result in serious price discrimination. Under block rates a customer's consumption is divided into a number of blocks, with different rates for each block. Typically lower rates are charged for the additional blocks. It might appear at first that such rates reflect the lower unit cost of delivering greater volumes of water to the customer. But in the short run the marginal cost of any particular consumer's usage would appear to be independent of his volume. It costs as much to deliver the thousandth unit as it does to deliver the hundredth. The fixed facilities such as pipes are already installed and do not enter into the marginal costs. Thus the block rates would appear to discriminate in favor of the high-volume users.

Gas and electricity. One of the most thorough studies of gas and electricity rates is that of the Consolidated Gas Electric Light and Power Company of Baltimore.[10] The rate schedules of the Baltimore company are probably representative of those in the gas and electricity industries in general. They incorporate several kinds of price discrimination, all with the approval of the regulatory agencies. One kind of discrimination is called "peak–off-peak discrimination," which involves a failure to relate rates to the differentials in costs between peak and off-peak periods. The simplest form of such discrimination is the charging of the same rate in both peak and off-peak periods. Even when higher rates are charged peak energy users, the methods of allocating costs often fail to apply as high a proportion of capacity costs to the peak periods as is warranted, resulting in a subsidy of peak production by off-peak sales. Another form of price discrimination in gas and electricity is in the use of block rates,

---

[10] See R. K. Davidson, *Price Discrimination in Selling Gas and Electricity* (Baltimore: The Johns Hopkins Press, 1955), especially chap. xi.

which not only violate the equimarginal rules but may even result in some rates below marginal costs. Such extremely low rates result in the use of resources in the production of services worth less than those resources could produce elsewhere. Nevertheless many economists and regulatory agencies have supported such rates as socially desirable.

The study of the Baltimore Consolidated Gas Electric Light and Power Company provides illustrations of other types of price discrimination. The company makes estimates of the "value of service" to customers; rates are frequently related to such values rather than to costs. During the depression of the thirties, for example, the company set prices to meet the competition of other energy sources, cutting rates sharply for large industrial and domestic consumers. As Davidson says, "value-of-service pricing is precisely what economists call monopolistic price discrimination, the results of which many regard as socially undesirable."[11]

The different types of rate structures which have been used in the gas and electric utilities vary in the degree of discrimination. The "simple flat rate," which was used in the early history of such utilities, was highly discriminatory, for it charged no more for high consumption than low. The "adjusted flat rate," which varied according to the number of electric lights and connected appliances, no doubt was better correlated with consumption, but it obviously did not reflect different rates of usage of the equipment.

The "straight-line rate," a uniform charge per unit of energy consumed, requires metering. The trouble with such straight-line rates is that they do not separate the charges for capacity and for customer costs from the charges for the use of energy. This rate thus discriminates against the large consumer (for whom the unit customer costs are low) and against the off-peak user. The utilities, recognizing that the straight-line rates did discriminate against large users, introduced discounts for quantity consumption. These discounts have taken several forms, the most popular of which today is the block rate already described. Many utilities using block rates require customers to pay a minimum bill to assure that at least part of the fixed customer costs are recovered. A main defect of the block rates is their failure to charge extra for consumption at the peak, discriminating against those with relatively uniform consumption over time.

To overcome some of the defects of the preceding systems, several more sophisticated rate structures have been introduced. These structures are known as "demand rate" structures. They separate the charge for energy from what is called the "demand." Note that the word "demand" in this context has an entirely different meaning from the usual one in economics. It refers to the maximum level of consumption. The "demand"

---

[11] *Ibid.*, p. 215.

rate charges separately for the *maximum* "demand," which is a measure of the maximum load placed on the system's capacity.[12] The best known of the "demand" structures is the Hopkinson rate introduced in England in 1892. The typical Hopkinson rate schedule appears as follows:[13]

"Demand" charge
First 200 kw. (or less) of demand $3.02
Next 1,800 kw. .... 1.51 per kw.
Over 2,000 kw. .... 1.28 per kw.

Consumption charge
First 50,000 kw.-hrs. .... 0.94¢ per kw.-hr.
Next 250,000 kw.-hrs. .... 0.83¢ per kw.-hr.
Next 300,000 kw.-hrs. .... 0.56¢ per kw.-hr.
All over 600,000 kw.-hrs. .... 0.47¢ per kw.-hr.

The Hopkinson rate has one major failing. It charges for the maximum rate of consumption of the individual but does not charge for the maximum strain the individual places on the system. If the customer's peak comes at the trough of the system's load, he should be rewarded rather than penalized for he is helping to improve the "load factor" (the ratio of actual consumption to capacity consumption). What is needed is a charge for the individual customer's contribution to the peak-load. A fuller discussion of peak-load pricing appears in a later section of this chapter.

Davidson's conclusion on all of the rate structures used in the gas and electricity industry is that "none" "conforms to the true costs of service" and "all are discriminatory."[14] Perhaps he has given too little weight to the metering costs and administrative difficulties involved in completely nondiscriminatory rates.

Railroads.   The railroads are perhaps best known of all industries for the practice of price discrimination. Several varieties of rail rate discrimination are prevalent or have prevailed in the past: (1) discrimination among commodities; (2) discrimination between localities; (3) personal discrimination. The existence of discrimination among commodities is clear from the fact that some rates are as much as eight times the rates for other commodities over the same distance, as shown in Table 8–1. Only a part of this difference reflects difference in cost; the remainder is related to the ability to pay. Table 8–1 shows rates on various com-

---

[12] Special demand meters record the maximum demand.
[13] Taken from R. K. Davidson, *op. cit.*, which contains an excellent discussion of gas and electricity rate structures. Most readers will recognize the distinction between kilowatts (kw.) and kilowatt-hours (kw.-hrs.), the first being a stock concept (power) and the second a flow concept (energy).
[14] *Ibid.*, pp. 96–97.

TABLE 8–1

COMPARISON OF CARLOAD FREIGHT REVENUE FROM SELECTED COMMODITIES AND
FULLY DISTRIBUTED COST, 1956*

Commodity	Percentage of Fully Distributed Cost	Commodity	Percentage of Fully Distributed Cost
Wheat	130	Iron ore	63
Corn	121	Gravel and sand (N.O.S.)	54
Flour, wheat	73	Lumber, shingles, lath	101
Cotton, in bales	135	Paint, putty, and varnish	157
Cottonseed	117	Drugs and toilet preparations	141
Cottonseed hulls	92	Agricultural implements	158
Oranges and grapefruit	78	Machinery and machines	207
Lettuce	62	Office machines	203
Potatoes	72	Automobiles, passenger	171
Cattle and calves (in single-deck cars)	74	Refrigerators	142
Eggs	100	Boots, shoes, etc.	157
Butter	112	Liquors, alcoholic	208
Anthracite coal	101	Sugar	127
Bituminous coal	80	Cigarettes	192

* Interstate Commerce Commission, Bureau of Accounts, Cost Finding and Valuation, Statement No. 6–58, *Distribution of the Rail Revenue Contribution by Commodity Groups—1956* (Washington, D.C.: U.S. Government Printing Office, 1958).

SOURCE: D. Philip Locklin, *Economics of Transportation* (5th ed.) (Homewood, Ill.: Richard D. Irwin, Inc., 1960), p. 136.

modities related to fully distributed cost (marginal cost would have been more suitable).

Local discrimination consists of differences in rates for equal distances, equal rates for unequal distances, and charging more for short hauls than for long hauls over the same line. One reason for such discrimination is to meet the competition of other forms of transportation, such as water and truck competition. The ICC regulates such discrimination but has made exceptions in a variety of cases.

Personal discrimination in railroad rates is rare today. In the early history of the American railroads it was a widespread practice, especially in the form of concessions or rebates to favored customers. Around the turn of the century the Standard Oil Company was able to extract such concessions and rebates by threatening to shift business to other lines or to pipelines. Apparently personal discrimination is still frequent on European railroads.

2. MULTIPLE PRODUCTS

The interrelatedness of commodities in production and in demand can take a great variety of forms. The tools of analysis introduced in Chapter 2 are adequate to deal with decision making on multiple products if they are fully understood and correctly applied. That is to say, the correct use of incremental reasoning and the full recognition of opportunity costs, with adequate attention to the problems of time perspective and discounting, are all that is necessary for the management of multiple products. The problem is to evaluate the impact of each decision on costs and revenues (and on the other objectives of the firm), both immediate and in the future.

It is well to recognize the great variety of ways in which products can be interrelated. We shall consider first relations on the production and cost side and then transfer attention to demand.

Output independent in production

The simplest case is one in which the firm produces several products completely independent from each other. Each product requires a separate plant. Each plant is specialized and unsuitable for the production of other products. It is true that there must be some common costs for all the products or we could hardly call this a firm; but let us assume that such common costs are relatively insignificant. In such a case it would be appropriate to treat each product division as a separate firm, applying the analysis for single-product firms.

Alternative products

Another relatively simple case is one in which the facilities may be readily shifted from one product to another, in which the total capacity is fixed but the marginal costs of each product are constant up to capacity. In such a case the marginal cost of one product is independent of the marginal cost of another at all ranges below capacity, but at capacity the increase in production of one involves a sacrifice of the production of others. We shall label such products "alternative products." The analysis for alternative products depends on whether the firm is operating at capacity or below.

1. Let us consider the case of excess capacity. All that is required is the measurement of the marginal cost or incremental cost of each product. In combination with the appropriate revenue measures, such costs will indicate the contribution to overhead and profit. Even here there is a complication, having to do with the longer-run impact of decisions. A decision based on short-run incremental costs with excess capacity may bind the firm to produce in the longer run when such excess capacity no longer exists. Thus the decision maker must make a forecast of the probable persistence of excess capacity, the probable sacrifice of alternative profit opportunities, and the probable need for added capacity in the future. In other words, such decisions require the proper blend of short-run and long-run incremental analysis. The acceptance of an order or establishment of a price on purely immediate cost considerations can lead to losses of profits in the future.

2. If the firm is operating at capacity, the issue becomes one of allocation of the given facilities. Linear programming is particularly suited to
this kind of decision, if the assumed linearity of costs and production
functions is a convenient approximation. Whether or not management
uses linear programming, decision making requires the comparison of the
contribution to overhead and profit of each decision with the sacrifices
required. Again the longer-run implications of the decision are relevant, a
point that the mechanical use of linear programming might neglect.

Joint products: fixed proportions

Let us turn next to the simplest case of *joint products*, the case in
which they must be produced in fixed proportions, with no possibility
of increasing one at the expense of another. In this situation the costs
are entirely joint costs. There is no sound logical basis for allocating costs
to the various products. And, indeed, it is best to think of production of
a package of products. If the total revenue from the package covers more
than the short-run incremental costs of the joint products, and thus makes
a contribution greater than alternatives to overhead and profits, the package is worth producing in the short run. If the total long-run revenue is
expected to cover all the long-run costs including the opportunity cost of
capital, the package is worth producing in the long run. This is true even
if part of the package results in no revenue or only a small revenue, in
which case it might be called a by-product.

Figure 8–2 illustrates the pricing of joint products.[15] Only one marginal
cost curve is shown, since the costs of the entire package are indivisible.
Two demand curves are shown, one for each of the two products. MR_1
indicates the marginal revenue derived from sales of the first product.
MR_2 shows the marginal revenue for the second product. MR_{1+2} is the
vertical sum of MR_1 and MR_2. The difference between Figures 8–2 and
8–1 (which illustrated price discrimination) is that the marginal revenues
are summed vertically rather than horizontally. The reason for this is that
an increase of one unit on the horizontal scale means an increase in the
package consisting of quantities of each product; added revenues result
from both products and the total of the two should be compared with
marginal costs. The optimum is at the point of intersection between marginal cost and the aggregate marginal revenue curve. P_1 and P_2 represent
the most profitable prices for the two commodities.[16]

Figure 8–3 represents a slight alteration in the situation. Here MR_2

---

[15] For a fuller analysis, see M. R. Colberg, "Monopoly Prices under Joint Costs:
Fixed Proportions," *Journal of Political Economy*, February, 1941, p. 109. Also see
M. R. Colberg, W. C. Bradford, and R. M. Alt, *Business Economics: Principles and
Cases* (rev. ed.; Homewood, Ill.: Richard D. Irwin, Inc., 1957), pp. 299–302.

[16] Note that the demand curves are here considered to be completely independent
of one another.

FIGURE 8–2
MAXIMIZATION OF PROFITS—TWO JOINT PRODUCTS

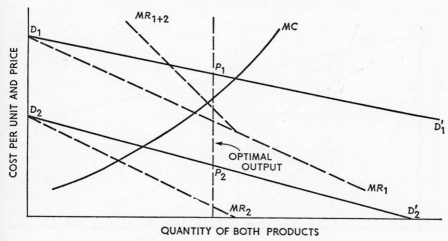

QUANTITY OF BOTH PRODUCTS

becomes negative before MR_{1+2} reaches the marginal cost curve. The firm will not maximize profits if it keeps on reducing the price on product 2 to get rid of it; the negative marginal revenue means a loss in total revenue. Product 2 will be sold up to the point at which its marginal revenue is zero, with P_2 the appropriate price. But it is profitable to produce more packages, because MR_1 still exceeds the marginal cost. The optimum is at the point at which MR_1 equals the marginal cost. The excess units of product 2 will be destroyed, since their appearance on the market will depress prices.

Other variations in the situation may be worked out by the reader. These could include a case in which one of the products is sold in a purely competitive market or one in which both are sold in such a market.

Joint products: variable proportions

Joint products are not always fixed in proportion. Management is capable of considerable ingenuity in adjusting the proportions to increase profits. For example, it is possible to breed sheep producing somewhat different ratios of wool and mutton to adjust to the relative profitability of those two products.[17] A single marginal cost curve for the two products together no longer suffices; and since it is no longer possible to consider a package of products in fixed ratios, a two-dimensional diagram, like Figure 8–2, no longer can handle all of the variables. One approach is to

---

[17] This illustration appears in J. M. Clark, *Studies in the Economics of Overhead Costs* (Chicago: University of Chicago Press, 1923), p. 98.

FIGURE 8–3

MAXIMIZATION OF PROFITS—JOINT PRODUCTS WITH DESTRUCTION
OF PART OF ONE

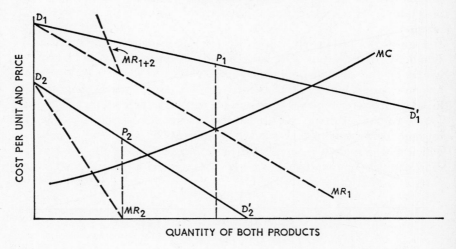

QUANTITY OF BOTH PRODUCTS

switch to another type of graph, showing transformation curves, also
known as production possibility curves.

Figure 8–4 shows the production possibility curves for two products.
The axes represent quantities of these products, with the output of product 1 on the horizontal axis and of product 2 on the vertical axis. Consider
one of the production possibility curves. It shows the various quantities
of products 1 and 2 that can be produced with a given quantity of a
variable input. The diagram indicates two ways of increasing the quantity
of product 1. One is to increase the quantity of the variable inputs moving

FIGURE 8–4

PRODUCTION POSSIBILITY CURVES TWO OUTPUTS

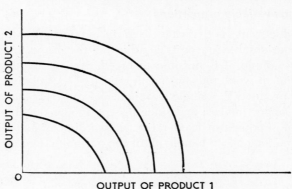

OUTPUT OF PRODUCT 1

in a northeast direction on the graph. In this case the output of product 2 will increase also. The second method would be to move along the production possibility curve (instead of moving to higher production possibility curves), increasing the output of product 1 at the expense of product 2.

Figure 8–5 brings price into the picture. Assume, for the sake of simplicity, that the prices are given and are independent of quantity, as would be the case in pure competition. We can draw a series of iso-revenue curves which, in this situation, are downward sloping straight lines. Each iso-revenue curve represents various combinations of products 1 and 2 that result in the same total revenue. For example, one iso-revenue curve might represent all combinations of the two products which will provide a revenue of $100; a second iso-revenue curve might represent all combinations returning $200 and so on. Figure 8–5 super-

FIGURE 8–5

Iso-Revenue Curves Superimposed on a Production Possibility Diagram

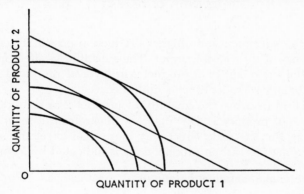

imposes a set of such iso-revenue curves on the same diagram with the production possibility curves. The reader will recognize readily that an optimal solution requires a tangency between a production possibility curve and an iso-revenue curve. At such a point of tangency the marginal costs of the products are proportional to the prices.

An increase in the price of one of the products will change the slope of the iso-revenue curves and the points of tangency. If the price of product 1 increases, the production of that product also increases for two reasons: the firm will hire a greater quantity of the variable input, and it will sacrifice some product 2 by moving along the production possibility curve. Figure 8–6 illustrates this situation.

These two reasons for the increase in product 1 are known in economics as the *scale effect* and the *substitution effect*. The scale effect has

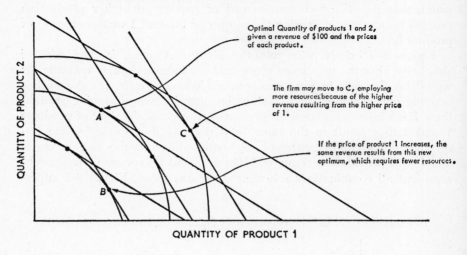

374   *Managerial economics*

FIGURE 8–6

EFFECTS OF AN INCREASE IN THE PRICE OF ONE PRODUCT

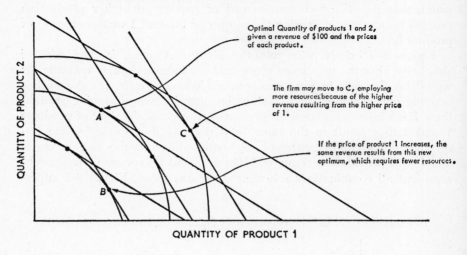

to do with the movement onto higher production possibility curves, with the greater use of the variable input. The substitution effect involves the curtailment of the quantity of product 2 in favor of product 1 (requiring a movement along a production possibility curve).

Will the firm decrease the quantity of product 2 as a result of the increased price of product 1? Our diagram illustrates a case in which this does happen. But the scale effect may more than offset the substitution effect with a net increase in product 2, as is indicated by Figure 8–7.

Joint products: mathematical notation[18]

Mathematical notation is useful in keeping the various types of joint production in order. (Note again that we are concerned here only with the technology of production and are ignoring demand and prices.) Let x represent the quantity of product 1, y the quantity of product 2, and v the quantity of the variable input.

It should be clear that v is a function of x and y, so that we have:

$$v = f(x, y)$$

The partial derivatives of v with respect to x and y respectively are known as *marginal coefficients of production*. The two marginal coefficients of production are:

$$\frac{\partial v}{\partial x} \text{ and } \frac{\partial v}{\partial y}$$

---

[18] Readers with inadequate training in calculus may wish to bypass this section.

FIGURE 8–7
EFFECTS OF AN INCREASE IN THE PRICE OF ONE OUTPUT
(scale effect exceeds substitution effect)

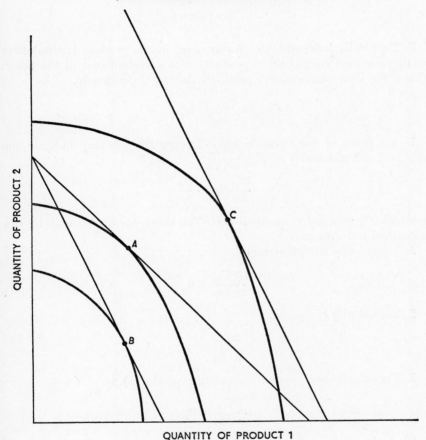

which are the inverse of the marginal productivities of v with respect to x and y.

We now use this notation to distinguish three classes of joint products:

1. *Technically complementary.* The increase of one product causes the marginal coefficient of the other to decrease.

$$\frac{\partial^2 v}{\partial x \; \partial y} \text{ is negative}$$

Another way of putting this case is that an increase in one product causes the marginal cost of the other to decline. (Remember, however, the assumption that the price of the variable input is given.)

2. Technically competitive. An increase in one product causes the marginal coefficient of production of the other to increase.

$$\frac{\partial^2 v}{\partial x \ \partial y} \text{ is positive}$$

3 Tecnically independent. An increase in one product has no effect on the marginal coefficient of production or marginal cost of the other. This is the case of alternative products discussed previously.

$$\frac{\partial^2 v}{\partial x \ \partial y} = 0$$

If the price of the variable input is constant we may indicate the marginal cost of x and y as

$$\frac{\partial C_T}{\partial x} \text{ and } \frac{\partial C_T}{\partial y}$$

in which C_T represents the total cost. The three cases then may be distinguished in terms of cost.

1. Technically complementary.

$$\frac{\partial^2 C_T}{\partial x \ \partial y} < 0$$

2. Technically competitive.

$$\frac{\partial^2 C_T}{\partial x \ \partial y} > 0$$

3. Technically independent (alternative products).

$$\frac{\partial^2 C_T}{\partial x \ \partial y} = 0$$

Some discussions of joint products restrict the term to the first case, the one in which an increase in one product reduces the marginal cost of the other. We use the term here more broadly to cover all cases of two or more products resulting from a single process. One reason for the broader definition is that products that may be technically complementary within a range may become competitive beyond that range.

Other complications on the production side

It is possible to complicate the analysis on the production side much more. For example, we may wish to drop the assumption that only one variable input is employed in producing the two outputs. Introduction of other variable inputs results in the possibility of varying the proportions among these inputs as we vary the outputs, a very likely possibility in actual practice. Then we may wish to move beyond the two-product cases to the more general multiple-product cases. We may go further and introduce the possibility that the prices of the inputs are not independent of their usage. All of these cases could be presented mathematically, but it is best for our purposes to stop short of the full elaboration of the theory. A manager who wishes to develop the complete analysis for this situation may refer to the fuller discussions in Carlson and other works on the theory of production and the theory of the firm.[19] Most managers will probably prefer a simple approach, even if it means a failure to take the full situation into account.

Relations on the demand side

Two situations present themselves on the demand side:
1. Commodities which are substitutes (competing commodities).
2. Commodities which are complements in demand.
The reader might at first consider a category of "independent in demand" to be appropriate, but further consideration would show that commodities are competing for the consumer's dollar if they are not complements. It is true that some pairs of commodities are much closer substitutes for each other than other pairs. Margarine is a closer substitute for butter than apples are for automobiles. Or Wheaties are a closer substitute for corn flakes than Ivory soap is for potatoes. The relation of substitution is more pervasive than that of complementarity, but both are important in managerial practice.

The definition of complementarity in demand is no easy task and, in fact, has been a stumbling block for economists.[20] For our purposes we are interested in a definition which is appropriate from the seller's point of view. (This is fortunate since the definition from the consumer's point of view is more complex.) We shall conclude that two commodities are complements if one of two conditions is met:

a) The availability of one stimulates the demand for the other (causes the demand for the other to increase), or

b) The reduction of the price of one stimulates the demand for the other.

The illustrations of complementary products are plentiful. The argument for maintaining a "complete line" or "full line" is really an argument that the availability of some products improves the marketability of others. The reduction of prices in special sales aims in part at increasing the purchases of items not on sale, or to increase familiarity with the

[19] Sune Carlson, *A Study on the Pure Theory of Production* (London: P. S. King, 1939).
[20] The treatment by J. R. Hicks in his classic, *Value and Capital*, differs from that in P. A. Samuelson's equally important *Foundations of Economic Analysis*. Still other definitions appear in other works.

selling outlet. The case of "loss leaders" is another clear illustration of an attempt to increase the demand for some products by lowering the price of others. Loss leaders attract customers into the store, where it is hoped he will buy his whole market basket of goods and will engage in a little "impulse buying." Holdren breaks the effect of an addition to a product line into two parts: a "transfer effect," consisting of increased sales at the expense of other stores and a "budget effect," consisting of a reduction in consumer saving.[21] Both effects are aspects of complementarity.

A glossary of terms

It is desirable to review the terms under discussion for they are difficult to keep in order. The key terms are:

a) *Alternative products*—commodities which can be produced in the same facilities when the marginal costs of one are independent of the outputs of others up to full capacity.

b) *Joint products*—commodities which are interrelated in production so that changes in the volume of one affects the marginal costs or availability of the others.

c) *By-products*—those joint products which for some reason are considered less "important" than other parts of the joint production.

d) *Technically complementary products*—increased output of one causes the marginal costs of others to decline or the availability of others to increase (one type of joint production).

e) *Technically competing products*—increased output of one causes the marginal cost of the others to increase or their availability to decrease (another type of joint production).

f) *Joint costs*—costs which are shared by joint products and which cannot easily be attributed to one product or another. (The term here is defined narrowly to exclude costs which are shared by "alternative products.")

g) *Common costs*—a broader term than "joint costs," including costs which are shared by alternative products as well as by joint products but which cannot be easily attributed to individual commodities.

h) *Commodities which are complementary in demand*—commodities whose availability or whose lower price stimulates the sale of the other commodities.

Multiple products and pricing

The multiple-product situations which we have reviewed require different pricing practices depending on the type of relationship among the

---

[21] Bob R. Holdren, *The Structure of a Retail Market and the Market Behavior of Retail Units* (Englewood Cliffs, N.J.: Prentice-Hall, Inc., 1960), pp. 121–22.

products. We have seen that for commodities absolutely fixed in proportion in production the most profitable solution is one of equating the vertical sum of the marginal revenues to the joint marginal cost (except when one of the marginal revenues drops below zero). In the case of alternative products under conditions of excess capacity, the most profitable price is at the point at which the marginal revenue of each product equals the marginal cost of that product. For alternative products at full capacity, the same rule applies, but care must be taken that the computation of each marginal cost makes provision for the opportunity costs of the alternative products. One way to approach this analysis is to compute the contributions to overhead and profits of each product under various assumptions about price until the most profitable price combinations are found. (More elaborate mathematical procedures would be appropriate but are beyond the scope of this book.)

Technically competing products, technically complementary products, or products which are complementary in demand require a more complex analysis. A change in the price of one product affects not only its output but also the costs and revenues of the other products. It should be clear that in principle the problem is solvable but that rather elaborate mathematical models are required for the solution.

Empirical studies and illustrations

The usual approach in practice to decisions on multiple products which are related in production or in demand is relatively unsophisticated. In the case of alternative products, linear programming provides a convenient method for bridging the gap between theory and practice. But in the more complex cases the construction of models which reflect the important interrelations is a difficult and costly task. Therefore, most managers rely mainly on experience and trial and error. We would expect that such a rough and ready approach will often provide approximations to the theoretical optima. However, it is also clear that confusion about the treatment of overhead costs may sometimes interfere with the attainment of those optima.

The classic example of joint costs is that of cattle production. The cattle rancher sells products to both the meat packers and the leather tanners. He has no way of determining the cost of each, and, in fact, his prices are governed by demand and not individual product costs. The objective is to set prices at levels that will clear the market for both meat and hides. Output will be at levels that will equate the marginal revenue from both meat and hides to the marginal cost of producing both. Similarly, the meat packer sells meat to grocery chains and other distributors along with by-products to other purchasers. Again, the "full" cost of the by-products cannot be determined; demand must govern the setting of the price of each by-product.

The grocery, in turn, must determine what price to charge for the different cuts of meat it obtains from the carcass. As Holdren states, "the elasticity of demand rather than carcass cost dominates the determination of the relative prices of different cuts of meat."[22] In the supermarkets which he studied, the average price of round steak was 85 cents per pound, rib roast was 55 cents per pound, chuck roast, 42 cents, and hamburger, 30 cents (July, 1954, prices). In all of the stores hamburger and chuck roast were sold below the average cost of the carcass. He found that as beef prices rose the range of prices on different cuts narrowed, the customer substituting cheaper cuts for more expensive ones. Such substitutionary relations in demand complicate the determination of the most profitable prices. Holdren found that the individual store managers tended to keep their prices on chuck, hamburger, and round steak competitive with prices in other stores. They followed "the get rid of" principle in pricing the other cuts. They bought enough carcasses to fill the demand for round steak and chuck roast and altered the prices of other cuts (except hamburger) until the market was cleared. In other words, the stores did not use anything approaching a mathematical model reflecting the demand and cost conditions. They instead followed a series of decision-making rules: imitate the price of other stores on some cuts; purchase quantities according to the demand for those cuts at the imitative prices; and price the other cuts to get rid of the quantity which results from the previous rules. These rules are rather uninformative on how the prices which are imitated are themselves established, a question which cannot be answered by studying one or a few stores at a time.

The pricing of pork follows a somewhat different pattern. The packer breaks down the carcasses and charges the grocery store for each part separately. In this situation, the packers rather than the stores practice the "get rid of" principle. At the time Holdren made his study the pricers were reducing prices on ham "butts" and "shanks," which were not selling in the summer climate. Holdren quotes one meat pricer as saying, "Well, I'll just raise the prices of center slices until I can afford to throw the 'shanks' and 'butts' out the back door."[23]

3. PUBLIC UTILITY RATE REGULATION

Pricing (rate making) in the public utilities presents a special problem in economic analysis. The utilities—electricity, gas, water, telephones, and public transportation—are "natural monopolies"; in any one locality a

---

[22] *Ibid.*, p. 80.
[23] *Ibid.*, p. 82.

single firm tends to drive out competing firms.[24] These are industries in which the technology of production and distribution results in substantial economies of scale, which means that one large firm can produce more cheaply than can several firms.[25] Legislatures have recognized these economies of scale and tendencies to monopoly in granting franchises protecting utility companies from competition and in subjecting them to rate control by regulatory commissions.

Basic pricing

Three alternative policies for pricing in the public utilities are possible: monopoly pricing, full-cost pricing, and marginal cost pricing. All are illustrated in Figure 8–8, which assumes a decreasing cost firm. Price *OA* is the monopoly price—the price which maximizes profit. Almost all observers agree that this price is intolerable to the public. It provides a monopoly profit to firms at the expense of consumers. It results in a misallocation of resources, since the value to consumers of additional output would exceed the value of resources such additional output would use up. A monopoly price is becoming more acceptable in the railroad industry, in which the demand curve has shifted back to the average total cost curve and in which competition has made the demand more elastic. But price *OA* in most public utilities would result in a waste of resources and in inequities in the distribution of income.

Price *OB* is the price sought in the usual utility regulation. It is based on full cost—it covers fixed as well as variable costs and includes a normal return on investment. Price *OB* is set to provide a "fair rate of return" on the investment in the utility. The history of rate regulation is a history of controversy over what rates of returns are fair and conducive to the growth and financial strength of the utilities. It is also a history of controversy over the "rate base"—the value of the property on which the rate of return should be allowed. In periods of inflation the utilities have a strong preference for valuation at reproduction cost. They argue that the original costs, or "book costs," do not reflect the true value

---

[24] Precision in the definition of a public utility is not necessary for our purpose. Bonbright prefers a definition close to ordinary usage: "any enterprise subject to regulation, including price regulation, of a type designed primarily to protect consumers." This definition suits the purpose of our discussion, if it is qualified to eliminate cases of temporary, wartime price regulation. See J. C. Bonbright, *Principles of Public Utility Rates* (New York: Columbia University Press, 1961), chap. 1, for a fuller discussion of definitions.

[25] It might seem that the telephone industry is an exception; a telephone company is subject to increasing costs as it expands the number of customers. But if one were to measure output in terms of the quantity and quality of service, such increasing costs would no longer appear. In any case, there are obvious advantages in having a single telephone company in any single locality.

FIGURE 8–8

ALTERNATIVE LEVELS OF PUBLIC UTILITY RATES

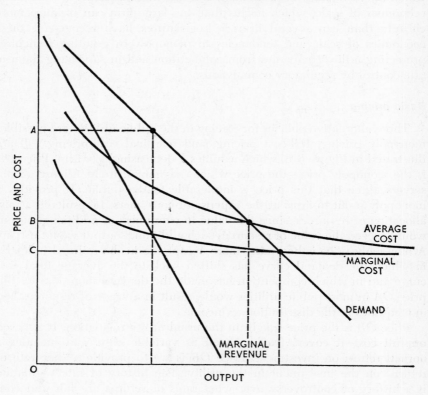

of the property and that returns on property valued at such costs are confiscatory. Some regulatory commissions, on the other hand, favor original cost, or a variation of original cost known as "prudent investment," not only because this practice holds down utility rates but also because original cost is easier to determine objectively. Considerable litigation often results from estimates of reproduction cost; accounting conventions reduce the amount of litigation that is possible over original cost.

The issue of original cost, reproduction cost, or other variations, such as "fair value," is still unsettled. The state regulatory commissions have not standardized their practices in establishing the rate bases; a full discussion of this issue must be left to books on public utility economics. It is necessary to note, however, that the exact level of *OB*, the price at full cost, depends somewhat on the particular regulatory agency which has jurisdiction over the utility.

Marginal cost pricing

Price *OC* is the price at marginal cost. Much of the literature on welfare economics expresses a preference for this price. The discussion of marginal cost pricing tends to become rather involved, but the argument can be summarized in nontechnical language. It is claimed that the welfare of society is increased if the price is lowered below *OB* because the value of the added service exceeds the marginal cost of added output, down to the point at which the demand curve intersects the marginal cost curve. At *OC* the value to the marginal user (measured by the price he pays for the last unit, which is also the price he pays for all units) is equal to the value of the resources used up to produce the last unit. Any higher price and lower consumption, it is argued, means a failure to maximize welfare.

Price *OC* has the disadvantage that it does not cover total costs in a decreasing cost firm. The economists who favor marginal cost pricing recommend that the government pay a subsidy to the utility so that it can cover all costs. Some of them even recommend public ownership on the grounds that the government is not required to cover all costs out of revenues.

If the utility is subject to increasing costs, as may be true of the telephone companies, marginal cost pricing may result in prices which exceed total costs. This result is shown in Figure 8–9. The firm earns excess profits in this case, but not as high profits as would be possible without regulation. Special taxes could siphon off a large part of the excess profit.

FIGURE 8–9

MARGINAL COST PRICING IN AN INCREASING COST INDUSTRY

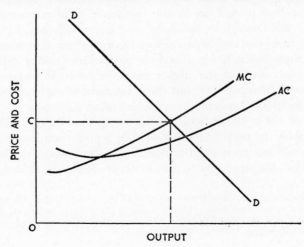

Marginal cost pricing is objectionable on several grounds. Subsidies mean the loss of the control advantages of rules that revenues must cover costs. Utilities may be distracted from their main business if they have to contend with political agencies for subsidies. Their profits may depend more upon their success in demonstrating the need for subsidies than in controlling costs. A subsidy is often a reasonable method for attaining certain social objectives, but the use of subsidies in the utilities should not be undertaken lightly. It is interesting that most nationalized utilities maintain the rule that revenues must cover costs.[26] Apparently most governments are unwilling to abandon the control advantages of requiring that costs be covered.

Multiple prices: price discrimination

The discussion of utility pricing up to this point has assumed a single, homogeneous service with a single price. Public utilities, however, supply a variety of services to various classes of customers and maintain complex structures of prices. Many of the pricing practices clearly are discriminatory in the economist's sense. The railroads charge higher prices for transporting high-value commodities even though the differences in marginal costs of transporting different commodities are negligible. The telephone companies charge more than twice as much for business telephones as for residential telephones, even though the higher usage of business phones can hardly add much to the total costs of the system. It seems likely that the higher prices on services with a less elastic demand are "subsidizing" the services with more elastic demands.

Some welfare economists would object to such discrimination on the grounds of the failure to equate marginal values to various users. Why should we penalize business phones by higher rates? The costs of those phones are part of the total costs of doing business; presumably most business costs are passed on to the consumer. The consumers are encouraged to use more telephones by the low residential rates but are discouraged from buying commodities incorporating telephone costs by the high business rates. Some telephone companies (and regulatory commissions) point out that the higher rates on business phones result in lower corporate income taxes, but these tax reductions must be made up somewhere by higher taxes on other goods and services.

In spite of these theoretical arguments, price discrimination in the utilities is likely to persist. In fact, a number of prominent economists have recommended such discrimination for the railroads; these economists state that the appropriate aim of the railroads is to determine the

---

[26] Nationalized utilities are often subsidized in subtle ways, through reduced taxes or lower interest rates. And some utilities, such as the British Railways, operate with large deficits not as a matter of policy but because they have not been able to bring costs and revenues in line.

margins above incremental costs, traffic volume considered, at which a rate produces the maximum total contribution toward fixed costs and net income. Such a policy would permit the railroads to lower rates on services with highly elastic demands, thus approaching marginal costs on those services.

Most authorities avoid a dogmatic stand on price discrimination in the utilities. Each case deserves an evaluation on its own merits. Probably few people would object to the high prices for colored telephones, even though those prices involve discrimination. If some consumers are willing to pay more for the appearance of their telephones and thus to subsidize the users of regular telephones, no great social loss results. On the other hand, if the utility is willing to provide special services below full cost in order to take advantage of the elastic demand for such services, both the company and the general public may benefit. Regulatory agencies probably are too cautious in rejecting rates below full cost on the grounds that the burden will then be placed on other services. If the marginal revenue accompanying a price reduction exceeds the marginal cost, so that the contribution to overhead and profit increases, there is no "burden" to transfer. For example, a reduction in rates on special services which make use of idle capacity may make possible the reduction of rates on other services.

Empirical studies and illustrations

The issue of marginal cost pricing has received considerable attention in the electric utilities. Few utilities apply marginal cost pricing on an overall basis, though some of them may approach marginal costs in pricing some special services. The low electricity rates of the TVA might be rationalized as moving toward marginal cost pricing, though it does not appear that the literature on the subject was a great influence on TVA rate making. The TVA's low rates result in large part from such subsidies as low tax rates (the payments in lieu of taxes made to local and state governments are far below the rates private utilities would be required to pay) and low interest rates on funds owed the federal government.

A survey of electricity pricing in Europe suggests that marginal cost pricing is still relatively unknown there.[27] France and Sweden are the leaders in attention to marginal cost pricing. The Électricité de France, a nationalized concern, has been a pioneer in this respect, though it has concentrated more on marginal costs in determining particular prices than on the general level of rates. It has even revised particular rates when there was a "deficit between income and expenditures." This suggests that the movement towards marginal cost pricing has been quite

---

[27] *The Theory of Marginal Cost and Electricity Rates* (Paris: Organisation for European Economic Co-operation, 1958).

cautious. Sweden apparently is more willing to apply the marginal cost principle when marginal cost is above average cost than in the opposite case. In explanation of this position, it is stated that it "may be true, theoretically, that electricity rates ought to correspond to marginal costs even when these are lower than average costs. But if this were applied in practice, the losses incurred would have to be borne by some agency other than the electricity undertakings, e.g., the State."[28]

In other countries covered by the survey—Austria, Belgium, Italy, Norway, the Netherlands, the United Kingdom, and Switzerland—average cost pricing (full-cost pricing) appears to predominate, modified by examples of price discrimination in favor of special segments of the market.

Turning now to the United States, all the regulatory agencies, federal and state, follow a full-cost rule for overall pricing. The objective in rate regulation is to allow revenues that will cover all expenses, including depreciation and leave a fair return on investment. The regulatory agencies vary, however, in the rates of return which they allow and in determination of the rate base.

American regulatory commissions consider four major criteria in determining the fair return.[29] The first is the capital-attraction criterion. Most commissions are concerned with allowing returns which permit the utilities to attract capital for needed expansions and which contribute to the financial soundness of those utilities. Another criterion is that of efficiency of management. Some commissions make it a policy to approve higher returns to utilities which demonstrate outstanding performance in controlling costs and improving services. Such a policy should stimulate greater managerial efficiency. A third criterion is that of stable rates. Commissions prefer not to revise rates with each change in demand and costs, on the grounds that constant changes would be inconvenient to both customers and management. The last criterion is that of fairness to investors. This criterion is perhaps the most nebulous and most difficult to apply in practice. Commissions are not in agreement, for example, on the extent to which public utilities should take part in the general increase in profits earned in competitive industries in periods of inflation. Some of them are quite restrictive in this respect, on the grounds that the owners of the utilities have, like the purchasers of bonds, taken the risk that their earnings might not keep up with prices. Questions of fairness will continue to lead to controversy and litigation in public utility regulation.

---

[28] *Ibid.*, p. 76.

[29] This discussion is based on Bonbright, *op. cit.*, pp. 151–58. Bonbright adds a fifth criterion—that of consumer rationing, which would lead to rates encouraging all consumption covering marginal costs. No American commissions are much influenced by this criterion since they do not accept the principle of marginal cost pricing.

Over the history of American public utility regulation, determination of the rate base has been even a greater source of litigation than has determination of the fair rate of return. The problem becomes especially acute in periods of inflation, in which book values (original costs) are below reproduction or replacement costs. The Federal Power Commission and most of the state commissions stress an original cost or prudent investment rate base and give little regard to increasing replacement costs until the utilities actually purchase a new plant at the higher costs. Their preference for original cost is based primarily on its administrative convenience. Original costs are readily determined from the accounts and make possible the rapid disposition of rate cases with reduced expenses and more precise results. The supporters of original cost claim that it reduces the costs of regulation and litigation. Another argument for original cost is that it reduces uncertainty and thus is more conducive to credit maintenance.

An important minority of American regulatory commissions lean toward what is known as the "fair value" rate base. The definition of "fair value" is rather difficult, in view of the long history of controversy over it since 1898 when the Supreme Court in *Smyth* v. *Ames* made it the law of the land.[30] (The Hope Natural Gas Case[31] of 1944 ended the supremacy of the "fair value" rule and left it to the individual jurisdictions to determine their own principles of rate base valuation.) In general, the "fair value" rate base is a compromise, incorporating both original cost and reproduction cost and still other considerations. In actual practice, however, some of the commissions which are bound by "fair value" statutes devote primary attention to original cost, with minor deviations to take other factors into account.

According to Bonbright, when it comes to actual practice, *all* of the commissions use versions of original cost, with minor deviations.[32] He claims that the important differences in regulation lie more in different degrees of liberality in rates of return than in determinations of the rate base. This conclusion suggests that regulation should concentrate on the determination of rates of return most appropriate for the growth and financial strength of the utilities and most conducive to the public interest, with a diminished attention to controversies over the valuation of the property. Nevertheless, some authorities would dissent and would argue for a valuation of property more in line with reproduction cost. It may at some time be possible to find an objective technique for determining reproduction cost which will reduce the costs of litigation and delay in administering rate changes.

---

[30] *Smyth* v. *Ames*, 169 U.S. 466 (1898).
[31] *Federal Power Commission* v. *Hope Natural Gas Company*, 320 U.S. 591 (1944).
[32] Bonbright, *op. cit.*, p. 283.

4. PEAK-LOAD PRICING

One of the most difficult applications of economic analysis is in the area of peak-load pricing. An illustration of peak loads is in the electricity industry, in which consumption varies over the day and over the seasons of the year but capacity must meet the peak consumption. The problem in this case is accentuated by the fact that electricity cannot be stored economically in significant quantities. The peak-load problem is also characteristic of the transportation industry, in which storage is impossible. It applies in the pipeline transportation of petroleum, in the distribution of gas, and in water supply, in which storage is expensive. The problem in all of these cases is determination of the "best" prices in both peak and off-peak periods.

A comment on what is meant by "best" or "optimal" in this context is in order. Most of the discussion in this book is based on the treatment of "optimal" as synonymous with "profit maximizing." We have broadened the definition of "optimal" at times to include objectives other than profit, but almost always we have been concerned with *private* objectives rather than *social* objectives. Fortunately, the maximization of profits and other private objectives is often, perhaps usually, consistent at least roughly with the attainment of social objectives, which is of course a major argument for the free enterprise system. In the case of the industries in which peak loads are a problem, such is not the case. These industries are usually "natural monopolies" and are given the status of public utilities. What is conducive to profit maximization is under these circumstances in conflict with social welfare, for the monopoly power of the utilities could be used to raise prices above competitive (and socially desirable) levels and to restrict production to an uneconomically low level.

Therefore, the problem of peak-load pricing is partly a problem in welfare economics. The "optima" with which we are concerned are social optima rather than profit maxima. The objective of the analysis is to guide utility managers and regulatory commissions to achieve price structures which lead to a more efficient allocation of resources.

Some general principles

It may be best to narrow our attention to electricity for the time being. The electric utilities must maintain capacity to meet peak loads. The question is whether they should vary rates from peak to off-peak periods. The answer of almost all economists who have studied the question is that they should charge higher rates at the peaks. The failure to vary rates over time results in price discrimination, since the cost of producing for the peak is clearly greater than the cost for other periods.[33] The failure to charge higher rates in peak periods means that the extra capacity built for those periods involves an economic waste—the waste of resources which would be more productive in other occupations. This results from the fact that the low peak prices will cause peak consumption to be even higher than it would be otherwise, so that the utility must construct extra capacity to meet this subsidized peak. Or, in the absence of such capacity, the utility must engage in "load shedding" (cutting off the electricity supply of some customers), a practice which is arbitrary and inefficient.

The economists who have written on peak-load pricing are in agreement on the following two propositions:

1. Peak prices should be higher than off-peak prices for two purposes: (*a*) to allocate the limited capacity available at the peak to those who are willing to pay most for it; and (*b*) to help cover the costs of providing the additional capacity to meet the peak consumption which remains at the higher prices.

2. The only relevant costs in the determination of both the peak and off-peak prices are the marginal costs. (Unfortunately, some difference of opinion remains on how to measure the marginal costs.)

The problem of peak loads appears at first to combine elements of both topics covered earlier in this chapter: price discrimination and joint products. Many writers on the subject appear to classify high prices at the peak as discriminatory. But if differential prices are proportional to marginal costs they are not discriminatory as we have defined discrimination. This issue will receive fuller attention below. The question of whether the services at different times of the day are joint products is similarly confusing. It is true that some of the same facilities are used in both peak and off-peak periods. But an increase in the output in one period does not require an increase in output in another. And it is not clear that the marginal cost of supplying in off-peak periods is affected by the volume of production at the peak or vice versa. Nevertheless, we shall see that one solution to the problem of peak-load pricing takes on some of the attributes of the pricing of joint products.

A graphic solution: firm peaks

Recently economists have developed what appears to be a logical solution to peak-load pricing.[34] For the sake of simplicity, it is best to

---

[33] As we shall see, the term "cost" in this connection has several alternative meanings, but the statement holds true for any of these alternatives. The statement would not hold true if we defined cost to be the energy costs plus a share of the capacity costs allocated equally to every kilowatt-hour of consumption, but this definition of cost is unacceptable to economists.

[34] The following discussion is based primarily on P. O. Steiner's "Peak Loads and Efficient Pricing," *Quarterly Journal of Economics,* November, 1957, pp. 585–610 and J. Hirshleifer's "Comment" in the August, 1958, issue of the same journal, pp. 451–62.

start with the case of firm peaks—where the peak is not shifted from one period to another by the differential prices under consideration. This is extreme. Even in subway traffic it is claimed that the peak would be shifted by differential rates over the day. And while the peak household use of electricity in lighting would appear to be nonshiftable, the use in washers, clothes dryers, water heaters, and other appliances would probably shift if the penalty for use at the peak were made high enough.

The solution to this problem is to equate price with marginal cost. The marginal cost in off-peak periods is simply the cost of the energy itself. The marginal cost in peak periods is the sum of the energy cost and the capacity cost. Figure 8–10 shows the solution for both peak and off-peak periods.

FIGURE 8–10

PEAK AND OFF-PEAK PRICING: THE FIRM PEAK CASE

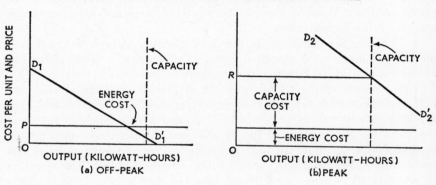

Assume for purposes of simplicity that for half of each day demand is at D_1D_1' and the other half at D_2D_2'. The charge in the low-demand period should include only the energy cost; no capacity cost enters into the marginal cost since there is no need to add to capacity for this period. The price should be at the marginal cost since it reflects the use of resources at the margin and thus the opportunity cost (the value of the resources in alternative occupations). The charge in the high-demand period is equal to the energy cost plus the capacity cost. The capacity cost is part of the marginal cost in this case, since capacity must be added to meet this demand. What we need is a measure of the added capacity cost as one more unit of consumption is added at the peak. We then add this amount to the energy cost.

Perhaps a more appropriate way of stating the rule for the peak is as follows: If the capacity falls short of what can be sold at a price equal to marginal energy cost plus marginal capacity cost, increase capacity until that position is reached.

The final solution might be called the long-run equilibrium solution in which the capacity has been adjusted to the level of demand. In the shorter run it is unlikely that the capacity will exactly fit this requirement, so that the rule must be restated. In the short run the price at the peak should be such as to clear the market—that is, it should be set to allocate the capacity which is available. If capacity is in short supply the price should be set at a level higher than the sum of the capacity and energy costs, to discourage consumption by those who place low marginal values on electricity and allocate the supply to those with high marginal values. Figure 8–11a illustrates that *OS* is the appropriate price. In the lower peak demand situation the price should be at *OT,* as shown in Figure 8–11b.

FIGURE 8–11

SHORT-RUN PEAK-LOAD PRICING: THE FIRM PEAK CASE

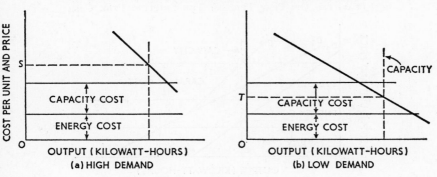

This price is not based on full cost, but it allocates the available capacity efficiently. In the first (high demand) case the utility should add capacity. In the second (low demand) case it should fail to replace capacity as it wears out. In both cases it should set the rate on off-peak consumption to cover only the energy cost. Is this solution a discriminatory one? The long-run solution in Figure 8–10 clearly is not, for it relates prices in both the peak and off-peak periods to marginal costs. The shorter run solution in Fig. 8–11 would at first appear to be discriminatory, for the off-peak price is at marginal cost while the peak price depends on the relation of demand to capacity and not on cost. Jack Hirshleifer, however, has argued that the price *is* at the marginal cost in the peak case, if we define the cost of the marginal unit in Figure 8–11 to be the failure to serve a customer who is willing to pay only slightly less than the specified price for an added unit of service. If we sell to the peak users at 10 cents per unit and we are operating at capacity, the cost of supplying the marginal user under this interpretation is the value of the service to a customer who is willing to pay 9.99999 cents but not 10 cents.

A more complete discussion would consider the possibility (some economist would say the inevitability) of curvilinear costs, with rising marginal costs. For such a discussion the reader should refer to Hirshleifer's article.[35]

A graphic solution: shifting peaks

The firm peak case is probably not typical. Where the peak may shift because of differential prices the analysis is more complex, looking more like the joint-product analysis earlier in this chapter. In this case it is necessary to plot both demand curves (the high demand and low demand) on the same graph. Figure 8–12 illustrates. This time we add

FIGURE 8–12

PEAK AND OFF-PEAK PRICING: THE SHIFTING PEAK CASE

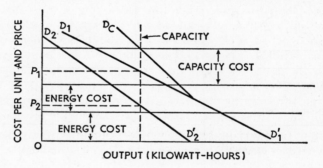

the two demands vertically to get D_C. This combined demand curve provides an estimate of how much buyers will pay for one unit of off-peak energy *plus* one unit of peak energy. The utility should expand capacity to the point at which D_C intersects the sum of the capacity cost plus *twice* the energy cost, for at this point the price will cover the marginal cost of the energy in the off-peak period plus the marginal cost of the energy in the peak period plus the marginal capacity cost (the capacity will be used in both periods). The prices OP_1 and OP_2 are again set to "clear the market" (use up the capacity). The result is that the capacity is fully utilized in both periods, the price mechanism acting to hold back consumption in periods of high demand and to stimulate the use of capacity in periods of low demand.

Note that capacity is added in this shifting demand case up to the point that the combined demands (D_C) will cover the costs of the energy

---

[35] *Ibid.*, p. 455.

and the costs of the added capacity. At that point prices are set to ration the capacity. This is a case of joint costs. As before, it is possible to define the marginal cost as the opportunity cost (value of the first unit not supplied), so that the result is not discriminatory.

This analysis can be generalized to more than two periods and to periods which are unequal in length. The theoretical literature on peak load pricing is in the process of extension and refinement to cover a wider range of considerations, such as indivisibilities in production and differences in plant costs.[36]

Some practical problems

To the practitioner the preceding analysis for peak-load pricing may seem theoretical and impractical. A number of obstacles stand in the way of actual application.

1. The demands in different periods cannot be predicted accurately in advance. Even more difficult is the prediction of the response of the quantities demanded to price. Therefore the setting of rates that will encourage use up to capacity in all periods (except in periods when capacity is not reached even when rates are reduced to energy costs) is an unattainable ideal. This objection is not as serious as it may at first appear, for all businesses under any pricing scheme must approximate rather than achieve their exact goals.

2. The measurement of the marginal energy and capacity costs is no simple problem. If it is safe to assume that these costs are linear, their measurement is simplified, but some economists would insist that the energy costs rise as capacity is approached.

3. The proposed scheme involves flexible prices. This results from the necessity of using trial and error in approximating the appropriate prices and from the shifts in demand which are inevitable. This poses serious problems for the administration of rate changes—problems which are compounded by the requirement of approval of changes by regulatory commissions.

4. The public would probably react unfavorably to prices which *seem* discriminatory even though they may not be. The public is not likely to understand that high rates for cooking their Thanksgiving turkeys are conducive to their welfare.

5. The public would probably also react unfavorably to the instability of prices which the pricing scheme, in an extreme form, would require. They would prefer to know the rates they will pay in advance rather than be subject to sharp shifts in such rates.

The utility managers and public service commissioners are in a diffi-

---

[36] O. E. Williamson, "Peak Load Pricing and Optimal Capacity under Indivisibility Constraints," *American Economic Review*, Sept., 1966, pp. 810–27, and M. A. Crew, "Comment," in the March, 1968, issue of the same journal, pp. 168–70.

394   *Managerial economics*

cult position in the sphere of peak-load pricing. If they heed the advice of economists on marginal cost pricing, they run the risk of public misunderstanding and attacks of "unfair" pricing. But if they base their prices on full costs and try to average out rates over peaks and troughs in consumption, they are responsible for a waste of resources. Furthermore, they will not find the construction of rate schedules which meet the theoretical criteria for optimization any easy task. The public will have to make up its mind whether it wants rates which seem "fair" or ones which actually are conducive to giving the most for the dollars spent. No complete solution to his dilemma is imminent.

Nonprice techniques for improving load factors

The use of pricing for the improvement of load factors has been shown to be complex and easily misunderstood. As a result, many companies have shown a preference for marketing and other nonprice techniques which accomplish the same purpose. These consist of increased advertising in off-peak periods and the development of new markets or new products to use facilities in off-peak periods. Electric utilities have engaged in promoting the use of appliances which consume energy in off-peak periods or at least have a more stable demand. Gas companies are presently promoting air conditioning.

These nonprice devices have the advantage of flexibility. Customers resent the frequent change of price but are tolerant of varying promotional activity. When advertising pushes consumption toward capacity it is easy to diminish the effort, but it is not so easy to take away a low price which has been used to promote a particular type of consumption.

Empirical studies and illustrations

Some public utilities and regulatory commissions have experimented with peak-load pricing over the years. The electric utilities used a peak-responsibility method of pricing in the early 1900's but abandoned it because of difficulties in allocating costs, in predicting when the peaks would come, and in dealing with the shift of sales to off-peak periods which created new peaks.[37] As might be expected from the intricacies of the problem, the theoretical solution was not understood. It is no wonder that the utilities found it difficult to apply the theory in practice.

Nevertheless, the electric utilities continued to experiment with methods which at least were moving in the right direction. In the 1920's, W. J. Greene introduced a schedule of rates which charged separately for consumption and "demand." "Demand" in this context referred, as we have noted above, to the customer's maximum rate of consumption. Obviously this method does not charge the customer exactly for his

---

[37] Davidson, *op. cit.*, p. 119.

contribution to the system's peak. His peak might come at the system's trough. But this method at least moved in the direction of charging for peak responsibility. The "noncoincident demand" method, which is used widely in allocating capacity cost for cost-of-service studies, is a variation of the same idea.[38] Davidson shows that under any of these methods a subsidy of peak users by off-peak customers is probable. Two comments are in order, however: more recent analysis suggests that Davidson went too far in allocating capacity costs to peak users, since he failed to recognize fully the joint-product character of the shifting peak case. Secondly, it is too much to expect that a practical rate schedule will exactly meet the theoretical needs.

The gas industry has long charged lower rates to interruptible customers (ones whose consumption can be cut off on short notice when capacity is reached). Such differentials in rates again move in the direction of the theoretical optimum for peak-load pricing. The storage of gas, however, makes it possible to even out the use of facilities and thus to spread the capacity costs over a wider range of consumption. A complete solution to the problem would have to recognize that storage costs are a substitute for added capacity costs, and that some allocation of capacity cost to interruptible customers is justified.[39]

Other examples of attempts to ease the peak-load problem through pricing are the low early morning fares of the British Railways (the fare for arrival in London before 8 A.M. is almost 50 percent below the regular fare) and the persistent experimentation of the airlines with off-season rates. An even more familiar example is the lower prices of motion pictures before 5 or 6 P.M.

Pricing is, of course, not the only way of dealing with the problem. Many firms are constantly developing new products and new markets to improve their load factors. The air-conditioning market smoothed out the demand curve for some utilities, though it created a new peak for others. The history of the electric utilities is marked by persistent efforts to increase the diversity of the market by bringing in new types of customers with peaks at different times of the day or year.

The use of advertising and other promotional activities to improve load factors is illustrated in many industries. The Florida hotels have made a great effort to stimulate occupancy in the off-season period. European countries have advertised the great advantages of travel in the spring and autumn when the tourists are not so much in each others' way. Universities advertise the advantages of their summer climates in the effort to obtain greater use of their facilities in their off-peak periods.

---

[38] These and other techniques are reviewed and analyzed in Davidson, *op. cit.*, pp. 127–38.

[39] See Davidson *op. cit.*, pp. 138–47 for a fuller discussion.

Cases for part four

Pricing has always been a central interest in managerial economics. Many managers who are engaged in pricing decisions are somewhat baffled by the problem. They find it difficult to organize their thoughts in some kind of pattern. A few managers may refer to the standard works on price theory but find little guidance there in bridging the gap between theory and practice.

The cases in this chapter provide an opportunity to develop skills in relating economic theory to pricing decisions. It will soon become apparent, however, that traditional economic theory by itself is not sufficient to deal with the complexities of the pricing situation. The cases involve environmental considerations such as antitrust and antidiscrimination legislation. They involve problems of internal organization. In all of them, the pervasiveness of uncertainty about demand, competition, and costs stands in the way of a simple application of theoretical concepts.

PRICING PRACTICES OF SIX SELECTED MANUFACTURERS*

Studies of the pricing practices of individual manufacturers reveal considerable variety in management's approach to the problem. Most

---

* Five of these case summaries are based on research sponsored by the Small Business Administration. The interviewers were W. W. Haynes and J. L. Gibson of the University of Kentucky. All names are disguised. The Small Business Administration is in no way responsible for the findings. The International Harvester Case is based on A. D. H. Kaplan, J. B. Dirlam, and R. E. Lanzillotti, *Pricing in Big Business* (Washington, D.C.: The Brookings Institution, 1958).

of the following cases are in small firms, but a study of pricing in one large firm, International Harvester, is included as a basis for comparison.

1. The Variety Press

The Variety Press is a small job-printing shop employing ten persons. The firm's general pricing policy is full cost plus a 20 percent markup. The management obtains full-cost estimates from a nationally published manual which provides regional breakdowns, but it checks these estimates against its own experience. For regular customers the firm usually does not quote a price in advance, but instead bases the final charge on the actual costs that have been accumulated on the order, plus the 20 percent markup. In such cases the management protects customer goodwill by carefully checking the actual costs. On a few orders on which the actual costs are running high, the management may reduce the markup.

The company's pricing policy leads to lower unit prices on large orders on which there is a "spreading" of make-ready costs, but this is not an exception to the cost-plus rule. The management infrequently charges more on rush jobs; this is more likely if the plant is busy than if there is idle capacity. The management does not charge more on jobs requiring special servicing by the president; such service contributes to company goodwill and to future sales.

One clear exception to the usual policy is the pricing of envelopes and letterheads. The markup on this business is only 10 percent. A higher markup would lead to a loss of this business. The president believes that the company must maintain this line as a part of its service to its customers, many of whom prefer to place all of their printing with one firm.

The president believes that prices either above or below those provided by the 20 percent markup are usually unsound. He is firmly opposed to pricing below full cost, stating that "profitable plants make a profit on every job." The president apparently has given little direct attention to demand elasticities or to estimates of what "the traffic will bear," but at the same time he believes that the ability to raise prices is limited by competition. He faces competition from at least 20 similar firms in the vicinity.

The president keeps a close watch on his equipment needs; if some equipment is chronically idle he will replace it with other equipment needed to handle the kind of business he can sell. For example, he has sold a press which can take care of large pages because the volume of such business does not justify such a machine. He can farm out this type of business to other firms. Similarly, the firm has given up some types of business that require too much time for quoting and servicing; the president rations his time so as not to allocate too much time to any particular order.

The estimates of full cost are based on an estimate of the machine time required by the job. If the firm is quoting on a job to be done in the future, it would use estimates of the machine time required on similar jobs in making the estimates on the particular job at hand. But if it instead is pricing a job already completed, it uses the actual times taken on the job. The hourly machine times include labor and overhead costs. Electricity, heat, and rent are allocated to particular machines on the basis of floor space occupied. The depreciation on each machine is included in the hourly charge on that machine. The hourly charge includes an estimate for idle time. For example, if it appears that a machine is normally idle 30 percent of the time, the hourly charge is higher by 130/100 of what is would be otherwise. But the president stated that it would be unreasonable to use this principle on a machine idle most of the time, for the result would be charges that would price the firm out of the market.

2. *Welburn Furniture Company*

The Welburn Furniture Company employs about 150 persons, and sells its products throughout the United States east of the Rocky Mountains. The company maintains a cost department, which costs each type of furniture. The normal way of estimating price is to follow this formula: direct labor cost + materials cost + indirect labor (distributed as a percent of direct labor) + factory overhead (distributed as a percent of direct labor) + a percentage of selling price to cover selling and administrative costs, interest, and a target return of 10 percent of sales.

The firm varies markups from one line to another and from one season to another. The target return on certain types of cabinets is only 6 percent of selling price because of the low prices of competitors. On the other hand, certain types of chests may permit a 15 percent return; these chests are a specialty of the Welburn Company that most competitors do not duplicate. The firm offers a 10 percent discount to distributors who have been customers for many years. These distributors buy in large volumes and help the company achieve the volume it needs. But the firm is not taking on any new distributors on this discount basis.

The company is often willing to sell at lower prices in June, when sales are usually low. It sometimes even goes below full cost in off-season periods. It follows a similar practice in recessions to try to maintain volume and employment; fortunately, however, the furniture business has been fairly stable since World War II, making such sacrifice sales infrequent. The company has been fortunate in introducing new popular lines just in time to offset a decline in the sales of old lines, making an overall price reduction unnecessary. Management did, however, reduce prices in the recession of 1954. Furthermore, management has reduced prices as much as 30 percent to close out lines no longer being manufactured.

In 1960, the management wished to increase prices by 3 percent to absorb cost increases. An analysis indicated that the time was not propitious for such an increase, for the furniture market was "soft." The management believed that the furniture buyers would have resisted any increase in price at this time and would have turned to alternative sources of supply.

3. Giffen Furniture Company

The Giffen Furniture Company is about the same size as the Welburn company. But instead of producing household furniture it specializes in large-volume contracts for motels, hotels, schools, and the armed forces. It produces very little for stock.

The company sells most of its furniture on a "bidding" basis. Usually the firm is asked to submit a bid to supply a certain volume of furniture of a particular style. The management bases its bid on full costs. It adds direct labor and materials to arrive at "basic cost." It then adds a 90 percent markup to cover selling costs, overhead, and profits. This system of pricing is kept simple to expedite bidding on new jobs on short notice.

The "bidding" in this situation is not necessarily highly competitive. Usually a customer will seek a bid from the Giffen company alone and will accept the company's bid if it seems reasonable. Such customers prefer to be supplied by one source. The bidding on government contracts is more competitive; the Giffen company considers such business to be a "filler," and expects to win only about one out of 15 government contracts on which it bids. It wins most of the motel contracts on which it bids.

Since World War II the firm has been operating at capacity. In 1960 the management claimed that it had not cut price below "basic" cost plus 90 percent for over five years. In a few cases the markup is set at 100 percent to cover the extra costs of working up special designs. The way in which management rations its capacity is simply not to bid on added business until the firm has caught up on back orders. The company stabilizes employment by the amount of effort devoted to seeking extra contracts.

The company produces its own lumber, which helps it meet its customers' delivery requirements. The management is not interested in expanding capacity to meet demand; it believes it has a greater chance of attaining stable employment and profits with its present capacity.

4. Case Concrete Products

Case Concrete Products is located in a medium-size city. Prior to June, 1956, the firm's principal product was concrete burial vaults. The product line also included lintels, patio stones, and bird baths. The firm enjoyed a local monopoly in the manufacture of these products. There was competition from metal burial vaults; however, the price differential was large enough to reduce the importance of price competition.

The basis for the price of burial vaults and other items was full cost plus a markup. The full-cost estimates were determined as follows:

```
Labor ............................................. $X
Materials ........................................... X
Overhead (10% of labor and materials) ................... X
        Total cost ....................................... $X
Markup (100% of total cost) ............................. X
Selling price ........................................ $X
```

The owner, Mr. Case, spent a great deal of time revising the cost estimates as costs changed. For example, he gave a general hourly wage increase and revised the costs estimates of all products and increased the selling prices.

In order to arrive at the cost estimates, Mr. Case ran crude time studies on the workmen, recording the time that each spent on a particular product. The overhead rate of 10 percent had been suggested at a trade association meeting which Mr. Case attended several years before. He had never verified that overhead was actually 10 percent of direct labor. The firm did not have a job order cost accounting system which would accumulate the cost of each product; rather the cost estimates were checked only periodically against actual costs.

In June, 1956, the firm was considering a new product, concrete septic tanks. The manufacture of this product was well suited to the present production scheme. Also there was only one supplier of septic tanks in the city at the time, and Mr. Case believed that the building boom was creating a market large enough to support two producers. The molds and a delivery truck would require an investment of $3,700, which would be financed from internal funds. In order to arrive at some estimate of costs, the firm manufactured a pilot model. The cost estimate was:

```
Materials .................. $26.85
Labor ......................   9.00
Overhead ...................   3.60
                            $39.45
```

Applying the same pricing policy used on the other products would result in a price of $78.90; however, the established producer's price was only $65. Mr. Case decided that his initial price should be the same as his competitor's. The competitor did not retaliate by lowering his price;

later, however, he did initiate discounts for certain customers. Mr. Case did not grant discounts, partly because the volume of sales was "satisfactory" and partly because he feared that if he were too aggressive the competitor might begin producing concrete burial vaults.

5. *Dandy Concrete Products*

Dandy Concrete Products is located in the same city as Case Concrete Products. The two firms do not compete with each other. Dandy Concrete produces precast concrete building items, such as cast stone trim (window sills, surrounds, and coping), lintels, wall panels, grill blocks, and other specialties. On most jobs, the firm is asked to submit a bid; however, there is seldom competition for the job; the bid is required by the contractor for inclusion in *his* bids. On one such job, the firm estimated the costs as follows:

Materials	$100.00
Labor	100.00
Contingency	50.00
Total cost	$250.00
Markup (25%)	62.50
Price	$312.50

The materials cost included the cost of the mold (which was to be constructed especially for the job) and the cost of concrete. An hourly overhead charge of about $3 was obtained by dividing the estimated daily overhead expense of $90 by the total of 32 hours per day of labor time of the four production men. The hourly labor charge of $4.25 consisted of $1.25 wages and $3 overhead. Multiplying the $4.25 by the 23½ hours of estimated labor time resulted in the labor charge of $100. The contingency charge was applied to every job at a variable rate depending upon the uncertainty of the cost estimate and the extent to which productive capacity would be tied up by the job. This particular job was a "first done" type on which the uncertainty was high. The plant would be tied up almost an entire day on the project; since this order would come during the busy season, it would interfere with the flow of other orders. The markup like the contingency charge was variable and depended upon several factors as follows: (1) possible future repeat business, (2) competition from cut stone which on some jobs was quite severe, (3) a feeling of what is fair to the customer (especially churches and schools). The firm could have priced much higher on many previous jobs, but preferred to take the lower price at the time in order to secure later business. In many instances, the firm was the only possible supplier of a needed product but refused to charge "what the traffic would bear."

In keeping with a desire to build a stable business, the owner refused to lay off his workmen during slack seasons—winter months. The work performed by these men required some training, and he believed that by offering job security he could encourage their interest in workman-ship and avoid retraining expenses. Thus the only variable cost was material expense.

6. *International Harvester Company*[1]

International Harvester has a diversified product line, consisting of agricultural equipment, construction machinery, motor trucks, and mis-cellaneous equipment. The company wishes to achieve several objectives in pricing these products: (1) a target return on investment of around 10 percent after taxes; (2) maintenance of a reputation for high quality and durable products; (3) growth, without becoming so dominant that price competition is undermined. The company succeeded in earning the target return in the years immediately after World War II, but more recently has experienced lower profits after taxes.

The company's position of leadership in the market varies from one product to another. In 1947 it led an effort to resist inflation by lowering prices on farm equipment; in other years its increases in farm equipment prices have been followed by competitors. On light trucks International Harvester has followed the product and price policies of the major automobile companies, and has been able to achieve only a low return on investment. On heavy trucks the company is in a stronger position. In 1955 the company abandoned the production of refrigerators and freezers because of an inability to obtain the volume that would provide a profit. The company's traditional emphasis on quality and durability appeared to be inconsistent with the need to cut costs so that the company could compete in the refrigerator and freezer market.

The company's market share of agricultural equipment had steadily declined from 44 percent in 1922 to 23 percent in 1948. Its share varied from about 20 percent on combines, and 30 percent on tractors, to 65 percent on cotton pickers. The company wished to maintain a reputation for quality on farm equipment. It also wished to set prices that would permit farmers to earn the initial investment in a satisfactory pay-back period, which varied from three to ten years, depending upon the product. The company also wished to keep prices on the various models in a reasonable proportion to each other, modified to some extent by the desire to meet competitive conditions in the different markets.

International Harvester's costing practices were similar to those of the large automobile companies. The main stress in pricing was on

---

[1] Based on Kaplan, Dirlam, and Lanzillotti, *ibid.*, pp. 69–79, 135–42.

"normal costs," which are full costs, including current material and labor, plus overhead computed on the basis of "normal" operations. The overhead was prorated on the basis of direct labor costs; sales, service, collection, and administrative costs were allocated in proportion to total sales value. In addition to the normal costs the company estimated the "season's costs," which were the "actual" unit costs accumulated during the season. If the season's costs indicated that the normal costs were unrealistic, the company might revise its prices. The company also measured "specific costs," especially for service parts. Specific costs included only the actual cost of material, direct labor costs, and the direct overhead resulting from the particular item.

The practice in pricing a new product is of interest. The management started with a price based on competitors' prices and the estimated value to the farmer. It then worked back to estimating a "target cost" which, at the given price, would provide the target return on investment. The equipment designers then tried to develop models consistent with such target costs. Exhibit 1 shows the actual experience with three products introduced in 1956.

While the company's profit objective of 10 percent on investment would suggest a target return on sales of about 7 percent (sales are usually about 40 percent higher than invested capital), the company modified the target on particular products according to the competitive situation, the originality of the product, and the value to the farmer. The company recognized the need to maintain a full line, which means carrying some products that do not permit the usual markup. The company also set higher prices when it had an advantage (perhaps because of a superior product) over competition.

As Exhibit 1 suggests, the company modified its introductory prices as it accumulated experience in the actual market. Competition might force it to lower price; costs might exceed the preliminary estimates. When the profit was as low as on product C in Exhibit 1, the company might redesign the product to reduce costs, might increase price, or might abandon the line.

Several specific examples will give insight into the company's pricing practices:

1. In May, 1957, it raised the retail price on a product from $218 to $228 because of dissatisfaction with the profit. The new price was still in line with competition. The profit position would still be unsatisfactory, but the management doubted the feasibility of even higher prices.

2. In March, 1957, the company reduced the price of another product from $525 ($397.17 to the dealer) to $490. The cost to manufacture was $264.35. Management was dissatisfied with the volume on this item and wished to reduce prices to the range charged by two smaller competitors.

EXHIBIT 1

PRICE-COST ANALYSIS, REPRESENTATIVE FARM IMPLEMENTS INTRODUCED IN 1956

	Product A			Product B			Product C		
	Target	Intro-ductory	Actual	Target	Intro-ductory	Actual	Target	Intro-ductory	Actual
List price	$592.60	$592.60	$592.60	$455.85	$455.85	$455.85	$687.40	$691.35	$691.35
Trade discount—23 percent	136.30	136.30	136.30	104.85	104.85	104.85	158.10	159.00	159.00
Dealer price	$456.30	$456.30	$456.30	$351.00	$351.00	$351.00	$529.30	$532.35	$532.35
Cash discount—2 percent	9.13	9.13	9.13	7.02	7.02	7.02	10.60	10.65	10.65
Net from dealer	$447.17	$447.17	$447.17	$343.98	$343.98	$343.98	$518.70	$521.70	$521.70
Sales and administrative expense*	67.08	67.08	67.08	51.60	51.60	51.60	77.81	78.26	78.26
Net	$380.09	$380.09	$380.09	$292.38	$292.38	$292.38	$440.89	$443.44	$443.44
Manufacturing cost†	270.00	274.97	359.43	214.00	217.42	232.62	380.00	395.33	462.38
Profit margin (dollars)	$110.09	$105.12	$ 20.66	$ 78.38	$ 74.96	$ 59.76	$ 60.89	$ 48.11	$ 18.94
Profit margin as percent of:									
Manufacturing cost	40.8%	38.2%	5.7%	36.6%	34.5%	25.7%	16.0%	12.1%	−4.5%
Total unit (6) + (8)	32.6	32.5	4.8	29.1	27.9	21.0	13.3	10.2	−3.1
Net from dealer	24.6	23.5	4.6	22.3	21.8	17.4	11.7	9.2	−3.6

* Allocated as normal percentages (15%) of net from dealer.
† Target and introductory prices based on normal manufacturing cost, including plant overhead.
SOURCE: A. D. H. Kaplan, J. B. Dirlam, and R. F. Lanzillotti, *Pricing in Big Business* (Washington, D.C.: The Brookings Institution, 1958), p. 72.

3. The company's cotton pickers sold at a price which yielded the target return or better. The product had a high value to potential users. The company was the first to introduce this product; the more recent entrance of competitors had not undermined the company's ability to obtain the target return.

4. The company priced "captive parts" (manufactured only by Harvester) at a price yielding a target return on normal unit costs.

5. The company priced other parts which competed with parts produced by General Motors, Ford, and Mack Truck at prices designed to meet competition. These prices did not show any consistent relationship to unit costs or target returns. The company might continue to produce and sell such parts even though the price covered only the specific costs; such a policy helped the company maintain a full line and spread its overhead burden.

The company gave the same discount from list prices to all dealers. It also gave volume discounts, which varied from 2¼ to 4 percent. The list price was a "suggested price," and some dealers sold at much less.

1. Compare and contrast the cases in the following respects:
   a) The extent to which pricing is cost oriented or demand oriented.
   b) The extent to which pricing is mechanical or flexible.
   c) The extent to which pricing appears to be consistent with marginalism.
2. Evaluate the pricing policies and practices of the Variety Press. The following questions may be helpful:
   a) Should the Press reduce markups when costs are running high?
   b) Should the Variety Press apply lower markups to envelopes and letterheads?
   c) Is it true that "profitable plants make a profit on every job"?
   d) Does the inclusion of an estimate for idle time in the cost estimate make economic sense?
   e) Would greater flexibility in pricing be more profitable?
3. Evaluate the pricing policies and practices of the Welburn Furniture Company. The following questions may be helpful:
   a) Does the company's pricing formula make economic sense?
   b) Should the company vary markups from one line to another?
   c) Should it vary markups from season to season?
   d) Is the company influenced by the elasticity of demand in its pricing?
4. Evaluate the pricing policies and practices of the Giffen Furniture Company.
   a) Does the company's pricing formula make economic sense?
   b) How do the company's practices differ from those of the Welburn Company?
   c) Would a more flexible price policy be profitable?
   d) Would it be more profitable to seek more business and to expand capacity to meet the additional business?
5. Evaluate the pricing policies and practices of the Case Concrete Company.
   a) Does the company's pricing formula make economic sense?

b) *Why did the firm abandon this formula in pricing septic tanks? Was this wise?*

c) *Why didn't the firm grant discounts on septic tanks? Was this wise?*

6. *Is the contingency charge in the Dandy Concrete case a sound practice? Should it depend upon the factors mentioned in the case?*

7. *What is the significance for pricing of the Dandy Concrete Company's policy of stabilizing employment?*

8. *What is the meaning of "normal costs" in the International Harvester case? Should such costs be the basis of pricing?*

9. *What is the meaning of "specific costs" in the International Harvester case? Should they be the basis of pricing?*

10. *How does the "target cost" practice of International Harvester differ from the usual approach described in theory?*

11. *Does International Harvester price to earn a "target return"? Or is the target return a measure of what competition permits it to earn?*

12. *Does International Harvester apply full-cost pricing? Does it apply marginalism in pricing? Is it influenced by market considerations and elasticities of demand?*

13. *Are the profit figures in Exhibit 1 consistent with full-cost pricing, target returns, profit maximization, or marginalism? Discuss.*

PRICING PRACTICES OF SIX RETAILERS*

The pricing practices of retailers are similar in some respects to those of manufacturers and different in others. The practices are far from uniform even among retailers. Five of the following cases cover relatively small firms; the other case is on the pricing practices of Sears, Roebuck and Company.

1. *Three Rivers Hardware Company*

This firm handles general hardware merchandise, radio and television sets, and appliances. The owner prices by applying a markup on wholesale cost. The percentage markup varies on different categories of merchandise, as follows:

1. The markup is low on high-turnover items, such as nails, hammers, and screwdrivers.

2. The markup is high on low-turnover items, such as special tools.

3. If considerable service is required in the sale of an item (as might be true in fitting a new handle to a tool), the markup is high to reflect the extra time required in the sale.

---

* Five of these case summaries are based upon research done for the Small Business Administration by B. Davis, J. L. Gibson, and W. W. Haynes. The Small Business Administration is in no way responsible for the findings. All names are disguised. The sixth summary is a condensation of a case study appearing in A. D. H. Kaplan, J. B. Dirlam, and R. F. Lanzillotti, *Pricing in Big Business* (Washington, D.C.: The Brookings Institution, 1958).

4. On appliances the markup is 25 percent on the wholesale price plus transportation cost. Such a low markup still results in a high dollar margin per unit of sales. The allowance of a high trade-in value on an old appliance may result in an even lower markup. The trade-in value may be reduced for a potential customer who seems to be a poor credit risk.

The owner of this store often follows the suggested list price of the manufacturer. In fact, he prefers to carry prepriced items, because he doesn't have to worry about pricing decisions so frequently on them. But he does not always follow such suggested prices, and he does not believe that his competitors do so. The price cutting of his competitors may force him to abandon the suggested list prices.

The owner has a policy of low prices on fad items such as hula hoops. He states that his fixed costs are not increased by carrying such items, and that he can achieve a high volume by setting a low price. The owner also believes in what he calls "magic prices." An example is a price of 88 cents, which he believes has a special appeal to the public.

The store faces competition from two nearby hardware stores, from furniture stores, variety stores, paint stores, and drugstores. The owner devotes considerable time to a study of competitors' prices. He reads their advertisements and listens to price comparisons made by his customers. He believes that price is the main drawing device, but also stresses advertising, sales effort, and maintenance of an adequate inventory. The owner tries to hold down the variety of merchandise he keeps in inventory by restricting the number of price lines. He also tries to clear out excess stock by holding annual sales, at which he may go below wholesale cost.

2. Main Street Hardware Store

The pricing practices of this store are similar to those of the Three Rivers Store, even though the line of merchandise is somewhat different (toys and sporting goods instead of appliances and television sets). For example the markup on Spic and Span, a high turnover item, is only 2 cents on wholesale cost. The markup on paint is 40 to 50 percent *on retail price* because of the large amount of selling time required.

The owner tries to increase his margin by purchasing at lower costs. When he finds bargains, he does not pass the savings on to his customers. He buys from a cooperative wholesaler which supplies only larger hardware stores and which offers a quantity discount. The result is lower wholesale costs and higher margins than would be possible in buying from a conventional jobber.

The owner makes no attempt to apportion his fixed costs to the various items, and thus does not try to relate his prices systematically to full cost. The monthly income statement does, however, indicate whether markups in general are resulting in the level of income he thinks necessary or desirable.

Unlike the Three Rivers Store, this firm does not conduct storewide sales. But three times a year the owner does mark down certain items that are overstocked. The firm distributes handbills advertising these specials. The price is seldom set below wholesale cost; the one exception is on an item that has become obsolete.

The firm maintains a special order service for customers who desire items not kept in stock. On such merchandise the markup is usually 50 percent on wholesale price plus a handling and postage cost.

3. Sprague College Store

Sprague College, a small private school, owns a store which competes with several groceries, clothing stores, drugstores, and stores specializing in school supplies. The store has a monopoly on the sale of textbooks in the town of 10,000 in which it is located.

The store management establishes a target return on sales for each of the four departments: books, groceries, clothing, and school supplies. An annual budget estimates the volume of business and the expenses necessary to handle that volume. On the basis of this budget, the management determines what departmental margins are necessary to cover overhead and allow the target return. Each department is given a margin to maintain which should result in the desired margin for the store as a whole. The departments report their achieved margins each week and this serves as an internal control. If a department's volume were to decrease, the average margin required on each item would increase, even though the department might be able to reduce some costs (by reducing the sales force, for example).

In 1960, at the time of the case interviews, the markup on textbooks was 13.6 percent of *selling price* for both new and used books. The cost of new books is 80 percent of list price, but the store sells below list. The store buys only used books that are to be reused; its markup on such used books is much lower than is usual in college bookstores. The margin in 1960 did not cover the estimated overhead (15½ percent of revenue). The manager gave this reason for his policy on textbooks: "If I am going to give students a break on anything, why not do it on something they must have?"

Margins on the other merchandise vary considerably. Coffee, for example, is a highly competitive item on which only a 3 to 5 percent margin is possible; higher prices would result in a transfer of business elsewhere. Higher margins on less competitive goods help compensate for the low margins on coffee and books. The store makes a careful survey of the grocery prices of competitors and tries to keep its prices in line with competition.

The target net profit on sales is approximately 2½ percent. This results in a return on investment which is higher than the average return on the other college investments. Inventory control, with an emphasis on maintaining the minimum inventory and the highest possible turnover, is essential in attaining the target return. The management maintains detailed inventory records on each item in stock; these records help the control of inventory and serve as a guide in buying.

4. Mason's Men's Shop

Mason's Men's Shop is located in a college city and is in active competition with several other retail outlets. The store was purchased in a bankrupt condition by a former employee of a national retail chain. The merchandising and pricing policies are designed to appeal to the middle-income group and college men. After several years of operation the store is now operating on a profitable basis.

The owner emphasizes price in his extensive advertising. He does not have specified times for sales, but he regularly advertises reductions in price and bargains. For example, a full wardrobe is advertised at $149, which if purchased separately would cost $189. The markups vary; the markup on suits usually is from 40 percent to 45 percent of selling price. The owner attempts to maintain a markup of 40 percent for the entire store, but the markup is different depending upon particular items. He does not consider it ethically wrong to charge what the traffic will bear.

The aggressive tactics of the owner have resulted in poor relations with other quality men's clothing stores in the city. He is not a member of the local men's clothing store association, the members of which frown on price competition and sales occurring at times other than when all stores are participating.

5. Bismarck Men's Shop

Bismarck Men's Shop is located in the same city as Mason's. However, the pricing policies are quite different. Bismarck specializes in only one style of suit and carries a line of shirts, overcoats, and accessories designed to complement the suit. The markup on suits and overcoats is an unvarying 46 percent of selling price. In buying merchandise for stock, an item may be rejected if after the usual markup is applied, the resulting price is too high in the manager's opinion.

The store attempts to cater to the upper-income group and to college students. The advertising appeal is directed to quality-conscious consumers who are willing and able to pay. The store defends the higher price on the grounds that the suit is long wearing and will not "go out of style" after one year. In addition, the three salesmen give a great deal of attention to each customer and consider themselves to be "advisors" rather than salesmen.

The owner does not have sales other than seasonal close-outs. He frowns on those retailers who do advertise bargains on clothing, stating that one "gets what he pays for." The owner also states that running continual sales on selected merchandise would destroy the image of the store that he has attempted to maintain.

6. Sears, Roebuck and Company[1]

The merchandising organization of Sears, Roebuck has the primary responsibility for pricing. The company's 420 buyers initiate prices under the supervision of the merchandise supervisors (in charge of the 50 buying departments) and the vice-president in charge of merchandising. The pricing for mail-order selling is more centralized than that for the retail stores. The buyers and merchandise supervisors generally add a predetermined percentage or dollar markup based on the custom of the trade, modified by attention to competitors' prices. The vice-president normally approves the price recommendations of the merchandise supervisors, though he does give more attention than they to the prospective return on investment that might result from larger volumes at lower prices or smaller volumes at higher margins.

At the same time, the buyers recommend retail prices for the 35 retail zones in which Sears operates. These prices are suggested retail prices; each store manager may revise prices to fit local conditions and competition. Over 90 percent of the time the store managers follow the recommendations of the parent organization. The central office determines the prices for the regular seasonal and special mail-order sales. The retail store managers determine the time of their sales. On the whole there is considerable centralization of the pricing decisions.

The objectives of the company's price policy are several: (1) to provide the maximum level of sales consistent with a target return on investment of 10 to 15 percent after taxes; (2) to maintain and increase the company's share of the national market; (3) to contribute to the company's reputation for low prices.

Pricing and buying are closely interwoven in the Sears organization. The objective of buying is to obtain merchandise at low costs that will permit low retail prices. The company owns about 22 factories, manufacturing commodities such as stoves and plumbing fixtures which at some previous time it could not obtain on satisfactory terms from outside manufacturers. The company also owns part interest in other suppliers. No doubt the company's ability to manufacture itself exerts a downward

---

[1] Based on Kaplan, Dirlam, and Lanzillotti, *ibid.*, pp. 188–98, 237–39.

pressure on costs. Sears' contracts with outside firms normally cover direct costs to the manufacturer and a margin to cover overhead plus a profit comparable to that of Sears. Even so these contracts include a "competitive clause" that permits a transfer to lower-cost suppliers. Sears works closely with the suppliers to help them hold down distribution costs and to aid them in technical and design problems. One objective is to obtain a large volume which will reduce unit costs.

The result of these practices is selling prices ranging from about 15 to 30 percent below the list prices of competitors. These competitors' prices, however, are suggested retail prices and are less rigidly maintained than Sears' suggested prices. In fact, in recent years the differential between Sears' prices and those of competitors has narrowed on many items. Sears tries to meet this competition by emphasis on brand name (the brand name is connected in the consumer's mind with low prices), by attracting customers with low-price "striped" models and "trading up" to more expensive models providing a higher margin, and by selling last year's models at lower prices.

Sears generally follows customary "price-points" on soft goods such as men's shirts and women's garments. Thus shirts sell at $2.95 or $3.95, rather than at some intermediate price such as $3.30, which many customers might interpret as a high price for a $2.95-quality shirt rather than a low price for a $3.95 shirt. The result is an inflexibility in price which may require a variation in quality to meet rising costs.

Sears generally maintains a differential on mail-order prices below retail prices to allow for differences in selling costs, mailing costs, and delays in delivery. Decisions on both retail and mail-order prices are based on knowledge of traditional markups and price-points, on estimates of the price differentials needed to obtain volume, expected price changes of competitors, comprehensive reviews of competitive prices, shopping surveys, quality testing, and changes in the company's share of the market for different products. On some lines of merchandise, such as tires, paint, refrigerators, and other large appliances, the company wishes to avoid starting price wars; it avoids price-slashing promotions on these lines.

1. *Compare the decision rules and pricing practices of the six companies.*
2. *Evaluate each decision rule and each pricing practice of the six companies. Which of these rules and practices appear to be consistent or inconsistent with marginalism?*
3. *Is the objective of the Sprague College Store one of profit maximization? Are there any special influences on this store's pricing?*
4. *Should Mason's Men's Shop be more cooperative with the other men's stores in pricing?*
5. *What are the arguments for and against the decentralization of pricing in Sears, Roebuck?*

PRICING IN FIVE SMALL SERVICE OUTLETS*

The pricing practices of service outlets, like those of manufacturers and retailers, are variable. The five cases which follow give an opportunity to compare and contrast the practices of widely differing service producers, with an evaluation of the influence of costs, demand, and market conditions on pricing.

1. The Ace Laundry Company

The Ace Laundry Company is one of the leading firms in a midwestern city of 150,000. It employs approximately 100 workers and competes against approximately 40 other firms, most of which are smaller. Because of its reputation for service and quality, the Ace company is able to charge prices averaging about 10 percent higher than for the market in general. The managers express the view that most consumers are unaware of these price differentials, but they believe that an increase in prices would lead to a long-run decline in volume and a loss of profits. The managers also state that Ace's higher prices are related to the higher costs arising from more expensive services.

The managers do not attempt to earn the same margin on all of their business. For example, the prices on the "family bundle" (on which all items are washed and ironed) permits only a low profit above costs including the allocated overhead costs. This service is maintained as a drawing card for other, more profitable business. On the other hand, dry cleaning permits a higher margin. The managers believe that such differentials in margins are typical of the industry. The firm also varies prices on large-volume hotel and motel business in the summer, when other sales are low. The managers are willing to go as low as full cost (including allocated overhead), but they have a firm policy against going any lower. In fact, the managers rejected an opportunity for a large motel order that would have helped fill in the summer lull in activity because the offered price was below full cost. They do not vary prices on their other business over the seasons.

In the interviews, the managers many times expressed the view that their prices were based upon competition and what the market would bear. They strongly doubted that price reductions would be profitable. They thought that the cutting of costs by the elimination of "extras" might temporarily raise profits but that it would lead to a gradual deterioration of business. They were concerned about the inroads of sev-

---

* These case summaries are based on research sponsored by the Small Business Administration. The interviewers were D. Osborne, W. W. Haynes, J. L. Gibson, and M. B. Solomon, Jr., of the University of Kentucky. All names are disguised. The Small Business Administration is in no way responsible for the findings.

eral types of competition, such as coin-operated laundries, and the possible establishment of coin-operated cleaning services. They were also concerned about the development of "wash-n-wear" fabrics, which not only cut the costs of laundering but also cut down on the delay in getting the garment back from a laundry.

The interviews indicated that the managers had not recently thought about price policy in a systematic manner.

2. The Thadeus Truck Leasing Firm

The Thadeus company leases trucks to small businesses and to the general public. Because of the difficulty of measuring the cost of operating a particular truck, the owner makes little effort to relate rentals to costs. He is concerned, however, with his overall fleet costs. The owner thinks of himself as a price follower, usually maintaining his prices at a level 10 percent below the rates of the leading competitor. He does not consider pricing a major problem, preferring to devote attention to cost control. When profits are unsatisfactory, he looks for ways to cut costs, such as the purchase of less-expensive vehicles.

In 1960 the owner stated that he had increased his rates only once in the previous three years, and that time it was within three months after the leading competitor had raised prices. One obstacle to more frequent rate changes was the cost of printing new rate schedules and the repainting of a large sign in the sales office.

Mr. Thadeus follows the industry practice of reduced rates per hour for longer leases. He quotes quantity discounts for large weekly volumes. He believes that long-term leases are more profitable than "over-the-counter" rentals. He restricts his business to the leasing of trucks; he believes that the car rental business is unprofitable because of rapid wear and tear and frequent replacement. Furthermore his finances are inadequate for an investment in automobiles.

The city where the firm is located supports 15 automobile and truck rental firms. Mr. Thadeus believes that only five of these compete directly with him on his kind of business. He fears that any price reductions on his part might lead to retaliation.

A later interview in 1961, after the above facts were obtained, revealed a change in some of the company's policies. The firm had moved to new quarters where the costs were higher. Furthermore there had been a cumulative increase in costs over the years. Mr. Thadeus stated that this had required an increase in rates; his profits would have been inadequate without such an increase. The higher rates had wiped out the 10 percent differential under the rates of the leading competitor. But Mr. Thadeus expected that the competitors would soon increase their rates also, because of the increased costs they were experiencing. Thus he was not worried about a loss of business to competitors. This interview indicated that Mr. Thadeus was not as consistent a price imitator as he had at first appeared to be.

3. *Thomas Denton, Contractor*

Thomas Denton is a small builder. He normally builds six to eight homes in the $20,000 to $30,000 price bracket each year, and gives his personal attention to the details of construction. He subcontracts much of the specialized work, such as plumbing and wiring, but he employs his own carpenters.

Mr. Denton classifies his business into two types from the point of view of pricing: (1) a house to be constructed in the future on which he is asked to submit a bid; (2) a house built "on speculation" to be sold when completed or partially completed. Approximately 70 percent of his business is in the second category. Mr. Denton normally charges more for the first type because of the probability that the customer will require many time-consuming changes before the house is complete.

Mr. Denton does not follow the practice of some other builders in pricing on a square footage basis. He believes that such pricing does not reflect the variations in materials, fixtures, and his own time required from house to house. Instead he makes a detailed estimate of the labor and materials required in a house, using the form shown as Exhibit 1. Mr. Denton does not charge a percentage markup on cost. Instead he adds a sum for his own time, indicated at the bottom of Exhibit 1.

Mr. Denton's charge for his own time varies from job to job. One consideration is the amount of time required in the construction of the particular house. He will vary this charge somewhat with business conditions. For example, in 1958, when business in this locality was slow, he reduced this charge to speed up the sale of houses already completed. The need to finance the construction of new houses out of the profits from those already built sometimes puts him under pressure to shade prices. In 1958, he had held two houses for over a year before reducing price. Mr. Denton is slow in starting new houses until he has sold old ones, largely because he does not like to be heavily in debt and does not like to be under extreme pressure to reduce prices because of a large inventory of unsold houses.

Mr. Denton also reduces his bids on houses to be constructed in the winter. He believes that his time is not so valuable in this period of low activity. He also wants to keep his force of carpenters together as much as possible on a full-year basis, since it is difficult to acquire first-grade carpenters. Furthermore he can hire workers at lower rates in the winter. One last consideration in pricing is Mr. Denton's estimation of the customer's personality. If he appears to be a person who is demanding of continual changes in the plan and details of the house, Mr. Denton will raise his bid.

EXHIBIT 1. THOMAS DENTON

JOB _____   DATE _____

LOCATION _____

Lot	Towel bars, etc.
Plans	Stone labor
Taxes	Plumbing
Insurance binder	Extras
Comprehensive insurance	Sump pump
Stamps	Wiring
Water	Extras
Gas	Light fixtures
Electricity	Painting
Excavation	Extras
Footings	Caulking
Labor	Sanding floors
Form work	Concrete front porch
Foundation	Steps
Waterproofing	Walk
Drain tile	Concrete back porch
Back fill	Steps
Concrete basement floor	Walk
Steel post	Plastering
Steel basement sash	Lath
Aeroways	Lath labor
Steel girders	Corner rite
Steel bolts	Furnace
Framing lumber	Duct work
3/4" Storm siding	Flashing and gutter work
Rock wool	Linoleum in kitchen
Inside doors	Linoleum in bath
Outside doors	Tile in bath
Windows	Medicine cabinets
Glazing	Kitchen cabinets
Screens	Ironing board
Storm and screen doors	Attic fan
Plywood	Exhaust fan
Kitchen and bath subfloor	Dishwasher
Flooring	Disposal
Building paper	Weatherstripping
Finish lumber	Grading and bulldozer
Carpenter labor	Extra dirt
Extras	Sod
Social security	Shrubs
Nails	Drive
Hardware	Venetian blinds
Roofing	Wall paper
Garage material	Labor
Garage doors	Cleaning house
Brick chimney	Coach light
Mantle	Fence
Fire brick and tile installation	Freight
Brixment	Hauling expense
Sand	Shutters
Cut stone sills	Flower box
Brick	Advertising
Brick labor	Real estate commission
Angle irons	Miscellaneous
Stone	Contractor's fee

     SUB TOTAL $ _____   GRAND TOTAL $ _____

Mr. Denton has never heard of incremental costs, opportunity costs, or demand elasticities. He faces the competition of 10 or 12 builders very much like himself. He is not fearful of retaliation to reductions in his prices from such competitors, for it is difficult to compare houses and most price reductions are secret. One way of reducing price is to offer to do additional work, such as paneling a basement, without charge. Mr. Denton does admit, however, that his prices are influenced by the prices he thinks other builders are asking. Mr. Denton frequently sells his houses through real estate agents, paying the normal commission on new houses. He sometimes reduces his price for a direct sale to a customer which avoids the real estate commission. The real estate agents claim that this practice is unethical, but they continue to do business with Mr. Denton.

4. Millville Theater

The Millville Theater is located in a city of 30,000 close to a city of over 400,000. The 40-year-old building has a 900-seat capacity. In 1961 its tickets sold for 25 cents for children and 65 cents for adults, with only infrequent increases for special films (at the insistence of the film distributors). The theater normally shows a loss or barely breaks even after the payment of salaries to the four owner-managers.

The theater owners do not believe that either price increases or decreases would increase total revenue. Other theaters would not retaliate to a price reduction (they are at too great a distance to pay much attention to the Millville Theater's prices), but few customers would be attracted by lower rates. The owners had increased the prices on children's tickets from 20 cents to 25 cents in 1958 and had experienced a decrease in volume; they doubted that the decrease resulted from the price change. The owners had considered instituting "bargain nights" in the summer months but were dissuaded by a trade association pamphlet stating that lower prices were ineffective in increasing volume. The owners had sold books of tickets to high school students at reduced rates.

The firm's costs were relatively simple in structure. On most films, the theater paid a percentage of receipts to the distributors; infrequently it paid a fixed guarantee plus a percentage of receipts. The other main costs were the salaries of the owners and depreciation on the building. The building itself would be of little value in any other activity and probably could not even be sold as a theater. The location itself is valuable, because of its central position in the city.

The owners believe they are in a semimonopoly position in the relatively low-income market in which they operate. The most serious competition is from television and drive-in theaters. They do not believe that the large theaters in the nearby city offer much competition; most of their customers would not travel that far to go to a movie.

5. Ben's Radio and TV Repair Company

Ben's repair shop is located in a town of 8,000. The firm maintains two prices for the labor involved in repairs. It charges $3 per service call, with an extra charge of 10 cents per mile outside the city limits. It charges a flat rate of $7.50 for "bench work" done in the shop, whether this takes 15 minutes or three hours. The firm prices parts according to the manufacturers' schedules of list prices.

The shop owner believes that these prices are as high as they can profitably be for most jobs. He might charge more than $7.50 for bench work for a wealthy customer but this is exceptional. He occasionally charges as much as $10 for rush jobs and a few exceptionally complicated jobs.

He opposes charging by the hour, since it leads to arguments and poor customer relations; the flat rate contributes to customer goodwill and repeat business.

The owner maintains this business as a sideline and does not consider it a lucrative full-time occupation. He states that if he were to engage in the business on a full-time basis he would be forced to resort to charging higher prices to wealthier clients.

1. *Compare and contrast the pricing practices of the five service outlets.*
2. *Evaluate the practices in each case.*
3. *To what extent are the practices of these companies influenced by market structure, demand, or cost?*
4. *Are these companies full-cost pricers?*
5. *Do these companies follow the precepts of marginalism?*

FALL RIVER NURSERY

The Fall River Nursery was the second largest garden nursery and landscaping firm in its locality, a city of 150,000. The firm was a family concern founded about 1910, with a continual reputation for quality and service. In 1961 four partners cooperated in managing the firm.

The firm grew most of its own materials on its 500-acre plot, but purchased a few plants from wholesalers. The firm also sold a small fraction of its materials at wholesale; the local climate and soil conditions gave it an advantage on some plant varieties. Most of the sales were at retail at the company's garden center. The mail-order business was relatively small. One of the partners was in charge of the landscaping service as well as service work and spraying, another in charge of growing and propagation, and a third in charge of the garden center.

Pricing policies and practices

The firm did not appear to have a definite policy on pricing. The officials were skeptical of systematic approaches to pricing. They did not maintain a cost accounting system and doubted that it would be useful. In fact one of the partners stated that most experiments in cost accounting in other nurseries had failed and had been abandoned. He claimed that uncertainity about the weather, plant diseases, and soil conditions made it impossible to predict the cost of growing a particular plant variety. The long period it took to produce plants also made it difficult to estimate costs.

The same official stated that the firm's plants are priced "according to the market, just as wheat and corn are priced." The firm's prices were a little higher than prices of nurseries to the south, where labor costs were lower, but lower than prices in the large metropolitan areas. The firm did not maintain systematic records of what other firms were charging, though it did have a file of catalogues of other nurseries. This file was not kept up-to-date, and it apparently was not used often. In fact the company officials did not appear to know except vaguely what the price differentials from firm to firm were. Thus, if the firm's prices were based on the market, it was on a subjective evaluation of market forces rather than on any kind of statistical analysis.

The officials believed that the firm's prices were slightly on the low side in the local market, if one excluded the prices at some of the large chain groceries. They pointed to some advertisements in the local newspaper showing higher prices at a competitive firm.

Changes in prices

Price changes on plants were infrequent. Prices were established in the summer for the coming year. These prices were published in a catalogue in September. The partners believed that price changes during the year were undesirable; they did not even revise their mimeographed wholesale price during the season. The main exception to this rule was pricing for the end-of-season sale in May, at which time two categories of plants were marked down:

1. Dormant materials that had been dug up the previous fall and winter. These materials including fruit trees, hedges, and shrubs would have to be destroyed if not sold in May.

2. Block clearance items, mostly evergreens. If a few evergreens are occupying a block of land, it is desirable to sell them off at reduced prices to clear the land. Some of these materials may be of lower quality, but usually this is not the case.

From one season to the next the partners revised prices. In 1959, for example, they took into account an increase in labor costs in changing their prices upward.

Round-number pricing and promotional pricing

The company officials have traditionally preferred round numbers in pricing, such as $6 or $7 per plant, though they often used prices such as $6.50 or $8.25. In 1959 they broke away from this policy when they adjusted prices for labor cost changes. For example, they increased one price from $6.75 to $6.95 in the belief that a $7 price would develop customer resistance. In 1960 the firm returned to prices such as $7.25 and $9.25. A plant's price was the same regardless of how the plant was sold —by telephone, by purchase at the garden store, or by mail order.

The partners believed that round-number pricing was consistent with the atmosphere of quality and dignity that the company tried to maintain. They did not want to be classified with the chain stores and mass mail-order firms which sometimes had a poorer reputation. In 1961, however, the firm experimented with prices of $1.11, $2.22, or $4.44 on distress items in oversupply. In 1961 the partners also experimented with a two-for-one sale which permitted a customer to purchase a second plant for $1 upon purchase of the first plant at the regular price. In addition, bulbs, fertilizers, and other items purchased on the outside were being sold at odd prices in 1961. Expert merchandisers and speakers at trade meetings had convinced the partners that some experimentation with promotional pricing might be desirable in building up volume. But the catalogue prices were kept on a round-number basis; the promotional odd prices were the exception rather than the rule.

In 1962, the partners were not yet certain that the experiments with promotional pricing had been successful. They were planning several new "traffic builders," however. For example, they planned to offer to give one popular rose bush free to the purchaser of five rose bushes. The trend appeared to be toward more specials of this sort, but these specials were still the exception.

The pricing of particular plants

The firm did not have control over all of its prices. Some plants were patented; the firm holding the patent set the price and collected a royalty from individual nurseries. The markups on such plants were usually higher than the Fall River Nursery's markups on plants of similar size and variety.

In spite of the general inflation in costs and prices in the 1950's, the prices on some plants were lower than in earlier years. For example, *Juniperus excelsa stricta* (15 to 18 inches) was selling at $2.50 instead of the $3 of a decade earlier. The reasons for the price decline were the reduction in demand for this variety and the fact that it was more readily available. The company officials were uncertain whether they were making money on this variety at such low prices, but they continued to grow it. One partner, however, stated that the company would not continue to grow a plant that did not return a profit in the long run.

Another plant that had fallen in price was *Taxus cuspidata browni*. This plant was in short supply in 1952–53, but supply had caught up with demand by 1960 and prices had reached a more normal level.

EXHIBIT 1

Prices of Selected Plants, 1948-60

Plant and Size	1948-49	1950-51	1952-53	1954-55	1956-57	1958-59	1959-60
Juniperus excelsa stricta							
15 to 18 inches	3.00	N.L.*	N.L.	2.50	2.50	2.50	2.50
18 to 24 inches	N.L.	3.00	3.00	3.00	3.00	3.00	3.00
2 to 2½ feet	N.L.	4.00	4.00	4.00	4.00	4.00	4.00
2½ to 3 feet	N.L.	5.50	N.L.	N.L.	N.L.	N.L.	5.00
3 to 3½ feet	N.L.	7.00	N.L.	N.L.	N.L.	N.L.	N.L.
Juniperus chinensis glauca hetzi							
15 to 18 inches	N.L.	3.50	3.50	3.00	N.L.	N.L.	N.L.
18 to 24 inches	N.L.	4.00	4.50	4.00	N.L.	N.L.	N.L.
2 to 2½ feet	N.L.	N.L.	5.50	5.00	5.50	N.L.	N.L.
2½ to 3 feet	N.L.	N.L.	7.00	6.50	7.00	7.00	N.L.
Taxus cuspidata							
15 to 18 inches	4.00	4.00	4.50	N.L.	N.L.	5.25	5.50
18 to 24 inches	5.00	5.00	6.00	6.00	6.50	6.95	7.25
2 to 2½ feet	6.50	7.00	8.00	8.00	8.50	8.95	9.25
2½ to 3 feet	8.00	9.00	11.00	11.00	12.00	12.00	12.50
3 to 3½ feet	N.L.	12.00	14.00	14.00	15.00	15.00	16.00
3½ to 4 feet	N.L.	N.L.	N.L.	18.00	20.00	20.00	22.50
4 to 4½ feet	N.L.	N.L.	N.L.	N.L.	N.L.	25.00	30.00
Taxus baccata repandens							
15 to 18 inches	N.L.	N.L.	N.L.	5.50	6.00	6.25	N.L.
18 to 24 inches	N.L.	7.00	N.L.	7.50	N.L.	8.25	8.50
2 to 2½ feet	N.L.	N.L.	N.L.	N.L.	10.00	N.L.	9.75
Taxus cuspidata browni							
15 to 18 inches	N.L.	N.L.	6.00	5.50	5.50	5.25	5.50
18 to 24 inches	5.00	5.00	6.00	7.00	7.00	6.95	7.25
2 to 2½ feet	6.50	8.00	10.00	9.00	9.00	8.95	9.25
2½ to 3 feet	8.00	N.L.	N.L.	N.L.	N.L.	N.L.	N.L.

* N.L.: not listed.

EXHIBIT 1—Continued

PRICES OF SELECTED PLANTS, 1948–60

Plant and Size	1948–49	1950–51	1952–53	1954–55	1956–57	1958–59	1959–60
Taxus cuspidata capitata							
2 to 2½ feet	N.L.*	N.L.	N.L.	N.L.	N.L.	8.00	8.00
2½ to 3 feet	7.00	7.00	7.50	7.50	N.L.	9.50	9.50
3 to 3½ feet	8.00	8.00	9.00	9.00	10.00	11.00	11.00
3½ to 4 feet	10.00	10.00	11.50	10.75	12.00	13.00	13.00
4 to 4½ feet	12.50	12.50	13.50	12.75	14.00	15.00	15.00
4½ to 5 feet	15.00	15.00	17.00	15.00	17.50	17.50	18.00
5 to 5½ feet	17.50	17.50	20.00	18.00	21.00	21.00	22.00
5½ to 6 feet	20.00	20.00	23.50	21.00	24.00	24.00	25.00
6 to 7 feet	25.00	25.00	27.50	25.00	28.00	28.00	30.00
7 to 8 feet	N.L.	N.L.	N.L.	N.L.	35.00	35.00	40.00
Columnar *Taxus hicksi*							
2½ to 3 feet	N.L.	7.00	8.00	8.00	N.L.	N.L.	N.L.
3 to 3½ feet	N.L.	8.00	10.00	10.00	N.L.	N.L.	N.L.
3½ to 4 feet	N.L.	12.50	12.50	12.50	N.L.	N.L.	N.L.
4 to 4½ feet	N.L.	15.00	15.00	15.00	N.L.	N.L.	N.L.
4½ to 5 feet	N.L.	17.50	17.50	N.L.	N.L.	N.L.	N.L.
5 to 6 feet	N.L.	20.00	20.00	N.L.	N.L.	N.L.	N.L.
Globe *Taxus*							
15 to 18 inches	N.L.	N.L.	N.L.	N.L.	N.L.	N.L.	6.50
18 to 24 inches	N.L.	7.00	N.L.	N.L.	8.00	8.00	8.00
2 to 2½ feet	N.L.	9.00	N.L.	N.L.	10.00	10.00	N.L.
2½ feet	N.L.	N.L.	N.L.	N.L.	15.00	15.00	15.00
3 feet	N.L.	N.L.	N.L.	N.L.	20.00	20.00	20.00
3½ feet	N.L.	N.L.	N.L.	N.L.	N.L.	25.00	25.00
4 to 4½ feet	N.L.	N.L.	N.L.	N.L.	N.L.	30.00	30.00

* N.L.: not listed.

EXHIBIT 1—Continued

PRICES OF SELECTED PLANTS, 1948–60

Plant and Size	1948–49	1950–51	1952–53	1954–55	1956–57	1958–59	1959–60
Tsuga hemlock							
2 to 2½ feet	3.50	N.L.*	N.L.	N.L.	N.L.	N.L.	N.L.
2 to 3 feet	N.L.	N.L.	N.L.	N.L.	N.L.	4.00	4.00
2½ to 3 feet	4.00	4.00	5.00	5.00	5.00	N.L.	N.L.
3 to 3½ feet	4.50	5.00	6.00	6.00	6.00	N.L.	N.L.
3 to 4 feet	N.L.	N.L.	N.L.	N.L.	N.L.	6.00	6.00
3½ to 4 feet	5.00	5.00	7.00	7.00	7.00	N.L.	N.L.
4 to 4½ feet	6.00	6.00	8.00	9.00	9.00	N.L.	N.L.
4 to 5 feet	N.L.	N.L.	N.L.	N.L.	N.L.	8.00	8.00
4½ to 5 feet	7.00	7.00	9.00	11.00	11.00	N.L.	N.L.
5 to 6 feet	8.00	8.00	10.00	N.L.	15.00	11.00	11.00
6 to 7 feet	10.00	10.00	12.50	N.L.	N.L.	15.00	15.00
7 to 8 feet	12.00	12.00	16.00	N.L.	N.L.	20.00	20.00
8 to 9 feet	N.L.	N.L.	20.00	N.L.	N.L.	N.L.	N.L.
11 to 12 feet	25.00	N.L.	N.L.	N.L.	N.L.	N.L.	N.L.

* N.L.: not listed.

Some of the company's prices were 25 percent or even 50 percent below prices in the large metropolitan markets. The company grew some plants especially adapted to the local climate in large blocks, with resultant economies of scale.

The prices of some plants at first appeared to be out of line with the size of the plant. An example was globe *Taxus*. The officials explained that this plant requires special shearing to give it the desired shape. Thus the labor costs were higher, and it took more years for the plant to grow to a given size. The officials doubted that they were making as great a profit on these plants as on the same variety left unsheared.

Exhibit 1 shows the record of prices of some selected items over the period from 1948 to 1960.

1. *Make a list of various possible changes in the nursery's pricing practices. Evaluate each of these possibilities.*
2. *Is the nursery's pricing cost oriented or demand oriented? Discuss.*
3. *Analyze the price changes in Exhibit 1. Why do some prices increase while others decrease?*
4. *Evaluate the company's experimentation with promotional pricing in 1961 and 1962.*
5. *What recommendations would you make to improve the nursery's pricing?*

AIR-INDIA (D)*

Tariffs

Air-India, like the other members of the International Air Transport Association (IATA), does not have full control over its own tariffs. Instead, the company and the Government of India have acceded to the decisions of the Traffic Conferences of IATA in which the rule of unanimity applies. Nevertheless Air-India does have a policy and a point of view with regard to tariffs. The Company *favors lower fares* and its representatives at the Traffic Conferences press for a fairly sharp reduction in tariffs, as opposed to the gradual reductions in fares favored by some other airlines and governments.

Air-India's position was expressed in its 1962–63 Annual Report as follows:

Air-India's voice at Traffic Conferences, such as it is, has generally been in favour of lower fares with the object of achieving a mass market. Because of its lean and efficient operations, resulting in almost the lowest costs in the industry, Air-India is well placed to absorb the initial impact of lower fares and benefit from the resulting expansion of the market.

---

* Case material of the Indian Institute of Management, Ahmedabad, is prepared as a basis for class discussion. Cases are not designed to present illustrations of either correct or incorrect handling of administrative problems. Copyright © 1964 by the Indian Institute of Management, Ahmedabad.

The International Air Transport Association

IATA was formed in 1945 by the International airlines of countries in most parts of the world. It was given a legal existence by a special Act of the Canadian Parliament in 1945. It was associated closely with another organization, the International Civil Aviation Organization (ICAO) which was established in 1945 as an agency for governments which wished to establish international standards for the regulation of civil aviation.

Membership in IATA is open to any airline providing scheduled air services licensed by a government eligible for membership in ICAO. The international airlines are active members, while the domestic airlines may join as associate members.

The voting procedures of IATA are unusual when compared with those of other international organizations. Each airline has a single vote regardless of its size. All decisions must be unanimous. No decisions are effective without the approval of the interested governments. Thus any single airline or any single government has the power to veto any decision.

IATA is concerned with much more than traffic matters. It has committees dealing continuously with technical, medical, legal, and financial issues. IATA, through these committees, promotes standards of safety, comfort, and efficiency. Rules and procedures govern airlines in all parts of the world. An effort is made to simplify and standardize the documents which must flow from one airline to another. The Association publishes manuals of *Revenue Accounting Practices* which aim at the standardization of the reporting of costs, profits, and losses. The IATA Clearing House in London settles monthly accounts for interline revenue transactions, making it possible for each airline to pay and collect debts in a single settlement. This case is concerned, however, with the rate-making aspects of IATA which are perhaps the most complicated and controversial matters with which the organization must deal.

The IATA traffic conferences

The steps in establishing tariffs on international routes are different from those of domestic routes. Before the tariffs are filed with the respective governments for approval, the airlines meet together to agree on a pattern of rates. These rates apply to all the carriers concerned. Unless all agree, no decision is binding. And the governments have the final say on whether the agreements can be maintained. The normal practice is for the airlines to reach an agreement after considerable give-and-take in the Traffic Conferences and for the governments to approve those agreements. Occasionally the Conferences fail to reach an agreement or one or more governments fail to sanction the agreements, but such failures are the exception rather than the rule. Furthermore, soon after a conference has failed to achieve an agreement, the airlines and governments become quite uncomfortable with the possible anarchy in rates which might ensue; thus they soon reconvene to avoid this possibility. It is also the practice of each airline to refrain from vetoing an agreement affecting territories outside its main routes.

The world is divided into three areas for the purposes of the Conferences. Area No. 1 covers the Americas. Area No. 2 covers Europe, the Middle East, and Africa; and Area No. 3 covers the rest of the world. Meetings deal separately with the relations between Area No. 1 and Area No. 2, No. 2 and No. 3, and No. 3 and No. 1. But the most important work takes place in the Composite Conference covering the whole world, usually held every two years. Individual airlines make recommendations of tariff changes at these Conferences. Traffic working groups and cost committees make careful studies of prospective traffic and costs of operation. The agreement reached by past conferences consists of over 1,000 resolutions covering rates between 60,000 pairs of points in the world network.

Among the criteria of rate-making considered by the Conferences are the following: (*a*) operating costs; (*b*) traffic potential; (*c*) local economic conditions; (*d*) type of traffic to be moved; (*e*) seasonal nature of the traffic; and (*f*) competition from non-IATA carriers such as the steamship companies.

Conference crises

From time to time crises over specific issues require the adjournment and reconvenement of the Conferences. In October, 1959, for example, the delegates failed to agree on fares and facilities in several parts of the world. Six months later the issue was resolved. As one commentator observed the agreement was "accomplished by special excursion and direction fares and group discounts on those international routes where they were needed, by applying cabotage fares on certain others, and sealing of the repercussive effects on other routes. . . . by measures of noncombinability and the like."[1]

Another crisis took place in 1960 and 1961 over cargo rates on the North Atlantic. It took three Conferences to settle this issue, but the fear of the consequences of an "open" rate system brought about an agreement.

The 1962–63 crisis on North Atlantic fares

Although the North Atlantic run was relatively new among Air-India routes, the Company took a great interest in the 1962–63 controversies

---

[1] W. Gordon Wood, "The IATA Traffic Conferences: An Airline Man's View," Montreal: IATA, n.d.

over rates from New York to Europe. The crisis arose from the failure of one Government to approve the agreements reached by the Traffic Conference of October, 1962, at Chandler, Arizona, on North Atlantic rates. Most of the 19 airlines involved on the transatlantic run favored a 5 percent increase in the round trip rates in the form of a reduction in the transatlantic return discount. The American and Canadian airlines did not oppose this rate increase. The crisis was brought to a head finally by the refusal of the United States Civil Aeronautics Board to accept the new rates. In fact the United States Civil Aeronautics Board threatened action against Pan American Airways and Trans World Airlines if they complied with the IATA recommendations. The American government was forced to back down when several European countries threatened not to permit American aircraft to land. Thus the new high rates went into effect in April, 1963.

In the period from April to October, 1963, various proposals for reduced fares were publicized. Pan American Airways proposed a "thrift-class" fare on the North Atlantic which would be over 40 percent below the existing rates. BOAC pressed for a 25 percent reduction in first-class fares and extensions of existing excursion rates.

One of the main factors contributing to the controversy over rates was the upsurge in capacity resulting from re-equipment with jet aircraft. The development of new national airlines added to the capacity. Some leaders in the industry argued that a restriction of capacity was essential to profitable operators. The shipping industry had been able to control capacity through a conference system; the same principle might be applied to the airlines.

The IATA Traffic Conference which reconvened in Salzburg on October 22, 1963, was faced with the following specific proposals: (a) reduce the one-way, first-class, transatlantic fare from $475 to $400; (b) reduce the one-way economy fare from $263 to $210; (c) introduce a round trip excursion fare, valid for 21 days, at $300.

Two of the smaller lines, Aer Lingus of Ireland and El Al of Israel, opposed these proposals, which included an abolition of "group rates" for members of clubs.

Air-India's position on passenger fares

As has already been mentioned, Air-India was a strong advocate of lower passenger fares. Company officials did not believe gradual decreases in fares would do much to stimulate traffic. They thought that the reductions must be substantial to be felt by the traveling public.

One reason for Air-India's position was the large amount of excess capacity on all of the airlines, including Air-India. Exhibit 1 presents information on the capacity offered and the capacity utilized since Air-India was established in 1953. In recent years the capacity had outrun the usage so that the load factor had fallen below 50 percent. It was hoped that lower fares would stimulate traffic and raise the load factor.

One might ask why the company continued to increase capacity when the load factor was so low. One reason company officials gave was that Air-India must increase its frequency of service if it was to win over customers. For example, they would like to build up a daily service across the Atlantic to New York so that potential customers would not have to worry about whether Air-India was operating on a particular day. Extension of the Bombay–London service to New York which took place in May, 1960, could be justified on several grounds: it would feed traffic into the other company lines; it would help establish the company's reputation as an international carrier; and to some extent it would use planes which otherwise would be idle in London waiting for the turn-around. Company officials also believed that an airline which failed to expand its capacity might stagnate. In any case the company had added rapidly to its capacity, as Exhibit 1 clearly demonstrates.

Another related argument for lower rates was that the added costs of filling up the aircraft would be negligible. Company officials believed that practically all of the costs were fixed. Exhibit 2 presents figures on the operating expenses in 1962–63.

On the revenue side, the company's position was that passenger traffic would respond very sharply to rate reductions. One company official expressed the view that the demand was highly elastic in all parts of the world if the rate reductions were large enough to be noticed. Perhaps Air-India would benefit more than the average airline for several reasons: The Asia market provided a great pool of potential customers who could not afford the higher rates. The large numbers of Indians in such places as East Africa would like to visit their homeland and would like to save travel time if they could pay the air fares.

Air-India did not have to worry quite so much as some other lines, such as KLM, about the impact on chartered services of lower fares on scheduled services. Only 1 percent of the company's revenues came from chartered services (see Exhibit 3).

At the same time, one company official noted a factor which was holding down the elasticity of demand for Air-India's passenger services. Under India's exchange controls Indian citizens could not travel abroad without P-forms. The number of P-forms issued by the Indian government was not influenced by whether fares were high or low. Approximately half of Air-India's traffic was by Indian nationals.

The arguments for higher fares emphasized the heavy capital outlay

EXHIBIT 1
Air-India (D)
(total capacity offered and utilized for schedules service only)

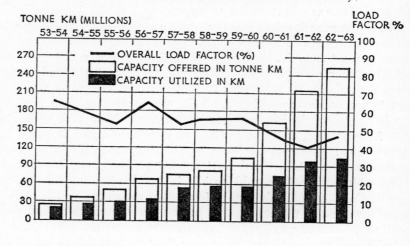

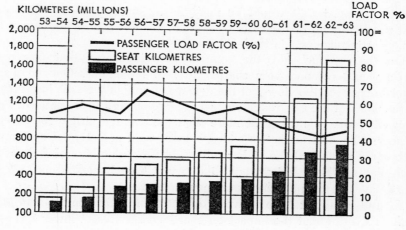

and rapid obsolescence involved in aircraft, the great economic and political uncertainties, the high cost of fuel, landing fees, taxes, and other expenses. In the late 1950's and early 1960's the international air fares were inadequate to provide a profit for most airlines—let alone to permit a profit which would compensate for the risks.

Air-India officials tended to prefer special discounts to stimulate traffic, including seasonal discounts and discounts for large groups. In the latter case it was necessary to provide special safeguards to assure that the group rates were used only by bona fide groups. In some cases, Air-

EXHIBIT 2
AIR-INDIA (D)
(operating expenses, 1962–63)

Particulars	In Indian Rupees	
1. A. Flying operations:		
a) Pay, allowances and provident fund contributions	7,639,978	
b) Staff and other general insurance	210,169	
c) Other staff costs	2,271,537	
d) Fuel and oil	31,384,512	
e) Aircraft insurance	8,894,439	
f) Aircraft landing, housing and parking fees	7,765,239	
g) Hire of aircraft	53,401	
h) Other operational expenses	1,612,537	
		59,831,812
B. Flying training:		
a) Pay, allowances and provident fund contributions	394,707	
b) Fuel, landing fees, cost of materials and insurance	1,028,405	
c) Training by third parties	—	
		1,423,112
2. Flight equipment maintenance and overhaul:		
a) Pay, allowances and provident fund contributions	12,132,569	
b) Staff insurance	11,012	
c) Other staff costs	795,163	
d) Materials consumed including outside repairs and services	14,042,794	
e) Charges for technical handling by other operators	1,034,763	
f) Insurance of equipment and stores	210,865	
g) Other engineering expenses	2,175,714	
		30,402,880
3. Traffic, sales and publicity:		
a) Pay, allowances and provident fund contributions	14,734,370	
b) Staff and other general insurance	59,839	
c) Other staff costs	2,832,873	
d) Booking agency commission	16,603,058	
e) Publicity and sales promotion	13,798,220	
f) Charges for traffic handling by other operators	5,363,622	
g) Other traffic expenses, including rent, rates, printing and stationery, postage and telegraphs, telephones, etc.	11,381,106	
		64,773,088
4. Passenger and cargo services:		
a) Pay, allowances and provident fund contributions	3,072,762	
b) Staff and other general insurance	55,657	
c) Other staff costs	2,727,549	

EXHIBIT 2 (*Continued*)

AIR-INDIA (D)

(operating expenses, 1962–63)

Particulars		In Indian Rupees	
d) Food service including hotel accommodation and cabin service amenities		7,345,444	
e) Liability insurance		1,021,309	
f) Other expenses		585,733	
			14,808,454
5. Surface transport:			
a) Pay, allowances and provident fund contributions		1,029,115	
b) Staff and other general insurance		134,672	
c) Other staff costs		47,572	
d) Fuel and oil		438,898	
e) Materials and outside repairs		357,030	
f) Hire of transport		749,649	
g) Other expenses		253,396	
			3,010,332
6. A. General administration:			
a) Pay, allowances and provident fund contributions:			
i) Finance and accounts	3,828,824		
ii) Personnel and security	653,947		
iii) Administrative and planning	614,144		
		5,096,915	
b) Staff and other general insurance		45,631	
c) Other staff costs		353,364	
d) Board members' fees and expenses		8,880	
e) Auditors' fees and expenses		46,235	
f) Legal charges		144,888	
g) Other expenses		1,552,815	
			7,248,728
B. Staff welfare:			
a) Pay, allowances and provident fund contributions		369,128	
b) Other expenses (Net)		102,695	
c) Depreciation		233,320	
			621,015
			182,119,421

India sometimes charged less for segments of a particular route than would be consistent with the rate over the entire route. IATA permitted this practice when the competition from non-IATA lines made it necessary.

Air-India's position on cargo rates was not so strong, partly perhaps because only 15 percent of its revenue came from that source. Air-India

EXHIBIT 3

Air-India (D)

Particulars	Rupees in Millions	Percent
How Every Rupee Was Earned		
What the corporation earned:		
Passengers	159.57	65.1
Mails	26.45	10.8
Freight including excess baggage	36.68	14.9
Charters	3.10	1.2
Contract services	4.09	1.7
Incidental revenues	15.37	6.3
Total operating revenue	245.27	100.0

Particulars	Rupees in Millions	Percent
How Every Rupee Was Spent		
What the corporation spent:		
Employees	44.42	21.1
Traffic and passenger service	44.04	20.9
Operations	44.04	20.9
Depreciation	25.94	12.3
Engineering	18.05	8.5
Booking agency commission	16.60	7.9
Insurance	10.72	5.1
Administration	5.07	2.4
Surface transport	1.85	0.9
Total operating expenses	210.73	100.0

favored the practice of relating the cargo rates to the value of the cargo and of providing special rates to move cargo which otherwise would not move by air. Company officials recognized that this last practice might lead to demands for rate reductions from other shippers. All in all, they seemed less convinced that cargo traffic would respond as much to rate reductions as passenger traffic would.

The issues in 1963

Air-India had made a profit in 1961–62 and 1962–63 despite the reduction of its load factor to 45 percent and despite the fact that most of the international airlines were unprofitable. The question was what stand the company should take on the North Atlantic fares, on fares in other parts of the world, on proposals to restrict capacity, and on the IATA system in general.

1. *What is the main issue in this case? What tools of economic analysis are applicable?*
2. *Should Air-India continue to support the IATA system?*

3. *What stand should Air-India have taken in October, 1963?*
4. *Should Air-India oppose or favor an "open" rate system?*
5. *Should Air-India cooperate in plans for restricting capacity on international airlines?*

STEEL PRICES IN 1962

The most famous pricing decision in recent years was that of the U.S. Steel Company on April 9, 1962, a decision that was rescinded on April 13, 1962. The strong opposition of President John F. Kennedy, along with the refusal of several steel producers to follow the lead of U.S. Steel, resulted in this rapid reversal of price policy.

The publicity at the time of the decision and its reversal stressed cost considerations. The United Steel Workers had signed a contract with the industry in early April which limited wage increases to the estimated rate of annual increase in national productivity. The agreement provided an increase in fringe benefits costing about 10.9 cents an hour, about a 2½ percent increase in hourly wage costs. The contract was widely hailed as noninflationary and as indicating a growing maturity of union-management relations. President Kennedy praised the agreement as "industrial statesmanship of the highest order" and said that it "should provide a solid base for continued price stability."* Steel officials, however, were concerned not merely with the 10.9 cent wage cost increase in 1962, but with the approximate 50 cents per hour increase in employment costs since 1958, the time of the last price increase. Furthermore, they noted that the increase in productivity in the steel industry had been only 1.7 percent per year since 1940, which was lower than the contemplated increase in employment costs. Steel officials were disturbed by their reduced profit position—the low profits resulted in part from the reduced demand in 1960 and 1961 but also from rising costs. The profits of U.S. Steel in 1961 were 36 percent below those in 1958, a recession year. Exhibit 1 presents data on steel output and prices in the years from 1957 to 1961.

The decision of U.S. Steel to increase steel prices by an average of $6 per ton, about 3½ percent, came as a surprise to many observers, who had assumed that the moderate union demands would mean no increase in prices. No doubt the officials of U.S. Steel tried to take into account not only the rising costs and reduced profits already mentioned, but also the political repercussions and the probable price policies of competitors. It is clear that these officials made an incorrect evaluation of the political

---

* In *Business Week*, April 7, 1962, p. 29, Mr. Roger Blough, Chairman of the Board of U.S. Steel, denied that U.S. Steel had made any commitment on prices before, during, or after the wage negotiations. See his article in *Look* magazine, January 29, 1963.

EXHIBIT 1

IMPORTANT STATISTICS ON THE STEEL INDUSTRY, 1951-61

	U.S. STEEL COMPANY (MILLIONS OF DOLLARS)							ENTIRE INDUSTRY			
	Products and Services Sold	Employ- ment Costs*	Income		Dividends		Reinvested in Business	Average Number of Employees	Steel Products Shipped (Net Tons)	Ingot Production (Net Tons)	Ingot Operating Rate
Year			Amount	% of Sales	Preferred Stock	Common Stock					
1951	3,524.1	1,374.5	184.3	5.2	25.2	78.3	80.8	670,700	78,928,950	105,199,848	100.9
1952	3,137.4	1,322.1	143.6	4.6	25.2	78.3	40.1	653,700	68,003,612	93,168,039	85.8
1953	3,861.0	1,569.2	222.1	5.8	25.2	78.3	118.6	682,800	80,151,893	111,609,719	94.9
1954	3,250.4	1,387.0	195.4	6.0	25.2	85.5	84.7	611,000	63,152,726	88,311,652	71.0
1955	4,097.7	1,614.9	370.1	9.0	25.2	122.9	222.0	657,600	84,717,444	117,036,085	93.0
1956	4,228.9	1,681.0	348.1	8.2	25.2	144.9	178.0	653,400	83,251,168	115,216,149	89.8
1957	4,413.8	1,862.0	419.4	9.5	25.2	161.3	232.9	656,700	79,894,577	112,714,996	84.5
1958	3,472.1	1,488.5	301.5	8.7	25.2	161.4	114.9	551,000	59,914,433	85,254,885	60.6
1959	3,643.0	1,576.2	254.5	7.0	25.2	161.8	67.5	538,800	69,377,067	93,446,132	63.3
1960	3,698.5	1,700.0	304.2	8.2	25.2	162.0	117.0	601,600	71,149,218	99,281,601	66.8
1961	3,336.5	1,622.7	190.2	5.7	25.2	162.3	2.7	N/A	66,125,505	98,014,492	N/A

* Employment costs include pensions and social security taxes and also include payments for insurance and other employee benefits.

SOURCE: United States Steel Corporation, *Annual Report 1961; Annual Statistical Reports*, American Iron and Steel Institute. The number of employees represents total wage and salaried employees engaged in the production and sale of iron and steel products reported to American Iron and Steel Institute by companies comprising 93 to 97 percent of the steelmaking capacity of the steel industry adjusted to 100 percent of the industry steelmaking capacity.

repercussions. But some observers would argue that they may also have misjudged the elasticity of demand.

The measurement of the elasticity of the demand for steel is complicated by the fact that steel is not a homogeneous product and that it is sold in a variety of markets at a variety of prices. The fact that steel can be stored means that a distinction must be made between the response to temporary price changes and permanent price changes. Secret price concessions mean that published price data are not always reliable.

Several bits of evidence would suggest that the demand for steel is inelastic. Theodore Yntema's statistical study for the U.S. Steel Corporation presented to the Temporary National Economic Committee (TNEC) in 1938 indicated extremely low demand elasticities.[1] The steel industry used this study to argue that a reduction in steel prices would make little contribution to employment in the depression of the 1930's. One might object to using a depression study in the evaluation of demand in 1962. But the fact that the demand for steel is a derived demand would support the argument that it is inelastic. For example, the price of steel would appear to be a minor factor in determining how much steel is used in the production of automobiles.

On the other hand, the growing competition from steel producers abroad, and from substitutes for steel might suggest that the demand for steel produced within the United States was becoming more elastic in the 1960's. In fact, this was one of the arguments used by the steel industry for moderation in wage demands—high domestic costs were hurting the United States' international trade position. In 1956 and 1957 the United States had exported four to five times the steel that it imported. Since 1958 imports had exceeded exports. Competition with Western Europe had become extremely severe, with the disappearance of most of the U.S. exports in Europe but with imports from Europe of over 2 million tons per year.[2] *Business Week* reported that companies in the European Coal and Steel Community were offering products at 10 to 15 percent below United States company prices in European markets. (Exhibits 2, 3, and 4 present data on the export situation.)

Probably even more important were the inroads that competing metals were making into steel markets. Aluminum had become particularly important as a substitute for steel; no doubt many purchasers made careful comparisons between the cost of aluminum and the cost of steel.

The elasticity of demand facing individual firms such as U.S. Steel was influenced in large part by the extent to which other steel companies followed the price increases of the leader. President Kennedy and other

---

[1] See United States Steel Corporation, *T.N.E.C. Papers*, Vol. I, pp. 169ff.
[2] *Business Week*, March 24, 1962, pp. 100–102.

EXHIBIT 2
TOTAL WORLD STEEL TRADE AND U.S. STEEL EXPORTS

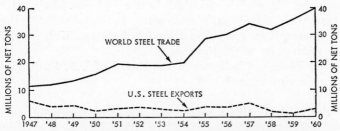

SOURCES: United Nations Economic Commission for Europe and U.S. Department of Commerce as reprinted in American Iron and Steel Institute, *The Competitive Challenge to Steel*, 1961.

EXHIBIT 3
RELATIVE IMPORTANCE OF DIRECT STEEL EXPORTS AND IMPORTS

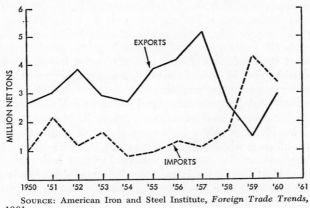

SOURCE: American Iron and Steel Institute, *Foreign Trade Trends*, 1961.

EXHIBIT 4
U.S. EXPORTS AND IMPORTS OF STEEL RELATED PRODUCTS

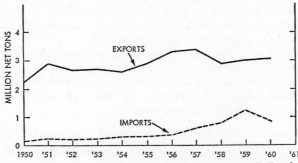

SOURCE: American Iron and Steel Institute, *Foreign Trade Trends*, 1961.

government officials exerted a great effort to prevent an industry-wide increase and thus had an important influence on the elasticity of demand. Two companies, the eighth and ninth in size, announced that they would not increase their prices. Soon thereafter, Bethlehem Steel, the second largest steel company, rescinded its price increase. U.S. Steel followed with restoration of its original prices.

Mr. Roger Blough, Chairman of the Board of U.S. Steel, made these comments on competition:[3]

There was no doubt that a price increase was necessary and we reviewed again all of the competitive factors involved. We did not—and could not—know, of course, whether other major steel producers would also raise their prices if we made the attempt; but from their published annual reports we could assume that they were suffering as we were from steadily rising costs and that they needed, as we did, the profits necessary to pay for the replacement and modernization of worn-out and obsolete facilities.

We were aware, too, that should other companies go along with the price increase, competition with substitute materials and foreign sources of steel might even add temporarily to our competitive difficulties. But the continued improvement in the economy as well as some improvement in the demand and consumption of steel indicated that a moderate price increase might be competitively possible; and, in view of the need, it was our judgment that we should delay no further in testing the market.

So on Tuesday, April 10, we announced an increase of three-tenths of a cent per pound in the general level of our steel prices. This amounted to about 3½ percent and would cover only a little more than half of the 6 percent net increase in over-all costs which had occurred since 1958. Therefore, it would not restore, by any means, the cost-price relationship that had existed four years ago; but it would at least assist in meeting the competitive needs of our company, as our President, Mr. Worthington, pointed out in his statement announcing the price action. He said:

"If the products of United States Steel are to compete successfully in the market place, then the plants and facilities which make those products must be as modern and efficient as the low-cost mills which abound abroad, and as the plants which turn out competing products here at home. Only by generating the funds necessary to keep these facilities fully competitive can our company continue to provide its customers with a dependable source of steel, and to provide its employees with dependable jobs. . . .

"The financial resources supporting continuous research and resultant new products as well as those supporting new equipment, are therefore vital in this competitive situation—vital not alone to the company and its employees, but to our international balance of payments, the value of our dollar, and to the strength and security of the nation as well."

In another article Mr. Blough commented on competitive pressures at the time of the steel price controversy. He stated that the competitive

---

[3] *The U.S. Steel Quarterly*, May, 1962, p. 5.

limitations of the market had restricted U.S. Steel to a 3½ percent price increase instead of the 6 percent increase in costs. The order by Secretary of Defense Robert S. McNamara to defense contractors to buy steel only from companies which had not raised prices, along with long-distance calls by the President and his associates urging other steel companies not to raise prices, had made it difficult to maintain the 3½ percent price increase. While eight of the companies had raised prices, the "rest of the steel companies were still selling at $6 lower, and manifold Government pressures were being exerted."[4] When Inland Steel and Kaiser Steel announced against price increases it was obvious that the "eight steel companies that had raised prices would have to lower them in order to survive." Mr. Blough also commented that no firm "has yet discovered a way to sell steel in a buyer's market at $6 a ton more than his competition."

Mr. Blough believed that one favorable outcome of the steel price controversy was a public awareness "that, in the absence of Government intervention, steel prices are determined by the competitive forces of the marketplace—not by the decision of one company. Perhaps the public also realized that the market alone is the infallible arbiter of prices, and if error is made, the market itself will correct it."

The steel controversy involved broad questions about the relationship between government and business. President Kennedy stated that a few steel executives had shown "utter contempt for the interests of 185 million Americans." He apparently believed that the government had the right to intervene to protect the "public interest." Mr. Blough, on the other hand, took the position that "it is the duty of Government to protect each [individual] . . . in the pursuit of his lawful interests, to insure that force and coercion do not intrude upon those interests, and to guarantee that each individual not intrude upon the lawful interests of others." He therefore denied that it was in the public interest for the President "to substitute his own action for the action of the marketplace by trying to set prices for any competitive products."

1. *Compare the elasticity of demand facing the American steel industry in general, the eight steel companies which raised prices in 1962, and U.S. Steel. How important were these elasticities as influences on steel prices in 1962?*
2. *Did the government influence these demand elasticities in 1962? If so, how?*
3. *How would you describe the structure of the steel industry in 1962? Did this structure influence the pricing patterns in that year?*
4. *Is the steel industry competitive? If so, how is it able to increase prices in the face of low demand and excess capacity? If not, why weren't the steel companies able to maintain their 1962 price increases?*

---

[4] "My Side of the Steel Price Story," *Look* magazine, January 29, 1963, by Roger Blough, as told to Eleanor Harris.

5. *Which position on the "public interest" was correct: that of President Kennedy or that of the steel companies?*
6. *Was the April 9, 1962, pricing decision of the U.S. Steel Company a wise one? Discuss.*
7. *Was the April 13, 1962, decision to rescind the price increase a wise one? Discuss.*

TELEPHONE CHARGES TO AUXILIARY ACTIVITIES*

In 1961 the Vice President of Business Administration at the University of Kentucky requested one of his assistants to make a study of telephone charges made to auxiliary activities attached to the University. These activities were not included in the regular University budget but were connected to the central campus PBX. It was desirable that these agencies be charged their share of the total bill paid by the University to the General Telephone Company of Kentucky.

The auxiliary agencies included the Campus Bookstore, the Athletics Department (which had a separate budget), the Experiment Station (largely financed out of federal funds), and the various dormitories. In 1960 the University billed each agency at the rate of $10 per month for each main extension (MEX) and $4 per month for each bridged extension (BEX). (A bridged extension is simply a second telephone attached to the same MEX with the same extension number.) In addition, each agency paid any special charges resulting from its operations, such as the cost of installing a telephone, and recurrent monthly charges for buzzer systems, wiring plans, horns, additional listings, and special illumination. The question was whether any revisions of these charges were warranted.

The assistant made a careful analysis of the telephone expenses paid by the University, which amounted to over $13,000 per month. He found that the costs common to the whole PBX system amounted to $3,609.65 per month, as shown in Exhibit 1.

The wages paid the PBX operators directly by the University were

EXHIBIT 1
COMMON COSTS

Central office trunks	$1,466.40
Toll terminals	112.80
Station lines	1,477.00
Attendants' cabinets (positions)	300.00
Other charges	253.45
Total common costs	$3,609.65

* This case was prepared by Bernard Davis under the supervision of W. W. Haynes of the University of Kentucky as a basis for class discussion.

another large expense which might be considered a common cost. These wages amounted to $3,647 per month.

In addition, the telephone company charged $1.85 per month for each main extension (MEX) and another $1.85 per month for each bridged extension (BEX). The system included 680 main extensions and 635 bridged extensions. Most of the special charges of $4,010 per month for buzzers, horns, and illumination were not at stake, since everyone agreed that each agency should pay those expenses for which it was directly responsible. The one exception was the substantial charge for "mileage," a charge proportional to the distance of the lines from the PBX to the main extensions. This charge (included in the $4,010) was $734 per month. It would be difficult to allocate this expense to individual extensions because of the difficult bookkeeping problem of recording the lengths of line and keeping up with changes as new extensions were added. Furthermore, it was not clear that an agency should be charged more because it was at a greater distance from the PBX. None of the above figures includes the costs to the University accounting office for recording and distributing these expenses.

The assistant making the study found that a special statistical study would be required to determine the impact of added bridged extensions. Most of the common costs would not be affected by adding more bridged extensions. In fact, the adding of 1 or 10 bridged extensions would result in only the extra charge of $1.85 per phone. But the addition of, let us say, 300 bridged extensions might require an added attendant's cabinet and, more important, additional PBX operators. There were no records to indicate how much bridged extensions added to the total load of telephone calls.

The addition of main extensions would have a clearer impact on costs, requiring added mileage, added attendants' cabinets, and added PBX operators. Again it would make a difference whether a few or a great number of main extensions were contemplated.

Of the total number of telephones in the system, 505 (or 38%) were being charged to auxiliary services. Of this total, 322 were main extensions and 183 bridged extensions.

1. *What are the objectives of the pricing in this case?*
2. *Estimate the marginal cost of an additional main extension, of an additional 300 main extensions, and of an additional 300 bridged extensions.*
3. *What is the relevance of marginal costs in this case?*
4. *Should the University charge what the market will bear? Should it adopt marginal cost pricing? Or should it attempt to compute a "fair" price covering a reasonable share of the fixed costs?*
5. *What revisions in telephone charges should be made by the University?*

GENERAL PASSENGER FARE INVESTIGATION*
CIVIL AERONAUTICS BOARD

Decided: November 25, 1960

OPINION

BY THE BOARD:

This proceeding was instituted in order to determine whether the general level of passenger fares of the domestic trunkline carriers is unjust or unreasonable, and if so, to determine what overall percentage change in the fare level should be permitted or required.

After due notice, extensive public hearings were held before Examiner Ralph L. Wiser, who, on May 27, 1959, issued his Initial Decision. The ultimate conclusion reached in the Initial Decision was that fares should be increased 12% above the pre-February 1958 fare level. The basic findings may be briefly summarized. With respect to the return element, the Initial Decision found that the carriers could attract capital and accomplish the required financing for their jet reequipment programs if allowed a rate of return on a prudent investment base, including equipment deposits, of 10.6% for the industry. The traffic, revenue, and load factor forecasts of the carriers were found to be reasonable, and the carriers' estimates of expenses, including their computation of normalized Federal income tax expense, were generally accepted as proper. However, the carriers' cash expense estimates were found to be somewhat high, and it was also found that their flight equipment depreciation estimates should be adjusted to reflect straight-line depreciation based upon specified service lives and residual values. The recommended 12% fare increase, to be accomplished by a $1 surcharge, and any necessary percentage adjustment, was found to bring fair earnings to the bulk of the industry, on a fulcrum-rate basis, and not substantially to affect the movement of traffic.

The original objective of this proceeding was "(1) to develop appropriate and well-defined standards as to the earnings which are required by the 12 domestic trunkline carriers for proper development consistent with the public interest; and (2) based on such standards, to require or permit such overall decreases or increases in domestic fares as circumstances may warrant."[1] Upon consideration of the record, the contentions of the parties, and Form 41 data for recent years, we conclude that the record before us is inadequate to permit the fixing of the fare level. However, the record does permit us to formulate significant standards which will contribute to the regulation of fares.

Our difficulty in attempting to prescribe the just and reasonable fare level from the present record is very basic. Neither the carriers nor Bureau Counsel have submitted forecasts of operations, revenues, and expenses which we find are reliable indicia of what future results will be. In addition, there is an absence of data in the record presenting the experience of operations with the new turbine-engine aircraft which are becoming an ever-larger element of the

---

* This case is a condensation of a Civil Aeronautics Board Decision.
[1] Annual Report of the Civil Aeronautics Board, 1956, p. 9.

industry's operations. In these circumstances, it would be futile to attempt to prescribe the appropriate fare level on the basis of the record herein.

However, much has been gained from this proceeding in the development of standards. Thus, we are setting standards herein for passenger fare regulation in four basic areas: profit element, rate base, depreciation, and taxes. These standards will be used in assessing future fare proposals of the carriers, and in assisting the Board in evaluating the reported results of the carriers so that the Board may determine when action on its own motion should be taken.

Rate of Return

The Examiner found that the industry return should be regulated by the conventional test of rate of return on investment. The carriers' proposal to measure earnings by the operating ratio or its complement, the return margin,[2] was considered but rejected. A primary contention of the carriers is that the operating ratio method provides the proper measure of risk for the investor. The carriers argue that airline risks are more closely associated with the magnitude of annual expenses and the width of return margins than with the long-term capital investment. However, we agree with the conclusion in the Initial Decision that "No other measure than rate of return on investment . . . provides a direct and positive measure of risk." Although he recognized that capital turnover[3] and return margin[4] affect the degree of risk, the Examiner correctly pointed out that the amount at risk is limited to the amount invested. Even as to the degree of risk, capital turnover and return margin alone were properly found to provide no meaningful measure of risk that is recognized in the market place.

A related contention made by the airlines is that they cannot safely afford to operate with the margin of return produced by an otherwise fair rate of return. Asserting that low return margins and rapid capital turnover mean variability of profits, the carriers insist that only the operating ratio approach can assure that their margin of return will not be eliminated by moderate changes in expenses or revenues. The Examiner, however, correctly declined to accept the carriers' contentions. He found that a fair return on investment will afford an adequate cushion against changes in business conditions by providing an opportunity to build up a surplus in good times which would be sufficient to tide the company over bad times. The Examiner also noted that variability of profits is not wholly dependent upon the width of profit margins, but is affected by variability in the volume of business and by ability to adjust costs to changes in revenues and revenues to changes in costs.

---

[2] The return margin, or margin of return, is the ratio of return to revenue, computing return after all expenses including depreciation and taxes but before interest on debt. The operating ratio, or all-expense ratio, is the ratio of expenses to revenue.

[3] The rate of capital turnover, or the ratio of annual revenues to capital employed to produce those revenues, is typically less than 0.5 for ordinary utilities, including railroads; averaged for the airlines 1.66 for the years 1946–56 and 1.78 for the years 1951–56; and was 1.76 for certain industrials for the years 1946–56.

[4] The return margin for the period 1950–56 was 14.4 percent for natural gas operating utilities, 10.2 percent for Class I railroads, 5.8 percent for 20 selected manufacturers, and 5.3 percent for the trunk airlines.

We find ourselves in basic agreement with the Initial Decision. The reasonableness of the decision is further underscored by recognition that the carriers' computed margin of return substantially understates their margin of safety between operating revenues and expenses. Although the carriers have figured the operating ratio with income tax included as an expense, the accurate measure of earnings protection is indicated by the operating ratio computed before, not after, taxes. The 52 percent corporate income tax expense declines as taxable income declines; and net income after taxes declines in an amount only about half that of net income before taxes. The result is that the real protective margin between revenues and expenses is nearly double that shown by the "all-expense" operating ratio.

Further exaggeration of the vulnerability of earnings stems from the failure to take account of the adaptability of revenues and expenses. For the airlines, significant factors in the protection of profits are the ability to offset increases in costs through revenue growth and to decrease costs to compensate for decreases in revenues. Thus the steady enlargement of the air traffic market has made the level of the margin of return less crucial, since it has meant that, over the long term, increases in expenses are accompanied by corresponding increases in revenues. Similarly, because a substantial portion of expenses is directly responsive to the volume of capacity offered and traffic carried, airlines are markedly able to blunt the effects of a slackening of revenue growth upon return margins by a substantial contraction of expenses. These considerations, in our view, lend persuasive weight to the Examiner's conclusion that the safety of airline earnings is not truly endangered by inadequate return margins.

A further contention of the carriers, not directly dealt with by the Examiner, relates to certain economic characteristics of airlines that are said to be more like those of unregulated industrials than like those of traditional utilities. Along with the asserted hazards of low return margin and high capital turnover mentioned above, special risks are attributed to such airline traits as vigorous competition, variable demand, and rapid technological change and obsolescence. These factors, according to the carriers, make inappropriate the rate-of-return approach to revenue regulation.

On the record before us, we cannot conclude that retention of the traditional rate-of-return approach conflicts with the economic realities of the air transport industry. Although comparative risk of different industries may be a consideration in determining the reasonableness of a specific return to capital, we find that the indicia of relative risk cited from this record furnish no guide in themselves to the particular formula that should be employed to reach that end result. The rate-of-return standard, in our view, is sufficiently flexible to permit pragmatic adjustments to account for all risk factors, and, as is clear from the Examiners' findings adopted herein, was applied to do so here.

In sum, we conclude that only the rate of return on investment indicates the appropriate end result: earnings sufficient to compensate for all costs of service, including a reasonable but not exorbitant return to capital. Although useful for certain limited purposes, the operating ratio fails to measure the full costs of service, for the cost of capital can be determined only with respect to the amount of capital invested.

The inability of the operating ratio to approximate the return required to attract capital is clear upon this record. As found by the Examiner, the investor's ultimate test of the adequacy of earnings, in the light of all risks, is the return on his capital commitment. This means that rate of return, which keys return to the capital investment, is directly related to the investor's criterion of earnings adequacy; in contrast, the operating ratio approach, which relates return to revenues, gives no clue to the supply price of capital. For the foregoing reasons, we cannot accept the operating ratio or its complement, the return margin, as a measure of fair and reasonable earnings.

Cost of Capital.   In determining the fair and reasonable return, as that term is judicially defined, the Board must reach an end result which provides earnings sufficient to cover all the costs consistent with the furnishing of adequate and efficient air transportation. Among these costs must be included a return to the owners of the enterprise which is not only comparable to the results of similar undertakings, but which will insure the retention and attraction of capital in amounts adequate to foster economic health and development.

Although the supply price of capital is a paramount consideration in finding the fair return, enlightened ratemaking for a future period depends not upon the application of any fixed historical formula, but upon the exercise of informed judgment. As the Board has stressed even with regard to rates for past periods, the cost of capital computation is only one of the elements upon which conclusions as to the proper rate of return may be based.

Following this basic approach, we have computed the fair rate of return with full regard for all the factors of record which affect the price at which capital can be retained and attracted. Our conclusion is that the industry requires a 10.5 percent rate of return. Although this result approximates the 10.6 percent figure reached by the Examiner, it rests upon different conclusions concerning the cost of equity and the appropriate capital structure for cost of capital computations. Set forth below are our findings concerning these matters, as well as the proper cost of debt.

Cost of Debt.   The Examiner concluded on a judgment basis that a reasonable estimate of the cost of debt during the future period is 4.5 percent for the Big Four and 5.5 percent for the Intermediate Eight. Higher as well as lower estimates made by four cost-of-capital witnesses were considered, but rejected.

Cost of Equity.   Considering all the data of record, the Examiner found on a judgment basis that the cost of equity is 15 percent for the Big Four and 17 percent for the Intermediate Eight. Weight was given to a number of factors, including the Big Four earnings-price ratios of approximately 13 percent, and the relative risk of the airlines.

After considering the contentions of the parties, we find ourselves in fundamental agreement with the Examiner's refusal to rely solely upon earnings-price ratios, and with his attempt to resolve the issue by resort to all the reliable evidence of record. Our examination, however, leads us to conclude that the supply price of equity is 16 percent for the Big Four and 18 percent for the smaller trunklines—a result for each group one point above that reached in the Initial Decision. The factors we have considered and our conclusions are set forth below.

1. Turning first to a consideration of airline earnings-price ratios, we begin with the finding that the Big Four earnings-price ratios centered about 13 per-

cent, including allowances for costs of acquisition. Although the Initial Decision accepted the earnings-price ratio as the "most significant single indicator of capital cost," it nonetheless found that the ratio "is subject to many deficiencies."

Bureau Counsel insists that "The Examiner erred in not accepting the cost of equity as developed by the method of earnings-price ratios." In essence this is a contention that the cost of equity is precisely equivalent to an adjusted earnings-price ratio. We believe this contention is unsound, and fails to assign a proper role to the earnings-price ratio in the determination of equity cost.

The first approximation of the cost of equity capital, or the rate of earnings which will retain or attract the investor's dollar, may be gained by relating the earnings of the enterprise to the contemporaneous market price for common stock. Although the resulting earnings-price ratio has the allure of mathematical exactitude, it may not reflect the investor's real asking price. For, while the basis upon which the investor pays the market price is not past but anticipated earnings, the ratio of current earnings to price does not reveal what prospective earnings rate the investor anticipates, or to what extent he is influenced by prospects of corporate growth or investment appreciation.

Nevertheless, for long-established utilities with stable earnings, a concurrent earnings-price ratio may furnish a rather precise indicator of the actual cost of capital. This is because the reported earnings are approximately the same as the prospective income which the investor expects at the time he purchases the stock, and the market price of the stock therefore represents the investor's evaluation of the present worth of prospective income.

In contrast, the instability of airline earnings has led to relatively erratic earnings-price ratios which do not invariably reflect a market appraisal of future earnings literally translatable into a cost of equity capital. The instability of airline earnings, as compared with those of long-established utilities, is evident from the following table.

ANNUAL EARNINGS PER SHARE

Year	Moody's 24 Public Utilities	12 Trunklines: Net Operating Income
1950	$2.62	$3.62
1951	2.44	5.64
1952	2.62	4.48
1953	2.78	4.19
1954	2.94	4.98
1955	3.21	5.30
1956	3.35	4.06
Year ended 6/30/57	3.34	2.82

The result of earnings instability is that the investor in airline securities does not rely upon reported earnings as the yardstick of future prospects and investment worth to the same extent as does the investor in utility stocks. This is shown by the failure of airline stock prices to respond closely to changing earning reports, with a consequent instability in airline earnings-price ratios. As illustrated in the table below, the airline earnings-price ratios fluctuated more widely in past years than did the ratios of the conventional utilities.

INDUSTRY EARNINGS–PRICE RATIOS

Year	12 Trunklines	Moody's 24 Public Utilities
1950	12.89%	8.39%
1951	12.33	7.50
1952	12.51	7.38
1953	14.17	7.35
1954	13.66	6.64
1955	8.78	6.52
1956	8.50	6.75
Year ended 6/30/57	7.20	6.71

The importance of stability in the earnings-price ratios was stressed by the expert witnesses, and even Bureau Counsel's rate-of-return expert agreed that "the more erratic an earnings-price ratio is over a period of time, the less reliable it is." Yet, as is evident from the foregoing discussion, airline earnings-price ratios are dissimilar, dispersed, and markedly changeable from year to year. The result is that, although analysis of the ratio is helpful as a starting point in determining the area of equity supply prices, any single average of these ratios is not reliable as the sole yardstick of the supply price of equity and can be meaningfully employed only as tempered by other available data concerning capital cost.

2. Having found that airline earnings-price ratios are not precise indicators of capital cost, we must decide whether the Examiner correctly concluded that the ratios substantially understate the cost of equity. For this purpose, we must relate the ratios to the risks of the enterprise which presumptively influence the price demanded by equity investors.

There is little controversy that investors have considered airline returns insufficient to compensate for the risks of the industry. Even apart from the abundant evidence that meager earnings caused "a flight of capital from the airlines" and left "airline stocks in disrepute among investors," the unanimous testimony of professional investors establishes that airline securities are not attractive investment opportunities at the yields expressed in the historic earnings-price ratios.

Inadequacies in the return shown by earnings-price ratios were found by witness Foster, a consulting economist who compiled a rate of return study which, among other things, appraised airline earnings-price ratios in the light of comparative risks. After examining airlines and other industries, witness Foster testified that "The earnings-price ratios for common stocks of trunklines, if averaged over a term of years, are below any reasonable rate of return required to compensate for risk of investment in airline stocks."

This conclusion was derived from a comparison of industries according to indicia of relative risk. Using a technique consistent with our goal of "a return to the owners of the enterprise which is . . . comparable to the results of similar undertakings," the witness compared airlines with other utilities and with industrials with regard to three indicia of risk: deviation of annual rates of return; ratio of retained earnings to total earnings; and fluctuation of common stock prices.

The results of this study tend to support the quoted conclusion of the witness which, in turn, rested upon his view that "The earnings-price ratio averages, equated for differences in investment risk, are below the averages for water and electric utility stocks." Thus, taking the 1950–56 percentage price fluctuations of common stock as one index of relative risk, the measure of risk for the Big Four trunklines exceeded that of seven electric and seven water utilities by more than three and less than four times, respectively, although Big Four earnings-price ratios were less than twice those of either group. Similar computations with other indicia of relative risk, and with other industries, yield conclusions differing in detail but still indicating that airlines earnings-price ratios do not reflect fully the risks which presumptively influence the rate of earnings required by investors.

3. Although computations of the bare costs of capital can delimit the range of reasonable returns, the precise point within that range can be fixed only after consideration of special traits which affect the trunklines' ability to attract capital. Some of these factors, including the $2 billion accelerated jet reequipment program, were adverted to by the experts and, in part, appear to have been taken into the account by the Examiner.

In addition, we believe that substantial weight must be accorded to the unique risk which arises from our decision to gear fare regulation generally to the needs of the bulk of the industry, rather than to the needs of each individual carrier. Our reasons for adopting an industry-wide unit of ratemaking are sound, are necessary, and are legally proper; but the result is the risk that, because of competitive disadvantages, an individual carrier will be unable to earn the weighted average return found reasonable. This is illustrated in the following table, showing the overall rates of return which individual carriers would have earned in 1958 under the Examiner's recommended 10.6 percent for the industry.

HYPOTHETICAL RATES OF RETURN RESULTING FROM
10.06 PERCENT INDUSTRY RATE OF RETURN: 1958

Carrier	Rate of Return
Northeast	3.30%
Continental	6.09
Eastern	7.64
National	8.13
Northwest	9.11
TWA	9.39
Western	9.83
Braniff	10.20
Capital	12.00
Delta	12.63
United	12.78
American	13.95
Industry weighted average	10.60%

The disparity in earning power shown above, in general, couples the carriers whose earnings needs are highest with the returns which are lowest. Although this paradox cannot be resolved through ratemaking alone, we believe that where rates are set for the industry as a whole but it is apparent that many of the member enterprises will fall below the line of the average rate of return, a rate of return at the upper limits of the range of reasonableness is fair and reasonable.

4. After reviewing the foregoing factors which point towards the cost of equity, we conclude that the appropriate supply price must be recognized at 16 percent for the Big Four and 18 percent for the Intermediate Eight.

Capital Structure. The Examiner found that the overall rate of return should be computed on the basis of the actual capital structure, rather than on a hypothetical or optimum structure. Adopting the study submitted by Bureau Counsel, the Examiner found that the debt ratios planned for the period covered by carrier estimates are 45 percent for the Big Four and 50 percent for the Intermediate Eight.

We conclude that the Initial Decision correctly based the overall return upon an actual capital structure; but we find that the actual debt ratio will exceed the estimate accepted. Examination of the record in the light of actual reported results, which we officially notice, satisfies us that the percentage of debt in the capital structure will approximate that present at the end of 1959. Accordingly, we will premise our rate of return upon a capital structure containing 50 percent debt for the Big Four and 55 percent debt for the Intermediate Eight.

Increased undertakings of debt will continue during the immediate future to exceed any increment to equity by way of retained earnings or otherwise. We will, therefore, modify the Examiner's conclusions concerning the precise debt ratios which will be typical for the carriers.

Overall Returns. Application of the costs for debt and equity to the capital structure found reasonable, results in overall rates of return of 10.25 percent for the Big Four and 11.125 percent for the Intermediate Eight. Based upon the Examiner's finding that the Big Four account for two-thirds of industry investment, the weighted average return appropriate for the industry is 10.5 percent. These computations are shown in the following table.

For the reasons stated, we find that these returns are fair and reasonable for the carriers.

OVERALL RATES OF RETURN

Industry Unit	Security	Capitalization	Security Cost	Weighted Cost
Twelve trunks				10.5%
Big Four				10.25
	Debt	50%	4.5%	2.25%
	Equity	50	16.0	8.00
Other Eight				11.125
	Debt	55	5.5	3.025%
	Equity	45	18.0	8.1

The foregoing analysis demonstrates that the determination of capital costs involves the exercise of judgment with respect to a substantial number of issues. In resolving each of these issues, we have done so, after full consideration of the evidence of record. While judgments can reasonably differ on the various subsidiary issues treated herein, it is the "end-result," in the last analysis, which must stand the test of reasonableness, and we are convinced that the overall returns determined herein fulfill that test.

Rate Base

In prescribing an appropriate rate base, the Initial Decision included all investments represented by the total capitalization of the enterprise, including equipment purchase deposits. The Examiner refused, however, to increase stated capitalization by adding thereto reserves for referred taxes or an increment for the effects of inflation.

After considering the exceptions filed by the parties, we find ourselves in disagreement with the Initial Decision's failure to adopt a depreciated assets rate base which excludes certain additional investments and special funds. Otherwise, we agree with the findings and conclusions.[5] We will limit our discussion to adjustments of the rate base and to certain exceptions.

Adjustments.   The Initial Decision adopted a rate base computed from the right-hand side of the balance sheet by adding net worth to long-term debt. It was held that exclusions from this invested-capital or prudent-investment rate base should be limited to dishonest, wasteful, or imprudent expenditures, and the entire domestic portion of the stated capitalization was included in the rate base since "There is no contention . . . that any investment . . . does not constitute exercise of reasonable judgment."

Bureau Counsel contends that stated capitalization is not the proper yardstick of rate base determination. Bureau Counsel advocates adoption of a depreciated assets rate base, figured from the left-hand side of the balance sheet. A rate base so computed would be less in amount than the sum of net worth plus long-term debt, since Bureau Counsel would limit recognized investment to the domestic allocation for net working capital (current assets and certain deferred charges less current liabilities and certain deferred credits), net operating property and equipment (after deducting depreciation and overhaul reserves), and other used and useful assets.

We find that Bureau Counsel's exception is well-taken. The stated capitalization method tends to result in burdening the rate base with investments not productively employed in the public service. Although exclusion of such assets from the rate base is not dependent upon the side of the balance sheet examined, adherence to the conventional depreciated assets technique properly focuses analysis upon the purpose to which investment is devoted by the enterprise.

The need for adjustment of the rate base is clear upon this record and uncontested by any party. Among the assets represented by the stated capitalization, and thus considered as part of the rate base by the Initial Decision, are a substantial number of investments which do not constitute contributions by

---

[5] As a matter of principle, we would classify notes due beyond three months as long-term debt.

corporate owners to the public service. These assets consist of several types: investments and special funds not used and useful to domestic certificated operation; nonoperating property and equipment not used and useful to domestic certificated operations; reserves accrued by charges to operating expense; unamortized discount and expense on debt; and property acquisition adjustments.

There can be no question that ratepayers should not be obliged to pay a return on investments and special funds or on nonoperating property and equipment which are not used and useful. Such assets, which include National's investment in a Miami television station, do not benefit air transportation or its ratepaying users. Although investors are free to receive a return on investments not beneficially dedicated to the utility enterprise, they must extract their profit from sources other than the traveling public. For this reason, we find that these investments must be excluded from the rate base, just as earnings from such assets must be excluded from calculation of carrier earnings.

Prevention of double-charging requires that we reduce the rate base by reclassifying as operating reserves those reserves, accrued by charges to operating expense, which appear on the balance sheet as surplus reserves. Through the expense allowance, these items have already been recovered by charges to the ratepayer. Since the investor is entitled to a return only upon his contributions to the enterprise, and not upon those supplied by the ratepayer, these reserves derived from charges to expense may not be included in the rate base.

Avoidance of duplicating charges to ratepayers also requires exclusion of unamortized discount and expense on debt. These expenses have already been recognized in the computations of debt costs and are compensated by inclusion in cost of capital. No further burden upon ratepayers is necessary or proper.

Rate Level

The unreliability of the expense and revenue forecasts in the record makes it impossible to determine the proper fare level in this proceeding. We have therefore confined ourselves in this opinion to the fixing of the standards which will be employed in regulating future fare levels. There remains for consideration the question of the method of employing these standards in future cases.

Essentially, the major problems of application of the standards fall into two categories: (*a*) the extent to which the fare level should be based upon results to be anticipated over an extended period, and (*b*) the extent to which fares should be regulated on an industrywide basis.

a) No party has suggested that we attempt to regulate fares so as to produce a particular rate of return for every 12-month period. It is manifest that in an industry in which costs and revenue factors tend to fluctuate and are difficult to forecast precisely for any short-term period, any attempt to maintain a constant rate of return would be futile. There is thus general agreement among the parties that the fare levels must be regulated to produce a reasonable return over an extended period of time.

This is not to say that short-term considerations need always be ignored. For example, if fare relief is necessary to prevent financial ruin to the bulk of the industry, we would clearly not be justified in refusing such relief on the ground that the adverse factors responsible for the industry's condition were merely of a temporary nature. Thus, the extent to which short-term factors would be influential in affecting the fare level must depend on the length of time those factors are expected to remain operative and the magnitude of their impact on the carriers' operating results.

From the foregoing it is apparent that the problem of determining when and for what periods fare adjustments should be made cannot be relegated for solution to any mechanical device. For this reason we do not believe that the five-year moving average formula proposed in the Initial Decision is practicable. Rather, the determination of when to permit fare adjustments and the length of the future period which should be considered in making these adjustments can be resolved only on a case-by-case basis, applying informed judgment to the task of balancing the relevant factors.

b) The second major problem in the application of standards relates to the so-called unit of ratemaking. Section 1002(e)(5) sets forth, as one of the factors to be considered in ratemaking, "the need of *each* air carrier for revenue sufficient to enable such air carrier under honest, economical, and efficient management, to provide adequate and efficient air service." While we are thus enjoined to take into consideration "each" carrier's need, we are also faced with the facts that a large part of the domestic route structure is served by two or more carriers in competition, and that fares must be uniform as between them, notwithstanding that one carrier's revenue need may be less than another's. In short, we must reckon with the vexing problem of how to reconcile the statutory mandate to consider the need of "each" carrier with the hard fact that fares cannot be regulated on an individual basis. Specifically, shall fares be fixed to meet the needs of the carriers as a group, of the smaller trunks, of the poorest situated carrier or possibly even of the most favorably situated?

The Initial Decision concluded that fares should be set at levels which would meet the average of the costs, including return, of the bulk of the industry. In effect, the entire domestic trunkline industry would be treated as a single unit and would be regulated so as to produce an over-all rate of return to the industry equal to 10.6 percent, the weighted average of the returns which were found reasonable in the Initial Decision for the Big Four and Medium Eight carriers, respectively. The parties disagree among themselves as to the propriety of this "bulk-line" approach. Some of the carriers and Bureau Counsel agree that the nature of the industry requires that fare levels be set on the basis of the industry as a whole, whereas other carriers and the GSA argue that the Initial Decision method violates the requirement of Section 1002(e)(5) that we consider the need of "each" carrier. We agree in general with the result, although we reach that result by somewhat different means and would subject it to some qualifications.

The Initial Decision is based in large part on the theory that regulation should strive toward achieving the same kind of results that would obtain in the open market-place, and upon the belief that fixing fares at the level proposed in the Initial Decision would substantially achieve that result. But conformance with results under hypothetical free competitive conditions is not one of the stated policy objectives of the Act, nor is it one of the statutory ratemaking standards. We would not be justified in refusing to consider the need of each individual carrier merely because a "bulk-line" concept may more nearly approach the results under free competition. Nor can we read Section 1002 (e) as authorizing the Board to ignore the need of each carrier in favor of the need of the carriers as a group. As the excepting parties have pointed out, the statute does not speak in terms of groups of carriers but rather of individual carriers. The fact that we cannot regulate fares so as to provide precisely for the need of each individual carrier does not authorize us to refuse to take such need into consideration.

On the other hand, we clearly are not required to establish fare levels to meet the need of the most poorly situated carrier as Eastern contends we must. The statutory requirements that we "consider" the need of each carrier is only one of five ratemaking factors which we are required to weigh. Consideration of the other ratemaking standards of Section 1002 (e), particularly the effect of rates on movement of traffic (Sec. 1002 (e) (1)) and the need in the public interest for transportation at the lowest cost (Sec. 1002 (e) (2)) militates against the adoption of the least profitable carrier as the standard for fixing rates. Moreover, the standard pressed upon us by Eastern would be inconsistent with the need factor itself. Thus, were we to base fares on the results of the poorest situated carrier we would of necessity be ignoring the need of every other carrier, contrary to the mandate that we consider the need of each of them. Finally, to use the most poorly situated carrier as the unit of ratemaking would result in the vast majority of the public paying rates greatly in excess of the cost of furnishing the transportation and would unjustly enrich the great majority of the air carriers.

By the same token, we obviously cannot fix fare levels on the basis of the need of the most favorably situated carrier. Such a standard could have a disastrous impact upon many of the other carriers and upon the development of transportation generally. It is thus clear that the proper fare level must be found at some point between the needs of the most profitable and least profitable carriers and that the determination of the unit to which the standards shall be applied must be based upon informed judgment. Insofar as the need standard is concerned, this determination can only be made after testing any fare proposal against the needs of the industry as a whole, smaller groups of carriers, and each individual carrier.

The approach recommended by Bureau Counsel appears to us to accommodate reasonably the practical problems of industrywide regulation with the requirements of the statute. The Bureau would first examine the results of the carriers as a group by taking the weighted average of the relationship of yield per passenger-mile to cost per passenger-mile (including return on investment). This industry average, although not controlling, is entitled to great weight. It indicates the extent of the general fare adjustment needed to produce a reasonable return for the industry as a whole. The Bureau would then test the resulting fare level against the needs of the individual carriers and of groups of carriers. Thus, consideration is given to the extent to which the fare level meets the costs of the Big Four and the Medium Eight carriers; the relative number of passenger-miles accounted for by the various carriers; the extent by which each carrier deviates from the norm; the effect of such deviation on the group and industry averages, etc.

In the absence of special circumstances, the record indicates that rates which meet the needs of the domestic trunkline industry as a whole would reflect a balancing of the needs of the high cost and low cost carriers. Where the bulk of the carriers fall within a reasonable range of the rates of return found herein to be proper, and industry figures are not distorted by the unrepresentative results of carriers who are in extremely poor or extremely favorable situations, fare adjustments should normally be based upon the results for the industry as a group.

Inevitably, under an industrywide system of regulation some carriers may fall below the standard rate of return. That a given carrier may earn less than the standard during a particular period is not by itself a cause for concern since, as we have previously discussed, the reasonableness of earnings must be judged over an extended period of time. On the other hand, even failure to earn the standard return for an extended period does not necessarily mean that the particular carrier will be unable to compete, grow, and prosper. Our findings on rate of return demonstrate that the rates of 10.25 and 11.125 percent which we have adopted as standards are not minimum returns below which confiscation would result. Rather, we have deliberately adopted rates of return which are above the minimum returns but within the broad range of reasonableness. In arriving at these rates, we have taken into consideration the circumstances that fares cannot be fixed on an individual carrier basis because of the competitive nature of our domestic rate structure and that some carriers will of necessity earn less than the average standard of return. Thus, in view of the level of the rate of return standards established, we would not regard a carrier's earnings to be deficient unless those earnings fell significantly below the standards for an extended period.

The problem of accommodating the requirements of the weak and strong carriers is, of course, one of the most difficult to be found in regulation. Clearly, general fare increases cannot be regarded as the panacea capable of solving the problem. There are other tools which are more appropriate for use in dealing with the less profitable carriers. First, an over-all examination of the general passenger fare structure, an issue excluded from this proceeding, might well result in bringing the costs and revenues of the individual carriers into closer alignment. Second, as the Examiner pointed out, carriers whose needs are not met by general fare level adjustments can seek higher fares, although competitive aspects would preclude them from charging such fares except on some few noncompetitive segments (assuming, of course, that such fares are otherwise lawful). A third tool is that of route realignments designed to produce a more balanced competitive structure. Finally, we are authorized by Section 406 of the Act to grant subsidy payments where we find that such compensation is required in the interests of commerce, the Postal service, and national defense. Whether, and to what extent, any of these approaches should be used will, of course, depend on all surrounding circumstances. Suffice it to say, however, that the Board has available to it a number of techniques for dealing with problems not amenable to solution by regulation of the general level of commercial fares.

We have considered all the exceptions to the Initial Decision, and we find that, except to the extent indicated, they should not alter our decision herein.

An appropriate order will be entered.

Gillilland, Chairman, Gurney, Vice Chairman, and Boyd, Member of the Board, concurred in the above opinion. Minetti, Member, filed the attached concurring and dissenting opinion. Bragdon, Member, did not take part in the decision.

MEMBER MINETTI, CONCURRING AND DISSENTING:

While I agree with most of the majority's determinations, I cannot concur in its resolution of three basic issues. The effect of the majority's decision on these issues is to burden the traveling public with (1) an excessive rate of return applied to (2) an inflated investment base, and (3) an allowance for fictitious federal incòme taxes. As a result, the users of air transportation will be charged in the neighborhood of $80 million annually in excess of a reasonable fare level, based upon 1958 results.

With respect to rate of return, I conclude that rates of approximately 8.75 percent for the Big Four and 9.6 percent for the Intermediate Eight would be

	Domestic Trunklines	
	Per Majority	Per Dissent
	(000)	(000)
Investment	$1,091,741	$ 923,691
Rate of return	(10.536%)	(9.04%)
Return element	$ 115,029	$ 83,483*
Interest expense	23,768	23,768
Income tax	98,866	50,827
Return and taxes	213,895	134,310
Operating costs, passenger	1,387,925	1,387,925*
Passenger revenue required	$1,601,820	$1,522,235

* Does not include provisions for return on, and amortization of, capitalized interest on purchase funds, the data being unavailable.

reasonable and ample and that the returns of 10.25 percent and 11.125 percent found by the Board are not supported by the record. With respect to the investment base, it is my opinion that, in recognizing equipment purchase funds and deposits which are related to airplanes not yet delivered, the Board is charging today's airline passengers with part of the costs of operating tomorrow's airplanes, a result which is at war with the weight of regulatory precedent, is unfair to present passengers, and may well impede the development of traffic.

1. *Rate of return.* The rates of return adopted by the Board in this proceeding, so far as I am aware, are higher than those allowed by any other government agency in history. This fact alone would be no more than an interesting sidelight to this proceeding if the high rates of return were in fact supported by the record. In my opinion they are not.

My basic disagreement with the majority is with respect to its findings on the cost of equity capital. The majority has found that the fair returns on equity are 16 percent for the Big Four and 18 percent for the Intermediate Eight. These rates exceed the recommendations of the Examiner and of every expert witness who testified on rate of return in this proceeding.

The majority constructs its cost of equity on the basis of the earnings-price ratios of airline common stocks to which the usual allowance for flotation costs and underpricing is added. According to all of the experts, this method produces a cost of equity of approximately 13 percent for the Big Four. Had the majority stopped at this point, I would have no cause to complain. But the majority adds three percentage points to the objectively determined 13 percent on the basis of "judgment." It is here that we part company. In my opinion, the three point allowance results in double compensation to the investor for risks which are actually reflected in the earnings-price ratios.

The majority supports its three point increment on the ground that the earnings-price ratios, while they provide an appropriate starting point for determining cost of equity, are nevertheless unreliable. According to the majority "the instability of airline earnings has led to relatively erratic earnings-price ratios which do not invariably reflect a market appraisal of future earnings literally translatable into a cost of equity capital." It may be conceded that the earnings-price ratios for airlines do not follow as consistent a pattern as the data for the more stable public utilities, and it is therefore incumbent upon us to use such data with the utmost care. But the fact that the data may have some infirmities does not prove that the data *understates* the cost of equity capital. On the contrary, the majority's conclusion that the earnings-price ratios must be adjusted upwards is not only unsupported by the record but is at war with the logic of the situation.

In reaching its conclusion that airline earnings-price ratios understate the cost of equity, the majority relies heavily upon the testimony of witness Foster who concluded that the earnings-price ratios "are below any reasonable rate of return required to compensate for risk of investment in airline stocks" and that "the earnings-price ratio averages, equated for differences in investment risk, are below the averages for water and electric utility stocks." Although the majority states that Foster's conclusions are supported by certain studies which he placed in the record, I have found nothing in these studies which would tend to support the conclusions. These studies merely show that in terms of common stock price fluctuations and other indicia of risks, airline equity securities are riskier than water and electric utility stocks. But this proves nothing, since the airline earnings-price ratios are in fact substantially higher than the utility ratios. Foster's studies in no way substantiate his bare assertion that the high airline earnings-price ratios do not fully reflect airline risks.

In my opinion, the record if anything supports the conclusion that the earnings-price ratio data used by the witnesses and the Board *overstates* rather than understates investor earning requirements. The crucial factor which leads me to this conclusion is the fact that the period from which the ratios were drawn was the period of the highest sustained earnings level in the history of the industry. As a result, the earnings-price ratios, which were also at peak levels during this period, overstate the cost of equity. This was so because, as the majority states, "the basis upon which the investor pays the market price is not past but anticipated earnings [and] the ratio of current earnings to price does not reveal what prospective earnings rate the investor anticipates. . . ." Therefore, when earnings in any particular period are higher than those which the investor can reasonably expect will be the long term average future earnings, the earnings-price ratio developed for such a period will tend to be excessive in relation to the actual investor earnings requirements. And yet, the period from which the earnings-price ratios are drawn was a period of unusual prosperity for the carriers.

The earnings-price ratio data was drawn primarily from the period 1950–1956. During a large part of this period, airline earnings were at a high level as a result of the Korean war boom and the post-Korean shortage of aircraft. For the period 1950 to 1956, the earnings on equity for the Big Four averaged 18.51 percent, *the highest sustained level of earnings in their history.* This compared to a loss of 1.94 percent during the post-war years 1946–49. In view of the economic conditions prevailing during most of 1950–56, the markedly inferior earnings of earlier periods and the characterization by this Board in 1953 of the then current earnings of the air carriers as "excessive when measured by any reasonable standard applicable to a regulated industry," it cannot be supposed that the investor expected Big Four earnings to maintain the high 1950–56 level indefinitely. It can only be concluded that the investor expected that the long term earnings of the carriers would average out to something less than the 1950–56 high. If the earnings-price ratios were adjusted for this factor a reduction of the rate of return somewhat below the majority's 13 percent starting point would be indicated.

1. *What are the most controversial issues in this case?*
2. *To what extent has the Civil Aeronautics Board followed the usual approaches to rate regulation discussed in Chapter 8?*
3. *Why was the Board unable to fix fare levels in this case?*
4. *Evaluate the operating rate method for fixing rates. Why did the airlines prefer this method?*
5. *Are the airlines more or less risky than other regulated industries? Should this factor influence rate decisions? Discuss.*
6. *Evaluate the estimates of the cost of capital in this case.*
7. *Why was there controversy about the determination of the rate base?*
8. *Was the decision of the Board generous or restrictive? Discuss.*

REPORT ON THE PRICING OF DRUGS

In 1961 the Subcommittee on Antitrust and Monopoly of the United States Senate (better known as the Kefauver Committee) published a report on the pricing of drugs.[1] The majority of the committee, led by the chairman, Senator Estes Kefauver, was extremely critical of the industry's pricing practices. A minority consisting of Senators Everett Dirksen and Roman Hruska, supported in part by Senator Alexander Wiley, dissented strongly to the majority's findings. This case consists mainly of extracts from the majority and minority reports.

---

[1] United States Senate, Subcommittee on Antitrust and Monopoly of the Committee on the Judiciary, *A Study of Administered Prices in the Drug Industry,* 87th Cong., 1st sess. (Washington, D. C.: U.S. Government Printing Office, June 27, 1961).

The behavior of price

The majority's view on pricing behavior in the drug industry is summarized in the following extracts:

. . . The difference in the behavior of administered versus market-determined prices, which has been noted in the subcommittee's earlier reports and hearings, is nowhere more dramatically illustrated than in the drug industry. Where the only sellers consist of one or a few of the major companies, prices tend to be unchanged over long periods of time, with the different companies selling at identical prices. While most antibiotics are sold by only one or a few of the large companies, there are two areas in which vigorous price competition exists in both bulk and packaged form. These consist of the older forms of penicillin, which are not patented, and streptomycin, which is produced by several firms operating as licenses under the patent held by Rutgers University.

The broad spectrum antibiotics, introduced in late 1948–50, were subject to a few price reductions during that early period. By 1951, however, the price of each had stabilized at the identical figure of $5.10 to the druggists, where it has been maintained through the third quarter of 1960. What appears to be a straight black line near the top of chart 1 is the price trend of the broad spectrums during this 10-year period. In contrast to the complete rigidity of the broad spectrums the bulk prices of penicillin and of streptomycin have fallen during the 10-year period about 90 percent—from $2.50 to 21 cents and from $3.24 to 36 cents, respectively.

A similar contrast between administered and market-determined prices appears in Chart 2, which compares the price trend of one of the newer patented forms of penicillin (V-Cillin), with the trends of the unpatented forms both in bulk and package. All of the prices relate to one company, Eli Lilly. To facilitate comparison they have been expressed on the basis of a common measure, 1 billion units.

As was true of the broad spectrums, the price trend of the patented penicillin is represented since its introduction in 1956 by a straight line. During that same period Lilly's price of the older type in tablet form declined by 14 percent while the bulk price dropped by 60 percent after an increase. The chart also reveals that up to very recent years the price trend of the older type closely paralleled that of the bulk price, after about a 1-year lag. Such parallelism, however, has recently been conspicuous by its absence, as the bulk price showed a further price decrease between 1958 and 1960 while the tablet price remained unchanged.

Small manufacturers sell the unpatented penicillin in finished form at prices substantially below those of the major companies. This is evident from Chart 3 which shows the price differences between selected small companies and large concerns for penicillin potassium G tablets; the horizontal scale is by size of company in terms of its total annual sales of all products. The smallest firm, Penhurst Pharmacal Corp., has a price of $3.30. The lowest price ($2.95) is that of the Bryant Pharmaceutical Corp., with annual sales of less than $1 million. Three other small companies whose sales range from $1 to $5 million quote prices in the area of $4 or $5. In contrast, two of the largest companies,

Merck and the Squibb Division of Olin Mathieson, have the highest price, $12. This is also the price quoted by Lilly while Abbott and Parke, Davis charge approximately a dollar less. Among the majors, Pfizer is a price cutter on this product, selling it for only about half the price charged by the other large companies.

The price differences among the major companies on unpatented penicillin are not to be found in the patented broad spectrum antibiotics. This is brought out by Table 1, which shows for the various dosage forms of tetracycline, Aureomycin and Terramycin, the price to the druggist of each of the sellers.

For each of the dosage forms the five companies selling tetracycline charge the same price, which also happens to be the price charged by American Cyanamid for Aureomycin and by Pfizer for Terramycin. From the 94 cents which each charges for a 100 milligram vial for intramuscular injection to the $18.36 for 16 ounces of 125 milligram syrup to the $30.60 for 100 capsules of 250 milligrams, not a single variation of more than 1 cent among the companies is to be found. Similar identity within 2 cents is to be found in the suggested resale prices to consumers.

SALES TO INSTITUTIONAL BUYERS

In addition to the usual prescription market, substantial quantities of drugs are sold to institutional buyers. In the regular market the customer, being limited to the brand name product usually prescribed for him, has little freedom to shop around for a lower price. This is true even where a product is sold by small manufacturers at prices substantially below those of the major companies. The essential difference between the two markets is that, unlike the physician, the institutional buyers frequently and increasingly have an acute interest in price. Faced with mounting drug costs the institutional buyers, consisting of private nonprofit hospitals, State and local governmental hospitals, clinics and dispensaries, and Federal agencies, are to an increasing extent using generic formularies and are purchasing from qualified suppliers on a price basis. An outstanding example of this market is provided by the U.S. Department of Defense through its procurement arm for medical supplies, the Military Medical Supply Agency. MMSA acts as a unified central purchasing agent for all hospitals and dispensaries operated by any of the armed services; it also purchases on request for the Office of Civil and Defense Mobilization, the U.S. Public Health Service and, under the military assistance program, for allied nations.

MMSA is required to purchase drugs by generic names at the lowest possible price from what are termed any "qualified suppliers." To provide the best possible medical treatment for patients, who may range from the newest Army recruit to Members of Congress and the President, MMSA insists that suppliers meet exacting standards. Not only must the quality of the particular product being delivered conform to rigid specifications but inspection is made of the supplier's entire operation including the "housekeeping" facilities of his plant, his production and quality control techniques and performance, his records system, the technical proficiency of his staff, and the competency and knowledge of the management itself. In short, every effort is made to assure that any company, large or small, which sells drugs to MMSA is capable of providing

TABLE 1

IDENTITY OF PRICES TO DRUGGISTS—TETRACYCLINE, AUREOMYCIN, AND TERRAMYCIN

	Tetracycline					Cyanamid Aureomycin	Pfizer Terramycin
	Cyanamid Achromycin	Pfizer Tetracyn	Bristol Polycycline	Squibb Steclin	Upjohn Panmycin		
Capsules							
100 mg. 25's	$ 3.61	$ 3.61	$ 3.61	$ 3.61	$ 3.61	$ 3.61	$ 3.60
100 mg. 100's	13.77	13.77	13.77	13.77	13.77	13.77	13.77
250 mg. 16's	5.10	5.10	5.10	5.10	5.10	5.10	5.10
250 mg. 100's	30.60	30.60	30.60	30.60	30.60	30.60	30.60
Intramuscular—100 mg. vial	.94	.94	.94	.94	.94		.94
Intravenous							
250 mg. vial	1.62	1.62	1.62	1.62	1.62	1.62	1.62
500 mg. vial	2.91	2.91	2.91	2.91	2.91	2.91	2.90
Ped. drops—100 mg./cc. 10 cc.	1.47	1.47	1.47	1.47	1.47	1.47	1.47
Oral susp.—250 mg./5 cc. 1 oz.	2.54	2.55	2.54	2.54	2.55	———	2.55
Syrup							
125 mg./5 cc., 2 oz.	2.54	2.55	2.54	2.54	2.55		2.55
125 mg./5 cc., 16 oz.	18.36	18.36	18.36	———	18.36	18.36	18.36

SOURCE: FTC, "Proposed Findings of Fact and Conclusions of Fact and Law," June, 1960, p. 375.

pharmaceutical products of fully acceptable quality. Given quality, MMSA endeavors to fill its requirements at the lowest possible cost.

The agency has provided the subcommittee with a complete record of its contracts, dating back as far as 1954, in a variety of areas (antibiotics, sulfa drugs, polio vaccine, steroids, insulin, tranquilizers, and vitamins). Here, also, a sharp differentiation between administered and market-determined prices emerges. The differentiation exists not only among drugs as a whole but within given product groups which are characterized by a general similarity of production methods and thus of costs.

MMSA has had little success in securing price concessions in the patented broad-spectrum antibiotics. A case in point is Chloromycetin available only from Parke, Davis. From May, 1954, to February, 1958, MMSA negotiated 16 contracts with the company; despite a wide variation in quantities, the price was rigid at $12.50 per bottle. In April, 1958, MMSA's purchase officer persuaded Parke, Davis to reduce the price to $11.25; from that date through June, 1959 there were 11 additional procurements—all at this same price, although there was again a wide range in quantities.

A similar pattern is presented by Aureomycin, also available only from a single supplier, American Cyanamid. From May, 1954, to February, 1956, MMSA made nine procurements in widely varying quantities, all at a price of $12 per bottle. In April, 1956, the price was reduced but only to $11 a bottle, which has prevailed for 11 procurements of widely varying quantities.

MMSA has had its greatest procurement difficulties with tetracycline, which is sold by five companies, though one of them (Upjohn) has not sought MMSA orders. Rear Adm. William L. Knickerbocker, USN, executive director of MMSA, described to the subcommittee his experience in trying to secure lower prices for this important drug:

> When the Government first purchased these tablets, it paid $11 per bottle of 100 in a procurement involving 94,176 bottles. Six months later in May, 1957, the unit price (from a different supplier) was still $11, even though the quantity purchased was about one-seventh that of the previous procurement. On the third procurement, 9 months later, the price rose, inexplicably, to $17.24—a 57 percent increase over the previous $11 price. As a matter of fact, in this latter procurement the low offeror refused to take more than one-half the quantity required by the Government, and the remainder had to go to the second low offeror at a price of $19.19 per bottle—or an increase of 74 percent over the initial low price.
>
> During 1958 there were 3 additional procurements of tetracycline hydrochloride for 93,476, 41,904, and 25,632 bottles, respectively. For the first two of these procurements, the price remained at $17.24 and for the third it was $17.15. In June, 1959, it seemed that this price "freeze" finally had been broken when the Government was able to buy 46,512 bottles at a unit price of $14.36. But no. This "thawing out" process was illusory, because 2 months later, in August, 1959, a solicitation for 28,000 bottles again produced an offered low price of $17.15 with 3 suppliers offering the identical price. This was the same price as quoted

TABLE 2

IDENTITY OF SUGGESTED RESALE PRICES TO CONSUMERS, TETRACYCLINE, AUREOMYCIN, AND TERRAMYCIN

	Tetracycline					Cyanamid Aureomycin	Pfizer Terramycin
	Cyanamid Achromycin	Pfizer Tetracyn	Bristol Polycycline	Squibb Steclin	Upjohn Panmycin		
Capsules							
100 mg. 25's	$ 6.02	$ 6.02	$ 6.02	$ 6.02	$ 6.02	$ 6.02	$ 6.00
100 mg. 100's	22.95	22.95	22.95	22.95	22.95	22.95	22.95
250 mg. 16's	8.50	8.50	8.50	8.50	8.50	8.50	8.50
250 mg. 100's	51.00	51.00	51.00	51.00	51.00	51.00	51.00
Intramuscular—100 mg. vial	1.56	1.56	1.56	1.57	1.57	—	1.57
Intravenous							
250 mg. vial	2.70	2.70	2.70	2.70	2.70	2.70	2.70
500 mg. vial	4.85	4.85	4.85	4.85	4.85	4.85	4.85
Ped. drops—100 mg./cc. 10 cc.	2.45	2.45	2.45	2.45	2.45	2.45	2.45
Oral susp.—250 mg./5 cc. 1 oz.	4.24	4.25	4.24	4.23	4.25		4.25
Syrup							
125 mg./5 cc. 2 oz.	4.24	4.25	4.24	4.23	4.25	———	4.25
125 mg./5 cc. 16 oz.	30.60	30.60	30.60	———	30.60	30.60	30.60

SOURCE: FTC, "Proposed Findings of Fact and Law," June, 1960, p. 372.

before the so-called price break. When this occurred, MMSA felt that it had no alternative but to cancel the procurement because of the unreasonably high price.

Over a period of 3 years, four independent suppliers participated in the Government procurement of this item. Nevertheless, in that time the price rose to a high of 174 percent of the initial low price, and thereafter, with one exception, became constant in the $17 bracket. Moreover, all price quotations to the Government bore no relationship to the quantities ordered . . .

Aside from the foregoing peculiar pattern of cost to the Government, there are other characteristics in the procurement history of tetracycline hydrochloride tablets which should be noted. On a number of procurements, more than one supplier initially offered the identical low price. Furthermore, even when only one supplier was low, others came in at higher but identical prices (i.e., either the specific prices offered were the same, or they became identical when the prompt payment discount was applied).

While Admiral Knickerbocker refused to hazard any guess as to the reason for this strange price behavior, an explanation was proffered by Mr. Lyman Duncan, manager of the Lederle Laboratories Division of American Cyanamid. According to his testimony the first MMSA tetracycline procurement was announced at a time when Mr. Duncan was still learning the drug business (shortly after his transfer to Lederle from Cyanamid's Organic Chemicals Division). As a result, he made a mistake and simply bid for the tetracycline contract at the same $11 price at which Cyanamid had been supplying Aureomycin to MMSA for some months:

> As I recall the circumstances, up to that time I think the buying had been entirely Aureomycin or Terramycin with some Chloromycetin, but the real competing products there were Aureomycin and Terramycin.
>
> Now what happened there was I was not fully aware of this, being new in the business, that the Army had never before bought tetracycline.
>
> It was brought to my attention that they had an order for tetracycline. Well, I guess I did not give it a great deal of consideration. . . .
>
> .   .   .   .
>
> So far as I can remember, when this came up, I said: "Well, I suppose we have been bidding $11 on Aureomycin. It is too low a price, but I guess we might as well bid the same price."

Mr. Duncan's uncertainty as to what Lederle should charge for tetracycline is surprising in view of the fact that for a full 2 years prior to the MMSA procurement, his company had been selling the same product to the Veterans' Administration at a price of $19.58, less 2 percent for prompt payment.

On the second procurement Pfizer apparently made a "mistake" in bidding $11 on the assumption that Cyanamid would be in that range. Since Cyanamid actually bid $19.58, the contract of course went to Pfizer. Thereafter, prices rose as described by Admiral Knickerbocker. As the subcommittee counsel pointed out: "I notice that $11 mistake never occurred after the first two times."

In a discussion of subsequent identical bids by several companies, Mr. Duncan was asked specifically about the MMSA procurement in September, 1958, for which Cyanamid, Pfizer, and Squibb all bid $17.24; he explained that this was a coincidence which "astounded" him.

> I had not the faintest idea, Mr. Dixon—it is very easy looking back, but in looking ahead, I had not the faintest idea. Actually, I was astounded that they bid $17.24. I expected someone to bid, with a different situation, to bid $15 or $16. I had no idea what those bids would be.

Another "astounding" coincidence is the mathematically precise division of the MMSA market for tetracycline. For the 3-year period, November, 1956–October, 1959, the patent holder, Pfizer, had 46.6 percent of the MMSA purchases of this drug. The remaining 53.4 percent was split almost exactly evenly among the other sellers, with the Lederle Division of American Cyanamid getting 17.8 percent, Bristol 17.6 percent, and Squibb 17.5 percent. (See Table 3.)

The division of the business in the two principal products, 250-milligram capsules and tetracycline for oral suspension, represents at the least an unusual coincidence. Pfizer supplied approximately 60 percent of MMSA's dollar purchases of tablets, while the remaining percentage was divided almost exactly evenly between Lederle and Squibb; none was furnished by Bristol. On the other hand, Bristol supplied the greater part of MMSA's requirements for the drug in oral suspension form, with relatively modest participation by Pfizer and Squibb and none at all by Lederle. This division of the oral suspension contracts cannot reflect any form of product specialization. Bristol, of course, makes tablets, while Pfizer, Lederle, and Squibb sell the oral suspension form to the regular trade and, indeed, entered bids on it during this period to the MMSA. What is most unusual is that the dollar volume of Bristol's oral suspension sales to MMSA is almost identical to the dollar shares of Lederle and Squibb in the procurement of tablets in which Bristol has not participated successfully.

The MMSA's experience for more than a year in buying drugs is summarized in the attached scatter diagram. Charts 1 through 4 were prepared from data for 44 products purchased in significant quantities by MMSA during 1959 and early 1960. In each case the lowest price at which MMSA was able to buy during the period has been expressed as a percentage of the price to the retail druggist for the same product sold under the brand names of the large companies. Inasmuch as the average sale is substantially larger and advertising and selling costs are considerably less on sales to MMSA, it is to be expected that prices to the Government will be noticeably lower than on sales to the retail druggist. What is of interest here is the extent of the difference as among products with differing numbers of bidders.

The scatter diagram clearly shows the existence of an inverse relationship between MMSA prices and the number of bidders; the greater the number of available suppliers, the lower the price. A freehand curve has been fitted to the plotted points to show the approximate relationship between MMSA prices and the number of bidders for contracts to supply the various products. It will

TABLE 3

MMSA Procurement of Tetracycline, All Forms, November, 1956–October, 1959
(in dollars)

	Pfizer	Lederle	Bristol	Squibb	Upjohn	Total
Tetracycline hydrochloride						
Tablets, 250 mg. 100's	3,572,922	1,397,148	—	1,330,219	42,000	6,342,289
Oral suspension	178,434	—	1,377,335	86,298	—	1,642,067
Powder, 250 mg.	56,131	7,540	74,313	33,408	—	171,392
Powder, 100 mg.	44,155	67,923	—	—	—	112,078
Total	3,851,642	1,472,611	1,451,648	1,449,925	42,000	8,267,826
Percent	46.6	17.8	17.6	17.5	.5	100.0

Source: MMSA, September 2, 1960.

CHART 1

ANTIBIOTIC PRICES

(broad versus narrow spectrum, 1951–60)

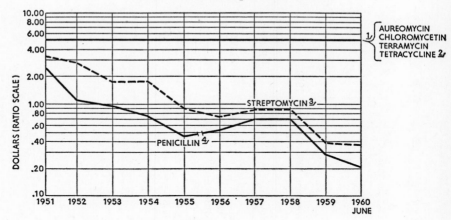

1 16 250-mg. capsules—price to druggists.
2 Tetracycline introduced in 1953.
3 10 grams, bulk prices.
4 10 million units, bulk prices.
SOURCES: Bulk prices of streptomycin: Open-market quotations; June figure, *Oil Paint and Drug Reporter*. Bulk prices of penicillin: 1951–55, Lilly prices compiled by FTC. Broad spectrum: American Druggist *Blue Book*.

be observed that the curve tends to fall sharply as the number of sellers rises—i.e., the effectiveness of competition in reducing prices when drugs are purchased by generic name is clearly illustrated. When its sources of supply are limited to a single firm or a very few companies, MMSA's procurement advantage over the retail druggist is far smaller than is the case when 10 or 12 firms are competing for the agency's contracts. The curve appears to break definitely at about five sellers. With fewer sellers the difference between the MMSA price and the commercial price may be noticeable, but arbitrary; with more sellers, a fairly uniform pattern of relatively low prices appears. . . .

The determination of price

In previous hearings the subcommittee has concerned itself with the standards employed by large corporations in concentrated industries to establish prices. This important issue, which has received considerable attention in economic literature, was also examined during the course of the drug inquiry. In the other industries examined by the subcommittee—steel, automobile, and bread—price leadership was found to be generally observed. Even though they might be more efficient, have lower costs, and show higher profit margins, companies in those industries tend to change their prices only after the leader has changed.

The same practice has been found to prevail in the drug industry, with,

CHART 2

PENICILLIN—LILLY

(bulk prices compared with prices to druggist per billion units, 1948–60)

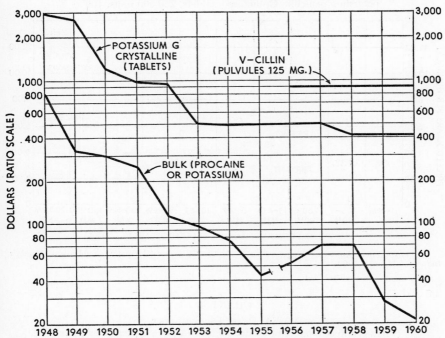

SOURCES: Bulk: 1948–55, Lilly prices compiled by FTC. 1956–60, Open-market quotations; June figures, *Oil, Paint and Drug Reporter*. Dosage forms: 1948, Drug Topics *Red Book*. 1949–60, American Druggist *Blue Book;* annual quotations.

however, an important further dimension. This is the extension of the principle to the introduction of new drugs. In an industry such as steel, price "followership" usually takes the form of matching the leader's prices on the industry's existing products. In drugs the practice is followed not only on existing products but on new drugs as well. When a new product is put on the market, the customary procedure is to introduce it at or very near the price charged for an existing drug used to treat the same general type of ailment. Inasmuch as most ailments are treated with a drug of some kind, there is usually no great difficulty in finding a product whose price can be matched. The practice, which is referred to by industry representatives and their legal spokesmen as "meeting competition," is the essence of simplicity; this, incidentally, makes it rather irrelevant to speculate on the complex variables that businessmen might have in mind in setting their prices. Whether so intended or not, the practice has the effect of automatically eliminating price rivalry. As long as a new drug is intro-

CHART 3

PENICILLIN
(wholesale prices by size of company, 1960—
potassium penicillin G, buffered, tablets, 250,000 units, 100's)

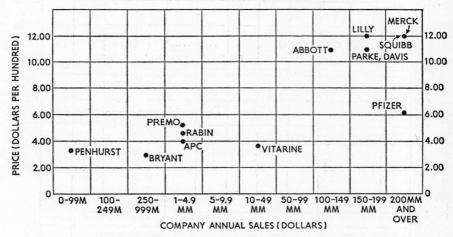

SOURCES: Price: American Druggist *Blue Book*, 1960–61. Size (Company annual sales); *Moody's Industrial Manual*, 1960; and companies.

CHART 4

MMSA DRUG PROCUREMENT
(relationship of number of bidders to MMSA price expressed as percent
of commercial price, 1959 and early 1960)

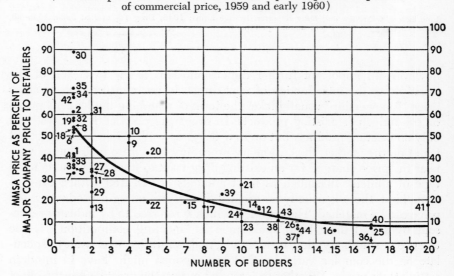

SOURCE: MMSA purchase records and American Druggist *Blue Book*.

duced at the same price as its predecessor, the manufacturer of the older drug is not faced with the necessity of lowering his price, which in turn might provoke a further price reduction of the new product, culminating in "disastrous" competition.

The broad spectrum antibiotics provide a striking example of the manner in which "meeting competition" resulted in price identity on different, though competing, products, as well as among the different sellers of a given product. Less than three years after the introduction of the first of these antibiotics, the price of each of the three broad spectrums then on the market, Aureomycin, Terramycin, and Chloromycetin, had been stabilized. On September 27, 1951, Pfizer adopted a price of $5.10 for Terramycin; four days later both Lederle and Parke, Davis announced the same price for Aureomycin and Chloromycetin, respectively. A little more than two years later Lederle became the first company to introduce the new broad spectrum antibiotic, tetracycline; the price which it adopted was the same as that of the earlier broad spectrums, $5.10. Shortly thereafter the four other sellers of tetracycline put their products on the market at the same price.

Gross margins

The committee majority stressed the high margins between production costs and prices on many drugs. For example, it presented evidence on tranquilizers.

The relationship between prices and production costs among the major brands of tranquilizers appears to bear many of the characteristics exhibited in corticosteroids. Computed unit production costs for meprobamate, one of the most widely used "mild" tranquilizers, may be taken as an example.

The patent rights to meprobamate were assigned to Carter Products, Inc., which sells the drug in finished form under the trademark "Miltown." Carter has licensed one other firm, American Home Products Corp., to sell finished meprobamate in the United States, and only two companies, American Home Products and American Cyanamid, have been licensed to sell throughout the world. American Home Products offers meprobamate through its Wyeth division under the trademark "Equanil." Wyeth's production role is confined to finishing and packaging, since the Carter license does not permit American Home Products to manufacture meprobamate itself; Wyeth's bulk meprobamate must be purchased from Carter to the extent that Carter is willing to supply it, with any additional amounts to be purchased from sources approved by Carter.

Interestingly enough, Carter does not manufacture meprobamate either. Bulk production is subcontracted to a number of other firms (seven in 1958), none of which is licensed to sell meprobamate in finished form.

Unit production costs were computed both for Carter's Miltown and for Wyeth's Equanil tablets containing 400 milligrams of meprobamate. As in the case of other similar computations, production costs include all of the costs of bulk powder, finishing, bottling, and packaging for shipment, but exclude selling and distribution costs.

Table 4 clearly illustrates Wyeth's cost disadvantage with respect to Carter. Carter, buying from its subcontractors who are barred from entering the finished product market, secured its meprobamate at an average cost in December, 1958, of $4.35 per pound. Wyeth, which had to secure bulk meprobamate from its only domestic competitor in the finished product market, had to pay Carter's price of $10 per pound. As a result, Carter could manufacture and package its Miltown tablets at a cost of 0.7 cent per tablet, while Wyeth's costs were twice as great, 1.5 cent per tablet. In either case, however, there appear to be substantial margins between total production costs and the selling prices of 5.2 cents to wholesaler, 6.5 cents to retailers, and nearly 11 cents to the ultimate buyer.

TABLE 4

COMPUTED PRODUCTION COST OF MEPROBAMATE—400 MG. TABLETS—BASED
ON BULK PRICE TRANSACTIONS AND CONTRACT PROCESSING CHARGES
(EXCLUSIVE OF SELLING AND DISTRIBUTION COSTS)
(100,000-tablet order)

	Per 1,000 Tablets	
	To Carter (Miltown)	To Wyeth (Equanil)
Material, 400 gm.		
At average cost to Carter in December, 1958, of $4.35 per pound	$3.84	—
At price Wyeth pays Carter of $10 per pound	—	$8.82
Wastage, at 2 percent	.08	.18
Tableting charge	2.00	2.00
Bottling charge (20 bottles of 50 tablets each)	1.40	1.40
Royalty to Carter at 5 percent of selling price	—	2.60
Total computed production cost per thousand	$7.32	$15.00

COMPARISON BETWEEN COMPUTED PRODUCTION COST AND ACTUAL PRICE

	Per 1,000	Per Tablet
Computed production cost, exclusive of selling and distribution costs		
Carter	$ 7.32	0.7¢
Wyeth	15.00	1.5
Actual prices, both brands		
To wholesaler at $2.60 for 50	52.00	5.2
To druggist at $3.25 for 50	65.00	6.5
To consumer at $5.42 for 50	108.40	10.8

SOURCE OF PRICES: 1959–60, American Druggist *Blue Book.*

It should be noted that the subcommittee's estimates of production costs were fully confirmed by Mr. Henry H. Hoyt, president of Carter Products, and by Mr. Alvin G. Brush, chairman of the board of American Home Products.

Mr. Hoyt, appearing before the subcommittee, offered in evidence a break-down of Miltown price and costs per tablet based upon his company's records. His price was 5.1 cents, rather than the subcommittee figure of 5.2 cents which made no allowance for trade discounts. His actual manufacturing cost of 0.7 cent per tablet was identical to the estimate of the subcommittee staff.

The committee made some comparisons of gross margins among the drug companies and selected firms in other industries. These are shown in Tables 5 and 6.

TABLE 5

Cost of Goods Sold and Gross Margin as Percentages of Sales
for 15 Drug Companies, 1959
(percent of sales)

Company	Cost of Goods Sold	Gross Margin
Norwich Pharmacal Co.	21.6	78.4
Schering Corp.	21.7	78.3
Bristol-Myers Co.	25.5	74.5
The Upjohn Co.	25.6	74.4
Smith Kline & French Laboratories	27.4	72.6
Carter Products, Inc.	27.8	72.2
G. D. Searle & Co.	31.3	68.7
U.S. Vitamin & Pharmaceutical Corp.	34.3	65.7
Sterling Drug, Inc.	36.4	63.6
Warner-Lambert Pharmaceutical Co.	36.6	63.4
Parke, Davis & Co.	36.8	63.2
American Home Products Corp.	37.3	62.7
Abbott Laboratories	40.1	59.9
Merck & Co., Inc.	41.1	58.9
Mead Johnson & Co.	41.4	58.6

SOURCE: *Moody's Industrial Manual*, 1960, and supplements.

The committee majority doubted that research expenditures could account for the high gross margins, since research costs of the 20 major drug companies represented only 6.4 percent of the total revenue.[2] The majority's conclusions on these comparisons were as follows:

No unique characteristic inherent in the economics of the drug industry suggests itself as a logical explanation for this startling difference in the break-down of the sales dollar of the drug producers as contrasted with large firms in other industries. It should be noted that the nondrug list contains a number of firms which are generally considered to rely very heavily on advertising and other promotional and selling expenses to create sales volume—e.g., General Motors, General Electric, Colgate-Palmolive, R. J. Reynolds, General Foods. The expectation, it will be recalled, would be that because the basic demand for drugs, namely the incidence of illness, cannot be significantly increased by advertising and selling expenditures, selling costs would be relatively smaller

---

[2] *Report*, p. 12.

TABLE 6. COST OF GOODS SOLD AND GROSS MARGIN AS PERCENTAGES OF SALES
FOR 50 COMPANIES IN 50 "3-DIGIT" INDUSTRY GROUPS, 1959
(percent of sales)

Industry (S.I.C. Group No.)	Company	Cost of Goods Sold	Gross Margin
208X	Coca-Cola Co.	$42.64	$57.36
284	Colgate-Palmolive Co.	53.33	46.67
383	Eastman Kodak Co.	59.82	40.18
211	R. J. Reynolds Tobacco Co.	60.95	39.05
281	E. I. DuPont de Nemours & Co.	61.57	38.43
324	Lehigh Portland Cement Co.	62.55	37.45
205	National Biscuit Co.	62.61	37.39
381	Minneapolis-Honeywell Regulator Co.	63.26	36.74
357	Burroughs Corp.	63.96	36.04
351	Outboard Marine Corp.	65.21	34.79
289	Hercules Power Co.	66.18	33.82
326	Johns-Manville Corp.	66.21	33.79
398	Armstrong Cork Co.	67.28	32.72
207	Hershey Chocolate Co.	67.36	32.64
271	Curtis Publishing Co.	68.53	31.47
203	General Foods Corp.	69.72	30.28
321	Pittsburgh Plate Glass Co.	70.30	29.70
266	Masonite Corp.	71.43	28.57
314	International Shoe Co.	71.91	28.09
287	Tennessee Corp.	72.05	27.95
285	Glidden Co.	72.81	27.19
204	Corn Products Co.	73.24	26.76
251	Simmons Co.	73.36	26.64
231	Cluett, Peabody & Co., Inc.	73.72	26.28
202	National Dairy Products Corp.	74.00	26.00
291	Socony Mobil Oil Co.	74.43	25.57
295	Flintkote Co.	74.61	25.39
331	United States Steel Corp.	74.90	25.10
333	Aluminum Co. of America	75.13	24.87
301	Goodyear Tire & Rubber Co.	76.79	23.21
241	Georgia-Pacific Corp.	77.05	22.95
356	Worthington Corp.	78.33	21.67
355	Food Machinery and Chemical Corp.	78.83	21.17
354	Blaw-Knox Co.	79.31	20.69
352	International Harvester Co.	79.41	20.59
343	American Radiator & Standard Sanitary Corp.	79.71	20.29
208	Schenley Industries	79.79	20.21
227	Bigelow-Sanford, Inc.	80.34	19.66
371	General Motors Corp.	80.90	19.10
365	Radio Corp. of America	81.10	18.90
374	Westinghouse Air Brake Co.	82.09	17.91
262	West Virginia Pulp & Paper Co.	82.29	17.71
341	American Can Co.	83.76	16.24
366	Raytheon Co.	85.15	14.85
221	Burlington Industries, Inc.	86.05	13.95
349	Combustion Engineering, Inc.	86.15	13.85
206	American Sugar Refinery Co.	87.83	12.17
361	General Electric Corp.	88.16	11.84
201	Swift & Co.	90.72	9.28
372	Douglas Aircraft Co., Inc.	95.40	4.60

SOURCES: Compiled by the Legislative Reference Service, Library of Congress, from directory of companies filing annual reports with the Securities & Exchange Commission, 1959; Moody's Industrial Manual, 1960; The Fortune Directory of the 500 largest U.S. industrial companies, August, 1960.

in drugs than in other industries. Moreover, because of the unique importance of the product to the public health, management might be expected to be content with lower profit margins. These expectations, it appears, find little support in the actual showings.

Profits

The committee also collected data on the profits of drug companies. Since the determination of the profits on individual products would require an arbitrary allocation of overhead, the committee stressed overall company profits. An exception is the tabulation of costs and profits on Miltown which will be cited. The following extracts summarize the viewpoints of the majority:

Perhaps the most commonly used test of the reasonableness of prices is the degree of profitability. Stated simply, total profits are the remainder when all costs and expenses are subtracted from receipts. The subtraction of the additional element, taxes, yields "net profits after taxes" which is the measure that will be used in this chapter.

Profit data are usually available in this country for any large corporation taken as a whole. Through special surveys of the type conducted by the subcommittee, they can be obtained for a subsidiary or division of a corporation. Profit figures relating to an individual product are not only something of a rarity; businessmen often contend that they are meaningless since in a multiple-product company they necessarily reflect arbitrary allocations of overhead, or indirect costs, among individual products. Not infrequently, however, businessmen themselves make such allocations in order to get some idea of the profitability of their various products.

The hearings contained two instances where drug companies did keep their accounting records in sufficient detail and did make the allocations necessary to arrive at their own estimates of costs and profits on individual drugs. Mr. Hoyt, president of Carter Products, Inc., presented a tabulation of costs, expenses, and profits for his company's most important product, Miltown, computed in terms of cents per pill:

MILTOWN COSTS AND PROFIT IN CENTS PER TABLET

Carter receives from wholesalers	5.1
Manufacturing costs (actual)	.7
Selling expenses and administration	.4
Advertising, promotion, and clinical samples	1.0
Research and royalties	.4
Income taxes	1.4
Total cost per tablet	3.9
Net profit	1.2

As compared to an actual production cost of .7 cents, net profit after taxes is 1.2 cents per pill or nearly a quarter of the sales dollar. Selling, advertising, and administration expenses are exactly double the cost of production.

As has been noted, all of the meprobamate produced in this country is made by seven companies under license from Carter. None is permitted to sell the product, except to Carter. In 1958 Carter purchased meprobamate at an average price of $4.77; it then kept part for its own needs and sold almost all the rest to American Home Products, which sells meprobamate in the United States and abroad under the trade name, Equanil, and to American Cyanamid which has the exclusive right to sell the product abroad under the trade name, Miltown. Carter's purchases in 1958 amounted to 983,000 pounds of meprobamate (nearly 500 tons) of which it sold 614,000 pounds in bulk, retaining 369,000 for its own Miltown pills. At 400 milligrams per tablet, Carter's 184 tons of powder would make 400 million pills after reasonable allowances for wastage. At a net profit after taxes of 1.2 cents per tablet, this would represent net profits of $4.8 million. Carter also made over $3 million before taxes on the sale of bulk meprobamate, and received some $3 million more in royalties, mostly from the same drug.

Charts 5 and 6 present some overall averages of profits in the drug industry as compared with manufacturing.

CHART 5

DRUG COMPANY PROFITS* COMPARED WITH ALL MANUFACTURING, 1959

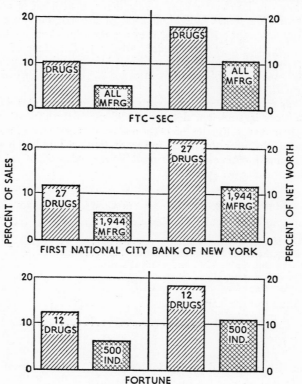

* Net profits after taxes.

CHART 6

COMPARISON OF RATES OF RETURN AFTER TAXES IN SELECTED INDUSTRIES, 1957

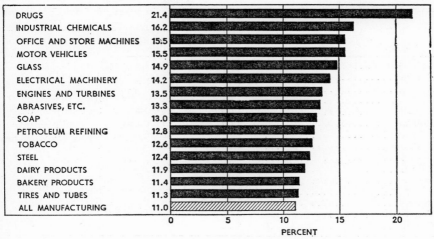

DRUGS	21.4	
INDUSTRIAL CHEMICALS	16.2	
OFFICE AND STORE MACHINES	15.5	
MOTOR VEHICLES	15.5	
GLASS	14.9	
ELECTRICAL MACHINERY	14.2	
ENGINES AND TURBINES	13.5	
ABRASIVES, ETC.	13.3	
SOAP	13.0	
PETROLEUM REFINING	12.8	
TOBACCO	12.6	
STEEL	12.4	
DAIRY PRODUCTS	11.9	
BAKERY PRODUCTS	11.4	
TIRES AND TUBES	11.3	
ALL MANUFACTURING	11.0	

PERCENT

SOURCE: Industries: Federal Trade Commission. All Mfg.: FTC-SEC.

International price comparisons

The committee stressed the lower prices charged for drugs in foreign markets as compared with American markets. It collected data on foreign drug prices from American consulates abroad. Some of the findings are summarized in Tables 7 and 8. The committee alleged that the patent protection afforded drugs in the United States was partly responsible for the high prices there. Table 9 presents comparisons of prices in countries with patent protection with those in countries without such protection.

The committee concluded that American drug firms sold their products at lower prices in countries without patent protection.

TABLE 7

PROMAZINE—COMPARATIVE U.S. AND FOREIGN PRICES, 1959
(25 mg. tablets, 50's)

Country	Brand Name	Company Marketing	Price to Druggist	Price as % U.S. Price
United States ...	Sparine	Wyeth	$3.00	100
Germany	Protacyl	Asche	.80	27
Germany	Verophen	Bayer	.83	28
Australia	Sparine	Wyeth International	.94	31
Brazil	Promazionon	Wyeth	1.26	42
Italy	Liranol	Wyeth	1.32	44
Holland	Prazine	Wyeth	1.59	53
Mexico	Liranol	Wyeth	1.66	55
Venezuela	Vipromazine	Wyeth	2.70	90
Canada	Sparine	Wyeth	3.15	105

SOURCES: U.S. price: American Druggist *Blue Book*, 1959–60.
Foreign prices: Collected by the U.S. Department of State through the American embassies in spring of 1959.

TABLE 8

SERPASIL—COMPARATIVE U.S. AND FOREIGN PRICES, 1959
(100's)

Country	0.25 mg. Tablets		1 mg. Tablets	
	Price to Druggist	Price as % U.S. Price	Price to Druggist	Price as % U.S. Price
United States	$4.50	100%	$12.00	100%
France	.83	18	1.21	10
Austria	1.03	23	2.78	23
Germany	1.05	23	3.42	28
England	1.06	24	3.94	33
Holland	1.09	24		
Belgium	1.89	42	4.24	35
Australia	1.35	30	4.41	37
Iran			4.87	41
Italy	1.83	41	4.90	41
India			5.29	44
Brazil	1.95	43	5.53	46
Japan	1.75	39	5.56	46
Venezuela	3.05	68	7.85	65
Canada	2.70	60	9.87	82

SOURCE: U.S. price: American Druggist *Blue Book*, 1959–60. Foreign prices: Collected by the U.S. Department of State through the American embassies in spring of 1959.

TABLE 9

COMPARISON OF AVERAGE PRICES IN COUNTRIES WITHOUT AND WITH PATENT
PROTECTION ON DRUG PRODUCTS, SPRING, 1959

Product	Without Patents (a)	With Patents (b)	$\frac{b}{a}$
Prednisone (Meticorten)	$14.75	$22.36	151.6%
Chlorpromazine (Thorazine)	1.24	1.89	152.4
Prochlorperazine (Compazine)	.80	2.84	355.0
Promazine (Sparine)	1.57	1.98	126.1
Meprobamate (Miltown)	2.53	3.31	130.8
Reserpine (Serpasil)	1.73	2.79	161.3
Tolbutamide (Orinase)	2.03	3.02	148.8
Chlorpropamide (Diabinese)	3.81	4.87	127.8
Penicillin V	10.87	13.19	121.3
Chloramphenicol (Chloromycetin)	3.17	3.77	118.9
Chlortetracycline (Aureomycin)	4.68	5.53	118.2
Tetracycline (Achromycin)	4.63	5.68	122.7

SOURCE: Foreign prices: Obtained by Department of State through U.S. embassies abroad in the spring of 1959. U.S. prices: Obtained from American Druggist *Blue Book*, 1959–60.

The committee's conclusions

The Kefauver committee argued that the drug industry was unusual in several respects. It held a special position in relation to public health and welfare. In addition, the consumer is not the one who orders the product, since he is dependent on the prescription of the physician. Thus the consumer is not in a position to "shop around" but in a sense is a "captive" of the market.

The committee majority also argued that the demand for drugs is inelastic, so that the companies are not checked by the decline in volume at high prices. It concluded that the monopoly power of the drug companies, supported by patent protection and large advertising expenditures, resulted in high profits and high prices. The consumers were not protected by the normal competitive processes.

Dissenting views

Senators Dirksen and Hruska were critical of the majority report on many points. They argued that the patent system had been supported by the founding fathers, including Jefferson and Hamilton, and had been basic to our economic growth. They complimented the drug industry on the great part it had made in improving the nation's health standards. They noted that drug prices had increased only 3 percent in the period from 1948 to 1958, a period in which wage costs had risen 70 percent.

The minority stressed the large expenditures of the drug industry on research, and the high degree of risk involved in such expenditures. They pointed out that prices would have to be high enough to cover the research that did not result in saleable products as well as the research that was successful. Similarly, the minority argued that the majority had paid too little attention to selling and distribution cost, as well as overhead and taxes. For example it was unreasonable to stress that the markup on cost on a product having a production cost of $1.57 and selling for $17.90 was 1,118 percent, when the $1.57 did not include rent, plant maintenance, depreciation, general overhead, or taxes.

The minority defended the practice of selling some drugs abroad at lower prices in the following words:

> It has always been known to every economist that if a sale is to be made, it is necessary to meet the prevailing price of a similar product in the marketplace. This fact controls the actions of American firms abroad as much as it does in their sales here at home. American drug producers, in order to assure themselves of world wide recognition and good relations with the medical profession in other lands, as well as securing a favorable patent position, have had no choice but to exploit their inventions and discoveries whenever possible. Furthermore, those who operate our major pharmaceutical firms have a strong personal motivation toward the improvement of health standards wherever possible, and in many cases there is a greater need for these drugs abroad than at home.
>
> The majority's report has attempted to attribute to sinister influences the fact that prices vary for the same product in different countries and that licensing agreements involving patents are not always uniform. It is again easy to criticize but far more difficult to develop a foreign market and build a reputation among the citizens of these countries favorable to American products, their producers, and our Government.

In order to attempt to discredit the efforts of American firms which have engaged in foreign promotional work, there has been a concerted effort on the part of the subcommittee to use the agencies of the executive branch of our Government, including the State Department, to collect data that would present the efforts of American firms overseas in an unfavorable light. This approach is detrimental not only to the drug industry but to the prestige of the Nation as a whole.

The committee also argued that the lower wage costs abroad made it necessary for American firms to charge less in foreign markets.

The minority was highly skeptical of the whole majority argument on administered prices. Some economists would support the minority in the position that the expression "administered prices" is not particularly useful. One economist expresses the following view of the entire series of hearings by the Kefauver Committee.[3]

The entire performance of the Kefauver Committee over the past four years has been a highly unsatisfactory one. The Committee has lacked focus—flitting from administered prices to the "fancification" of automobiles to local price discrimination to the accuracy of advertisements for drugs, and where not. Vulgar digressions into the stock options of witnesses are symptomatic of the fishing expedition the Committee had turned into. The levels of evidence have been low, and the selection of academic economists has been somewhat less than representative.

The American economy still has a good deal of monopoly power, and much of it is within reach of the Sherman Act. The Committee, by drawing attention to the drug industry and to identical bids on contracts, has made a contribution in this area. But its chief results were to popularize the erroneous beliefs that there is an important phenomenon called administered prices, and that if such prices existed they would have something to do with inflation.

1. *Suppose that you have been employed as an economist to the drug industry to defend the pricing of drugs. Write a report presenting such a defense.*
2. *Do you think that the expression "administered prices" is a useful one? Give your reasons.*
3. *Is there evidence of collusion in the drug industry? If not, how do you account for the identical prices?*
4. *Are the price patterns in the drug industry desirable from the social point of view? Discuss.*
5. *Would it be better from the social point of view if congressional committees and other government agencies stayed out of the internal pricing practices of industry? Discuss.*
6. *Do risk and high research and distribution costs account for the high margins in the drug industry? Discuss.*

---

[3] See George J. Stigler, "Administered Prices and Oligopolistic Inflation," *Journal of Business,* January, 1962, pp. 1–13.

7. *If you were an official in one of the drug companies what kind of price policy would you recommend?*

FEDERAL TRADE COMMISSION v.
THE PROCTER & GAMBLE COMPANY*

This case was argued Feb. 13, 1967, decided April 11, 1967. Mr. Justice Douglas delivered the opinion of the Court.

This is a proceeding initiated by the Federal Trade Commission charging that respondent, Procter & Gamble Co., had acquired the assets of Clorox Chemical Co. in violation of § 7 of the Clayton Act, as amended by the Celler-Kefauver Act, 64 Stat.[1]

The charge was that Procter's acquisition of Clorox might substantially lessen competition or tend to create a monopoly in the production and sale of household liquid bleaches.

Following evidentiary hearings, the hearing examiner rendered his decision in which he concluded that the acquisition was unlawful and ordered divestiture. On appeal, the Commission reversed, holding that the record as then constituted was inadequate, and remanded to the examiner for additional evidentiary hearings. After the additional hearings, the examiner again held the acquisition unlawful and ordered divestiture. The Commission affirmed the examiner and ordered divestiture. The Court of Appeals for the Sixth Circuit reversed and directed that the Commission's complaint be dismissed. We find that the Commission's findings were amply supported by the evidence, and that the Court of Appeals erred.

As indicated by the Commission in its painstaking and illuminating report, it does not particularly aid analysis to talk of this merger in conventional terms, namely, horizontal or vertical or conglomerate. This merger may most appropriately be described as a "product-extension merger," as the Commission stated. The facts are not disputed, and a summary will demonstrate the correctness of the Commission's decision.

At the time of the merger, in 1957, Clorox was the leading manufacturer in the heavily concentrated household liquid bleach industry. It is agreed that household liquid bleach is the relevant line of commerce. The product is used in the home as a germicide and disinfectant, and, more importantly, as a whitening agent in washing clothes and fabrics. It is a distinctive product with no close substitutes. Liquid bleach is a low-price, high-turnover consumer product sold mainly through grocery stores and supermarkets. The relevant geographical market is the Nation and a series of regional markets. Because of high shipping costs and low sales price, it is not feasible to ship the product more than

---

* 87 *Supreme Court Reporter,* 1226; 386 U.S. 568.

1 "No corporation engaged in commerce shall acquire, directly or indirectly, the whole or any part of the stock or other share capital and no corporation subject to the jurisdiction of the Federal Trade Commission shall acquire the whole or any part of the assets of another corporation engaged also in commerce, where in any line of commerce in any section of the country, the effect of such acquisition may be substantially to lessen competition, or to tend to create a monopoly."

300 miles from its point of manufacture. Most manufacturers are limited to competition within a single region since they have but one plant. Clorox is the only firm selling nationally; it has 13 plants distributed throughout the Nation. Purex, Clorox's closest competitor in size, does not distribute its bleach in the northeast or mid-Atlantic States; in 1957, Purex's bleach was available in less than 50% of the national market.

At the time of the acquisition, Clorox was the leading manufacturer of household liquid bleach, with 48.8% of the national sales—annual sales of slightly less than $40,000,000. Its market share had been steadily increasing for the five years prior to the merger. Its nearest rival was Purex, which manufactures a number of products other than household liquid bleaches, including abrasive cleaners, toilet soap, and detergents. Purex accounted for 15.7% of the household liquid bleach market. The industry is highly concentrated; in 1957, Clorox and Purex accounted for almost 65% of the Nation's household liquid bleach sales, and, together with four other firms, for almost 80%. The remaining 20% was divided among over 200 small producers. Clorox had total assets of $12,000,000; only eight producers had assets in excess of $1,000,000 and very few had assets of more than $75,000.

In light of the territorial limitations on distribution, national figures do not give an accurate picture of Clorox's dominance in the various regions. Thus, Clorox's seven principal competitors did no business in New England, the mid-Atlantic States, or metropolitan New York. Clorox's share of the sales in those areas was 56%, 72% and 64% respectively. Even in regions where its principal competitors were active, Clorox maintained a dominant position. Except in metropolitan Chicago and the west-central States Clorox accounted for at least 39%, and often a much higher percentage, of liquid bleach sales.

Since all liquid bleach is chemically identical, advertising and sales promotion are vital. In 1957 Clorox spent almost $3,700,000 on advertising, imprinting the value of its bleach in the mind of the consumer. In addition, it spent $1,700,000 for other promotional activities. The Commission found that these heavy expenditures went far to explain why Clorox maintained so high a market share despite the fact that its brand, though chemically indistinguishable from rival brands, retailed for a price equal to or, in many instances, higher than its competitors.

Procter is a large, diversified manufacturer of low-price, high-turnover household products sold through grocery, drug, and department stores. Prior to its acquisition of Clorox, it did not produce household liquid bleach. Its 1957 sales were in excess of $1,100,000,000 from which it realized profits of more than $67,000,000; its assets were over $500,000,000. Procter has been marked by rapid growth and diversification. It has successfully developed and introduced a number of new products. Its primary activity is in the general area of soaps, detergents, and cleansers; in 1957, of total domestic sales, more than one-half (over $500,000,000) were in this field. Procter was the dominant factor in this area.

It accounted for 54.4% of all packaged detergent sales. The industry is heavily concentrated—Procter and its nearest competitors, Colgate-Palmolive and Lever Brothers, account for 80% of the market.

In the marketing of soaps, detergents, and cleansers, as in the marketing of household liquid bleach, advertising and sales promotion are vital. In 1957, Procter was the Nation's largest advertiser, spending more than $80,000,000 on advertising and an additional $47,000,000 on sales promotion. Due to its tremendous volume, Procter receives substantial discounts from the media. As a multi-product producer Procter enjoys substantial advantages in advertising and sales promotion. Thus, it can and does feature several products in its promotions, reducing the printing, mailing, and other costs for each product. It also purchases network programs on behalf of several products, enabling it to give each product network exposure at a fraction of the cost per product that a firm with only one product to advertise would incur.

Prior to the acquisition, Procter was in the course of diversifying into product lines related to its basic detergent-soap-cleanser business. Liquid bleach was a distinct possibility since packaged detergents—Procter's primary product line—and liquid bleach are used complementarily in washing clothes and fabrics, and in general household cleaning. As noted by the Commission:

"Packaged detergents—Procter's most important product category—and household liquid bleach are used complementarily, not only in the washing of clothes and fabrics, but also in general household cleaning, since liquid bleach is a germicide and disinfectant as well as a whitener. From the consumer's viewpoint, then, packaged detergents and liquid bleach are closely related products. But the area of relatedness between products of Procter and of Clorox is wider. Household cleansing agents in general, like household liquid bleach, are low-cost, high-turnover household consumer goods marketed chiefly through grocery stores and pre-sold to the consumer by the manufacturer through mass advertising and sales promotions. Since products of both parties to the merger are sold to the same customers, at the same stores, and by the same merchandising methods, the possibility arises of significant integration at both the marketing and distribution levels."

The decision to acquire Clorox was the result of a study conducted by Procter's promotion department designed to determine the advisability of entering the liquid bleach industry. The initial report noted the ascendancy of liquid bleach in the large and expanding household bleach market, and recommended that Procter purchase Clorox rather than enter independently. Since a large investment would be needed to obtain a satisfactory market share, acquisition of the industry's leading firm was attractive. "Taking over the Clorox business . . . could be a way of achieving a dominant position in the liquid bleach market quickly, which would pay out reasonably well." The initial report predicted that Procter's "sales, distribution and manufacturing setup" could increase Clorox's share of the markets in areas where it was low. The final report confirmed the conclusions of the initial report and emphasized that Procter would make more effective use of Clorox's advertising budget and that the merger would facilitate advertising economies. A few months later, Procter acquired the assets of Clorox in the name of a wholly owned subsidiary, the Clorox Company, in exchange for Procter stock.

The Commission found that the acquisition might substantially lessen competition. The findings and reasoning of the Commission need be only briefly summarized. The Commission found that the substitution of Procter with its huge assets and advertising advantages for the already dominant Clorox would dissuade new entrants and discourage active competition from the firms already in the industry due to fear of retaliation by Procter. The Commission thought it relevant that retailers might be induced to give Clorox preferred shelf space since it would be manufactured by Procter, which also produced a number of other products marketed by the retailers. There was also the danger that Procter might underprice Clorox in order to drive out competition, and subsidize the underpricing with revenue from other products. The Commission carefully reviewed the effect of the acquisition on the structure of the industry, noting that "[t]he practical tendency of the . . . merger . . . is to transform the liquid bleach industry into an arena of big business competition only, with the few small firms that have not disappeared through merger eventually falling by the wayside, unable to compete with their giant rivals." Further, the merger would seriously diminish potential competition by eliminating Procter as a potential entrant into the industry. Prior to the merger, the Commission found, Procter was the most likely prospective entrant, and absent the merger would have remained on the periphery, restraining Clorox from exercising its market power. If Procter had actually entered, Clorox's dominant position would have been eroded and the concentration of the industry reduced. The Commission stated that it had not placed reliance on post-acquisition evidence in holding the merger unlawful.

The Court of Appeals said that the Commission's finding of illegality had been based on "treacherous conjecture," mere possibility and suspicion. It dismissed the fact that Clorox controlled almost 50% of the industry, that two firms controlled 65%, and that six firms controlled 80% with the observation that "[t]he fact that in addition to the six . . . producers sharing 80 percent of the market, there were two hundred smaller producers . . . would not seem to indicate anything unhealthy about the market conditions." It dismissed the finding that Procter, with its huge resources and prowess, would have more leverage than Clorox with the statement that it was Clorox which had the "knowhow" in the industry, and that Clorox's finances were adequate for its purposes. As for the possibility that Procter would use its tremendous advertising budget and volume discounts to push Clorox, the court found "it difficult to base a finding of illegality on discounts in advertising." It rejected the Commission's finding that the merger eliminated the potential competition of Procter because "[t]here was no reasonable probability that Procter would have entered the household liquid bleach market but for the merger." "There was no evidence tending to prove that Procter ever intended to enter this field on its own." Finally, "[t]here was no evidence that Procter at any time in the past engaged in predatory practices, or that it intended to do so in the future."

The Court of Appeals also heavily relied on post-acquisition "evidence" . . . to the effect that the other producers subsequent to the merger were selling more bleach for more money than ever before" and that "[t]here [had] been no significant change in Clorox's market share in the four years subsequent to the merger" and concluded that "[t]his evidence certainly does not prove anticompetitive effects of the merger." The Court of Appeals, in our view, misapprehended the standards for its review and the standards applicable in a § 7 proceeding.

Section 7 of the Clayton Act was intended to arrest the anticompetitive effects of market power in their incipiency. The core question is whether a merger may substantially lessen competition, and necessarily requires a prediction of the merger's impact on competition, present and future. The section can deal only with probabilities, not with certainties. And there is certainly no requirement that the anticompetitive power manifest itself in anticompetitive action before § 7 can be called into play. If the enforcement of § 7 turned on the existence of actual anticompetitive practices, the congressional policy of thwarting such practices in their incipiency would be frustrated.

All mergers are within the reach of § 7, and all must be tested by the same standard, whether they are classified as horizontal, vertical, conglomerate[2] or other. As noted by the Commission, this merger is neither horizontal, vertical, nor conglomerate. Since the products of the acquired company are complementary to those of the acquiring company and may be produced with similar facilities, marketed through the same channels and in the same manner, and advertised by the same media, the Commission aptly called this acquisition a "product-extension merger":

> "By this acquisition, Procter has not diversified its interests in the sense of expanding into a substantially different, unfamiliar market or industry. Rather, it has entered a market which adjoins, as it were, those markets in which it is already established, and which is virtually indistinguishable from them insofar as the problems and techniques of marketing the product to the ultimate consumer are concerned. As a high official of Procter put it, commenting on the acquisition of Clorox, 'While this is a completely new business for us, taking us for the first time into the marketing of a household bleach and disinfectant, we are thoroughly at home in the field of manufacturing and marketing low priced, rapid turn-over consumer products.' "

The anticompetitive effects with which this product-extension merger is fraught can easily be seen: (1) the substitution of the powerful acquiring firm for the smaller, but already dominant, firm may substantially reduce the competitive structure of the industry by raising entry barriers and by dissuading the smaller firms from aggressively competing; (2) the acquisition eliminates the potential competition of the acquiring firm.

The liquid bleach industry was already oligopolistic before the acquisition, and price competition was certainly not as vigorous as it would have been if the industry were competitive. Clorox enjoyed a dominant position nationally, and its position approached monopoly proportions in certain areas. The existence of some 200 fringe firms certainly does not belie that fact. Nor does the fact, relied upon by the court below, that, after the merger, producers other than Clorox "were selling more bleach for more money than ever before." In the same period, Clorox increased its share from 48.8 to 52 percent. The inter-

---

[2] A pure conglomerate merger is one in which there are no economic relationships between the acquiring and the acquired firm.

jection of Procter into the market considerably changed the situation. There is every reason to assume that the smaller firms would become more cautious in competing due to their fear of retaliation by Procter. It is probable that Procter would become the price leader and that oligopoly would become more rigid.

The acquisition may also have the tendency of raising the barriers to new entry. The major competitive weapon in the successful marketing of bleach is advertising. Clorox was limited in this area by its relatively small budget and its inability to obtain substantial discounts. By contrast, Procter's budget was much larger; and, although it would not devote its entire budget to advertising Clorox, it could divert a large portion to meet the short-term threat of a new entrant. Procter would be able to use its volume discounts to advantage in advertising Clorox. Thus, a new entrant would be much more reluctant to face the giant Procter than it would have been to face the smaller Clorox.[3]

Possible economies cannot be used as a defense to illegality. Congress was aware that some mergers which lessen competition may also result in economies but it struck the balance in favor of protecting competition.

The Commission also found that the acquisition of Clorox by Procter eliminated Procter as a potential competitor. The Court of Appeals declared that this finding was not supported by evidence because there was no evidence that Procter's management had ever intended to enter the industry independently and that Procter had never attempted to enter. The evidence, however, clearly shows that Procter was the most likely entrant. Procter had recently launched a new abrasive cleaner in an industry similar to the liquid bleach industry, and had wrested leadership from a brand that had enjoyed even a larger market share than had Clorox. Procter was engaged in a vigorous program of diversifying into product lines closely related to its basic products. Liquid bleach was a natural avenue of diversification since it is complementary to Procter's products, is sold to the same customers through the same channels, and is advertised and

---

[3] The barriers to entry have been raised both for entry by new firms and for entry into new geographical markets by established firms. The latter aspect is demonstrated by Purex's lesson in Erie, Pennsylvania. In October, 1957, Purex selected Erie, Pennsylvania—where it had not sold previously—as an area in which to test the salability, under competitive conditions, of a new bleach. The leading brands in Erie were Clorox, with 52%, and the "101" brand, sold by Gardner Manufacturing Company, with 29% of the market. Purex launched an advertising and promotional campaign to obtain a broad distribution in a short time, and in five months captured 33% of the Erie market. Clorox's share dropped to 35% and 101's to 17%. Clorox responded by offering its bleach at reduced prices, and then added an offer of a $1-value ironing board cover for 50¢ with each purchase of Clorox at the reduced price. It also increased its advertising with television spots. The result was to restore Clorox's lost market share and, indeed, to increase it slightly. Purex's share fell to 7%.

Since the merger Purex has acquired the fourth largest producer of bleach, John Puhl Products Company, which owned and marketed "Fleecy White" brand in geographic markets which Purex was anxious to enter. One of the reasons for this acquisition, according to Purex's president, was that:

"Purex had been unsuccessful in expanding its market position geographically on Purex liquid bleach. The economics of the bleach business, and the strong competitive factors as illustrated by our experience in Erie, Pennsylvania, make it impossible, in our judgment, for us to expand our market on liquid bleach."

merchandised in the same manner. Procter had substantial advantages in advertising and sales promotion, which, as we have seen, are vital to the success of liquid bleach. No manufacturer had a patent on the product or its manufacture, necessary information relating to manufacturing methods and processes were readily available, there was no shortage of raw material, and the machinery and equipment required for a plant of efficient capacity were available at reasonable cost. Procter's management was experienced in producing and marketing goods similar to liquid bleach. Procter had considered the possibility of independently entering but decided against it because the acquisition of Clorox would enable Procter to capture a more commanding share of the market.

It is clear that the existence of Procter at the edge of the industry exerted considerable influence on the market. First, the market behavior of the liquid bleach industry was influenced by each firm's predictions of the market behavior of its competitors, actual and potential. Second, the barriers to entry by a firm of Procter's size and with its advantages were not significant. There is no indication that the barriers were so high that the price Procter would have to charge would be above the price that would maximize the profits of the existing firms. Third, the number of potential entrants was not so large that the elimination of one would be insignificant. Few firms would have the temerity to challenge a firm as solidly entrenched as Clorox. Fourth, Procter was found by the Commission to be the most likely entrant. These findings of the Commission were amply supported by the evidence.

The judgment of the Court of Appeals is reversed and remanded with instructions to affirm and enforce the Commission's order. It is so ordered. Reversed and remanded.

Mr. Justice Stewart and Mr. Justice Fortas took no part in the consideration or decision of this case. Mr. Justice Harlan, concurring, stated:

I agree that the Commission's order should be sustained, but I do not share the majority opinion's view that a mere "summary will demonstrate the correctness of the Commission's decision" nor that "[t]he anticompetitive effects with which this product-extension merger is fraught can easily be seen." I consider the case difficult within its own four corners, and beyond that, its portents for future administrative and judicial application of § 7 of the Clayton Act to this kind of merger important and far-reaching. From both standpoints more refined analysis is required before putting the stamp of approval on what the Commission has done in this case.

1. *Did the Procter & Gamble acquisition of Clorox raise the barriers to entry? Did it lessen competition or tend to create monopoly?*
2. *Did the acquisition have any significance for the pricing of Clorox or other bleaches?*
3. *Were the volume discounts available to Procter & Gamble a form of price discrimination? Did they contribute to barriers to new competition with Clorox? Should these kinds of volume discounts be permitted?*
4. *Do the principles in this case apply to other conglomerate mergers?*

FEDERAL TRADE COMMISSION v. ANHEUSER-BUSCH, INC.*

This case was argued March 2, 1960; decided June 20, 1960. Mr. Chief Justice Warren delivered the opinion of the Court.

The question presented is whether certain pricing activities of respondent, Anheuser-Busch, Inc., constituted price discrimination within the meaning of § 2(a) of the Clayton Act, as amended by the Robinson-Patman Act,
Section 2(a) provides in pertinent part:

> That it shall be unlawful for any person engaged in commerce, in the course of such commerce, either directly or indirectly, to discriminate in price between different purchasers of commodities of like grade and quality, where either or any of the purchases involved in such discrimination are in commerce, where such commodities are sold for use, consumption, or resale within the United States or any Territory thereof or the District of Columbia or any insular possession or other place under the jurisdiction of the United States, and where the effect of such discrimination may be substantially to lessen competition or tend to create a monopoly in any line of commerce, or to injure, destroy, or prevent competition with any person who either grants or knowingly receives the benefit of such discrimination, or with customers of either of them. . . .

This controversy had its genesis in a complaint issued by the Federal Trade Commission in 1955, which charged respondent, a beer producer, with a violation of § 2(a). The complaint alleged that respondent had "discriminated in price between different purchasers of its beer of like grade and quality by selling it to some of its customers at higher prices than to other [s]"; that, more specifically, respondent had lowered prices in the St. Louis, Missouri, market, without making similar price reductions in other markets; that this discrimination had already diverted substantial business from respondent's St. Louis competitors; that it was "sufficient" to have the same impact in the future; that there was a "reasonable probability" it would substantially lessen competition in respondent's line of commerce; and that it might also tend to create a monopoly or to injure, destroy, or prevent competition with respondent. Thus the complaint described a pricing pattern which had adverse effects only upon sellers' competition, commonly termed primary-line competition, and not upon buyers' competition, commonly termed secondary-line competition.

Both the hearing examiner and, on appeal, the Commission held that the evidence introduced at the hearing established a violation of § 2(a). The Commission found the facts to be as follows:

Respondent, a leading national brewer,[1] sells a so-called premium beer, which is priced higher than the beers of regional and local breweries in the great majority of markets, although both the price of respondent's beer and the

---

* 80 *Supreme Court Reporter* 1267; 363 U.S. 536; and 4 L. Ed. 2nd, 385.
[1] Anheuser-Busch ranked second nationally in gross sales in 1952 and 1955, and first in 1953 and 1954.

premium differential vary from market to market and from time to time. During the period relevant to this case, respondent had three principal competitors in the St. Louis area, all regional breweries: Falstaff Brewing Corporation, Griesedieck Western Brewing Company, and Griesedieck Brothers Brewery Company. In accord with the generally prevailing price structure, these breweries normally sold their products at a price substantially lower than respondent's.

In 1953, most of the national breweries, including respondent, granted their employees a wage increase, and on October 1, 1953, they put into effect a general price increase. Although many regional and local breweries throughout the country followed suit by raising their prices, Falstaff, Griesedieck Western, and Griesedieck Brothers maintained their pre-October price of $2.35 per standard case. Although respondent's sales in the St. Louis area did not decline, its national sales fell, along with industry sales in general.

On January 4, 1954, respondent lowered its price in the St. Louis market from $2.93 to $2.68 per case, thereby reducing the previous 58¢ differential to 33¢. A second price cut occurred on June 21, 1954, this time to $2.35, the same price charged by respondent's three competitors. On January 3, 1954, the day before the first price cut, respondent's price in the St. Louis market had been lower than its price in other markets,[2] and during the period of the price reductions in the St. Louis area, respondent made no similar price reductions in any other market. In March, 1955, respondent increased its St. Louis price 45¢ per case, and Falstaff, Griesedieck Western, and Griesedieck Brothers almost immediately raised their prices 15¢, which re-established a substantial differential. This ended the period of alleged price discrimination.

The Commission concluded:

As a result of maintaining higher prices to all purchasers outside of the St. Louis area and charging the lower prices, as reduced in 1954, to only those customers in the St. Louis area, respondent discriminated in price as between purchasers differently located.

Since, as will appear, it is this aspect of the decision which concerns us, it is necessary only to sketch summarily the remaining elements in the Commission's decision. The Commission's finding of competitive injury was predicated to a substantial degree upon what it regarded as a demonstrated diversion of business to respondent from its St. Louis competitors during the period of price discrimination. For example, by comparing that period with a similar period during the previous year, the Commission determined that respondent's

---

[2] The following table discloses the degree of this price spread:

St. Louis, Mo.	$2.93	Bronx, N.Y.	3.68
Chicago, Ill.	3.44	Kearney, Nebr.	3.68
Cincinnati, Ohio	3.75	St. Joseph, Mo.	3.17
Houston, Tex.	3.70	Buffalo, N.Y.	3.60
Baltimore, Md.	3.62	St. Paul, Minn.	3.53
Washington, D.C.	3.65	Sioux Falls, S. Dak.	3.50
Detroit, Mich.	3.55	Denver, Colo.	...
Boston, Mass.	3.69	San Francisco, Calif.	3.79
Kansas City, Mo.	3.15	Los Angeles, Calif.	3.80

sales had risen 201.5%, Falstaff's sales had dropped slightly, Griesedieck Western's sales had fallen about 33%, and Griesedieck Brothers' sales had plummeted about 41%. In tabular form, the relative market positions of the St. Louis sellers were as follows:

	Dec. 31, 1953	June 30, 1954	Mar. 1, 1955	July 31, 1955
Respondent	12.5%	16.55%	39.3%	21.03%
Griesedieck Brothers	14.4	12.58	4.8	7.36
Falstaff	29.4	32.05	29.1	36.62
Griesedieck Western	38.9	33.	23.1	27.78
All others	4.8	5.82	3.94	7.21

The Commission rejected respondent's contention that its price reductions had been made in good faith to meet the equally low price of a competitor within the meaning of the proviso to § 2(b) of the Act, and also found respondent's attack upon the examiner's cease-and-desist order to be meritless. The Commission thereupon adopted and issued that order, with only slight modification.[3]

On review, the Court of Appeals set aside the order. 265 F.2d 677. We granted certiorari 361 U.S. 880, 80 S.Ct. 151, 4 L.Ed.2d 117, because a conflict had developed among the Courts of Appeals on a question of importance in the administration of the statute.

The limited nature of our inquiry can be fully appreciated only in the light of the correspondingly narrow decision of the Court of Appeals, which rested entirely upon the holding that the threshold statutory element of price discrimination had not been established. Thus the Court of Appeals did not consider whether the record supported a finding of the requisite competitive injury, whether respondent's good faith defense was valid, or whether the Commission's order was unduly broad. We have concluded that the Court of Appeals erred in its construction of § 2(a) and that the evidence fully warranted the Commission's finding of price discrimination. Respondent would have us affirm nonetheless on any of the alternative grounds it strongly urged below. While this is, to be sure, an appropriate course of action under proper circumstances, we believe that it would be unwise for us to grapple with these intricate problems, the solution to which requires a careful examination of a voluminous record, before they have been dealt with by the Court of Appeals. Therefore, the case will be remanded, and of course nothing in this opinion should be interpreted as intimating a view upon the remaining aspects of the controversy.

---

[3] "It Is Ordered that the respondent, Anheuser-Busch, Inc., a corporation, and its officers, representatives, agents and employees, directly or through any corporate or other device, in the sale of beer of like grade and quality, do forthwith cease and desist from discriminating, directly or indirectly, in price, between different purchasers engaged in the same line of commerce, where either, or any, of the purchases involved in such discrimination are in commerce, as 'commerce' is defined in the Clayton Act, by a price reduction in any market where respondent is in competition with any other seller, unless it proportionally reduces its prices everywhere for the same quantity of beer."

A discussion of the import of the § 2(a) phrase "discriminate in price," in the context of this case, must begin with a consideration of the purpose of the statute with respect to primary-line competition. The Court of Appeals expressed some doubt that § 2(a) was designed to protect this conception at all, but respondent has not undertaken to defend that position here. This is entirely understandable. While "precision of expression is not an outstanding characteristic of the Robinson-Patman Act," it is certain at least that § 2(a) is violated where there is a price discrimination which deals the requisite injury to primary-line competition, even though secondary-line and tertiary-line competition are unaffected. The statute could hardly be read any other way, for it forbids price discriminations "where the effect . . . may be substantially to lessen competition or tend to create a monopoly *in any line of commerce,* or to injure, destroy, or prevent competition with any person *who either grants or knowingly receives* the benefit of such discrimination, or with customers of either of them." (Emphasis added.)

The legislative history of § 2(a) is equally plain. The section, when originally enacted as part of the Clayton Act in 1914, was born of a desire by Congress to curb the use by financially powerful corporations of localized price-cutting tactics which had gravely impaired the competitive position of other sellers. It is, of course, quite true—and too well known to require extensive exposition— that the 1936 Robinson-Patman amendments to the Clayton Act were motivated principally by congressional concern over the impact upon secondary-line competition of the burgeoning of mammoth purchasers, notably chain stores. However, the legislative history of these amendments leaves no doubt that Congress was intent upon strengthening the Clayton Act provisions, not weakening them, and that it was no part of Congress' purpose to curtail the pre-existing applicability of § 2(a) to price discriminations affecting primary-line competition.

The federal courts, both before and after the amendment of § 2(a), have taken this view of the scope of the statute in cases involving impairment of primary-line competition. In fact, the original focus of § 2(a) on sellers' competition was so evident that this Court was compelled to hold explicitly, contrary to lower court decisions, that the statute was not *restricted* to price discriminations impeding primary-line competition, but protected secondary-line competition as well.

Thus neither the language of § 2(a), its legislative history, nor its judicial application countenances a construction of the statute which draws strength from even a lingering doubt as to its purpose of protecting primary-line competition. But the rationale of the Court of Appeals appears to have been shaped by precisely this type of doubt. The view of the Court of Appeals was that, before, there can be a price discrimination within the meaning of § 2(a), "[t]here must be some relationship between the different purchasers which entitles them to comparable treatment." Such a relationship would exist, the court reasoned, if different prices were being charged to *competing* purchasers. But the court observed that in this case all *competing* purchasers paid respondent the same price, so far as the record disclosed. Consequently, the court concluded that, even assuming the price cuts "were directed at [Anheuser-Busch's] local competitors, they were not *discriminatory.*"

This qualification upon the applicability of § 2(a) to primary-line competition cases is in no way adumbrated by the prevailing line of relevant decisions. More important, however, is the incompatibility of the Circuit Court's rule with the purpose of § 2(a). The existence of competition among buyers who are charged different prices by a seller is obviously important in terms of adverse effect upon secondary-line competition, but it would be merely a fortuitous circumstance so far as injury to primary-line competition is concerned. Since, as we have indicated, an independent and important goal of § 2(a) is to extend protection to competitors of the discriminating seller, the limitation of that protection by the alien factor of competition among purchasers would constitute a debilitating graft upon the statute.

Although respondent's starting point is the same as that of the Court of Appeals—that a price discrimination is not synonymous with a price difference—its test of price discrimination is somewhat broader. Respondent concedes that a competitive relationship among purchasers is not a prerequisite of price discrimination, but maintains that at least there must be "proof that the lower price is below cost or unreasonably low for the purpose or design to eliminate competition and thereby obtain a monopoly." Since such a finding is lacking here, respondent argues that it cannot be said that there was price discrimination.

Respondent asserts that its view is supported by legislative history, court decisions, and reason. Respondent relies heavily, as did the Court of Appeals, upon a statement made during Congress' consideration of the Robinson-Patman legislation by Representative Utterback, a manager of the conference bill which became § 2(a). In this rather widely quoted exegesis of the section, Representative Utterback declared that "a discrimination is more than a mere difference," and exists only when there is "some relationship . . . between the parties to the discrimination which entitles them to equal treatment." Such a relationship would prevail among competing purchasers, according to the Congressman, and also "where . . . the price to one is so low as to involve a sacrifice of some part of the seller's necessary costs and profit," so that "it leaves that deficit inevitably to be made up in higher prices to his other customers." Respondent also cites expressions in the legislative history of the Clayton Act which reflect Congress' concern over classic examples of predatory business practices. Moreover, respondent maintains that the principle it advances has found expression in the decisions of the federal courts in primary-line-competition cases, which consistently emphasize the unreasonably low prices and the predatory intent of the defendants. Respondent also urges that its view is grounded upon the statutory scheme of § 2(a), which penalizes sellers only if an anticompetitive effect stems from a *discriminatory* pricing pattern, not if it results merely from a low price. Thus, the argument goes, unless there is proof that high prices in one area have subsidized low prices in another, the price differential does not fall within the compass of the section. In such a case, it is contended, § 3 of the Robinson-Patman Act, 49 Stat. 1528, 15 U.S.C. § 13a, 15 U.S.C.A. § 13a, may be applicable, but not § 2(a).[4] Finally, respondent argues that, unless its position is

---

[4] Section 3 provides:
"It shall be unlawful for any person engaged in commerce, in the course of such commerce, to be a party to, or assist in, any transaction of sale, or contract to sell, which discriminates to his knowledge against competitors of the purchaser, in that any

accepted, the law will impose rigid price uniformity upon the business world, contrary to sound economics and the policy of the antitrust laws. The trouble with respondent's arguments is not that they are necessarily irrelevant in a § 2(a) proceeding, but that they are misdirected when the issue under consideration is solely whether there has been a price discrimination. We are convinced that, whatever may be said with respect to the rest of §§ 2(a) and 2(b) —and we say nothing here—there are no overtones of business buccaneering in the § 2(a) phrase "discriminate in price." Rather, a price discrimination within the meaning of that provision is merely a price difference.

When this Court has spoken of price discrimination in § 2(a) cases, it has generally assumed that the term was synonymous with price differentiation. In Federal Trade Comm. v. Cement Institute, the Court referred to "discrimination in price" as "selling the same kind of goods cheaper to one purchaser than to another." And in Federal Trade Comm. v. Morton Salt Co., the Court said, "Congress meant by using the words 'discrimination in price' in § 2 that in a case involving competitive injury between a seller's customers the Commission need only prove that a seller had charged one purchaser a higher price for like goods than he had charged one or more of the purchaser's competitors." The commentators have generally shared this view. ˙

These assumptions, we now conclude, were firmly rooted in the structure of the statute, for it is only by equating price discrimination with price differentiation that § 2(a) can be administered as Congress intended. As we read that provision, it proscribes price differences, subject to certain defined defenses,[5] where the effect of the differences "may be substantially to lessen competition or tend to create a monopoly in any line of commerce, or to injure, destroy, or prevent competition with any person who either grants or knowingly receives the benefit" of the price differential, "or with customers of either of them." In other words, the statute itself spells out the conditions which make a price

---

discount, rebate, allowance, or advertising service charge is granted to the purchaser over and above any discount, rebate, allowance, or advertising service charge available at the time of such transaction to said competitors in respect of a sale of goods of like grade, quality, and quantity; to sell, or contract to sell, goods in any part of the United States at prices lower than those exacted by said person elsewhere in the United States for the purpose of destroying competition, or eliminating a competitor in such part of the United States; or, to sell, or contract to sell, goods at unreasonably low prices for the purpose of destroying competition or eliminating a competitor."

[5] In addition to the statutory provisions regarding injury to competition, set out at page 537 of 363 U.S., page 1268 of 80 S.Ct., supra, there are other relevant portions of the statute, such as the seller's § 2(b) defense of "showing that his lower price . . . was made in good faith to meet an equally low price of a competitor . . ." And a proviso to § 2(a) states:

"That nothing herein contained shall prevent differentials which make only due allowance for differences in the cost of manufacture, sale, or delivery resulting from the differing methods or quantities in which such commodities are to such purchasers sold or delivered . . ." And still another proviso to § 2(a) states:

"That nothing herein contained shall prevent price changes from time to time where in response to changing conditions affecting the market for or the marketability of the goods concerned, such as but not limited to actual or imminent deterioration of perishable goods, obsolescence of seasonal goods, distress sales under court process, or sales in good faith in discontinuance of business in the goods concerned."

difference illegal or legal, and we would derange this integrated statutory scheme were we to read other conditions into the law by means of the non-directive phrase, "discriminate in price." Not only would such action be contrary to what we conceive to be the meaning of the statute, but, perhaps because of this, it would be thoroughly undesirable.

The other materials adduced by respondent do no more than indicate that the factors in question—predatory intent and unreasonably low local price cuts—may possibly be relevant to other matters which may be put in issue in a § 2(a) proceeding. For example, it might be argued that the existence of predatory intent bears upon the likelihood of injury to competition, and that a price reduction below cost tends to establish such an intent. Practically all of the legislative materials and court decisions relied upon by respondent are explicable on this basis, since hardly any of them are concerned specifically with the meaning of price discrimination. Moreover, many of the legislative expressions cited by respondent may merely be descriptive of the prototype of the evil with which Congress dealt in § 2(a) rather than delineative of the outer reach of that section. A possible exception is the statement of Representative Utterback. But the primary function of statutory construction is to effectuate the intent of Congress, and that function cannot properly be discharged by reliance upon a statement of a single Congressman, in the face of the weighty countervailing considerations which are present in this case.

Nothing that we have said, of course, should be construed to be the expression of any view concerning the relevance of the factors stressed by respondent to statutory standards other than price discrimination. We wish merely to point out, on the one hand, why respondent's arguments in our view are not pertinent to the issue at bar, and, on the other, that we are not foreclosing respondent from urging in the Court of Appeals that such arguments are material to issues not now before us.

What we have said makes it quite evident, we believe, that our decision does not raise the specter of a flat prohibition of price differentials, inasmuch as price differences constitute but one element of a § 2(a) violation. In fact, as we have indicated, respondent has vigorously contested this very case on the entirely separate grounds of insufficient injury to competition and good faith lowering of price to meet competition. Nor is it relevant that the Commission did not proceed upon the basis of the respondent's price differentials which existed prior to the period in question in this case. This choice is committed to the discretion of the Commission; and it may well be that the Commission did not believe the remaining statutory elements could be established with respect to other differentials. Our interest is solely with this case, and at this stage of the litigation that interest is confined exclusively to identifying and keeping distinct the various statutory standards which are part of the § 2(a) complex.

The judgment of the Court of Appeals is reversed and the case is remanded to that court for further proceedings not inconsistent with this opinion.

Reversed.

1. *In your opinion was there price discrimination in the economic sense in this case? Give your reasons.*
2. *Was there price discrimination in the legal sense? Discuss.*

3. *According to Chief Justice Warren's opinion is price discrimination, as defined by statute, illegal?*
4. *In your opinion what was the purpose of the price reductions in this case? Were these price reductions desirable from the point of view of the consuming public?*
5. *Were the price reductions profitable from the point of view of Anheuser-Busch?*
6. *List some of the legal issues that are likely to arise in cases of price discrimination.*

UTAH PIE COMPANY v. CONTINENTAL BAKING CO. (et al.)*

This case was argued Jan. 17, 1967; decided April 24, 1967; a rehearing was denied June 5, 1957. Mr. Justice White delivered the opinion of the Court.

This suit for treble damages and injunction under §§ 4 and 16 of the Clayton Act, 38 Stat. 731, 737, 15 U.S.C. §§ 15 and 26[1] was brought by petitioner, Utah Pie Company, against respondents, Continental Baking Company, Carnation Company and Pet Milk Company. The complaint charged a conspiracy under §§ 1 and 2 of the Sherman Act, 26 Stat. 209, as amended, 15 U.S.C. §§ 1 and 2, and violations by each respondent of § 2(a) of the Clayton Act as amended by the Robinson-Patman Act, 49 Stat. 1526, 15 U.S.C. § 13(a).[2] The jury found for respondents on the conspiracy charge and for petitioner on the price discrimination charge.[3] Judgment was entered for petitioner for damages and attorneys' fees and respondents appealed on several grounds. The Court of Appeals reversed, addressing itself to the single issue of whether the evidence against each of the respondents was sufficient to support a finding of probable

---

* 87 *Supreme Court Reporter* 1327; 386 U.S. 687.

[1] 15 U.S.C. § 15 provides that:
"Any person who shall be injured in his business or property by reason of anything forbidden in the antitrust laws may sue therefor in any district court of the United States in the district in which the defendant resides or is found or has an agent, without respect to the amount in controversy, and shall recover threefold the damages by him sustained, and the cost of suit, including a reasonable attorney's fee."
15 U.S.C. § 26 provides injunctive relief for private parties from violation of the antitrust laws.

[2] The portion of § 2(a) relevant to the issue before the Court provides:
"That it shall be unlawful for any person engaged in commerce, in the course of such commerce, either directly or indirectly, to discriminate in price between different purchasers of commodities of like grade and quality, where either or any of the purchases involved in such discrimination are in commerce * * * where the effect of such discrimination may be substantially to lessen competition or tend to create a monopoly in any line of commerce, or to injure, destroy, or prevent competition with any person who either grants or knowingly receives the benefit of such discrimination, or with customers of either of them . . .

[3] Respondent Continental by counterclaim charged petitioner with violation of § 2(a) in respect to certain sales. On this issue the jury found for Continental, and although petitioner failed to move for a directed verdict on the counterclaim before its submission to the jury, the trial judge granted petitioner's motion for judgment notwithstanding the verdict. The Court of Appeals reversed the judgment notwithstanding the verdict on the counterclaim, and remanded the issue for a new trial. No question concerning the counterclaim is before the Court.

injury to competition within the meaning of § 2(a) and holding that it was not. We reverse.

The product involved is frozen dessert pies—apple, cherry, boysenberry, peach, pumpkin, and mince. The period covered by the suit comprised the years 1958, 1959, and 1960 and the first eight months of 1961. Petitioner is a Utah corporation which for 30 years had been baking pies in its plant in Salt Lake City and selling them in Utah and surrounding States. It entered the frozen pie business in late 1957. It was immediately successful with its new line and built a new plant in Salt Lake City in 1958. The frozen pie market was a rapidly expanding one: 57,060 dozen frozen pies were sold in the Salt Lake City market in 1958, 111,729 dozen in 1959, 184,569 dozen in 1960, and 266,908 dozen in 1961. Utah Pie's share of this market in those years was 66.5%, 34.3%, 45.5%, and 45.3% respectively, its sales volume steadily increasing over the four years. Its financial position also improved. Petitioner is not, however, a large company. At the time of the trial, petitioner operated with only 18 employees, nine of whom were members of the Rigby family, which controlled the business. Its net worth increased from $31,651.98 on October 31, 1957, to $68,802.13 on October 31, 1961. Total sales were $238,000 in the year ending October 31, 1957, $353,000 in 1958, $430,000 in 1959, $504,000 in 1960 and $589,000 in 1961. Its net income or loss for these same years was a loss of $6,461 in 1957, and net income in the remaining years of $7,090, $11,897, $7,636, and $9,216.

Each of the respondents is a large company and each of them is a major factor in the frozen pie market in one or more regions of the country. Each entered the Salt Lake City frozen pie market before petitioner began freezing dessert pies. None of them had a plant in Utah. By the end of the period involved in this suit Pet had plants in Michigan, Pennsylvania, and California; Continental in Virginia, Iowa, and California; and Carnation in California. The Salt Lake City market was supplied by respondents chiefly from their California operations. They sold primarily on a delivered price basis.

The "Utah" label was petitioner's proprietary brand. Beginning in 1960, it also sold pies of like grade and quality under the controlled label "Frost 'N' Flame" to Associated Grocers and in 1961 it began selling to American Food Stores under the "Mayfresh" label. It also, on a seasonal basis, sold pumpkin and mince frozen pies to Safeway under Safeway's own "Bel-air" label.

The major competitive weapon in the Utah market was price. The location of petitioner's plant gave it natural advantages in the Salt Lake City marketing area and it entered the market at a price below the then going prices for respondents' comparable pies. For most of the period involved here its prices were the lowest in the Salt Lake City market. It was, however, challenged by each of the respondents at one time or another and for varying periods. There was ample evidence to show that each of the respondents contributed to what proved to be a deteriorating price structure over the period covered by this suit, and each of the respondents in the course of the ongoing price competition sold frozen pies in the Salt Lake market at prices lower than it sold pies of like grade and quality in other markets considerably closer to its plants. Utah Pie, which entered the market at a price of $4.15 per dozen at the beginning of the relevant period, was selling "Utah" and "Frost 'N' Flame" pies for $2.75 per dozen when the instant suit was filed some 44 months later.⁴ Pet, which was offering pies at $4.92 per dozen in February 1958, was offering "Pet-Ritz" and "Bel-air" pies at $3.56 and $3.46 per dozen respectively in March and April 1961. Carnation's price in early 1958 was $4.82 per dozen but it was selling at $3.46 per dozen at the conclusion of the period, meanwhile having been down as low as $3.30 per dozen. The price range experienced by Continental during the period covered by this suit ran from a 1958 high of over $5 per dozen to a 1961 low of $2.85 per dozen.⁵

We deal first with petitioner's case against the Pet Milk Company. Pet entered the frozen pie business in 1955, acquired plants in Pennsylvania and California and undertook a large advertising campaign to market its "Pet-Ritz"

---

⁴ The prices discussed herein refer to those charged for apple pies. The apple flavor has been used as the standard throughout this case, without objection from the parties, and we adhere to the practice here.

⁵ The Salt Lake City sales volumes and market shares of the parties to this suit as well as of other sellers during the period at issue were as follows:

1958

Company	Volume (in doz.)	Percent of Market
Carnation	5,863	10.3
Continental	754	1.3
Utah Pie	37,969.5	66.5
Pet	9,336.5	16.4
Others	3,137	5.5
Total	57,060	100.0

1959

Company	Volume	Percent
Carnation	9,625	8.6
Continental	3,182	2.9
Utah Pie	38,372	34.3
Pet	39,639	35.5
Others	20,911	18.7
Total	111,729	100.0

1960

Company	Volume	Percent
Carnation	22,371.5	12.1
Continental	3,350	1.8
Utah Pie	83,894	45.5
Pet	51,480	27.9
Others	23,473.5	12.7
Total	184,569	100.0

1961

Company	Volume	Percent
Carnation	20,067	8.8
Continental	18,799.5	8.3
Utah Pie	102,690	45.3
Pet	66,786	29.4
Others	18,565.5	8.2
Total	226,908	100.0

brand of frozen pies. Pet's initial emphasis was on quality, but in the face of competition from regional and local companies and in an expanding market where price proved to be a crucial factor, Pet was forced to take steps to reduce the price of its pies to the ultimate consumer. These developments had consequences in the Salt Lake City market which are the substance of petitioner's case against Pet.

First, Pet successfully concluded an arrangement with Safeway, which is one of the three largest customers for frozen pies in the Salt Lake market, whereby it would sell frozen pies to Safeway under the latter's own "Bel-air" label at a price significantly lower than it was selling its comparable "Pet-Ritz" brand in the same Salt Lake market and elsewhere. The initial price on "Bel-air" pies was slightly lower than Utah's price for its "Utah" brand of pies at the time, and near the end of the period the "Bel-air" price was comparable to the "Utah" price but higher than Utah's "Frost 'N' Flame" brand. Pet's Safeway business amounted to 22.8%, 12.3%, and 6.3% of the entire Salt Lake City market for the years 1959, 1960, and 1961, respectively, and to 64%, 44%, and 22% of Pet's own Salt Lake City sales for those same years.

Second, it introduced a 20-ounce economy pie under the "Swiss Miss" label and began selling the new pie in the Salt Lake market in August 1960 at prices ranging from $3.25 to $3.30 for the remainder of the period. This pie was at times sold at a lower price in the Salt Lake City market than it was sold in other markets.

Third, Pet became more competitive with respect to the prices for its "Pet-Ritz" proprietary label. For 18 of the relevant 44 months its offering price for Pet-Ritz pies was $4 per dozen or lower, and $3.70 or lower for six of these months. According to the Court of Appeals, in seven of the 44 months Pet's prices in Salt Lake were lower than prices charged in the California markets. This was true although selling in Salt Lake involved a 30- to 35-cent freight cost.

The Court of Appeals first concluded that Pet's price differential on sales to Safeway must be put aside in considering injury to competition because in its view of the evidence the differential had been completely cost justified and because Utah would not in any event have been able to enjoy the Safeway custom. Second, it concluded that the remaining discriminations on "Pet-Ritz" and "Swiss Miss" pies were an insufficient predicate on which the jury could have found a reasonably possible injury either to Utah Pie as a competitive force or to competition generally.

We disagree with the Court of Appeals in several respects. First, there was evidence from which the jury could have found considerably more price discrimination by Pet with respect to "Pet-Ritz" and "Swiss Miss" pies than was considered by the Court of Appeals. In addition to the seven months during which Pet's prices in Salt Lake were lower than prices in the California markets, there was evidence from which the jury could reasonably have found that in 10 additional months the Salt Lake City prices for "Pet-Ritz" pies were discriminatory as compared with sales in western markets other than California. Likewise, with respect to "Swiss Miss" pies, there was evidence in the record from which the jury could have found that in five of the 13 months during which the "Swiss Miss" pies were sold prior to the filing of this suit, prices in Salt Lake City were lower than those charged by Pet in either California or some other western market.

Second, with respect to Pet's Safeway business, the burden of proving cost justification was on Pet and, in our view, reasonable men could have found that Pet's lower priced, "Bel-air" sales to Safeway were not cost justified in their entirety. Pet introduced cost data for 1961 indicating a cost saving on the Safeway business greater than the price advantage extended to that customer. These statistics were not particularized for the Salt Lake market, but assuming that they were adequate to justify the 1961 sales, they related to only 24% of the Safeway sales over the relevant period. The evidence concerning the remaining 76% was at best incomplete and inferential. It was insufficient to take the defense of cost justification from the jury, which reasonably could have found a greater incidence of unjustified price discrimination than that allowed by the Court of Appeals' view of the evidence.[6]

With respect to whether Utah would have enjoyed Safeway's business absent the Pet contract with Safeway, it seems clear that whatever the fact is in this regard, it is not determinative of the impact of that contract on competitors other than Utah and on competition generally. There were other companies seeking the Safeway business, including Continental and Carnation, whose pies may have been excluded from the Safeway shelves by what the jury could have found to be discriminatory sales to Safeway. What is more, Pet's evidence that Utah's unwillingness to install quality control equipment prevented Utah from enjoying Safeway's private label business is not the only evidence in the record relevant to that question. There was other evidence to the contrary. The jury would not have been compelled to find that Utah Pie could not have gained more of the Safeway business.

Third, the Court of Appeals almost entirely ignored other evidence which provides material support for the jury's conclusion that Pet's behavior satisfied the statutory test regarding competitive injury. This evidence bore on the issue of Pet's predatory intent to injure Utah Pie. As an initial matter, the jury could have concluded that Pet's discriminatory pricing was aimed at Utah Pie; Pet's own management, as early as 1959, identified Utah Pie as an "unfavorable factor," one which "d[u]g holes in our operation" and posed a constant "check" on Pet's performance in the Salt Lake City market. Moreover, Pet candidly admitted that during the period when it was establishing its relationship with

---

[6] The only evidence cited by the Court of Appeals to justify the remaining 76% of Pet's sales to Safeway was Safeway's established practice of requiring its sellers to cost justify sales that otherwise would be illegally discriminatory. This practice was incorporated in the Pet-Safeway contract. We are unprepared to hold that a contractual obligation to cost justify price differentials is legally dispositive proof that such differentials are in fact so justified. Pet admitted that its cost-justification figures were drawn from past performance, so even crediting the data accompanying the 1960 contract regarding cost differences, Pet's additional evidence would bring under the justification umbrella only the 1959 sales. Thus, at the least, the jury was free to consider the 1960 Safeway sales as inadequately cost justified. Those sales accounted for 12.3% of the entire Salt Lake City market in that year. In the context of this case, the sales to Safeway are particularly relevant since there was evidence that private label sales influenced the general market, in this case depressing overall market prices.

Safeway, it sent into Utah Pie's plant an industrial spy to seek information that would be of use to Pet in convincing Safeway that Utah Pie was not worthy of its custom. Pet denied that it ever in fact used what it had learned against Utah Pie in competing for Safeway's business. The parties, however, are not the ultimate judges of credibility. But even giving Pet's view of the incident a measure of weight does not mean the jury was foreclosed from considering the predatory intent underlying Pet's mode of competition. Finally, Pet does not deny that the evidence showed it suffered substantial losses on its frozen pie sales during the greater part of the time involved in this suit, and there was evidence from which the jury could have concluded that the losses Pet sustained in Salt Lake City were greater than those incurred elsewhere. It would not have been an irrational step if the jury concluded that there was a relationship between price and the losses.

It seems clear to us that the jury heard adequate evidence from which it could have concluded that Pet had engaged in predatory tactics in waging competitive warfare in the Salt Lake City market. Coupled with the incidence of price discrimination attributable to Pet, the evidence as a whole established, rather than negated, the reasonable possibility that Pet's behavior produced a lessening of competition proscribed by the Act.

Petitioner's case against Continental is not complicated. Continental was a substantial factor in the market in 1957. But its sales of frozen 22-ounce dessert pies, sold under the "Morton" brand, amounted to only 1.3% of the market in 1958, 2.9% in 1959, and 1.8% in 1960. Its problems were primarily that of cost and in turn that of price, the controlling factor in the market. In late 1960 it worked out a co-packing arrangement in California by which fruit would be processed directly from the trees into the finished pie without large intermediate packing, storing, and shipping expenses. Having improved its position, it attempted to increase its share of the Salt Lake City market by utilizing a local broker and offering short-term price concessions in varying amounts. Its efforts for seven months were not spectacularly successful. Then in June, 1961, it took the steps which are the heart of petitioner's complaint against it. Effective for the last two weeks of June it offered its 22-ounce frozen apple pies in the Utah area at $2.85 per dozen. It was then selling the same pies at substantially higher prices in other markets. The Salt Lake City price was less than its direct cost plus an allocation for overhead. Utah's going price at the time for its 24-ounce "Frost 'N' Flame" apple pie sold to Associated Grocers was $3.10 per dozen, and for its "Utah" brand $3.40 per dozen. At its new prices, Continental sold pies to American Grocers in Pocatello, Idaho, and to American Food Stores in Ogden, Utah. Safeway, one of the major buyers in Salt Lake City, also purchased 6,250 dozen, its requirements for about five weeks. Another purchaser ordered 1,000 dozen. Utah's response was immediate. It reduced its price on all of its apple pies to $2.75 per dozen. Continental refused Safeway's request to match Utah's price, but renewed its offer at the same prices effective July 31 for another two-week period. Utah filed suit on September 8, 1961. Continental's total sales of frozen pies increased from 3,350 dozen in 1960 to 18,800 dozen in 1961. Its market share increased from 1.8% in 1960 to 8.3% in 1961. The Court of Appeals concluded that Continental's conduct had had only minimal effect, that it had not injured or weakened Utah Pie as a competitor, that it had not substantially lessened competition and that there was no reasonable possibility that it would do so in the future.

We again differ with the Court of Appeals. Its opinion that Utah was not damaged as a competitive force apparently rested on the fact that Utah's sales volume continued to climb in 1961 and on the court's own factual conclusion that Utah was not deprived of any pie business which it otherwise might have had. But this retrospective assessment fails to note that Continental's discriminatory below-cost price caused Utah Pie to reduce its price to $2.75. The jury was entitled to consider the potential impact of Continental's price reduction absent any responsive price cut by Utah Pie. Price was a major factor in the Salt Lake City market. Safeway, which had been buying Utah brand pies, immediately reacted and purchased a five-week supply of frozen pies from Continental, thereby temporarily foreclosing the proprietary brands of Utah and other firms from the Salt Lake City Safeway market. The jury could rationally have concluded that had Utah not lowered its price, Continental, which repeated its offer once, would have continued it, that Safeway would have continued to buy from Continental and that other buyers, large as well as small, would have followed suit. It could also have reasonably concluded that a competitor who is forced to reduce his price to a new all-time low in a market of declining prices will in time feel the financial pinch and will be a less effective competitive force.

Even if the impact on Utah Pie as a competitor was negligible, there remain the consequences to others in the market who had to compete not only with Continental's 22-ounce pie at $2.85 but with Utah's even lower price of $2.75 per dozen for both its proprietary and controlled labels. Petitioner and respondents were not the only sellers in the Salt Lake City market, although they did account for 91.8% of the sales in 1961. The evidence was that there were nine other sellers in 1960 who sold 23,473 dozen pies, 12.7% of the total market. In 1961 there were eight other sellers who sold less than the year before— 18,565 dozen or 8.2% of the total—although the total market had expanded from 184,569 dozen to 226,908 dozen. We think there was sufficient evidence from which the jury could find a violation of § 2(a) by Continental.

The Carnation Company entered the frozen dessert pie business in 1955 through the acquisition of "Mrs. Lee's Pies" which was then engaged in manufacturing and selling frozen pies in Utah and elsewhere under the "Simple Simon" label. Carnation also quickly found the market extremely sensitive to price. Carnation decided, however, not to enter an economy product in the market, and during the period covered by this suit it offered only its quality "Simple Simon" brand. Its primary method of meeting competition in its markets was to offer a variety of discounts and other reductions, and the technique was not unsuccessful. In 1958, for example, Carnation enjoyed 10.3% of the Salt Lake City market, and although its volume of pies sold in that market increased substantially in the next year, its percentage of the market temporarily slipped to 8.6%. However, 1960 was a turnaround year for Carnation in the Salt Lake City market; it more than doubled its volume of sales over the preceding year and thereby gained 12.1% of the market. And while the price structure in the market deteriorated rapidly in 1961 Carnation's position remained important.

We need not dwell long upon the case against Carnation, which in some respects is similar to that against Continental and in others more nearly resembles the case against Pet. After Carnation's temporary setback in 1959 it instituted a new pricing policy to regain business in the Salt Lake City market. The new policy involved a slash in price of 60¢ per dozen pies, which brought Carnation's price to a level admittedly well below its costs, and well below the other prices prevailing in the market. The impact of the move was felt immediately, and the two other major sellers in the market reduced their prices. Carnation's banner year, 1960, in the end involved eight months during which the prices in Salt Lake City were lower than prices charged in other markets. The trend continued during the eight months in 1961 that preceded the filing of the complaint in this case. In each of those months the Salt Lake City prices charged by Carnation were well below prices charged in other markets, and in all but August 1961 the Salt Lake City delivered price was 20 to 50¢ lower than the prices charged in distant San Francisco. The Court of Appeals held that only the early 1960 prices could be found to have been below cost. That holding, however, simply overlooks evidence from which the jury could have concluded that throughout 1961 Carnation maintained a below-cost price structure and that Carnation's discriminatory pricing, no less than that of Pet and Continental, had an important effect on the Salt Lake City market. We cannot say that the evidence precluded the jury from finding it reasonably possible that Carnation's conduct would injure competition.

Section 2(a) does not forbid price competition which will probably injure or lessen competition by eliminating competitors, discouraging entry into the market or enhancing the market shares of the dominant sellers. But Congress has established some ground rules for the game. Sellers may not sell like goods to different purchasers at different prices if the result may be to injure competition in either the sellers' or the buyers' market unless such discriminations are justified as permitted by the Act. This case concerns the sellers' market. In this context, the Court of Appeals placed heavy emphasis on the fact that Utah Pie constantly increased its sales volume and continued to make a profit. But we disagree with its apparent view that there is no reasonably possible injury to competition as long as the volume of sales in a particular market is expanding and at least some of the competitors in the market continue to operate at a profit. Nor do we think that the Act only comes into play to regulate the conduct of price discriminators when their discriminatory prices consistently undercut other competitors. It is true that many of the primary line cases that have reached the courts have involved blatant predatory price discriminations employed with the hope of immediate destruction of a particular competitor. On the question of injury to competition such cases present courts with no difficulty, for such pricing is clearly within the heart of the proscription of the Act. Courts and commentators alike have noted that the existence of predatory intent might bear on the likelihood of injury to competition. In this case there was some evidence of predatory intent with respect to each of these respondents. There was also other evidence upon which the jury could rationally find the requisite injury to competition. The frozen pie market in Salt Lake City was highly competitive. At times Utah Pie was a leader in moving the general level of prices down, and at other times each of the respondents also bore responsibility for the downward pressure on the price structure. We believe that the Act reaches price discrimination that erodes competition as much as it does price discrimination that is intended to have immediate destructive impact. In this case, the evidence shows a drastically declining price structure which the jury could rationally attribute to continued or sporadic price discrimination. The jury was entitled to conclude that "the effect of such discrimination," by each of these respondents, "may be substantially to lessen competition . . . or to injure, destroy, or prevent competition with any person who either grants or knowingly receives the benefit of such discrimination. . . ." The statutory test is one that necessarily looks forward on the basis of proven conduct in the past. Proper application of that standard here requires reversal of the judgment of the Court of Appeals.

Since the Court of Appeals held that petitioner had failed to make a prima facie case against each of the respondents, it expressly declined to pass on other grounds for reversal presented by the respondents. 349 F.2d 122, 126. Without intimating any views on the other grounds presented to the Court of Appeals, we reverse its judgment and remand the case to that court for further proceedings. It is so ordered. Reversed and remanded.

The Chief Justice took no part in the decision of this case. Mr. Justice Stewart and Mr. Justice Harlan joined in dissenting:

I would affirm the judgment, agreeing substantially with the reasoning of the Court of Appeals as expressed in the thorough and conscientious opinion of Judge Phillips.

There is only one issue in this case in its present posture: Whether the respondents engaged in price discrimination "where the effect of such discrimination may be substantially to lessen competition or tend to create a monopoly in any line of commerce, or to injure, destroy, or prevent competition with any person who either grants or knowingly receives the benefit of such discrimination. . . ."[1] Phrased more simply, did the respondents' actions have the anticompetitive effect required by the statute as an element of a cause of action?

The Court's own description of the Salt Lake City frozen pie market from 1958 through 1961, shows that the answer to that question must be no. In 1958 Utah Pie had a quasi-monopolistic 66.5% of the market. In 1961—after the alleged predations of the respondents—Utah Pie still had a commanding 45.3%, Pet had 29.4%, and the remainder of the market was divided almost equally between Continental, Carnation, and other, small local bakers. Unless we disregard the lessons so laboriously learned in scores of Sherman and Clayton Act cases, the 1961 situation has to be considered more competitive than that of 1958. Thus, if we assume that the price discrimination proven against the respondents had any effect on competition, that effect must have been beneficial.

That the Court has fallen into the error of reading the Robinson-Patman Act as protecting competitors, instead of competition, can be seen from its unsuccessful attempt to distinguish cases relied upon by the respondents. Those

---

[1] Section 2(a) of the Clayton Act as amended by the Robinson-Patman Act, 15 U.S.C. § 13(a).

cases are said to be inapposite because they involved "no general decline in price structure," and no "lasting impact upon prices." But lower prices are the hallmark of intensified competition.

The Court of Appeals squarely identified the fallacy which the Court today embraces:

". . . a contention that Utah Pie was entitled to hold the extraordinary market share percentage of 66.5, attained in 1958, falls of its own dead weight. To approve such a contention would be to hold that Utah Pie was entitled to maintain a position which approached, if it did not in/fact amount to a monopoly, and could not exist in the face of proper and healthy competition."

I cannot hold that Utah Pie's monopolistic position was protected by the federal antitrust laws from effective price competition, and I therefore respectfully dissent.

1. *The ruling in the Utah Pie Case has been attacked as reducing competition rather than protecting it. What are your views?*
2. *Does the fact that the Utah Pie Company is a small, independent firm influence your opinion of the case? Should it influence your opinion?*
3. *How would you describe the pricing practices of the various competitors in this case? Did they resort to price discrimination? Were their practices illegal in your opinion? Should they be considered illegal?*

PART FIVE / Capital budgeting and uncertainty

9 / Capital budgeting

Capital budgeting, one of the main topics of managerial economics, is also known as investment decision making, equipment replacement analysis, or the analysis of capital expenditures. The problem in capital budgeting is one of choosing among investment alternatives available to the firm —with acceptance of the most profitable investments and rejection of those with low or negative profitability.

Capital budgeting requires an application of the basic concepts introduced in Chapter 2. It requires an estimation of the incremental profits which will arise from each investment alternative; the correct determination of such profits requires the use of incremental reasoning, with special care in the treatment of overhead costs. The analysis must take into account the full long-run impact of each alternative—not merely the impact on first-year profits. The future profits expected from each investment must be discounted according to the time period that will elapse before receipt of those profits. And the results of each investment must be compared with those of alternatives—the opportunity cost of capital must be taken into account.

Capital budgeting quite clearly involves the equimarginal principle. The objective is to assure the most profitable use of funds, which means that funds must not be applied where the marginal returns are less than in other uses.[1] All capital budgeting systems include some kind of measuring stick, or cut-off rate which, at least roughly, prevents the use of funds in projects with low profitability.

---

[1] When profit maximization is not the sole objective, there must be ways of taking the other goals into account, either as a part of the formal analysis or as an adjustment before the final decisions are made.

1. STEPS IN CAPITAL BUDGETING

The tendency in the literature of capital budgeting is to stress the quantifiable part of the decision-making process: the measurement of investment worth. Capital budgeting has become one of the mathematical branches of economics—a branch characterized by elegant mathematical models which give the impression of precision. There is, however, much more to actual capital budgeting than the mere jamming of numbers into formulas; for one thing one might wish to know where the numbers came from in the first place; he might then wish to know whether the formulas at hand are relevant or useful.

A complete study of capital budgeting must recognize at least six steps in investment decision making. These steps are:

1. The search for investment opportunities.

2. A forecast of the changes in cash flows that will result from each investment.

3. A method of computing the cost of capital which will take into account the availability of funds.

4. A method of converting the changes in future cash flows into a common unit that will reflect the discounting principle.

5. The selection of the most profitable investments.

6. A postaudit of the results of previous investments.

This section is devoted to steps number 1 and 2, which normally receive little attention in the literature of capital budgeting. Later sections will take up the other steps in the capital budgeting process.

The search for investment opportunities

Before any computations are possible, management must first discover the investment opportunities that are to be compared. Some opportunities are obvious and require no search effort—the need to replace a worn-out machine or to expand the capacity of an over-worked department. But one of the greatest errors that can be made is to restrict attention to such obvious alternatives. An accumulation of a large pool of opportunities is more likely to contain highly profitable alternatives. It is also more likely to raise the "aspiration levels" of management, helping to prevent complacency with an ordinary selection of alternatives.

The organizational structure should be one which minimizes obstacles to the search for investment opportunities and which stimulates the discovery of such alternatives. The managers of small firms may often find it wise to delegate the routine detail of day-to-day management which distracts them from the more important tasks of discovery. Larger firms often institute suggestion systems, bonuses for cost-saving innovations, and "brain storming" sessions to encourage the flow of investment ideas.

Research departments, marketing researchers, product development departments, purchasers, and other specialized officials and divisions have responsibilities for initiating and fostering investment proposals.

Forecasting changes in cash flows

The forecast of the impact of each investment requires a second type of search activity: the search for information. In some cases the accounting system may provide the data that are required. But in view of the fact that investments often involve a rearrangement of inputs, it is unlikely that accounting based on historical data can automatically supply complete information on the impact of a new investment. Engineering data may provide insight into physical capacities of new equipment, but it is necessary to convert these physical attributes into dollars and cents. *Ad hoc* or nonprogrammed economic analysis would seem to be required for the measurement of the full impact of the investment on costs and revenues.

It is useful to distinguish between two types of investments. One type consists of cost-reduction investments. An example would be the replacement of one machine by another more productive machine. The "cash flow" with which we are concerned on this type of investment consists of the expenses which would have been paid without the investment but which are escaped as a result of the change. The other type consists of revenue-increasing investments, such as the expansion of plant facilities or additional advertising expenditures. The "cash flows" in this case may consist of both changes in revenues and changes in costs. Many investments may combine elements of cost reduction and revenue increase.

Perhaps it is no longer necessary to repeat that the relevant revenues and costs in the study of investment proposals are the incremental revenues and costs. We are interested in the changes in profits that new investments will bring about. The fact that some existing procedures ignore such incremental reasoning, and make use of arbitrary overhead allocations and historical relationships, suggests that some stress on the incremental principle is not entirely misplaced. It is foolish to apply an extreme degree of mathematical precision to the wrong information; the failure to apply sound incremental reasoning will result in the wrong information.

It is essential to distinguish clearly between two kinds of cash flow analysis. The usual cash forecasting or cash budgeting—also known as source and application of funds analysis—is concerned with the cash position of the entire firm or activity and is not restricted to a particular investment decision. This is a major topic in courses in finance, which are of necessity faced with forecasting the cash needs arising from the whole complex of factors affecting the firm. The cash flows which are estimated in capital budgeting are much narrower. They are the increases and decreases in cash inflows and cash outflows which result from individual investment decisions.

Obviously considerable uncertainty surrounds most forecasts of the profit impact of investment. Tastes may change and demands shift before the plant is built or the equipment installed. Costs may rise in unexpected ways. One of the most perplexing of the uncertainties is that concerning obsolescence—the rate at which the new investment will be replaced by even superior investments in the future. No one wants to invest in a new jet airplane today, if a less costly and safer model will be available tomorrow—but the trouble is that management usually does not know when the better model will be available and how superior it will be. It can deal only with probabilities.

In conclusion, the forecast of the results of investments is a much more difficult and conjectural part of the decision-making process than is often recognized. It is also a crucial step in the process, for no refinements in the later steps can overcome errors in these forecasts.

A numerical illustration

The points just made about cash flows may not become completely clear until they are illustrated by a numerical example. Suppose that we are considering a labor-saving machine. Its purchase price is $23,000. It costs $2,000 to install the machine. Thus the total investment is $25,000. Suppose that the total annual revenue is expected to increase by $1,500 because the machine will provide a higher quality product and more dependable production. The machine is expected to reduce direct labor costs by $5,500 per year, but maintenance labor costs will increase by $500 per year. Normally the firm allocates indirect labor costs at the rate of 30 percent of direct labor costs and overhead at the rate of 110 percent of direct labor. But it is clear that neither the indirect labor costs nor the overhead will be affected by the decision. Straight-line depreciation on the machine is estimated at $5,000 per year, but depreciation is not a cash expense and can be ignored in the cash flow estimates.

Tax considerations complicate the cash flow analysis. Assume that taxes are at the rate of 50 percent of profits. The new machine will increase profits and will thus increase taxes; the incremental taxes must be deducted in obtaining the net incremental cash flow. Depreciation *is* deductible as an expense for tax purposes. Thus the incremental tax will be considerably less than half of the incremental cash flow.

The machine is expected to last seven years and in this simplified illustration will have no salvage value at the end of this time. The cash flows for each of the seven years would be as shown in Table 9–1.

The results are a net posttax cash inflow of $5,750 in each of the first five years and $3,250 in the sixth and seventh years. The total cash inflow over time is estimated at $35,250, which is more than the initial $25,000 investment. But those who remember the discussion of the discounting concept in Chapter 2 will realize that these two figures cannot be com-

TABLE 9-1

CASH FLOWS: HYPOTHETICAL MACHINE

Year 1:

Incremental revenue	$1,500
Net labor savings	5,000
Pretax net cash inflow	$6,500
Less: Taxes at 50% ($6,500–$5,000)	750
Posttax cash inflow	$5,750

Years 2, 3, 4, and 5:

Same as Year 1

Year 6:

Incremental revenue	$1,500
Net labor savings	5,000
Pretax net cash inflow	$6,500
Less: Taxes at 50%	3,250
Posttax cash inflow	$3,250

Year 7:
Same as Year 6

pared as they now stand, for they ignore the time value of money. A major problem in capital budgeting is the treatment of this problem.

Empirical studies and illustrations

The chief empirical question raised so far in this chapter is the extent of the search activity in actual investment decision making. Do firms go to a great deal of trouble in searching for investment opportunities? Do they search carefully for the right kinds of information? No systematic study of these issues is available, but we shall cite some examples indicating a wide variety of behavior.

Large firms usually have a great number of channels through which investment proposals may flow. Line administrators and foremen consider investment proposals part of their responsibility. Specialized research and development departments, engineering departments, methods study departments and similar units are in a continual process of developing new proposals. Suggestion systems provide a means through which the whole work force may contribute to the backlog of investment opportunities. It would appear, therefore, that the problem in large firms is not the search for opportunities but instead the screening of proposals and the rationing of capital. Yet casual observation suggests that some large firms are less successful than others in the same industry in discovering the investments which contribute to profitable growth or even to survival.

It is obvious that the suggestion systems of some firms are much more effective than others in producing sound proposals. Few firms can match the record of the Lincoln Electric Company of Cleveland, Ohio, in which motivation for suggestions is high.[2] The Lincoln Electric Company pays high rewards for cost-saving suggestions. But the success of its system appears to result also from the high level of participation of employees in decision making, with a resultant strong interest in the company's progress. The company's management emphasizes the recognition of the individual employee's contribution to the total results, and to the sharing of company profits. The Lincoln Electric case suggests that the discovery of investment opportunities is closely entwined with the whole system of management and is tied in with questions of morale and motivation.

The subject of research and development is too large to be treated adequately here. Companies with research departments have to face up to problems of budgeting for research itself, in addition to questions of the amount of autonomy to be allowed research workers, and methods of motivating high-level research. Such companies must also make decisions about the extent of fundamental research as opposed to applied research.

Perhaps it would be more profitable to concentrate on some of the observable deficiencies in capital budgeting practice. A study of small business suggests that many small firms neglect the discovery of investment opportunities. The owner-managers of small firms often appear to be so involved in day-to-day affairs, such as selling or ordering replacements for inventory or handling routine telephone calls, that they have little time to think about the larger decisions.[3] When routine activities compete with the nonprogrammed, imaginative search for investments, the routine takes priority—a sort of "Gresham's Law" of management that most of us observe in our own lives. Some managers of small firms make a conscious effort to divest themselves of these routines, to release time for long-run planning. Imitation of this practice would undoubtedly be profitable to other firms.

Similarly, managers vary in the intensity of their search for information about the investment alternatives which do come to their attention. Some managers make a thorough study of the probable outcome of a project, investigating the outcomes of similar investments in other firms, gathering data from every possible source, internal or external, and projecting the probable outcome into the future. But other managers are content with the vague impressions or hunches.

Some serious errors in the organization of information appear in the practices of many firms. The treatment of overhead costs is a common example of the erroneous treatment of information. Suppose that a firm introduces a labor-saving machine. Suppose, also, that this firm custom-

[2] See James F. Lincoln, *Incentive Management* (Cleveland, Ohio: Lincoln Electric Company, 1951).

[3] Martin B. Solomon, Jr., *Investment Decisions in Small Business: Theory and Practice* (Lexington: University of Kentucky Press, 1963).

arily allocates overhead at 90 percent of direct labor costs. Often the analysis of such a proposal will assume implicitly that for every dollar of saving in direct labor costs there will be an added 90 cents of overhead saving. But such an overhead saving is unlikely. Similarly, many systems of analyzing proposals for expansion permit no distinction between expansions that make use of idle facilities and those that require added floor space. Some systems try to include estimates of the added working capital required by an expansion; other systems neglect expected changes in working capital. Such major deficiencies in the collection and organization of information will inevitably result in a misallocation of resources within the firm.

2. "THEORETICALLY CORRECT" METHODS OF EVALUATING INVESTMENTS

The fourth step in the capital budgeting process is the measurement of "investment worth."[4] It requires the determination of a common denominator into which all investment impacts can be converted. Without such a common denominator it is impossible to compare and rank investment opportunities. Take two hypothetical examples: (1) an investment which costs $1,000 and which will return $500 each year for three successive years and (2) an investment which costs $7,500 and which will return $5,000 the first year, $2,000 the second, $500 the third, and $100 the fourth. Which is more profitable? Since the future profit flows occur at different points in time, no direct comparison of the two examples is possible; it is necessary to convert the flows into units that are comparable.

Another element is also required in the evaluation of investment alternatives: the cost of capital. Only if the two investments provide profits that exceed the cost of capital can they be deemed desirable.

Two measurements are known as the "theoretically correct" criteria for measuring investment worth. They are: (1) the present value of the investment and (2) the discounted rate of return of the investment, also known as the internal rate of return. Both measurements are based firmly on the discounting principle.

Present value

The simplest formula for computing the present value is:

$$V = \frac{R_1}{1+i} + \frac{R_2}{(1+i)^2} + \cdots + \frac{R_n}{(1+i)^n} + \frac{S}{(1+i)^n} \qquad (9\text{-}1)$$

[4] A full discussion of the computation of the cost of capital, the third step, is postponed until a later point in the chapter.

in which

$$V = \text{present value}$$
$$i = \text{the interest rate or cost of capital}$$
$$R_1 R_2, \ldots, R_n = \text{cash inflow after taxes in years 1, 2, \ldots, } n$$
$$n = \text{life of the asset}$$
$$S = \text{salvage value of the asset in year } n.$$

Some readers may be familiar with such computations of present value as "capitalization." The result is a "capitalized present value" measured in current dollars.

The investment decision requires a comparison of V, the present value, with C, the supply price or cost of the asset. If the present value exceeds the supply price, that is if

$$V > C \tag{9–2}$$

the investment is worthwhile.

Note that the unknown in this approach is V, the present value. All the other information must be given before a computation of V is possible.

Use of the discount tables

The computations in a formula like

$$V = \frac{R_1}{1 + i} + \frac{R_2}{(1 + i)^2} + \cdots + \frac{R_n}{(1 + i)^n} + \frac{S_n}{(1 + i)^n}$$

are cumbersome. In the illustration given in Table 9–1 these would look as follows, assuming a 15 percent cost of capital.

$$V = \frac{\$5,750}{1.15} + \frac{\$5,750}{(1.15)^2} + \frac{\$5,750}{(1.15)^3} + \frac{\$5,750}{(1.15)^4}$$
$$+ \frac{\$5,750}{(1.15)^5} + \frac{\$3,250}{(1.15)^6} + \frac{\$3,250}{(1.15)^7}$$

The arithmetic involved in this example is simple in principle but time-consuming. The arithmetic in a more realistic example would be even more involved.

Fortunately the availability of discount tables (present value tables) simplifies the computations. Discounting is such a widespread phenomenon, in banks and other lending institutions as well as in capital budgeting, that such tables are readily available. A set of discount tables appears at the back of this book, in Appendix A.

Let us proceed year by year. The cash inflow in Year 1 of $5,750 can be discounted by multiplying the figure appearing in the next column. This figure is 0.86957, so let us say 0.87. The result is $5,002.50. The discounted cash inflow for Year 2 is obtained from the 15 percent column opposite an N of 2. It is

$$\$5,750 \times 0.76 = \$4,460.00$$

The results for all seven years are summarized in Table 9–2.

TABLE 9–2

DISCOUNTED CASH FLOWS: HYPOTHETICAL EXAMPLE

Year 1	$5,750 × 0.87 =	$ 5,002.50
Year 2	5,750 × 0.76 =	4,460.00
Year 3	5,750 × 0.66 =	3,795.00
Year 4	5,750 × 0.57 =	3,277.50
Year 5	5,750 × 0.50 =	2,875.00
Year 6	3,250 × 0.43 =	1,397.50
Year 7	3,250 × 0.38 =	1,235.00
Total Present Value		$22,042.50

Note that the present value is $22,042.50, much less than the total undiscounted cash inflow of $35,250 obtained earlier. It now appears that the investment is undesirable, unless we consider the discount rate of 15 percent to be too high.

It should also be noted that the arithmetic can be simplified even more by using discount tables which cumulate the results over a period of years. These tables are known as annuity tables. In the same example of the labor-saving machine, the estimated net cash inflow is the same for the first five years. The table in Appendix A shows that a cash inflow of one dollar for each of five years has a present value of $3.35 if the discount rate is 15 percent. Note that the figure 3.35 is the sum of the first five present value multipliers in the previous computation.

$$3.35 = 0.87 + 0.76 + 0.66 + 0.57 + 0.50$$
$$\text{(except for rounding)}$$

Therefore the computation in Table 9–2 can be simplified as shown in Table 9–3.

TABLE 9–3

DISCOUNTED CASH FLOWS: HYPOTHETICAL EXAMPLE

Years 1–5	$5,750 × 3.35 =	$19,262.50
Year 6	3,250 × 0.43 =	1,397.50
Year 7	3,250 × 0.38 =	1,235.00
Total Present Value		$21,895.00

The discrepancy between Tables 9–2 and 9–3 is a result of rounding.

The discounted rate of return

The definition of the discounted rate of return is cumbersome. It is the rate of discount which when applied to the future cash flows will equate their sum to the supply price of the asset. The formula is probably easier to follow than is the verbal definition.

It is

$$C = \frac{R_1}{1+r} + \frac{R_2}{(1+r)^2} + \cdots + \frac{R_n}{(1+r)^n} + \frac{S}{(1+r)^n} \qquad (9\text{-}3)$$

in which r is the discounted rate of return (the marginal efficiency of capital or internal rate of return).

Note that the one unknown in this formula is r, the discounted rate of return. It is necessary to know the R's, the future cash inflows; the C, the supply price of the asset; and the S, the salvage value, before it is possible to solve for r.

After the computation of r, it is necessary to compare the result with i, the cost of capital. If

$$r > i$$

the investment is desirable, since its discounted return exceeds the opportunity cost of capital.

In general, one would expect that when $V > C$ it will also be true that $r > i$. And when $V < C$ it follows that $r < i$. Thus it would appear that the two methods give exactly the same result. For most practical purposes this is true, but unfortunately the two methods do not always *rank* investments in the same order.

Use of the discount tables to find the discounted rate of return

The equation for the discounted rate of return can be applied to our example of the labor-saving machine. The equation would appear as follows:

$$\$25{,}000 = \frac{\$5{,}750}{1+r} + \frac{\$5{,}750}{(1+r)^2} + \frac{\$5{,}750}{(1+r)^3} + \frac{\$5{,}750}{(1+r)^4}$$

$$+ \frac{\$5{,}750}{(1+r)^5} + \frac{\$3{,}250}{(1+r)^6} + \frac{\$3{,}250}{(1+r)^7}$$

There is only one unknown in this equation, as there was in the present value equation. As stated before the unknown is the internal rate of return, r, and not the present value, v. Obviously an algebraic solution of this equation would be difficult, since the r's will be raised to the seventh, sixth, fifth, fourth, third, second, and first powers. The usual procedure is to find an approximate solution by trial and error. Even an electronic computer would reach the solution by the process of successive approximation.

We already know that the discounted rate of return must be below 15 percent, since we have already found that the 15 percent rate produces a present value less than the original investment cost. By inspection, we know that the present value at 15 percent is only about $3,000 less than the investment cost. This suggests that we try a somewhat lower discount rate, let us say 14 percent. The computation is shown in Table 9–4.

TABLE 9–4
TRIAL OF 14% DISCOUNT RATE: HYPOTHETICAL EXAMPLE

Years 1–5	$5,750 × 3.43 =	$19,722.50
Year 6	3,250 × 0.46 =	1,495.00
Year 7	3,250 × 0.40 =	1,300.00
Total		$22,517.50

The reduction from the discount rate of 15 percent to 14 percent raised the result by only $500 approximately. This suggests that we should make a larger jump this time, let us say down to 10 percent. This rate is tried out in Table 9–5.

TABLE 9–5
TRIAL OF 10% DISCOUNT RATE: HYPOTHETICAL EXAMPLE

Years 1–5	$5,750 × 3.79 =	$21,792.50
Year 6	3,250 × 0.56 =	1,820.00
Year 7	3,250 × 0.51 =	1,657.50
Total		$25,270.00

The result is very close to the investment cost of $25,000. We can conclude that the discounted rate of return is close to 10 percent. Whether this rate is sufficient depends on the cost of capital—the opportunity cost. If 10 percent is better than could be expected on alternative investments, the investment is a sound one.

Comparison of present value and discounted rate of return

As already stated, we normally expect the present value and discounted rate of return to produce the same results on acceptance or rejection of projects. But exceptions are possible; such exceptions have received considerable attention in the literature.[5] Take, for example, the following estimated net cash inflows from two proposals.

---

[5] For example, in Ezra Solomon, *The Theory of Financial Management* (New York: Columbia University Press, 1963), pp. 134–35.

Year	Proposal A	Proposal B
1	$100,000	$ 0
2	100,000	50,000
3	100,000	300,000

Suppose that each proposal requires an investment of $198,000. Suppose also that the cutoff rate of return is 10 percent. The present value of Proposal A is approximately $248,680. The present value of Proposal B is $266,716. By the present value criterion, Proposal B is superior. But the discounted rate of return on Proposal A is 24 percent, while that on Proposal B is 22 percent. This kind of possibility seems to fascinate the specialists, but it should be clear that the cash flows on Proposal B had to be made rather unusual to produce this result. Even so the degree of error is small, for the choice between Proposal A and Proposal B is a close one. The profits of the company will not be affected markedly by selecting one rather than the other. The real problem in capital budgeting is to avoid selecting, let us say, seven percent proposals at the expense of 15 percent ones; it takes a great deal of manipulation of numbers to find an illustration in which the present value method would select the first at the expense of the second.

The reason that the two methods may produce a different ranking of projects is that they implicitly carry different assumptions about the alternative rates of return available. The present value method in the above illustration assumes that the reinvestment rate, or opportunity cost, is 10 percent. But the discounted return method implicitly assumes that the earnings each period can be reinvested at 24 percent on Proposal A or 22 percent on Proposal B.

If the cut-off rate is a fairly accurate measure of opportunity costs—if it reflects the approximate rate of return on alternative investments, the present value would appear to be the correct criterion for investment decisions. The general opinion among specialists on the subject is that the present value approach is superior for ranking projects.

Profitability index

It should be clear that a comparison of present values on different projects cannot be based on the dollar amount of present value alone. If two projects require the same amount of investment, as in the preceding illustration of Proposals A and B each costing $198,000, the problem is easy. But if one project costs $10,000 and has a present value of $20,000, it is superior to another project with a very large present value of $300,000 but costing $250,000. Clearly it is necessary to compute an index reflecting the ratio between present value to investment cost. The formula for such an index is

$$PI = \frac{V}{C}$$

in which *PI* represents the profitability index, *V* is the present value, and *C* is the cost of the investment. The indexes for the two examples just given would be

$$PI_1 = \frac{\$20,000}{\$10,000} = 2$$

$$PI_2 = \frac{\$300,000}{\$250,000} = 1.2$$

Up to now, we have assumed that the investment cost is concentrated in one period at the beginning. In practice, the investment cost may be spread over several periods and in complicated cases may fall and then rise again when some new component is required or old component must be replaced. In such cases the profitability index compares the present value of the outflows.[6]

$$PI = \frac{\text{Present value of cash inflows}}{\text{Present value of cash outflows}}$$

Economic life of an investment[7]

Up to now it has been assumed that the economic life of the investment, *n*, is given. At first it might appear that the expected life of the asset is a technological issue and a matter of engineering information. Further thought on the matter should make it clear that the optimum life is an economic question rather than a strictly technological one.

The principle governing the economic life of an asset is concerned with two sacrifices resulting from retaining the asset: the sacrifice of the interest on the funds tied up in the asset—funds which could be recovered by its sale—and the sacrifice due to the loss in the market value of the asset as it is retained for longer periods of time. The first sacrifice is the opportunity cost of the funds tied up in the asset; the second is the "economic" depreciation (not the accounting depreciation).

The principle to be followed is to retain the asset as long as its cash inflow (excess of revenues over costs) exceeds the sum of the two sacrifices just enumerated. A mathematical formulation of this principle is convenient, appearing as an inequation

---

[6] See James C. Van Horne, *Financial Management and Policy* (Englewood Cliffs, N.J.: Prentice-Hall, 1968), chap. 3, for a discussion of this and related issues.

[7] If the reader wishes to avoid some of the mathematical refinements in capital budgeting, he may skip the rest of this section without loss of continuity. He probably will wish to read the material on empirical studies which comes at the end of the section.

$$R(t) > iS(t) + S'(t) \qquad (9\text{--}4)$$

in which $S(t)$ is the market value of the asset in period t and $S'(t)$ is the loss in that market value in the period t. The market value is a function of time. The rule can be expressed in terms of an equality rather than an inequality. What is needed is to determine the time, n, when

$$R(n) = iS(n) + S'(n) \qquad (9\text{--}5)$$

at which time the asset should be sold.

If the asset has no market or salvage value, it should be retained as long as $R(t)$ is positive. This follows from the fact that the asset is still making a contribution to profit without any sacrifices or opportunity costs.

The formulas presented in this section have two uses. If an asset is presently in use, they indicate whether it should be retained. If, instead, the asset is a new one under consideration, the formulas provide an estimate of the length of life that should be used in the present value or discounted rate of return formulas.

Several refinements

Unfortunately, the matter of determining the theoretically correct method of evaluating investments is not quite so simple as suggested so far. There seems to be almost no end to how far refinement of the present value and discounted rate of return formulas may be carried. Several of the major refinements are discussed here.

Conversion from a discrete to a continuous formulation. The formulas (9–1) and (9–3) are discrete in character. Implicitly they assume that the entire cash flows (R_1, R_2, etc.) come at the end of particular periods—at the end of the first period, the second period, or the nth period. Obviously in actual practice such an assumption is unrealistic, for the revenues and costs are spread over time rather than being concentrated at the end of periods.

Calculus is necessary to convert from the discrete to a continuous formulation of the problem. The formula for the present value becomes

$$V = \int_o^t R(t)e^{-it}\, dt + Se^{-in} \qquad (9\text{--}6)$$

in which $R(t)$ now represents a continuous equation for the cash inflow resulting from the proposal, t represents time, n represents the time period when the asset is sold, e is 2.71828 (the base of natural logarithms), and i is the cost of capital.

Several comments on this equation may be helpful. The effect of integrating the function in $R(t)$ is to sum up the discounted cash flows over the life of the asset. Those familiar with calculus are aware of this summation feature of integration. The effects of multiplying the continuous function by e^{-it} or the salvage value by e^{-in} is to discount the future cash flows according to the cost of capital. In other words, multiplying by e^{-i5} has approximately the same discounting effect as dividing by $(1 + i)^5$.

Normally the error in applying the discrete formula rather than the continuous one is small. Mathematically the continuous formula is less cumbersome, but its interpretation does require at least an elementary understanding of calculus.

"Planning horizon" and the "chain of machines" formula. The formulas presented so far focus attention on a single life of an investment. This way of looking at the problem oversimplifies it in a respect that may result in an important error. If one project lasts for 10 years but a second lasts 1 year before it must be replaced, the computation of the present value based on one cycle of each no longer suffices. In principle, the firm should use a "chain of machines" formulation on each of the investment opportunities, projecting revenues and costs to infinite time or, at least, to the firm's "planning horizon"—the point beyond which it does not look at the outcome of any of its prospective investments.

The formula that would apply for an infinite chain of machines (applicable when the planning horizon extends indefinitely into the future) is

$$V_E = \left[\frac{R_1}{1+i} + \frac{R_2}{(1+i)^2} + \cdots + \frac{R_n + S}{(1+i)^n} - C \right]$$

$$\left[1 + \frac{1}{(1+i)^n} + \frac{1}{(1+i)^{2n}} + \cdots \right] \quad (9\text{-}7)$$

in which V_E is the excess present value over the supply price of the asset. Note that the total inside the first bracket will give the difference between V, the present value of one life of the machine, and the supply price. The multiplication by the terms in the second bracket totals up the discounted excess of present value over cost for the first cycle of the machine, the second cycle, and so on.

Since the second bracket is a geometric progression, the mathematically inclined reader will not be surprised to find that the formula simplifies into the following form:

$$V_E = \left[\frac{R_1}{1+i} + \frac{R_2}{(1+i)^2} + \cdots + \frac{R_n + S}{(1+i)^n} - C \right] \left[\frac{(1+i)^n}{(1+i)^n - 1} \right] \quad (9\text{-}8)$$

In practice, most firms overlook this refinement, being content to compare the first cycle of each investment. Yet in some cases the refinement may be important. Take the case of a garden nursery considering alternative uses of an acre of land. The nursery wishes to maximize the present value of the uses of that land. If it plants trees which take 15 years to mature, the firm will receive revenues only once in the 15 years. If it plants fast-growing flowering shrubs it may expect revenues every two years. Obviously it would be erroneous to compare the present value expected from the 15-year trees with the present value of only one round of two-year shrubs, for the land will be free for a replanting of shrubs in the third, the fifth, the seventh, and so on, years. Without projecting the full sequence of the "chain of flowering shrubs" no accurate comparisons are possible. It is necessary to project the revenues and costs on both plantings to the full planning horizon.

Perhaps the "chain of machines" refinement is still inadequate. One advantage of the short-lived asset is that it ties up funds for a shorter period of time. At the end of the life of the asset, the firm is in a more flexible position than with the longer lived asset. It can consider transfer to entirely new investments. In a world of rapid technological change and shifting tastes, this added flexibility may be of considerable importance. Another way of expressing the same idea is to state that the risk on the longer lived investment is greater, due to its inflexible character. There are several ways of dealing with such risks: one may adjust the cash inflows (the R's) to reflect the degrees of risk or one may use a higher discounting factor (a higher i). There is no completely satisfactory way of treating varying risks on alternative investments.[8]

Empirical studies and illustrations

To what extent do firms actually use the "theoretically correct" methods just described? The empirical evidence is that these methods are hardly ever applied in small firms and are applied in big business in only a minority of cases.

A study covering approximately 60 small firms uncovered no cases of the use of present value or discounted rate of return formulations.[9] One manager, who happened to have a master's degree in economics, was aware of such formulations. Despite this knowledge, he applied subjective, nonquantitative methods, with a rough consideration of the payback period in some cases. This manager stated that "when things settled down" he would introduce the present value method, but that present demands on investment were so urgent that no refinement in analysis was warranted. The firm was relatively new and the backlog of investment needs was great. Probably few of the managers of the other firms in the study were even aware of such abstract concepts as present value or the discounted rate of return.

Surveys of investment decisions in big business are more numerous. A study by the Machinery and Allied Products Institute in 1948 found that only 1 out of 70 firms determined the discounted rate of return. A second study in 1956 found that 2 out of 133 firms determined the discounted

---

[8] Myron J. Gordon, *The Investment, Financing, and Valuation of the Corporation* (Homewood, Ill.: Richard D. Irwin, Inc., 1962) is an advanced work on these problems.

[9] Martin B. Solomon, Jr., *op. cit.*

rate of return.[10] These surveys found a fairly wide use of the MAPI formula (to be discussed in the next section) but an even wider use of cruder methods.

A more recent survey by James H. Miller concentrated on 127 "well-managed" firms.[11] Only 38 of these used the discounted cash flow in making investment decisions. Even so, it seems likely that such surveys exaggerate the degree to which large firms resort to sophisticated techniques; the interviewees may often report what they would like to see done or what they consider to be company policy rather than actual practice.

Other studies confirm the infrequent use of the "theoretically correct" techniques. Walter W. Heller found that most of his sample of firms used the payback formula or qualitative judgment.[12] A personal interview study of 48 large firms found that 5 used the discounted rate of return.[13] The only conclusion one can reach is that there is a wide gap between the theory of capital budgeting and actual practice, unless one can show that the cruder and more subjective methods do in fact approximate the results of the theoretically correct methods.

3. SHORTCUTS IN EVALUATING AND RANKING INVESTMENTS

It is clear that most firms do not apply the "theoretically correct" formulas in evaluating investments. They resort to a variety of shortcuts which simplify investment decision making with the loss of some of the precision of the refined formulas. It is not possible here to discuss every method in use; attention focuses on a few of the most widely applied approaches.

Qualitative rankings of alternatives

Many small firms go to little effort to quantify their comparisons of investment alternatives. Managers of such firms rely on their subjective evaluations of the alternatives that come to their attention. They believe that they are close enough to the situation to determine with little effort that some investments are profitable and others unwarranted.

Such subjective evaluations often stress the urgency of various alternatives. Some investments appear to require immediate action; an example

---

[10] *Equipment Replacement and Depreciation—A Survey of Policies and Practices* (Washington, D.C.: Machinery and Allied Products Institute, 1956).

[11] James H. Miller, "A Glimpse at Practice in Calculating and Using Return on Investment," *N.A.A. Bulletin*, June, 1960, p. 73.

[12] Walter W. Heller, "The Anatomy of Investment Decisions," *Harvard Business Review*, March, 1951, pp. 95–103.

[13] D. F. Istvan, "The Capital Expenditure Decision Making Process in Forty-Eight Large Corporations" (Ph.D. dissertation, Indiana University, 1959).

would be the replacement of a broken-down machine. Other investments are more easily postponed. While it is probable that most of the "urgent" proposals are likely to be profitable ones, there is a danger that the "postponable" projects may in some cases be even more profitable. For example, investment in facilities for a new product line may not be considered urgent, but such an investment may be more profitable than any conceivable plowing back of funds into existing product lines.

The difficulty with the nonquantitative approach to capital budgeting is that the "hunches" or "guesses" on which it relies may not conform to the realities revealed by a more careful analysis. This is the argument against any subjective comparison of alternatives, whether it concerns the setting of a price, the purchase of a home, or the selection of a college course. Yet all of us make hundreds of decisions in this way, and rightly so. The decision to apply a quantitative approach to any problem of choice is in itself an investment decision; and it is not true that the payoff for quantification always justifies the expenditure of time and money it requires. Up to the present time there has been little research which would help the manager decide when more elaborate analysis will or will not be profitable.

The payback period

The most widely applied quantitative approach to investment decisions involves computation of the payback or payout period. The payback period is simply the time it takes the firm to recover the initial investment out of the earnings resulting from the investment.

The formula for the payback period is

$$P = \frac{C}{R} \tag{9-9}$$

in which P is the payback period, C is as before the supply price of the investment, and R is the annual cash inflow expected from the investment. If an investment costs \$5,000 and results in a cash inflow of \$2,000 per year, the payback period is two and one-half years.

It is important to recognize several features of this formula. First, the formula implicitly assumes a uniform cash inflow over the years. The formula cannot handle the case in which R_1 differs from R_2, etc. Secondly, the cash inflow, R, consists of the earnings *without* a deduction for depreciation. (Note that this is also true of the R's in the formulas for the present value and the discounted rate of return.) Since the formula is concerned with the recovery of the initial investment, it would be improper to subtract depreciation as an expense, for depreciation is also concerned with capital recovery.

The payback technique is incomplete without a comparison of the payback period, *P*, with some standard. What is needed is a payback criterion. The firms using the method usually establish a maximum period, let us say three years; investments that take longer than this to pay off are rejected. More sophisticated approaches recognize that the payback criterion should vary according to the type of investment under consideration. It would be foolish to require that a new building pay off in as short a period as new jigs and fixtures.

The payback period after taxes

Any of the formulas in this chapter may be revised to take into account the impact of the corporate income tax on the added earnings resulting from the investment. Such revisions are complicated by the fact that the tax applies not to the entire cash inflow, but only to the inflow *less* depreciation. If the corporate income tax is 50 percent of earnings after depreciation the payback formula becomes

$$P' = \frac{2C}{R + D} \tag{9-10}$$

in which *P'* is the payback period after taxes, and *D* is the annual depreciation charge. Straight-line depreciation is assumed in this formula.

The mathematically inclined student will find it easy to derive the after-tax payback formula from the pre-tax formula.

Limitations of the payback formula

The payback period would appear to be an extremely crude measure of investment profitability. Its most obvious limitation is that it ignores profits earned after the initial investment has been recovered. Take two investments, each costing $10,000 and each returning a cash inflow of $5,000 per year. The first is expected to provide earnings for ten years, the second for three years. Obviously the first is much more profitable, but both would pass equally well the requirement of a three-year payback.

A second limitation is that the formula ignores discounting altogether. Or perhaps it is more accurate to say that it discounts returns beyond the payback period at an infinite rate. Lastly, it rests on the assumption, already noted, of a uniform cash inflow. If the rates of cash inflow on different investments vary from year to year, the formula may not provide an accurate comparison of the alternatives.

Recent literature on the payback approach suggests that some of these limitations are not so serious as they first appear. First, we must not forget that investment decisions are made under conditions of high uncertainty. If the uncertainty is greater for earnings in the distant future than in the near future, it may not be completely foolish to ignore earnings beyond a certain period. The payback formula involves a simplification very much like that of the break-even chart; it ignores certain complications, but it may provide a convenient shortcut for dealing with the world of uncertainty.

A second argument in favor of the payback formula is mathematical in character. If the cash inflow is uniform, the formula for the discounted rate of return may be written as[14]

$$r = \frac{R}{C} - \frac{R}{C} \left(\frac{1}{1+r} \right)^n \qquad (9\text{--}11)$$

The expression $\frac{R}{C}$ is known as the payback reciprocal. It is simply the formula for the payback period turned upside down. Now it is clear from the above formula that the expression for r consists of two parts: $\frac{R}{C}$, the payback reciprocal, and a correction factor which depends on n. The larger n, the life of the project, the smaller this correction factor. When n is more than double the payback period, the correction factor becomes small and the payback reciprocal becomes a good estimate of the rate of return.

Another point to note is that the larger r, the smaller the correction factor. If a firm restricts its attention to highly profitable investments with long lives, the payback reciprocal becomes an excellent estimator of the rate of return.[15] Thus the reputation of the payback criterion, which has suffered from the attacks of the capital budgeting experts in the past, has recently enjoyed a recovery.

First-year performance

Some managers evaluate investment opportunities by estimating their impact on revenues and expenses in the first year. If the increased revenues resulting from added sales, or the savings in expenses resulting from the improved equipment, exceed all of the added expenses including interest and depreciation, the investment may be accepted. It is customary in this approach to include depreciation as an expense; without such a deduction no account would be taken of the cost of the asset. It should also be customary, but is not always so in actual practice, to charge interest on the funds tied up in the investment, or at least interest on the average investment (the initial investment will be recovered over the years, so that the funds tied up on the average will be less than those required initially). This "interest" would, as before, be a measure of the cost of capital.

---

[14] A mathematical proof is given in Milton H. Spencer and Louis Siegelman, *Managerial Economics* (Homewood, Ill.: Richard D. Irwin, Inc., 1959), p. 389.

[15] See M. J. Gordon, "The Payoff Period and the Rate of Profit," *The Journal of Business,* October, 1955, pp. 253–60.

It is unnecessary to dwell on the inadequacies of this approach. It may be desirable to compare it with the payback reciprocal. The payback reciprocal might start with first-year performance, but it would compute it as a percentage of the initial investment. The payback reciprocal would *not* involve a deduction for interest or depreciation.

Many variations on this type of formula are found in practice. One variation, sometimes known as the "accountant's rate of return," takes the annual posttax cash inflow *minus depreciation* as a percentage of *average* investment. One may prefer to use the average cash inflow over the life of the asset to the first-year performance, though often the first year is taken to be representative of the whole life of the asset.

The MAPI formula

George Terborgh, a well-known economist with the Machinery and Allied Products Institute, has developed a formula for evaluating investment decisions known as the MAPI formula. In a way, this method does not belong in a section on "shortcuts," for it is based on highly sophisticated reasoning. But MAPI has made the method available in a simplified form.[16]

The MAPI formula compares investing in a project with going without it for one more year. It is aimed primarily at evaluating replacements, with an explicit recognition of gradual deterioration and obsolescence. It incorporates the reasonable assumption that as a machine ages, it faces decreasing efficiency and becomes obsolete as compared with newer machinery. The formula may be summarized in the following equation:

$$r_m = \frac{(R_1 + Y)\,(1 - X) - (Z - TX)}{C}$$

in which r_m is the MAPI rate of return, R_1 is the first-year "operating advantage" of the proposal before taxes, Y is the loss in salvage value that the existing project will incur in the next year plus capital additions planned for the existing project, X is the tax rate, Z is the next-year capital consumption of the proposal, T is the next-year tax deductions on the new project, and C is the cost (supply price) of the proposal.

The capital consumption element of the formula, Z, is a complicated idea in the MAPI approach—perhaps too complicated for the present discussion. This component of the MAPI formula incorporates adjustments for taxes. It also permits alternative assumptions about the rate of obsolescence and deterioration, so that the manager can select the assumptions suited to his operations.

---

[16] George Terborgh, *Business Investment Policy* (Washington, D.C.: Machinery and Allied Products Institute, 1958).

It is unnecessary for our purposes to go into the other assumptions underlying the MAPI approach. The interested reader can find a full discussion in Terborgh's various publications. The manager is saved from having to deal with the complexities of the system by a series of charts which permit a simple application of the method to particular proposals. Figure 9–1 presents one such chart, the one based on the assumption of

FIGURE 9–1

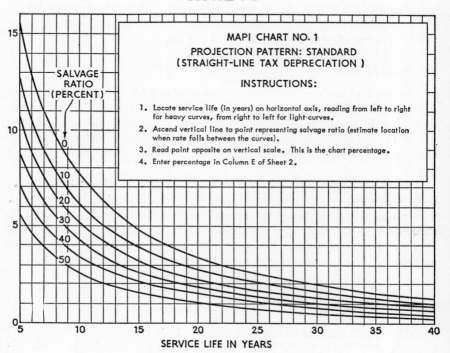

constant capital consumption. The manager must estimate the service life in years and the salvage ratio (the ratio of the value of the asset at the end of its service life to its initial value). He may then read on the chart the resultant capital consumption percentage (a figure which, as has been stated, includes an adjustment for taxes).

Table 9–6, which is the standard form for evaluating a proposal by the MAPI method, indicates the steps required in the analysis. Note that the capital consumption (and tax adjustment) charge appears on line 33 of this worksheet.

The result of the MAPI formula is an estimate of the rate of return. This return approximates the "theoretically correct" return discussed

TABLE 9–6

```
┌─────────────────────────────────────────────────────────────────────────────┐
│ PROJECT NO.  5                                              SHEET I           │
│                      SUMMARY OF ANALYSIS                                      │
│              (SEE ACCOMPANYING WORK SHEETS FOR DETAIL)                         │
│                                                                               │
│                     I.  REQUIRED INVESTMENT                                   │
└─────────────────────────────────────────────────────────────────────────────┘
```

1	INSTALLED COST OF PROJECT	$ 112,000	1
2	DISPOSAL VALUE OF ASSETS TO BE RETIRED BY PROJECT	$	2
3	CAPITAL ADDITIONS REQUIRED IN ABSENCE OF PROJECT	$ 48,000	3
4	INVESTMENT RELEASED OR AVOIDED BY PROJECT (2+3)	$ 48,000	4
5	NET INVESTMENT REQUIRED (1−4)	$ 64,000	5

II. NEXT-YEAR ADVANTAGE FROM PROJECT

A. OPERATING ADVANTAGE
(USE FIRST YEAR OF PROJECT OPERATION)*

		Increase	Decrease	
6	ASSUMED OPERATING RATE OF PROJECT (HOURS PER YEAR)		2,000	6
	EFFECT OF PROJECT ON REVENUE			
7	FROM CHANGE IN QUALITY OF PRODUCTS	$	$	7
8	FROM CHANGE IN VOLUME OF OUTPUT			8
9	TOTAL	$ A	$ B	9
	EFFECT OF PROJECT ON OPERATING COSTS			
10	DIRECT LABOR	$	$ 1,280	10
11	INDIRECT LABOR			11
12	FRINGE BENEFITS		155	12
13	MAINTENANCE		3,500	13
14	TOOLING		2,000	14
15	SUPPLIES			15
16	SCRAP AND REWORK			16
17	DOWN TIME		1,675	17
18	POWER			18
19	FLOOR SPACE		500	19
20	PROPERTY TAXES AND INSURANCE	1,680		20
21	SUBCONTRACTING			21
22	INVENTORY			22
23	SAFETY			23
24	FLEXIBILITY		3,000	24
25	OTHER			25
26	TOTAL	$ 1,680 A	$ 12,110 B	26
27	NET INCREASE IN REVENUE (9A−9B)		$	27
28	NET DECREASE IN OPERATING COST (26B−26A)		$ 10,430	28
29	NEXT-YEAR OPERATING ADVANTAGE (27+28)		$ 10,430	29

B. NON-OPERATING ADVANTAGE
(USE ONLY IF THERE IS AN ENTRY IN LINE 4)

30	NEXT-YEAR CAPITAL CONSUMPTION AVOIDED BY PROJECT:		30
	A DECLINE OF DISPOSAL VALUE DURING THE YEAR	$	
	B NEXT-YEAR ALLOCATION OF CAPITAL ADDITIONS	$ 10,000	
	TOTAL	$ 10,000	

C. TOTAL ADVANTAGE

31	TOTAL NEXT-YEAR ADVANTAGE FROM PROJECT (29+30)	$ 20,430	31

* For projects with a significant break-in period, use performance after break-in.

(*Table 9–6 continued on next page.*)

earlier, but, as has been noted, it incorporates some factors not normally taken into account. The next section will compare its evaluations with those resulting from the other methods.

Comparison of the methods[17]

How close do the shortcuts just discussed come to the "theoretically correct" discounted rate of return? Figures 9–2 to 9–4 provide comparisons for several types of investments. The first chart, Figure 9–2 examines the

---

[17] The discussion in this section is based on Martin B. Solomon, Jr., *op. cit.*, pp. 30–45.

TABLE 9–6—*Continued*

PROJECT NO. ___5___   SHEET 2

III. COMPUTATION OF MAPI URGENCY RATING

32 TOTAL NEXT-YEAR ADVANTAGE AFTER INCOME TAX (31 — TAX) $ 10,215

33 MAPI CHART ALLOWANCE FOR PROJECT (TOTAL OF COLUMN F, BELOW) $ 2,576 *

(ENTER DEPRECIABLE ASSETS ONLY)

Item or Group	Installed Cost of Item or Group A	Estimated Service Life (Years) B	Estimated Terminal Salvage (Percent of Cost) C	MAPI Chart Number D	Chart Percentage E	Chart Percentage × Cost (E × A) F
Gear Shapers	$112,000	20	20	1	2.3	$ 2,576
					TOTAL	$ 2,576

34 AMOUNT AVAILABLE FOR RETURN ON INVESTMENT (32—33) $ 7,639

35 MAPI URGENCY RATING (34÷5) · 100   %   12

* Since the chart allowance does not cover future capital additions to project assets, add an annual proration of such additions, if any, to the figure in Line 33.

outcome for an asset with constant annual pre-tax returns. As might be expected from the preceding discussion, the payback reciprocal provides a good approximation to the discounted rate of return for long lengths of life. Surprisingly, the rate of return on total investment does better than the return on average investment for long lengths of life. The MAPI formula gives a low estimate of the return throughout.[18]

---

[18] The way to read Figures 9–2, 9–3, and 9–4 is to consider a single length of life at a time. For example, consider a length of life of six years. Then construct a vertical line at that length of life. This line will cross the various estimates of returns and will indicate the amount of dispersion in the estimates obtained by different methods.

FIGURE 9–2

COMPARISONS OF ALTERNATIVE COMPUTATIONS OF RATES OF RETURN
(constant annual returns)

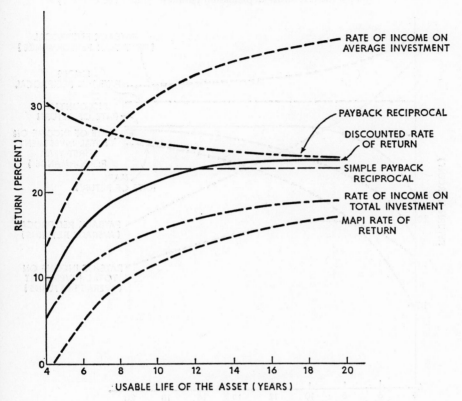

Figure 9–3 considers a case of declining annual returns over the life of the asset. It is assumed that the pre-tax returns decline as in Table 9–7.

The results shown in Figure 9–3 cover proposals of varying lives. A proposal with a 2-year life would have a return of $2,000 the first year, and $1,900 the second. An asset with a 20-year life would provide all of the returns shown in Table 9–7. In this case the payback reciprocal still provides a fairly good estimate of the discounted rate of return. Even closer in most years is the first-year performance as a percentage of total investment.

The third chart, Figure 9–4, differs from the second only in that depreciation charges for tax purposes are concentrated in the first five years, a fact that affects the outflow of taxes over the life of the asset. Again the payback reciprocal provides a close estimate for long lengths of life.

These comparisons cover several hypothetical cases with varying lengths of life. They do not cover the whole range of possibilities. They do

FIGURE 9–3

COMPARISONS OF ALTERNATIVE COMPUTATIONS OF RATES OF RETURN
(declining annual returns—depreciation period = usable life of asset)

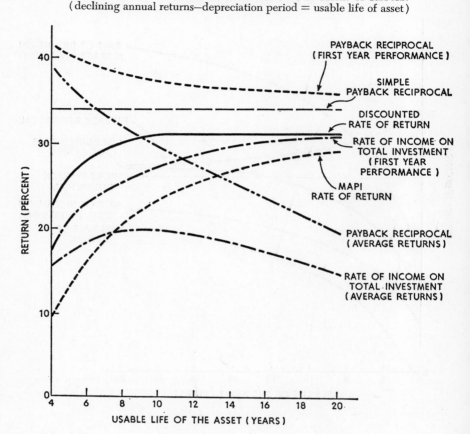

suggest, however, that the "shortcuts" provide reasonably accurate estimates of the discounted rate of return. The "crudest" of all of the quantitative approaches appears to provide the closest estimates in most cases.

It is also possible to check the "shortcuts" by determining how they
rank alternative investments. Table 9–8 presents such a comparison on a
set of six hypothetical investments with constant annual returns and
another set of investments with declining annual returns. Unfortunately,
the payback reciprocal does not fare so well in ranking investments in
order of profitability when investments of both short and long life are
considered at the same time. The MAPI return and the first-year performance measures do rank proposals in almost the same order as tne discounted rate of return. For a fuller discussion of these issues, the reader is

TABLE 9-7

HYPOTHETICAL PROPOSALS WITH DECLINING ANNUAL RETURNS

Year	Pre-Tax Returns	Year	Pre-Tax Returns
1	$2,000	11	$1,000
2	1,900	12	900
3	1,800	13	800
4	1,700	14	700
5	1,600	15	600
6	1,500	16	500
7	1,400	17	400
8	1,300	18	300
9	1,200	19	200
10	1,100	20	100

TABLE 9-8

RANKING RESULTS OF ALTERNATIVE FORMULAS: 12 HYPOTHETICAL INVESTMENTS

Proposal	Excess Present Value as Percent of Cost (Discounted at 10 Percent)	Discounted Rate of Return	Using First-Year Performance to Compute Net Return		Using Average Annual Returns to Compute Net Return		Simple Payback Reciprocal	MAPI
			Rate of Income on Total Investment	Payback Reciprocal	Rate of Income on Total Investment	Payback Reciprocal		
Constant Annual Returns								
K ..	.887	.238	.181	.248	.181	.248	.226	.157
I ..	.450	.197	.136	.236	.136	.236	.226	.096
C ..	.299	.166	.111	.211	.111	.211	.179	.071
A ..	.131	.151	.098	.298	.098	.298	.234	.022
G ..	.102	.140	.091	.291	.091	.291	.226	.015
E ..	−.148	.074	.045	.112	.045	.112	.090	.021
Declining Annual Returns								
L ..	.853	.266	.257	.324	.151	.218	.302	.232
J ..	.353	.182	.147	.247	.115	.215	.214	.107
D ..	.133	.139	.175	.275	.066	.166	.242	.135
F ..	.086	.120	.136	.203	.057	.123	.181	.111
H ..	.041	.118	.136	.336	.068	.268	.272	.060
B ..	−.048	.080	.106	.306	.045	.245	.241	.030

referred to more detailed discussions in other books.[19] The main point to remember here is that the deficiencies of the shortcut formulas as com-

---

[19] M. B. Solomon, Jr., *op. cit.*, pp. 30–45. Harold Bierman and Seymour Smidt, *The Capital Budgeting Decision* (New York: The Macmillan Co., 1960), pp. 16–32 differ somewhat from Solomon in their evaluation of the ranking ability of the "shortcuts." The differences result from the selection of different hypothetical examples.

FIGURE 9–4

COMPARISONS OF ALTERNATIVE COMPUTATIONS OF RATES OF RETURN
(declining annual returns—depreciation period = 5 years)

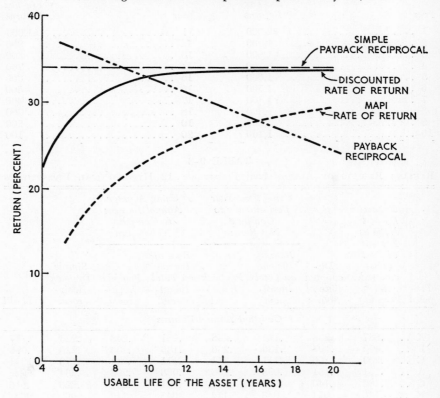

pared with the "theoretically correct" methods may be less in actual practice than they appear to be in the abstract. If one remembers that any
formula must deal with estimates of uncertain outcomes in the future
which inevitably involve a margin of error, he may be more tolerant of the
imprecision of some of the shortcuts.

Empirical studies and illustrations

Earlier sections of this chapter have made it clear that the "shortcut"
methods of evaluating decisions predominate in practice over the discounted rate of return or present value approaches. One can point to no
definitive study of the relative uses of various methods, but the following
summary of surveys of relatively large firms will give a rough idea of
prevailing practice.

MAPI studies. The Machinery and Allied Products studies cited earlier indicate widespread use of the payback period, as the following table shows:[20]

Methods	1948 Survey (*Percent of Firms*)	1956 Survey (*Percent of Firms*)
Payback	42	60
Minimum average cost	8	24
MAPI	19	47
Discounted rate of return..............	1	2

Perhaps it is more than a coincidence that this survey found such a widespread use of the MAPI formula; no other survey seems to confirm this finding.

James H. Miller's survey. The survey by James H. Miller enumerates a variety of different rationing formulas used in 127 companies.[21] Some of the firms apply more than one formula.

Method	No. Companies Using
Payback	66
Discounted cash flow	38
Return on total assets at original cost	59
Return on total assets at original cost less current liability	15
Return on total assets at replacement cost less current liability	1
Return on net worth	2
Other methods	6

This survey mixes two things together: methods for evaluating *new* investments and methods for evaluating performance of investments already installed or even whole departments or companies. Consequently the results must be interpreted with caution, though they clearly confirm the widespread use of the payback formula.

N.A.A. study. The National Association of Accountants has made a survey of 44 large companies.[22] Forty-two of these firms use the rate of

---

[20] *Equipment Replacement and Depreciation—A Survey of Policies and Practices* (Washington, D.C.: Machinery and Allied Products Institute, 1956). The fact that the percentages for 1956 add to more than 100 indicates the use of more than one method by some firms.

[21] James H. Miller, "A Glimpse at Practice in Calculating and Using Return on Investment," *N.A.A. Bulletin,* June, 1960, p. 73.

[22] *Return on Capital as a Guide to Managerial Decision,* Research Report No. 35 (New York: National Association of Accountants, December, 1959).

income on investment as a capital budgeting criterion. Again it may be more than a coincidence that a survey by accountants should find the method best known among accountants in widest use. This study found some rather sophisticated use of the discounted rate of return among an unspecified number of firms.

Istvan's study. In an interview study of 48 large corporations, Donald F. Istvan found that 5 used the discounted rate of return rather consistently, while 9 others used it for large projects.[23] Two firms used the MAPI formula, 32 the rate of income on total investment, and 34 the payback period. A number of the firms used more than one method. This study like the others, indicates that while there may be a trend toward more sophisticated capital budgeting devices, the "shortcuts" still predominate.

4. THE COST OF CAPITAL

So far this chapter has concerned itself mainly with the demand side of the capital budgeting problem—with the discovery and evaluation of investment opportunities. But the very expression "capital budgeting" implies that there is also a supply side, concerned with the limited supply of funds available for investment and the rationing of those funds.

In both the present value and discounted rate of return formulas the need for a measure of the cost of capital is explicit. We cannot determine present value without inserting a discounting rate into the formula, and this discounting rate should clearly be a measure of the cost of capital. Similarly, the mere fact that the discounted rate of return on a particular project is, let us say, 9 percent is insufficient in determining whether the project is a sound one; we must compare the rate of return with some standard, and the appropriate standard quite clearly is the cost of capital. Even the cruder methods of evaluting investments must somehow take into account the availability and cost of funds or no rational selection of alternatives is possible.

But just what is the cost of capital? The first point to make is that it is an opportunity cost. The cost of funds applied to internal investments is surely a measure of the sacrifice of alternative opportunities for earnings. Unfortunately, determination of the opportunity cost of capital is in practice no easy matter. Outside investment opportunities vary in the degree of risk. It seems appropriate to restrict attention to investments equivalent in risk to those available internally. The rate of return on outside investments is itself difficult to estimate. One might start with the earnings yield on the stock of other companies—the ratio of earnings to

---

[23] D. F. Istvan, *op. cit.*

the price of the stock on the market. It is not current or past earnings that are relevant but earnings expected in the future. For example, the fact that the earnings on IBM stock are only 1 or 2 percent of the current market price does not mean that the yield in the mind of the purchaser is that low; the buyer is obviously betting on increased earnings and capital gains. The exact determination of the relevant earnings-price ratio on IBM stock or any other stock is thus no simple matter.

It may be profitable to review some of the complications that stand in the way of measuring the cost of capital:

1. The capital structure of a firm—that is, the ratio among common stock equity, preferred stock, and debt—may affect the cost of capital.[24] Some writers suggest that the cost of capital should be defined as the earnings-price ratio when the firm has an "optimum" capital structure. An optimum capital structure would be one balancing debt and owners' equity in such a way as to minimize the cost. Determination of such an optimum is in itself difficult. Tax considerations add a further complication; the corporate income tax is a factor in favor of debt financing, since interest is deductible as an expense.

2. The determination of the future earnings of any company is highly conjectural, making it difficult to compute the relevant earnings-price ratio.

3. Important subjective considerations have an influence on the cost of capital. Some managers have an aversion to debt, apparently adding a high subjective cost of indebtness to the market rates of interest when considering financing. Other firms favor "trading on the equity," aiming at increasing the earnings of the existing common stockholders by borrowing at rates below expected earnings. Some small-firm owners are concerned about the dilution of ownership and control that might result from the issuance of more common stock. Incorporation of such considerations into an exact measure of the cost of capital would be complicated.

4. A company's policy on retained earnings may influence its cost of capital. Retained earnings are not subject to the personal income tax. Retained earnings thus appear to involve a lower cost of capital to the ultimate stockholders than do dividends that are paid out and returned in the form of new stock purchases. But different stockholders fall into different personal income tax brackets and experience varying degrees of urgency for dividend payments, making the impact of taxes on the cost of capital difficult to evaluate.

One procedure for determining the cost of capital takes it to be a weighted average of the cost of each type of financing—common stock,

---

[24] Modigliani and Miller deny that the capital structure does affect the cost of capital. See F. Modigliani and M. Miller, "The Cost of Capital, Corporation Finance and the Theory of Investment," *American Economic Review*, June, 1958, pp. 261–97.

preferred stock, bonds, retained earnings, and other sources of funds.[25] The cost of common stock financing is obtained by computing the earnings-price ratio on common stock. The earnings included in this computation must not be the current earnings alone—they must reflect the future trend in earnings expected by stockholders. One way of obtaining the trend in earnings is to project the past annual rate of increase into the future. The cost of long-term debt may be found by finding the yield on the present market value of the bonds.

Unfortunately, the foregoing discussion is more informative on the obstacles in the way of measuring the cost of capital than it is on techniques for making such measurements. A few large firms may be able to afford the extensive research required for refined estimates of the cost of capital. But most managers will for some time have to remain content with a rough, subjective answer to the following question: "What sacrifice of earnings in alternative investments are we making by investing in the proposal at hand?" Or they may put the question even more simply: "What rate of return shall we establish as a cut-off rate?" It seems unlikely at our present state of knowledge that any two managers will reach precisely the same answer.

Empirical studies and illustrations

How does one compute the cost of capital for a specific company? We shall use the DuPont Company as an illustration of both the procedures and limitations of the results. The liabilities and net worth of DuPont were as follows on December 31, 1961:

Total current liabilities	$ 139,296,487
Provisions for bonuses	39,105,286
Reserves for insurance and contingencies	7,726,104
Preferred stock $4.50 cum.	168,885,000
Preferred stock $3.50 cum.	70,000,000
Common stock ($5.00)	229,863,480
Earned surplus	1,214,746,509
Paid-in surplus	166,319,452
Revaluation surplus	1,093,942,355

Computations of the cost of capital are usually concerned only with the long-term debt and net worth. Since the DuPont Company avoids long-term debt, we are concerned with the preferred stock and common stock (including surplus) sections of the balance sheet.

The data presented so far are book figures, while the cost of capital is concerned with market values and current yields. The relevant data for 1961 are as follows:

---

[25] Harold Bierman, Jr. and Seymour Smidt, *op. cit.*, chap. x.

	Market Value (Approx. Average)	Yield in Percentage
Cumulative preferred $4.50	$105	4.3%
Cumulative preferred $3.50	84	4.2
Common stock (paid dividends of $7.50 in 1961)	220	3.4

What we now require is a weighted average of these three cost of capital figures. Market values are more appropriate than book values as weights. The computation of the market value weights involves multiplication of the number of shares by the market values.

	Number of Shares	Market Value per Share	Total Market Value
Preferred ($4.50)	1,668,850	$105	$ 175,229,250
Preferred ($3.50)	700,000	84	58,800,000
Common	45,972,696	220	10,113,992,240

It should be clear that the common stock is of overwhelming importance so that the yields on the preferred stock have little influence on the overall computation. The computation is as follows:

$$\frac{\$175,229,250 \times .043 + \$58,800,000 \times .042 + \$10,113,992,240 \times .034}{\$175,229,250 + \$58,800,000 + \$10,113,992,240} = .034$$

The use of book value weights would have had little effect on the computation. In any case the cost of capital comes out to around 3.4 percent. It seems unlikely, however, that DuPont or any other company would use a cost of capital as low as 3.4 percent in the evaluation of investment proposals. No doubt a large safety margin would be required. Furthermore, the fact that the stockholders were expecting increases in earnings in the future (and capital gains) is not reflected in the computation. The current yields understate the "true" cost of capital, especially in a year like 1961 when stock prices are governed much more by trend projections than by current yields. Such considerations destroy the mathematical precision of the computation.

The controversy over the influence of methods of financing on the cost of capital continued throughout the 1960's.[26] The subject is one of the most advanced ones in the area of corporate finance and applied statistics and it is too involved for a full elaboration here.

---

[26] A review of these issues appears in John Lintner, "The Cost of Capital and Optimal Financing of Corporate Growth," *Journal of Finance*, May, 1963, pp. 292–310.

The best known statistical study of the cost of capital is that done by Miller and Modigliani in the electric utilities. Their study of 1947–48 data published in 1958 appeared to confirm their hypothesis that the cost of capital was relatively independent of the capital structure of the firm.[27] The results are shown in Figure 9–5. Their study of the oil industry pro-

FIGURE 9–5

COST OF CAPITAL IN RELATION TO FINANCIAL STRUCTURE FOR
43 ELECTRIC UTILITIES, 1947–48

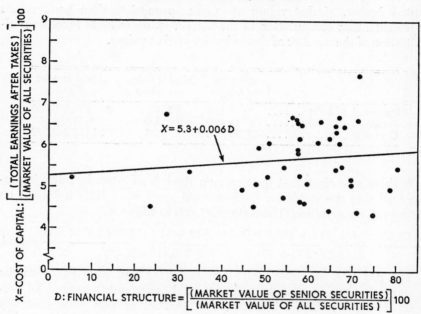

duced similar results, shown in Figure 9–6. The authors recognized that the data were crude and that the scatter was wide, but found that the statistical tests were favorable to their hypotheses. The high cost of capital (8.5 percent) in the oil companies as compared with the electric utilities (5.3 percent) is in line with a priori expectations, since the oil industry is more uncertain and variable.

Miller and Modigliani have continued their research in the electric utilities in more recent years.[28] They have defined the cost of capital as "that minimum prospective rate of yield that a proposed investment in real assets must offer to be just worthwhile undertaking from the stand-

---

[27] Modigliani and Miller, *op. cit.*, pp. 282–88.
[28] M. H. Miller and F. Modigliani, "Some Estimates of the Cost of Capital to the Electric Utility Industry, 1954–57," *The American Economic Review,* June, 1966, pp. 333–91.

FIGURE 9–6

COST OF CAPITAL IN RELATION TO FINANCIAL STRUCTURE FOR
42 OIL COMPANIES, 1953

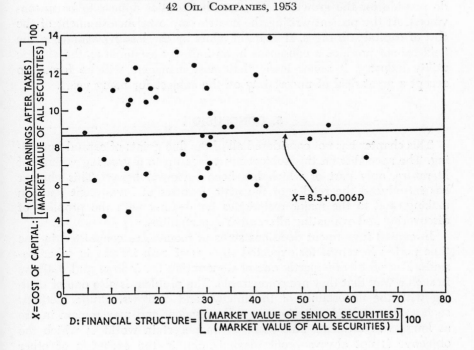

point of the current owners of the firm." They have followed the recent tendency of experts on the subject in stressing that the objective of investment is to maximize the market value of the shares held by current owners of the firm. Thus the cost of capital may be looked upon as the minimum prospective yield on a new investment which will increase the value of such shares. On the basis of an extremely elaborate procedure they found the after-tax cost of capital was .036, .045, and .046 in 1954, 1956, and 1957 respectively. Critics of their procedure have been skeptical of the low level of those figures which were barely above AAA bond yield for those years. A major criticism has been that their method did not adequately provide for the expected growth of earning which should logically be a part of the cost of capital. A prospective shareholder in a utility may be willing to buy a share at $100 if it pays only a 4 or 5 percent return, but, it is argued, only if he expects the earning to grow in the future. Somehow the cost of capital should be adjusted for this growth factor.[29]

---

[29] Jean Crockett and Irwin Friend, "Some Estimates of the Cost of Capital to the Electric Utility Industry: Comment," *The American Economic Review,* December, 1967, pp. 1258–67.

The before tax estimates for 1954, 1956, and 1957 were .079, .094, and .098, according to Miller and Modigliani. They argue that these estimates do provide for the growth factor, but their critics appear to be unconvinced. At the present writing the controversy over measurement of the cost of capital still rages. If years of effort by the leading experts in the field cannot produce a consensus in an industry as stable as the electric utility industry, it seems likely that most managers will be forced to accept a great deal of uncertainty on the subject for many years.

5. CONCLUSION

This chapter has not considered all of the fine points of capital budgeting. The specialist on this subject must face up to a growing volume of literature, only part of which has been reviewed here.[30] This chapter has introduced the reader to the main features of investment decision making, and to the major techniques for dealing with the problem of discovering and evaluating alternative opportunities.

In capital investment decisions sums of money are committed in one time period in return for expected streams of cash inflows in other periods. The problem is partly one of discounting the inflows and outflows in such a way that they are comparable. The problem is also one of dealing with the uncertainty of the inflows and outflows. Crude methods such as the payback criterion are still prevalent and may remain in use as long as investments take place in an uncertain world in which the objective is not always profit maximization to the exclusion of other goals.

One point should be stressed in this conclusion, for it has barely been mentioned in the preceding discussion. It is the need for the evaluation of the results of investment proposals. Only by making a systematic comparison of the actual cost savings and revenue gains against the predictions, can the efficacy of the procedure be determined. Unfortunately, many firms have no procedures for the systematic review of the results of capital expenditures. Without such a follow-up they are in no position to prevent future cases of overoptimism, overpessimism, or empire building at the expense of the overall objectives of the firm.

---

[30] See Ezra Solomon (ed.), *The Management of Corporate Capital* (Chicago: The University of Chicago Press, 1959), for a collection of articles on many aspects of the problem. James C. Van Horne has edited a collection of readings, *Foundations for Financial Management: A Book of Readings* (Homewood, Ill.: Richard D. Irwin, Inc., 1966), which includes many articles related to capital budgeting and the cost of capital.

10 / Risk and uncertainty

All business decisions are made under conditions of uncertainty. Management does not know and cannot know all the future events which will affect the outcome of each alternative. It cannot know how consumer tastes and demands will change in the future. It cannot know what new competition will enter the market, how the present competitors will behave, what new substitutes will appear, or what new technological developments will alter the environment. It cannot predict exactly the impact of political changes which may result in changes in regulations, subsidies, fiscal policies, or international trade policies. It cannot even be certain of its own internal cost structure, for it does not have control over raw material prices, wage changes, or rates of obsolescence of equipment. Rates of productivity may respond to improvements in management and working conditions, but not by precisely predictable amounts.

Most of this book has proceeded as though management does have perfect information about the outcome of decisions, though it has faced up to the implications of uncertainty at several points. We have noted that decisions on prices are frequently the outcome of reasoning or experimentation which might be called partial marginalism—management accommodates to uncertainty by going only part way in incremental reasoning. We have also commented that the shortcuts which are widespread in actual capital budgeting are reasonable adjustments to uncertainty. But we have taken the position that it is often useful to ignore uncertainty, at least in the early stages of analysis.

In recent years the analytical tools for dealing with uncertainty have been refined and sharpened. The problem in an introductory book in managerial economics is to determine how far to go into this analysis. The following discussion tries to avoid two extremes: on the one hand the attempt to boil a whole course in probability and Bayesian statistics into one chapter; on the other hand the mere repetition of the cliché that risk and uncertainty are important without saying anything significant about them.

1. A VARIETY OF APPROACHES TO UNCERTAINTY

It is well to recognize that management can deal with uncertainty in a variety of ways. The choice of the appropriate approach is itself an important business decision. Information varies in degree from the situations at one extreme, in which uncertainty is so insignificant that it is convenient to ignore it, to the situations at the other extreme, in which it is so great that choices can be little more than random selections. The analysis of uncertainty becomes more profitable between those extremes.

Some writers make a distinction between risk and uncertainty.[1] Risk refers to relatively objective probabilities which can be computed on the basis of past experience or some a priori principle. Examples of the use of past experience are the actuarial probabilities in the insurance business that certain proportions of fires of various magnitudes will take place or that certain numbers of people of various ages will die. Examples of the a priori type are the odds that a coin will turn up heads or that an ace will be drawn from a deck of cards. In any of these cases the probability of the outcomes can be computed with considerable precision. In risk situations experience is repetitive and provides a frequency distribution about which inferences can be drawn by objective statistical procedures. Uncertainty, on the other hand, is relatively subjective, there being insufficient past information or insufficient stability in the structure of the variables to permit exact prediction. Most business decisions take place under conditions of uncertainty, for each decision is made in somewhat a different environment. Sometimes the term objective probability is used in connection with risk and subjective probability in connection with uncertainty.

A few writers have taken the position that risk and uncertainty are completely different phenomena which require completely different treatments. Where risk is involved it is convenient to compute the whole probability distribution. In cases of uncertainty the parameters of the probability distribution itself are unknown. In such instances it is common to simplify the problem and focus on only a few of its elements. The recent tendency, however, is to treat subjective probabilities as different from objective probabilities only in degree. There is a continuum from

---

[1] Frank H. Knight, *Risk, Uncertainty and Profit* (Boston: Houghton Mifflin Company, 1921), p. 233.

high uncertainty to low uncertainty. What is called risk is toward one end of the continuum; complete ignorance is at the other. Most problems in management fall in between. In the remainder of this chapter we shall use the term uncertainty to refer to the whole continuum and to include risk as part of uncertainty.

What are the alternative methods for dealing with uncertainty? There are at least nine approaches: (*a*) avoidance of analysis by following rules of thumb, tradition, or external suggestions; (*b*) simplification of the problem through break-even analysis; (*c*) application of the insurance principle; (*d*) hedging; (*e*) the search for additional information; (*f*) sampling; (*g*) the stress on flexibility; (*h*) the stress on diversification; and (*i*) increased control over the future.

Avoidance of analysis by following rules of thumb, tradition, or external suggestions

One way to deal with uncertainty is to "escape" from it by avoiding analysis as much as possible. Rules of thumb provide a way of making decisions without much thought. The adherence to traditional "decision rules," such as those on markups and markdowns in department stores, can convert decision making into mechanical routine requiring little analysis. Many retail store managers prefer to stock commodities on which prices have been suggested by manufacturers, for they can thus avoid making pricing decisions. (They still must make decisions on which items to stock.) Still another way of avoiding analysis is through the simple imitation of the prices of others.

It is wrong to conclude that these rules of thumb and shortcuts are devoid of any economic meaning. In a competitive society firms do not survive unless they make some kind of adjustment to market forces. The decision rules which do survive must represent ways of dealing with cost, demand, and competitive factors. For example, manufacturers' suggested prices are undoubtedly based on experience with what retailers can live with. Imitative prices may enable a firm to learn from the experience of others, or it may be a kind of price followership which cuts down on cutthroat competition in the industry.[2]

---

[2] The argument here is a modification of Alchian's views on uncertainty. See Armen A. Alchian, "Uncertainty, Evolution and Economic Theory," *The Journal of Political Economy* (Chicago: The University of Chicago Press, 1950), pp. 211–21. Alchian states that economic analysis is useful for predicting the behavior of an aggregate of competing firms, even when uncertainty precludes profit maximization for the individual firm. The firms which survive may have used decision rules which appear to be "nonrational," but they have by luck or imitation made viable choices which are consistent with economic forces. "Like the biologist, the economist predicts the effects of environmental changes on the surviving class of living organisms; the economist need not assume that each participant is aware of, or acts according to, his cost and demand situation." Alchian does not deny that many managers do make an analysis of the situation but argues that some may survive without such analysis.

Break-even analysis and similar simplifications

Break-even charts, which show total cost and total revenue curves, are only one of a family of similar devices which simplify analysis. The payback criterion is quite similar to the break-even chart, for it focuses attention on the probability of doing better than a certain predetermined standard or criterion. While our earlier discussion of break-even charts argued that management should concern itself with the whole cost-revenue relationship and not merely a single point, it is clear that many managers do take great interest in the break-even point itself. Their reasoning seems to be as follows: It is impossible under conditions of uncertainty to determine the exact volume that will be attained. It is possible, however, to determine roughly the chance that the future volume will exceed that at the break-even point. If the probability of exceeding the break-even volume is extremely high, the manager may be satisfied without knowing the probabilities of specific volumes. If, however, the chances of falling below the break-even point are too high, the manager may reject the proposal outright. Such a use of the break-even point may seem unreasonable, since it places a proposal which may provide a 90 percent expected return on the same level as one with a 10 percent expected return, if both have about the same probability of being above the break-even point. Or, looking at the matter in another way, this approach ignores the desirability of risking losses if the chances for large gains are great. If the manager is extremely conservative—if his marginal utility of income falls sharply—this approach may make sense, for the large gains result in a smaller proportional change in utility than in dollars.

The payback criterion is similar to the break-even point as a way of avoiding a full analysis of uncertainty. Managers who use the payback criterion are satisfied with determining that the probability of the investment paying for itself in less than the predetermined time is extremely high. But they avoid the hard work of determining the probabilities that the rates of return will be 10 percent, 20 percent, and so on. They are satisfied with a strong assurance that the investment will pay off without knowing exactly how profitable it might be.

The two approaches to uncertainty discussed so far are consistent with Herbert Simon's "satisficing theory," which argues that businessmen are often satisfied with less than the optimum. As long as results come up to predetermined ideas of what is satisfactory these businessmen will seek no further for better solutions. High degrees of uncertainty increase this temptation to "let well enough alone" or, at least, not to spend a great deal of effort in finding the very best.[3] In fact, under conditions of un-

---

[3] The same kind of reasoning may help explain Baumol's finding that many firms try to maximize total revenue rather than total profit. See W. J. Baumol, *Business Behavior, Value and Growth* (New York: The Macmillan Co., 1959), pp. 45–53.

certainty the concept of the "best," "most profitable," or "optimum" becomes fuzzy, since managers must choose among probability distributions which overlap, rather than among single-point estimates.

The insurance principle

In the case in which it is possible to compute "objective" probabilities on the basis of past experience (the case some economists have labeled "risk"), the insurance principle may be applicable. Even in this situation there is still high uncertainty about the event faced by each individual firm. No one knows which particular worker will suffer an injury. No one knows which buildings will burn in fires. But by pooling these uncertainties it is possible to compute the probabilities for the mass, if not for the individuals. Insurance converts the high uncertainty about individual losses into a high degree of certainty about pooled losses.

The "law of large numbers" helps explain this conversion of high uncertainties about individual events into objective probabilities for the mass of events. The law observes that certain mass phenomena have a tendency toward regularity in behavior. Examples are the number of aces that will be drawn from complete decks of cards if the draws are repeated many times, the numbers of houses that will burn down in a year nationally, the number of deaths in each age category, and so on.

Only when the law of large numbers applies is a sound insurance program possible. The regularity in mass phenomena makes it possible to transfer risks. An individual can pay premiums to an insurance company in return for a promise to compensate for losses. Sometimes self-insurance is feasible. A firm owning 1,000 trucks might, instead of paying premiums to an outside insurance firm, establish a reserve for covering the losses in accidents which will inevitably occur. The predictability of accidents would be stable enough so that the reserve would absorb the losses without much danger of an unusual financial drain in a single year.

Insurance differs from the methods of dealing with uncertainty discussed so far in that it actually reduces uncertainty for the individual. The insured replaces a high degree of uncertainty about the occurrence of a particular event with the certainty of a definite premium. The insurance company reduces uncertainty by pooling risks and applying the law of large numbers.

Hedging

The traditional definition of hedging has been the "matching of one risk with an opposing risk." By holding two opposite positions the firm can avoid the risk of loss, though simultaneously it loses part of the opportunity for gain. If, for example, the firm holds a large inventory of raw materials as an incident to doing business, it may wish to avoid the danger of declining prices. In some industries a decline in the prices of raw materials might more than wipe out any profits that might be earned through normal operations. An opposite example is the firm which operates in a "short" rather than a "long" position, as would be the case if it has made a contract to deliver a commodity at a future date at a predetermined price. By the time such a firm is ready to manufacture and deliver it may find that raw material prices have risen, wiping out any profit that might be earned.

Futures markets provide one means of hedging against price increases or decreases. Such markets permit the purchase or sale of contracts for future delivery, especially in the case of storable commodities such as grain, cotton, and metals. Normally the buyers of futures contracts do not actually want to take delivery on the contracts, nor do the sellers want to make the delivery. Some of the buying and selling of these contracts is done by speculators who are betting on rising prices or falling prices in the future. Such speculation is somewhat the opposite of hedging, for it involves the assumption of risk rather than its avoidance.

More specifically, the hedging operation could proceed as follows. A flour-milling firm is worried that prices may change before it has processed and delivered its flour. It holds large inventories of wheat; a decline in the price of wheat and flour could wipe out the processing profits. Since it is "long" on wheat the firm might sell futures on wheat for delivery about the time the flour would be ready for delivery. If the price of wheat and flour goes down the firm loses on the flour it delivers, but it gains from buying wheat at "spot" (current cash) prices to fulfill the futures contract.[4] If the price of wheat and flour go up, the margin on the flour actually milled increases, but this increased profit is offset by a loss in the futures market.

Another illustration involves the purchase of futures. A manufacturer may make a contract to deliver finished goods six months later at specified prices. The danger is that rising prices will wipe out the profit. The purchase of futures will enable a firm to profit on the price rise in the futures market at the same time it loses on the higher prices it must pay on the materials actually used in manufacture. If the prices fall, the firm loses in the futures market but earns a higher profit margin in manufacture.

A fuller discussion of hedging is unnecessary for our purposes, except to note that it can take many forms. The "put and call" options on the stock market may take the form of hedges. Some writers even classify insurance as a type of hedge. But recent research cited in the empirical studies section which follows shortly suggests that the use of the futures market for risk avoidance is rare. Perhaps hedging does not deserve the central position in discussions of uncertainty it has traditionally received.

---

[4] The firm normally would never see the wheat bought and sold in the hedging transactions. The discussion considers only the simplest type of hedging and neglects some of the complications which might be met in practice.

The search for additional information

Another way to reduce uncertainty is to gather more information. If a firm is uncertain about price-volume relationships (the elasticity of demand) it may collect more data about the past response of purchases to price. It may refine its analysis, taking a larger number of variables into account. If it is uncertain about the marginal cost of increased output it may install better accounting methods for separating costs into appropriate categories. It may run statistical correlations between cost and output.

The methods of forecasting discussed in Chapter 4 contribute to better information for decision making. General economic forecasts, industry forecasts, and forecasts of the demand for individual products should reduce the uncertainty about future sales. Econometric studies of the variables affecting the sales of individual products along with analyses of the psychological and sociological determinants of consumer behavior should contribute to more accurate predictions of demand. One of the great needs at the present time is for follow-up studies which would show how successful the forecasting and statistical studies have been in actual practice in improving decisions.

The collection of information is costly. Like any other managerial activity it produces benefits which must be weighed against the added expenses. The improvement of computers is making it possible to process larger quantities of data economically. The growing knowledge of operations research, statistics, and managerial economics is increasing skills in making better use of information. But there will always be a point at which added information will no longer pay for itself.

Sampling

Sampling provides a way of cutting costs in the collection of information. Instead of attempting to obtain complete information about a problem, management may make use of systematic sampling techniques to obtain sufficient information for the purposes at hand. The theory of sampling provides a basis for inferring characteristics of the total population of data from selected observations. The arguments in favor of sampling are several: it reduces the cost of data collection; it reduces the time to make the study required as background for the decision; and sometimes the systematic collection of samples will result in more accurate information than the haphazard collection of more information. In cases in which the collection of information requires the destruction of the product, as might be the case in testing radio tubes, sampling is the only feasible approach. When the information which is sought concerns a continuing process, the collected observations are necessarily a sample taken from this infinite, continuing population.

Economic considerations should govern decisions on sampling. Let us consider the problem of controlling quality in manufacturing. Suppose we are interested in holding down the proportion of defects. Sometimes the cost of defects is so high and the cost of observations so low that complete measurement is desirable. Such is the case in the inspection of parachutes—no one would advocate that management rely on sampling to determine the proportion of defects since no level is tolerable. As the benefits from the information decrease or the costs of sampling increase, it becomes economical to reduce the size and frequency of the samples.

Sequential sampling provides a way of reducing the cost of sampling. Suppose the problem is one of accepting or rejecting a lot. One approach is to take a single sample from the lot and to make the decision on the basis of the number of defects in the sample. An alternative is to take a smaller sample the first time, with three possible outcomes. If the number of defects in the sample is small enough, management will accept the lot without further investigation. If the number of defects is larger than some predetermined level, management will reject the lot. If the defects lie somewhere in between, management should take another sample (with possibly a third or fourth sample if the number of defects still lies in the intermediate zone). The advantage of sequential sampling is that it may require a smaller sample size, on the average, to reach a decision on acceptance of a lot.

The notion of sequential decision making is much broader than the use of sequential samples in quality control. Management has a certain amount of information pertinent to a decision at hand. It must make a choice between deciding now on the basis of the limited information available or to collect additional information. For example, management may decide to introduce a new product now on the basis of limited information, or it may decide to hire a marketing research firm to collect data on the demand for the product. When it receives the findings of the marketing research, it may still be dissatisfied and may experiment with trial runs before the final decision. At each step the value of the added information in reducing uncertainty and providing better estimates must be weighed against the costs of research and the costs of delay. In the past managers have used rough judgments in determining whether they should act now or wait for added data; in the future more systematic uses of probability theory may replace such broad judgments, but some subjective judgment will always remain.

Flexibility

Flexibility provides another way of reducing the unfavorable effects of uncertainty. Rather than build facilities which will minimize costs at the mean expected level of demand or for some other specified level, it may be better to adopt more flexible methods which are more costly at the mean level but less subject to rising costs away from the mean. In Chapter 6 we graphed the effects of flexibility in the form of a cost curve which is more horizontal as compared with a more specialized U-shaped curve.[5]

The break-even chart can also portray the comparison between a high fixed cost plant (which produces high profits beyond the break-even point and high losses if sales fall short) and a more flexible plant which may be more moderate on both the profit and loss sides. The specialized plant may mean a higher break-even point, which is a sensible choice if the certainty of being beyond that point is high enough.

Illustrations of flexibility are numerous. A digital computer is more flexible than the more specialized analog computer but sometimes is more costly in handling a specialized computing task. Assembly line production techniques are less flexible than "functional" plant layouts, but are more productive in turning out a predetermined product. (Methods have been found to combine some of the advantages of the specialization of the assembly line with some of the flexibilities of functional layouts.) A new bowling alley may involve the construction of a specialized building little suited for any other purpose or may make use of a general-purpose building which could be converted to use as a grocery store if the bowling enterprise were to fail. A firm may choose to maintain a high level of current assets to fixed assets to be able to meet changing economic conditions, at the sacrifice of higher earnings on more fixed assets. A farmer may select a type of barn which is easily converted from the storage of hay to a shed room for feeding cattle or to dairying. Some breeds of cows are better suited to switching back and forth from milk and beef products, but are less productive of milk.

Diversification

Still another way of preparing for uncertainty is by diversifying activities. The ancient warning against putting one's eggs in one basket shows that this principle has a long history, though it is only in recent years that a systematic theory of diversification has appeared.[6] The principle of diversification is well known among stock purchasers, who tend to mix together stocks from a variety of industries with different economic characteristics. It is also known in manufacturing, in which some firms wish to avoid being tied to the vicissitudes of one or two product lines. Especially when the firm is interested in the stability of earnings as well as the magnitude of earnings it looks to diversification to average out the impacts of uncertain changes in particular markets. Also the stress on survival of the firm rather than on maximum short-run profits leads to a search for variety.

---

[5] See Figure 6–14 on p. 261.

[6] See, for example, H. M. Markowitz, *Portfolio Selection: Efficient Diversification of Investments* (New York: John Wiley & Sons, Inc., 1959).

Control over the future

Still another way of dealing with uncertainty is to try to control the variables which bring it about. Often management has no control over external events and must take the consequences. But if the firm is large enough it may be able to bring outside economic forces into some kind of order. For example, collusion among oligopolists has as its aim not only the monopoly profits that may result from price control but also the reduction of uncertainty. The perennial attempts by trade associations to win acceptance of pricing formulas and accounting systems is similar. Price leadership is a way of reducing uncertainty about the reactions of rivals to a firm's price changes. And it is possible that a firm may manipulate advertising and other promotional devices to reduce the instability and uncertainty of sales and production volumes.

Empirical studies and illustrations

Recent research suggests that hedging is not as common a device for avoiding risks as was formerly assumed. There is no doubt that hedging does take place widely in the grain market, in flour milling, in the markets for butter and eggs, and so on. And the very word hedge has come to take on the meaning of avoidance of risk. One dictionary definition is "to counterbalance a sale or purchase of one claim by making a purchase or sale of another." But most of the activity that goes under the name of hedging in actual practice has purposes quite different from the dictionary definitions or ordinary usage.

Holbrook Working and other writers have shown that hedging serves multiple purposes.[7] One purpose is to profit from anticipated changes in price relationships, which is quite a different thing from avoiding the risks due to price changes. Another purpose is to facilitate merchandising and processing operations and to simplify the decision-making process. For example, flour mills find it easier to judge prices offered by future purchasers of flour by relating those prices to current futures prices rather than to estimates of the prices that may be paid on later wheat purchases.[8]

The other ways of dealing with uncertainty are so pervasive that the reader can fill in his own illustrations. Earlier chapters have presented illustrations of imitative prices, payback criteria, and other shortcuts used to evade uncertainty. Examples of insurance, sampling, diversification and flexibility are too well known to require further substantiation as ways of dealing with uncertainty.

---

[7] Holbrook Working, "New Concepts Concerning Futures Markets and Prices," *The American Economic Review,* June, 1962, pp. 431–59.

[8] Several other purposes receive attention in Working's article.

2. BASIC TOOLS FOR THE ANALYSIS OF UNCERTAINTY

The analysis of uncertainty is a major topic in itself—one which could easily take up this full volume. Nevertheless it is desirable to introduce the basic concepts which are part of the language of management. Most managers cannot be experts in statistical analysis, but they can develop skills in identifying situations when expert advice is appropriate.

The frequency distribution

Masses of data which at first appear chaotic can often be arranged by grouping them into frequency distributions. This is done by tabulating the numbers of observations which fall into certain class intervals. Table 10–1 provides an illustration of arrivals of vehicles at a toll booth.

TABLE 10–1

FREQUENCY DISTRIBUTION: ARRIVALS AT TOLL BOOTH PER HOUR

Number of Vehicles Arriving Each Hour	Frequency of Occurrences	Percent of Total Occurrences
0– 3.9	2	4
4– 7.9	7	13
8–11.9	12	22
12–15.9	17	31
16–19.9	10	18
20–23.9	6	11
24–27.9	1	2
	55	101*

* Not 100 because of rounding.

One way of communicating such data is to present them graphically, as in Figure 10–1. Many kinds of data show a gradual increase of frequencies up to a peak and then a gradual decline as is true of the data in that diagram.

If there were some reason for one to assume that the observations were representative and highly likely to repeat themselves, one might use these past observations as the basis for estimates in the future. Thus, one might say that the probability of the number of arrivals being between 8 and 11.9 was 0.22 or 22 percent. The probability of 24 or more arrivals would be 0.02 or 2 percent.

Unfortunately most problems of interest to the manager do not present themselves in such a simple form. Past data do not serve so easily as a basis for establishing probabilities for the future, though inferences can be drawn from past observations. In fact, many decisions must be based on a heterogeneous collection of information of great variety—last period's

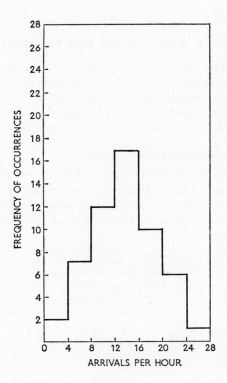

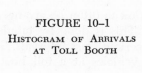

FIGURE 10–1
HISTOGRAM OF ARRIVALS
AT TOLL BOOTH

sales, the average seasonal pattern of sales, surveys of buyers' attitudes, forecasts of business conditions, and the manager's own assessment of the situation. Still, it is convenient to summarize the final estimates of what may happen in the form of a probability distribution. This forces the manager to think systematically about his estimates rather than permit his emotions to overwhelm him. The election forecaster who thought in 1968 that the probability of a Nixon victory was 80 percent had probably done more homework than those who were "certain" of a Nixon victory, though neither was as well informed as those who were analyzing the actual results as they came in from the polls. (The ability of the analysts to be almost 100 percent confident of the outcome in a particular state on the basis of data from a few precincts was based of course on a sophisticated use of sampling and probability analysis.)

The normal distribution and other distributions

Most readers of this volume will be familiar with the fitting of a normal curve to a frequency distribution like that shown in Table 10–1 and Figure 10–1. The normal curve is a bell-shaped curve with well-defined mathematical properties. Many actual distributions in industry and nature approximate the normal distribution, but not all. The arrival of vehicles at toll booths is, in fact, not to be expected to follow a normal pattern for theoretical reasons developed in books on queuing theory. Actual observations of vehicle arrivals do not follow the normal distribution. The actual distributions tend toward the theoretical distributions which are Poisson at lower volumes and normal at higher volumes.

The fact is that several different theoretical distributions are available to deal with a variety of problems. Among them are the exponential distribution, the gamma distribution, the binomial distribution, and the Pascal distribution.[9] In the discussion which follows, attention will be concentrated on normal distributions or cases in which normal distributions provide close approximations to reality.

A frequency distribution can be specified by the identification of its parameters. A normal distribution is specified if the central value (the mean) is given along with a measure of dispersion (such as the standard deviation). The arithmetic mean $\bar{y}$ is computed from the formula:

$$\bar{y} = \frac{\sum\limits_{i=1}^{n} y_i}{n} = \frac{y_1 + y_2 + y_3 + \cdots + y_{n-1} + y_n}{n}$$

The standard deviation σ is given by the formula:

$$\sigma = \sqrt{\frac{\sum\limits_{i=1}^{n} (y_i - \bar{y})^2}{n-1}}$$

Roughly this is the square root of the average deviations of observations from the means squared. One point of significance about the standard deviation is that we can use it to generalize about the probabilities of occurrences at certain ranges from the mean, as indicated in Figure 10–2.

Applications of normal distributions

The break-even analysis in earlier chapters of the book tended to gloss over the problem of uncertainty. The fact is, however, that the sales volume plotted along the horizontal axis of a break-even chart is almost always uncertain. Indeed, the costs themselves may be uncertain. Let us assume here that the cost estimates are dependable enough to use in the form of certainty equivalents and concentrate on the uncertainty of sales volume.

---

[9] An excellent, relatively nonmathematical, presentation of these distributions appears in Robert Schlaifer, *Probability and Statistics for Business Decisions* (New York: McGraw-Hill Book Co., 1959).

FIGURE 10–2
AREAS UNDER THE NORMAL CURVE

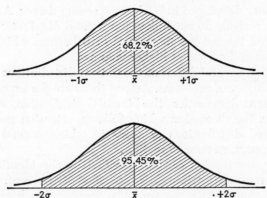

Suppose that two factories encounter the same cost functions and the same mean estimates of sales. It might appear that the optimum decision for one also applies to the other. But if the dispersion (standard deviation of sales) for one is greater than that for the other, this is not true. If the costs are at all curvilinear or if they include discrete "stairsteps," it is by no means clear that the gains at high sales will exactly compensate for lower sales at the lower end of the probability distribution. The corporate income tax also creates a degree of complexity into the analysis; losses are not treated precisely as negative profits for tax purposes. Lastly, attitudes toward risk vary from firm to firm. A highly uncertain sales situation might be avoided if the disutility of losses is considered high.[10]

Uncertainty becomes a more important consideration in the area of capital budgeting, but it is seldom given specific attention in the usual discussions of capital budgeting. Sometimes higher cut-off rates (costs of capital) are applied to riskier investments but this procedure is rather subjective. Still another approach is to apply sensitivity analysis. Such analysis attempts to determine how much difference to profits or other objectives a shift in cash flows will make. This analysis fails, however, to examine the probabilities of such shifts in sufficient detail. It may be useful to apply probability analysis more directly. The procedures for doing so using standard deviation analysis have been developed.[11]

---

[10] A fuller development of these issues appears in R. K. Jaedicke and A. A. Robichek, "Cost-Volume-Profit Analysis Under Conditions of Uncertainty," *Accounting Review*, October, 1964, pp. 917–26, reprinted in James C. Van Horne (ed.), *Foundations for Financial Management*, pp. 11–24.

[11] F. S. Hillier, "The Derivation of Probabilistic Information for the Evaluation of Risky Investments," *Management Science*, pp. 443–57. John Lintner has carried the

The payoff table

The payoff table is a useful device for organizing one's ideas when choice is to be made among a number of *acts,* the outcomes of which depend on *events* which are uncertain. The expressions "acts" and "events" are used frequently in modern treatments of uncertainty.

Suppose the question is to stock some level of inventory of an item without knowing what the level of sales will be. The acts are the number of items to stock. The events are the various levels of sales which are possible. Table 10–3 illustrates such a possibility.

TABLE 10–3

PAYOFF TABLE

Events (Level of Sales)	Acts (Units to be Stocked)				
	0	1	2	3	4
0	$0	−$ 5	−$10	−$15	−$20
1	0	+ 20	+ 15	+ 10	+ 5
2	0	+ 20	+ 40	+ 35	+ 30
3	0	+ 20	+ 40	+ 60	+ 55
4 or more	0	+ 20	+ 40	+ 60	+ 80

The cells in Table 10–3 indicate various levels of profits resulting from combinations of acts and events—that is, from combinations of different levels of sales. If no units are stocked the profit is of course zero. If one unit is stocked but not sold, a loss of $5 is suffered. If one unit is stocked and sold, the profit is $20. The table shows that the highest profit within the range shown results when four units are stocked and all of them sold. But the problem is that all of the four units may not be sold. We need to know the probabilities of the various levels of sales before we can find the optimum.

This is much simpler than the usual problem faced by management. Probabilistic analysis in more realistic cases is likely to become confused unless some devices like the payoff table are used to keep one's ideas in order.

Decision trees

Decisions involving uncertainty are not usually simple cases of choosing among five separate acts, such as those in the inventory example, when

---

analysis further, with attention to the significance of uncertainty for the cost of capital, in "The Valuation of Risks Assets and the Selection of Risky Investments," *Review of Economics and Statistics,* November, 1963, and in "Cost of Capital and Optimal Financing," *Journal of Finance,* May, 1963, pp. 292–310.

each has a simple payoff which can be specified by a single number. In some cases the decision about what is to be done now will determine the options which will be open at the next stage. The initial decision cannot be made until these later options are evaluated. The decision tree is a useful device for analyzing this kind of problem.

Suppose that a firm has an opportunity to purchase one of two other firms, but cannot buy both. If the first purchase is highly successful in producing a sufficient cash inflow, the second purchase might be possible at a later date unless the firm is sold elsewhere in the meantime. The tree diagram would look as in Figure 10–3.

FIGURE 10–3

Tree Diagram

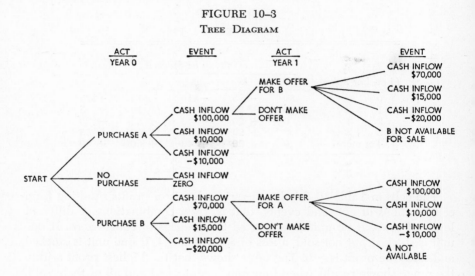

At first glance the purchase of A may appear clearly best because it produces the higest cash inflow; but if the probability of the cash inflow of $100,000 is low, not only may the purchase of A be less satisfactory on its own merits, it may also limit the chances of making the second purchase.

Let us assume that a cash inflow of $40,000 is sufficient to finance a second purchase. Let us also assume that the objective is to maximize the net cash inflow over the first three years without regard to discounting, the cost of capital or other considerations stressed by more sophisticated capital budgeters.

The probabilities for Purchase A are as follows:

Cash inflow	$100,000	—	Probability 0.8
Cash inflow	10,000	—	Probability 0.1
Cash inflow	10,000	—	Probability 0.1

For Purchase B:

Cash inflow	$ 70,000 —	Probability 0.7
Cash inflow	15,000 —	Probability 0.2
Cash inflow	20,000 —	Probability 0.1

If the purchase of A is delayed one year the probability it will not be available the next year is 0.5. If the purchase of B is delayed, this probability of nonavailability would be 0.2.

The analysis requires working backwards, from the right hand side to the left hand side. It requires attaching probabilities to all of the events. Even with this structuring of the problem some ambiguities remain, for it is not really rational to allow undiscounted cash inflows to govern the decision.

3. ECONOMICS AND PROBABILITY ANALYSIS

At this point it is appropriate to consider some well-known applications of probability analysis to managerial problems. We are now concerned with subjective probabilities, for the objective risks can be treated as ordinary expenses by applying the insurance principle. Many managers are skeptical about applying formal probability analysis to cases of uncertainty; indeed, many statisticians are doubtful about the theoretical basis for such analysis. The trend, however, appears toward a more formal analysis; a growing literature supports the use of payoff tables, Bayes' theorem, tree diagrams, Monte Carlo simulation methods, queuing theory, and other techniques for making use of probability theory in decision making.

In the discussion which follows we shall avoid the mathematics of probability. We shall neglect the methods used to obtain particular probability distributions—for example, we shall gloss over the ways in which newly acquired sample information is combined with prior subjective probabilities to reach revised subjective probabilities. These are problems better left for more formal courses in statistics. We shall assume that the reader knows what we mean by a statement that the probability of a particular event is 0.15 or that the cumulative probability that a magnitude exceeds a particular level is 0.63. Such terminology is part of the language of business and should be familiar to all.

What we want to demonstrate now is that the economic concepts developed throughout this book can be combined with probabilities in a variety of managerial problems. It is best to consider a variety of examples; unfortunately the illustrations must be kept simple to make the discussion clear. In real business situations a number of complications are likely to appear.

Inventory control models

One of the best known and simplest probability models goes under the name of the "newsboy problem." A newsboy is faced with the decision of how many newspapers to stock at the beginning of the day. Let us assume that the paper sells for five cents but costs the newsboy two cents. Every sold newspaper results in a profit of three cents; every unsold paper results in a loss of two cents. How many papers should he stock? The newsboy cannot make a decision unless he has some idea of demand, and his notions of demand are likely to be in the form of probabilities. Let us suppose that his subjective probability distribution for sales on this particular day are as shown in Table 10–4. Note that the probabilities in Table 10–4 are cumulative probabilities.

TABLE 10–4

SUBJECTIVE PROBABILITIES OF VARIOUS LEVELS OF NEWSPAPER SALES

Level of Sales	Probability That Sales Will Exceed or Equal That Level
0	1.0
50	1.0
100	.99
200	.90
300	.75
350	.40
400	.25
500	.10
600	.02
700	.01
800	.00

One way of gaining insight into this simple problem is to think of it in terms of incremental costs and incremental gains. The incremental gain from stocking one more newspaper is three cents multiplied by the probability that sales will equal or exceed the amount carried in stock. The incremental cost of adding that newspaper is the two cents multiplied by the probability that sales will fall below the amount carried in stock.

If we start with zero newspapers the incremental gain is clearly three cents, for there is no doubt that the newspaper will sell. The incremental cost is zero, for the probability that the paper will not sell is nil. The newsboy should increase the size of his stocks up to the point at which the incremental cost equals the incremental gain. Equation 10–1 presents the condition for the optimum:

$$mP(d \geqq s) = cP(d < s) \tag{10–1}$$

in which

$$m = \text{margin per newspaper}$$
$$d = \text{demand (quantity of sales)}$$
$$s = \text{amount stocked}$$
$$c = \text{cost of each newspaper}$$
$$P(d \geqq s) = \text{cumulative probability that demand}$$
$$\text{will exceed or equal stocks}$$

Since the two probabilities in equation 10–1 must add to unity, the equation may be rewritten in the form

$$mP(d \geqq s = c\,[1 - P(d \geqq s)] \tag{10–2}$$

The left-hand side of this equation is the incremental gain and the right-hand side is the incremental cost. Often this equation is rewritten in the form

$$P(d \geqq s) = \frac{c}{m + c} \tag{10–3}$$

which indicates that the newsboy should keep increasing his stocks up to the point at which the cumulative probability that sales will exceed or equal the stocks declines to the ratio of the unit cost to the sum of the unit cost and the unit margin.[12]

Let us apply this reasoning to the probability schedule in Table 10–4. Since the ratio of c to $m + c$ is 0.40, it follows that the newsboy should stock 350 newspapers. At this point the incremental gain is $.012 (the probability of 0.40 that sales will equal or exceed 350 multiplied by the margin of $.03) and the incremental cost is also $.012 (the probability of 0.60 that the newspaper sales will be less than 350 multiplied by the unit cost of $.02).

Unfortunately most inventory problems are more difficult than the one described. Even the newsboy might want to take other factors into account, such as the loss of customer goodwill if he runs out of stock very often. In manufacturing, the problem is often one of maintaining an inventory continuously over time and of weighing the carrying costs (interest, storage space, insurance, obsolescence, deterioration, and so on) against the cost of stockouts. The problem is complicated by the need to determine the economic lot size (or economic purchase quantity). The type of model developed for this problem is sometimes known as the order-point order-quantity model, since it determines both the reorder point and the quantity to order. (The model also goes under the name

---

[12] The full derivation of the formulas cited here appears in most books on operations research.

of max-min inventory control.) The development of this model lies beyond the scope of this book; it is sufficient to state that incremental reasoning applies to it as well as to our simple newsboy problem.

Scrap allowances

The analysis of scrap allowances is similar to that in some inventory control models. The problem is one of producing a specified quantity of nondefective pieces. The uncertainty arises from not knowing how many defects to expect. The firm may build up a probability distribution on the number of defects, making use of past experience or of current knowledge about the production process. An increase in the size of the production run reduces the risk of running short and of having to set up the process to fill out requirements. On the other hand, the increased production run increases the chances of producing too many units, with the loss of the labor and materials that go into the excess production.

The scrap allowance problem differs from the newsboy problem in that the cost of running short is a lump-sum cost—the cost of setting up for a second run.[13] The cost of overages is proportional to the number of units of overage (or can be assumed to be so in most cases).

The optimum scrap allowance is given by the equation[14]

$$K_u P(n = j) = k_o P(n < j) \qquad (10\text{–}4)$$

in which

n = the serial number of the required last good piece
j = the specified number of units planned in a run
k_o = the unit cost of overages
K_u = the lump-sum cost of setting up a second run

The left-hand side of this equation is the expected gain from scheduling the jth unit. The right-hand side is the expected cost of the jth unit. The variable which can be manipulated by management is j, the number of units to be scheduled in the first run. As j is increased, the probability of overages (the probability that n is less than j) increases, and the expected cost of overages rises. Eventually the expected cost of overages will catch up with the expected gain from scheduling the jth unit. At this point the incremental profit of increasing j by one unit is zero; beyond this point the incremental profit becomes negative.[15]

---

[13] We shall ignore the possibility of a third or subsequent setup.

[14] The notation follows closely that of Robert Schlaifer in *Probability and Statistics for Business Decisions* (New York: McGraw-Hill Book Co., 1959), p. 140.

[15] These statements depend on a smooth, single-humped probability distribution, which is what one would normally expect in practice.

The formula for the economical scrap allowance can be rewritten

$$\frac{P(n=j)}{P(n<j)} = \frac{k_o}{K_u} \qquad (10\text{-}5)$$

which is a simpler form for practical use, though it is less easy to interpret in incremental terms. In this formula the ratio of the probabilities is made equal to the ratio of the costs. Note that $P(n=j)$ is the probability that the number of units scheduled is *exactly* the number of units required—the probability that this particular level of j will be the one to preclude having to set up a second time.

A bidding model

This book has devoted considerable space to pricing but no space up to this point to the special form of pricing known as bidding. Bidding takes place when several sellers compete for a given contract, each establishing his bid without communication with the others.[16] This problem is necessarily probabilistic in character; each bidder must somehow evaluate the probability that he will win the contract at various bids. In the past, bidders have no doubt relied on informal evaluations of the probabilities. In the future, the formal application of probability theory may become more widespread.

The first step in the analysis is to determine the probabilities that the lowest opponent bid will involve various percentage markups. For the sake of simplicity let us assume that the markup must be in discrete jumps of 5 percent and that the probabilities are as follows:

Markup on Cost	Probability That Lowest Opponent Bid Will Be at This Markup
0%	.05
5	.10
10	.20
15	.30
20	.20
25	.10
35	.05
40	.00

The manufacturer could use past experience in setting up this probability distribution. He might also make use of his current knowledge as to how desperate his opponents are to win the bid and how many opponents are likely to enter bids. The discussion here assumes that

---

[16] Other forms of bidding, such as auction bidding, require an entirely different analysis.

the opponents' bidding habits will not change. If the manufacturer sets his markup low enough, the probability that he will win the bid becomes high, but he sacrifices profits on the job. Maximization of his expected profit involves a compromise between getting the most profit out of each job and increasing the chances of getting the job.

Let us consider a job which will cost $20,000. Let z represent the decision variable, the markup on the manufacturer's bid, and x the markup on the lowest bid. Let π represent the profit in dollars. Then

$$E(\pi) = \$20,000z \, P(x > z)$$

which means that the expected profit is equal to the $20,000 multiplied by the markup and by the probability that the lowest opponent bid will exceed the markup. The objective is to maximize $E(\pi)$. As we increase the markup from 0 percent to 5 percent the expected profit increases from $0 to $20,000 × .05 × .85 or $850.[17] As we increase the markup to 10 percent the expected profit increases to $20,000 × .10 × .65 or $1,300. The results are summarized below:

z	$E(\pi)$
0%	$ 0
5	850
10	1,300
15	1,050
20	600
25	250
30	0

The bid with the highest expected profit is at 10 percent, which means that the bid should be at $22,000. If the manufacturer were to quote bids with fractional markups, a markup of 14.99 percent would be preferable, but our model should then also recognize fractional bids by the opponents. (Calculus and continuous probability distributions would be more appropriate in this more realistic case.)

Oil drilling decisions[18]

A somewhat different problem presents itself when the alternatives open to management are limited in number but substantially different

---

[17] We assume that a bid equal to that of opponents will mean loss of the contract. We also assume that the cost is the same for all bidders. More sophisticated models can overcome the limitations of these assumptions. See Lawrence Friedman's discussion in Churchman, Ackoff, and Arnoff, *Introduction to Operations Research* (New York: John Wiley & Sons, Inc., 1957), pp. 599–73.

[18] This illustration is based on C. Jackson Grayson, Jr., *Decisions Under Uncertainty: Drilling Decisions by Oil and Gas Operators* (Boston: Harvard Business School, Division of Research, 1960).

in character. In the newsboy and scrap allowance problems the decision is about a magnitude—the number of newspapers to stock or the number of units to schedule for production. Frequently, however, management is concerned with a choice among a small number of alternatives. Such might be the case when the choice is between drilling and not drilling for oil. The decision maker does not know whether the outcome will be successful or not; he must face up to uncertainty. He might do better to resort to some formal analysis of probabilities than to depend on intuition or rough guesses.

The first step is to determine the probabilities of the outcomes. At this point the decision maker will want to use as much information on past experience and geological data as possible. Suppose that the subjective probabilities are:

$$
\begin{array}{ll}
\text{Dry hole} & 0.70 \\
\text{100,000 barrels} & 0.20 \\
\text{500,000 barrels} & 0.10
\end{array}
$$

Suppose that the incremental net revenues (after discounting and after the deduction of all expenses including the initial drilling costs of $50,000) are:

$$
\begin{array}{ll}
\text{Dry hole} & -\$\ 50,000 \\
\text{100,000 barrels} & \$\ 50,000 \\
\text{500,000 barrels} & \$450,000
\end{array}
$$

It is now possible to compute the expected monetary value of drilling or not drilling. The expected monetary value of drilling is

$$0.70 \times (-\$50,000) + 0.20 \times (\$50,000) + 0.10 \times (\$450,000) = \$20,000$$

The expected monetary value of not drilling is $0. The analysis indicates that it is profitable to drill. It is true that this particular hole might well turn up dry, but in the long run the losses will more than offset the gains if this type of analysis is followed consistently.

The oil drilling illustration provides an opportunity to introduce two modifications which are receiving considerable attention in the current literature. The first has to do with personal risk preferences. The expected monetary value does not take such personal attitudes toward risk into account and might lead to the wrong conclusion. For example, one oil driller might place a lower marginal utility on added income than on reduced income. A loss of $50,000 might mean bankruptcy and disgrace; a gain of 450,000 might be worth much less than it seems because of the driller's diminishing marginal utility of income. Thus, while the expected monetary value of drilling in the illustration just described is $20,000, the expected utility might be negative. For a different driller with a greater fondness for risk the chance of profits of $450,000 might be most attractive, and he might be willing to drill under even less favorable conditions. Before a sound decision is possible each driller must measure his marginal utility of income at various income levels. (The feasibility of such utility measurements is still a matter of controversy.) In large corporations, in which the utilities of thousands of stockholders might be involved, the expected monetary value would probably be an adequate measuring stick.[19]

The other modification is concerned with the value of additional information. The oil driller is not required to make a choice between drilling and not drilling on the basis of the probabilities with which he starts. He can collect additional information which will enable him to revise his probabilities. For example, he can employ someone to make seismographic soundings. Figure 10–4 is a tree diagram showing alternative acts and the probabilities of various events. The seismographic recordings show whether or not subsurface structure usually associated with oil pools exists. If the structure does exist the probability of dry holes is reduced.

FIGURE 10–4

Tree Diagram for Oil Drilling Problem

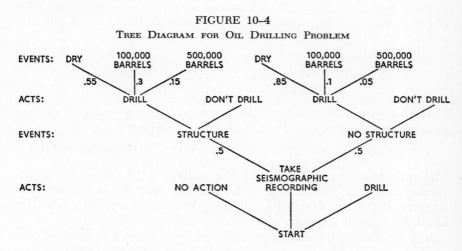

We already know the value of no action is $0. We know that the expected monetary value of drilling is $20,000. A small amount of arithmetic will show that the expected value with the seismographic sounding is $32,500, minus the cost of the sounding. Thus the value of the sounding is $12,500. It is in this way that the value of additional information can be determined.

---

[19] Even if a firm uses expected monetary value as the criterion it still might want to investigate the risk preferences of individual managers within the firm to determine whether those preferences can be reconciled with the objectives of the firm.

The practicality of probability models

Some managers may have difficulty reconciling the requirements of practicality with the theoretical models under discussion. They may object that the models are too general and overly simple. One answer to the objection of overgenerality is that management must develop models to fit their specific problems; the simple models are valuable in giving insight into a problem, but they must be adapted to each specific situation. Another reply is that analysis always requires simplification, for the human mind (even with the aid of computers) is incapable of dealing with all of the factors bearing on a problem. The whole history of science is one of deriving simple generalizations about a complex world. The whole history of management is one of focusing on the key variable the manipulation of which will achieve practical results.

In some applications the usefulness of probability analysis is well established. Statistical quality control has shown its worth for several decades. Queuing models have produced savings which are known to be substantial. But there is a shortage of systematic, scientific studies which have evaluated the results of the great variety of models that have been proposed. Some researchers are careful to estimate in advance the dollar savings which will result from their proposals, but fewer take the trouble to present studies of the savings that have actually materialized. In many cases the absence of follow-up studies is a result of managerial secrecy—there is no reason to let one's competitors in on a good thing. In other cases the paucity of findings results from the failure to put the recommendations into effect—at least not in the original form. Human resistance to change, failures of educating the work force to the new methods, conflicts with established procedures, and many other obstacles stand in the way of application. Even more serious is the general failure of managers throughout industry to study the results of decisions systematically.

Sensitivity analysis is one way of bridging the gap between probability theory and the practical needs of management. Management can use the models to measure the sensitivity of the results to errors in the estimates. For example, it has been found that the present value of a chain of trucks is relatively insensitive to variations in the replacement period.[20] For one type of truck, a replacement period anywhere between 2.2 years and 4.4 years will produce approximately the same results in minimizing costs. In such a situation, errors in estimates are not likely to result in seriously unprofitable decisions. Similarly, the

---

[20] Vernon L. Smith, "Economic Valuation Policies: An Evaluation," *Management Science*, October, 1957, republished in E. H. Bowman and R. B. Fetter, *Analyses of Industrial Operations* (Homewood, Ill.: Richard D. Irwin, Inc., 1959), pp. 444–62.

use of queuing theory in decisions on the number of work stations to install are not likely to be greatly affected by the usual errors of estimate that result from uncertainty. Formal models for determining such sensitivities of profits or costs to errors will help management to focus attention on areas in which it will pay to accumulate more information to reduce the errors. Sensitivity analysis is merely one of a number of ways of making it easier for management to cope with uncertainty.

Conclusions

This chapter has presented only a few of the simplest models of combining probability and economic analysis. More complex problems might require the application of waiting-line (queuing) theory or Markov chains. Probability analysis has been applied to a great variety of management problems: determination of the optimal number of toll collectors at a toll bridge or tunnel, analysis of brand loyalty and brand switching, analysis of the work load on various employees, determination of an economic sampling plan for the inspection of purchased parts or for manufactured parts, the evaluation of the results of industrial experimentation, and many others.

It should be clear that the formal analysis of probabilities has come first in cases in which a fairly steady flow of information is available. Applications are more common in production than in marketing, presumably because information from within the firm on production costs is more accessible and reliable than information on external consumer demands. Management seldom applies formal probability theory to relatively nonrepetitive decisions, such as plant expansions or the employment of new top executives.

It seems likely that managers will make greater use of probability and statistical analysis in the future, even under conditions of high uncertainty. The intuitions on which managers have relied so heavily in the past are susceptible to wide margins of error. It is too easy for managers to make errors in calculation when a complex chain of probabilities is at issue. The student who wishes to progress to more advanced work in managerial economics should obtain a thorough training in mathematics and statistics, for the models which are likely to be important in the future will require considerable sophistication in the use of quantitative methods. Mathematical and statistical methods will not, however, replace the need to understand the fundamentals of economics stressed throughout this book.

Cases for part five

Most of the cases in this section focus attention on capital budgeting. The analysis of actual capital investment problems supplies insights which no text discussion can provide. In the abstract it is easy to be dogmatic about what type of analysis is correct; in practice one must compromise with theory to make it applicable to the complexities and uncertainties of reality.

While all of the cases in this chapter involve uncertainty, only one— The State University Press (B)—is appropriate for a formal evaluation of probabilities. A fuller treatment of uncertainty in decision making must be left to texts in statistics or in operations research.

WALDO, SMITH, AND MAXEY

Fred Waldo, John Smith, and Thomas Maxey were partners in a sign business. Each had other business interests; the sign firm was a sideline for all of them. After they returned from the Armed Forces in 1946, they started buying up small sign companies in towns of populations under 15,000. This venture had proved highly successful, as shown in Exhibit 1. A comparison of Exhibits 1 and 2 indicates an extremely high return on the original investment (most of the capital consisted of plowed-back earnings). Exhibits 3 and 4 provide additional information on company operations.

In 1959 and 1960 several major decisions were required of the partners. One concerned the purchase of additional sign companies located in several towns scattered in nearby states. The partners knew that such companies were available at prices of from five to six times earnings. On the basis of past experience the partners had established a rule of

EXHIBIT 1

COMPARATIVE STATEMENT OF INCOME AND EXPENSE
(years ended December 31, 1954 through 1959)

	Dec. 31, 1959	Dec. 31, 1958	Dec. 31, 1957	Dec. 31, 1956	Dec. 31, 1955
Income					
Gross sales	$109,790	$114,163	$104,212	$79,124	$68,675
Other income	3,068	742	340	0	1,139
Capital gains	396	5,046	2,210	658	0
Total income	$113,254	$119,951	$106,762	$79,782	$69,814
Operating Expenses					
Cost of material	$ 4,385	$ 2,698	$ 4,264	$ 4,066	$ 4,329
Wages and salaries	20,043	25,698	19,878	13,467	12,142
Agency commissions	12,830	13,591	11,060	10,106	9,042
Transportation expenses	4,823	5,050	5,433	4,059	3,806
Insurance	7,049	1,719	1,306	915	934
Depreciation	13,237	14,223	10,148	8,309	7,920
Rent	6,240	4,894	4,509	2,827	2,268
Office supplies	2,338	2,066	918	834	849
Maintenance	1,442	2,116	2,429	1,919	1,890
Taxes and licenses	2,960	2,275	1,814	1,202	901
Professional services	366	6,123	804	200	249
Travel expenses	346	303	6,316	3,036	2,546
Other expenses	8,360	13,446	12,093	6,532	2,893
Total material cost and expense	$84,419	$94,202	$80,972	$57,472	$49,769
Net profit before manager's salary	28,835	25,749	25,790	22,310	20,045
Manager's salary	4,800	4,800	4,213	4,160	4,160
Net profit	$24,035	$20,949	$21,577	$18,150	$15,885

thumb that they would not pay more than five times earnings. They had never paid more than this amount in the past.

The partners knew of one small company which was available at a price of five times earnings. The company had allowed its equipment to run down, so that considerable repairs might be necessary. Mr. Waldo believed that the profits could be increased by raising rentals from the existing level by 20 percent immediately and by another 20 percent at a later date. For example, the company might raise the rate on a medium-size sign from $10 per month to $12 per month and eventually to $15 per month. The firm's experience in the past was that improved service would permit increased rates.

In establishing rates the company was influenced somewhat by the rates in other small towns. The prevailing rate on the size sign already discussed was $15 per panel, though some rates went as low as $12. Rates were almost double in cities of 50,000 population or above.

Before purchasing a new sign company, the partners did research into its potential volume and costs. Outside organizations supplied

EXHIBIT 2

BALANCE SHEETS, 1955–59
(March 31)

	1959	1958	1957	1956	1955
ASSETS					
Cash	$ 4,756	$ 4,630	$ 2,182	$ 3,337	$ 1,626
Accounts receivable	11,384	8,446	12,366	6,150	7,419
Notes receivable	824	0	0	0	0
Inventories	2,450	2,711	3,349	3,359	2,698
Total current assets	$19,414	$15,787	$ 17,897	$12,846	$11,743
Fixed assets	77,819	77,546	88,334	45,854	43,084
Other assets	1,333	1,995	1,748	1,257	477
Total Assets	$98,566	$95,328	$107,978	$59,957	$55,304
LIABILITIES AND CAPITAL					
Current liabilities					
Notes payable	$14,293	$14,088	$ 20,800	$ 5,000	$10,000
Accounts payable	2,718	3,382	3,730	1,692	474
Accrued expenses	780	989	1,162	178	142
Federal tax withheld	311	311	264	130	154
Other	45	21	827	12	155
Total current liabilities	$18,147	$18,791	$26,777	$ 7,012	$10,925
Long-term notes	4,400	8,800	17,688	0	0
Total liabilities	$22,547	$27,591	$ 44,465	$ 7,012	$10,925
Capital					
Mr. Maxey	$25,340	$22,579	$ 21,171	$17,648	$14,793
Mr. Waldo	25,339	22,579	21,171	17,648	14,793
Mr. Smith	25,339	22,579	21,171	17,648	14,793
Total capital	$76,018	$67,737	$ 63,514	$52,945	$44,378
Total Liabilities and Capital	$98,566	$95,328	$107,978	$59,957	$55,304

EXHIBIT 3

ADDITIONS TO FIXED ASSETS

	1958–59	1957–59	1956–57	1955–56
Land	$ 0	$ 0	$ 3,800	$ 0
Signs	12,800	10,860	48,608	9,770
Trucks	902	820	1,720	1,142
Buildings	0	101	142	214
Machinery	356	0	1,039	302
Office equipment	97	337	558	118
Total Additions	$14,154	$12,118	$55,867	$11,546

traffic data which could be used to establish average daily circulation. It was necessary to obtain cost and profit data from the potential seller or from an analysis of Waldo, Smith, and Maxey's own experience.

Mr. Waldo expressed the view that six times earnings was too much

EXHIBIT 4
FIXED ASSETS AND RESERVES FOR DEPRECIATION

	Balance 4–1–58	Additions	Retirements	Balance 3–31–59
Assets:				
Land	$ 6,193	$ 0	$ 0	$ 6,193
Signs	104,182	12,800	10,148	106,834
Autos and trucks	8,281	902	2,400	6,783
Buildings	8,316	0	0	8,316
Machinery and equipment	2,338	356	0	2,694
Office equipment	2,155	97	62	2,190
Totals	$131,465	$14,155	$12,610	$133,010
Reserves for Depreciation:				
Signs	$43,274	$11,273	$ 9,620	$44,926
Autos and trucks	6,149	713	2,300	4,563
Buildings	2,023	438	0	2,461
Machinery and equipment	1,325	538	0	1,863
Office equipment	1,148	274	46	1,376
Totals	$53,919	$13,236	$11,966	$55,189

to pay for sign companies in small towns. He knew of some companies that might be available at that price but wasn't much interested in following up on such opportunities.

In 1960 another issue arose. Mr. Maxey wished to sell his interest in the firm to the other partners. The partners wished to set a price that was fair and that recognized Mr. Maxey's one-third financial contribution to the firm.

1. *Is the rule of buying companies at five times earnings but not at six times earnings a reasonable one? Discuss.*
2. *The partners were able to borrow large sums of money for new ventures at 6 percent. Assuming this to be the cost of capital and assuming a 15-year life of a sign business beyond the time of the case, estimate the present value of the Waldo, Smith, and Maxey firm. Compare this value with a price of five times earnings.*
3. *The partners had access to investment opportunities which in recent years had returned more than 20 percent profit (before taxes). Assuming the opportunity cost of capital to be 20 percent, estimate the present value of the firm. Compare this value with a price of five times earnings.*
4. *Which cost of capital estimate (6 percent or 20 percent) is appropriate? Discuss.*
5. *Discuss the way in which you handled depreciation in your computation.*
6. *Should Waldo, Smith, and Maxey buy the small sign company mentioned in the case? Discuss.*
7. *What would be a fair price to pay Mr. Maxey for his one-third interest in the company?*

WALDO AND SMITH*

In 1962, several years after the events in the preceding case, a new opportunity for the purchase of billboard companies presented itself. A large merchandising corporation was offering to sell local billboard companies which it had acquired. One group of these companies was located in the same region as the Waldo and Smith operations. Waldo and Smith were interested in purchasing this group, though it involved a much larger investment than they had ever considered before.

The price set on the group of billboard companies was $2,512,500. Waldo and Smith would be able to borrow almost all of this sum from a bank without much difficulty. Exhibit 1 shows projected income

EXHIBIT 1
PROJECTED INCOME ON NEW COMPANIES AND THE OLD COMPANY

	New (000)	New (% Sales)	Old (000)	Old (% Sales)	Old and New (Eight-Year Depreciation) (000)	Old and New (Eight-Year Depreciation) (% Sales)
Sales	$1,350	100%	$228	100%	$1,578	100%
Less expenses	928	69	158	69	1,061*	67
Profit before tax, interest, depreciation ...	422	31	70	31	501†	32
Less depreciation	100	7	38	16	320	20
Profit before tax and interest	322	24	32	15	181	12

* Figure has been adjusted as follows: wages are to be increased by $5,000 and "Home office expense" of $20,000 is to be eliminated.
† Figure includes additional $9,000 income derived from commercial business by the old firm.

statements on the new companies, the old firm, and on the new and old consolidated. Depreciation in the consolidated part of the exhibit is accelerated to an eight-year basis, which accounts for the lower profit figure. By writing off the full amount of the investment over a period of eight years, the company could pay for the business out of depreciation. The company would also avoid most of the federal income tax liability in this period by accelerating the depreciation.

Exhibit 2 presents the computation of payback periods on two bases: the first averages the interest payment over eight years, while the second charges the total first year's interest as an expense in the first year. Exhibit 3 shows a schedule for the repayment of the loan that would be required.

___
* This case was prepared by James Ledford under the supervision of W. W. Haynes.

EXHIBIT 2

COMPUTATIONS OF PAYBACK PERIODS

	Eight-Year Depreciation (000)	First-Year Performance (000)
Average annual interest	$ 75*	$150
Profit before tax	106	32
Less federal income tax	48	11
Profit after tax	58	21
Add back depreciation	320	320
Cash available	378	341
Deduct 25 per cent (contingencies)	94	85
Cash available for payback	284	256
Payback period	8.84 years	9.81 years

* Figure arrived at by using 3 percent as the average interest rate over eight years.

EXHIBIT 3

SCHEDULE FOR LOAN REPAYMENT

Payment Number	Date	Cash Required	Cash Available	Excess
1	4–1–63	$232,406	$177,405*	($55,001)
2	10–1–63	227,694	293,400	63,706
3	1–1–64	111,717	121,215	9,498
4	4–1–64	110,539	86,490	(24,049)
5	7–1–64	109,266	144,990	35,724
6	10–1–64	108,170	148,410	40,240
7	1–1–65	106,992	121,215	14,323
8	4–1–65	105,814	86,490	(19,324)
9	7–1–65	104,650	144,990	45,340
10	10–1–65	103,473	148,410	44,937
11	1–1–66	102,296	121,215	18,909
12	4–1–66	101,118	86,490	(14,628)
13	7–1–66	99,940	144,990	45,050
14	10–1–66	98,763	148,410	49,647
15	1–1–67	97,584	121,215	23,631
16	4–1–67	96,406	86,490	(9,916)
17	7–1–67	95,229	144,990	49,761
18	10–1–67	94,052	148,410	54,358
19	1–1–68	92,872	121,215	28,343
20	4–1–68	91,682	86,490	(5,192)
21	7–1–68	90,502	144,990	54,488
22	10–1–68	89,340	148,410	59,070
23	1–1–69	88,162	121,215	33,053
24	4–1–69	86,985	86,490	(495)
25	7–1–69	85,808	144,990	59,182
26	10–1–69	84,630	148,410	63,780
27	1–1–70	83,452	121,215	37,763
28	4–1–70	82,275	86,490	4,215
29	7–1–70	81,098	144,990	63,892
30	10–1–70	79,920	148,410	69,490

* First payment due at the end of six months (from time of purchase). Cash available at the end of six months has been adjusted for $30,000 of accounts receivable which buyer must pay for out of earnings.

The companies under consideration owned real estate which had recently been appraised at $361,000. Waldo and Smith might be able to sell this property and apply the proceeds to the cost of the investment. This would make it easier to obtain the loan and would speed up repayments.

1. *Since the company can borrow large sums of money at 6 percent interest, one might argue that the cost of capital is 6 percent. What is the present value of the new investment at a rate of 6 percent? (Assume the investment will have a life of 15 years. It will be useful to use discount tables. Be certain to take taxes into account.)*
2. *The partners have been successful in their other investment ventures in making returns of 20 percent or higher. Would it be reasonable to use 20 percent as the rate of discount in computing the present value? Compute the present value on this basis, assuming a life of 15 years. (Discount tables will simplify the computation). Which present value figure (the one at 6 percent or the one at 20 percent) is more reasonable?*
3. *Which of the two ways of computing the payback period seems more appropriate? Is either computation helpful in the decision to buy or not?*
4. *Evaluate the treatment of depreciation in Exhibits 1 and 2. Is it correct to speed up depreciation in Exhibit 1? Is it sound to add back depreciation in Exhibit 2?*
5. *Exhibit 2 shows only a $58,000 profit after tax on one basis and a $21,000 profit after tax on the other basis. These represent returns of less than 3 percent and 1 percent respectively on the original investment. Do such low returns show that the investment is unsound?*
6. *Should Waldo and Smith invest the $2,512,500?*

AVELLA, INC.*

Avella, Inc. was a well-established company engaged in the manufacture of various rubber and plastic goods. The products were generally inexpensive, and a high volume of sales had to be maintained to enable the company to recover its fixed costs. The management consciously avoided taking on any products which could be characterized as novelties or fads likely to have a relatively brief period of prosperity. Avella had been fortunate in maintaining a stable pattern of sales over the years and had developed a strong customer loyalty. The company had gained a reputation through its production of a relatively complete line of quality products. There was some competition from the producers of specialties, but no other business in the industry offered competition with such a complete line.

---

* This case was prepared by Professor Carl L. Moore of Lehigh University as a basis for class discussion. This case is not designed to present illustrations of either correct or incorrect handling of administrative decisions. Copyright 1959 by Carl L. Moore.

Mr. Edgar A. Gordon, who had recently retired as chairman of the board, was firmly convinced that the company should maintain a strong working capital position and finance its resources primarily with equity capital. This policy, he believed, would place the company in a favorable position to exploit opportunities when they arose and would have the further advantage of providing protection during prolonged periods of general economic decline.

This policy was being carefully reviewed. Many of the officers and directors believed that a restrictive cash policy had checked the growth of the company and had resulted in the loss of many favorable opportunities for profitable investment. There was no desire, however, to make rapid changes. The position of the firm and its policies and procedures were being currently examined.

The company had maintained a minimum cash balance of approximately $1,500,000 at all times. Throughout the year, cash needs were carefully budgeted and plotted on a broken-line graph as shown in Exhibit 1.

EXHIBIT 1

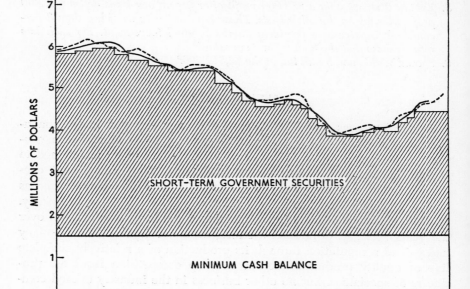

CASH POSITION BUDGET
(AS OF SEPTEMBER 20)

———————— ACTUAL CASH AND SECURITIES
------------ BUDGETED CASH AND SECURITIES
//////////// INVESTMENT IN SHORT-TERM GOVERNMENT SECURITIES

Any cash flow in excess of what was required in order to finance current operations was invested in short-term government securities. This investment was adjusted up or down according to the seasonal needs for cash. Careful budgeting had resulted in stabilizing the cash balance at about the desired level.

During 19—, Avella, Inc., increased its working capital by $1,310,000.

Source of net working capital	
Net income before depreciation charges of $1,302,994	$3,510,050
Uses of net working capital	
Dividend payments	$1,250,100
Fixed asset additions	959,950
Total	$2,200,050
Net increase in working capital	$1,310,000

The statement of financial position at December 31, 19—, and the condensed operating statement for the year 19—, as given in Exhibit 2, were considered by the controller to be typical. The gross cost of the plant and equipment at the end of the fiscal year was $24,362,130. After deducting the accumulated depreciation of $16,740,630, there was a remaining net book value of $7,621,500.

The controller of the company, Mr. Charles A. Penberthy, was in the process of reviewing the way in which business investment opportunities were evaluated to determine their economic feasibility. Mr. Penberthy was well acquainted with the various activities of the company through his long years of service in production, sales, and financial administration.

Investment proposals were initiated by a new products committee which worked closely with the director of research. Possible projects were carefully screened as to market potential, their relationship to existing product lines, and production possibilities. The controller and his staff assisted in this screening process. As a general rule, a project was not accepted unless analysis revealed that the project would probably yield a rate of return upon investment of at least 30 percent before taxes. The 30 percent rate of return had been established as a guide on the basis that the company had been earning approximately that rate on its investment in machinery and equipment over the years. For example, the company earned $4,686,073 before taxes during 19—. The total cost of the machinery and equipment (without allowance for depreciation) at the end of the year was $15,654,257. Relatively insignificant acquisitions or replacements and obvious cost saving possibilities did not go through such a rigorous screening process.

After the project had been accepted by the new products committee, it was reviewed by the marketing committee of the board of directors.

EXHIBIT 2

STATEMENT OF FINANCIAL POSITION
(December 31, 19—)

Current assets
Cash	$ 1,707,269
U.S. government securities at cost including accrued interest	3,111,398
Accounts receivable	7,818,592
Inventories	8,616,133
Prepaid expenses	309,380
Total current assets	$21,562,772

Current liabilities
Accounts payable	$ 1,141,834
Accrued taxes, wages, and miscellaneous expenses	1,788,636
Estimated federal income tax liability less U.S. Treasury notes. . of $1,080,000	183,301
Total current liabilities	$ 3,113,771

Net working capital	$18,449,001

Other assets
Miscellaneous investments	$ 590,417
Real estate, machinery, and equipment at cost less depreciation	8,420,152
Net assets	$27,459,570

Capital
Common stock	$ 7,413,480
Capital in excess of par value	2,527,242
Reinvested earnings	17,518,848
	$27,459,570

STATEMENT OF EARNINGS
(for the year ended December 31, 19—)

Sales and other income	$48,654,260

Cost and expenses
Cost of products sold	$30,232,458
Selling, administrative and general expenses	13,535,720
Federal income tax, estimated	2,479,017
Total costs and expenses	$46,447,204
Net earnings	$ 2,207,056

Ordinarily the marketing committee would approve the projects received from the new products committee and would recommend that the facilities committee of the board appropriate the funds necessary to carry out the project. The new products committee, well aware of the company policy established while Mr. Gordon was chairman of the board, did not bother to submit projects which could not show a potential rate of return of at least 30 percent.

The rate of return as computed by the company was the net dollar advantage before taxes divided by the average annual investment.

$$\frac{\text{Net dollar advantage before taxes}}{\text{Average annual investment}} = \text{Rate of return}$$

Both the net additional revenue and the direct cost savings to be derived from the project were considered in arriving at the net dollar advantage before taxes. The net additional revenue was the gross revenue anticipated from the project as reduced by the cost of goods sold and estimated selling and administrative expenses. The cost of goods sold was computed in the conventional manner, including the cost of direct materials, direct labor, and manufacturing overhead. Manufacturing overhead, including depreciation, was applied to the products on a predetermined rate basis as a percentage of direct labor cost. An allowance of 17 percent of the estimated gross revenue was deducted for selling and administrative expenses. This percentage had been established from past experience studies which showed that the selling and administrative expenses which should be identified with a product were approximately 17 percent of sales. Finally, depreciation computed on a straight-line basis on the facility cost and on what was called the capital corollary was deducted to arrive at the net dollar advantage before taxes.

The capital corollary represented the allocated investment in floor space used. Mr. Penberthy maintained that each machine had to absorb a portion of the cost of space used. If the allocated plant costs such as depreciation, taxes, and insurance were not considered, the building expansion required to accommodate additional equipment would be unfairly charged against the last piece added, when in reality all additional pieces helped bring about the need for building expansion. The corollary investment was estimated to amount to 70 percent of the cost of the equipment. Some time in the past a study was made over a period of time to determine the relationship between plant costs and investment. As a result of this study, it was found that the allocated plant costs would amount to about 70 percent of the investment in equipment.

The total average annual investment was then computed. The cost of the equipment itself was divided in half to arrive at an average. The

NET DOLLAR ADVANTAGES BEFORE TAXES

1. Direct cost savings before depreciation .... $
2. Increased revenue
   Sales .... $
   Cost of goods sold ....
   Gross profit .... $
   17 percent allowance for selling and administrative expenses ——————
   Net revenue addition ....
3. Gross dollar advantage [(1) + (2)] .... $
4. Less depreciation of facility cost and capital corollary ......
5. Net dollar advantage before taxes [(3) − (4)] .... $

capital corollary cost amounting to 70 percent of the equipment cost was similarly averaged. Furthermore, a provision was made for the increase in working capital which would be required to support the project.

A study had been made showing that approximately 9 percent of the estimated gross revenue was held as accounts receivable, 21 percent of the estimated cost of goods sold was invested in inventories, and 5 percent of the estimated cost of goods sold was held as a minimum cash balance.

Accordingly, these percentages were applied to the expected gross revenue and cost of goods sold resulting from the project to arrive at the additional investment held in the form of working capital.

INVESTMENT

One-half facility estimated cost .... $
One-half capital corollary ....
Total working capital .... ———
    Total average annual investment .... $

As an example, an evaluation of a proposal to manufacture a certain type of air mattress to be used in swimming pools is given in Exhibit 3.

Projects which were accepted were subject to a postcompletion audit. If the results did not come close to expectations, a decision was reached as to whether or not an additional audit was to be made. In certain cases it was believed that if more time were allowed, the project would eventually meet the requirements. On the other hand, some projects might show that there was little opportunity for improvement and that additional audits would not be justified. An unsuccessful project might be liquidated, or it might be continued as a sort of necessary evil which had to be tolerated. For example, a project might be maintained, which did not justify itself, in order to round out the product line.

Mr. Penberthy and his staff were actively investigating the possibility of improving the method by which business investment proposals were evaluated. Both Mr. Penberthy and his staff had been reading current literature on the subject and had attended various conferences dealing with this topic.

1. *Evaluate the capital budgeting procedures of the Avella Company, including the following specific considerations:*
   a) *The amount of working capital on hand.*
   b) *The cut-off rate.*
   c) *The cost of capital to the company.*
   d) *The formula for computing the rate of return.*
   e) *The treatment of overhead in the computations.*
   f) *The treatment of depreciation in the computations.*
   g) *The use of capital corollary concept.*
   h) *The provision for working capital.*

EXHIBIT 3

ECONOMIC EVALUATION OF FACILITY ACQUISITION PROPOSAL
(net dollar advantages before taxes)

Increased revenue
Sales $793,278
Cost of goods sold 558,774

Gross profit $234,504
17% allowance for selling and administrative expenses 134,857

Net revenue increase .... $ 99,647

Gross dollar advantage .... $ 99,647
Less depreciation of facility cost and capital corollary 25,730

Net dollar advantage before taxes .... $ 73,917

INVESTMENT

One-half facility estimated cost .... $ 75,675
Capital corollary
One-half other fixed assets 52,973
Total working capital 216,677

Total average annual investment $345,325

$$\frac{\text{Net dollar advantage before taxes—\$73,917}}{\text{Total average annual investment—\$345,325}} = 21.4\% \text{ Rate of return}$$

Explanatory notes
Total facility cost $151,350
(Est. life of 10 years, no residual salvage value)
Capital corollary (70% of $151,350) $105,945
Sales $793,278
Cost of goods sold $558,774
Selling and administrative expenses (17% of $793,278) $134,857
Total working capital
Accounts receivable (9% of $793,278) .... $ 71,395
Inventories (21% of $558,774) 117,343
Cash (5% of $558,774) 27,939

Total working capital 216,677
Depreciation [10% of ($151,350 + $105,995)] 25,730

2. *Would the capital budgeting procedures described in this case be equally applicable to replacement investments and to investments in entirely new facilities? Discuss.*

WHITE CASTLE TRUCKING CO.*

"I'm sorry I can't agree with you Jim. I still believe we should pay for the trucks we have before we go out on a limb and over-extend our-

* This case was prepared by Professor Frederic A. Brett of the University of Alabama as a basis for class discussion.

selves by committing most of our revenue to meeting time payments."
George Pike and his brother, Jim, thus continued their argument over
the expansion policy of the White Castle Trucking Company.

This company had come into existence in the spring of 1958 as the
result of a casual remark made by the owner of a ready-mix concrete
company: "I surely could use some extra 12-yard dump trucks this
summer."

Following upon this remark, George and Jim Pike made a study of
the costs and revenues involved in the dump-truck leasing business with
the following results:

1. New 12-yard 10-wheel dump trucks cost between $15,000 and
$22,000 each. Used trucks in fair operating condition could be pur-
chased for between $3,500 and $10,000 depending upon their age and
condition. Many methods were used to depreciate used trucks. The most
common method was to depreciate them on an eight-year basis from
January 1 of the model year (i.e., a 1953 truck purchased on April 1,
1957, would be depreciated over three and three quarter years from April
1, 1957).

2. State license fees and insurance would amount to about $625 per
truck per year.

3. As each truck had 10 wheels, tire repair and replacement costs
would be a major consideration. Trucks were used over rough ground
and the experiences of other truck leasing companies indicated that
about half of the tires had to be replaced each year. Some of the tires
could be recapped which would reduce replacement costs. New tires
cost about $225 each. It was estimated that with careful driver main-
tenance it would cost approximately $800 a year for tires on a per truck
basis.

4. At current prices, the cost of gasoline and oil to operate a truck
on an eight-hour basis amounted to between $15 and $18.

5. There were no general figures available for repair and maintenance
costs with the exception that a complete overhaul of a truck engine
would cost between $1,000 and $1,300. Other truck leasing companies
had found a direct relationship between repair costs and the care given
to trucks by drivers. Some companies found it necessary to completely
overhaul each truck on an annual basis. Other companies, using a wage
incentive plan, had reduced the annual repair and maintenance costs
to as little as 40 percent of the cost of a complete overhaul.

6. Truck-with-driver lease rates were $8.50 to $9.50 per hour depending
upon location (county) and road surface conditions. Road construction
companies usually paid $75 per truck on a daily lease basis. It was com-
mon practice for ready-mix concrete companies to lease truck with driver
for $60 per day when gasoline and oil were supplied by the lessee.

7. In order to lease trucks to most companies in the area, it was necessary to employ only union drivers. The going rate for drivers was $3.12½ per hour or $25 for an eight-hour day. However, because of competition for jobs, many union drivers worked for a flat $20 per day. These "cut-rate" drivers were considered a risk by many of the companies, which found that repair costs mounted when these drivers were used.

The Pike brothers discussed their findings and decided to start a dump-truck leasing business if they could get a firm contract from one of the concrete ready-mix companies. They contacted Carl Manning who had given them the idea of starting the business by his casual remark earlier in the year. Manning agreed to give them a contract for five trucks at $60 per truck per day (five days a week) for the period May 15 to October 15 and that he would supply gasoline and oil for the trucks. It was further agreed that if a truck started work on a particular day and, at the option of the lessee, worked less than four hours it would be paid for on the basis of one-half day; if it worked more than four hours, it would be considered as having worked a full day. If a truck broke down due to mechanical trouble, it would be docked on an hourly rate ($7.50) until repaired and put back in service. Time required for tire changes or minor repairs would not be charged against the truck unless down time ran over one hour at which time the $7.50 deduction rate would go into effect.

On May 7, 1958, four used trucks were bought from Eastern Mack Trucks Inc., a local truck dealer, for $16,500. Terms of the purchase contract called for a down payment of $4,000 and monthly payments of $754 for 18 months. A used three-quarter ton pickup truck was also purchased for $500 cash. This vehicle was to be outfitted and used as a service truck. State license plates for the four trucks amounted to $960 and one year premiums for liability and property damage insurance cost $1,527.84. The license plate for the pickup cost $24.50 and the insurance premium amounted to $151.70.

On May 10, a fifth truck was purchased for $7,500. Time payments of $388 per month for 18 months and a down payment of $1,000 was the best deal they could make. The annual insurance premium for this truck amounted to $381.96 and the license plate cost $240.

Drivers were hired for four of the trucks and Jim decided to give up his job as an automotive parts salesman and drive the fifth truck as well as manage the company. George would devote only part of his time to the new business. The drivers agreed to work for $20 a day until the new firm got on its feet, at which time they would expect to receive union wages. Jim decided to drive a 1954 International which was in pretty poor condition with the hope that he could "baby it along" until the cash account was improved and funds were available for needed repairs.

All five trucks reported for work on Wednesday, May 14. During the next month and a half, total revenue amounted to $8,160 of which $240 was receivable due to the practice of lease payments being made on Saturday of each week. During this same period of time, cash payments amounted to $6,458 of which $1,142 went for time payments on the trucks, $2,720 for driver's pay, $1,230 for tire repair and replacement, and $816 for truck repairs.

Analyzing the operations for the first six weeks, George and Jim came to the following conclusions:

1. Trucks had operated at only 83 percent efficiency due to down time for repairs. On a total basis, this had resulted in the loss of 29 truck-days at $40 per day or $1,160 ($60 rental less $20 driver pay).

2. The calculated risk of buying the cheaper trucks which were in rather poor operating condition had resulted in high repair costs as well as reducing potential revenue. This condition would have a reverse trend as soon as trucks were overhauled.

3. The high cost of tire repair and replacement would not continue once all worn tires had been replaced.

4. One driver had quit because he lost too much time while his truck was being repaired. The other drivers were not too happy about losing time when their trucks broke down. They felt that as long as they were working for less than union wages they should have full-time trucks to drive.

After a lengthy discussion, George and Jim decided on a new operating policy as follows:

1. Drivers would be hired at $20 a day on a five-day week basis. If their trucks were out of service due to mechanical breakdown, they would be paid at half-rate to assist in the repair work. It was believed that this policy would encourage drivers to take better care of their trucks in order to earn full pay. Another benefit would be that driver morale would be higher because of the minimum $10 per day wage rate.

2. Repair costs had been high, and it was thought that if a suitable location could be had at a reasonable price, it would be cheaper in the long run to employ a full-time mechanic to work on the trucks at a company-owned garage.

George surveyed the area and on August 1 a service station, located near the edge of town on a little-traveled road, was leased for one year. The station was equipped with a grease rack and a wash shed which could be used as an enclosed repair shop. The station was on a large lot which could park about 50 vehicles. It was thought some revenue could be earned through leasing parking space to independent truckers and thus reduce the overhead for the operation.

On September 30, 1958, the following financial data were taken from the books of the company:

Truck rental income $23,688
Operating expenses:
    Drivers' wages (1) $8,460
    Tire repair and replacement 2,389
    Truck repair (2) 2,178
    Insurance (3) 2,337
    Interest and bank charges 363
    Gasoline and oil, etc. (4) 274
    Taxes (5) 1,998
    Other cash expenses 966
Total expenses before depreciation   18,965
Profit before depreciation .... $ 4,723

  (1) Includes regular driver pay for Jim.
  (2) Includes rent on service station and mechanic's pay.
  (3) Includes annual insurance premiums on trucks.
  (4) Supplied for special jobs worked on Saturdays.
  (5) Includes annual truck license fees and social security taxes.

Jim was elated over the $4,723 profit the company had made since it was formed in May. George, however, was a bit worried when he realized that the cash account had increased only $501 due to the principal payments on the trucks of $4,222 ($4,568 less $346 interest included in above statement). George was also concerned about the contract running out on October 15 with no assured work for the trucks during the winter months.

The weather during October and the early part of November was favorable for work and White Castle was able to work 32 days after October 1 before Manning closed down operations for the winter. During this period, $8,060 was collected for truck rentals. The remainder of the winter was a very trying time for the new company. On an overall average, only one truck was kept busy from November 17 until May 4, 1959, resulting in rental income of only $6,420. Operating expenses before depreciation charges for the period October 1, 1958, to May 4, 1959, were:

Drivers' wages (1) .... $ 4,880
Tire Repair and replacement 737
Truck repairs (2) 3,160
Taxes (3) 1,682
Other cash expenses (4) 1,442
Total cash expenses $11,901

  (1) Drivers hired on a daily basis during winter months.
  (2) The winter months were used to overhaul trucks. Other independent truckers used repair shop and receipts from these jobs were used to offset repair costs.
  (3) Includes trucks license fees due January 1 of each year.
  (4) Includes interest payments of $641.

The company had been in a very poor cash condition during the winter months and George had had to borrow a total of $1,500 from a local bank to make the March and April payments on the trucks. George was further concerned about the insurance premiums of $2,061.50 and time payments of $1,142 due in May.

On May 4, 1959, all five trucks were leased out to Manning at the same rates as the previous year. Manning stated that he could use twice as many trucks and Jim thought it would be a good idea to refinance the old trucks, which were in good operating condition after the winter repair work was completed, and buy several more trucks for the 1959 season. He reasoned that with only six more payments to be made on the trucks, they could cut the payments to a point where three or four new trucks would not be any more of a burden than the five trucks had been the previous year. In addition, the added revenue from the additional trucks would ease the entire cash position of the company.

George was very much against the idea and voiced his opinion that the old trucks should be paid for before any new time payment commitments were made. If no new obligations were undertaken, the old trucks would be paid for before the slack winter season set in and they wouldn't have to worry about the heavy drain on cash during the winter months.

Jim believed that this conservative approach would stunt the growth of the company and favored a policy of rapid expansion for the new company. To prove his point of view, Jim had their accountant project their cash position for the period June 1, 1959, to May 31, 1960, using the following assumptions:

1. Three additional trucks would be purchased for a total of $15,000. The down payment would amount to $3,000 and monthly payments of $776 for 18 months would complete the contract.

2. The five old trucks would be refinanced for a total of $412 per month for 18 months.

3. Trucks would rent for $60 a day (gasoline and oil to be supplied by lessee) and drivers would be paid on the same basis as last year.

4. Truck repair expense, which would include net service station operations, would not cost more than an estimated $300 per month.

5. Tire repair and replacement would not run more than $500 per truck per year. This lower than average estimate was based on the fact that trucks were used on hard surface roads about 90 percent of the time.

6. An additional $2,500 would be used during the winter months to overhaul the new trucks. This amount was in addition to repair costs considered under #4 above.

7. All trucks would operate at 85 percent efficiency between June 1 and September 30. Two trucks would be kept busy for the other months on a five-day week basis. This estimate was based upon last year's experience and a snow removal and sanding contract which Jim was assured of for the coming winter.

Jim considered these estimates very conservative since revenue was being understated for May and October when the company had a good chance of operating above 25 percent efficiency.

1. *Was the original investment in the company a sound one? Discuss. What criteria are relevant in evaluating this question?*
2. *Would the company have been better off to have invested in new rather than second-hand trucks? Discuss.*
3. *Estimate the economic profit for the company in the period up to September 30, 1958. Estimate the economic profit for the period up to May 4, 1959.*
4. *Should the company have purchased additional trucks in May, 1959?*
5. *Develop a cash budget based on the assumptions listed at the end of the case. Is this budget useful in making the decision on the purchase of additional trucks?*
6. *Would it be useful to compute the present value or discounted rate of return in this case? What cost of capital would be relevant?*

ECONOMIC LIFE AND PRESENT VALUE OF AN AUTOMOBILE

Most of the cases in this book are based on actual decision-making situations. The present case, however, is based not on a particular situation but upon a general decision problem faced by most Americans. It is the problem of how long to retain an automobile and how much value to place upon it.

To determine the economic life of an automobile it is necessary for each individual to determine certain magnitudes for each year lying ahead:

1. The value of the annual benefits expected from the automobile. This would be a sum of the bus fares, taxi fares, train fares, and airplane fares which will be saved, plus the convenience value of the automobile (including the advantage of not having to wait for public transportation), plus the value of other satisfactions one may get from owning the car (the status satisfaction, conspicuous consumption, keeping up with the Joneses, or other sociological gratifications). The annual benefits are likely to decline over the years, as the car becomes older, less dependable, and less satisfactory as a status symbol.

2. The expected annual expenses including gas, oil, tires, batteries, maintenance and repairs. Depreciation should not be included among these costs. The expenses will rise as the automobile becomes older.

3. The expected net benefits after deduction of expenses.

4. The expected salvage value (market value) of the automobile year by year. The decline in market value varies from one automobile to another. It might be convenient to express the salvage value in the form of an equation such as

$$S(t) = C(\tfrac{3}{4})^t$$

in which

S(t) = salvage value at the end of year *t*
C = original cost of the automobile
t = the year of life of the automobile (first year, second year, etc.)

5. The loss in salvage value expected year by year. This can be obtained by subtracting the expected salvage value at the end of a year from the expected salvage value at the beginning of that year. Or it may be obtained by computing the derivative of the expression for the salvage value.

$$S'(t) = \frac{dS(t)}{dt}$$

These two methods will not give exactly the same answer. The first method estimates the discrete drop in salvage value over a year while the other gives the instantaneous rate of loss in salvage value at a moment in time.

6. The cost of capital. This should be an estimate of the opportunity cost of the money to be tied up in the automobile.

Once one has determined each of the above variables or functions he is ready to determine the economic life of the automobile. He then can compute the present value of the automobile to determine whether it is worth its price.

Because of the subjective element in the benefits received from an automobile, each person will obtain a somewhat different economic life and present value for the same automobile. When different automobiles at different prices are under consideration, considerable variations in the answers are to be expected.

1. *Compute the economic life of a new automobile costing $2,500. Does your computation of economic life appeal to your common sense? Discuss. (The reader may wish to try out other price lines and experiment with alternative assumptions about expenses, the cost of capital, etc.)*
2. *Often there will be two lengths of life at which* R(t) = iS(t) + S'(t). *Explain. Which is the economic life? What is the significance of the other "solution"?*
3. *Determine the present value of the automobile based on the economic life you have computed for Question 1.*
4. *Would the determination of the present value of a factory machine be as subjective as in this automobile illustration? Explain.*

AMERICAN TELEPHONE AND TELEGRAPH COMPANY*

The Federal Communications Commission has jurisdiction over interstate telephone services and rates. In this area it has been able to follow,

* This case is based primarily on official FCC proceedings on September 19 and 20, and December 13, 1962, and January 4, 1963.

for many years, a policy of regulation based on continuous surveillance. The Commission has maintained continuing studies of extensive financial and operating data which it requires the Bell System companies to submit in monthly, annual, and special reports. Through its field offices located in New York City, St. Louis, and San Francisco, the Commission's staff conducts on-the-spot investigations of the companies' books and associated records. The Commission also keeps itself informed of the companies' plans for new constructions and financing, as well as of the Commission Staff and the Bell System views concerning the level of earnings required, by means of periodic informal meetings.

Following this process the Commission has taken action to secure overall rate reductions where it thought such reductions warranted. Since 1934, numerous rate reductions have been made and one general rate increase has been allowed. Based on 1962 volumes of traffic the net effect of the major rate changes during this period have resulted in savings to the public of over $1 billion annually.

The Commission has not been committed, however, exclusively to informal procedures. In several instances where agreement could not be reached informally, the Commission instituted formal rate reduction proceedings through show-cause orders. In each instance, this action led to a satisfactory resolution of the matter without the need to proceed with the hearings. The Commission also has initiated formal hearings dealing with specific rates and services. At one time recently, there were 31 formal cases involving the Bell System before the Commission.

The Commission held a series of informal conferences between September, 1962, and January, 1963, concerning the level of earnings required from the interstate telephone operations of the Bell System. In addition to explaining its plans for new construction and financing, the company presented testimony supporting its view that an 8 percent return was both within the range of reasonableness and required to encourage the greatest development of its communications services at the lowest cost to the users over the long term. Conversely, an expert retained by the Commission staff testified that a rate of return of 6.1 percent would be adequate.

The cost of capital: Professor Friend's testimony

One of the Company's expert witnesses, Professor Irwin Friend of the Wharton School of Finance and Commerce, testified that the cost of capital to the AT&T was more than 7½ percent. Such a figure would cover the 3.9 percent of "embedded" debt cost and a 9.2 percent cost of equity, assuming a capital structure of 35 percent debt and 65 percent equity.

Professor Friend concentrated most of his analysis on the cost of equity. He rejected both past earnings-price ratios and past dividends-price ratios as measures of the cost of capital. These measures, he said, would apply only if investors were expecting no change in earnings, dividends, or market prices. The fact is that investors buy common stocks in the expectation of growth in earnings and dividends, so that a provision for growth must be included in the cost of capital.

Professor Friend presented a formula for the computation of the cost of equity capital. The formula is

$$i_e = g + \frac{E}{P}(1 + g)d$$

in which i_e is the cost of equity capital, g is the expected growth in earnings per share, $\frac{E}{P}$ is the earnings-price ratio, and d the expected dividend payout ratio. One assumption Dr. Friend made with respect to AT&T stock is that the investor expects the $\frac{E}{P}$ ratio will be the same at the termination of his investment as at the beginning. Therefore he found that the cost of equity for AT&T is the sum of the expected growth rate in earnings plus the dividend-price ratio adjusted for growth.

Professor Friend stated as a fundamental that the price-earnings ratio used in the formula must be consistent with the growth rate. Exhibit 1 shows a relationship between growth rates and price-earnings ratios for a group of income stocks, growth stocks, and utility stocks. This demonstrates that a low growth rate is accompanied by a low price-earnings multiple (a high earnings-price ratio). It would be "improper to combine a high growth rate with a low price-earnings multiple or on the other hand a high price-earnings ratio with a low rate of growth."

Exhibit 2 provides some evidence on AT&T growth rates and price-earnings multiples. The period from 1946 to 1950 was atypical, being a period of depressed earnings and low interest rates. The price in 1947 seemingly was held up by the expectation of increased earnings; when the increased earnings did not materialize the price-earnings multiple declined.

The price-earnings multiple for the period 1950–58 averaged about 13½ times. Earnings per share in this period increased about 4 percent per annum. In the period 1958–62 the growth rate in earnings per share was 5½ percent which goes far to explain the rise in the price-earnings multiple in that period. Professor Friend concluded from this analysis that a 1962 investor would expect an average price-earnings multiple of 18 times and a growth rate of 5 percent for the foreseeable future. Even higher expected growth rates, he believed, might be justified on the basis of the postwar evidence.

Exhibit 3 shows Professor Friend's computation of the cost of equity capital. He assumed a 65 percent payout even though the recent AT&T payout had been somewhat below that figure. In the bottom half of the

EXHIBIT 1

RELATIONSHIP BETWEEN GROWTH AND PRICE/EARNINGS MULTIPLES,
MOODY'S INDEXES[*]

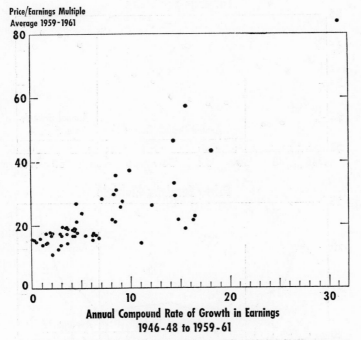

* Moody's "20 Income Stocks, 20 Growth Stocks and 24 Utility Stocks."

exhibit, he made an adjustment for the "underpricing" of the stock—that
is for the fact that the proceeds to the company on a sale of new stock
would be 10 percent below the market price. The result was an estimated
cost of equity capital of 9.2 percent.

Professor Friend used a cost of debt capital of 3.9 percent in his computation of the overall cost of capital. This estimate was low because it
was well below the current costs of *new* debt. These are higher than the
"embedded" costs which are weighted heavily by the low interest rates in
the 1940's and early 1950's. A weighted average of the 9.2 percent cost
of equity and the 3.9 percent cost of debt resulted in an overall cost of
7.4 percent. An adjustment for the low cost of debt and for the use of
book value weights instead of market value weights would raise the
estimate to over 7½ percent.

Professor Friend denied that an increase in debt financing would lower
the cost of capital. While it is true that debt carries a lower cost than

EXHIBIT 2

AT&T Stock: Earnings per Share and Price/Earnings Multiples

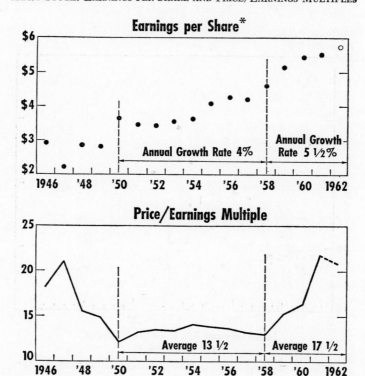

* Adjusted for 1959 stock split and rights offerings.

EXHIBIT 3

Cost of AT&T Common Equity

Investors' Capitalization Rate

Reasonable expectations for AT&T stock:

annual growth in earnings per share 5%
price earnings multiple 18
dividend payout 65%

$$\text{Capitalization rate} = 5\% + \frac{1.05 \times 65\%}{18} \text{ or } 8.8\%$$

Cost to Company

Investors' capitalization rate adjusted for difference between market price and proceeds to company on sale of new shares.

Reasonable expectations for AT&T stock:

Proceeds on new shares 10% below market price

$$\text{Cost} = 5\% + \frac{1.05 \times 65\%}{18 \times 90\%} \text{ or } 9.2\%$$

equity, any attempt to increase the debt-equity ratio would bring an increase in investor risk, and thus in both the interest rate and the cost of equity. The tax-exempt status of interest on debt would not result in a significant saving in cost.

The cost of capital: Mr. Kosh's testimony

One of the FCC's consultants, Mr. Kosh, differed from Professor Friend in two major respects. First, he made use of recent earnings-price ratios with only a minor provision for growth. Second, he used a debt ratio of 50 percent on the grounds that the Commission should use a theoretical "optimum" capital structure in its computations even though the actual ratio was 35 percent. In his opinion a 50 percent debt ratio was safe for the telephone company even under conditions of depression. The failure to increase the debt to that level meant a failure to take full advantage of the "leverage" principle. The result of his computations was a 6.1 percent overall cost of capital instead of over 7.5 percent which Dr. Friend found.

The comparable earnings test

Another AT&T argument for an 8 percent of return presented by Mr. J. J. Scanlon, a vice-president of AT&T, was based on a comparison of equity earnings with a broad cross-section of both regulated and unregulated companies. Exhibit 4 shows how these companies were selected.

They were the firms whose growth both in dividends and the book equity per share was greater than the increase in the Consumer Price Index, but did not exceed the growth in real GNP. The claim was that the long-term risk for AT&T is at least as great as the risk in these companies and that differences in short-term risks are equated by their differing capital structures. On this basis comparable rates of return on equity would be justified. Exhibits 5 and 6 show that the selected firms earned an average of 10.4 to 12.5 percent on equity, leading to the conclusion that the Bell System requires equity earnings at least of 10½ to 11 percent.

Professor James C. Bonbright of Columbia University, another consultant retained by the FCC, was critical of the comparable earnings test. He admitted that the Bell System did face competition for many of its services, but he noted that consumers had no choice but to use the Bell System if they were to make telephone calls. He also argued that industrial companies are subject to greater risks and therefore did not provide a sound basis for comparison.

Other considerations

The hearings on AT&T's earnings also covered several other issues. Professor Bonbright was concerned with the ratio of market value to book value of the AT&T stock. He would concede a rate of return which in prosperity would allow the company a market value "well in excess of

EXHIBIT 4

225 MANUFACTURING COMPANIES AND 96 ELECTRICS
(classified by growth in book equity and dividends per share)

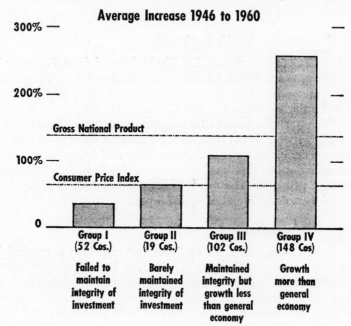

Average Increase 1946 to 1960

	Group I (52 Cos.)	Group II (19 Cos.)	Group III (102 Cos.)	Group IV (148 Cos)
	Failed to maintain integrity of investment	Barely maintained integrity of investment	Maintained integrity but growth less than general economy	Growth more than general economy

book value." But when the market value reached a price double that of book value, as was the case in 1962, he became skeptical.

Witnesses at the hearings also went into the effects of rate regulation on the national economy. Dr. Paul W. McCracken, of the University of Michigan, who was formerly on the President's Council of Economic Advisors, expressed fear that a reduction in the rate of return, with a consequent reduction in the market value of AT&T stock, would have an unsettling effect on the national economy. He, as well as Dr. Joseph Kieper of New York University, also claimed that an adequate return would stimulate the AT&T construction and equipment program which would help bolster the economy. The profitable companies, they claimed, were the ones making the greatest contribution to economic growth. This position would mean that the FCC should be concerned with much more than the cost of capital. Professor Bonbright, however, maintained that the FCC should confine itself mainly to the task of finding a rate of return which would attract capital.

The record on the FCC proceedings was closed out on January 4, 1963. It resulted in an announcement that interstate station to station toll rates

EXHIBIT 5

AVERAGE EARNINGS ON COMMON EQUITY, 1946–60
(groups of companies per chart 2)

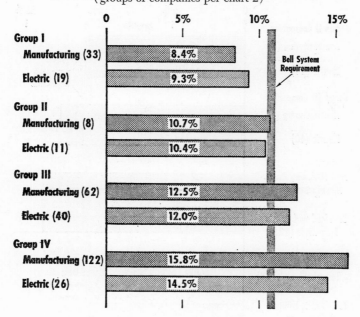

would be reduced to a maximum of $1.00 coast to coast after 9:00 P.M. This reduction, offset in part by an increase in person to person rates which had gotten out of line with increasing labor costs, resulted in a net $30 million annual saving to the public and a cutback of about 0.3 percent in the return the company was earning. The FCC believed, however, that technological change and an increased market for telephone service would permit the company to maintain a level of earnings within the 7 to 8 percent range realized by it since the last rate reduction in 1959.

1. *In your opinion what was the cost of capital to AT&T in 1962–63? Discuss.*
2. *What is the significance of Exhibit 1? What is its relevance in determining the cost of capital?*
3. *What is the relevance of Exhibit 2 in determining the cost of capital?*
4. *Develop the logic behind the computations in Exhibit 3.*
5. *Evaluate the comparable earnings test. In that connection evaluate Exhibits 4 and 5 as to pertinence in rate regulation.*
6. *Make a list of the other factors considered in this rate case and give your opinion on their significance and relevance.*
7. *Should the reduction of "after 9" long-distance rates have been instituted in 1963?*

EXHIBIT 6

AVERAGE EARNINGS ON COMMON EQUITY

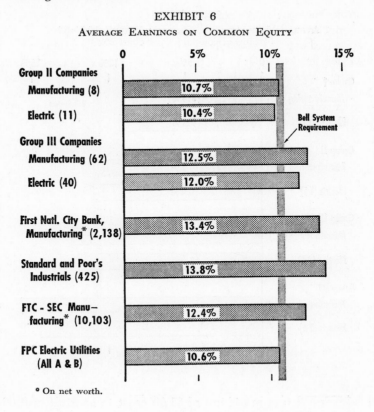

* On net worth.

THE STATE UNIVERSITY PRESS (B)

The State University Press is engaged in producing scholarly books and monographs for which the demand is relatively limited. The objective is not profit; if it were the Press would select more popular works with a wider market. The Press must operate within the limits of its budget, including subsidies from outside foundations, and must therefore control costs.

One important decision affecting costs is the length of run for each publication. If the first run of a book is too small, the Press takes the risk of running out of stock and losing sales. It also must meet the extra setup costs required by a second run. But if the run is too large, the Press encounters storage costs and losses from unsold books.

Before publication of each book, one of the Press's editors makes an estimate of costs based primarily on past experience with similar books.

For example, the cost of publishing 1,000 copies of a monograph in business administration planned for November 15, 1962, was $1,300 for composition and printing, $550 for binding, and $40 for freight.

Sometimes the estimates were considerably in error, especially if the author's alterations were numerous. The estimates tended to be on the low side. In the case of the business monograph under dicussion, however, the actual costs were close to the estimates, as is shown in Exhibit 1 (many of the figures have been rounded).

EXHIBIT 1
ACTUAL COSTS ON MONOGRAPH
(publication date—November 15, 1962)

Text

Stock	$138.00	
Composition	638.00	(98 hours)
Press	141.40	(20 hours)
Ink	3.10	
Miscellaneous	10.00	
Overhead (15% of above)	140.50	
Total cost of text		$1,071.00

Jacket

Stock	$ 10.00	
Composition	39.20	(5 hours)
Press	37.80	(5.4 hours)
Miscellaneous	1.50	
Ink	2.00	
Overhead (15% of above)	13.50	
Total cost of jacket		104.00
Binding		506.83
Freight		40.72
Total actual cost		$1,722.55

The stock cost was a completely variable cost. The composition and press costs were a mixture of direct labor costs and allocations of equipment and space charges.

A second run of 1,000 copies would be considerably cheaper than the first run. A second run of the text would require 11 offset lithographic plates, costing $18 per plate. The stock would cost about $138, as before. The offset press run would take about 11 hours at $9 per hour. The ink would be $3.10. The jacket would require $10 for stock, $2 for ink, $18 for one offset plate, $9 for one offset press run, and $7 for one letterpress run. Binding costs would again be approximately $507. If the second run were smaller than 1,000 copies, the costs would be about the same except for the stock and binding costs. The stock costs would be proportional to the run, but the binding costs include a fixed element of about $100 per run.

Sometimes the Press would print extra sheets of a book in the first run, postponing binding the sheets until the first batch of bound copies were sold. On the business monograph under discussion no extra sheets were printed.

Decisions on the length of run were influenced by the shortage of storage space. No one had made an estimate of storage costs. Probably the rental value of the space used for storage would be $1,000 per annum. The space had a capacity for about 16,000 volumes and was constantly overcrowded. Copies of some old books were stored in a basement room and finally discarded after any hope of further sales had passed.

The retail price of the monograph was set at $3. The Press could expect to receive an average of $2.10 per copy after discounts to distributors. The greatest uncertainty concerned the level of sales. One purchaser had guaranteed to buy 500 copies. The Press had no previous experience with monographs in the business area and thus had little basis for estimating sales beyond the 500 copies. Sales of monographs in other subject matter areas usually ran below 500, and sometimes as low as 200. The Press could make fairly accurate estimates of sales of books on historical subjects and of monographs in archeology and anthropology, because it had published a number of works in those areas, but its estimates on other books were subject to considerable error.

1. *Construct a model for the determination of the economic length of run on books.*
2. *What economic principles are incorporated in your model?*
3. *Apply your model as best you can to the problem of the business monograph.*
4. *Did the Press make a sound decision in running off 1,000 copies? Explain. Should it have run some extra sheets?*
5. *Is a formal analysis of uncertainty helpful in this case? Discuss.*

AIR-INDIA (E)*

Purchase of Boeing 707's

In early 1956 the Chairman of Air-India, Mr. J. R. D. Tata, visited the United States to discuss the purchase of jet aircraft with the Douglas Aircraft Co. and the Boeing Co. Up to that time, Air-India had also been considering turbo-propeller aircraft but had determined that they were uneconomical and less acceptable to the travelling public as compared with the jets. The management had also investigated the Comet IV type jet, but had found that it did not have the range required for the Bombay–Cairo or Atlantic sectors. Mr. Tata found that most of the international airlines of the world were placing orders for either the DC–8 or the Boeing 707 for delivery in the period from 1959 to 1961 (see Exhibit 1).

---

* Copyright 1964 by the Indian Institute of Management, Ahmedabad.

EXHIBIT 1
Orders Booked as of End of April, 1956

Boeing 707

Customer	No.	Option		Model	Delivery Date
Pan American	23		(6)	120	December, 1958, to
			(17)	320	November, 1959
American Airlines	30	5		120	From March, 1959
Braniff	5			120	From October, 1959
Continental	4	1		120	1959
Air France	10	7		320	November, 1959, to
					November, 1960
Sabena	4			320	From December, 1959
TWA	8	22		120	From April, 1959
Lufthansa	4	4		320	Spring, 1960
Total	88 +	39 options			

Douglas DC–8

Customer	No.	Option		Model	Delivery Date
Pan American	21			J–57 & J–75	From December, 1959
United Airlines	30		(15)	J–57	From May, 1959
			(15)	J–75	
National	6			J–57	Midsummer, 1959
K.L.M.	8	4		J–75	From March, 1960
Eastern Airlines	18	8	(6)	J–57	May, 1959
			(12)	J–75	March, 1960
JAL	4			J–75	1960
SAS	7			J–75	1960
Panagra	4			J–75	Early 1960
Swissair	2			J–75	Spring, 1960
Delta Airlines	6			J–57	June, 1959
TCA	6			RR–505	
Total	112 +	12 options			

Mr. Tata discussed the jet purchase proposal at the Board meetings on March 5, 1956, and May 25, 1956. He noted that the carrying capacity of the jets would be equivalent to three or three-and-a-half Super-Constellations, the type of aircraft which the airline was using in 1954. They would cruise at about 500 miles per hour. Mr. Tata noted that introduction of the new aircraft would raise a number of difficult operational and economic problems, but nevertheless came out strongly for the purchase in these words:

If the Corporation was to remain in business in competition with the other carriers on its routes, it would seem to be left with no option but to place an order for one of these two makes in the very near future in order to have a reasonable place in the queue. If orders were placed within the next three months or so, the Corporation would be able to get its aircraft in the second half of 1960 at approximately the same time as other carriers who had already placed their orders.

Mr. Tata also remarked that the minimum number of jets which should be purchased was three, which would be the equivalent to 10 of the existing Super-Constellations. The total cost including spare engines would be about Rs. 120 million. The Corporation could give consideration to the sale of some of its present fleet.

The Second Five-Year Plan made provision for Rs. 100 million for new aircraft. Of this amount over Rs. 20 million were committed to Super-Constellations on order. Thus, not enough was left to finance the purchase of three jets. Mr. Tata believed that the problem could be met by deferred payments or by a loan from the Import-Export Bank, the World Bank, or some other financial institution. Furthermore, delivery of even the first of the jets would come near the end of the Second Five-Year Plan period.

There appeared to be little to choose technically between the DC–8 and the Boeing 707. It would be difficult, however, to get delivery of a DC–8 before 1961. The Boeing Company had three positions open for delivery in 1960. Other airlines were in the market for these three, but Air-India could secure the three positions if it acted rapidly.

As of May 25, 1956, Air-India was one of the few international lines not to have placed an order. Mr. Tata stated that the issue was urgent since the only alternatives were to go out of business or to give up first- and tourist-class traffic and concentrate on third-class or coach traffic.

On June 6, 1956, company officials circulated a formal memorandum on purchase of the jets, most of which appears below:

Proposal for the purchase of jet aircraft— Boeing 707 Intercontinental model

1. Ever since its inception in 1947, and with the approval of the Government of India both before and after nationalization, Air-India International have followed the consistent policy of equipping their fleet with the latest and most competitive type of aircraft available. The original Constellation 749's were changed within three years for 749A's. This was followed by the purchase of 1049 Super-Constellations, culminating with the order for three 1049G's and for two Mark III Comets (subsequently cancelled). This policy has enabled Air-India International to be from the start and to remain fully competitive with much larger, older, and better known carriers. In the view of the management, such a policy is essential to the success of any small international airline operating in a highly competitive market. In pursuance of this policy, the development of commercial jet aircraft has been closely watched by the Corporation and its predecessor ever since the early 1950's when the de Havilland Comet first came on the scene.

2. During the [preceding] nine months or so, two much larger types of American jet aircraft, almost identical in design, price, and technical characteristics, have been announced for delivery from 1959 onwards. One is the Douglas

DC–8 and the other is the Boeing 707. In carrying capacity and all-up weight these American jets will be approximately twice the size of the Mark IV Comet and approach a take-off weight of 300,000 pounds. Their four engines will total over 60,000 pounds of thrust as against about 40,000 for the Comet. Their range will be such as to enable pay-loads in excess of 30,000 pounds to be carried on non-stop services over such extreme sections as the Atlantic. They will be capable of carrying up to 140 passengers although the number will be restricted to about 118 in the mixed configuration (28 standard and 90 tourist) of the aircraft proposed to be ordered by the Corporation.

3. Since October, 1955, when the first orders were announced by Pan American Airways, practically every major airline in the world has ordered one or the other of these two types and a total of well over 200 has been ordered up to now with correspondingly lengthening deliveries.

4. The advent of this new generation of great jet airplanes offers to the air transport industry immense potentialities for profitable expansion and, at the same time, poses some serious problems. Substantial increases in cruising speed in air transport have in the past invariably generated new strata of air traffic which did not exist before and these increases in traffic have been achieved without any decrease in surface transport. There is every reason to expect that this greatest of all jumps in cruising speeds—from about 300 to 500 mph—will have the same effect. The fact that the increased speed will be coupled with the elimination of intermediate landings on extra long sections will still further accelerate travel from the passengers' point of view. Other features which will attract passengers will be the extraordinarily smooth conditions of flying at extreme altitudes and the freedom from vibration inherent in turbine engines.

5. From the operational point of view, the higher speeds will produce important economies in flight personnel, out-station expenses and overhead expenses, while the elimination on the one hand of propellers, with their heavy gearing, complicated controls, and feathering devices, and on the other of vibration, which is one of the principal causes of wear and tear will result in considerable simplification and lower maintenance costs. As against these favorable factors are admittedly some unfavorable ones, amongst which are (a) heavy capital cost, (b) high fuel consumption at low altitudes, and (c) need for long runways for take-off at high all-up weights.

6. While the cost of these aircraft is high, the capital cost per unit of transportation produced will actually be lower than in the case of Super-Constellation or DC–7 aircraft. In annual ton miles of capacity, one of these jet aircraft will be equivalent to approximately 3.75 Super-Constellations, whereas its capital cost is only 2.5 times that of the Super-Constellation.

7. Although fuel consumption per mile is undoubtedly high at low altitudes, jet aircraft spend very little time at such altitudes while the combination of high cruising speed and low turbine fuel prices results in fuel cost per seat-mile or ton-mile being lower than that of piston-engined, propeller-driven airplanes. It is true that potentially the propeller-driven turbine engine (Turbo-prop) aircraft have a fuel consumption considerably below that of the pure jets under almost all comparable flight conditions, but no long-range turbo propeller aircraft, competitive with the coming big jets, is available.

8. The need for long runways for take-offs at high all-up weight, particularly

in the Tropics where conditions of high temperature and humidity prevail, places some financial burden on Government, but this is a problem which every country must eventually face. In the case of India, the additional expenditure will be heavy only at Bombay where a good deal of cutting, filling, and culvert construction will be required. The only other cities at which relatively small expenditure will be required are Delhi and Calcutta. The Director-General of Civil Aviation and his experts have been informed of the requirements, and estimates of cost are under preparation. It is respectfully submitted that with the whole world entering the Jet Age in civil aviation, India cannot possibly remain out of it on the ground of the extra expenditure of 20 or 30 million rupees on aerodrome.

9. With the general background, the main features of the project may now be specifically discussed. On the main principle of jet operation, there is today no choice before Air-India International. The matter was generally discussed at the two last meetings of the Board and it was agreed in principle that the Corporation must enter the field of jet operations if it is to remain in business at all. The possible alternative of giving up first- and tourist-class traffic on the Corporation's main routes and concentrating exclusively on coach or third-class traffic, is not considered either a practical proposition or a financially prudent one, as coach operations are likely to be extremely marginal. Assuming therefore, that Government accept the view recommended by the Corporation that jet aircraft must be ordered, the main points to be decided are (*a*) the number of aircraft to be ordered, (*b*) the type to be purchased, (*c*) the type of engines to be fitted, (*d*) deliveries, and (*e*) financial arrangements.

10. *Number of aircraft:* The minimum number of aircraft in a fleet which it is practical to operate on long routes is three, four being a more satisfactory figure. In view of the heavy cost of these aeroplanes and their high work capacity, it is proposed to limit the initial fleet to three.

11. *Type of aircraft:* The technical personnel of the Corporation, assisted by a Government of India expert, have recently undertaken a fairly detailed comparative study of both the Douglas DC–8 and the Boeing 707 on the basis of specifications and explanations furnished by representatives of the two manufacturers. Simultaneously, confidential enquiries were made with a number of other international airlines which have ordered jets. From the Corporation's own studies and the confidential reports received from other airlines, it is clear that there is, to all intents and purposes, nothing to choose between the two types on technical grounds and that either will be suitable for operation on the Corporation's main present and future routes. There is also nothing to choose in price as the price of both the types is almost identical. The choice of engines in both cases is also the same. Consequently, it has become clear that the ultimate choice must depend on other than technical or financial considerations, such as the reputation and experience of the manufacturer and delivery.

12. *Comparison of Douglas and Boeing Companies:* The Douglas Aircraft Company, one of the world's three giants in aircraft production, has an unequalled reputation in the civil transport field, having since 1934 brought out a series of transports, beginning with the DC–2 and ending with the DC–7, all of which have proved an operational and commercial success. On the other hand, they have never produced a large jet aircraft of their own although they

have built a large number of Boeing Jet bombers under license. Their immense technical and other resources, however, are such that no doubt is entertained as regards the technical and operational soundness of the DC–8 when built.

13. The Boeing Company is also one of the largest aircraft manufacturers in the world. While they have produced only three multi-engined transport types in their history, including the Stratocruiser which is still in use on intercontinental routes, they have for years been one of the largest producers of heavy military aircraft—bombers, tankers, and freighters—and are today the only producers of heavy and super-heavy jet bombers. They have built themselves over a thousand B–47 jet bombers, the all-up weight of which approximates or exceeds that of the proposed transports and are today in full production of the B–52 bomber which is a considerably bigger and heavier aircraft than the 707 jet transport. Their unique experience in the heavy jet field is, in the management's opinion, more than adequate to compensate for their small experience in the civil aircraft field.

14. *Delivery:* As the reputation and experience of both manufacturers are found equally satisfactory, the final choice would seem to boil down to considerations of delivery and here there is a considerable difference between the two. While DC–8 aircraft will be available for delivery only in the winter of 1960–61, three Boeing 707 aircraft, equipped with Rolls Royce Conway engines, are today offered, subject to prior sale, for delivery in the first quarter of 1960. A reference to engine types will be made later in this memorandum.

15. As in the past, the Corporation is anxious to initiate operations with an entirely new type at the beginning of summer and not in the winter when flying conditions are more difficult and traffic less abundant. Delivery in early 1960 would, therefore, enable the Corporation to inaugurate jet operations a whole year ahead than originally thought possible. The advantages of the time gained would be enormous as the Corporation would have virtually no competition on its U.K. route for at least a year, during which it would be able to establish a strong position while securing highly profitable payloads from the start. The only drawback to the early delivery offered is that, being subject to prior sale and having been offered also to other airlines, like BOAC and Qantas, it necessitates an almost immediate decision on the part of the Corporation and Government if the three open positions in January, February, and March, 1960, are to be secured. Because the advantages of the earlier delivery are so great, while the risks involved are so small, the management of Air-India International and the undersigned have no hesitation in recommending to the Board and to Government the grant of the earliest possible sanction to the issue to the Boeing Company of a Letter of Intent for the purchase of three Boeing 707/420 aircraft for delivery in the months mentioned above. The reason why an immediate decision is considered to involve no risk whatsoever is that in the unlikely event that within the next two or three years the Corporation or Government were to change their mind in regard to jet operations in general or to the purchase of these aircraft in particular, there would be no difficulty in disposing of the order to some other airlines not only at no loss but, in view of the past experiences, with the probability of a considerable profit.

16. *Choice of engines:* Both the manufacturers have offered their aircraft

with a choice of two engines—the American Pratt & Whitney J–75 and the British Rolls Royce Conway. Both the engines have about the same thrust rating of about 16,000 pounds. In favor of the Conway are the facts that (*a*) it is about 1,400 pounds lighter in weight, (*b*) it has a specific fuel consumption lower by 2 to 4 percent, (*c*) it is paid for in sterling, and (*d*) it is available earlier. In favor of the J–75 is the fact that the large majority of the airlines which have ordered Boeing and Douglas jet transport have preferred it to the Conway. The main reason for this is attributed to the fact that the bulk of the orders are from American operators who naturally prefer an American engine. The J–75 will, however, not be available with full thrust for delivery in time for the Corporation to begin operations during the summer of 1960. Up to now, Trans-Canada Airlines alone have ordered the Conway engine but it is considered certain that when BOAC and Qantas finalize their orders for one or the other of these jet transports, they will specify the Conway engine.

17. While the Corporation is anxious to start operations with jets in 1960 rather than 1961, it attaches great importance to the engine chosen for its aircraft being in use in sufficiently large numbers to ensure that the resale value of its aircraft is not adversely affected and also to ensure the maximum of future improvement and development. It is recommended, therefore, that the Conway engine be ordered on the condition, if Boeing and Rolls Royce can be induced to accept it, that it will, within a period of one year, have the right to switch its order to the Pratt & Whitney J–75 at the cost of delayed delivery if necessary. Such a condition would give sufficient time to the Corporation to satisfy itself thoroughly about the Conway engine and about its adoption by other airlines.

18. *Terms of payment and finance:* The Second Five-Year Plan, as approved by Government in Parliament, has made a provision of Rs. 100 million for purchase by Air-India International of new aircraft during the period of the Plan. Out of this amount, a sum of about Rs. 25 million will be utilized for meeting a part of the cost of two 1049G's on order.

19. The total cost of the Boeing jet project will be a little over Rs. 110 million, as detailed in Exhibit 2. This exceeds capital funds available for the Second Five-Year Plan period by about Rs. 35 million. About two thirds of the total expenditure will actually be incurred during the last year of the Plan period and the aircraft will be used throughout the Third Five-Year Plan period. If the Government finds it impossible to make the additional amount available prior to the Third Five-Year Plan period, it is considered that there would be no difficulty in arranging for short- to medium-term credit facilities, either in India or abroad, for the amount of Rs. 35 million to Rs. 40 million. Such a loan could, for instance, be obtained from the Export-Import Bank, the amount being repayable over a period of three to five years. Such an arrangement would in effect carry over the project into the Third Five-Year Plan period.

20. *Profitability:* As will be seen from the summarized data and estimates covering the projects appended to this memorandum (see Exhibits 2, 3 and 4), a net profit subject only to taxes and interest on capital, of about Rs. 9.51 million per year is expected to be made from the operation of three aircraft proposed to be purchased. These estimates have been prepared on a conservative

EXHIBIT 2

Air India (E)

(estimates of capital cost for Boeing 707 & DC–8)

Particulars	Boeing 707		DC–8	
	$	Rs.	$	Rs.
Cost of aircraft	15,450,000	73,388,000	15,750,000	74,812,000
Cost of 9 spare engines @ $225,000 each	2,025,000	9,619,000	2,025,000	9,619,000
Radio, galley, etc.	200,000	950,000	200,000	950,000
Cost of special equipment including engine overhaul facilities and test cell	1,800,000	8,550,000	1,800,000	8,550,000
Cost of simulator	1,000,000	4,750,000	1,000,000	4,750,000
Initial provisioning for rotational units and other spares for a one period	2,000,000	9,500,000	2,000,000	9,500,000
	22,475,000	106,757,000	22,775,000	108,181,000
Import duty @ 2.5% (preferential rates of duty as applicable to aircraft and engines have been assumed)	562,000	2,669,000	569,000	2,704,000
Flight and ground training expenses	239,000	1,135,000	239,000	1,135,000
Delivery charges of 3 aircraft @ $26,300 or Rs. 125,000 per aircraft	79,000	375,000	79,000	375,000
Total Capital Cost	23,355,000	110,936,000	23,662,000	112,395,000

EXHIBIT 3

Air-India (E)

(estimates of operating cost of the Boeing 707)

A. *Operational Summary*

1. Frequencies: 6 times weekly Bombay/London/Bombay and 2 times weekly London/New York/London *during season* (once weekly during off-season)
2. Hours: 8,135
3. Miles: 3,687,000
4. Cargo Ton Miles: 61,400,000

B. *Summary of Operating Cost*

	Total Cost Rs.	Cost per Hour Rs.	Cost per Hour Rs.
1. Crew	1,857,000	228.27	0.504
2. Fuel & oil	19,386,000	2,383.04	5.258
3. Engineering labor for maintenance & overhaul of aircraft & engines	4,653,000	572.00	1.262
4. Materials & spares for maintenance of aircraft & engines	10,331,000	1,270.00	2.802
5. Landing fees	1,592,000	195.70	0.432
6. Depreciation & obsolescence	9,990,000	1,228.03	2.710
7. Insurance of aircraft	3,869,000	475.60	1.049
8. Route diversions, practice & test flights	1,050,000	129.07	0.285
9. Total direct operating cost	52,728,000	6,481.71	14.302
10. Indirect cost at 100% of the direct operating cost excluding fuel & oil item 2: (This percentage is generally applied in preparing cost estimates. In case of 1049 operations the indirect cost ratio is 82.5%)	33,342,000	4,098.59	9.043
11. Total operating cost	86,070,000	10,580.30	23.345
Revenue (see Exhibit 4)	95,580,000	11,749.23	25.924
Estimated profit	9,510,000	1,168.93	2.579
Comparative Unit cost for Super-Constellation 1049's		3,775	14.953

basis. For instance, the estimated cost of fuel, which forms the biggest single item of operating expenditure, has been increased by a safe margin for tolerances and increased consumption and, in addition, 20 percent has been added to the existing price per gallon of this type of fuel. Similarly, the estimated cost of stores, materials, and labor per hour of operation has been increased by about 20 percent. On the revenue side, estimates have been based on an average passenger load of 15 first class and 49 tourists, as against 28 first class and 90 tourist seats available, equivalent to a passenger load factor of 55 percent. With the estimates for mail and cargo calculated on the basis of what we actually expect to carry in the light of our existing experience, the overall load

EXHIBIT 4

AIR-INDIA (E)
(estimates of revenue for operation of
jet aircraft Boeing 707 or DC–8)

	Millions of Rs.	Millions of Rs.
Passenger revenue:		
1. Bombay/London		
15 Std. passengers × Rs. 4080 × 312 flights	19.09	
49 Tourist passengers × Rs. 2834 × 312 flights 43.33		
Less off-season fare differential on tourist revenue for 5 months, est. Rs.		
18,050,000 @ 15% 2.71	40.62	
2. London/New York		
15 Std. passengers × Rs. 3564 × 78 flights 4.17		
49 Tourist passengers × Rs. 2348 × 78 flights 8.97		
13.14		
Less off-season differential on total revenue for 5 months or a pro rata revenue of Rs. 550,000 @ 7.5% .... .41		12.73
Mails:		
1. Bombay/London 3000 lbs. × Rs. 12.5 × 312 flights	11.70	
2. London/New York 1000 lbs. × Rs. 7.5 × 78 flights		.59
Cargo:		
1. Bombay/London 8000 lbs. × Rs. 4.10 × 312 flights	10.23	
2. London/New York 3200 × Rs. 2.46 × 78 flights		.61
Total Bombay/London Revenue 81.65		
Total London/New York Revenue		13.93
Total Revenue .... 81.65 + 13.93		
= 95.58		

* Passenger fares: single fares less 15% to cover round trip rebate, concessional fares, etc. Double the amount is taken for a round trip fare.

factor has been estimated at only 49 percent. Considering the very large carrying capacity and revenue earning potentiality of these big jets during peak seasons, the management believe that the estimated financial results will be improved upon in practice.

21. The annual turnover of the jet fleet of three Boeings, shown in the estimates at Rs. 95 million, is higher than the total turnover of the Corporation in the current year, estimated at Rs. 80 million with a fleet of five Super-Constellations and three Constellations. With the addition of the 1049G to replace the Constellation lost in the China Sea, and the possible retention of one of the two 1049C's, for the replacement of which two 1049G's have been ordered, the estimated revenues for 1957–58 will probably be about Rs. 100 to 105 million. Thus the addition of the three jets in 1960 will require doubling the Corporation's turnover. While this may at first appear optimistic, no serious difficulty is expected in reaching such a target for the following reasons:

a) Unless there is a significant change in the existing traffic trends, which have lasted for many years, the normal growth of traffic may be expected to account for an increase of 50 percent to 60 percent in the next four years.

b) The rapid development of tourist passengers and the introduction of a third-class or "coach" fare on main routes in the next year or two are expected to create an additional demand. By the time the big jets come into operation it is anticipated that the pattern of international air transport will be that first-class and tourist services on main trunk routes will be operated with jets, while "coach" traffic and traffic on secondary routes will be operated with turbo-propeller and piston-engined aircraft.

c) The Corporation intends, before 1960, to open some new routes, including the Atlantic.

If, however, the Corporation's expectations were not to materialize to the full extent and the Corporation finds that it could not economically use the whole of its piston-engined fleet with the addition of the jets, there should be no difficulty in the disposal, at prices well above their then value in the Corporation's books, of some of its Constellations or Super-Constellations.

22. In conclusion, the Government is requested kindly to grant urgent approval to the following proposals:

a) General approval to the project for the purchase of three 707/420's equipped with Rolls Royce Conway engines or three Boeing 707/320's equipped with Pratt & Whitney J–75, at a total estimated cost (including spare engines, initial spares, customer-finished equipment, flight simulator, import duty, delivery, and training expenses and contingencies) not exceeding Rs. 115 million is requested.

b) Authority is requested to issue a Letter of Intent to the Boeing Company for the purchase of the above aircraft at a cost ex-factory, excluding customer-finished and radio equipment, of $15,450,000, payable as follows:[1]

5% within 10 days of issuing the Letter of Intent	$ 772,500
28% in 12 quarterly installments terminating six months prior to delivery	$ 4,326,000
67% on delivery	$10,351,500
100%	$15,450,000

The above figures are based on aircraft equipped with Pratt & Whitney J–75 engines and are subject to a slight downward revision, and substitution of sterling for dollars, in respect of the engines if Rolls Royce Conway engines are purchased.

c) Sanction is requested of an advance by the Government during the current financial year of a sum of Rs. 8,806,000 made up as follows:

5% down payment	$ 772,500	Rs. 3,669,000
Three quarterly payments	$1,081,500	Rs. 5,137,000
Total requirement for 1956–57	$1,854,000	Rs. 8,806,000

[1] $1.00 = Rs. 4.76 at the time of this case. It is simpler to use the rate $1.00 = Rs. 5.00; the resulting error is not large.

1. *What criteria were used by Air-India in evaluating the purchase of jets? Were these criteria quantitative or qualitative in character? Should a more exact quantitative approach have been applied?*
2. *In evaluating the jets from the financial point of view what measure did Air-India use: payback period, discounted rate of return, present value, or some other alternative? Was this the appropriate measure?*
3. *What attention was given the cost of capital in the decision? Should more or less attention have been given this factor?*
4. *What revisions in the capital budgeting procedures of Air-India might be appropriate?*
5. *At the time of this case, foreign exchange was in extremely short supply in India. In fact, one could call the situation a foreign exchange crisis. How is your analysis influenced by this fact?*
6. *Should Air-India have purchased the Boeing 707's as outlined in the proposal of June 9, 1956?*
7. *How would you evaluate Air-India procedures in dealing with large equipment purchases?*

AIR-INDIA (F)*

Seventh and eighth aircraft

One of the major issues facing Air-India in late 1962 and early 1963 concerned the purchase of additional aircraft. In 1962 Air-India had six Boeing 707's in operation. The top company officials favored increasing the number to eight by adding one Boeing 707-320B in April, 1964, and a second in early 1965. Several arguments against this proposal were presented by members of Air-India's Board of Directors. One was that the required investment exceeded what had been provided in the Third Five-Year Plan. A second was that the investment would require substantial amounts of foreign exchange. The low load factors of the airline industry in general and of Air-India in particular raised doubts about the need for additional capacity.

Despite these arguments the top executives of Air-India were firmly convinced that the investment in the two additional planes was desirable.

Profitability analysis

The investment in the two aircraft would total $19.246 million (Rs. 91,600,000). Approximately 70 percent of this would be payable by March, 1964 and the remainder by March, 1965. The foreign exchange content of the investment amounted to $18.5 millions (Rs. 88,100,000), most of which could be borrowed from U.S. commercial banks or the World Bank at a 5¾ percent rate of interest and a ¾ percent commitment fee on all undrawn balances. It was assumed that repayment could take place over a period of five years after delivery of the second aircraft.

---

* Copyright © 1964 by the Indian Institute of Management, Ahmedabad.

Exhibit 1 summarizes the estimates of additional costs resulting from the two new aircraft for the year 1964–65 and 1965–66. Within the Tripartite Group 1 (London to Hong Kong or Sydney) no additional revenue would result from the new planes since the revenue was determined on the basis of the total revenue of all three members of the Tripartite Pool: BOAC, Qantas, and Air-India. But the failure to purchase the new aircraft would make it necessary for Air-India to purchase capacity from BOAC and Qantas in order to maintain its share of total capacity under the Pool Agreement. It was estimated that these purchases of capacity would amount to Rs. 16,400,000 in 1964–65 and Rs. 48,700,000 in 1965–66.

EXHIBIT 1

AIR-INDIA (F)

(economics of operation with two additional aircraft in 1964–65 and 1965–66)*

Year	Operations	Additional Revenue Anticipated	Additional Cost of Operating 320B	Cost of Purchasing Capacity if Not Operating	Net Loss by Not Operating
1964–65	Tripartite: Group I	†	9.9	16.4	6.5
	Tripartite: Group II (London–New York);				
	3 flights for 21 weeks ...	6.3	7.6	—	(−) 1.3
	Delhi–Moscow	7.1	5.0	—	2.1
	Charters	6.0	5.1	—	0.9
	Total	19.4	27.6	16.4	8.2
1965–66	Tripartite: Group I	†	29.3	48.7	19.4
	Tripartite: Group II (London–New York);				
	3 flights for 21 weeks ...	6.9	7.6	—	(−) 0.7
	Tripartite: Group III				
	(Hong Kong–Tokyo) ...	1.5	3.3	—	(−) 1.8
	Delhi–Moscow	8.5	5.0	—	3.5
	Bombay–Nairobi	4.8	5.6	—	(−) 0.8
	Charters	6.0	5.1	—	0.9
	Total	27.7	55.9	48.7	20.5

* In million Rs.
† Constant

The addition of the two aircraft would permit Air-India to increase its number of flights from London to New York, one of the primary objectives of top management, but the added cost of the New York expansion would exceed the added revenues by Rs. 1,300,000 in 1964–65 and Rs. 700,000 in 1965–66. The additional capacity would permit an increase in the profitable Delhi–Moscow operation and charter flights and would make possible in 1965–66 an expansion of the Hong Kong–Tokyo and Bombay–Nairobi operations, both of which were expected to be unprofitable in the development stages.

The additional costs listed in Exhibit 1 included crew costs, fuel and oil, landing fees, insurance, depreciation, the cost of spares, and engineering labor. The sum of these costs was increased by 50 percent to cover indirect costs. Actually the company's indirect expenses far exceeded 50 percent of the direct costs, but company officials believed that certain economies in the indirect costs would be realized. The bulk of the standing costs were not expected to increase proportionately. Exhibit 2 presents a more detailed breakdown of the cost estimates on a per-hour basis. No increase in charges for the ground staff, headquarters, or office rentals were included. In other words, it was expected that the ratio of indirect to direct costs for the entire fleet would decrease from about 93 to 80 percent as the fleet was increased from six to eight.

Exhibit 3 presents the cash flow forecast for the period 1963 to 1970. Several features of this forecast deserve attention. First it was assumed

EXHIBIT 2

AIR-INDIA (F)

(cost analyses: cost of operating two Boeing 707's—foreign exchange contents)

	Rs. per Hour	Foreign Exchange Content	Rs. Costs
A. Direct Operating Costs			
Crews salary	430	143(33⅓%)	287
Fuel	1,620	1,215(75%)	405
Landing fees	485	437(90%)	48
Insurance	570	570(100%)	——
Depreciation	1,160	1,160(100%)	——
Spares consumption	955	955	——
Engineering labor	450	45(10%)	405
	5,670	4,525	1,145
B. Indirect Costs			
Handling fees	315	315(100%)	——
Booking agents' commission (net)	575	385(66⅔%)	190
Food service and passenger amenities	445	355(80%)	90
Insurance for L. D. of passengers	100	100(100%)	——
Obsolescence of spares	100	100(100%)	——
Cabin crews salary	85	17(20%)	68
Expenditure	140	140(100%)	——
Publicity	400	320(80%)	80
Other indirect expenses	670	335(50%)	335
	2,830*	2,067	763
Total A + B ...... Rs.	8,500	6,592	1,908

* The total indirect cost at present is Rs. 5,260 per hour.

EXHIBIT 3

Air-India (F)

(statement of cash flow* for fiscal years 1963 through 1970†)

	1963	1964	1965	1966	1967	1968	1969	1970
SOURCE OF FUNDS								
Opening cash balance on April 1	54,861	78,115	79,764	83,045	89,280	121,765	154,137	186,856
Operating profit after depreciation but before interest and taxes	18,500	18,500	18,500	18,500	18,500	18,500	18,500	18,500
Depreciation and obsolescence	26,504	27,294	31,971	35,031	35,681	35,681	35,681	35,681
Capital funds from government	16,139	—	—	—	17,600	17,600	16,400	—
Proposed dollar loans	3,170	34,976	28,684	21,230	—	—	—	—
Sale proceeds of 1049 fleet	32,618	—	—	—	—	—	—	—
Total Cash Inflow (A)	151,792	158,885	158,919	157,806	161,061	193,546	224,718	241,037
APPLICATION OF FUNDS								
Boeing project payments:								
5th & 6th Boeings	26,218	—	—	—	—	—	—	—
7th & 8th Boeings (320Bs)‡	3,170	34,976	31,204	22,230	—	—	—	—
Administrative building	—	4,000	8,000	8,000	—	—	—	—
Expansion of workshops including ground support equipment	4,700	—	—	3,000	—	—	—	—
Normal replacements	2,500	2,500	2,500	2,500	2,500	2,500	2,500	2,500
Repayment of loans:								
Previous loans	17,136	18,276	18,278	8,015	2,284	1,142	—	—
Proposed dollar loans	—	—	—	8,806	17,612	17,612	17,612	26,418§
Interest and commitment fees	3,405	4,238	5,284	5,450	7,300	9,810	9,000	7,987
Increase in inventories	6,000	5,000	2,500	2,500	2,500	2,500	2,500	2,500
Predevelopment and training costs	3,000	3,000	—	3,000	—	—	—	—
Provision for deferred taxes	6,048	5,631	6,608	6,525	5,600	4,345	4,750	5,256
Unforeseen contingencies	1,500	1,500	1,500	1,500	1,500	1,500	1,500	1,500
Total Cash Outflow (B)	73,677	79,121	75,874	68,526	39,296	39,409	37,862	46,161
Year-end Cash Balance (A) − (B)	78,115	79,764	83,045	89,280	121,765	154,137	186,856	194,876

* In thousand Rs.

† Years ending March 31.

‡ The total of these payments for Boeings would have been less if a lump sum had been paid at the beginning. In other words, these project payments include interest and commitment fee on the money tied up.

§ It is assumed that the last installment of Rs. 8,806,000, maturing in April 1970, would be repaid before March 31 1970.

that by selling its fleet of Super-Constellation (1049) aircraft and spare parts Air-India would receive cash proceeds of over Rs. 32,400,000. This sum would make it less necessary to rely completely on foreign loans. The operating profit before interest and taxes was assumed to be constant at the 1963 level, despite the addition of the two new planes. To maintain the Corporation's reputation for conservatism with the banks, the cash forecast took into account the drain on cash required by the payments on the loans to finance the new aircraft but did not include the extra profits which would result.

The cash flow statement assumed that in the Fourth Five-Year Plan years of 1967, 1968, and 1969, the Indian government would supply finance of Rs. 17,400,000, Rs. 17,400,000, and Rs. 16,400,000 respectively, as is indicated in Exhibit 3.

Foreign exchange analysis

Company officials argued that rather than the purchase of the two new Boeings being a drain on foreign exchange, it would permit the company to avoid losses in foreign exchange which otherwise would take place. Returning to Exhibit 1 it should be noted that the estimated loss of not operating the extra plane in 1964–65 was Rs. 8,200,000 and of not operating the extra two planes in 1965–66 was Rs. 20,500,000. Almost all of that loss would consist of foreign exchange. Note that the additional cost figures in Exhibit 1 include depreciation on the new plane.

Exhibit 2 also casts some light on the foreign exchange requirements, by showing the proportion of the direct and indirect costs coming from foreign exchange. Of the total costs per hour of Rs. 8,500, Exhibit 2 indicates that Rs. 6,592 or 77 percent would require foreign exchange. But looking at the matter more positively, the addition of these planes would mean a net addition of India's foreign exchange as a result of two factors: the added profits (or avoidance of losses) made possible by the two new aircraft; and the payment by foreigners for a large part of the Indian expenses incurred by the aircraft.[1] (The reader might wish to give special attention to how the foreign exchange on the initial investment and on the depreciation were handled in this analysis.)

Expanding operations

Air-India's officials argued that the six Boeing 707's were already fully scheduled and could not be expected to provide greater service. The utilization per plane for 1963–64 was expected to be 3,500 hours, excluding

---

[1] In addition, Indians who would otherwise fly on foreign aircraft requiring foreign exchange would now be able to travel by Air-India. Company officials claimed, for example, that the total Air-India revenue (less selling expenses) on the Bombay–Nairobi run would amount to savings in foreign exchange. The same reasoning applied to other routes.

the operation of charter flights. This was considered to be about optimum. In fact, it was a somewhat higher utilization than was general in the industry. Therefore operations in 1964–65 and 1965–66 would have to remain at the 1963–64 level without additional aircraft. But forecasts indicated a probable increase of 15 percent per year in passenger traffic, with much higher rates of growth in South East Asia. To maintain the required additional capacity in the Tripartite Pool it would be necessary to purchase capacity from the partners, BOAC and Qantas. The costs of such purchases have already been discussed. The whole of these capacity purchases would require foreign exchange.

Similarly a failure to expand capacity on the Delhi–Moscow route would mean a reduction in Air-India's share of that profitable business, since Aeroflot would be expected to increase its capacity. The failure to maintain a daily service to New York would be a serious sales deterrent, in the view of company officials. The company wanted to look forward to the possibility of a Pacific operation in 1965–66. All these factors would place pressure on the facilities of the airline.

A variety of objections

Some members of Air-India's Board and some government officials concerned with exchange controls raised a series of questions about the proposed investment.

1. *Restrictions on travel:* It was argued that the P-form regulation on foreign travel would reduce the traffic from India—or at least would keep it from increasing at the projected rates. Company officials replied that in fact the Indian traffic had grown despite the regulations and furthermore defense needs and foreign aid programs would continue to stimulate air travel. (Company officials denied that the P-form was used to put pressure on Indian nationals to use Air-India flights, though Indian government officials were expected to use Indian facilities.)

2. *Other priorities:* One government official noted that the highest priority in using foreign exchange belonged to defense requirements and to crucial sectors like power, coal, steel, oil, and transport. The use of foreign exchange for the purpose of aircraft would be at the expense of other needs. Management's reply was that the project would generate its own foreign exchange.

3. *Low load factors:* Representatives of a government department raised the question of whether the low load factors on Air-India aircraft did not provide enough cushion to handle additional traffic. Company officials replied that Air-India's load factors were no lower than those of most of its competitors, as is shown in Exhibit 4. The introduction of large jets had reduced load factors throughout the world. The big jets had a lower breakeven point (in the low 40's) than previous aircraft. Airlines were planning their operations at much lower load factors to take advan-

EXHIBIT 4

AIR-INDIA (F)

(air transport industry capacity and traffic data—1958–59 to 1961–62—area: Europe/Far East)

	AF	AI	AZ	BOAC	KLM	LH	PAA	PIA	QEA	SAS	SR	TWA
Available Seats Kilometers (Millions)												
1958–59	469	*	*	1,037	733	*	748	93	510	295	152	*
1959–60	582	623	62	1,332	964	22	739	104	516	508	158	285
1960–61	610	898	78	1,797	1,177	137	1,374	212	636	535	196	364
1961–62	1,166	1,053	147	2,035	1,261	323	1,622	*	815	620	272	369
Seat Factor												
1958–59	56.0	*	*	60.8	53.3	*	49.0	42.0	62.0	51.6	53.1	*
1959–60	56.5	55.8	34.9	65.4	52.2	21.4	49.0	50.0	60.0	43.9	53.0	50.9
1960–61	49.5	50.2	42.4	61.7	51.6	34.5	41.0	38.2	65.0	44.9	43.3	44.4
1961–62	42.0	48.6	33.9	52.5	52.3	45.6	47.0	–	58.0	37.9	43.2	36.1
Available Ton Kilometers												
1958–59	58,092	*	*	146,794	103,328	*	97,319	13,616	77,990	41,200	20,313	*
1959–60	72,929	83,743	7,445	166,203	128,791	2,967	100,736	14,279	76,619	69,200	20,017	32,033
1960–61	76,358	123,844	9,632	208,748	143,353	18,332	182,324	27,097	92,440	71,200	24,926	42,034
1961–62	140,525	148,617	17,833	232,636	165,290	42,565	213,545	*	120,081	73,200	33,323	44,191
Load Factor (Overall)												
1958–59	63.0	*	*	62.8	52.0	*	47.0	33.0	63.0	49.2	61.0	*
1959–60	61.0	57.6	35.0	68.8	53.6	24.2	48.0	45.5	62.0	46.8	65.2	54.2
1960–61	53.0	49.2	44.9	65.9	56.2	34.5	42.0	43.0	65.0	50.0	56.7	47.9
1961–62	46.0	48.3	35.2	58.6	53.7	49.6	39.0	*	58.0	31.2	56.2	41.8

* Not reported.
SOURCE: IATA Cost Committee Reports 1960, 1961, and 1962.

tage of seasonal variations and directional flows of traffic. The failure of one line to increase its capacity would leave the market to the other lines, and would not achieve the objective of increasing the load factor. It would, instead, merely reduce the company's share of the market.

4. *The discrepancy between the cost of purchasing capacity versus the cost of operating:* The estimated total cost of the expected purchases of capacity in 1964–65 would be Rs. 16,400,000; in 1965–66 it would be Rs. 48,700,000. The cost of operating the two new Boeings were estimated at only Rs. 9,900,000 and Rs. 2,930,000. The question was raised on how the management could account for this large difference, when presumably the same type of equipment would be used. One reply to this question was that the overheads on the pool arrangement were of necessity higher than the 50 percent rate used in the international computations. As explained earlier, this 50 percent rate was based on the assumption that standing costs would not rise in proportion to the number of aircraft. Furthermore Air-India's costs were below those which generally prevailed in the industry.

PART SIX / Advanced topics and comprehensive cases

11 / Advanced topics

The basic concepts introduced at the beginning of this book are applicable to many subjects not fully covered in earlier chapters. Some of the most significant developments in management theory and practice fall into an area which might be called advanced managerial economics; the present chapter is concerned with some apects of this subject.

An advanced study of managerial economics can proceed in three directions. First, certain specialized applications, such as transfer pricing or lease-back arrangements, provide opportunities to adapt the techniques to a wider range of topics and thus to strengthen skills in the diversified application of the basic concepts. Second, advanced techniques of a mathematical character indicate ways in which the analysis is being formalized and quantified to facilitate applications to a range of problems not readily amenable to nonmathematical treatment. Third, managerial economics can be applied to a range of multidimensional problems much more complex than the usual textbook illustrations. Management is seldom confronted with problems which are simple exercises in capital budgeting or probability analysis or linear programming. Quantifiable aspects are often interwoven with organizational and motivational issues less easily quantified. Sometimes the issues themselves are not clear or the objectives of the choices to be made are not precisely defined. Managerial economics is not a set of models into which problems neatly fit. Rather, it is a tool kit of techniques, chains of logic, insights, and models which are useful in creating order out of part of the complexity of reality.

The present chapter introduces the first two types of advanced topics: specialized applications and quantitative techniques. It is followed by a chapter which includes comprehensive cases in which the application of economic analysis is conditioned by considerations which go beyond the narrow confines of economics.

1. TRANSFER PRICING

One of the more difficult problems of managerial economics is the costing of intermediate products which pass from one division or department of a company to another. This is known as the problem of transfer pricing. A wrong transfer price will motivate erroneous decisions by understating or overstating values and costs.

The correct approach to transfer pricing requires application of the basic concepts introduced in Chapter 2. A mastery of those concepts should clear up most of the uncertainities on the subject. The fact is, however, that a great deal of the literature on transfer pricing has undergone revision in even the recent past. It seems reasonable to suppose that most companies concerned with the problem are making questionable decisions because of confusion about transfer prices.

Many companies need not worry about the problem. If the company is small or if it consists of relatively independent divisions, the application of the concepts introduced in earlier chapters is relatively straightforward. In the modern complex integrated concern, however, transfers of intermediate products may be of major significance. The multidimensional conglomerate has become increasingly important in the United States and is beginning to expand in other parts of the world; the problem of transfer pricing is consequently becoming more significant.

The simplest case: a specialized intermediate product with excess capacity in the supplying department

Let us consider a hypothetical company with two departments—a supplying department and a using department. The letter S will represent the supplying department and U the using department. P_s will represent the price charged by the supplying department—this is the transfer price. P_u will represent the final price charged by the using department to outside purchasers. In the present example we assume excess capacity in S, the supplying department. That is, S can meet all the needs of U for the intermediate product.

This simplest case of transfer pricing requires an additional assumption. The intermediate product is specialized and is used only within the company. All of it is transferred to the using department. None of it is sold on the outside. Another way of stating this assumption is that no market for the intermediate product exists.

Under these assumptions, the solution for the transfer price is clear. It is the marginal cost (unit incremental cost) in the supplying department.

$$P_s = MC_s$$

in which

$$MC_s = \text{marginal cost in the supplying department.}$$

This transfer price will motivate the using department to order as many units as it can use and still make a contribution to overhead and profit on each unit, including the last (marginal) unit.

Let us consider a hypothetical example. The supplying department, S, produces at a constant marginal cost of $10.

$$MC_s = \$10$$

The using department, U, can produce five different products each of which makes use of the same intermediate product. The five products sell at five different prices and incur different marginal costs within the using department.

$$P_{u1} = \$25.00 \qquad MC_{u1} = \$\ 7.00$$
$$P_{u2} = \$24.00 \qquad MC_{u2} = \$\ 7.50$$
$$P_{u3} = \$23.00 \qquad MC_{u3} = \$\ 7.50$$
$$P_{u4} = \$22.00 \qquad MC_{u4} = \$10.00$$
$$P_{u5} = \$21.00 \qquad MC_{u5} = \$13.00$$

It is clear that the company is adding to its profits as long as the final prices exceed the sum of the marginal costs in the using and supplying departments. This is true of the first four products.

$$P_{u1} > MC_{u1} + MC_s \qquad \$25.00 > \$\ 7.00 + \$10.00$$
$$P_{u2} > MC_{u2} + MC_s \qquad \$24.00 > \$\ 7.50 + \$10.00$$
$$P_{u3} > MC_{u3} + MC_s \qquad \$23.00 > \$\ 7.50 + \$10.00$$
$$P_{u4} > MC_{u4} + MC_s \qquad \$22.00 > \$10.00 + \$10.00$$

But the final price of the fifth product ($P_{u5} = \$21$) is less than the sum of the marginal costs

$$P_{u5} < MC_{u5} + MC_s \qquad \$21.00 < \$13.00 + \$10.00$$

The first four products should be accepted and the fifth rejected, assuming of course that there is sufficient capacity.

Another way of stating this is that the contributions of the first four products are positive and of the fifth product negative.

$$C_1 = \$25.00 - (\$\ 7.00 + \$10.00) = \quad \$8.00$$
$$C_2 = \$24.00 - (\$\ 7.50 + \$10.00) = \quad \$6.50$$
$$C_3 = \$23.00 - (\$\ 7.50 + \$10.00) = \quad \$5.50$$
$$C_4 = \$22.00 - (\$10.00 + \$10.00) = \quad \$2.00$$
$$C_5 = \$21.00 - (\$13.00 + \$10.00) = -\ \$2.00$$

It should be clear that a transfer price which includes an allocation of the supplying department's overheads or fixed costs will lead to the wrong results. If these allocated overheads were $6, the transfer price on the intermediate product would become $16 instead of $10 and the "contributions" of the third and fourth products would be negative rather than positive. The result would be a rejection of the third and fourth products and a loss of contributions on both.

A graph is useful in summarizing the discussion up to this point. This graph is unusual in one respect. The quantity (horizontal) axis is measured in units of the intermediate product, not of the final products. This is because the final products are different and their quantities cannot be measured along a single axis. The intermediate product is homogeneous. We shall assume that the quantities of sales of the five products could be as high as follows:

Product 1—2,000 units
Product 2—1,000 units
Product 3—1,500 units
Product 4—1,000 units
Product 5—1,500 units

The vertical axis is the usual cost and price axis. The prices of the five products are shown. The total marginal cost in both S and U is shown.

If the overheads (fixed costs) were included in the marginal costs of the supplying department, the graph would appear as in Figure 11–2.

This graph shows that the apparent optimum would include only Products 1 and 2 and would eliminate the contributions which could be earned from Products 3 and 4.

How could a company make such an error as to select the false optimum in Figure 11–2 in preference to the more profitable set of products shown in Figure 11–1? This error, which in practice must be fairly common, is a result of mixing two functions of accounting: the measurement of performance and the guidance of decisions. In measuring performance it seems reasonable at first glance that the transfer price should be at a level to permit the supplying department to cover its overheads and to earn a profit. Therefore, full cost transfer pricing, including overhead allocation seems appropriate. At the end of each accounting period a rate of return which reflects the capacity of the department's management to control both variable and fixed costs would seem to measure performance. To allow the supplying department a transfer price which covers only its marginal costs would appear to give all the profit and all the credit to the using department.

This reasoning, attractive as it may at first be, is wrong. The profitability which is important is the company-wide profitability. To allow mere paper allocations of costs to take priority over this company-wide profitability cannot be permitted. The creation of departmental or divisional profit centers, each with its own responsibility for the control of costs, would appear to be consistent with modern ideas on decentralization of

FIGURE 11–1

OPTIMUM QUANTITY, FIVE PRODUCTS
USING THE SAME INTERMEDIATE PRODUCT*

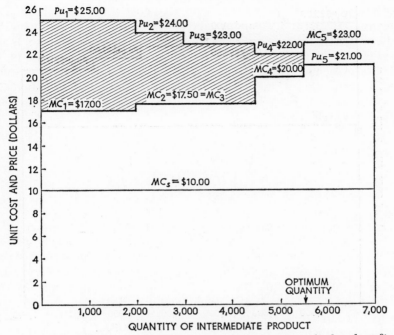

* The shaded area on the graph is the contribution to overhead and profit resulting from the four accepted products. The fifth product is rejected because its marginal cost is higher than its price.

responsibility and control. But the purpose of bringing departments together under a single company framework is to achieve the advantages of integration. Decentralization must be interpreted in a way which does not defeat the very purposes of integration.

One way of making the using department contribute to the fixed expenses of the supplying department, even when the transfer price is at the marginal cost, is to require a lump sum payment for the right of access to the supplying department. The lump sum could be determined in advance; the essential point is that it must not depend on the actual volume of purchases from the supplying department.

The case of a marketable intermediate product

The first case we have discussed is that of a specialized intermediate product for which there is no external market. Now let us turn to a case in which the intermediate product is bought and sold in a competitive

FIGURE 11–2
FALSE OPTIMUM, SAME FIVE PRODUCTS
USING COMMON INTERMEDIATE PRODUCT

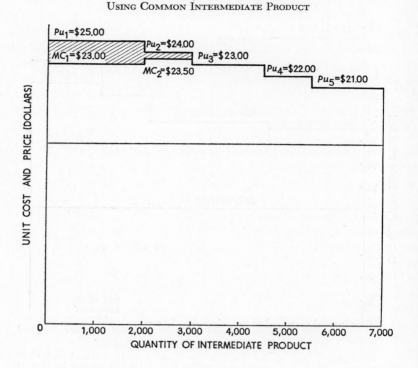

market. Now the opportunity cost concept becomes of paramount importance. In this case, the supplying department, S, should produce all of the units it can as long as it earns contributions to its overhead and profits; this includes units to be sold externally.

If, as we assumed before, the marginal cost to the supplying department is $10 ($MC_S = \$10$), production should be increased up to full capacity as long as the market will take units of the product at prices above that level.

Suppose that the market price is $16. Let us temporarily assume that transportation and outside selling costs are zero. Then the supplying department should expand production to capacity, with the result that a contribution of $6 is earned on every unit.

In this case, the rule for the transfer price is changed. It becomes $16 rather than $10. The opportunity cost of not being able to sell to the market replaces the internal marginal cost.

Figure 11–2 now becomes the governing graph. Only Products 1 and 2 should be produced. Products 3, 4, and 5 require costs which exceed prices. The marginal costs of these products now reflect the opportunity cost of sales on the outside. The supplying department allocates its supply of intermediate product to those uses which can pay the market price, whether these uses are internal departments or external buyers.

If external sales require certain transportation and selling costs and also risks in incurring bad debts, these should be taken into account. If the net sales price after deduction of incremental transportation and selling costs is only $13, this becomes the governing opportunity cost. In this case it will be profitable to produce Products 1, 2, and 3. The transfer price is now $13 and the first three products all make a contribution after taking this transfer price into account.

Imperfect market for final product—perfect market for intermediate product

Unfortunately, the most significant cases of transfers occur in imperfect markets. Market imperfections complicate the analysis to the point that implementation of theoretical solutions becomes almost unmanageable. It will not be possible to deal with all of the possible variations here; those who wish to study the subject in greater detail must be referred elsewhere.[1]

Let us start with a one-product firm which sells its final product in an imperfect market but can buy or sell its intermediate product in a competitive market. Figure 11–3 portrays this situation.

FIGURE 11–3

IMPERFECT MARKET FINAL PRODUCT
PERFECT MARKET INTERMEDIATE PRODUCT

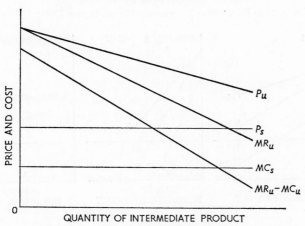

---

[1] The fundamental articles are Jack Hirshleifer's, "On the Economics of Transfer Pricing," *Journal of Business*, July, 1956, pp. 172–84, and "Economics of the Divisionalized Firm," *Journal of Business*, April, 1957, pp. 96–108. An excellent exposition of the problem, both theoretical and practical, appears in David Solomons', *Divisional Performance: Measurement and Control* (New York: Financial Executives Research Foundation, 1965).

In this case the demand curve facing the using department slopes down-ward to the right, as indicated by P_u. The marginal revenue curve, MR_u, lies below the demand curve and slopes more steeply for reasons developed in Chapter 3. In this graph it is convenient to subtract the marginal cost within the using department, MC_u, from the marginal revenue to obtain the net marginal revenue, $MR_u - MC_u$.

If there were no market for the intermediate product, the optimum would be where $MR_u - MC_u$ intersects MC_s. On all units up to that point a contribution to company-wide overhead and profits is made. The transfer price should in this subcase be MC_s. If a perfect market for the intermediate product exists at a price of P_s, the optimum is at the inter-section of $MR_u - MC_u$ and P_s. If excess capacity still exists in the using department, extra units can be sold in the open market more profitably than they can be sold to the using division. The transfer price should be at the level P_s.

The reader should work out solutions for the case in which the capacity of the supplying department is less than the using department's require-ment or the case in which the marginal cost in the supplying department is increasing as output increases.

Competing demands for the intermediate product

The next step is to consider an intermediate product used by several competing using departments, each facing an imperfect market. Figure 11–4 illustrates this case.

FIGURE 11–4

COMPETING DEMANDS—IMPERFECT MARKETS FOR FINAL PRODUCT

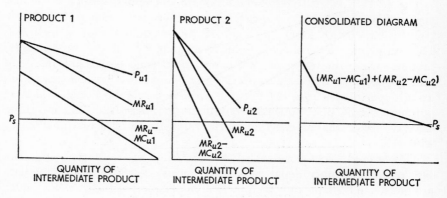

On the consolidated diagram, we sum horizontally the quantities on the $MR_{u1} - MC_{u1}$ and $MR_{u2} - MC_{u2}$ curves. The total quantity of inter-mediate product is determined where this aggregate curve ($MR_{u1} -$

MC_{u1}) + ($MR_{u2} - MC_{u2}$) cuts P_s. The resultant quantity of intermediate product is then allocated to the two products. This is an application of the equimarginal principle introduced in Chapter 2.

Again the reader can work out solutions when the capacity of the supplying department is limited or when its marginal cost is rising. The marginal cost of the supplying department has been left out of Figure 11–4 for purposes of simplicity. But if MC_s is rising, the analysis is changed slightly and the company may find it profitable to buy part of its supply on the outside.

Imperfect market for the intermediate product

In the preceding section we were saved from having to determine the price of the intermediate product by the fact that a perfect market did that job for us. When the market for intermediate products is imperfect, the problem is complicated by the need to solve a large number of problems simultaneously—the quantity and price of the intermediate product as well as the quantity and price of the final products. The solution requires an application of the concepts introduced in Chapter 2— marginal costs, opportunity costs and the equimarginal principle.

It is tempting to leave this problem for more advanced treatises. But the fact appears to be that this case is the most relevant one; to abandon the subject at this point would give a misleading impression of the ease with which transfer prices can in fact be established.

For the present discussion it is desirable to introduce an additional assumption: that the marginal cost of the intermediate product MC_s, is rising. A solution to the problem when the marginal cost is constant up to capacity can be introduced later.

Figure 11–5 summarizes the solution to the imperfect market, rising marginal cost case. The net marginal revenues are summed horizontally but this time the marginal revenue in the outside market is included. The supplying department produces a quantity of the intermediate product where the aggregate net marginal revenue equals the marginal cost. It should be noted that P_s is the transfer price to be charged to the using departments; it is *not* the price which should be charged outside purchasers. The price to outsiders will be found on the demand curve directly above the intersection of the transfer price (marginal cost) with MR_σ.

This example does not exhaust the discussion of transfer pricing. The case of the assembly department which uses a variety of intermediate products is too complex for the practical application of the methods under discussion. The case in which marginal costs are constant up to capacity is best handled by mathematical programming, which will be introduced later in this chapter. The case in which the demands for final products are interdependent, as would be the case of an automobile company

FIGURE 11–5

Imperfect Markets for Both Final and
Intermediate Product—Rising Marginal Costs

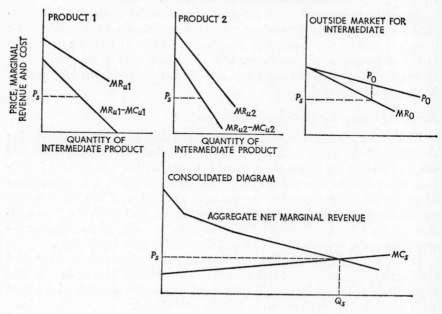

producing competing brands, has apparently not been solved in a form which can be used in practice. All of which suggests that transfer pricing remains a field for pioneering effort.

Empirical studies and illustrations

An excellent study of transfer pricing appears in a study by David Solomons.[2] Solomons not only reviews the theoretical literature but supplies a number of illustrations of sound and unsound practices in the area of transfer pricing. He provides several illustrations of companies which attempt to treat each department as if it were a separate business. The transfer prices from manufacturing to sales departments were computed on the basis of full cost without regard to whether the manufacturing department was operating at capacity. One company in this group raised the transfer price if the firm was not provided with "optimum production runs," apparently without regard to external prices. Solomons comments that this "is not how independent businesses operate. As an

---

[2] David Solomons, *Divisional Performance: Measurement and Control* (New York: Financial Executives Research Foundation, 1965), p. 163.

independent concern the factory would probably charge lower, not higher prices if it were short of work."

Solomons also cites the case of an oil company which faced the allocation of the impact of gasoline price wars. A firm transfer price was established between the refining and the marketing departments, roughly at market price less a small deduction per gallon negotiated between the two departments. This meant that the marketing department suffered the impact of price wars. At an earlier date a fixed unit margin was guaranteed the marketing department, which left the production department with the problem of fluctuating prices.

Another oil company found the problem of transfer pricing so difficult that it treated three departments, refining, marketing and marine transportation, as a single profit center. In this way it helped make certain that arbitrary transfer prices did not stand in the way of sound decisions.

Another company set transfer prices at the "best price given any outside customer, less (*a*) division selling expense and (*b*) freight, allowances, cash discount, etc., allowed such customer."[3] This rule applied when the product was sold "regularly and in reasonable volume to outside customers." This rule was reasonable, but a similar rule was applied even when the product was not sold on the outside—in this case a deduction from the competitive price was not made for selling expenses. As a result, using divisions might buy on the outside even when internal supplying division costs were lower. An "escape clause," however, permitted the negotiation of lower prices.

Studies of the problem show that determination of the "market price" is far from simple. For differentiated products no markets in the usual sense may exist. Discounts and terms of payment make comparisons difficult. Apparently the market price solution to the transfer pricing problem can be applied in only a minority of cases. Nevertheless, the marginal cost solution is still relatively unused. This suggests that considerable progress is yet to be made in the area of transfer pricing. Many companies achieve something in the direction of marginal cost solutions by encouraging their divisions to negotiate prices between them.

2. LINEAR PROGRAMMING APPLIED TO PRODUCT MIX DECISIONS

Earlier chapters have introduced aspects of linear programming as these relate to some of the main topics of managerial economics. They have shown that linear programming is in fact a way of applying some of the fundamental economic concepts, such as the contribution to overhead and profits, the equimarginal principle, and opportunity costs. It is now

---

[3] Solomons, *op. cit.*, p. 175.

appropriate to develop the subject of linear programming in a more systematic way. First we shall consider its application to the product mix problem.[4]

Conditions when linear programming is appropriate

The product mix problem is one of maximizing the total contribution to overhead and profit through the choice of the appropriate set of products. Certain conditions must be met if linear programming is to be applied.

1. The contribution to overhead and profits of each alternative product must be known and must be independent of the volume produced. In other words, the contribution function must be linear—10 units of a product results in 10 times the contribution resulting from one unit.

2. In order for the contribution to be linear, the price of each product must be independent of the volume produced and sold. This means that demand is assumed to be perfectly elastic—a large quantity can be sold at the same price as a small quantity. If, in fact, the price must be reduced to increase sales, more complex systems of programming must be applied, or the problem must be solved by nonmathematical methods.

3. Also, the linear contribution condition means that the incremental cost of each product must be linear. It costs as much to raise production from 20 to 30 units as from 10 to 20.

4. The use of the capacity in various departments or on various machines must be known for each product and must be linear. This means that 15 units of a product will use up 15 times as much capacity time as one unit.

5. Capacities in all departments (on all machines) must be definite and known.

6. Any limits on the quantities of the various products which can be sold must be known. In some cases it may be appropriate to assume that any quantity can be sold at the given price; in other cases the maximum level of sales may be stated.

It should be clear that these conditions are not the ones assumed in traditional economic analysis. The economist treats the perfectly elastic demand curve as a special case applicable only under conditions of pure competition and perfect knowledge. Imperfections in the market and differentiation of products will result in downward sloping demand curves. This limitation is not as damaging as it might first appear. Under conditions of oligopoly, for example, the individual firm may well take prices to be given until the price leader changes them. Similarly, while the assumed independence of unit cost from volume appears to ignore

---

[4] A review of the graphical approach to the product mix problem as reviewed in Chapter 8 might be useful at this point.

the law of diminishing returns, this may be a close enough approximation to reality for practical purposes. The capacity constraints may be
modified by adding extra shifts or overtime work, or by investing in new
facilities, but these factors may be introduced into more complex linear
programming models. In fact, linear programming can be used to determine the value of added capacity and therefore to provide a basis for
investment analysis. (This requires the solution of the "dual," which
will not be discussed here but which appears in more advanced treatments of linear programming.)

Setting up the equations and inequations

If the actual conditions seem to approximate the assumptions of linear
programming, it is then fairly easy to set up the appropriate equations
and inequalities. We shall use an illustration that appeared earlier in the
book.[5] This illustration assumes five possible products with three departmental capacities. The basic data are summarized in Tables 11–1 and
11–2.

TABLE 11–1

CAPACITY REQUIREMENTS AND UNIT CONTRIBUTIONS

| Product | Time Required per Unit | | | Contribution per Unit |
	Dept. A	Dept. B	Dept. C	
1	3	4	5	$10
2	5	4	10	18
3	4	4	4	9
4	8	4	10	15
5	4	6	7	12

TABLE 11–2

CAPACITIES AVAILABLE IN THE THREE DEPARTMENTS

Department	Hours of Capacity per Week
A	310
B	300
C	500

It may facilitate the discussion and indicate its generality if symbols as
well as numbers are used. Thus, let us indicate the quantities of the
five products as follows:

---

[5] See Table 2–2, page 34.

$$x_1 = \text{quantity of Product 1}$$
$$x_2 = \text{quantity of Product 2}$$
$$x_3 = \text{quantity of Product 3}$$
$$x_4 = \text{quantity of Product 4}$$
$$x_5 = \text{quantity of Product 5}$$

The contributions of the five products may be indicated as follows:

$$c_1 = \text{contribution per unit of Product 1}$$
$$c_2 = \text{contribution per unit of Product 2}$$
$$c_3 = \text{contribution per unit of Product 3}$$
$$c_4 = \text{contribution per unit of Product 4}$$
$$c_5 = \text{contribution per unit of Product 5}$$

The time required per unit of each product in each department may be indicated as follows:

$$a_1, b_1, c_1 = \text{time required to produce 1 unit of Product 1 in}$$
departments A, B, C, respectively.

$$a_2, b_2, c_2 = \text{time required for Product 2}$$
$$a_3, b_3, c_3 = \text{time required for Product 3}$$
$$a_4, b_4, c_4 = \text{time required for Product 4}$$
$$a_5, b_5, c_5 = \text{time required for Product 5}$$

Lastly the capacities in the three departments may be indicated by K_a, K_b, and K_c.

The first equation to be drawn up is the objective function. It is assumed that the objective is to maximize the contributions resulting from the products. If the actual objective is more complex than this, the simple linear programming approach breaks down. If, for example, the products are complementary in demand—the availability of one product stimulates the sale of another—more complicated tools of analysis may be required.

The objective function may now be drawn up in both abstract and numerical form. If we let Z represent the contribution from all the products, the function becomes

$$\text{Maximize } Z = c_1x_1 + c_2x_2 + c_3x_3 + c_4x_4 + c_5x_5$$

or

$$\text{Maximize } Z = \$10x_1 + \$18x_2 + \$9x_3 + \$15x_4 + \$12x_5$$

Next, we express each of the constraints in the form of an inequality. The sum of the capacities used up by the five products must be less than or equal to the capacity available. Three inequalities express these three capacity constraints. Again we shall express the constraints in both abstract and numerical form.

$$a_1x_1 + a_2x_2 + a_3x_3 + a_4x_4 + a_5x_5 \leqq K_A$$
$$b_1x_1 + b_2x_2 + b_3x_3 + b_4x_4 + b_5x_5 \leqq K_B$$
$$c_1x_1 + c_2x_2 + c_3x_3 + c_4x_4 + c_5x_5 \leqq K_C$$

or

$$3x_1 + 5x_2 + 4x_3 + 8x_4 + 4x_5 \leqq 310$$
$$4x_1 + 4x_2 + 4x_3 + 4x_4 + 6x_5 \leqq 300$$
$$5x_1 + 10x_2 + 4x_3 + 10x_4 + 7x_5 \leqq 500$$

The system of equations and inequalities is not complete unless non-negativity restrictions are placed on the outputs. In the real world it is impossible to produce a negative quantity of any of the products. This fact is expressed in the form of the following inequalities:

$$x_1 \leqq 0, \quad x_2 \leqq 0, \quad x_3 \leqq 0, \quad x_4 \leqq 0, \quad x_5 \leqq 0$$

These non-negativity constraints will not be mentioned in the discussion which follows, but they are an essential part of a complete mathematical statement of the problem.

Note that the only unknowns are the quantities of the five products (x_1, x_2, x_3, x_4, and x_5) and the total contribution (Z). Once the objective function and the constraints have been set up, the problem becomes a relatively mechanical one. An electronic computer which has been programmed to solve linear programming problems can find the solution of a far more complex problem in a fraction of a minute. But it is useful to run through a solution to learn more about the logic of linear programming and its relation to managerial economics.

The simplex method

Several approaches to the solution of the set of equations and inequalities are available. The best known of these is the simplex method. The simplex method makes use of the opportunity cost reasoning introduced in Chapter 2.

The first step is to convert the capacity constraint inequalities into equations. This is done by adding what is called a "slack variable" to each. Since the slack by definition takes up all the capacity not used up by the products, the result is an equation. The slack in Department A may be represented by x_A, in Department B by x_B, and Department C by x_C. The result is three equations:

$$a_1x_1 + a_2x_2 + a_3x_3 + a_4x_4 + a_5x_5 + x_A = K_A$$
$$b_1x_1 + b_2x_2 + b_3x_3 + b_4x_4 + b_5x_5 + x_B = K_B$$
$$c_1x_1 + c_2x_2 + c_3x_3 + c_4x_4 + c_5x_5 + x_C = K_C$$

or

$$3x_1 + 5x_2 + 4x_3 + 8x_4 + 4x_5 + x_A = 310$$
$$4x_1 + 4x_2 + 4x_3 + 4x_4 + 6x_5 + x_B = 300$$
$$5x_1 + 10x_2 + 4x_3 + 10x_4 + 7x_5 + x_C = 500$$

The simplex method now proceeds in the form of a series of Tableaus which move from an initial feasible solution to the optimum solution. Normally the number of products in the optimum solution is equal to the number of constraints.[6] In the case under discussion we expect to obtain three products in the solution, exactly equal to the number of capacity constraints. The first Tableau is a feasible solution with three products in the solution. One such feasible solution is:

$$x_A = 310 \qquad x_1 = 0 \qquad x_4 = 0$$
$$x_B = 300 \qquad x_2 = 0 \qquad x_5 = 0$$
$$x_C = 500 \qquad x_3 = 0$$

Note that when we substitute these quantities into the capacity equations we obtain

$$(3)(0) + (5)(0) + (4)(0) + (8)(0) + (4)(0) + (1)(310) = 310$$
$$(4)(0) + (4)(0) + (4)(0) + (4)(0) + (6)(0) + (1)(300) = 300$$
$$(5)(0) + (10)(0) + (4)(0) + (10)(0) + (7)(0) + (1)(500) = 500$$

The reader may ask why we started with this particular solution. The initial choice of x_A, x_B, and x_C, all of which are slack variables, will clarify the later exposition. Experts in the use of the simplex method can introduce shortcuts, but it is well to ignore these in this introduction to the subject. The first Tableau can now be drawn up.

TABLEAU 1

	$10	$18	$9	$15	$12	$0	$0	$0	
	x_1	x_2	x_3	x_4	x_5	x_A	x_B	x_C	
$0 x_A	3	5	4	8	4	1	0	0	310
$0 x_B	4	4	4	4	6	0	1	0	300
$0 x_C	5	10	4	10	7	0	0	1	500

On the left-hand side of the Tableau are shown the three variables in the feasible solution—the slack variables. Along the top are shown all the variables in the solution or not. Above or alongside the variables are shown the respective contributions of each. In the cells are shown the *rates of substitution* between variables in the solution on the left and all the variables shown along the top. Thus, the first cell indicates that 3 units of slack must be given up to obtain one unit of Product 1. The last column shows the total capacity of each department.

Now we are ready to evaluate the introduction of a new variable into the solution. Let us evaluate Product 1. We must compute the opportunity cost of introducing Product 1 at the expense of giving up slack in the three departments. One unit of Product 1 will cost three units of slack in Department A, four units of slack in Department B, and five units of slack

---

[6] See R. Dorfman, P. A. Samuelson, and R. M. Solow, *Linear Programming and Economic Analysis* (New York: McGraw-Hill Book Co., 1958), pp. 74–78 for a precise statement of the conditions when this will hold.

in Department C. But the opportunity cost of slack is zero—slack produces no contribution. Therefore, we find that the opportunity cost of one unit of Product 1 is:

$$3 \times \$0 + 4 \times \$0 + 5 \times \$0 = \$0$$

Since Product 1 provides a contribution of $10 per unit and has an opportunity cost of zero, we introduce it into the solution. In fact, we introduce as much as possible. We must find which department is the bottleneck. Department A has capacity for 310/3 units of Product 1; Department B for only 300/4 or 75 units; Department C for 500/5 or 100 units. Department B is the bottleneck and 75 units of Product 1 can be introduced into the solution at the same time that the slack from Department B disappears from the solution.

Before we can construct Tableau 2, several computations are required. First, we must compute how much capacity in Departments A and C will remain after introduction of 75 units of Product 1.

$$\text{Remaining capacity in Department A} = 310 - (75)(3) = 85$$
$$\text{Remaining capacity in Department C} = 500 - (75)(5) = 125$$

On the basis of these computations we can draw up part of the new Tableau.

TABLEAU 2a

	$10	$18	$9	$15	$12	$0	$0	$0	
	x_1	x_2	x_3	x_4	x_5	x_A	x_B	x_C	
$10 x_1	—	—	—	—	—	—	—	—	75
$ 0 x_A	—	—	—	—	—	—	—	—	85
$ 0 x_C	—	—	—	—	—	—	—	—	125

Second, we must compute new rates of substitution. This is done by returning to Tableau 1 and noting that the rates of substitution for Product 1 shown in the first column were 3, 4, and 5. We express this relationship between inputs of capacity and output of Product 1 as an equation:

$$x_1 = 3x_A + 4x_B + 5x_C$$

Since x_B is being removed from the solution, we can re-express this equation with x_B on the left-hand side.

$$x_B = 1/4x_1 - 3/4x_A - 5/4x_C$$

We now express all the other columns in Tableau 1 as equations, but substitute for x_B, since x_B no longer appears in the solution.

$$x_2 = 5x_A + 4x_B + 10x_C$$

which becomes, when we substitute for x_B,

$$x_2 = 5x_A + x_1 - 3x_A - 5x_C + 10x_C = 2x_A + x_1 + 5x_C$$

The same procedure is now applied in expressing each of the variables in terms of the new variables in the solution.

$$
\begin{aligned}
x_3 &= 4x_A + 4x_B + 4x_C \\
&= 4x_A + x_1 - 3x_A - 5x_C + 4x_C \\
&= x_A + x_1 - x_C \\
x_4 &= 8x_A + 4x_B + 10x_C \\
&= 8x_A + x_1 - 3x_A - 5x_C + 10x_C \\
&= 5x_A + x_1 + 5x_C \\
x_5 &= 4x_A + 6x_B + 7x_C \\
&= 4x_A + 3/2x_1 - 9/2x_A - 15/2x_C + 7x_C \\
&= -\tfrac{1}{2}x_A + 3/2x_1 - \tfrac{1}{2}x_C
\end{aligned}
$$

The coefficients in these new equations become the rates of substitution in our new Tableau.

TABLEAU 2b

	$10 x_1	$18 x_2	$9 x_3	$15 x_4	$12 x_5	$0 x_A	$0 x_B	$0 x_C	
$10 x_1	1	1	1	1	3/2	0	1/4	0	75
$ 0 x_A	0	2	1	5	-1/2	1	-3/4	0	85
$ 0 x_C	0	5	-1	5	-1/2	0	-5/4	1	125

Now we are in a position to consider Product 2 as an entry into the solution. The opportunity cost of a unit of Product 2 is $10 since it requires a sacrifice of one unit of Product 1 ($10.1 = $10) and of slack in Departments A and C. But Product 2 provides a contribution of $18. The net contribution above opportunity cost is $8. Therefore, it increases profits to bring it into the solution.

By inspection it can be seen that Products 3, 4, and 5 are less desirable entries at this time. Product 4 would give a net contribution but not so great as that of Product 2. Products 3 and 5 involve opportunity costs greater than their contributions. For example, Product 5 contributes $12 but its opportunity cost is $\frac{3}{2}$ ($10) or $15.

The bottleneck in introducing Product 2 is Department C. The 125 units of slack there (x_8) are only sufficient to produce 25 units of Product 2. We start to construct Tableau 3.[7]

---

[7] For those who do not understand the new numbers in the last column, the following explanation may be helpful. Since x_C restricts the production of x_2 to 25 units and 25 units of x_2 requires the reduction of 25 units of x_1, x_1 becomes $75 - 25$ or 50. Similarly the 25 units of x_2 requires the reduction of 50 units of x_A, since the rate of substitution is 2:1; this leaves a residue of $85 - 50$ or 35.

TABLEAU 3a

	$10	$18	$9	$15	$12	$0	$0	$0	
	x_1	x_2	x_3	x_4	x_5	x_A	x_B	x_C	
$10 x_1	—	—	—	—	—	—	—	—	50
$18 x_2	—	—	—	—	—	—	—	—	25
$ 0 x_A	—	—	—	—	—	—	—	—	35

Now comes the task of computing the new rates of substitution.

$$x_2 = x_1 + 2x_A + 5x_C$$
$$x_C = 1/5x_2 - 1/5x_1 - 2/5x_A$$
$$x_3 = x_1 + x_A - x_C$$
$$= x_1 + x_A - 1/5x_2 + 1/5x_1 + 2/5x_A$$
$$= 6/5x_1 + 7/5x_A - 1/5x_2$$
$$x_4 = x_1 + 5x_A + 5x_C$$
$$= x_1 + 5x_A + x_2 - x_1 - 2x_A$$
$$= x_2 - 3x_A$$
$$x_5 = 3/2x_1 - 1/2x_A - 1/2x_C$$
$$= 3/2x_1 - 1/2x_A - 1/10x_2 + 1/10x_1 + 1/5x_A$$
$$= 8/5x_1 - 3/10x_A - 1/10x_2$$
$$x_B = 1/4x_1 - 3/4x_A - 5/4x_C$$
$$= 1/4x_1 - 3/4x_A - 1/4x_2 + 1/4x_1 + 1/2x_A$$
$$= 1/2x_1 - 1/4x_2 - 1/4x_A$$

We are now able to complete the Tableau.

TABLEAU 3b

	$10	$18	$9	$15	$12	$0	$0	$0	
	x_1	x_2	x_3	x_4	x_5	x_A	x_B	x_C	
$10 x_1	1	0	6/5	0	8/5	0	1/2	−1/5	50
$18 x_2	0	1	−1/5	1	−1/10	0	−1/4	1/5	25
$ 0 x_A	0	0	7/5	3	−3/10	1	−1/4	−2/5	35

Next we must select another product for consideration as an addition to the product line. Product 3 has an opportunity cost of:[8]

$$6/5 \times \$10 - 1/5 \times \$18 + 7/5 \times \$0 = \$8.40$$

and a net contribution after opportunity cost of

$$\$9 - \$8.40 = \$0.60$$

Product 4 has an opportunity cost of:

$$\$0 + \$18 + \$0 = \$18$$

but a net contribution after opportunity cost of

---

[8] The opportunity cost arises from the fact that units of Products 1 and 2 must be given up to make possible the production of units of Product 3.

$$\$15 - \$18 = -\$3$$

Product 5 has an opportunity cost of

$$8/5 \times \$10 - 1/10 \times \$18 - 3/10 \times \$0 = \$14.20$$

which exceeds its contribution of $12.

Clearly Product 3 is the most promising entry. The bottleneck is x_A which permits only 25 units of Product 3 to be introduced.

Tableau 4 appears below. The detailed computations are left to the reader.

TABLEAU 4

	$10	$18	$9	$15	$12	$0	$0	$0	
	x_1	x_2	x_3	x_4	x_5	x_A	x_B	x_C	
$10 x_1	1	0	0	$-18/7$	$13/7$	$-6/7$	$5/7$	$1/7$	20
$18 x_2	0	1	0	$10/7$	$-1/7$	$1/7$	$-2/7$	$1/7$	30
$ 9 x_3	0	0	1	$15/7$	$-3/14$	$5/7$	$-5/28$	$-2/7$	25

Results of the simplex method

Tableau 4 represents the optimum solution to the problem. This solution calls for the production of 20 units of Product 1, 30 units of Product 2, and 25 units of Product 3.

The introduction of Product 4 or Product 5 would reduce the total contribution to overhead and profit. The opportunity cost of Product 4 is

$$-18/7 \times \$10 + 10/7 \times \$18 + 15/7 \times \$9 = \$19.29$$

This exceeds Product 4's contribution of $15. Similarly the introduction of Product 5 would reduce profits. The opportunity cost of Product 5 is

$$13/7 \times \$10 - 1/7 \times \$18 - 3/14 \times \$9 = \$14.07$$

This exceeds Product 5's contribution of $12.

It can be shown that the introduction of slack in any of the three departments will reduce total profits.

Now we are ready for an interpretation of the results. Five products were available for production. Each of the five products earned a contribution in excess of its incremental costs. Each placed a strain on the three departmental capacities available. The products could not be selected on the basis of their contributions, for a high contribution product might also be a high user of capacity. The products could not be selected on the basis of the mere inspection of contributions and capacities, for the products were interdependent in production in a complicated way. The strain a particular product placed on one of the three bottlenecks was dependent on what other products were already scheduled for production.

A solution to this particular problem of five products and three capacities could be solved by trial and error. One could try out various combinations until he found the largest contribution. He would be helped by the knowledge that the optimum would probably consist of three products equal to the number of constraints. Clearly, however, when the number of products and capacities is increased, the solution by trial and error is time consuming beyond endurance. The simplex method, and other methods like it, provide a systematic path to the optimum. The simplex method does this by constantly computing the opportunity cost of making a change in a previous feasible solution. As long as the net contribution above opportunity cost is positive, the solution can be improved.

3. OTHER APPLICATIONS OF LINEAR PROGRAMMING

The approach just described can be applied to a variety of problems in which the objective is clearly defined, in which the constraints are determined, and in which input-output relationships are linear. Several illustrations of such problems will provide insight into the versatility of linear programming as an analytical tool.

Selection of production processes

The product mix problem described above assumed that certain inputs, (the department capacities) were fixed and others completely variable (the inputs which entered into the incremental costs before contributions were computed). The proportions of the outputs (the five products) were completely flexible within the departmental constraints. The problem was to find the optimum mix of these products.

The problem now under consideration is somewhat different. One product is to be produced. The prices of the inputs are known. But a finite number of production processes or technologies is available. Each of these processes requires a specific ratio between the inputs; if output is doubled the usage of inputs is doubled.

The situation is illustrated in Figure 11–6. Along the axes are measured the quantities of the inputs to be used in production. The lines radiating from the origin represent the alternative production processes—in this case four processes are available.

Let us examine the ray representing production process A. Various quantities of the product may be produced by moving along this ray. Moving from A_{10} to A_{20}, for example, represents an increase in output from 10 units to 20 units. This requires a doubling of the quantities of inputs x and y employed. We ignore the possibility of diminishing returns; the quantity of output is proportional to the quantities of inputs as long as the proportion of the inputs is maintained. This assumed proportionality of inputs and output is another illustration of linearity.

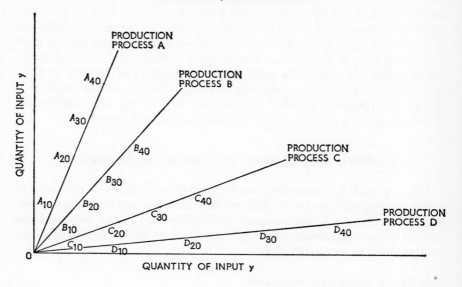

FIGURE 11–6

ONE PRODUCT, FOUR PROCESSES

Product process B requires proportionally more of input x and less of input y. But it also represents a linear relationship between output and input. The same is true of processes C and D.

In Figure 11–7 we join the points representing equal quantities of output. Thus A_{10} is joined with B_{10}, C_{10}, and D_{10}. Also A_{20} is joined with B_{20}, C_{20}, and D_{20}. We use straight lines to join these points representing equal outputs.

The "curves" which result from joining A_{10}, B_{10}, C_{10}, and D_{10} or similar sets of points representing equal levels of output are known as *isoproduct* curves. Along the isoproduct curves processes may be substituted for each other to produce the same level of output. The four isoproduct curves shown in Figure 11–7 are

$$A_{10}\, B_{10}\, C_{10}\, D_{10}$$
$$A_{20}\, B_{20}\, C_{20}\, D_{20}$$
$$A_{30}\, B_{30}\, C_{30}\, D_{30}$$
$$A_{40}\, B_{40}\, C_{40}\, D_{40}$$

but of course a large number of isoproduct curves could be drawn, each at a different level of output.

The next step is to construct a series of *isocost* curves, each representing a given amount of expenditure on the two inputs. Figure 11–8 shows a set of parallel isocost curves; the higher curves represent higher budgets of expenditures of the two inputs. The prices of the inputs are given—we

FIGURE 11-7
ISOPRODUCT CURVES

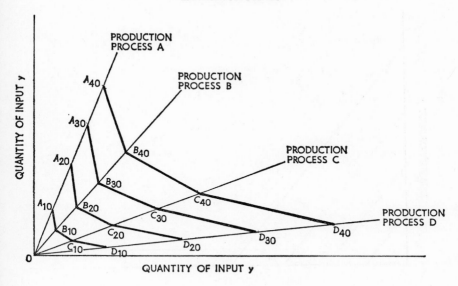

assume that these prices are beyond the control of management and are independent of the decisions under consideration.

The scales of the two axes in Figure 11-9 are the same as in the preceding graphs. As before, they represent quantities of the two inputs. Therefore it is easy to superimpose Figure 11-8 on Figure 11-7 to reproduce a graph showing both the isoproduct curves and the isocost curves. This is done in Figure 11-9.

Two kinds of optimal positions can be found in Figure 11-9. If we take the budget to be fixed and predetermined, the objective becomes one of maximizing the output. This is done by moving to the position at which the isocost curve representing that budget touches the corner of one of the isoproduct curves. This is the optimum—the greatest output for the given expenditure.

The other approach is to take the output as a given predetermined amount and to find the lowest isocost curve making that output available. Again this is found at one of the corners of the isoproduct curve. In exceptional cases an isocost curve might lie on a segment of an isoproduct curve so that more than one optimum is possible, but we shall not concern ourselves here with these exceptions.

Increasing marginal costs

In the illustrations up to this point the assumption has been that marginal costs (unit incremental costs) are constant. This assumption is roughly

FIGURE 11–8

COMBINATION OF ISOPRODUCT CURVES AND ISOCOST CURVES

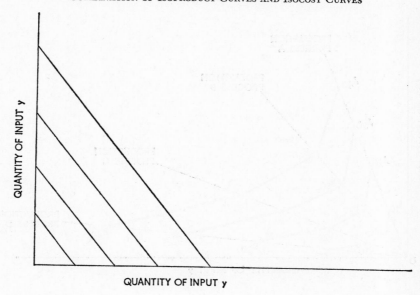

QUANTITY OF INPUT y

FIGURE 11–9

COMBINATION OF ISOPRODUCT CURVES AND ISOCOST CURVES

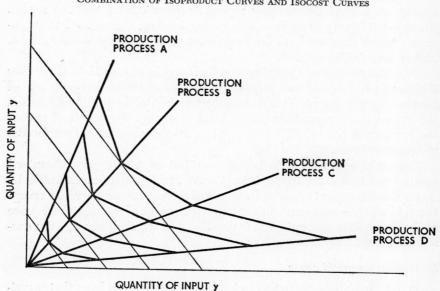

PRODUCTION PROCESS A

PRODUCTION PROCESS B

PRODUCTION PROCESS C

PRODUCTION PROCESS D

QUANTITY OF INPUT y

consistent with many of research findings described earlier in the book, but it is nevertheless a limitation. Linear programming can still be applied if the cost curve is broken into linear segments in a stairstep fashion. Figure 11–10 illustrates such a possibility.

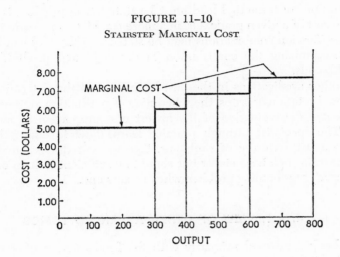

FIGURE 11–10
STAIRSTEP MARGINAL COST

In this case, the first 300 units are produced on regular time at a unit cost of $5. The next 100 units must be produced on overtime requiring time-and-a-half payments to labor. The next 200 units must be produced in a standby plant with less productive equipment and more damage to materials. The last 200 units are produced on a second shift which suffers from low productivity and extra bonuses.

The precise way in which such increasing costs can be handled need not be developed here. The point is that linear programming can cope with the increasing cost situation provided that discontinuities in the cost function are an acceptable approximation to reality.

A variety of applications

The earliest applications of linear programming were to the "transportation problem." Suppose m factories are to supply n destinations. If the freight and storage costs are known and if definite quantities demanded at the various destinations are given, the problem becomes one of minimizing cost. A set of equations and inequalities can be found which will express the objective of minimizing costs, within the constraints of demand requirements and productive capacities. The minimization of costs creates no conceptual problems which are different from the maximization of profits. In the case in which both capacities and destination requirements are involved, the problem can be solved not only by the simplex method but also by the well-known "transportation technique."

Linear programming has long been applied to the problem of blending gasoline. The prices and chemical qualities of various inputs must be known. The specifications in terms of octane ratings, vapor pressures, and concentrations of tetraethyl lead must be stated. The problem is to minimize the cost of a given grade. Or, in a more complete application, various price-specification combinations may be stated and the problem becomes one of maximizing the contribution to overhead and profits from the selected blends.

Still other applications in the past have been to the determination of the optimal rotation of crops, the scheduling of production, optimal bombing patterns, determination of the lowest cost proportion of metals for alloys. The specialist through practice learns how to adapt the technique to a wide variety of problems. The present discussion does not suffice to train such a specialist but should be sufficient to help one identify a linear programming problem when he sees one.

4. A REVIEW OF OTHER ADVANCED TOPICS

In a book concerned primarily with the fundamentals of managerial economics, it is well not to become deeply enmeshed in topics which are highly specialized and complex. But it may be well to introduce these problems and indicate how the fundamental concepts do provide insight into their solution.

Replacement decisions

Chapter 9 provided a brief introduction to the MAPI formula for making replacement decisions. But a full development of the subject was avoided, for it is in itself a subject for full books. The problem is much more complicated than that of a simple one-shot investment decision for several reasons. It is necessary to determine the optimal time to make the new investment. But the optimal time depends not only on a comparison of the existing equipment with available replacements; it depends also on forecasts of the rate of technological advance which determines the rate of obsolescence of equipment. It would be foolish to replace a piece of equipment today if it is known that a far superior substitute will be available tomorrow. A decision to invest in a replacement today may increase the net cash inflow at once but it reduces flexibility in making even better replacements in the near future.

The analysis is complicated even further by the fact that the present value of the replacement depends upon its economic life. But the optimal economic life of new replacements depends upon the very considerations just mentioned which influence the optimal time to scrap existing assets and purchase replacements.

Potential inflation is still another complication. Replacements today may help avoid higher replacement costs next year, though even higher costs may be encountered on later rounds of replacement.

A full exposition of these topics is to be found in the publications of George Terborgh and the Machinery and Allied Products Institute. Books on engineering economics also develop this topic more fully than is possible here. A British publication by A. J. Merrett and Allen Sykes called *Capital Budgeting and Company Finance* (London: Longmans, Green and Co. Ltd., 1966) contains several short chapters on the subject.

Lease or buy decisions

An ordinary lease which does not involve a fixed long-term commitment does not present any special problems beyond those already discussed. The monthly or annual payments can be treated as ordinary expenses. If the equipment is available on either a lease or purchase basis, the problem is a straightforward one in capital budgeting. A purchase will result in lower cash outflows in the form of monthly or annual payments. The savings in cash outflows may be discounted in the usual fashion to determine the present value of the purchase. The present value may then be compared with the purchase price. Or, alternatively, the discounted rate of return may be computed on the basis of the cash savings and purchase price.

Recent interest in leases arises, however, from what is called the "financial lease." This lease involves a fixed commitment to make certain payments over a period of years. The total of the payments exceeds the purchase price. The availability of the financial lease arrangement is an alternative source of finance.

Suppose that the choice is between borrowing to finance the purchase and a lease arrangement. The two alternatives involve the payment of an implicit interest rate arising from the fact that the total repayments exceed the original purchase price (and, thus, the original amount borrowed). The two alternatives also involve tax deductions arising from the fact that depreciation and interest are deductable for tax purposes.

The procedure recommended in a leading analysis of this problem requires a number of steps which involve opportunity cost estimates and present value computations. The details of the computations and of the reasoning behind these computations is again too involved for the purposes of this book. But we have introduced the basic concepts required in this kind of analysis.

Comprehensive cases

The cases in this last chapter cut across the various topics in this book and provide an opportunity to apply analysis in situations in which the issues are complex and not clearly defined. The Birch case is concerned with transfer pricing, but the other cases are not easily classified into any single category. The practitioner must be prepared to deal with situations in which the issues themselves must be defined before analysis can be applied.

RADFORD CORPORATION

The Radford Corporation was involved primarily in making wooden handles—broom handles, mop handles, and the like. The company had 60 employees. It had been highly successful over the years, building up its equity to $250,000. There were seven directors on the board, one of whom was Mr. John Caldwell, another his brother-in-law. Mr. Caldwell's mother and his uncle were also among the directors.

Formulation of the bowling alley idea

In 1959 the president of the company, the secretary, and the engineer developed the idea of investing in a bowling alley. They did the preliminary research on such an investment and were strongly in favor of it. Only Mr. Caldwell was hesitant about the idea. Mr. Caldwell felt two other alternatives were preferable:

1. Invest more money in the advertising business.
2. Build a new handle factory in another part of the country.

He believed that these were the areas in which the company officials had experience and special skills. He felt that almost anyone was qualified to establish a bowling alley and that competition would be more severe in that field. He doubted that the rate of return would be as high in the bowling alley alternative.

Originally it was planned to set up the bowling alley, if it were established, as a subsidiary corporation. The possibility of creating two corporations, one to own the land and buildings, the other to run the bowling alley itself was considered. This might have had the advantage of keeping both corporations in lower corporate income tax brackets. On the other hand, if the bowling alley were not successful, all the earnings would be in the land and building, so that this would no longer be an advantage. The idea of two subsidiary corporations was dropped.

Two alternative types of equipment for the bowling alley were considered. The first involved equipment by AMF. Later the Brunswick Company took an interest, and offered to deduct the $5,000 that had been deposited with the other supplier from its charges. Thus the decision involved an analysis of the proposals of these two possible suppliers. In this case the figures are all based on the AMF alternative.

Several members of the board of directors committed themselves to the bowling alley idea early in the game before the full analysis had been made.

First version considered

The first estimates of cost and revenue based on the AMF alternative, including an analysis of fixed and variable costs, are shown in Exhibit 1. The fixed costs were estimated to total $81,900. The variables costs were estimated at $.116 per customer. The revenue was estimated at $.53 per customer (of which $.42 was the average charge per line and the remainder the revenue from shoe rentals and the sale of food.) This gave a break-even point of 184,000 customers which would be at about two-thirds of the estimated level of business. The profit would be about $22,000 at the expected level of 250,000 customers (lines). Exhibit 2 is a break-even chart based on some early revisions of the estimates in Exhibit 1. This exhibit reflects higher fixed costs and thus a higher break-even point. But it also indicates greater optimism about sales, with revenues of $140,000 instead of $132,500.[1]

Refinements on first version

Exhibits 3, 4, 5, 6, and 7 show various refinements of the analysis. Considerable thought went into the financing. The Radford Corporation would purchase $50,000 of stock in the subsidiary corporation. Even this $50,000 would be borrowed. These exhibits show a higher net income than

---

[1] The minor discrepancies in the figures are a result of rounding and the roughness of certain compilations. These discrepancies are insignificant.

EXHIBIT 1
FIRST VERSION OF COST AND REVENUE
(16 alleys, 350-day operation)

			Fixed	Variable
Income ($.53/customer)				
Gross bowling income @ 42¢	$105,000			
Restaurant, soft drinks, candy (net) ...	12,800			
Shoe rental	7,800			
Net sales—Balls, bags, shoes	1,900			
Amusements, cigarettes, ball cleaning ..	5,000	$132,500		
Expenses				
Salaries	$ 20,000		$20,000	
Pin spotter rental	23,000			.092
Service cost	7,200		7,200	
Replacement reserve	1,800		800	.004
Utilities	4,500		4,500	
Advertising and promotion	2,400		2,400	
Insurance	2,200		2,200	
Federal and state taxes	4,900			.02
Federal and state licenses	1,100		1,100	
FICA and payroll taxes	1,500		1,500	
AMF payments	14,300		14,300	
Interest on alleys	2,000		2,000	
Interest on building	2,200		2,200	
Depreciation on building (20 years) ...	5,000		5,000	
Depreciation on alley (5 years)	18,600		18,600	
	$110,700		$81,800	.116

Paid in capital .... $50,000 from Radford 6%
Loan .... $80,000 to $100,000—@ 6% insurance company
Depreciation first year $11,300

in the original estimates in Exhibit 1. A slightly higher volume is estimated —252,000 customers instead of 250,000 customers. The restaurant is eliminated, but some revenue from a snack bar is included. The total effect of these changes is to decrease the revenue figures. On the expense side, the salaries, rental and service costs remain the same. The depreciation expenses are lower, being spread over 40 years and 10 years rather than 20 years and 5 years. The advertising and promotion expenses are cut in half. The insurance estimates are $700 lower. The tax estimates are over $1,000 lower. The social security taxes are also estimated at a considerably lower figure. No interest expense is deducted in arriving at net income, so that this exhibit is not directly comparable with the first. On the other hand, $10,000 of parent company overhead expenses are shown in Exhibit 4.

Further revisions

Exhibits 8, 9, 10, and 11 show further consideration of the AMF alternative. One important difference at this stage was that estimated operations

EXHIBIT 2
BREAK-EVEN CHART

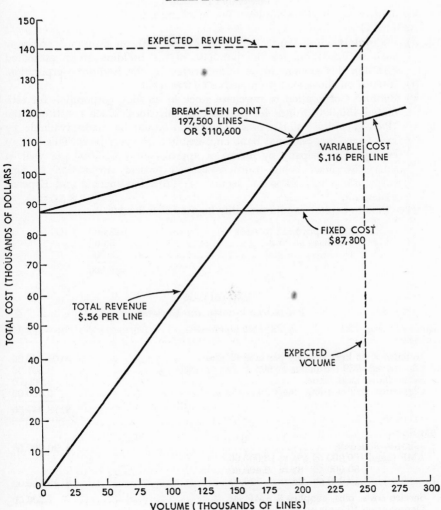

for only 300 days were considered, on the assumption that the business would be closed on Sunday. Two of the directors, Mr. Caldwell's mother and his uncle, insisted on Sunday closing, on religious grounds. Thus the number of customers was reduced by about 25,000. This reduced revenue in proportion and reduced the rental charges and service costs. Another difference in this later estimate was a complete revision of the estimates of fixed and variable costs.

EXHIBIT 3

Proposed Financing

1. Set up new corporation—"Radford Bowling Lanes, Inc."
   Radford Corporation to hold all stock.
2. *a*) Radford Bowling Lanes to negotiate loan with an insurance company such as Prudential for the purchase of the building at an estimated $85,000, this amount to be underwritten by the Radford Corporation.
   b) Interest on above loan presumed to be 6 percent.
   c) Radford Corporation to purchase stock in bowling corporation for estimated $50,000. Funds for purchase of this stock which constitutes the "Paid-in-capital" of the new corporation would be made available by loan from First National Bank on possibly a five-year basis. This loan to be repaid principally by means of approximately $10,000 per year in salary overhead being transferred from present corporation to new corporation. See "Expense" section of "Projected Income and Expense Statement."

The "Paid-in-capital" would probably be used as follows:

Down payment to AMF	$22,000
Purchase of land	15,000
Operating capital	13,000
	$50,000

EXHIBIT 4

Projected Income and Expense

Lines per Day—720	*A 350-Day Operation*	*Customers per Year—252,000*

Income

16 lanes × 45 lines per day per lane @ 42¢	$105,840.00
Shoe rental—239 customers × 60% = 143 @ 15¢	7,507.50
Sales—Balls, bags, shoes	2,000.00
Cigarettes, ball cleaning, snack bar—Net	3,000.00
	$118,347.50

Expense

Salaries—Schedule		$ 20,000.00
AMF rental 160,000 @ 10¢ = 16,000.00		
80,000 @ 8¢ = 6,400.00		
12,000 @ 6¢ = 720.00		$ 23,120.00
Service costs, pins, supplies ½ AMF est.		7,200.00
Depreciation 40 years on 100,000 = 2,500.00		
10 years on 88,000 = 8,800.00		$ 11,300.00
Utilities		4,500.00
Advertising and promotion		1,200.00
Insurance, (fire) on $188,000		1,500.00
Taxes—Ad valorem		3,300.00
Federal and state local license		1,000.00
Social security tax		600.00
Overhead absorbed from Radford		10,000.00
		$ 84,220.00
Net Income		$ 34,127.50*

* Interest expense not included above. Included with principal payments in another schedule (Schedule "A").

EXHIBIT 5
Schedule "A"

AMF Equipment Loan—Approximately	$88,000.00	
16 lanes @ $5,500.00 each	$88,000.00	
Less 25% down payment	22,000.00	
Balance to be paid in 5 years	$66,000.00	Principal

	Interest/Year
Total $66,000.00 × 6%	$ 3,960.00
— 23,760.00 (36%) Principal—1st year	
42,240.00 × 6%	2,534.00
— 15,840.00 (24%) Principal—2d year	
26,400.00 × 6%	1,584.00
— 10,560.00 (16%) Principal—3d year	
15,840.00 × 6%	950.00
— 7,920.00 (12%) Principal—4th year	
7,920.00 × 6%	475.00
Total interest 5 years	$ 9,503.00

Loan for Building—Insurance Company—Approximately $85,000.00
On 15-year term
    Payments $844.00 month per $1,000.00 (including interest), year $8,608.80
    (1st year—Each $1,000.00 of principal only reduced to $957.50)

Total Cash Payments—Principal and Interest

1st Year	Insurance Company	$ 8,608.80
	AMF	27,720.00
		$36,328.80
2d Year	Insurance Company	$ 8,608.80
	AMF	18,374.00
		$26,982.80
3d Year	Insurance Company	$ 8,608.80
	AMF	12,144.00
		$20,752.80

EXHIBIT 6
Schedule "B"
(source and disposition of funds)

Estimated profit per statement		$34,127.50	
Add—expense charges which do not require cash outlay		11,300.00	
Total funds available annually		$45,427.50	

	1st Year	*2d Year*	*3d Year*
Available cash	$45,427.50	$45,427.50	$45,427.50
Repayment schedule	36,328.80	26,982.80	20,752.80
To surplus	$ 9,098.70	$18,444.70	$24,674.70
Less estimated income taxes (Schedule "D")	8,676.00	8,676.00	8,676.00
Unappropriated surplus	$ 422.70	$ 9,768.70	$15,998.70

EXHIBIT 7
SCHEDULE "C"
estimated ad valorem taxes

City Taxes

Real—Property at $15,000 × 30% = 4,500.00 @ .4612 .... $ 207.45
Personal—Max. $188,000 × 30% = 56,400 @ .4612 .... 2,600.00
                                                                    $2,807.45

County Taxes

Real—Same valuation 4,500.00 @ .3 .... $ 135.00
Personal—Estimated ½ of city assessed 28,000 @ .3 .... 840.00
                                                                    $ 975.00

Total ad valorem tax $3,782.45

SCHEDULE "D"

(estimated income tax)

Earnings per operating statement $34,129.50
Interest payments not included on statement .... 7,100.00 (average/year)*
                                                       $27,029.50
Estimated federal tax $7,605.00
Estimated state tax 107.00
    Total $8,676.00

* This is an average amount of interest per year over the life of the notes. Total interest paid
first few years would be somewhat higher than the average of $7,100.00 per year.

1st year interest	AMF	$3,960.00
	Insurance company	5,003.00
		$8,963.00

Outside investigations

As part of the analysis for this decision, Mr. Caldwell and other members of the firm tried to learn about the profitability of bowling alleys elsewhere. They were able to obtain copies of a confidential national report covering 370 bowling alleys, which gave information on form of ownership, number of lanes, charge per lane, proportion of business in various categories (open, league, tournament, junior), the volume of automatic pin setters, extent to which these are leased, ownership of building, size of investment, etc. This report also gave a breakdown of receipts and expenses as percentages. The report included a special collection of statistics on 16-lane establishments. Most of the data were for 1958, but data on receipts and profits for 1955, 1956, 1957, and 1958 were summarized.

Mr. Caldwell spent considerable time interviewing the owners of two bowling alleys in a nearby location. He also telephoned an alley in a small town in Illinois, where the situation was more like the situation the new alley would face. For example, he found that the company in Illinois charged 45 cents per line (30 cents for children). This company did $300

EXHIBIT 8
BREAK-EVEN CHART

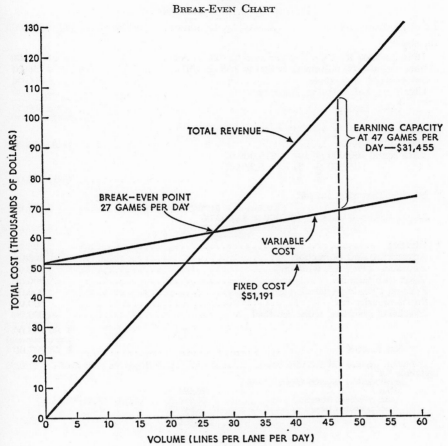

to $400 business per day, which would be slightly more than the estimates for the Radford Corporation. The company used Brunswick pin setters. The total investment was $650,000, which was more than the Radford Corporation had in mind. It operated on Sunday. The company also provided information on nearby bowling lanes within 35 to 40 miles.

Similar information was obtained from other bowling alleys. One of these companies expressed a preference for Brunswick equipment because of better maintenance and greater experience. This company suggested that it might be possible to get a franchise from the town to keep other establishments from coming in. One company official suggested that there must be a thousand population per lane within the trade area. It suggested that the break-even point was at 42 to 43 lines per lane per day. Another

EXHIBIT 9
PROJECTED INCOME AND EXPENSE

Lines per Day—752   A 300-Day Operation   Customers per Year—225,600

Income

16 lanes × 47 lines per day per lane @ 42¢	$ 94,752.00
Shoe rental—250 customers × 60% = 150 @ 15¢	6,750.00
Sales—Balls, bags, shoes	2,000.00
Cigarettes, ball cleaning, snack bar—Net	3,000.00
Gross income	$106.502.00

Expense

Salaries—Schedule .... $ 20,000.00
AMF rental 160,000 @ 10¢ = $16,000.00
              65,600 @ 8¢ =   5,248.00
                  —   @ 6¢ = _____ .... $ 21,248.00

Service costs, pins, supplies
                      (Total 5.5 % gross) 5,857.00
Depreciation 40 years on 100,000 = $2,500.00
            10 years on 80,000 =   8,000.00 .... $ 10,500.00

Utilities	4,500.00
Advertising and promotion	1,200.00
Insurance (fire) on $188,000	1,500.00
Taxes—ad valorem	3,800.00
Federal, state local license	1,000.00
Social security tax	600.00
Overhead absorbed from Radford	10,000.00
	$ 80,205.00

Net income .... $ 26,297.00*

* Interest expense not included above. Included with principal payments on another schedule (Schedule "A").

Actual earning capacity 5-year average
Above	$26,297.00	
Add overhead absorbed	+ 10,000.00	$1,800 net/expense line
Less interest average	− 4,842.00	
	$31,455.00	

EXHIBIT 10
SOURCE AND DISPOSITION OF FUNDS

Estimated profit per statement $26,297.00
Add: expense charges which do not
    require cash outlay—Depreciation 10,500.00
        Total funds available annually $36,797.00

	1st Year	2d Year	3d Year
Available cash	$36,797.00	$36,797.00	$36,797.00
Repayment schedule	36,328.80	26,982.80	20,752.80
To surplus	$ 468.20	$ 9,814.20	$16.044.20
Less estimated income taxes (Schedule "D")	—	5,770.00	6,237.67
Unappropriated surplus	$ 468.20	$ 4,044.20	$ 9,806.53

EXHIBIT 11

SCHEDULE "C"
(estimated ad valorem taxes)

City Taxes
Real—Property at $15,000 × 30% = 4,500.00 @ 0.4612 .... $ 207.45
Personal—Max. $188,000 × 30% = 56,400.00 @ 0.4612 .... 2,600.00
$2,807.45

County taxes
Real—Same valuation 4,500.00 @ 0.3 .... $ 135.00
Personal—Estimated ½ of city assessed 28,000 @ 0.3 .... 840.00
$ 975.00

Total ad valorem tax $3,782.00

SCHEDULE "D"

(estimated income tax—first year only)

Earnings per operating statement $26,297.00
Interest payments not included on statement ... 8,963.00 (average for 5 years—
4,842.00)*

Taxable income $17,344.00
Estimated federal tax $5.203.00
Estimated state tax 567.00
$5,770.00

* This is the actual amount of interest the first year (average first five years is $4,842.00).
Total interest paid first few years would be somewhat higher than the average of $4,842.00 per year.

1st year interest   AMF $3,960.00
Insurance company 5,003.00
$8,963.00

company put the break-even point at 30 lines a day. Officials of this company believed that there was no difference between AMF and Brunswick equipment. One of these companies charged 40 cents (children 35 cents) while the other stated that it could not do business below 45 cents. All of these companies gave considerable detailed information on operations.

Exhibit 12 is illustrative of the kinds of correspondence that took place among members of the board as the bowling alley plan was being formulated.

Demand and potential competition

The location of the alley was to be Pikeville, Missouri, a town of 10,000 where the broom handle plant was located. Mr. Caldwell believed that the town could support only one alley, making it unlikely that a competitor would move in. Nevertheless, he continued to worry about what would

EXHIBIT 12

Springfield, Illinois
February 24, 1960

Mr. J. C. Frederick, President
Radford Corporation
Pikeville, Missouri

Dear John:

I am enclosing the results of my investigation on the bowling situation. I visited three establishments and called another.

Most everything I heard would encourage one to go into the business. However, I learned that many, many mistakes were made by people not being able to see into the future. The most common was, "Parking Lot Too Small." As an example, one alley has a 6:30 p.m. league and a 9:00 p.m. league. Sixty bowlers in each league plus spectators and substitutes, etc. All the nine o'clock crowd comes before the six thirty crowd leaves, so he needs at least 120 spaces at this time. The lot looks awfully big, but he says it is much too small.

Another mistake he made--he can call his pin jumper over the speaker system, but the pin jumper has no mike with which to reply, and many trips to the back of the alleys are necessary.

I believe our estimated costs are too low. One owner said it would take $15,000 to cut 3 feet from a plot of land 150 x 200 and put a good base and black top the area. Then I believe we left out entirely the lights for the parking lot, and tall towers or poles and big lights are necessary for this.

The same owner also told me that his cash register, desk, chairs, and necessary equipment of this kind cost him $5,000.

He put in tile and wishes he didn't have it, and put in carpet on the lobby and is glad he did. (Tile under the spectators' and bowlers' seats.)

One thing I picked up should bear investigating--one man rents his pins and finds that more satisfactory than owning them.

One man told me Brunswick will also lease the pin spotters now.

EXHIBIT 12—*Continued*

page 2

However, I am about convinced that AMF is better. Evansville, Indiana has 4 or 5 big places, all with AMF. I looked at the Brunswick and AMF in operation, and could see or find out nothing wrong with either one. One man said AMF was extremely nice to do business with. They all said both Brunswick and AMF would treat you right.

My recommendation is:

Go slow and be very careful about Sunday, as this is decidedly the second best day in the week for the people with whom I talked. I cannot say I am against the plan, but I believe we will be at a very definite disadvantage without the Sunday income, possibly enough to make the difference between a highly successful operation and a mediocre one. Looking ahead a little, I believe the pressure for Sunday operation would mount after the opening and a situation might develop between those who want to run on Sunday and those who do not.

If, however, you and the rest of the board think it is all right to do so, I will be in favor of it.

One more thing I think of: I'd suggest a review of the cost estimates to arrive at good figures for the parking lot, lights, signs, cash register, furniture, etc., and that a safety factor be put in to take care of unforeseen contingencies. (A rather liberal one.)

I'm enclosing an expense sheet on the traveling and phone calls I made. The phone is an estimate, but I believe it is close.

Sincerely,

(signed)   John Caldwell

John Caldwell

happen if a second alley were to locate in the town or if the bowling fad were to diminish. No towns within a radius of 50 miles were large enough to support a bowling alley, so that the Pikeville location should draw customers from other towns.

The estimates of revenue were based on the experience of other bowling alleys in similar locations and the advice of the equipment producers. Mr. Caldwell believed that if the bowling alley were to prove unprofitable the building would be useful as a grocery store. The possibility of renting the building to the grocery business would reduce the risk somewhat.

Other alternatives

None of the directors had made an analysis of the probable results of expansion of broom handle manufacturing. Mr. Caldwell did give considerable attention to the possibility of expanding the advertising activities in which he and his brother-in-law were engaged as partners. He believed that the Radford Corporation might do better by purchasing some advertising companies which were located in towns with a population of 15,000 or less. Mr. Caldwell knew that some such companies were available for purchase. He and his brother-in-law had operated similar advertising companies with great success over the past 15 years.

Exhibits 13 and 14 show Mr. Caldwell's estimates if the Radford Corporation were to invest $206,000 (an amount comparable with the proposed investment in the bowling alley) in the advertising business. Exhibit 14 differs from Exhibit 13 only in that it is more optimistic about potential revenues for the advertising alternative.

EXHIBIT 13

ESTIMATE FOR ADVERTISING OPERATIONS—COMPANY A

	$206,000 Investment
12,360	Per month
12	Months
148,320	Potential
80%	
118,656.00	Estimated annual revenue
20%	
23,731.20	Profit
20,600	Depreciation
44,331.20	Available to pay off (gross)
12,331.20	Tax
32,000	Available to pay debt and interest
6,000	Interest
26,000	Apply to debt
7.9 Years	

EXHIBIT 14

ESTIMATE FOR ADVERTISING OPERATIONS—COMPANY B

	$206,000 Investment
16,524	Per month
12	Months
198,288	Potential
80%	
158,630.40	Estimated annual revenue
20%	
31,726.08	Profit
20,600	Depreciation
52,326	Available to pay off (gross)
16,000	Tax
36,326	Available to pay debt and interest
6,000	Interest
30,326	Apply to debt
6.8 Years	

1. *Evaluate the use of break-even charts in the major decisions in this case.*
2. *How would the discount structure on rentals (shown in Exhibit 9) affect the shapes of the curves on the break-even chart?*
3. *Should Mr. Caldwell and his associates invest in the bowling alley?*
4. *Evaluate the types of information Mr. Caldwell and his associates collected to make this decision.*

BIRCH PAPER COMPANY*

"If I were to price these boxes any lower than $480 a thousand," said James Brunner, manager of Birch Paper Company's Thompson division, "I'd be countermanding my order of last month for our salesmen to stop shaving their bids and to bid full cost quotations. I've been trying for weeks to improve the quality of our business, and if I turn around now and accept this job at $430 or $450 or something less than $480, I'll be tearing down this program I've been working so hard to build up. The division can't very well show a profit by putting in bids which don't even cover a fair share of overhead costs, let alone give us a profit."

Birch Paper Company was a medium-size, partly integrated paper company, producing white and kraft papers and paperboard. A portion of its paperboard output was converted into corrugated boxes by the Thompson division, which also printed and colored the outside surface of the boxes.

* This case was prepared by William Rotch under the direction of Neil E. Harlan of the Harvard University Graduate School of Business Administration as a basis for classroom discussion rather than to illustrate either effective or ineffective handling of administrative situations. Copyright © 1956 by the President and Fellows of Harvard College. Used by specific permission.

Including Thompson, the company had four producing divisions and a timberland division, which supplied part of the company's pulp requirements.

For several years each division had been judged independently on the basis of its profit and return on investment. Top management had been working to gain effective results from a policy of decentralizing responsibility and authority for all decisions but those relating to over-all company policy. The company's top officials believed that in the past few years the concept of decentralization had been successfully applied and that the company's profits and competitive position had definitely improved.

Early in 1957 the Northern division designed a special display box for one of its papers in conjunction with the Thompson division, which was equipped to make the box. Thompson's staff for package design and development spent several months perfecting the design, production methods, and materials that were to be used; because of the unusual color and shape, these were far from standard. According to an agreement between the two divisions, the Thompson division was reimbursed by the Northern division for the cost of its design and development work.

When the specifications were all prepared, the Northern division asked for bids on the box from the Thompson division and from two outside companies. Each division manager was normally free to buy from whatever supplier he wished; and even on sales within the company, divisions were expected to meet the going market price if they wanted the business.

In 1957 the profit margins of converters such as the Thompson division were being squeezed. Thompson, as did many other similar converters, bought its paperboard and its function was to print, cut, and shape it into boxes. Although it bought most of its materials from other Birch divisions, most of Thompson's sales were made to outside customers. If Thompson got the order from Northern, it probably would buy its linerboard and corrugating medium from the Southern division of Birch. The walls of a corrugated box consist of outside and inside sheets of linerboard sandwiching the fluted corrugating medium. About 70 percent of Thompson's out-of-pocket cost of $400 for the order represented the cost of linerboard and corrugating medium. Though Southern had been running below capacity and had excess inventory, it quoted the market price, which had not noticeably weakened as a result of the oversupply. Its out-of-pocket costs on both liner and corrugating medium were about 60 percent of the selling price.

The Northern division received bids on the boxes of $480 a thousand from the Thompson division, $430 a thousand from West Paper Company, and $432 a thousand from Eire Papers, Ltd. Eire Papers offered to buy from Birch the outside linerboard with the special printing already on it, but would supply its own inside liner and corrugating medium. The outside liner would be supplied by the Southern division at a price equivalent of $90 a thousand boxes, and would be printed for $30 a thousand by the Thompson division. Of the $30, about $25 would be out-of-pocket costs.

Since this situation appeared to be a little unusual, William Kenton, manager of the Northern division, discussed the wide discrepancy of bids with Birch's commercial vice president. He told the vice president, "We sell in a very competitive market, where higher costs cannot be passed on. How can we be expected to show a decent profit and return on investment if we have to buy our supplies at more than 10 percent over the going market?"

Knowing that Mr. Brunner had on occasion in the past few months been unable to operate the Thompson division at capacity, it seemed odd to the vice president that Mr. Brunner would add the full 20 percent overhead and profit charge to his out-of-pocket costs. When asked about this, Mr. Brunner's answer was the remark that appears at the beginning of the case. He went on to say that having done the developmental work on the box, and having received no profit on that, he felt entitled to a good markup on the production of the box itself.

The vice president explored further the cost structures of the various divisions. He remembered a comment that the controller had made at a meeting the week before to the effect that costs that for one division were variable, could be largely fixed for the company as a whole. He knew that in the absence of specific orders from top management, Mr. Kenton would accept the lowest bid, which was that of the West Paper Company for $430. However, it would be possible for top management to order the acceptance of another bid if the situation warranted such action. And though the volume represented by the transactions in question was less than 5 percent of the volume of any of the divisions involved, other transactions could conceivably raise similar problems later.

1. *What price should Mr. Brunner set on the special display boxes? Discuss.*
2. *How does the theory of transfer pricing reviewed in Chapter II relate to this case?*
3. *Is there a conflict in this situation between the needs of decisions on pricing and the requirements of profit reporting? Explain.*

MAHANAGAR MUNICIPAL DAIRY (A)*

On September 10, 1962, the municipal commissioner, the chairman of the milk committee, and the dairy manager met together to discuss the operating results of the Mahanagar Municipal Dairy. They discussed various policy implications of recent losses, with the intent of minimizing future losses.

---

* Copyright © 1965 by the Indian Institute of Management, Ahmedabad.

Events leading to the establishment of the municipal dairy

In the early 1950s the state government had realized the need for assuring an adequate supply of quality milk at reasonable prices to the growing city of Mahanagar. Consequently it set up a small milk dairy in Mahanagar in the year 1951. After about one and a half years of operation, that dairy business had to be wound up due to heavy financial losses.

During the same period another (privately owned) dairy was also set up in Mahanagar with a capital investment of Rs. 400,000. This dairy initially sold 500 liters of milk per day, a figure which subsequently rose to 7,000 liters. This dairy was closed down by its operators in the year 1954.

During this period, milk of uncertain quality was being sold throughout the city by local cow and buffalo keepers. Apart from its poor quality, another disadvantage of this milk was its highly variable prices. The state government, therefore, continued to cast about for a solution to the problem; it suggested that the municipal corporation initiate a milk scheme for ensuring a supply of quality milk at reasonable prices to the Mahanagar consumers.

In the beginning the municipal corporation authorities resisted the idea on the grounds that the activity was beyond the functional scope of the corporation. The authorities also were concerned over whether such a scheme would be competently carried out as a government department. The municipal authorities were nonetheless convinced that some satisfactory source of milk must be found. The municipal corporation finally decided in early 1955 to take charge of supplying quality milk to the city consumers at a reasonable price on a no-profit no-loss basis.

Initially the dairy acted as a distributor of pasteurized milk purchased from a milk plant located about 45 miles away. The dairy sold milk at a margin of 11.5 paise per liter,[1] which covered transportation, storage, and distribution expenses. At this margin, the dairy's operations resulted in a loss of Rs. 61,000[2] in the year 1955–56 but showed a net profit of Rs. 19,000 in the year 1956–57.

In 1957 the milk plant that supplied milk to the dairy expressed its inability to continue to supply pasteurized milk indefinitely because of its commitment to supply milk to another milk scheme at a very attractive price. Consequently this left the municipal corporation with no alternative except to set up its own pasteurization plant immediately and to find a source of raw milk. At that time, the average daily sale of the municipal

---

[1] One paise = .01 rupee.

[2] The dairy officials did not view this loss seriously. They felt that the loss arose on account of initial establishment; certain expenses, though of capital nature, were charged to profit/loss account in that year.

dairy's milk amounted to 5,000 liters. The total milk consumption in the city was, however, estimated at about 1.25 million liters per day and it was expected to increase because of the growing population. Many corporators favored installation of a "pilot plant" capable of pasteurizing about 15,000 liters per day. They believed that the plant would repay its costs within a short period. They also recommended that the municipal corporation request help from the state government in securing money from UNICEF[3] and the central government before committing itself to the capital expenditure involved in installing a full-scale plant. Accordingly, a pilot plant capable of pasteurizing and storing 15,000 liters of milk per day was set up in January, 1958.

By the end of 1958, the government of India and UNICEF came forward with financial aid to the municipal corporation for putting up a larger plant. The government of India agreed to provide an outright grant of Rs. 3,080,000, and UNICEF contributed plant and machinery worth Rs. 2,600,000 under an agreement with the corporation that the dairy would provide free or subsidized low fat milk on a continuing basis to needy children, nursing and pregnant women, and to selected needy families in the city. It was expected that within 10 years from the date of inauguration of the distribution program, the cumulative contribution of subsidized and free milk would not be less than 1½ times the landed value of machinery provided by UNICEF. The municipal corporation agreed to make the necessary funds available for free and/or subsidized milk supply in their overall budget. The municipal corporation also allotted Rs. 2,800,000 for the project.

The new plant, capable of processing 70,000 liters of milk per day, commenced operations in November, 1961, in a newly constructed building involving the following outlay:

Plant and Machinery:*
  a) Imported by utilizing funds
      provided by UNICEF .... Rs. 2,600,000
  b) Indigenous equipment 954,000   Rs. 3,554,000

Building:
  a) Factory .... Rs. 2,430,000
  b) Office 561,000   Rs. 2,991,000

Fixtures and fittings 183,000
Auto-rickshaws 133,000
Miscellaneous 26,000

    Total .... Rs. 6,887,000

   * The funds for this plant were made available by the following agencies:
               UNICEF .... Rs. 2,600,000
               Central government grant 3,080,000
               Municipal corporation 1,207,000
                           Rs. 6,887,000

---

[3] United Nations International Children's Emergency Fund.

Certain plant and machinery of the pilot project (by then written down to Rs. 325,000) was abandoned on November 15, 1961, but its building, valued at Rs. 177,000, was used for another purpose by the municipal corporation. Other equipment of the pilot plant valued at Rs. 120,000 was transferred to the new plant.

Organization

The municipal corporation was a body which was provided for in the state government statutes, which meant that it had permanence. The corporation consisted of such number of councillors elected at ward elections as the state government might fix from time to time. These councillors held office generally for a term of four years. The corporation body approved the budget and decided policy matters as defined in the Act.

The elected councillors appointed 12 persons out of their own members to form a committee (also provided for by statute) called the standing committee. This committee was responsible for the proper appropriation of funds and for framing budget estimates. The standing committee was also charged with most of the policy decision making in the overall activities of the corporation.

The corporation also appointed various special committees to formulate policies in specific areas. Some of the policy-setting powers of the standing committee were delegated to these communities. In the initial period, the policy matters regarding the municipal dairy's operation and milk supply were assigned to the health committee. With the increasing tempo of the dairy's work, the corporation realized the need to have a separate committee for milk and its distribution. Consequently, a milk committee was formed in 1961 for determining policy matters of the dairy.

Under the Municipal Corporation Act, the entire executive power for the purposes of carrying out the functions of the corporation was vested in the municipal commissioner. The municipal commissioner was assisted by the three deputy commissioners in discharging his responsibilities. The powers to carry out routine matters regarding the municipal dairy had been delegated to the dairy manager, but for decisions like the revision of prices, opening and closing of centers, he was required to seek the approval of the municipal commissioner through the deputy municipal commissioner.

Sources of milk supply to the dairy

In late 1957, when the milk plant that supplied pasteurized milk to the Mahanagar municipal dairy expressed its inability to continue to supply milk, the municipal authorities were faced with the problem of finding an alternate source of milk. By this time, some of the political and social workers of Mahanagar district had been successful in organizing a number of milk producers' cooperative societies at the village level, with a district union at their apex. The union had started selling milk in Mahana-gar through a number of milkmen and milkvendors on a commission basis. On a suggestion from the state government (which was inclined to en-courage the cooperative movement in the state) and some of the citizens, the municipal authorities negotiated with the union, and it was agreed that the union would supply buffalo milk to the municipal dairy. The dairy started purchasing milk from the union in December, 1957, and, after getting it pasteurized at another dairy for a fee, sold this milk to city consumers. After January, 1958, this milk was processed and pasteurized in the municipal dairy's own pilot plant.

In 1959 the municipal dairy also started purchasing buffalo milk from another district union at the same prices, terms, and conditions as were applicable to Mahanagar district milk producers' cooperative union. In the same year, the dairy had agreed to purchase cow and buffalo milk in the proportion of 50:50 from the Gopalak Sangh, which was an organiza-tion established for the protection of cattle (especially cows). Because of political and social considerations the dairy executives did not refuse to accept more cow milk than the proportion agreed for cow-milk supply. Consequently in 1961–62 the dairy received 2320 liters of cow milk and 1300 liters of buffalo milk per day, in the proportion of 16:9.

The dairy was also required to purchase some cow and buffalo milk from the ghosies' (local milkmen) colonies. The average milk purchases from this source in 1961–62 amounted to 3800 liters of buffalo milk and 1210 liters of cow milk per day. Milk from ghosies' colonies had to be collected directly by the diary under an agreement entered into with them by the municipal corporation. The corporation had built special, residen-tial colonies for shifting the ghosies with a view to improving sanitary conditions in the city, and had, therefore, agreed to collect their milk directly at the dairy's cost, which amounted to approximately 1.4 paise per liter.

Purchase price, terms and conditions

In 1958, the municipal corporation agreed to vest power to decide on purchase policies and prices for the milk supply to the dairy in a rating committee consisting of five representatives—two from the corporation, two from the milk suppliers and one from the state government. Any pur-chase issues which could not be settled by the committee were to be referred to arbitration.

This committee had decided that amounts of milk in the ratio of 3:4:5 for the three seasons, summer (April to July), monsoon (August to November), and winter (December to March) would be accepted by the dairy under purchase contracts. The summer months were taken as the base, as this was the period when milk yields were the lowest and supply was generally less than demand. The object in fixing the ratio was twofold: (1) to ensure a supply of milk to the dairy in all seasons, and (2) to assure the suppliers of a market for most of their milk. The actual ratio in total milk yields of cows and buffalos from season to season varied from year to year. The agreed upon 3:4:5 ratio established the minimum, but there was no ceiling on the total quantity of milk the dairy could purchase from the suppliers if it were available.

The rating committee had also decided that sour milk should be accepted by the dairy, up to a maximum of 7 percent of volume of the sweet, fresh milk supplied daily. For such sour milk, which could not be used in fluid milk products, the dairy would pay a price based on butterfat content only. This price was Rs. 1.50 per kilogram of butterfat less than the regular price for one kilogram of butterfat contained in fresh buffalo milk.

Up to March 31, 1961, the purchase price of buffalo milk was fixed by the rating committee, taking into account the price paid to the milk producers plus the overhead expenses of primary cooperative societies and the unions. This not only entailed a seasonal variation in the purchase cost of milk but also resulted in a purchase cost to the dairy over which it had no control. Realizing the impact of an unpredictable cost of milk on the financial results of the dairy, the rating committee agreed to fix the purchase cost of milk from April 1, 1961, on the basis of the realized retail price for milk minus a fixed amount which was expected to compensate the dairy for its costs. The initial formula was based on the April 1, 1961, price of 74.7 paise per liter paid by the consumers to the dairy, minus a deduction for processing and selling charges calculated at 16.8 paise, based on expected operating costs of the new dairy plant (Exhibit 1). On this basis, the rating committee fixed the purchase price for buffalo milk containing 6 percent and 9 percent solid non-fat (SNF) at 57.9 paise per liter (74.7 paise less 16.8 paise). For the additional fat content in the milk the producer was paid an extra amount pro rata, without taking into account SNF. For cow milk, the purchase price was fixed by linking it with the purchase price of the buffalo milk on the total solid contents (fat as well as SNF) basis. The cow milk was assumed to contain 12 percent solid contents (3.5 percent fat and 8.5 percent SNF) while the assumption for buffalo milk was 15 percent solid contents (6 percent fat plus 9 percent SNF). Accordingly, the purchase price for cow milk was fixed at 46.3 paise per liter (12/15 x 57.9). However, the fat content in both types of milk received by the dairy was generally found to be more than the base taken for determining the purchase price. The buffalo milk received by the dairy in the year 1961–62 contained an average of 7.1 percent fat and accordingly the purchase price paid for it was 66.8 paise per liter (7.1/6 x 57.9). Similarly, cow milk on an average contained 13 percent solid contents (4.2 percent fat plus 8.8 percent SNF) and therefore the purchase price paid for it was 50.2 paise per liter (13/15 x 57.9).

EXHIBIT 1

MAHANAGAR MUNICIPAL DAIRY (A)
(estimates of expenses for running the full-scale plant)

Quantities of Milk:

Per day	63,350	liters
Per annum	23,122,750	liters

Expenses per annum:

Establishment	Rs.	853,000
Power and fuel		180,000
Transportation		200,000
Insurance and taxes		200,000
Repair and maintenance		380,000
Depreciation		550,000
Interest		199,000
Conversion and handling loss		350,000
Reserve 2.5% on Rs. 8,580,000		214,500
Aluminum foils		170,000
Bottles breakage		95,000
Commission		447,500
Total	Rs.	3,839,000

Expenses per liter of milk	16.6 paise
Expenses allowed by agreement for determining the purchase price of milk	16.8 paise

NOTE: Out of 63,350 liters of milk per day to be handled, 37,000 liters were expected to be sold in bottles.

Product

The dairy sold whole milk, cow milk, toned milk, and double-toned milk. The toned and double-toned milk contained low percentages of fat. They were prepared by adding reconstituted milk (skimmed milk powder and water), or skimmed milk to whole milk, and were sold at a cheaper rate. The double-toned milk (containing 1.5 percent fat and 10 percent SNF) was mostly sold to the municipal corporation for free distribution in the municipal schools. The toned milk (containing 3 percent fat and 9 percent SNF) had been received well in the market at a reduced price below whole milk and cow milk (see Exhibit 2 for breakup of milk sales and Exhibit 3 for prices in effect).

The dairy converted excess milk into byproducts like butter and ghee. Sour milk received by the dairy was also converted into byproducts.

Sale and distribution

The dairy sold milk on a commission basis in bottles and in bulk (called "loose" milk) in the ratio of 2:5 through 195 centers spread all over the city. Besides these centers, the dairy had six shops of its own which sold only bottled milk and served as coordinating points for the centers operating on commission basis. The marketing of byproducts was arranged by the dairy at its central shop.

EXHIBIT 2

MAHANAGAR MUNICIPAL DAIRY (A)

(break up of milk procured, utilized and sold during the year 1961–62)

Particulars	Quantity (liters)*
Procurement:	
Total milk in terms of 6.6%† fat	7,414,600
Utilization:	
For various types of milk	5,096,000
Conversion into byproduct	2,318,600
	7,414,600
Sale of milk:	
Whole milk (6% fat‡)	3,627,200
Toned milk (3% fat‡)	2,458,000
Double-toned milk (1.5% fat‡)	892,000
Cow milk (3.5% fat‡)	42,400
	7,019,900

* Figures rounded off to the nearest hundred.
† 6.6% was the average fat content in the buffalo and cow milk taken together.
‡ Guaranteed fat.

EXHIBIT 3

MAHANAGAR MUNICIPAL DAIRY (A)

(selling prices of milk prevailing at different periods)

Particulars	1955 to 1960	1960 to 1962	1962 to date
Whole milk			
Bottled	68.2*	77*	80*
Loose	61.6	70	76
Cow milk			
Bottled	—	66	70
Loose	—	—	50
Toned milk			
Bottled	52.8	53	56
Loose	44.0	44	50
Double-toned milk†	33.0	34	40

* Prices given in paise per liter.
† Prices for double-toned milk were paid to the dairy from another corporation account; in essence this meant that the corporation was undertaking to make good the guarantee to UNICEF, rather than taxing the dairy's current operations with the subsidy for distribution of double-toned milk.

Except for schools and hospitals, which were supplied with milk directly from the dairy on credit, all sales were on a cash basis. The collection of cash sale proceeds from centers was done by cash collectors appointed by the dairy.

The selling price of milk was not changed frequently. Since its inception, the dairy had revised the price only three times, including the revision in August, 1962 (Exhibit 3). The selling price of byproducts was revised according to the market conditions, but in effecting these revisions, a delay of three to four weeks occurred because of the need to secure proper sanctions from the milk committee, through the municipal commissioner and his deputy.

Finance

Each year on or before such date as the corporation fixed from time to time, the municipal commissioner submitted to the standing committee an estimate of the following year's income and expenditures of the dairy.

These estimates and proposals, after being considered in detail by the standing committee were included in the budget estimate of the municipal corporation. After this was approved by the general body of the corporation, the municipal commissioner was empowered to incur expenditures from municipal funds. All receipts from the dairy's operations were required to be credited to the municipal fund account. In the Municipal Corporation Act, there was provision for revision of the budget estimate once framed and adopted, if the need arose. But such revision required a lengthy procedure. The municipal chief auditor, independent of the municipal commissioner, audited the dairy's deposits to and receipts from the municipal fund.

The detailed accounts of the dairy's operation were maintained at the dairy and these accounts were also audited by the municipal auditor. Cash payments and cash receipts, except for petty amounts, were handled at the municipal corporation's office. The dairy prepared its profit and loss account and balance sheet annually, which were then placed before the general body of the corporation.

At the meeting on September 10, 1962, the following points of view were expressed:

MUNICIPAL COMMISSIONER: From the financial statements (Exhibit 4), I find that out of the funds of Rs. 4,225,000 provided by the municipal corporation up to March 31, 1962, the dairy has lost outrightly Rs. 2,138,000. Besides that, Rs. 325,000 are locked up in the pilot plant which is lying defunct. I do not believe any recovery is possible out of it. Dairy operations thus have resulted in a loss of municipal funds amounting to Rs. 2,463,000. This is really a sad state of affairs.

DAIRY MANAGER: I have given considerable thought to it. There are certain basic defects in our purchase and sale policies which account to a great extent for these heavy losses. If you refer to the income statement for the year 1961–62 (Exhibit 5), the cost of milk and powder purchased appears more than the sales. On the other hand, one could expect a gross profit of about Rs. 1,250,000 on the procurement of 7,420,000 liters of milk during the year 1961–62, as a margin of 16.8 paise per liter had been allowed by the rating committee. But the dairy was not in a position to sell all the milk procured by it. In 1961–62, it had to convert much milk into butter and ghee, which is a

EXHIBIT 4

Mahanagar Municipal Dairy (A)
(balance sheets for 1958 through 1962 in thousands of rupees)

ASSETS*

	1958	1959	1960	1961	1962
Fixed:					
Building (net)	189.3	184.7	180.1	180.0	3,140.3
Cabins (net)	6.6	12.9	16.5	20.1	24.0
Machinery (net)	344.9	360.7	339.4	319.0	3,772.3
Other equipment (net)	36.3	62.7	70.4	66.6	258.4
Car & auto rickshaw (net)	43.6	50.7	91.4	90.4	160.7
Total	620.7	671.7	697.8	676.1	7,355.7
Current:					
Milk inventory	35.0	32.5	43.6	188.1	229.7
General stores inventory	—	95.4	299.6	533.7	473.8
Receivables	23.5	77.9	33.5	231.0	411.2
Total	58.5	205.8	306.7	952.8	1,114.7
Losses	29.6	38.3	235.2	832.1	2,138.4
Grand total	708.8	915.8	1,239.7	2,461.0	10,608.8

LIABILITIES†

	1958	1959	1960	1961	1962
Current liabilities:					
Creditors for milk	53.4	42.7	172.9	339.1	258.4
Creditors for other	26.1	31.9	49.9	322.0	418.2
Total	79.5	74.6	222.8	661.1	703.6
Municipal corporation fund	629.3	841.2	1,016.9	1,799.9	4,225.2
Central government subsidy	—	—	—	—	3,080.0
UNICEF loan	—	—	—	—	2,600.0
Grand total	708.8	915.8	1,239.7	2,461.0	10,608.8

* Net fixed assets also included the pilot dairy building and machinery—which had been abandoned with effect from November, 1961. The value on that date was as follows:

Pilot dairy building	Rs. 177,200
Pilot dairy machinery	324,600
Total	Rs. 501,800

† Depreciation provided:

1955–56	Rs. 4,700
1956–57	17,200
1957–58	21,300
1958–59	61,600
1959–60	74,100
1960–61	107,600
1961–62	234,900
Total	Rs. 521,400

losing line of products for the dairy. The buffalo milk cost for preparing one kilogram of ghee amounts to Rs. 9.40, whereas realization from that ghee and the resulting separated milk is Rs. 6.50. This involves a loss of about 16 paise per liter of milk besides the expenses involved in the preparation of ghee.

Secondly, the dairy had to purchase 3530 liters of cow milk per day against its daily sale of 125 liters. The rest of this milk was mixed with buffalo milk. The mixed milk was sold as whole milk or was utilized either in making other types of milk or by converting it into byproducts.

EXHIBIT 5

MAHANAGAR MUNICIPAL DAIRY (A)

(income statement for the years ending on March 31 in thousands of rupees)

	1957–58	1958–59	1959–60	1960–61	1961–62*	1962–63
Sales of milk & milk products	1,270.3	2,267.9	2,847.9	4,143.9	5,045.4	6,660.4
Cost of milk & milk powder	946.3	1,674.4	2,358.8	3,897.6	5,072.5	5,517.3
Gross profit/ loss	324.0	593.5	489.1	246.3	−27.1	1,143.1
EXPENSES						
Establishment	118.8	297.9	263.5	348.7	514.1	539.0
Power & fuel	13.1	35.2	62.1	43.4	104.2	147.1
Bottles & cabin loss, etc.	7.4	2.9	20.6	47.9	50.6	87.0
Aluminum foils	—	—	16.5	31.0	28.6	24.3
Transportation	98.5	100.7	97.0	112.6	128.6	198.6
Commission	29.8	77.7	118.5	130.5	135.3	174.7
Insurance and taxes	9.6	—	—	12.8	31.0	92.1
Total	277.2	513.5	578.2	726.9	992.4	1,262.8
Depreciation	21.3	61.6	74.1	107.6	234.9	465.1
Interest	13.0	27.1	33.6	45.8	80.4	222.4
Total	311.5	602.2	685.9	880.3	1,307.7	1,950.3
Profit/loss on operation	12.5	−8.7	−196.8	−634.0	−1,334.8	−807.2
Other income	—	—	—	37.0	28.5	30.1
Net profit/ loss	12.5	−8.7	−196.8	−597.0	−1,306.3	−777.1

* On November 15, 1961, the new dairy involving a capital expenditure of Rs. 16,887,000 went into operation. The depreciation on the new dairy was provided only for 4½ months, i.e, from November 15, 1961, to March 31, 1962. Although the machinery worth Rs. 1,200,000 was not utilized, the depreciation was charged on the total cost of the project.

Thirdly, the loss arose because of the supply of higher fat milk to the consumers. On an average, 7.1 percent fat was received in the buffalo milk and even after mixing cow milk, the average fat content in the milk remained as high as 6.6 percent. Most of this milk was sold as our "whole milk" in which we guarantee only 6 percent fat.

At present we are paying about 13 paise per liter for buffalo milk more than is being paid by other dairies in the nearby area. Out of this excess paid to the unions, 5 paise constitutes the higher price paid for milk by the Unions to the village milk producers' cooperative societies and the balance is kept by the unions for meeting their expenses. The dairy, in fact, should purchase milk directly from these co-operative societies in order to save at least the 8 paise per liter now being paid to the unions for rendering hardly any useful service. Their function at present involves merely an overlapping with the dairy's work of testing, weighing, etc. The transportation of milk from villages can very well be arranged by the dairy itself.

I would also recommend a revision in the purchase price of buffalo milk as regards the additional fat content over 6 percent in the milk purchased. Recently, we have taken a decision to extract the excess fat over 6 percent in the milk and sell it separately, but this extracted fat will bring only ghee price, on which we lose roughly 16 paise per liter of milk. We should, therefore, pay for the excess fat content in the milk over 6 percent on the basis of the recovery of ghee.

As I have pointed out, we have to purchase cow milk under political pressure. Some effective steps should be taken either by curtailing the purchase quantity of cow milk or by increasing the sale of cow milk to municipal and state institutions such as hospitals and schools.

Finally, the rating committee has become ineffective. It has become merely a committee for referring matters to arbitration. The producer-unions' representatives, having a considerable political influence, get a maximum purchase price fixed without caring for consumers' interest and the economic operation of the dairy. It would be better if there were one committee comprising members representing consumers, corporation, State government, milk producers, general interests like an economist and a financial expert, instead of having two committees—i.e., the rating committee for fixation of purchase price and the milk committee for setting operational policies, and fixation of selling price to consumers.

MILK COMMITTEE CHAIRMAN: I do not think that the dairy executives can economically manage the work of collecting milk from the milk producers' societies at village level. This requires an efficient organization. Besides, the societies at village level also require leadership for their existence. I do not feel that this leadership can be provided by the dairy's executives while they also perform their proper management functions at the dairy.

Extraction of excess fat content over 6 percent from the buffalo milk procured by the dairy may not be a wise step. Whole buffalo milk contains roughly from 6.5 to 7 percent butter fat. The supply of lower fat to consumers is likely to shake the consumers' confidence in the dairy's whole milk. We have already seen that citizens have not responded enthusiastically to the dairy's whole milk, even though it has more than 6 percent fat content. The supply of more than 6 percent fat content, of course, will require a revision of price, which can be possible only after creating a good reputation for the quality of milk supplied by the dairy.

Our new plant is being operated only at a third of its milk-handling capacity; roughly 30 percent of the milk procured is being converted into byproducts which do not constitute the main line of the dairy. Under such circumstances, what are your proposals to increase the sale of milk?

DAIRY MANAGER: We are confronted with two problems in sales. In the first place, the sale of milk by local vendors at a cheap rate (which they perhaps manage by adulteration) is hampering our sales. These vendors, at present, are selling milk at about 65 paise per liter whereas the dairy's whole milk is sold at 80 paise per liter after the recent revision. These vendors supply all kinds of milk without caring for quality or hygienic conditions. They do not incur high overhead expenses. If effective steps are taken by the municipal corporation in checking the quality of milk sold by these vendors, the supplies from such sources are likely to be discouraged, providing an impetus to the sales of the dairy's milk.

Secondly, the dairy sells milk on a cash payment. Since indigenous sources allow credit, most of the consumers prefer to buy milk from them.

MUNICIPAL COMMISSIONER: The dairy's realization on byproducts—butter and ghee—is quite low. I also find that overhead expenses of the dairy are too high. They need immediate attention for proper control.

DAIRY MANAGER: We can have better realization on byproducts. But because of the long procedure that we go through for revising prices,[1] we often lose the opportunity to sell our byproducts at higher prices.

As for overhead expenses, the fact that they are high is largely due to the high cost incurred on fixed assets. We have installed a plant of large capacity involving a heavy capital expenditure. Our actual overhead expenses compare favorably with the estimates made at the time the margin of 16.8 paise per liter was set up.

1. What is the main issue in this case? Discuss.
2. Should the dairy be expected to make a profit?
3. What should be the dairy's objectives? Are these objectives affected by the fact that it is owned by the public?
4. On the basis of the data for 1961–62, what would be the break-even volume for the dairy? On the basis of 1962–63 data, make a similar estimate of the break-even volume. What is the significance of this analysis, if any?
5. Why is it that the dairy is making losses, when the pricing formula appears to assure that the dairy's expenses will be covered?
6. How does the political environment affect the dairy's operations?
7. What recommendations would you make to the dairy's manager? to the municipal commission?
8. Is this a case in managerial economics?

MAHANAGAR MUNICIPAL DAIRY (D)*

In 1964 the executives of the Mahanagar municipal dairy were concerned about the losses which the dairy had been incurring during the last few years. Their consensus was that the dairy could show better results by increasing the sales volume of milk and by cutting back on the conversion of milk into ghee and butter. Some of the executives were of the opinion that the existing distribution system presented many opportunities for improvements, both in terms of service to the consumers and of sales volume to the dairy. They were also concerned whether the dairy should continue to sell both bottled and loose milk in future. This matter was, therefore, discussed in a meeting of the executives held on April 15, 1964.

---

[1] Price revision proposals were usually originated by the dairy manager. These were submitted through the deputy municipal commissioner to the municipal commissioner who had to take sanction from the milk committee.

* Copyright © 1964 by the Indian Institute of Management, Ahmedabad.

Sales and distribution

At times, the dairy purchased more milk than could be sold as fluid milk, and the excess was converted into butter and ghee on which the dairy typically did not recover even the cost of the milk.[1] This problem was intensified during the monsoon and winter months when the dairy, by the terms of purchase agreement, had to accept more milk from its suppliers than it did in the summer months (see Exhibit 1). On the other

EXHIBIT 1

MAHANAGAR MUNICIPAL DAIRY (D)
(sales of milk by seasons and type* in thousands of liters)

	Summer	Monsoon	Winter	Total	% of Total
1962–63					
Whole milk					
Loose†	574	454	343	1,371	13.9
Bottled	738	935	812	2,485	25.2
Toned milk					
Loose	1,548	1,526	1,072	4,146	42.2
Bottled	128	143	124	395	4.0
Cow milk, bottled	83	78	113	174	2.8
Double-toned milk	47	512	608	1,167	11.9
Total	3,118	3,648	3,072	9,838	100.0
1963–64					
Whole milk					
Loose†	356	360	329	1,045	10.8
Bottled	871	1,130	1,099	3,100	31.8
Toned milk					
Loose	927	1,321	1,253	3,501	36.0
Bottled	128	161	170	459	4.7
Cow milk, bottled	118	136	139	393	4.0
Double-toned milk	81	507	649	1,237	12.7
Total	2,481	3,615	3,639	9,735	100.0

* The dairy also sold small amounts of syrup milk, cold coffee milk, and higher fat milk in 1963–64.

† The dariy sold excess loose cow milk to another dairy; such sales amounted to 558,000 liters in 1962–63 and 210,000 liters in 1963–64, at approximately 50 paise per liter.

hand the demand for milk in the monsoon and winter months was considered to be lower than it was in the summer months. However, in the winter and monsoon months of the year 1963–64, the suppliers of milk

[1] To describe the situation:

Average purchase price of 100 liters of cow-cum-buffalo milk in 1963–64 .... Rs.	64.30
Less credit for skimmed milk computed at the rate of equivalent price for skimmed milk powder ..	9.60
Cost of fat recovery, i.e., 6.5 kg. fat	54.70
Average realization for fat	40.62
Loss on 100 liters of milk	14.08

were not offering as much excess milk as they did in the previous year (see Exhibit 2).

The dairy sold whole milk,[2] cow milk and toned milk[3] in half liter and 200 milliliters bottles. Whole milk and toned milk were also sold in unbottled form; such loose milk sales constituted 46.8 percent of the total sales volume in the year 1963–64 (Exhibit 3). In addition, the dairy sold double-toned milk[4] in amounts limited by the commitment between the municipal corporation and UNICEF.

The purchases of the dairy's milk fell into two categories—institutions which made bulk purchases (such as hospitals, schools, hotels, and cafeterias), and individual consumers. The milk supplies to institutions accounted for 15 percent of the dairy's total volume of milk in terms of value.

The rating committee usually set the purchase price for the procurement of milk at a fixed price for an entire year. In the year 1962–63, it fixed the rate for buffalo milk (containing 6 percent fat and 9 percent SNF) at 57.8 paise per liter. For additional fat content, a premium was payable at the rate of 0.77 paise per 0.1 percent fat content over 6 percent. In the year 1963–64, the base rate was reduced to 56.7 paise per liter. However, the premium payable for additional fat content was fixed at 0.94 paise per 0.1 percent on excess over 6 percent up to a figure of 7 percent, and 0.77 paise for every 0.1 percent thereafter. The committee had fixed the purchase price for the year 1964–65 at 56.1 paise per liter. The premium for additional fat content was set at 1.05 paise per 0.1 up to 7 percent and at 0.77 paise per 0.1 percent thereafter. During the year 1963–64, the fat content in buffalo milk received by the dairy averaged 7 percent.

The purchase price for cow milk in 1962–63 was fixed at 46.4 paise per liter for 12 percent solid content (3.5 percent fat and 8.5 percent SNF). A premium for additional solid content in the cow milk was set at 0.39 paise per 0.1 percent. In the year 1963–64, the base price was reduced to 44.5 paise per liter. However, the premium was payable at the same rate as in the year 1962–63. In the year 1964–65, there was no change in the base rate, but the premium for the additional solid content was raised to 0.5 paise per 0.1 percent. Cow milk purchased by the dairy during

---

[2] Whole milk was any milk which contained a minimum of 6 percent fat and 9 percent SNF. Most of it was buffalo milk since milk from this source contained solid ingredients in those approximate proportions.

[3] Toned milk contained a low percentage of fat (3 percent fat and 9 percent SNF). It was prepared by adding skimmed milk powder and water, or skimmed milk to the fresh milk, and was sold at a cheaper rate.

[4] Double-toned milk contained roughly 1.6 percent fat and was distributed free to municipal school children who were between the ages of 7 and 12, and to nursing and pregnant women. The municipal corporation paid a subsidy to the dairy for the free distribution of milk and for the reduced price distribution to low income families.

EXHIBIT 2

MAHANAGAR MUNICIPAL DAIRY (D)
(quantities of milk purchased and milk converted into butter and ghee
in thousand liters)

	Fresh Milk Purchases			Sour Milk Purchases	Converted to
	Buffalo	Ratio	Cow	Both Cow & Buffalo	Ghee & Butter
1962–63					
Summer:					
April	497		93		—
May	398		81		—
June	375		87		—
July	446		115		—
	1,716	3:0	376	NA	—
Monsoon:					
August	586		135		2
September	601		83		19
October	635		82		133
November	640		100		189
	2,462	4:3	400	NA	343
Winter:					
December	759		129		372
January	755		149		379
February	631		131		268
March	694		147		244
	2,839	4:9	556	NA	1,263
Grand Total ..	7,017	—	1,332	506	1,606
1963–64					
Summer:					
April	554		127	56	173
May	462		121	55	91
June	352		111	43	1
July	361		86	36	—
	1,729	3:0	445	190	265
Monsoon:					
August	455		94	42	3
September	502		84	45	—
October	540		75	48	7
November	515		71	45	9
	2,012	3:5	324	180	19
Winter:					
December	611		73	40	—
January	634		77	13	3
February	524		62	34	2
March	472		90	51	—
	2,241	3:9	302	138	5
Grand Total ..	5,982		1,071	508	289

EXHIBIT 3

MAHANAGAR MUNICIPAL DAIRY (D)

(realization, direct variable costs, and contribution per liter of milk)

Type of Milk	Realization	Direct Variable Costs of Milk Sold					
		Milk & Milk Powder*	Power, Coal & Chemicals†	Bottle Breakage & Aluminum Foils	Commission	Total	Contribution
Whole							
Bottled	80.9	60.6	1.2	2.8	3.8	68.4	12.5
Loose	76.0	60.6	0.6	—	2.2	63.4	12.6
Cow, bottled	70.0	47.5	1.2	2.8	3.8	55.3	14.7
Toned							
Bottled	58.5	36.3	1.2	2.8	1.6	41.9	16.6
Loose	51.8	36.3	0.6	—	1.6	38.5	13.3
Double-toned							
For schools	40.0	15.2	0.6	—	1.3‡	17.1	22.9
For low income families	40.0	25.0	0.6	—	1.3‡	26.9	13.1

* Cost of milk and milk powder includes process and handling losses with adjustment for fat and SNF content.
† This refers to power, coal and chemicals consumed in washing and filling of bottles and cans.
‡ Expense incurred on selling double-toned milk through self-operated centers.
SOURCE: Casewriter's calculation based on information supplied by the dairy's executives.

1963–64 contained on average 12.8 percent solids (4.2 percent fat and 8.6 percent SNF). The dairy purchased a large quantity of cow milk, although sales of such milk were meager. The unsold cow milk was principally utilized for standardization of whole milk.

The main sources of buffalo milk supply to the dairy were two milk producers' unions. Purchases from these two unions represented roughly 70 percent of the dairy's total purchases of milk (both buffalo and cow). Cow milk was supplied mainly by the Gopalak Sangh, an organization for the protection of cows.

The dairy experienced a shortage of milk supplies in the summer season and on many occasions was not in a position to cope with the demand.

Individual consumers received milk through a network of nine depots and 226 centers.[5] The depots were run by the dairy employees on a permanent basis at a monthly salary of around Rs. 50 to 100 per month. For home delivery from the depots the dairy employed delivery boys on a commission basis. In April, 1964, there were 32 such boys employed. The daily sale of milk from these depots on an average was 700 liters. In contrast to the depots, centers were run by individuals, who operated them under terms laid down by the dairy and received a commission calculated on sales (see Exhibits 4 and 5). The dairy ran some centers on a temporary basis when people could not be found to run them on a commission basis. In such cases, the dairy employed temporary workers at a daily wage

EXHIBIT 4

MAHANAGAR MUNICIPAL DAIRY (D)

(selling prices of the dairy's milk in paise per liter)

Milk	August 20, 1960 to August 19, 1962	August 20, 1962 to April 14, 1963	April 15, 1963 to July 14, 1963	July 15, 1963 to March 31, 1964
Whole				
Bottled*	77	80	80	80
Loose	70	76	76	76
Cow, bottled*	66	70	70	70
Toned				
Bottled*	53	56	62	56
Loose	44	50	60	50
Double-toned	34	40	40	40

* The bottled milk prices were for half-liter filling. For 200 milliliters filling the dairy charged slightly higher prices.

---

[5] The depots and centers served an area of 36 square miles and a population of about 1,300,000. The majority of the population drank tea regularly. There were no official statistics on the numbers of persons in various income groups, their milk consumption, etc. However, the Third Five-Year plan estimated the all-India per capita daily consumption of milk at roughly 0.14 liters.

EXHIBIT 5

MAHANAGAR MUNICIPAL DAIRY (D)
(commission rates for center operators*)

1. For home delivery of whole and cow milk in bottles ...... 75 paise for 20 liters
2. For whole milk and cow milk in bottles sold along
   with straw and ice, if required by the consumer
   for drinking at the spot .... 80 paise for 20 liters
3. For selling whole milk and cow milk (loose and
   bottled both) at the center .... 44 paise for 20 liters
4. For selling toned milk (loose and bottled both)
   at the center .... 31 paise for 20 liters

   * Delivery boys attached to the depots were paid a commission of 75 paise per 20 liters on
bottles actually delivered by them.

of Rs. 1.50 for running the center; in case the center also undertook home delivery, they were paid Rs. 3 per day. The daily average sales of the temporarily self-operated centers were in the range of 20 to 30 liters. The number of temporarily self-operated centers and centers on commission basis is shown in Exhibit 6.

EXHIBIT 6

MAHANAGAR MUNICIPAL DAIRY (D)
(number of centers selling dairy's milk in April, 1964)

Centers	On Commis- sion Basis	Temporarily Self-operated Centers	Total
Selling whole loose milk	24	1	25
Selling toned loose milk	92	11	103
Selling double-toned loose milk	—	22	22
Selling toned bottled only	6	1	7
Selling both loose and bottled milk	12	—	12
Selling bottled milk of all types	41	16	57*
	175	51	226

   * Of these centers, 26 also sold milk to be drunk on the spot from bottle. The persons in charge of such centers were required to supply ice and straws at their own cost to the consumers without additional charge. The ice box was, however, supplied by the dairy free of charge on a returnable basis. The commission on such sales was 80 paise for 20 liters.

Most of the persons operating centers on a commission basis took up milk distribution work as a part-time job. They got help from their children or hired people (generally at a salary of Rs. 30 to 40 per month) to run the center. These operators were responsible for the maintenance of cabins, for keeping accounts of the milk supplied, and for arranging home delivery of bottled whole and cow milk. The dairy required a cash security of Rs. 250 (repayable without interest) and a surety bond for Rs. 500 from these operators. The monthly earnings ranged between Rs. 20 and 500, the average being about Rs. 60.

The dairy had constructed approximately 100 wooden cabins of five-foot size for the depots and centers at an average cost of Rs. 700 each. The rest were open-air centers, generally shaded by a tree and reached by footpaths. If the demand for milk in a particular place was expected to be greater than 30 liters per day a new center was opened. It was the general practice of the dairy to separate distribution of bottled and loose milk in the centers, in order to minimize the chances of fraudulent practices by the operators of the centers (Exhibit 5). The nine depots operated by the dairy sold only bottled milk.

The depots and centers sold milk at the cabins or at fixed distribution points. In addition, bottled whole and cow milk was sold (at the same price as in the depots and centers) by home delivery. The bottled, toned milk was also delivered at homes with a one paise delivery charge per bottle regardless of size.[6] The one paise was retained by the delivery boys. The sale of milk was on a cash basis and the consumer was required to pay the money at the time of delivery. The consumer had to return the bottles immediately. This meant that most consumers had to transfer the milk into their own vessels at the point of buying. However, the consumer could purchase empty bottles (at 50 paise each) which could be exchanged for the filled ones at the time of delivery.

The dairy dispatched its milk daily between 2 and 5 A.M. and P.M. by five trucks and 17 auto-rickshaws, to fixed distribution points where the milk was sold between 5 and 7 in the morning and 5 and 6:30 in the evening. Home delivery was also made during these hours. The delivery boys generally used bicycles and carried 15 to 30 liters of milk in bags at a time.

The loose milk was supplied to the centers in sealed cans. The seal of the lid was to be opened by the person in charge of the center only in the presence of at least three customers. Although the capacity of a can was 40 liters, the center could order a smaller quantity down to a minimum of 20 liters in a can.

The empties and unsold bottled milk were collected by the dairy vehicles after sales hours in the morning and evening. The dairy did not accept unsold loose milk from the centers. The returns of unsold milk varied in different seasons. In the summer months such returns were hardly 1 percent to 2 percent of bottled milk sales whereas in the winter months it ranged between 5 percent and 8 percent. The returned milk was re-used by the dairy if its condition warranted. If found in good condition, it was sent for distribution as such or, if necessary, after re-

---

[6] For the supply of toned milk the dairy had fixed the commission (payable to persons operating centers on commission and to their own employed delivery boys) on the basis of sales at the cabins/fixed distribution points. The dairy, therefore, allowed them to charge 1 paise extra per bottle if the consumer wanted home delivery.

processing. If the milk was sour or showed signs of becoming sour, it was converted into butter or ghee.

The dairy had appointed eight cash collectors for collecting cash daily from the centers between 8 A.M. and 12:30 P.M. The cash collected at each depot, however, was deposited with the dairy's cashier at the dairy by the depot in charge.

The dairy had two inspectors and six subinspectors to supervise the milk distribution and to attend to the complaints of the public as well as of the centers and depots. These inspectors made frequent rounds of the centers and depots and visited each cabin at least twice a week. They also checked to insure that hygienic conditions were maintained. The depots and centers were required to maintain a complaint book on which consumers recorded their complaints.

Pricing the dairy's milk

In the past the authorities had adopted a policy of uniform selling prices for the whole year for each variety of milk. However, the executives believed that the dairy could charge a higher price for the summer season when there was an overall shortage in milk supply and when local milkmen and milk vendors generally charged higher prices. Selling prices prevailing in the years 1962–63, and 1963–64, are set out in Exhibit 4.

The nature of competition

Besides the sale of pasteurized milk by the dairy, a very large number of milkmen and milk vendors sold milk in the city. The milkmen had either their own cattle or purchased milk from villages and sold it direct to consumers or to milk vendors who in turn sold it to consumers in their own shops. Most of the milk vendors also arranged home delivery to their regular customers. Virtually all of these vendors held licenses for sale of cow milk; the fat content in such milk ranged between 3.5 percent and 5 percent. Either through deliberate oral misrepresentation or the general ignorance of the average customer, most of this milk was accepted as "buffalo milk." The prices charged depended on demand and supply position. In the summer, the milk prices shot up to 82 paise per liter. In the winter months the prices dropped to 55 paise per liter. Practically all milkmen and milk vendors sold their milk on a credit basis to their regular customers and payment was collected at the end of the month.

Highlights of the April meeting

In the April 15th meeting the executives of the dairy considered in detail the distribution practices being followed in order to determine whether improvements were possible. The highlights of the deliberations are summarized below:

The scope for penetrating the middle and uppermiddle class market was quite impressive inasmuch as these consumers in the higher brackets of income would buy quality milk at prices even slightly higher than the existing rates. But a penetration of this kind could hardly be achieved with the existing distribution arrangements.

The delivery boys did not make "home delivery" in the real sense of the term. The consumers living in the first and second floors were required to take delivery of the milk at the foyer of the house on the ground floor. This caused considerable hardship to the housewives.

The time schedule of delivery was not strictly adhered to by the delivery boys. It was also not uncommon for the delivery boys to skip over regular customers. When a delivery boy came to a customer's house, he would shout or ring his bicycle bell once or twice and if the housewife did not answer immediately he would leave.

The daily payment system had its own aspects of practical inconvenience. It was not only the question of keeping the money on hand daily for buying milk; when a housewife did not have the exact change it sometimes resulted in considerable inconvenience. Moreover, there was no guarantee of getting additional milk in adequate quantities as the delivery boys carried with them only a small excess quantity of milk to meet the additional requirement of regular customers. The boys rarely were willing to make a second trip from the cabin to meet the additional requirement of a customer.

In regard to the sale of loose milk, the centers ordered only that quantity which could be sold definitely so as to ensure no left over supply.

Apart from the inconveniences to the customers, the delivery boys indulged in practices which were undesirable from the hygienic point of view. If a customer wanted to buy a 200 milliliters milk bottle, it was not uncommon for the boys to open a half-liter milk bottle and pour part of it into a 200 milliliters bottle.

Some of the executives suggested the discontinuance of centers on a commission basis and recommended the setting up of self-owned depots, roughly 50, from which milk could be distributed throughout the day. The operating time of two hours in the morning and one and a half hours in the evening was considered to be inadequate. It was also suggested that a coupon system or monthly card system[7] could be introduced along with the cash system. Some of the persons operating these centers had already started their own system of issuing coupons privately. But the executives were not in favor of such private arrangements for which the dairy did not assume any responsibility whatsoever.

A few executives were also not in favor of selling whole milk in loose quantity. They felt that by selling whole milk in this manner, the dairy could not

---

[7] Under the coupon system, customers can purchase coupons of various denominations in advance according to their requirements for a certain period. The milk is then supplied daily against these coupons and in this way the daily handling of cash is eliminated. Under the card system, instead of issuing coupons, a monthly card is issued (against cash payment in advance) for the daily milk supply. For any "extra" milk on any particular day, the consumer is required to pay cash on delivery. If a consumer does not want to draw milk supply on a particular day, he is required to inform the center/depot in advance; money for such non-delivery is refunded at the end of the month.

have an effective control on the check points for maintaining hygiene and purity of the milk supplied. In their opinion the sale of loose milk should be stopped.

One of the senior executives, however, did not favor any change in the present pattern of distribution system. He felt that the solution to the dairy's problem did not lie in changing the distribution system. He did concede that these might be desirable to provide additional facilities to consumers. Nevertheless, he was against the implementation of these measures while the dairy was running at a loss. He believed that the dairy's efforts to increase sales would not bear any fruit until the dairy could assure regular and adequate supplies of milk throughout the year. Under the present circumstances, he thought that the only solution was the installation of an ice cream plant so that the excess supply of milk to the dairy could earn a profit. Moreover the suggested changes in the distribution system at this juncture would make the system unwieldy, giving rise to innumerable complaints from the public. His comments to the various suggestions were:

If the delivery boys supplied the milk on the first or second floor, they would have to leave the bicycle and milk bottles in the bags on the foyer of the ground floor where chances of theft could not be ruled out. Besides, mischievous small children could play tricks like taking air from the bicycle's wheels and thereby put the delivery boy to a great inconvenience.

The coupon or card system would mean maintenance of innumerable accounts by the dairy. Unless the dairy installed an effective system of checks and audit, it would lead to frauds, manipulation and counterfeiting of coupons etc. To set up such a system would be both costly and cumbersome.

The dairy's own shops would not be economical in the current state of affairs. Depots would increase the administrative difficulties, but could not be expected to perform better services to the consumers. The incentive of a person on commission should be greater than that of an employee getting fixed monthly salary.

The executive also pointed out the problem of the dairy's location in the milk-producing tract where local milkmen could supply raw milk at cheaper rates. However, he was optimistic about the future and felt that the problem would be automatically solved in a year or so with the coming of another cooperative dairy in the adjacent district. That dairy would then purchase milk which currently competed for the customers within the municipal limits. He also believed that the municipal dairy would also be in a position to purchase milk in the summer months from that dairy, thereby affecting a seasonal adjustment in the milk supply. This would lead to an increased sales volume and removal of the dairy's loss.

1. *The dairy continued to lose money in 1963–64, despite an increase in sales to Rs. 7,250,000. The loss amounted to Rs. 250,000. How do you explain these losses?*
2. *In 1963–64 the dairy's fixed costs were about Rs. 1,350,000 and variable costs about Rs. 6,150,000. Construct a break-even chart. Would it be difficult for the dairy to reach the break-even point? Explain.*

3. *Why were the dairy's sales far below capacity? Could anything be done to improve sales and, if so, should the dairy take such action?*
4. *Why were losses in 1963–64 below those in 1962–63?*
5. *Are there further ways the dairy could reduce losses?*
6. *What is the significance of Exhibit 3?*
7. *Some nutritional experts claim that toned milk is preferable to whole milk because of its lower fat content. What is the significance of this claim in this case?*
8. *What recommendations would you make to the dairy's management? to the municipal commission?*

KERN COUNTY LAND COMPANY*

Inventory management in large-scale cattle operations

Dene Pruett, marketing analyst, was putting the finishing touches on a large wall chart designed to depict the current position and plans for the various cattle operations of the Cattle Division at the Bakersfield, California, office of the Kern County Land Company's Agriculture and Cattle headquarters. Ordinarily visitors wouldn't see this part of the operation. "But since you aren't a competitor or a customer I think it's all right," he told his visitor from the east. (See Chart 1.)

Pruett explained:

With a throughput at our Gosford feedlot alone that may run to 10 or 12 million dollars a year, and an inventory value for cattle of all ages on our breeding ranches, grazing lands and feedlots amounting to over half that amount at a given time, we have a handful to look after.

The western large-scale cattle business is typically divided into three, often separate, operations. Our breeding herds, some ranging up to 10,000 or more cow units are maintained at several locations in Arizona, New Mexico and California. Then there are stocker operations, which are often seasonal, where calves moved from breeding herds are fed on grass ranges, sometimes with supplemental feed. There, the young steers and heifers gain perhaps 200 to 300 pounds in weight, from 400 or 500 pounds per head up to, say, 700 pounds, ready to be put on "hot feed." Finally, the feedlot "finishes" the cattle on a concentrated high nutrition ration in corrals holding, in the case of the large KCL Gosford Feedlot near Bakersfield, as many as 20,000 to 24,000 head at a time. There in 120 to 150 days they reach a weight of 1,000 pounds or more and are ready for slaughter.

Our Cattle Division, under Charles M. Quarre, is responsible for coordinating all these operations. Each ranch unit, the stocker operations, and the Gosford Feedlot, however, are managed independently. Each is a profit and loss

* This case was prepared by Henry B. Arthur of the Harvard University Graduate School of Business Administration as a basis for classroom discussion rather than to illustrate either effective or ineffective handling of administrative situations. Copyright © 1962 by the President and Fellows of Harvard College. Used by specific permission.

CHART 1

KERN COUNTY LAND COMPANY

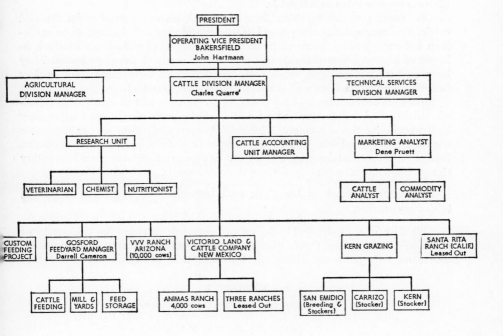

operation. Each buys and sells independent of the others. We found a number of years ago that for reasons of transportation, selection, availability and trading opportunities, we'd lose a lot of good opportunities if we tried to move our cattle only within our own company units.

This whole thing is complicated further by the fact that you have to do a lot of buying and selling ahead. Calves may be contracted for as much as six months, or even a year sometimes, ahead of the time they are ready to be delivered. Such purchases are customarily tied down with a deposit, perhaps $20 a head with the balance to be paid on delivery. This gives the seller some cash and seals the deal. The same goes for the stockers and the feeders. To make the situation even more involved, the feedlot owns part of its cattle, feeds some on a custom basis for others, and may have booked various kinds of forward sales to meatpackers. We sometimes help finance cattle we are custom feeding for others.

To top it off, the prices of cattle at various weights and grades are subject to wide fluctuations. Prices move sometimes 10 or 20 percent in a few months. There's no organized futures market, except this forward contracting, and no assurance as to the exact rate of gain or the ability of many cattle to "make" the choice grade at the time they reach the desired weight.

You can see that dates are one of the variables we have to keep somewhat flexible. Some years the grass isn't ready for stockers as early as others. Sometimes pasturage dries up too soon. Yet we want to keep the feedlot well filled, because this part of the business is almost as dependent for its efficiency on high occupancy rates as a hotel is.

One thing you can be fairly sure of, there's always a market for finished cattle. You may not like the price, but you can always sell. In fact, most cattle-men tell me the experience of holding back cattle once they are finished, in hopes of a recovery in price, is one of the best roads to the poor house. They keep on eating more feed, while their desirability to buyers is fading as they become overweight. It's a saying that they eat their heads off.

Now here's what's back of my chart. I can set up a sort of reservation sched-ule to show all our forward plans and commitments, our present occupancy and prospective out movement. That's fairly easy. But when we try to choose the time to buy and sell, whether to increase or reduce the number we custom feed, or whether to take penalties for low occupancy, we have a real inventory risk problem and a tough forecasting job on our hands.

Here Pruett went to his desk and brought out a group of charts, tables and forms.

This first one (Exhibit 1) shows the seasonal variation in shipments of cattle and calves into California and placements in California feedlots. Of course no two years are alike, but the pattern is pretty reliable, so far as

EXHIBIT 1

SEASONAL VARIATIONS IN CALIFORNIA MOVEMENT OF CATTLE
INTO FEEDLOTS, AND INSHIPMENTS OF STOCKERS AND FEEDERS
(average monthly movements 1959–62)

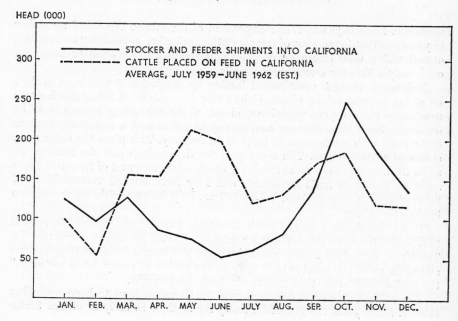

HEAD (000)

movement from out of state goes. The seasonal flows would be very tough to deal with if it weren't for a large movement within the state. Our grass is lush during the winter months when most other areas—except perhaps the winter wheat areas around Kansas and Oklahoma—are likely to be dry or snowed in. This helps account for the high calf movement in the months from September through December.

Our feedlot can draw on a good many sources, fortunately. We used to be tied much more closely to our own KCL breeding and stocker operations before top management put all units on their own profit-and-loss basis. In those days cattle were shipped in and the transfer price was whatever the general cattle manager wanted to make it. A cheap transfer made the feedlot look better and the ranches worse, but after all, the San Francisco office held him responsible for total cattle operations. Now we let the market decide the transfer price, and we have more dealings in both stockers and feeders with outsiders than we do with our own units.

Fortune magazine published an article a while ago that suggested we're pulling in our horns on the cattle operations (see Appendix A), but this isn't true, particularly of feedlot operations where we can now take advantage of more flexibility and a higher rate of turnover.

As an additional piece of background information a sample copy of the Western Feedlots Report appears as Appendix B. It records movements on a weekly basis for practically all major cattle feedlots in the three southwestern states.

At this point the visitor from the East raised a question:

Jack Ahearn up in San Francisco (Planning and Coordination Division at KCL head office) told me that each ranch and operation is standing on its own feet commercially, just as you have. But he also said the company now has eight or nine people concerned with problems like making forward commitments, increasing and reducing herds and the like. With 30,000 cattle on the ranches and a feedlot turnover of 45,000 finished cattle a year this isn't peanuts. In rough terms, a finished 1,000 pound steer is running $250 a head, and prices can go up or down a cent a pound or more in a month. The fluctuations of cattle prices I've seen look pretty violent (see Exhibit 2, giving Chicago prices for choice steers). Can all these men do a good job in such markets?

Dene replied:

There are two or three things that help out in handling the buying and selling. Charlie Quarre keeps mighty close to the fellows on their market operations. Doesn't interfere with their responsibility, so long as they do all right, but he gives them a lot of information and help. That fellow has to know the national market. Some idea of the margins we work with can be gained from the relative price levels (and the seasonal variations in price) shown on this chart (see Exhibit 3). My job fits in here too. Each lot we buy for the feedlot has to be planned and an estimate made of the prospective result. Not only this, we have developed a followup analysis of the actual outcome, and we study the deviations from the estimate, good or bad. We've been learning a lot

EXHIBIT 2

AVERAGE MONTHLY PRICES OF CHOICE SLAUGHTER STEERS
(ALL WEIGHTS) CHICAGO, 1957–61

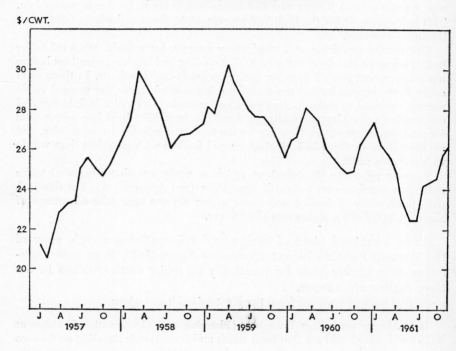

of things this way, partly about our own estimating ability and partly about our actual operations. We're even running some cattle on other people's feed-lots with experimental custom feeding projects in Washington, Idaho, Colorado and Texas.

But perhaps the major part of the answer to your question is that a man on the ground often has opportunities in the market that just wouldn't be known to a headquarters office. Shortages here, a drought there, or a herd liquidation by a neighbor. We want our men to be profit-conscious businessmen, not just cowboys.

The forms used in estimating results for a proposed cattle purchase are attached as Exhibits 4 and 5. Dene continued:

The figures are hypothetical but they aren't unrealistic in today's market. The first sheet tells what authority we had and our estimate of results. It's a sort of head office report. The other, you can see, is much more analytical. It shows a number of the factors that reflect good and bad performance in selection of the cattle, in the efficiency of their feed conversion, the death loss experience and so on. Feed costs are also taken into account. I suppose we ought

EXHIBIT 3

SEASONAL PRICE PATTERNS, 1957–61
(choice all weight slaughter steers, Chicago;
good 500–800# feeder steers, Omaha;
good & choice 300–500# steer calves, Kansas City)

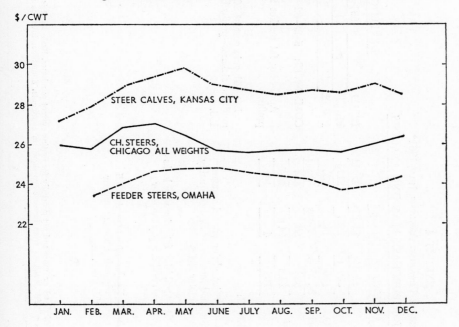

to separate the commercial from the operating elements, but this isn't easy in a single summary. We do it by looking at the separate items, like feed conversion ratios, daily rates of gain and the like. But the prices of the cattle and the feed ingredients have to be reckoned with, as well as physical operating factors.

There are no quoted historical series relating to prices of cattle for future delivery. From the date at which sale is made, delivery for what we call contracts can run from one month to as long as a year in the future. From the records we have developed within the company of sales for future delivery reported on livestock market news teletype, prices for these sales show no consistent pattern in relation to prices current when contract was negotiated; i.e., at times, contract prices are above current prices and at other times are below.

EXHIBIT 4

MAJOR PURCHASE PLANNING ANALYSIS, JULY, 1961*
FEEDYARD MAJOR PURCHASE PLANNING ANALYSIS

AUTHORIZED

DATE 10/23/61 for Nov.-Dec. Delivery
HEAD up to 5,000
SOURCE AREA Southwest
CLASS Ch. Strs.   WT. 650 #
PRICE $24.5 or below @ G

PRO FORMA P & (L)

Nov.-Dec.			
BUY	650 #	24.5/cwt.	$159
GAIN	350 #	25.0/cwt.	$88
Apr.-May			
SELL	1000 #	25.5/cwt.	$255
BREAK-EVEN	1000 #		$247
P & L			$8

COMMENTS: 10-23-61

Will be fed during winter with higher gain costs. Conversion ratio at 10:1 on $50/ton feed or 25.0 ¢/lb. gained. Sell in April-May at $25.5/cwt. market.

ACTUAL PURCHASES

DATE	11-10	11-27	12-11
HEAD	350	1867	2115
LOT NO.	136	141	153
SOURCE	N. Mex.	Texas	Texas
WT.	686	667	634
PRICE	24.3	24.6	24.7
P & L	10	4	14

COMMENTS:

11-5-61—Price edging up and appears doubtful if head numbers of desired quality will be available at $24.5 cwt.

12-3-61—April-May fat price now looks above $25.5 cwt. and can pay more for feeders.

12-28-61—Feeder price now at $25.5 cwt. for cwt. and quality. Do not appear profitable at this price.

DEVIATION

HEAD	(668)
PRICE	(.1)
P & L	1

COMMENTS: 5-28-62

April-May fat market 26+ for increased profits.

Lot 141 gain cost at 26.5¢ per lb. due to mud and sickness—profits below lots 136 and 153.

* This analysis, as labeled, is done for major purchases—say 3,000 head or more and not generally for routine current purchases. Basically it is a type of short-term budget compared with a review of the actual outcome. Reasons for actual deviation from forecast are shown in comments. Sometimes involves several lots, this one includes lot No. 153, Purchase Decision Form for which is included in this study (Exhibit 5).

The reason that people contract cattle for future delivery, both buyers and sellers, is that they feel the price negotiated for the contract is advantageous over the price they expect to be prevailing at delivery time. In other words, the buyer thinks the contract price will be below the market price at delivery; conversely, the seller thinks the contract price will be above the market price. It is, of course, possible for the market price at delivery time to be the same as the negotiated contract price, in which case neither party was hurt nor particularly benefited by entering into the contract.

Company results in the past, both as seller and as buyer, will show that contracting cattle can be very profitable—and also very unprofitable; results, of course, depend on which party to the contract you happen to be and the relationship of the contract price to the market price prevailing when delivery is made.

The decisions we have to make require that we have as good a record as possible of the following price statistics (expressed in terms of f.o.b. Gosford): (*a*) our forecast of prices for 700 pound choice feeder steers for the next six to 12 months, (*b*) our forecast of prices for 1,000 pound U.S. choice steers, (*c*) and (*d*) actual current market prices for feeder and fed steers described above, and (*e*) a price series representing our contracting prices. The occupancy statistics will (in addition to the data on lots of cattle shown in Exhibits 4 and 5) include the following which we can classify according to individual months: (*a*) actual occupancy divided between cattle we own and cattle on which we don't carry the ownership risk either because we are custom feeding them for others or have already contracted their sale, (*b*) number of head we have contracted to buy in particular forward months, (*c*) number of head contracted to feed on a forward basis. Supplementing these data we need to have (*d*) open authority to make purchase commitments, and (*e*) a general plan for ownership and feedlot occupancy extending over the next six to 12 months. Here's an idea of what some of these figures might look like (see Exhibit 6).

The guest was impressed with the number of variables confronting the feedlot management. He wondered, however, how these data could be set up to enable the management to make decisions regarding (1) when to buy and when to sell, (2) what devices to use in adhering to a planned ownership-risk program, (3) how to appraise management's performance in departing from a constant net ownership position, or from strictly spot purchases and sales in all livestock trading.

In addition, a number of questions ran through his mind. How should Pruett transmit to others the best advice and suggestions he could derive from the data at hand. He would have to take into account the specific responsibilities of the individuals involved at each level. What, for instance, would he do if he expected fed cattle to fall from today's price of $27.50 per hundredweight to $22.50 five or six months from now? Assume for completeness that 700 pound feeders would also fall, from $26 to $22 and that feed costs wouldn't change.

EXHIBIT 5
PURCHASE DECISION FORM

PURCHASE DECISION FORM dated 12/11/61

Lot # 153
From Ft. Worth, Texas   Broker No. Cattle Commission Co.—Current

2115 Head
12/11/61 Date In

	Management Forecast	Forecast Computation – Total Costs	Forecast Computation – Var. Costs	Actual Performance	Deviation – Actual is Better (+) or Worse (−) than Forecast	Effect on P & (L) ($/hd.)	Comments on Lot
Purch. Price (Delv.)		$24.7		$24.7	— %	—	At Forecast 12-11-61
Purch. Wt. (Delv.)	634 #			634 #	— %	—	Last purchase on major planning analysis # 7-61.
Purch. Cost/Hd.		$156		$156			
Feed Efficiency	10.0:1			9.7:1	+3 %	3	At Finish 5-27-62
Feed & Feeding Cost/Ton	$50		44	$48.5	+3 %	3	
Cost Per Lb. Prod.		25.0¢	22.0	23.5¢	+6 %	6	Good production results—fed more silage than planned. Price forecast fair.
Feed & Feeding Cost/Hd.		$ 91	80	$85			
Property Taxes/Hd.		$ 2	2	2			
Gain H/D	2.7 #			2.6 #	−4 %		Increased profits due to increased efficiency and higher sales price.
Head Days	135			139	−3 %		

	%	Price/cwt.	%	Price/cwt.	Grade Var.	Price Var.	%
Gain/Hd.		364 #					
Sale Wt. (Net)		998 #		995 #			—
Cost of Sales		$249		$243			6
Sales Forecast		238					
Month of Sale May	—		—				
Choice	70	$ 25.5	55	$26.2	−15	+3%	
Good & Choice	30	25.0	40	25.9	+10	+4	
Good	—	—	4	25.0	+4	—	
Other	—	—	—	—	—	—	
Deaths	—	—	1	—	—	—	
Average Selling Price		$ 25.4		$25.8		+2%	4
Selling Price/Hd.		$253		$257			4
Profit Head		$ 4	15	$ 14	$ 10		10
Profit H/D		3 ¢		10 ¢			
Break-Even Selling Price (choice)		$ 25.1	24.0	$24.8			
Forecasted by /s/ DC							

* Ideally, this analysis should be made before actual purchase, but this is very difficult and is usually done as soon as possible after placement for each lot of KCL-owned cattle. Very helpful tool in scheduling inventory flow and may indicate advantageous change in feeding pattern or sales timing. Analyzed to determine most advantageous source area, broker, weight, timing, etc.

EXHIBIT 6

PROJECTED FEEDYARD INVENTORY OWNERSHIP AND FLOW AS OF MAY 31, 1962

	June Head	Price	July Head	Price	August Head	Price	September Head	Price	October Head	Price	November Head	Price	December Head	Price
IN														
Forward Contracts														
KCL	1,200	25.0	500	24.8	2,000	24.5	600	24.0	800	24.0				
Finance	2,100		600		800		400							
Spot purchase capacity availability														
If not purchased previously	900		3,500		5,600		7,200		10,400					
If previous purchases made	—		2,600		2,100		1,600		3,200					
OUT														
KCL	3,800	26.2	2,000	26.0	3,100	25.5	3,800	25.0	3,200	24.5	2,600	24.5	1,000	25.0
Finance	600		1,700		1,800		800		2,800		3,100		700	
Est. ending inventory														
KCL	12,400		10,900		9,800		6,600		4,200		1,600		600	
Finance	10,700		9,600		8,600		8,200		5,400		2,300		1,600	
Total	23,100		20,500		18,400		14,800		9,600		3,900		2,200	
Total ending inventory capacity	24,000		24,000		24,000		22,000		20,000		18,000		18,000	

APPENDIX A—KERN COUNTY LAND COMPANY

Fortune magazine in March, 1961, characterized the KCL Co. as "one of the oddest-looking contraptions in the U.S. business world.[1]" Following are excerpts from the *Fortune* article, confined largely to things relating to the company's agricultural activities:

Offhand, KCL looks like a real estate mammoth with ranches in several western states besides California. The property now sprawls over 2,800 square miles, an area more than twice the size of Rhode Island. On that land KCL breeds calves and fattens steers, sells irrigation water through almost 1,000 miles of its own canals and ditches, farms 11,000 acres, collects and markets a share of the cotton, sugar beets, potatoes, and other crops raised by some very wealthy tenants, and makes deals with oil companies that bring it quite fancy royalties when, as happens with gratifying frequency, oil is found. This is the general pattern of land-and-royalty companies, and this was KCL for decades.

· · · · ·

Happily, the company had the wherewithal to turn itself around. In 1953, as in the past, it owed nothing to anybody. It had about $16 million in cash. (It still has virtually no debt and has never issued preferred stock.) By this time the chief executive officer, President John T. Pigott, had a strong sense that something must be done, not only with the cash but also with an increasing proportion of future profits, in order to bring KCL out of the doldrums.

Another career for Montgomery

Pigott was, however, on the point of retirement. The way the company had lived, not much management of a broad, corporate character had been required or developed. In fact, the other senior officer, Herbert L. Reid, was an oil specialist who preferred to stay with his specialty rather than to get into general company matters. So Pigott and two other directors set out to find a man with corporate experience deep enough and broad enough to lead the old company into a new and livelier career.

The man they found was a genial, unhurried, native Californian, George Granville Montgomery, who is 66, is now chairman of the board. His experience had equipped him both to ride herd on KCL's old operations and to make the new deals it was seeking. After briefly practicing law, Montgomery had spent a dozen years in factoring and securities companies. Then, as San Francisco vice president of Castle & Cooke, one of Hawaii's corporate "Big Five," he became familiar with agriculture and irrigation (major C & C interests are sugar and pineapple plantations), food processing, ocean shipping, and oil production. Montgomery was also a director of Bankers Trust, General Electric, Pacific Lumber, Matson Navigation, and American Trust. At 59, after 20 years with Castle & Cooke, he was not sure he needed a new career. But the job of finding

---

[1] Herbert Solow, "The Company Twice as Big as Rhode Island," *Fortune,* March, 1961, p. 138. Reproduced by courtesy of *Fortune* magazine.

one for KCL looked intriguing, and early in 1954 he signed on as president and chief executive officer.

. . . . .

Since KCL's top echelon was still frighteningly thin, he also began hunting for his "Number Two." He found him in Dwight M. Cochran, now 57, a former Safeway Stores manufacturing and marketing executive. In 1956, Cochran became a member of KCL's board and a paid consultant and, in 1957, executive vice president for everything except oil.

Montgomery saw that before KCL could profitably lead the strenuous life he had outlined for it, there would have to be some important internal changes —in administrative structure and methods, which were antiquated; in public relations, which had been purely defensive and secretive; and in employee relations, which had evolved haphazardly at a time when KCL employees were largely cowpunchers and *zanjeros* (irrigation ditch tenders). He hired Booz, Allen & Hamilton, which tailored a fat manual on organization and procedure; Ivy Lee & T. J. Ross, which sketched a public relations policy for a company that suddenly wanted to make itself visible; and Industrial Relations Counselors, Inc., which initiated the company into the mysteries of modern health and welfare programs. KCL acquired its first controller, its first public relations director, responsible managers for its farm, cattle, and real estate divisions, and specialized executives for various phases of its minerals program. Today KCL is settled in new offices, with computers at work on a variety of tasks: for example, controlling the cattle-feed components as their prices fluctuate so as to get optimum nutrition at minimum cost. And the company is operating under a top management team that, with few exceptions, is post-Montgomery. Cochran is now president and chief executive.

. . . . .

A major Pigott contribution was to improve part of KCL's rangeland in California for farming use. In 1941, for example, KCL spent about $2 million to level 10,000 acres to grade, and to install water supply equipment. The company used some of the new farmland to enlarge production of forage crops for its cattle, but Pigott decided to emphasize leasing on a share-of-the-crop basis. As the expansion into farming continued, Pigott's leasing policy justified itself in various ways. Political attacks on KCL as an outsize company-farm operation were avoided; so were some overhead costs. And KCL benefited from the fact that individual farmers, its tenants, enjoy tax advantages over a corporate farmer that also has sizable nonfarm income. Today the company itself farms 11,000 acres but leases 116,000.

Improved by precision watering and careful soil treatment, what KCL calls "the best land outdoors" has come alive with a variety of crops. Leading profit makers today include potatoes (Kern is the second biggest U.S. potato county after Maine's Aroostook), sugar beets, alfalfa hay, and, above all, cotton. Aided by a long growing season and close control of water, which is impossible in most cotton-growing areas, Kern County cotton farmers produce two and one-half times the national crop average per acre.

KCL's farm tenants—there are about 250—are technically sharecroppers, since their rent is paid in kind. The usual rent is 25 percent of the cotton crop and last year KCL marketed almost 14,000 bales of tenant-grown cotton, in addition to 1,300 from its own farm operation. The share of other crops is somewhat less. But the tenants look less like sharecroppers than like "agri-businessmen." Many of them work through partnerships or corporations, and about four-fifths of them farm other land in addition to their KCL leaseholds. Several own as many as 10,000 acres, which, with their leased lands, make them bigger farm producers than KCL itself. A number of tenants are KCL stockholders. Several, including the family of W. B. Camp, treasurer of the U.S. Chamber of Commerce, have private planes. Tenant operations are heavily mechanized, and the capital investment of some runs to $250,000.

In addition to making farm leasing a major aspect of KCL's career in the 1940's, Pigott made an important improvement in the company's cattle operations, which had been the heart of its first career. He put KCL into the most profitable phase of the cattle business—a feed lot. In 1948, as Gosford, he began building an installation that now can turn over more than 20,000 head twice a year. Attached to it is a feed mill with a capacity of 30 tons of mixed feed hourly. To expand the cattle operation, Pigott acquired a 492,000-acre Arizona breeding ranch.

Montgomery and Cochran, however, have pulled in their horns so far as the cattle business is concerned. Since they took over, KCL has sold an unprofitable 171,000-acre Oregon ranch; it has leased out part of a ranch in New Mexico and another in Arizona; it has reduced its breeder and stocker herds from 75,000 to 50,000 head; and it is still shifting some Kern County land to farm use. This retrenchment in cattle followed on a survey by Cochran which showed that the cattle operation as a whole was earning less than 1 percent on the current value of assets committed to it. Yet the company remains one of the biggest integrated producers of beef cattle in the U.S., and it is not abandoning cattle, in which it has, at worst, a way of holding its land at minimal cost. KCL has no desire to quit being a land company, whatever else it may become. Moreover, there is a tax problem about selling off land—unless it can be shown that the land can no longer be used profitably for cattle or farming. Selling land in the fashion of a real-estate company would subject KCL to straight income tax, instead of capital-gains tax.

In addition to cutting down their cattle operation and diversifying kaleidoscopically, Montgomery and Cochran have been shaking up KCL internally. After fortifying management by hiring a whole battery of specialists that KCL never had before, Montgomery and Cochran have decentralized the control of operations at Bakersfield. Before Montgomery took over, the farming, cattle, and water operations were all responsible to a general manager at Bakersfield, who made all operational decisions except those concerning oil. This concentration of power was not very efficient and has been abandoned. Now each major KCL operation is a division under a fully responsible local head.

Within the cattle division itself, decentralization has gone even further. As a result, the four breeding ranches, three stocker ranches, and the feed lot are managed as eight separate units, each responsible for its own net profits. A breeding-ranch manager may sell to a company stocker ranch or outside the company, depending on prices, and the same goes for stocker managers with cattle to sell to a feed lot.

KCL's cattle operation is still no bonanza in most years, but gains may come from a growing research program. This includes an effort to breed animals that are more uniform than existing strains, that yield more meat and less waste, and that can be "finished" faster. Montgomery and Cochran are acutely conscious in general of the value of spending money on research.

1. *The case describes a complex situation which is difficult to understand without organization of the key variables in the form of a model or other simplified picture of the operation. What would be the key variables in such a model? What purposes would it serve? How could it be useful in decision making?*
2. *Answer the questions mentioned in the case concerning organization of data for buying and selling and for management appraisal.*
3. *What organizational considerations should be taken into account in setting up systems for decision making?*
4. *What should Pruett do if he expected fed cattle prices to fall from $27.50 to $22.50 per hundredweight in six months? Make the assumptions mentioned at the end of the case.*

APPENDIX

APPENDIX / Tables useful
for capital budgeting

2% PER PERIOD

Period	(1) Present Value of $1	(2) Amount to Which $1 Will Accumulate	Present Value of $1 per Period		Amount to Which $1 per Period Will Accumulate	
			(3) Received at End	(4) Received Continuously	(5) Received at End	(6) Received Continuously
1	98039E 00	10200E 01	98039E 00	99016E 00	10000E 01	10100E 01
2	96117E 00	10404E 01	19416E 01	19609E 01	20200E 01	20401E 01
3	94232E 00	10612E 01	28839E 01	29126E 01	30604E 01	30909E 01
4	92385E 00	10824E 01	38077E 01	38457E 01	41216E 01	41627E 01
5	90573E 00	11041E 01	47135E 01	47604E 01	52040E 01	52559E 01
6	88797E 00	11262E 01	56014E 01	56573E 01	63081E 01	63710E 01
7	87056E 00	11487E 01	64720E 01	65365E 01	74343E 01	75084E 01
8	85349E 00	11717E 01	73255E 01	73985E 01	85830E 01	86685E 01
9	83676E 00	11951E 01	81622E 01	82436E 01	97546E 01	98518E 01
10	82035E 00	12190E 01	89826E 01	90721E 01	10950E 02	11059E 02
11	80426E 00	12434E 01	97868E 01	98844E 01	12169E 02	12290E 02
12	78849E 00	12682E 01	10575E 02	10681E 02	13412E 02	13546E 02
13	77303E 00	12936E 01	11348E 02	11461E 02	14680E 02	14827E 02
14	75787E 00	13195E 01	12106E 02	12227E 02	15974E 02	16133E 02
15	74301E 00	13459E 01	12849E 02	12977E 02	17293E 02	17466E 02
16	72845E 00	13728E 01	13578E 02	13713E 02	18639E 02	18825E 02
17	71416E 00	14002E 01	14292E 02	14434E 02	20012E 02	20212E 02
18	70016E 00	14282E 01	14992E 02	15141E 02	21412E 02	21626E 02
19	68643E 00	14568E 01	15678E 02	15835E 02	22841E 02	23068E 02
20	67297E 00	14859E 01	16351E 02	16514E 02	24297E 02	24540E 02
21	65978E 00	15157E 01	17011E 02	17181E 02	25783E 02	26040E 02
22	64684E 00	15460E 01	17658E 02	17834E 02	27299E 02	27571E 02
23	63416E 00	15769E 01	18292E 02	18475E 02	28845E 02	29132E 02
24	62172E 00	16084E 01	18914E 02	19102E 02	30422E 02	30725E 02
25	60953E 00	16406E 01	19523E 02	19718E 02	32030E 02	32350E 02
26	59758E 00	16734E 01	20121E 02	20322E 02	33671E 02	34006E 02
27	58586E 00	17069E 01	20707E 02	20913E 02	35344E 02	35697E 02
28	57437E 00	17410E 01	21281E 02	21493E 02	37051E 02	37420E 02
29	56311E 00	17758E 01	21844E 02	22062E 02	38792E 02	39179E 02
30	55207E 00	18114E 01	22396E 02	22620E 02	40568E 02	40972E 02

Source: J. Bracken and C. J. Christenson, *Tables for Use in Analyzing Business Decisions* (Homewood, Ill.: Richard D. Irwin, Inc., 1965) pp. 24, 26, 28, 30, 32, 34, 37, 40, 42, 47, 52.

4% PER PERIOD

Period	(1) Present Value of $1	(2) Amount to Which $1 Will Accumulate	Present Value of $1 per Period		Amount to Which $1 per Period Will Accumulate	
			(3) Received at End	(4) Received Continuously	(5) Received at End	(6) Received Continuously
1	96154E 00	10400E 01	96154E 00	98064E 00	10000E 01	10199E 01
2	92456E 00	10816E 01	18861E 01	19236E 01	20400E 01	20805E 01
3	88900E 00	11249E 01	27751E 01	28302E 01	31216E 01	31836E 01
4	85480E 00	11699E 01	36299E 01	37020E 01	42465E 01	43308E 01
5	82193E 00	12167E 01	44518E 01	45403E 01	54163E 01	55239E 01
6	79031E 00	12653E 01	52421E 01	53463E 01	66330E 01	67648E 01
7	75992E 00	13159E 01	60021E 01	61213E 01	78983E 01	80552E 01
8	73069E 00	13686E 01	67327E 01	68665E 01	92142E 01	93973E 01
9	70259E 00	14233E 01	74353E 01	75831E 01	10583E 02	10793E 02
10	67556E 00	14802E 01	81109E 01	82721E 01	12006E 02	12245E 02
11	64958E 00	15395E 01	87605E 01	89345E 01	13486E 02	13754E 02
12	62460E 00	16010E 01	93851E 01	95715E 01	15026E 02	15324E 02
13	60057E 00	16651E 01	99856E 01	10184E 02	16627E 02	16957E 02
14	57748E 00	17317E 01	10563E 02	10773E 02	18292E 02	18655E 02
15	55526E 00	18009E 01	11118E 02	11339E 02	20024E 02	20421E 02
16	53391E 00	18730E 01	11652E 02	11884E 02	21825E 02	22258E 02
17	51337E 00	19479E 01	12166E 02	12407E 02	23698E 02	24168E 02
18	49363E-00	20258E 01	12659E 02	12911E 02	25645E 02	26155E 02
19	47464E-00	21068E 01	13134E 02	13395E 02	27671E 02	28221E 02
20	45639E-00	21911E 01	13590E 02	13860E 02	29778E 02	30370E 02
21	43883E-00	22788E 01	14029E 02	14308E 02	31969E 02	32604E 02
22	42196E-00	23699E 01	14451E 02	14738E 02	34248E 02	34928E 02
23	40573E-00	24647E 01	14857E 02	15152E 02	36618E 02	37345E 02
24	39012E-00	25633E 01	15247E 02	15550E 02	39083E 02	39859E 02
25	37512E-00	26658E 01	15622E 02	15932E 02	41646E 02	42473E 02
26	36069E-00	27725E 01	15983E 02	16300E 02	44312E 02	45192E 02
27	34682E-00	28834E 01	16330E 02	16654E 02	47084E 02	48020E 02
28	33348E-00	29987E 01	16663E 02	16994E 02	49968E 02	50960E 02
29	32065E-00	31187E 01	16984E 02	17321E 02	52966E 02	54019E 02
30	30832E-00	32434E 01	17292E 02	17636E 02	56085E 02	57199E 02

6% PER PERIOD

Period	(1) Present Value of $1	(2) Amount to Which $1 Will Accumulate	Present Value of $1 per Period		Amount to Which $1 per Period Will Accumulate	
			(3) Received at End	(4) Received Continuously	(5) Received at End	(6) Received Continuously
1	94340E 00	10600E 01	94340E 00	97142E 00	10000E 01	10297E 01
2	89000E 0C	11236E 01	18334E 01	18879E 01	20600E 01	21212E 01
3	83962E 00	11910E 01	26730E 01	27524E 01	31836E 01	32782E 01
4	79209E 00	12625E 01	34651E 01	35680E 01	43746E 01	45046E 01
5	74726E 00	13382E 01	42124E 01	43375E 01	56371E 01	58046E 01
6	70496E 00	14185E 01	49173E 01	50634E 01	69753E 01	71825E 01
7	66506E 00	15036E 01	55824E 01	57482E 01	83938E 01	86432E 01
8	62741E 00	15938E 01	62098E 01	63943E 01	98975E 01	10192E 02
9	59190E 00	16895E 01	68017E 01	70038E 01	11491E 02	11833E 02
10	55839E 00	17908E 01	73601E 01	75787E 01	13181E 02	13572E 02
11	52679E 00	18983E 01	78869E 01	81212E 01	14972E 02	15416E 02
12	49697E-00	20122E 01	83838E 01	86329E 01	16870E 02	17371E 02
13	46884E-00	21329E 01	88527E 01	91157E 01	18882E 02	19443E 02
14	44230E-00	22609E 01	92950E 01	95711E 01	21015E 02	21639E 02
15	41727E-00	23966E 01	97122E 01	10001E 02	23276E 02	23967E 02
16	39365E-00	25404E 01	10106E 02	10406E 02	25673E 02	26435E 02
17	37136E-00	26928E 01	10477E 02	10789E 02	28213E 02	29051E 02
18	35034E-00	28543E 01	10828E 02	11149E 02	30906E 02	31824E 02
19	33051E-00	30256E 01	11158E 02	11490E 02	33760E 02	34763E 02
20	31180E-00	32071E 01	11470E 02	11811E 02	36786E 02	37878E 02
21	29416E-00	33996E 01	11764E 02	12114E 02	39993E 02	41181E 02
22	27751E-00	36035E 01	12042E 02	12399E 02	43392E 02	44681E 02
23	26180E-00	38197E 01	12303E 02	12669E 02	46996E 02	48392E 02
24	24698E-00	40489E 01	12550E 02	12923E 02	50816E 02	52325E 02
25	23300E-00	42919E 01	12783E 02	13163E 02	54865E 02	56494E 02
26	21981E-00	45494E 01	13003E 02	13389E 02	59156E 02	60914E 02
27	20737E-0C	48223E 01	13211E 02	13603E 02	63706E 02	65598E 02
28	19563E-00	51117E 01	13406E 02	13804E 02	68528E 02	70564E 02
29	18456E-00	54184E 01	13591E 02	13994E 02	73640E 02	75828E 02
30	17411E-00	57435E 01	13765E 02	14174E 02	79058E 02	81407E 02

8% PER PERIOD

Period	(1) Present Value of $1	(2) Amount to Which $1 Will Accumulate	Present Value of $1 per Period		Amount to Which $1 per Period Will Accumulate	
			(3) Received at End	(4) Received Continuously	(5) Received at End	(6) Received Continuously
1	92593E 00	10800E 01	92593E 00	96249E 00	10000E 01	10395E 01
2	85734E 00	11664E 01	17833E 01	18537E 01	20800E 01	21621E 01
3	79383E 00	12597E 01	25771E 01	26789E 01	32464E 01	33746E 01
4	73503E 00	13605E 01	33121E 01	34429E 01	45061E 01	46840E 01
5	68058E 00	14693E 01	39927E 01	41504E 01	58666E 01	60983E 01
6	63017E 00	15869E 01	46229E 01	48054E 01	73359E 01	76256E 01
7	58349E 00	17138E 01	52064E 01	54120E 01	89228E 01	92751E 01
8	54027E 00	18509E 01	57466E 01	59736E 01	10637E 02	11057E 02
9	50025E 00	19990E 01	62469E 01	64936E 01	12488E 02	12981E 02
10	46319E—00	21589E 01	67101E 01	69750E 01	14487E 02	15059E 02
11	42888E—00	23316E 01	71390E 01	74209E 01	16645E 02	17303E 02
12	39711E—00	25182E 01	75361E 01	78337E 01	18977E 02	19726E 02
13	36770E—00	27196E 01	79038E 01	82159E 01	21495E 02	22344E 02
14	34046E—00	29372E 01	82442E 01	85698E 01	24215E 02	25171E 02
15	31524E—00	31722E 01	85595E 01	88975E 01	27152E 02	28224E 02
16	29189E—00	34259E 01	88514E 01	92009E 01	30324E 02	31522E 02
17	27027E—00	37000E 01	91216E 01	94818E 01	33750E 02	35083E 02
18	25025E—00	39960E 01	93719E 01	97420E 01	37450E 02	38929E 02
19	23171E—00	43157E 01	96036E 01	99828E 01	41446E 02	43083E 02
20	21455E—00	46610E 01	98181E 01	10206E 02	45762E 02	47569E 02
21	19866E—00	50338E 01	10017E 02	10412E 02	50423E 02	52414E 02
22	18394E—00	54365E 01	10201E 02	10604E 02	55457E 02	57647E 02
23	17032E—00	58715E 01	10371E 02	10781E 02	60893E 02	63298E 02
24	15770E—00	63412E 01	10529E 02	10945E 02	66765E 02	69401E 02
25	14602E—00	68485E 01	10675E 02	11096E 02	73106E 02	75993E 02
26	13520E—00	73964E 01	10810E 02	11237E 02	79954E 02	83112E 02
27	12519E—00	79881E 01	10935E 02	11367E 02	87351E 02	90800E 02
28	11591E—00	86271E 01	11051E 02	11487E 02	95339E 02	99103E 02
29	10733E—00	93173E 01	11158E 02	11599E 02	10397E 03	10807E 03
30	99377E—01	10063E 02	11258E 02	11702E 02	11328E 03	11776E 03

10% PER PERIOD

Period	(1) Present Value of $1	(2) Amount to Which $1 Will Accumulate	Present Value of $1 per Period		Amount to Which $1 per Period Will Accumulate	
			(3) Received at End	(4.) Received Continuously	(5) Received at End	(6) Received Continuously
1	90909E 00	11000E 01	90909E 00	95382E 00	10000E 01	10492E 01
2	82645E 00	12100E 01	17355E 01	18209E 01	21000E 01	22033E 01
3	75131E 00	13310E 01	24869E 01	26092E 01	33100E 01	34729E 01
4	68301E 00	14641E 01	31699E 01	33258E 01	46410E 01	48694E 01
5	62092E 00	16105E 01	37908E 01	39773E 01	61051E 01	64055E 01
6	56447E 00	17716E 01	43553E 01	45696E 01	77156E 01	80953E 01
7	51316E 00	19487E 01	48684E 01	51080E 01	94872E 01	99540E 01
8	46651E-00	21436E 01	53349E 01	55974E 01	11436E 02	11999E 02
9	42410E-00	23579E 01	57590E 01	60424E 01	13579E 02	14248E 02
10	38554E-00	25937E 01	61446E 01	64469E 01	15937E 02	16722E 02
11	35049E-00	28531E 01	64951E 01	68147E 01	18531E 02	19443E 02
12	31863E-00	31384E 01	68137E 01	71490E 01	21384E 02	22437E 02
13	28966E-00	34523E 01	71034E 01	74529E 01	24523E 02	25729E 02
14	26333E-00	37975E 01	73667E 01	77292E 01	27975E 02	29352E 02
15	23939E-00	41772E 01	76061E 01	79803E 01	31772E 02	33336E 02
16	21763E-00	45950E 01	78237E 01	82087E 01	35950E 02	37719E 02
17	19784E-00	50545E 01	80216E 01	84163E 01	40545E 02	42540E 02
18	17986E-00	55599E 01	82014E 01	86050E 01	45599E 02	47843E 02
19	16351E-00	61159E 01	83649E 01	87765E 01	51159E 02	53676E 02
20	14864E-00	67275E 01	85136E 01	89325E 01	57275E 02	60093E 02
21	13513E-00	74003E 01	86487E 01	90743E 01	64003E 02	67152E 02
22	12285E-00	81403E 01	87715E 01	92031E 01	71403E 02	74916E 02
23	11168E-00	89543E 01	88832E 01	93203E 01	79543E 02	83457E 02
24	10153E-00	98497E 01	89847E 01	94268E 01	88497E 02	92852E 02
25	92296E-01	10835E 02	90770E 01	95237E 01	98347E 02	10319E 03
26	83905E-01	11918E 02	91609E 01	96117E 01	10918E 03	11455E 03
27	76278E-01	13110E 02	92372E 01	96917E 01	12110E 03	12706E 03
28	69343E-01	14421E 02	93066E 01	97645E 01	13421E 03	14081E 03
29	63039E-01	15863E 02	93696E 01	98306E 01	14863E 03	15594E 03
30	57309E-01	17449E 02	94269E 01	98908E 01	16449E 03	17259E 03

12% PER PERIOD

Period	(1) Present Value of $1	(2) Amount to Which $1 Will Accumulate	Present Value of $1 per Period		Amount to Which $1 per Period Will Accumulate	
			(3) Received at End	(4) Received Continuously	(5) Received at End	(6) Received Continuously
1	89286E 00	11200E 01	89286E 00	94542E 00	10000E 01	10589E 01
2	79719E 00	12544E 01	16901E 01	17895E 01	21200E 01	22448E 01
3	71178E 00	14049E 01	24018E 01	25432E 01	33744E 01	35730E 01
4	63552E 00	15735E 01	30373E 01	32161E 01	47793E 01	50607E 01
5	56743E 00	17623E 01	36048E 01	38170E 01	63528E 01	67268E 01
6	50663E 00	19738E 01	41114E 01	43534E 01	81152E 01	85929E 01
7	45235E-00	22107E 01	45638E 01	48324E 01	10089E 02	10683E 02
8	40388E-00	24760E 01	49676E 01	52601E 01	12300E 02	13024E 02
9	36061E-00	27731E 01	53282E 01	56419E 01	14776E 02	15645E 02
10	32197E-00	31058E 01	56502E 01	59828E 01	17549E 02	18582E 02
11	28748E-00	34786E 01	59377E 01	62872E 01	20655E 02	21870E 02
12	25668E-00	38960E 01	61944E 01	65590E 01	24133E 02	25554E 02
13	22917E-00	43635E 01	64235E 01	68017E 01	28029E 02	29679E 02
14	20462E-00	48871E 01	66282E 01	70183E 01	32393E 02	34299E 02
15	18270E-00	54736E 01	68109E 01	72118E 01	37280E 02	39474E 02
16	16312E-00	61304E 01	69740E 01	73845E 01	42753E 02	45270E 02
17	14564E-00	68660E 01	71196E 01	75387E 01	48884E 02	51761E 02
18	13004E-00	76900E 01	72497E 01	76764E 01	55750E 02	59032E 02
19	11611E-00	86128E 01	73658E 01	77994E 01	63440E 02	67174E 02
20	10367E-00	96463E 01	74694E 01	79091E 01	72052E 02	76294E 02
21	92560E-01	10804E 02	75620E 01	80072E 01	81699E 02	86508E 02
22	82643E-01	12100E 02	76446E 01	80947E 01	92503E 02	97948E 02
23	73788E-01	13552E 02	77184E 01	81728E 01	10460E 03	11076E 03
24	65882E-01	15179E 02	77843E 01	82426E 01	11816E 03	12511E 03
25	58823E-01	17000E 02	78431E 01	83048E 01	13333E 03	14118E 03
26	52521E-01	19040E 02	78957E 01	83605E 01	15033E 03	15918E 03
27	46894E-01	21325E 02	79426E 01	84101E 01	16937E 03	17934E 03
28	41869E-01	23884E 02	79844E 01	84544E 01	19070E 03	20192E 03
29	37383E-01	26750E 02	80218E 01	84940E 01	21458E 03	22721E 03
30	33378E-01	29960E 02	80552E 01	85294E 01	24133E 03	25554E 03

15% PER PERIOD

Period	(1) Present Value of $1	(2) Amount to Which $1 Will Accumulate	Present Value of $1 per Period (3) Received at End	Present Value of $1 per Period (4) Received Continuously	Amount to Which $1 per Period Will Accumulate (5) Received at End	Amount to Which $1 per Period Will Accumulate (6) Received Continuously
1	86957E 00	11500E 01	86957E 00	93326E 00	10000E 01	10733E 01
2	75614E 00	13225E 01	16257E 01	17448E 01	21500E 01	23075E 01
3	65752E 00	15209E 01	22832E 01	24505E 01	34725E 01	37269E 01
4	57175E 00	17490E 01	28550E 01	30641E 01	49934E 01	53592E 01
5	49718E-00	20114E 01	33522E 01	35977E 01	67424E 01	72363E 01
6	43233E-00	23131E 01	37845E 01	40617E 01	87537E 01	93950E 01
7	37594E-00	26600E 01	41604E 01	44652E 01	11067E 02	11877E 02
8	32690E-00	30590E 01	44873E 01	48160E 01	13727E 02	14732E 02
9	28426E-00	35179E 01	47716E 01	51211E 01	16786E 02	18015E 02
10	24718E-00	40456E 01	50188E 01	53864E 01	20304E 02	21791E 02
11	21494E-00	46524E 01	52337E 01	56171E 01	24349E 02	26133E 02
12	18691E-00	53503E 01	54206E 01	58177E 01	29002E 02	31126E 02
13	16253E-00	61528E 01	55831E 01	59921E 01	34352E 02	36868E 02
14	14133E-00	70757E 01	57245E 01	61438E 01	40505E 02	43472E 02
15	12289E-00	81371E 01	58474E 01	62757E 01	47580E 02	51066E 02
16	10686E-00	93576E 01	59542E 01	63904E 01	55717E 02	59799E 02
17	92926E-01	10761E 02	60472E 01	64901E 01	65075E 02	69842E 02
18	80805E-01	12375E 02	61280E 01	65769E 01	75836E 02	81392E 02
19	70265E-01	14232E 02	61982E 01	66523E 01	88212E 02	94674E 02
20	61100E-01	16367E 02	62593E 01	67178E 01	10244E 03	10995E 03
21	53131E-01	18822E 02	63125E 01	67749E 01	11881E 03	12751E 03
22	46201E-01	21645E 02	63587E 01	68245E 01	13763E 03	14771E 03
23	40174E-01	24891E 02	63988E 01	68676E 01	15928E 03	17094E 03
24	34934E-01	28625E 02	64338E 01	69051E 01	18417E 03	19766E 03
25	30378E-01	32919E 02	64641E 01	69377E 01	21279E 03	22838E 03
26	26415E-01	37857E 02	64906E 01	69660E 01	24571E 03	26371E 03
27	22970E-01	43535E 02	65135E 01	69907E 01	28357E 03	30434E 03
28	19974E-01	50066E 02	65335E 01	70121E 01	32710E 03	35107E 03
29	17369E-01	57575E 02	65509E 01	70308E 01	37717E 03	40480E 03
30	15103E-01	66212E 02	65660E 01	70470E 01	43475E 03	46659E 03

18% PER PERIOD

Period	(1) Present Value of $1	(2) Amount to Which $1 Will Accumulate	Present Value of $1 per Period		Amount to Which $1 per Period Will Accumulate	
			(3) Received at End	(4) Received Continuously	(5) Received at End	(6) Received Continuously
1	84746E 00	11800E 01	84746E 00	92163E 00	10000E 01	10875E 01
2	71818E 00	13924E 01	15656E 01	17027E 01	21800E 01	23708E 01
3	60863E 00	16430E 01	21743E 01	23646E 01	35724E 01	38851E 01
4	51579E 00	19388E 01	26901E 01	29255E 01	52154E 01	56719E 01
5	43711E-00	22878E 01	31272E 01	34009E 01	71542E 01	77803E 01
6	37043E-00	26996E 01	34976E 01	38037E 01	94420E 01	10268E 02
7	31393E-00	31855E 01	38115E 01	41451E 01	12142E 02	13204E 02
8	26604E-00	37589E 01	40776E 01	44344E 01	15327E 02	16668E 02
9	22546E-00	44355E 01	43030E 01	46796E 01	19086E 02	20756E 02
10	19106E-00	52338E 01	44941E 01	48874E 01	23521E 02	25580E 02
11	16192E-00	61759E 01	46560E 01	50635E 01	28755E 02	31272E 02
12	13722E-00	72876E 01	47932E 01	52127E 01	34931E 02	37988E 02
13	11629E-00	85994E 01	49095E 01	53392E 01	42219E 02	45914E 02
14	98549E-01	10147E 02	50081E 01	54464E 01	50818E 02	55266E 02
15	83516E-01	11974E 02	50916E 01	55372E 01	60965E 02	66301E 02
16	70776E-01	14129E 02	51624E 01	56142E 01	72939E 02	79323E 02
17	59980E-01	16672E 02	52223E 01	56794E 01	87068E 02	94688E 02
18	50830E-01	19673E 02	52732E 01	57347E 01	10374E 03	11282E 03
19	43077E-01	23214E 02	53162E 01	57815E 01	12341E 03	13421E 03
20	36506E-01	27393E 02	53527E 01	58212E 01	14663E 03	15946E 03
21	30937E-01	32324E 02	53837E 01	58549E 01	17402E 03	18925E 03
22	26218E-01	38142E 02	54099E 01	58834E 01	20634E 03	22440E 03
23	22218E-01	45008E 02	54321E 01	59075E 01	24449E 03	26588E 03
24	18829E-01	53109E 02	54509E 01	59280E 01	28949E 03	31483E 03
25	15957E-01	62669E 02	54669E 01	59454E 01	34260E 03	37259E 03
26	13523E-01	73949E 02	54804E 01	59601E 01	40527E 03	44074E 03
27	11460E-01	87260E 02	54919E 01	59725E 01	47922E 03	52116E 03
28	97119E-02	10297E 03	55016E 01	59831E 01	56648E 03	61606E 03
29	82304E-02	12150E 03	55098E 01	59920E 01	66945E 03	72804E 03
30	69749E-02	14337E 03	55168E 01	59996E 01	79095E 03	86017E 03

20% PER PERIOD

Period	(1) Present Value of $1	(2) Amount to Which $1 Will Accumulate	Present Value of $1 per Period		Amount to Which $1 per Period will Accumulate	
			(3) Received at End	(4) Received Continuously	(5) Received at End	(6) Received Continuously
1	83333E 00	12000E 01	83333E 00	91414E 00	10000E 01	10970E 01
2	69444E 00	14400E 01	15278E 01	16759E 01	22000E 01	24133E 01
3	57870E 00	17280E 01	21065E 01	23107E 01	36400E 01	39929E 01
4	48225E-00	20736E 01	25887E 01	28397E 01	53680E 01	58885E 01
5	40188E-00	24883E 01	29906E 01	32806E 01	74416E 01	81632E 01
6	33490E-00	29860E 01	33255E 01	36480E 01	99299E 01	10893E 02
7	27908E-00	35832E 01	36046E 01	39541E 01	12916E 02	14168E 02
8	23257E-00	42998E 01	38372E 01	42092E 01	16499E 02	18099E 02
9	19381E-00	51598E 01	40310E 01	44218E 01	20799E 02	22816E 02
10	16151E-00	61917E 01	41925E 01	45990E 01	25959E 02	28476E 02
11	13459E-00	74301E 01	43271E 01	47466E 01	32150E 02	35268E 02
12	11216E-00	89161E 01	44392E 01	48697E 01	39580E 02	43418E 02
13	93464E-01	10699E 02	45327E 01	49722E 01	48497E 02	53199E 02
14	77887E-01	12839E 02	46106E 01	50576E 01	59196E 02	64936E 02
15	64905E-01	15407E 02	46755E 01	51288E 01	72035E 02	79020E 02
16	54088E-01	18488E 02	47296E 01	51882E 01	87442E 02	95921E 02
17	45073E-01	22186E 02	47746E 01	52376E 01	10593E 03	11620E 03
18	37561E-01	26623E 02	48122E 01	52788E 01	12812E 03	14054E 03
19	31301E-01	31948E 02	48435E 01	53131E 01	15474E 03	16974E 03
20	26084E-01	38338E 02	48696E 01	53417E 01	18669E 03	20479E 03
21	21737E-01	46005E 02	48913E 01	53656E 01	22503E 03	24684E 03
22	18114E-01	55206E 02	49094E 01	53855E 01	27103E 03	29731E 03
23	15095E-01	66247E 02	49245E 01	54020E 01	32624E 03	35787E 03
24	12579E-01	79497E 02	49371E 01	54158E 01	39248E 03	43054E 03
25	10483E-01	95396E 02	49476E 01	54273E 01	47198E 03	51775E 03
26	87355E-02	11448E 03	49563E 01	54369E 01	56738E 03	62239E 03
27	72796E-02	13737E 03	49636E 01	54449E 01	68185E 03	74797E 03
28	60663E-02	16484E 03	49697E 01	54515E 01	81922E 03	89866E 03
29	50553E-02	19781E 03	49747E 01	54571E 01	98407E 03	10795E 04
30	42127E-02	23738E 03	49789E 01	54617E 01	11819E 04	12965E 04

25% PER PERIOD

Period	(1) Present Value of $1	(2) Amount to Which $1 Will Accumulate	Present Value of $1 per Period		Amount to Which $1 per Period Will Accumulate	
			(3) Received at End	(4) Received Continuously	(5) Received at End	(6) Received Continuously
1	80000E 00	12500E 01	80000E 00	89628E 00	10000E 01	11204E 01
2	64000E 00	15625E 01	14400E 01	16133E 01	22500E 01	25208E 01
3	51200E 00	19531E 01	19520E 01	21869E 01	38125E 01	42714E 01
4	40960E-00	24414E 01	23616E 01	26458E 01	57656E 01	64595E 01
5	32768E-00	30518E 01	26893E 01	30129E 01	82070E 01	91948E 01
6	26214E-00	38147E 01	29514E 01	33066E 01	11259E 02	12614E 02
7	20972E-00	47684E 01	31611E 01	35416E 01	15073E 02	16888E 02
8	16777E-00	59605E 01	33289E 01	37296E 01	19842E 02	22230E 02
9	13422E-00	74506E 01	34631E 01	38799E 01	25802E 02	28908E 02
10	10737E-00	93132E 01	35705E 01	40002E 01	33253E 02	37255E 02
11	85899E-01	11642E 02	36564E 01	40965E 01	42566E 02	47689E 02
12	68719E-01	14552E 02	37251E 01	41735E 01	54208E 02	60732E 02
13	54976E-01	18190E 02	37801E 01	42351E 01	68760E 02	77035E 02
14	43980E-01	22737E 02	38241E 01	42843E 01	86949E 02	97414E 02
15	35184E-01	28422E 02	38593E 01	43237E 01	10969E 03	12289E 03
16	28147E-01	35527E 02	38874E 01	43553E 01	13811E 03	15473E 03
17	22518E-01	44409E 02	39099E 01	43805E 01	17364E 03	19453E 03
18	18014E-01	55511E 02	39279E 01	44007E 01	21804E 03	24429E 03
19	14412E-01	69389E 02	39424E 01	44168E 01	27356E 03	30648E 03
20	11529E-01	86736E 02	39539E 01	44298E 01	34294E 03	38422E 03
21	92234E-02	10842E 03	39631E 01	44401E 01	42968E 03	48140E 03
22	73787E-02	13553E 03	39705E 01	44484E 01	53810E 03	60286E 03
23	59030E-02	16941E 03	39764E 01	44550E 01	67363E 03	75470E 03
24	47224E-02	21176E 03	39811E 01	44603E 01	84303E 03	94450E 03
25	37779E-02	26470E 03	39849E 01	44645E 01	10548E 04	11817E 04
26	30223E-02	33087E 03	39879E 01	44679E 01	13195E 04	14783E 04
27	24179E-02	41359E 03	39903E 01	44706E 01	16504E 04	18490E 04
28	19343E-02	51699E 03	39923E 01	44728E 01	20640E 04	23124E 04
29	15474E-02	64623E 03	39938E 01	44745E 01	25809E 04	28916E 04
30	12379E-02	80779E 03	39950E 01	44759E 01	32272E 04	36156E 04

30% PER PERIOD

Period	(1) Present Value of $1	(2) Amount to Which $1 Will Accumulate	Present Value of $1 per Period		Amount to Which $1 per Period Will Accumulate	
			(3) Received at End	(4) Received Continuously	(5) Received at End	(6) Received Continuously
1	76923E 00	13000E 01	76923E 00	87958E 00	10000E 01	11434E 01
2	59172E 00	16900E 01	13609E 01	15562E 01	23000E 01	26299E 01
3	45517E-00	21970E 01	18161E 01	20766E 01	39900E 01	45624E 01
4	35013E-00	28561E 01	21662E 01	24770E 01	61870E 01	70745E 01
5	26933E-00	37129E 01	24356E 01	27849E 01	90431E 01	10340E 02
6	20718E-00	48268E 01	26427E 01	30218E 01	12756E 02	14586E 02
7	15937E-00	62749E 01	28021E 01	32041E 01	17583E 02	20105E 02
8	12259E-00	81573E 01	29247E 01	33442E 01	23858E 02	27280E 02
9	94300E-01	10604E 02	30190E 01	34521E 01	32015E 02	36607E 02
10	72538E-01	13786E 02	30915E 01	35350E 01	42619E 02	48733E 02
11	55799E-01	17922E 02	31473E 01	35988E 01	56405E 02	64497E 02
12	42922E-01	23298E 02	31903E 01	36479E 01	74327E 02	84989E 02
13	33017E-01	30288E 02	32233E 01	36857E 01	97625E 02	11163E 03
14	25398E-01	39374E 02	32487E 01	37147E 01	12791E 03	14626E 03
15	19537E-01	51186E 02	32682E 01	37370E 01	16729E 03	19128E 03
16	15028E-01	66542E 02	32832E 01	37542E 01	21847E 03	24981E 03
17	11560E-01	86504E 02	32948E 01	37674E 01	28501E 03	32590E 03
18	88924E-02	11246E 03	33037E 01	37776E 01	37152E 03	42481E 03
19	68403E-02	14619E 03	33105E 01	37854E 01	48397E 03	55340E 03
20	52618E-02	19005E 03	33158E 01	37914E 01	63017E 03	72056E 03
21	40475E-02	24706E 03	33198E 01	37961E 01	82022E 03	93787E 03
22	31135E-02	32118E 03	33230E 01	37996E 01	10673E 04	12204E 04
23	23950E-02	41754E 03	33253E 01	38024E 01	13885E 04	15876E 04
24	18423E-02	54280E 03	33272E 01	38045E 01	18060E 04	20651E 04
25	14172E-02	70564E 03	33286E 01	38061E 01	23488E 04	26857E 04
26	10901E-02	91733E 03	33297E 01	38073E 01	30544E 04	34926E 04
27	83855E-03	11925E 04	33305E 01	38083E 01	39718E 04	45415E 04
28	64504E-03	15503E 04	33312E 01	38090E 01	51643E 04	59051E 04
29	49618E-03	20154E 04	33317E 01	38096E 01	67146E 04	76778E 04
30	38168E-03	26200E 04	33321E 01	38100E 01	87300E 04	99823E 04

INDEXES

Index of cases

Subject index

T

Taylor, L. D., 93
Technically competitive products, 376, 378–79
Technically complementary products, 376, 378–79
Technically independent products, 376
Technological suitability, 107–8
Telephone rates; *see* Public utilities
Tennessee Valley Authority rate reductions, time perspective concept, 27
Terborgh, George, 523–24, 641
Theil, H., 120 n, 158 n
Thematic Apperception Test, 117
Theoretical cost functions, 226–31
Time perspective concept, 25–29
  empirical studies and illustrations, 27–29
  printing company's refusal to price below full cost, 27–29
  Tennessee Valley Authority rate reductions, 27
Tinbergen, J., 111
Tintner, G., 244, 245 n
Total costs, 227–28
Traditional cost curves, 226–27
Transfer pricing, 616–25
  competing demands for intermediate product, 622–23
  empirical studies and illustrations, 624–25
  imperfect market for final product, 621–22
  imperfect market for intermediate product, 623–24
  marketable intermediate product, 610–21
  perfect market for intermediate product, 621–22
  specialized intermediate product with excess capacity, 616–19
Transformation curves, 246; *see also* Production possibility curves
Transitory income, 114–15
Transportation problem, linear programming applied to, 639–40
Troughton, F., 230 n
Turner, Robert C., 135 n
Turnover and pricing, 339–40
Two-part tariff, 196

U

Unavoidable costs, 202–3
Uncertainty, 539–40; *see also* Probability analysis
  additional information, search for, 545
  analysis of, tools for, 549–55
  approaches to, 540–48

Uncertainty—*Cont.*
  avoidance of, 541
  basic tools for analysis of, 549–55
  break-even analysis, 542
  control over the future, 548
  decision trees, 553–55
  distributions for analysis of, 550–51
  diversification, 547
  empirical studies and illustrations, 548
  escape from, 541
  external suggestions, 541
  flexibility, 546–47
  frequency distribution, 549–50
  hedging, 543–44, 548
  insurance principle, 543
  normal distribution, 550–51
    applications of, 551–52
  payback criterion, 542
  payoff table, 553
  profits, source of, 11–13
  risk distinguished, 540–41
  rules of thumb, 541
  sampling, 545–46
  sequential sampling, 546
  tools for analysis of, 549–55
  tradition, 541
  variety of approaches to, 540–48
Uncontrollable costs, 204
Unit cost curves, 229
Unit costs, 226–27
United States economy, econometric model of, 143–51
  empirical checks on, 151–54
U-shaped cost curves, 226–30
Utilities; *see* Public utilities

V

Van Horne, James C., 515 n, 538 n
Variable costs, 195–201
Variable proportions, law of, 38
Variables
  control of, 548
  econometric model equations, 143–48
    symbols used in, 148–51
  endogenous, 144
  exogenous, 120–21, 143
  predetermined, 143
Vatter, W. J., 202 n
Veblen, 113
Villers, Raymond, 221
Volatility of demand, 110–11
von Szelski, V., 91 n

W

Wage expense, 206
Wales, Hugh G., 116 n
Walker, S. H., 267 n
Warner, Aaron W., 93 n

This book has been set in 10 and 9 point Caledonia, leaded 2 points. Part numbers and titles and chapter numbers and titles are in 14 point Helvetica Bold. The size of the type page is 27 by 45½ picas.